Gretchen Bitterlin
Dennis Johnson
Donna Price
Sylvia Ramirez
K. Lynn Savage, Series Editor

Ventures 1

TEACHER'S EDITION

with **Arlen Gargagliano**
Lois Miller

CAMBRIDGE UNIVERSITY PRESS
Cambridge, New York, Melbourne, Madrid, Cape Town, Singapore, São Paulo, Delhi, Dubai, Tokyo

Cambridge University Press
32 Avenue of the Americas, New York, NY 10013–2473, USA

www.cambridge.org
Information on this title: www.cambridge.org/9780521683142

First published 2007
3rd printing 2009

Printed in the United States of America

A catalog record for this publication is available from the British Library.

ISBN 978-0-521-54838-0 pack consisting of Student's Book and Audio CD
ISBN 978-0-521-67958-9 Workbook
ISBN 978-0-521-68314-2 pack consisting of Teacher's Edition and Teacher's Toolkit Audio CD / CD-ROM
ISBN 978-0-521-67726-4 CDs (Audio)
ISBN 978-0-521-67727-1 Cassettes
ISBN 978-0-521-67583-3 Add Ventures

Art direction, book design, photo research, and layout services: Adventure House, NYC

Contents

Introduction

Teaching Notes

Additional Resources

To the teacher

What is Ventures?

Ventures is a five-level, standards-based, integrated-skills series for adult students. The five levels, which are Basic through Level Four, are for low-beginning literacy to high-intermediate students.

The ***Ventures*** series is flexible enough to be used in open enrollment, managed enrollment, and traditional programs. Its multilevel features support teachers who work with multilevel classes.

What components does *Ventures* have?

Student's Book with Self-study Audio CD

Each **Student's Book** contains a Welcome Unit and ten topic-focused units, plus five review units, one after every two units. Each unit has six skill-focused lessons. Projects, self-assessments, and a reference section are included at the back of the Student's Book.

- **Lessons** are self-contained, allowing for completion within a one-hour class period.
- **Review lessons** recycle, reinforce, and consolidate the materials presented in the previous two units and include a pronunciation activity.
- **Projects** offer community-building opportunities for students to work together, using the Internet or completing a task, such as making a poster or a book.
- **Self-assessments** are an important part of students' learning and success. They give students an opportunity to evaluate and reflect on their learning as well as a tool to support learner persistence.
- The **Self-study Audio CD** is included at the back of the Student's Book. The material on the CD is indicated in the Student's Book by an icon SELF-STUDY AUDIO CD.

Teacher's Edition with Teacher's Toolkit Audio CD/CD-ROM

The interleaved **Teacher's Edition** walks instructors step-by-step through the stages of a lesson.

- Included are learner-persistence and community-building tasks as well as teaching tips, expansion activities, and ways to expand a lesson to two or three instructional hours.
- The Student's Book answer key is included on the interleaved pages in the Teacher's Edition.
- The Teacher's Toolkit Audio CD / CD-ROM contains additional reproducible material for teacher support. Included are picture dictionary cards and worksheets, tests with audio, and student self-assessments for portfolio assessment. Reproducible sheets also include cooperative learning activities. These activities reinforce the materials presented in the Student's Book and develop social skills, including those identified by SCANS[1] as being highly valued by employers.
- The unit, midterm, and final tests are found on both the Teacher's Toolkit Audio CD / CD-ROM and in the Teacher's Edition. The tests include listening, vocabulary, grammar, reading, and writing sections.

Audio Program

The ***Ventures*** series includes the ***Class Audio*** and the ***Student Self-study Audio*** SELF-STUDY AUDIO CD. The Class Audio contains all the listening materials in the Student's Book and is available on CD or audiocassette. The Student Self-study Audio CD contains all the unit conversations, readings, and picture dictionary words from the Student's Book.

Workbook

The **Workbook** has two pages of activities for each lesson in the Student's Book.

- The exercises are designed so learners can complete them in class or independently. Students can check their own answers with the answer key in the back of the Workbook. Workbook exercises can be assigned in class, for homework, or as student support when a class is missed.
- Grammar charts at the back of the Workbook allow students to use the Workbook for self-study.
- If used in class, the Workbook can extend classroom instructional time by 30 minutes per lesson.

Add Ventures

Add Ventures is a book of reproducible worksheets designed for use in multilevel classrooms. The worksheets give students 15–30 minutes additional practice with each lesson and can be used with homogeneous or heterogeneous groupings. These

[1] The Secretary's Commission on Achieving Necessary Skills, which produced a document that identifies skills for success in the workplace. For more information, see wdr.doleta.gov/SCANS.

worksheets can also be used as targeted homework practice at the level of individual students, ensuring learner success.

There are three tiered worksheets for each lesson.

- **Tier 1 Worksheets** provide additional practice for those who are at a level slightly below the Student's Book or who require more controlled practice.
- **Tier 2 Worksheets** provide additional practice for those who are on the level of the Student's Book.
- **Tier 3 Worksheets** provide additional practice that gradually expands beyond the text. These multilevel worksheets are all keyed to the same answers for ease of classroom management.

Unit organization

Within each unit there are six lessons:

LESSON A Get ready The opening lesson focuses students on the topic of the unit. The initial exercise, ***Talk about the picture,*** involves one "big" picture. The visuals create student interest in the topic and activate prior knowledge. They help the teacher assess what learners already know and serve as a prompt for the key vocabulary of each unit. Next is ***Listening***, which is based on short conversations. The accompanying exercises give learners the opportunity to relate vocabulary to meaning and to relate the spoken and written forms of new theme-related vocabulary. The lesson concludes with an opportunity for students to practice language related to the theme in a communicative activity, either orally with a partner or individually in a writing activity.

LESSONS B and C focus on grammar. The sections move from a ***Grammar focus*** that presents the grammar point in chart form; to ***Practice*** exercises that check comprehension of the grammar point and provide guided practice; and, finally, to ***Communicate*** exercises that guide learners as they generate original answers and conversations. The sections on these pages are sometimes accompanied by a *Culture note*, which provides information directly related to the conversation practice (such as the use of titles with last names), or a *Useful language* note, which provides several expressions that can be used interchangeably to accomplish a specific language function (such as greetings).

LESSON D Reading develops reading skills and expands vocabulary. The lesson opens with a ***Before you read*** exercise, whose purpose is to activate prior knowledge and encourage learners to make predictions. A *Reading tip*, which focuses learners on a specific reading skill, accompanies the ***Read*** exercise. The reading section of the lesson concludes with ***After you read*** exercises that check students' understanding. In the Basic Student's Book and Student's Books 1 and 2, the vocabulary expansion portion of the lesson is a ***Picture dictionary***. It includes a *word bank*, pictures to identify, and a conversation for practicing the new words. The words are intended to expand vocabulary related to the unit topic. In Student's Books 3 and 4, the vocabulary expansion portion of the lesson occurs in ***Check your understanding***.

LESSON E Writing provides writing practice within the context of the unit. There are three kinds of exercises in the lesson: prewriting, writing, and postwriting. ***Before you write*** exercises provide warm-up activities to activate the language students will need for the writing and one or more exercises that provide a model for students to follow when they write. A *Writing tip*, which presents information about punctuation or organization directly related to the writing assignment, accompanies the ***Write*** exercise. The Write exercise sets goals for the student writing. In the ***After you write*** exercise, students share with a partner using guided questions and the steps of the writing process.

LESSON F Another view has three sections.

- **Life-skills reading** develops the scanning and skimming skills that are used with documents such as forms, charts, schedules, announcements, and ads. Multiple-choice questions that follow the document develop test-taking skills similar to CASAS[2] and BEST.[3] This section concludes with an exercise that encourages student communication by providing questions that focus on some aspect of information in the document.
- **Fun with language** provides exercises that review and sometimes expand the topic, vocabulary, or grammar of the unit. They are interactive activities for partner or group work.
- **Wrap up** refers students to the self-assessment page in the back of the book, where they can check their knowledge and evaluate their progress.

---

[2] The Comprehensive Adult Student Assessment System. For more information, see www.casas.org.

[3] The Basic English Skills Test. For more information, see www.cal.org/BEST.

Scope and sequence

UNIT TITLE TOPIC	FUNCTIONS	LISTENING AND SPEAKING	VOCABULARY	GRAMMAR FOCUS
Welcome Unit **pages 2–5**	• Identifying the letters of the alphabet • Identifying numbers • Identifying days and months	• Saying the alphabet and numbers • Clarifying spelling • Saying days and months	• The alphabet with capital and lowercase letters • Numbers • Months and days • Holidays	
Unit 1 **Personal information** **pages 6–17** **Topic:** Introductions	• Identifying names • Identifying numbers • Using greetings • Identifying countries of origin • Exchanging personal information	• Clarifying spelling • Using greetings • Using appropriate language to introduce self and others	• Personal information • Countries and nationalities • Personal titles	• Possessive adjectives • Subject pronouns • Simple present of *be* • Contractions
Unit 2 **At school** **pages 18–29** **Topic:** The classroom	• Describing location • Finding out location	• Asking and giving location of things • Saying *excuse me*	• Classroom furniture • Classroom objects	• Prepositions of location (*in, on*) • *Where is*? • Singular and plural nouns • *Yes / No* questions • Contractions
Review: Units 1 and 2 **pages 30–31**		• Understanding a conversation		
Unit 3 **Friends and family** **pages 32–43** **Topic:** Family	• Describing actions • Talking about family members	• Asking and answering questions about current activities • Answering questions about your family	• Family relationships • Daily activities • Descriptive adjectives	• Present continuous • *Wh-* questions • *Yes / No* questions
Unit 4 **Health** **pages 44–55** **Topic:** Health problems	• Describing health problems and suggesting remedies • Expressing sympathy	• Asking about someone's health • Expressing sympathy • Suggesting a remedy	• Body parts • Health problems • Descriptive adjectives	• Simple present of *have* • Questions with *have* • Contractions
Review: Units 3 and 4 **pages 56–57**		• Understanding a narrative		
Unit 5 **Around town** **pages 58–69** **Topic:** Places and directions	• Describing location • Giving directions • Asking for directions • Confirming by repetition	• Asking about a location • Describing your neighborhood • Clarifying directions	• Building and place names • Imperatives for directions	• Prepositions of location (*on, next to, across from, between, on the corner of*) • *Where* questions • Imperatives

READING	WRITING	LIFE SKILLS	PRONUNCIATION
• Reading the alphabet • Reading numbers	• Writing the alphabet • Writing numbers	• Understanding dates • Understanding holidays	• Pronouncing the alphabet • Pronouncing numbers
• Reading a paragraph describing a student's personal information	• Writing sentences giving personal information • Identifying and using capital letters • Understanding alphabetical order	• Reading a registration form • Understanding cultural differences in names • Using personal titles • Using a directory • Reading an ID card	• Pronouncing key vocabulary • Saying telephone numbers • Saying addresses
• Reading sentences describing a classroom • Using pictorial cues	• Writing sentences about the location of items in the classroom • Using capitalization and periods	• Reading an inventory list • Counting objects	• Pronouncing key vocabulary
			• Recognizing syllables
• Reading a paragraph describing a family birthday party • Using a passage's title for comprehension	• Writing sentences about your own family • Writing number words	• Completing an insurance application form • Using family trees • Using formal and informal family titles	• Pronouncing key vocabulary
• Reading a paragraph describing a sick family's visit to a health clinic • Interpreting exclamation points	• Writing an absence note to a child's teacher • Writing dates	• Using an appointment card • Matching remedies to ailments • Showing concern for someone's health	• Pronouncing key vocabulary
			• Pronouncing strong syllables
• Reading a personal letter describing a neighborhood • Interpreting pronoun referents	• Writing a description of your neighborhood • Capitalizing proper nouns	• Reading and drawing maps • Giving and getting directions • Understanding what a DMV is	• Pronouncing key vocabulary

UNIT TITLE TOPIC	FUNCTIONS	LISTENING AND SPEAKING	VOCABULARY	GRAMMAR FOCUS
Unit 6 Time **pages 70–81** **Topic:** Daily activities and time	• Describing habitual activities • Asking for dates and times • Giving information about dates and times	• Using *usually* vs. *always* • Using *has* vs. *goes to* for classes	• Times of day • Habitual activities	• Simple present tense • *Wh-* questions • Prepositions of time (*at, in, on*)
Review: Units 5 and 6 **pages 82–83**		• Understanding a conversation		
Unit 7 Shopping **pages 84–95** **Topic:** Food and money	• Asking about quantity • Reading prices • Asking the location of items	• Asking and answering *How many?* and *How much?*	• Grocery store items • U.S. currency	• Count and non-count nouns • *How many? / How much?* • *There is / There are* • Quantifiers with non-count nouns
Unit 8 Work **pages 96–107** **Topic:** Jobs and skills	• Identifying past and present jobs • Describing work and life skills	• Talking about your job • Talking about job skills	• Occupations • Work locations	• Simple past of *be* (statements and questions) • *Can* • Contractions
Review: Units 7 and 8 **pages 108–109**		• Understanding a narrative		
Unit 9 Daily living **pages 110–121** **Topic:** Home responsibilities	• Describing past actions • Discussing chores • Expressing appreciation	• Talking about household activities	• Chores • Household items • Time words	• Simple past tense of regular and irregular verbs
Unit 10 Leisure **pages 122–133** **Topic:** Free time	• Describing past actions • Describing future actions • Discussing plans	• Talking about leisure activities	• Leisure activities • Sports	• Simple past tense of irregular verbs • Future with *be going to*
Review: Units 9 and 10 **pages 134–135**		• Understanding a conversation		

READING	WRITING	LIFE SKILLS	PRONUNCIATION
• Reading a paragraph describing a person's schedule • Using *Wh-* questions to interpret a reading	• Writing a description of your schedule • Using indents for paragraphs	• Using class and other schedules • Understanding Parent-Teacher Associations • Understanding volunteerism • Using calendars • Understanding holidays • Reading clocks	• Pronouncing key vocabulary
			• Understanding intonation in questions
• Reading a paragraph describing a shopping trip • Looking for clues to understand new words	• Writing a note about a shopping list • Using commas in a list	• Reading supermarket ads • Reading receipts and using basic consumer math • Understanding the food pyramid • Using U.S. currency • Using multiple payment methods	• Pronouncing monetary values
• Reading a letter describing a person's job and work history • Interpreting narrative time through verb tense	• Writing a paragraph about your life and work skills • Checking spelling	• Completing job applications • Identifying work and life skills • Understanding job certification • Reading e-mail	• Pronouncing key vocabulary
			• Pronouncing the *-s* ending with plural nouns
• Reading a letter describing daily events • Interpreting the narrative voice	• Writing a letter describing household chores • Using the past tense in writing	• Using a job-duties chart • Understanding household chores and tools used for them • Reading clothing-care labels	• Pronouncing key vocabulary
• Reading a letter describing a vacation • Interpreting time words in a passage	• Writing a letter describing a family's weekend activities • Creating new paragraphs as the tense changes	• Reading a TV schedule • Using schedules • Understanding the cultural features of sports	• Pronouncing key vocabulary
			• Pronouncing the *-ed* ending in the simple past

Correlations

UNIT/PAGES	CASAS	EFF
Unit 1 **Personal information** pages 6–17	0.1.2, 0.1.3, 0.1.4, 0.1.5, 0.1.6, 0.2.1, 0.2.2, 2.1.1, 2.1.8, 2.4.1, 2.5.5, 2.7.2, 4.8.1, 6.0.1, 7.2.4, 7.4.3, 7.5.6	Most EFF Standards are met, with particular focus on: • Conveying ideas in writing • Listening actively • Practicing lifelong learning skills • Reading with understanding • Seeking feedback and revising accordingly • Speaking so others can understand • Testing learning in real-life applications • Understanding and working with numbers
Unit 2 **At school** pages 18–29	0.1.2, 0.1.4, 0.1.5, 2.5.5, 4.5.3, 4.6.2, 4.6.5, 4.7.2, 4.7.4, 4.8.1, 6.0.1, 6.0.2, 6.1.1, 7.1.4, 7.4.5	Most EFF Standards are met, with particular focus on: • Assessing the needs of others • Attending to visual sources of information • Interacting with others in positive ways • Offering input • Organizing and presenting information • Seeking feedback and revising accordingly • Understanding and working with numbers
Unit 3 **Friends and family** pages 32–43	0.1.2, 0.1.4, 0.2.1, 0.2.4, 1.4.1, 2.6.1, 2.7.1, 2.7.2, 6.0.1, 6.0.2, 7.1.4, 7.2.4, 7.4.7, 7.4.8, 7.5.6, 8.1.3, 8.2.1, 8.3.1	Most EFF Standards are met, with particular focus on: • Cooperating with others • Listening actively • Making inferences, predictions, or judgments • Monitoring comprehension • Organizing and relaying information effectively • Paying attention to the conventions of the English language • Seeking feedback and revising accordingly
Unit 4 **Health** pages 44–55	0.1.1, 0.1.2, 0.1.3, 0.1.4, 0.2.1, 0.2.3, 2.1.8, 2.3.2, 2.5.3, 2.5.5, 3.1.1, 3.1.2, 3.1.3, 3.2.1, 3.2.3, 3.3.1, 3.4.1, 3.4.3, 3.5.7, 4.6.1, 4.8.1, 6.0.1, 7.2.2, 7.2.4, 7.2.6, 7.3.2, 7.5.5, 7.5.6	Most EFF Standards are met, with particular focus on: • Anticipating and identifying problems • Attending to oral communication • Defining what one is trying to achieve • Gathering facts and supporting information • Organizing and relaying spoken information effectively • Selecting appropriate reading strategies • Taking responsibility for learning
Unit 5 **Around town** pages 58–69	0.1.1, 0.1.2, 0.1.3, 0.1.4, 0.2.1, 0.2.3, 1.1.3, 1.3.7, 1.4.1, 1.9.2, 1.9.4, 2.2.1, 2.2.3, 2.2.5, 2.5.4, 2.6.3, 4.8.1, 5.2.4, 6.0.1, 6.6.5, 7.1.2, 7.1.4, 7.2.2, 7.2.4, 7.2.7, 7.3.2, 7.3.4, 7.4.8, 7.5.6, 8.3.2	Most EFF Standards are met, with particular focus on: • Assessing interests, resources, and the potential for success • Attending to visual sources of information • Defining what one is trying to achieve • Establishing goals based on one's own current and future needs • Identifying and using strategies appropriate to goals and tasks • Organizing and relaying spoken information effectively • Understanding, interpreting, and working with symbolic information

SCANS	BEST Plus Form A	BEST Form B
Most SCANS standards are met, with particular focus on: • Acquiring and evaluating information • Improving basic language skills • Interpreting and communicating information • Organizing and maintaining information • Working with diversity	Overall test preparation is supported, with particular impact on the following items: Locator: W1–W7 Level 1: 2.2, 2.3 Level 2: 4.1 Level 3: 5.1	Overall test preparation is supported, with particular impact on the following areas: • Directions/Clarification • Envelopes • Greetings • Housing • Oral interview • Personal background forms • Telephone directories • Time/Numbers
Most SCANS standards are met, with particular focus on: • Acquiring and evaluating information • Allocating material and facility resources • Knowing how to learn • Monitoring and correcting performance • Participating as a member of a team • Solving problems	Overall test preparation is supported, with particular impact on the following items: Level 2: 4.1, 4.2, 5.1, 5.2	Overall test preparation is supported, with particular impact on the following areas: • Calendar • Employment • Oral interview • Personal information • Reading passages • Writing notes
Most SCANS standards are met, with particular focus on: • Interpreting and communicating information • Knowing how to learn • Participating as a member of a team • Practicing self-management • Understanding social systems	Overall test preparation is supported, with particular impact on the following items: Locator: W1–W7 Level 1: 2.1, 2.2, 2.3, 4.1, 4.2, 4.3 Level 2: 1.2, 1.3, 4.2 Level 3: 1.3, 4.1, 4.2	Overall test preparation is supported, with particular impact on the following areas: • Home environment • Oral interview • Personal information • Reading signs, ads, and notices • Time
Most SCANS standards are met, with particular focus on: • Acquiring and evaluating information • Improving basic skills • Interpreting and communicating information • Organizing and maintaining information • Practicing reasoning • Working with diversity	Overall test preparation is supported, with particular impact on the following items: Level 2: 4.2 Level 3: 1.2	Overall test preparation is supported, with particular impact on the following areas: • Accidents • Doctor/Health • Oral interview • Personal information • Telephone directory
Most SCANS standards are met, with particular focus on: • Interpreting and communicating information • Organizing and maintaining information • Solving problems • Understanding systems • Working with diversity	Overall test preparation is supported, with particular impact on the following items: Locator: W2, W6, W8 Level 1: 1.3, 2.3, 3.1, 3.2, 3.3, 4.1, 4.2, 4.3 Level 2: 2.1, 3.1, 4.1, 5.2 Level 3: 4.1, 4.2, 5.1	Overall test preparation is supported, with particular impact on the following areas: • Directions • Oral interview • Personal information • Reading passages

UNIT/PAGES	CASAS	EFF
Unit 6 **Time** pages 70–81	0.1.2, 0.1.4, 0.2.4, 2.3.1, 2.3.2, 2.5.5, 2.6.1, 2.6.3, 2.7.1, 4.1.6, 4.1.7, 4.2.1, 4.3.1, 6.0.1, 6.0.3, 7.1.2, 7.1.4, 7.2.4, 8.1.1, 8.1.2, 8.1.3	Most EFF Standards are met, with particular focus on: • Attending to visual sources of information • Communicating using a variety of mathematical representations • Paying attention to the conventions of spoken English • Setting and prioritizing goals • Understanding, interpreting, and working with numbers and symbolic information
Unit 7 **Shopping** pages 84–95	0.1.2, 0.2.4, 1.1.6, 1.1.7, 1.2.1, 1.2.2, 1.2.5, 1.3.1, 1.3.6, 1.3.8, 1.5.1, 1.5.3, 1.6.4, 1.8.1, 1.8.2, 2.6.4, 6.0.1, 6.0.2, 6.0.3, 6.0.4, 6.1.1, 6.1.2, 6.2.1, 6.2.2, 6.2.5, 6.5.1, 6.6.7, 6.9.2, 7.1.3, 7.1.4, 7.2.3, 7.5.6, 8.2.1	Most EFF Standards are met, with particular focus on: • Cooperating with others • Determining the reading purpose • Integrating information with prior knowledge • Monitoring the effectiveness of communication • Seeking feedback and revising accordingly • Speaking so others can understand • Using math to solve problems and communicate
Unit 8 **Work** pages 96–107	0.1.2, 0.2.1, 0.2.2, 1.9.6, 4.1.1, 4.1.2, 4.1.5, 4.1.6, 4.1.8, 4.4.2, 4.4.4, 4.4.7, 4.5.1, 4.6.2, 7.1.1, 7.1.4, 7.2.3, 7.2.4, 7.5.1, 7.5.6, 8.2.1, 8.2.6	Most EFF Standards are met, with particular focus on: • Conveying ideas in writing • Cooperating with others • Listening actively • Speaking so others can understand • Taking stock of where one is
Unit 9 **Daily living** pages 110–121	0.1.2, 0.2.4, 1.4.1, 1.7.4, 2.3.2, 4.6.3, 7.1.4, 7.2.2, 7.4.8, 7.5.1, 7.5.5, 8.1.1, 8.1.4, 8.2.1, 8.2.2, 8.2.3, 8.2.4, 8.2.5, 8.2.6, 8.3.1	Most EFF Standards are met, with particular focus on: • Attending to visual sources of information • Cooperating with others • Integrating readings with prior knowledge • Monitoring the effectiveness of communication • Organizing and presenting written information • Setting and prioritizing goals
Unit 10 **Leisure** pages 122–133	0.1.2, 0.1.4, 0.2.4, 2.3.2, 2.6.1, 2.6.2, 2.6.3, 5.2.4, 6.0.1, 6.0.3, 7.1.4, 7.5.1, 7.5.6	Most EFF Standards are met, with particular focus on: • Determining the communication purpose • Interacting with others in positive ways • Monitoring listening comprehension • Reflecting and evaluating • Seeking feedback and revising accordingly • Speaking so others can understand

SCANS	BEST Plus Form A	BEST Form B
Most SCANS standards are met, with particular focus on: • Allocating time • Interpreting and communicating information • Organizing and maintaining information • Participating as a member of a team • Practicing reasoning • Seeing things in the mind's eye	Overall test preparation is supported, with particular impact on the following items: Locator: W5–W7 Level 1: 3.3, 4.1, 4.2, 4.3 Level 2: 2.2, 4.2 Level 3: 4.1, 4.2, 5.2	Overall test preparation is supported, with particular impact on the following areas: • Oral interview • Personal information • Reading passages • Reading signs, ads, and notices • Time
Most SCANS standards are met, with particular focus on: • Allocating money • Organizing and maintaining information • Participating as a member of a team • Practicing arithmetic and mathematics • Understanding social and organizational systems	Overall test preparation is supported, with particular impact on the following items: Level 1: 1.2, 1.3, 3.3 Level 2: 3.1, 3.2, 3.3 Level 3: 1.1, 1.2, 1.3	Overall test preparation is supported, with particular impact on the following areas: • Checks • Food labels • Oral interview • Reading signs, ads, and notices • Shopping and money
Most SCANS standards are met, with particular focus on: • Assessing knowledge and skills • Interpreting and communicating information • Knowing how to learn • Participating as a member of a team • Practicing self-management	Overall test preparation is supported, with particular impact on the following items: Locator: W1–W7 Level 2: 1.2 Level 3: 2.3	Overall test preparation is supported, with particular impact on the following areas: • Calendar • Employment • Oral interview • Personal information form
Most SCANS standards are met, with particular focus on: • Allocating time • Improving basic skills • Interpreting and communicating information • Seeing things in the mind's eye • Working with diversity	Overall test preparation is supported, with particular impact on the following items: Locator: W6 Level 1: 2.3 Level 2: 1.2, 1.3	Overall test preparation is supported, with particular impact on the following areas: • Home environment • Oral interview • Personal information • Reading passages • Reading signs, ads, and notices
Most SCANS standards are met, with particular focus on: • Interpreting and communicating information • Participating as a member of a team • Practicing reasoning • Practicing self-management • Seeing things in the mind's eye	Overall test preparation is supported, with particular impact on the following items: Locator: W6 Level 1: 4.1, 4.2, 4.3 Level 3: 4.1, 4.2	Overall test preparation is supported, with particular impact on the following areas: • Notes • Oral interview • Personal information • Reading passages • Reading signs, ads, and notices • Shopping and money

Features of the Student's Book

The ***Ventures*** Student's Book is based on high-interest topics that reinforce the vocabulary and language adult language learners need in their daily lives. Not only are skills integrated throughout a lesson, but ***Ventures*** also teaches listening, speaking, reading, and writing individually in every unit.

To encourage learner persistence, the ***Ventures*** series is designed so that the one-hour lessons in the Student's Book are self-contained; each lesson moves from presentation to guided practice to communicative activities.

The self-study audio CD at the back of the Student's Book provides a way for students to practice at home.

The core philosophy of ***Ventures*** is:
Hear it before you say it.
Say it before you read it.
Read it before you write it.

Before producing language, students need input that can be internalized and understood. This holistic approach is essential to successful language acquisition and is the foundation of the ***Ventures*** series.

The Student's Book, combined with the ***Workbook***, ***Teacher's Edition Toolkit Audio CD / CD-ROM***, and ***Add Ventures***, offers maximum flexibility of use in multilevel classrooms, classes of various duration, and classes that encourage independent learning.

The "Big" Picture

- Introduces the unit topic
- Activates students' prior knowledge
- Previews unit grammar and vocabulary

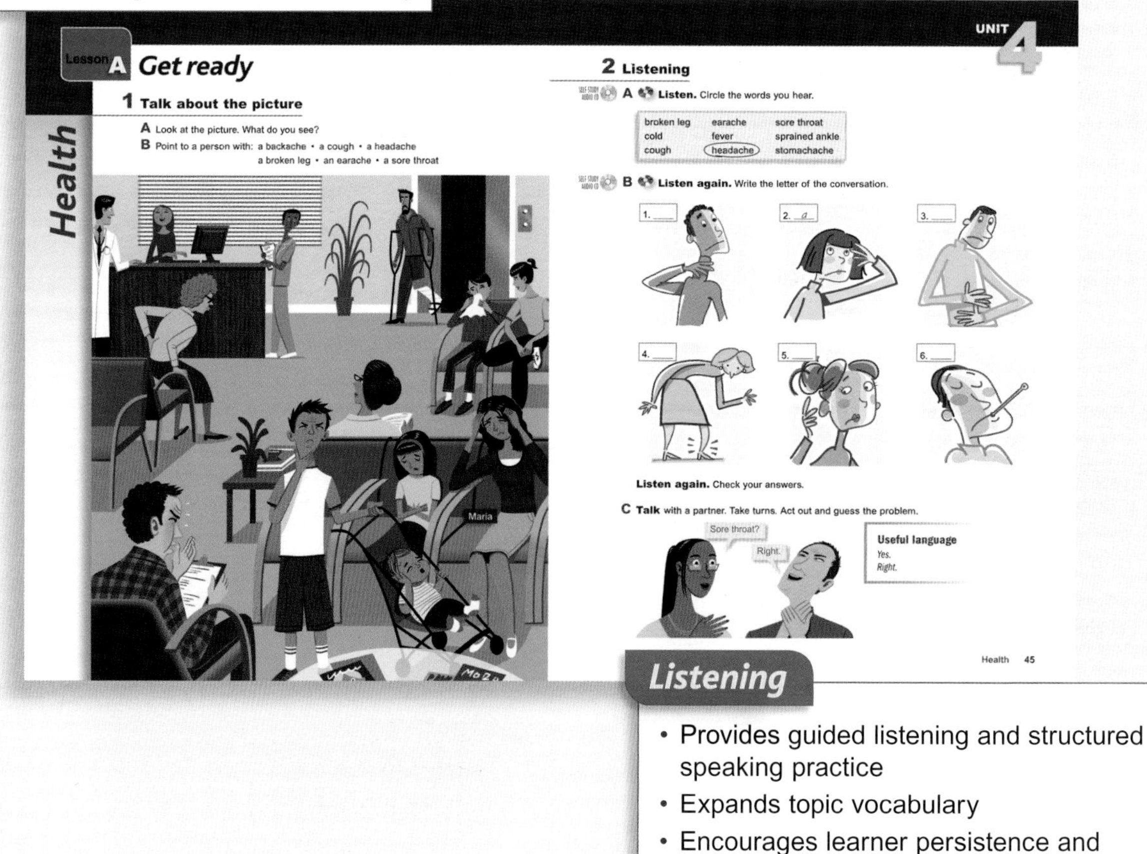

UNIT 4

Health

Lesson A **Get ready**

1 Talk about the picture

A Look at the picture. What do you see?

B Point to a person with: a backache • a cough • a headache • a broken leg • an earache • a sore throat

2 Listening

A Listen. Circle the words you hear.

broken leg	earache	sore throat
cold	fever	sprained ankle
cough	headache	stomachache

B Listen again. Write the letter of the conversation.

1. ____ 2. _a_ 3. ____ 4. ____ 5. ____ 6. ____

Listen again. Check your answers.

C Talk with a partner. Take turns. Act out and guess the problem.

Useful language
Yes.
Right.

Health 45

Listening

- Provides guided listening and structured speaking practice
- Expands topic vocabulary
- Encourages learner persistence and autonomy with self-study audio CD

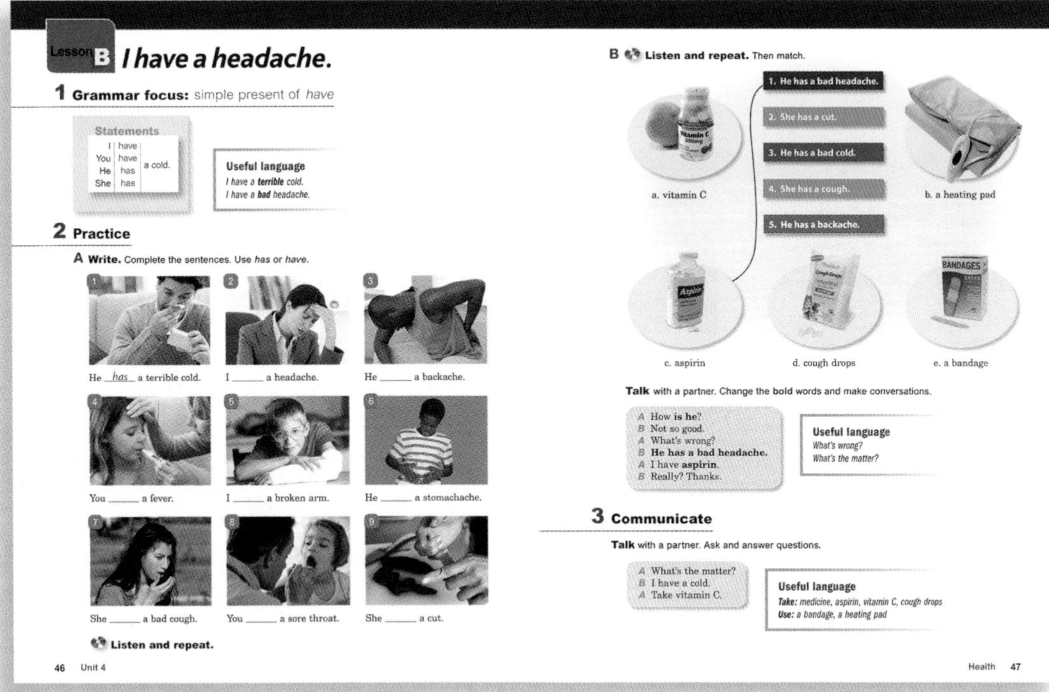

Lesson B I have a headache.

1 Grammar focus: simple present of *have*

Statements		
I	have	a cold.
You	have	
He	has	
She	has	

Useful language
I have a ***terrible*** *cold.*
I have a ***bad*** *headache.*

2 Practice

A Write. Complete the sentences. Use *has* or *have.*

1. He *has* a terrible cold.
2. I ____ a headache.
3. He ____ a backache.
4. You ____ a fever.
5. I ____ a broken arm.
6. He ____ a stomachache.
7. She ____ a bad cough.
8. You ____ a sore throat.
9. She ____ a cut.

Listen and repeat.

B Listen and repeat. Then match.

1. He has a bad headache.
2. She has a cut.
3. He has a bad cold.
4. She has a cough.
5. He has a backache.

a. vitamin C
b. a heating pad
c. aspirin
d. cough drops
e. a bandage

Talk with a partner. Change the bold words and make conversations.

A How **is he**?
B Not so good.
A What's wrong?
B **He has a bad headache.**
A I have **aspirin**.
B Really? Thanks.

Useful language
What's wrong?
What's the matter?

3 Communicate

Talk with a partner. Ask and answer questions.

A What's the matter?
B I have a cold.
A Take vitamin C.

Useful language
Take: *medicine, aspirin, vitamin C, cough drops*
Use: *a bandage, a heating pad*

46 Unit 4 Health 47

Grammar

- Builds fluency through two grammar lessons
- Moves from guided practice to communicative activities
- Includes *Useful language* notes
- Includes audio to check comprehension and practice pronunciation

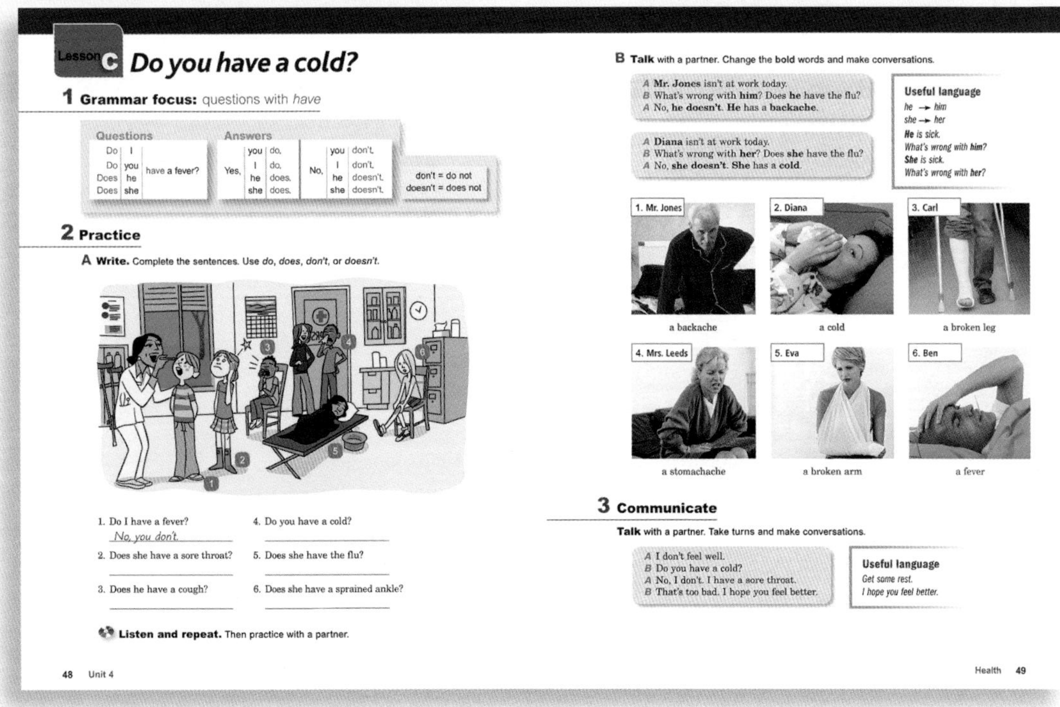

Lesson C Do you have a cold?

1 Grammar focus: questions with *have*

Questions			Answers					
Do	I	have a fever?	Yes,	you	do.	No,	you	don't.
Do	you			I	do.		I	don't.
Does	he			he	does.		he	doesn't.
Does	she			she	does.		she	doesn't.

don't = do not
doesn't = does not

2 Practice

A Write. Complete the sentences. Use *do, does, don't,* or *doesn't.*

1. Do I have a fever? *No, you don't.*
2. Does she have a sore throat? ____
3. Does he have a cough? ____
4. Do you have a cold? ____
5. Does she have the flu? ____
6. Does she have a sprained ankle? ____

Listen and repeat. Then practice with a partner.

B Talk with a partner. Change the **bold** words and make conversations.

A **Mr. Jones** isn't at work today.
B What's wrong with **him**? Does **he** have the flu?
A No, **he doesn't. He** has a **backache.**

A **Diana** isn't at work today.
B What's wrong with **her**? Does **she** have the flu?
A No, **she doesn't. She** has a **cold.**

Useful language
he → him
she → her
He *is sick.*
What's wrong with ***him****?*
She *is sick.*
What's wrong with ***her****?*

1. Mr. Jones – a backache
2. Diana – a cold
3. Carl – a broken leg
4. Mrs. Leeds – a stomachache
5. Eva – a broken arm
6. Ben – a fever

3 Communicate

Talk with a partner. Take turns and make conversations.

A I don't feel well.
B Do you have a cold?
A No, I don't. I have a sore throat.
B That's too bad. I hope you feel better.

Useful language
Get some rest.
I hope you feel better.

48 Unit 4 Health 49

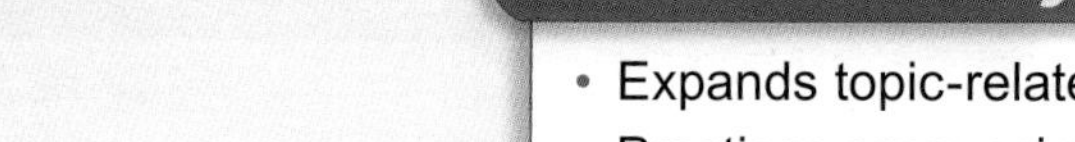

Reading

- Features three-step approach to reading: **Before you read**, **Read**, **After you read**
- Highlights reading strategies and skills
- Contextualizes unit vocabulary and grammar
- Integrates four skills: speaking, listening, reading, writing
- Presents a variety of reading texts on audio

Picture dictionary

- Expands topic-related vocabulary
- Practices pronunciation of new vocabulary
- Reinforces vocabulary through writing and conversation

Lesson **D** *Reading*

1 Before you read

Talk. Maria is at the health clinic. Look at the picture. Answer the questions.

1. Who is with Maria?
2. What's wrong?

2 Read

Listen and read.

The Health Clinic

Poor Maria! Everyone is sick! Maria and her children are at the health clinic today. Her son, Luis, has a sore throat. Her daughter, Rosa, has a stomachache. Her baby, Gabriel, has an earache. Maria doesn't have a sore throat. She doesn't have a stomachache. And she doesn't have an earache. But Maria has a very bad headache!

Look at the exclamation points (!) in the reading. An exclamation point shows strong feeling.

3 After you read

A Read the sentences. Are they correct? Circle *Yes* or *No*.

1. Maria and her children are at school. Yes No
2. Luis has a backache. Yes No
3. Rosa has a headache. Yes No
4. Gabriel has an earache. Yes No
5. Maria has a bad headache. Yes No
6. Everyone is happy today. Yes No

Write. Correct the sentences.

1. Maria and her children are at the health clinic.

B Write. Answer the questions about Maria.

1. Where are Maria and her three children today? ______
2. What's wrong with her baby? ______
3. What's the matter with Maria? ______

50 Unit 4

4 *Picture dictionary* *Parts of the body*

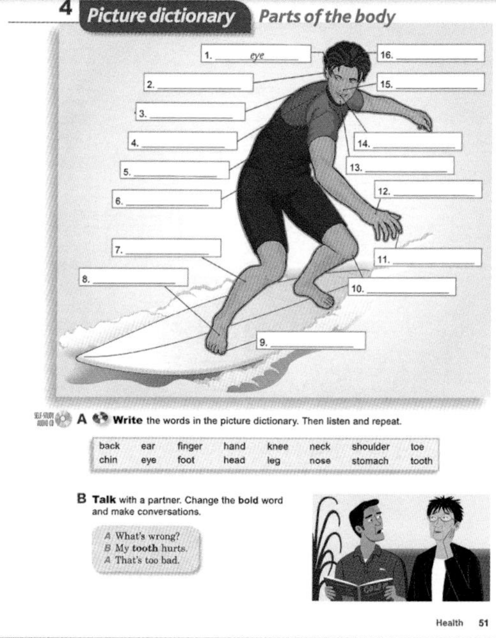

A Write the words in the picture dictionary. Then listen and repeat.

back	ear	finger	hand	knee	neck	shoulder	toe
chin	eye	foot	head	leg	nose	stomach	tooth

B Talk with a partner. Change the **bold** word and make conversations.

A What's wrong?
B My **tooth** hurts.
A That's too bad.

Health 51

Writing

- Includes a process approach to writing: prewriting, writing, and peer review
- Contextualizes unit vocabulary and grammar
- Features integrated skills: speaking, listening, reading, writing
- Moves from guided practice to personalized writing

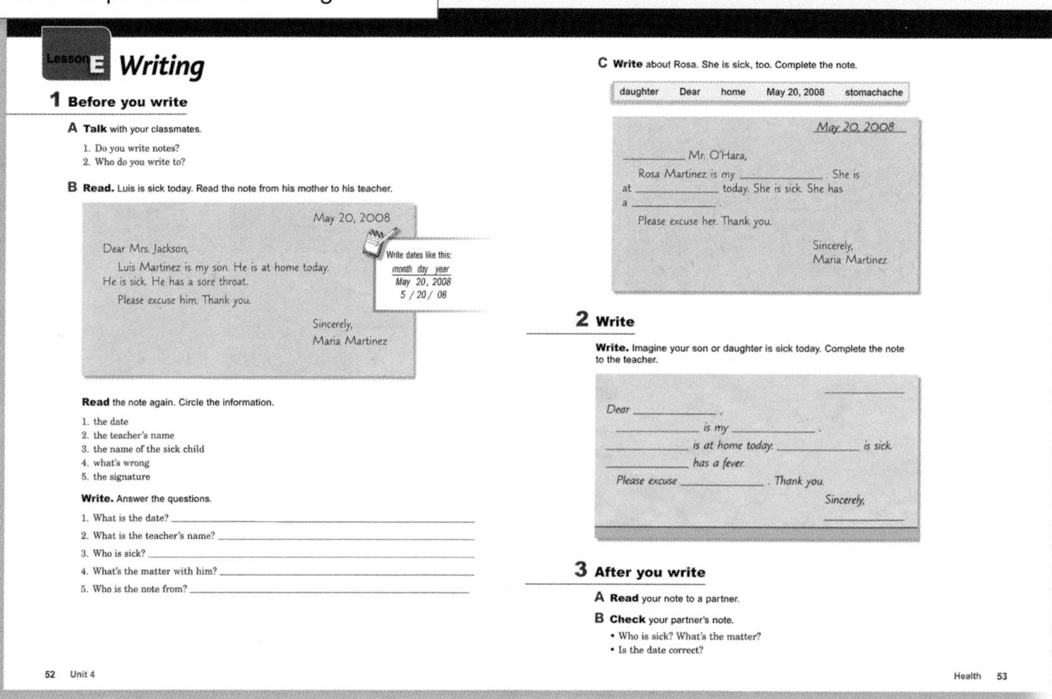

Lesson **E** *Writing*

1 Before you write

A Talk with your classmates.

1. Do you write notes?
2. Who do you write to?

B Read. Luis is sick today. Read the note from his mother to his teacher.

May 20, 2008

Dear Mrs. Jackson,
Luis Martinez is my son. He is at home today. He is sick. He has a sore throat.
Please excuse him. Thank you.

Sincerely,
Maria Martinez

Write dates like this:
month day year
May 20, 2008
5 / 20 / 08

Read the note again. Circle the information.

1. the date
2. the teacher's name
3. the name of the sick child
4. what's wrong
5. the signature

Write. Answer the questions.

1. What is the date? ______
2. What is the teacher's name? ______
3. Who is sick? ______
4. What's the matter with him? ______
5. Who is the note from? ______

C Write about Rosa. She is sick, too. Complete the note.

daughter Dear home May 20, 2008 stomachache

May 20, 2008

______ Mr. O'Hara,
Rosa Martinez is my ______. She is at ______ today. She is sick. She has a ______.
Please excuse her. Thank you.

Sincerely,
Maria Martinez

2 Write

Write. Imagine your son or daughter is sick today. Complete the note to the teacher.

______

Dear ______,
______ is my ______.
______ is at home today. ______ is sick.
______ has a fever.
Please excuse ______. Thank you.
Sincerely,
______

3 After you write

A Read your note to a partner.

B Check your partner's note.

- Who is sick? What's the matter?
- Is the date correct?

52 Unit 4

Health 53

Assessment and consolidation

- Concludes unit with practical and playful practice
- Familiarizes students with real-life documents
- Reviews unit content
- Provides test-taking practice and self-assessment
- Motivates students as they see progress

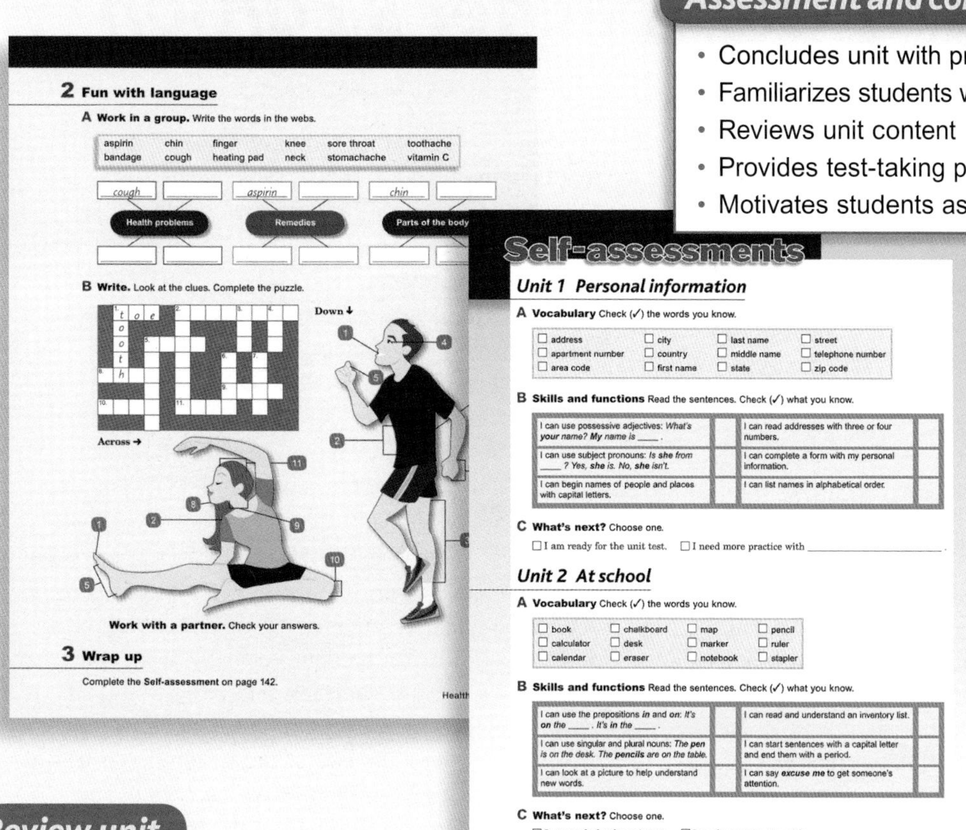

2 Fun with language

A Work in a group. Write the words in the webs.

aspirin	chin	finger	knee	sore throat	toothache
bandage	cough	heating pad	neck	stomachache	vitamin C

B Write. Look at the clues. Complete the puzzle.

Work with a partner. Check your answers.

3 Wrap up

Complete the **Self-assessment** on page 142.

Self-assessments

Unit 1 Personal information

A Vocabulary Check (✓) the words you know.

☐ address	☐ city	☐ last name	☐ street
☐ apartment number	☐ country	☐ middle name	☐ telephone number
☐ area code	☐ first name	☐ state	☐ zip code

B Skills and functions Read the sentences. Check (✓) what you know.

I can use possessive adjectives: *What's your name? My name is ____.*		I can read addresses with three or four numbers.	
I can use subject pronouns: *Is she from ____? Yes, she is. No, she isn't.*		I can complete a form with my personal information.	
I can begin names of people and places with capital letters.		I can list names in alphabetical order.	

C What's next? Choose one.

☐ I am ready for the unit test. ☐ I need more practice with ____________.

Unit 2 At school

A Vocabulary Check (✓) the words you know.

☐ book	☐ chalkboard	☐ map	☐ pencil
☐ calculator	☐ desk	☐ marker	☐ ruler
☐ calendar	☐ eraser	☐ notebook	☐ stapler

B Skills and functions Read the sentences. Check (✓) what you know.

I can use the prepositions *in* and *on*: *It's on the ____. It's in the ____.*		I can read and understand an inventory list.	
I can use singular and plural nouns: *The pen is on the desk. The pencils are on the table.*		I can start sentences with a capital letter and end them with a period.	
I can look at a picture to help understand new words.		I can say *excuse me* to get someone's attention.	

C What's next? Choose one.

☐ I am ready for the unit test. ☐ I need more practice with ____________.

141

Review unit

- Reinforces language of previous two units
- Focuses on listening, grammar, and pronunciation

Review

1 Listening

Read the questions. Then listen and circle the answers.

1. What's wrong with Connie?
   a. She has a backache.
   b. She has a headache.
2. What's wrong with Robert?
   a. He has an earache.
   b. He has a headache.
3. What's Robert doing?
   a. He's talking to the doctor.
   b. He's talking to the children.
4. What's Connie's daughter doing?
   a. She's sleeping.
   b. She's watching TV.
5. What's Connie's son doing?
   a. He's eating.
   b. He's watching TV.
6. What's wrong with Eddie?
   a. He has an earache.
   b. He has a stomachache.

Talk with a partner. Ask and answer the questions. Use complete sentences.

2 Grammar

A Write. Complete the story.

At the Hospital

This week, everyone in Anthony's family is sick. Anthony *has* (1. have / has) a wife, a son, and a daughter. Right now, they ______ (2. is / are) sitting in a hospital room. Anthony's wife ______ (3. have / has) a backache. The nurse ______ (4. is / are) giving her medicine. The doctor ______ (5. is / are) talking to Anthony. He ______ (6. is / are) asking questions about the children. They ______ (7. have / has) the flu.

B Write. Unscramble the words. Make questions about the story.

1. Is / home / family / at / Anthony's / ? *Is Anthony's family at home?*
2. is / doing / the nurse / What / ? ____________
3. wrong / the children / with / What's / ? ____________

Talk with a partner. Ask and answer the questions.

56 Review: Units 3 & 4

Project

- Builds community among students
- Enhances learner persistence
- Exposes students to simple Internet searches
- Reinforces the theme of the unit

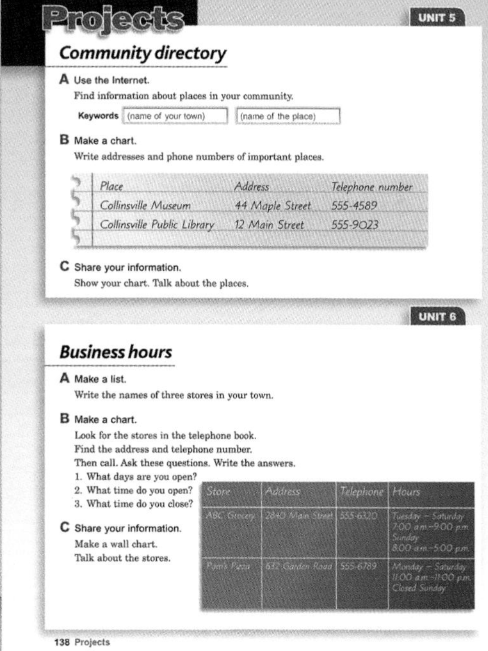

Projects

UNIT 5

Community directory

A Use the Internet.
Find information about places in your community.
Keywords (name of your town) (name of the place)

B Make a chart.
Write addresses and phone numbers of important places.

Place	Address	Telephone number
Collinsville Museum	44 Maple Street	555-4589
Collinsville Public Library	12 Main Street	555-9023

C Share your information.
Show your chart. Talk about the places.

UNIT 6

Business hours

A Make a list.
Write the names of three stores in your town.

B Make a chart.
Look for the stores in the telephone book.
Find the address and telephone number.
Then call. Ask these questions. Write the answers.
1. What days are you open?
2. What time do you open?
3. What time do you close?

C Share your information.
Make a wall chart.
Talk about the stores.

Store	Address	Telephone	Hours
ABC Grocery	2840 Main Street	555-6320	Tuesday – Saturday 7:00 a.m.–9:00 p.m. Sunday 8:00 a.m.–5:00 p.m.
Pam's Pizza	632 Garden Road	555-6789	Monday – Saturday 11:00 a.m.–11:00 p.m. Closed Sunday

138 Projects

Features of the Teacher's Edition

Introduction

Ventures **Teacher's Edition** includes step-by-step teaching notes for each lesson. The teaching notes divide the lesson into six stages. Each lesson begins with a warm-up and review followed by a presentation stage. The practice, comprehension, application, and evaluation stages do not follow a strict sequence in the Teacher's Edition. They vary depending on the content of the lesson being presented.

Stages of a lesson

Warm-up and review Each lesson begins with a review of previous material and connects that material to the present lesson. Quick review activities prompt students' memory. Warm-up activities at the beginning of class introduce the new lesson. These activities may take many forms, but they are quick, focused, and connected to the new material to be introduced. A warm-up also helps teachers ascertain what students already know about the topic and what they are able to say.

Presentation During this stage of the lesson, the teacher presents new information, but it should not be a one-way delivery. Rather, it is a dynamic process of student input and interaction – a give-and-take between the teacher and students as well as students and students. The teacher may give examples rather than rules, model rather than tell, and relate the material to students' experiences.

Practice It is important that students have enough time to practice. A comfortable classroom environment needs to be created so that students are not afraid to take risks. The practice needs to be varied and interesting. There should be a progression from guided to independent practice. In the ***Ventures*** grammar lessons, for example, practice begins with mechanical aspects such as form, moves to a focus on meaning, and ends with communicative interactions.

Comprehension check Asking, "Do you understand?" is not enough to ascertain whether students are following the lesson. The teacher must ask concrete questions and have students demonstrate that they understand. In this stage, students are asked to repeat information in their own words. Students are also invited to come to the board or to interact with other students in some way.

Application A teacher must provide opportunities for students to practice newly acquired language in more realistic situations. These situations could be in class or out of class. The important point is that students use what they have learned in new ways. In the grammar lessons, for example, the *Communicate* section asks students to role-play, interview, share information, or ask questions.

Evaluation An ongoing part of the lesson is to determine whether students are meeting the lesson objectives. This can be done formally at the end of a unit by giving a unit test and having students complete the self-assessment, but it can also be done informally toward the end of the lesson. Each lesson in the Teacher's Edition ends with a review and verification of understanding of the lesson objectives. Any in-class assignment or task can serve as an evaluation tool as long as it assesses the objectives. Having students complete ***Add Ventures*** worksheets or **Workbook** pages can also serve as an informal evaluation to gauge where students may be having difficulty.

The following chart presents the most common order of each stage and suggests how long each stage could take within a one-hour class period.

Stages of the lesson	Approximate time range
Warm-up and review	5–10 minutes
Presentation	10–20 minutes
Practice	15–20 minutes
Comprehension check	5–10 minutes
Application	15–20 minutes
Evaluation	10–15 minutes

The Teacher's Edition includes:

- Interleaved Student's Book pages with answers
- Lesson objectives and step-by-step teaching instructions
- Expansion activities, extra teaching tips, and culture notes
- Activities to encourage learner persistence and community building
- Tests, games, self-assessments, and projects
- Ideas for multilevel classroom management
- ***Teacher's Toolkit Audio CD / CD-ROM*** with a wealth of supplemental materials for teachers and students
- Class audio listening scripts

I have a headache.

Presentation

- Books closed. Draw a vertical line down the middle of the board. On the left side, write *Health problems*. On the right side, write *Remedies*. Under *Health problems*, write *headache*. Under *Remedies*, write *aspirin*. Make a list of health problems and remedies on the board.

Teaching tip
Help Ss understand the meaning of *remedies* by translating the word into a common language Ss understand; by explaining that remedies help a problem go away; by asking for additional examples; or by showing real products that help health problems.

- Books open. Direct Ss' attention to the pictures in Exercise **2B**. Add the health problems and remedies to the list on the board if they are not already there. Explain any words Ss don't understand.
- [Class Audio CD1 track 36] Read the instructions aloud. Play or read the audio program (see audio script, page T-154). Listen to Ss and correct pronunciation as needed.

Practice

- Read aloud the second part of the instructions for Exercise **2B**. Ask two Ss to read the example conversation aloud.
- Point to *She has a cut* in Exercise **2B**. Ask another S to read the conversation with you, substituting the correct words for the bold words. Check that Ss understand the task.
- Have Ss complete the exercise in pairs. Walk around and help as needed.
- Ask pairs to perform their conversations in front of the class.

Useful language
Read the tip box aloud. Ask Ss to repeat the questions after you. Have Ss practice the conversation using the useful language: *What's wrong?* and *What's the matter?*

Application

- Write on the board:

Use	*Take*
a heating pad	*vitamin C*
a bandage	*aspirin*
	cough drops

- Point to the first column. Say the complete phrase for each item: *Use a heating pad; use a bandage*. Ask Ss to repeat.
- Point to the second column. Say: *Take*. Gesture to your mouth to indicate that *take* is used for medicine a person swallows, eats, or drinks. Then say the complete phrase for each item: *Take vitamin C; take cough drops*. Ask Ss to repeat.
- Direct Ss' attention to Exercise **3**. Read the instructions aloud. Model the exercise by reading the example aloud with a S. Model the exercise again by working with a different S and using different language, for example: *What's the matter? How are you? What's wrong? I have a cough. I have a backache. Take cough drops. Use a heating pad*. Check that Ss understand the task.
- Have Ss complete the exercise in pairs, taking turns asking and answering. When they finish, have them switch partners and make different conversations. Walk around and help as needed.

Community building *(small groups)*

- Ask Ss to name stores where they find remedies for their health problems. As Ss brainstorm different places in town, write the names of the stores on the board.

Evaluation

- Direct Ss' attention to the phrases with *have* and *has*, which you wrote on the board at the beginning of the lesson. Ask Ss to look at the pictures on page 45 and make sentences using *has*. Ask students to act out health problems and elicit *I have, you have*.
- Check off each phrase as Ss demonstrate an understanding of what they have learned in the lesson.

More Ventures *(whole group, pairs, individual)*
Assign appropriate exercises from the *Teacher's Toolkit Audio CD / CD-ROM*, *Add Ventures*, or the *Workbook*.

T-47 Unit 4

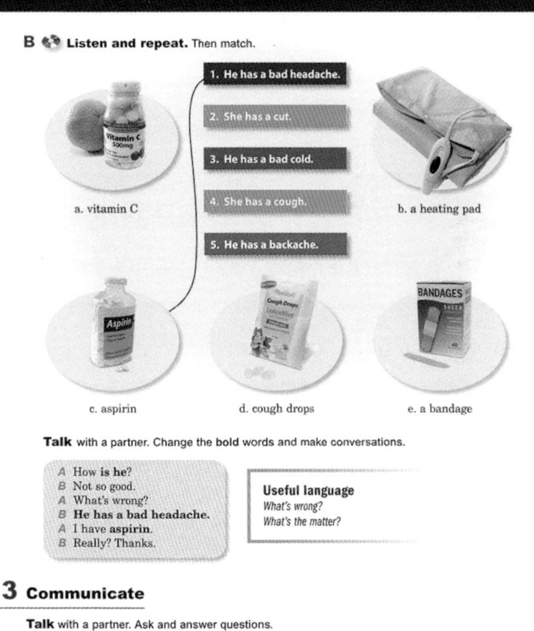

3 Communicate

Talk with a partner. Ask and answer questions.

A What's the matter?
B I have a cold.
A Take vitamin C.

Useful language
Take: *medicine, aspirin, vitamin C, cough drops*
Use: *a bandage, a heating pad*

Health 47

Class time guidelines

Class time varies in different educational settings. The flexibility of the *Ventures* series provides for the expansion of a one-hour class into a two- or three- hour class. For longer class periods, the expansion activities, teaching tips, culture notes, and community building and learner persistence activities in the Teacher's Edition offer ample material to expand the lesson. The Projects at the back of the Student's Book as well as the Games suggested in the Teacher's Edition offer further ways to enrich the two- or three-hour class. In addition, the materials on the ***Teacher's Toolkit Audio CD/CD-ROM*** as well as in the other components of the series can be used in class or as homework to satisfy the needs of the longer class period.

The chart below illustrates how the ***Ventures*** series might be used in a one-hour, two-hour, and three-hour class.

A one-hour class
Follow *Teacher's Edition* step-by-step lessons for the *Student's Book.*
Assign *Workbook* for homework.
Assign appropriate level *Add Ventures* worksheets for homework.
Optional: Projects and Games; Collaborative Activities on the *Teacher's Toolkit Audio CD / CD-ROM*

A two-hour class
Follow *Teacher's Edition's* step-by-step lessons for the *Student's Book*.
Assign *Workbook* for homework.
Use appropriate level *Add Ventures* worksheets as an in-class activity.
Optional: Projects and Games; Collaborative Activities and Picture Dictionary Cards on the *Teacher's Toolkit Audio CD / CD-ROM*

A three-hour class
Follow *Teacher's Edition's* step-by-step lessons for the *Student's Book.*
Use *Workbook* as an in-class activity.
Use appropriate level *Add Ventures* worksheets as an in-class activity.
Optional: Projects and Games; Collaborative Activities, Picture Dictionary Cards, and Picture Dictionary worksheets on the *Teacher's Toolkit Audio CD/CD-ROM*

Meet the *Ventures* author team

Gretchen Bitterlin has been an ESL instructor and ESL department instructional leader with the Continuing Education Program, San Diego Community College District. She now coordinates that agency's large noncredit ESL program. She was also an ESL Teacher Institute Trainer and Chair of the TESOL Task Force on Adult Education Program Standards. She is a co-author of *English for Adult Competency*.

Dennis Johnson has been an ESL instructor at City College of San Francisco, teaching all levels of ESL, since 1977. As ESL Site Coordinator, he has provided guidance to faculty in selecting textbooks. He is the author of *Get Up and Go* and co-author of *The Immigrant Experience.*

Donna Price is Associate Professor of ESL and Vocational ESL/Technology Resource Instructor for the Continuing Education Program, San Diego Community College District. She has taught all levels of ESL for 20 years and is a former recipient of the TESOL Newbury House Award for Excellence in Teaching. She is also the author of *Skills for Success*.

Sylvia Ramirez is a professor at MiraCosta College, where she coordinates the large noncredit ESL program. She has more than 30 years of experience in adult ESL, including multilevel ESL, vocational ESL, family literacy, and distance learning. She has represented the California State Department of Education in providing technical assistance to local ESL programs.

K. Lynn Savage, Series Editor, is a retired ESL teacher and Vocational ESL Resource teacher from City College of San Francisco, who trains teachers for adult education programs around the country. She chaired the committee that developed *ESL Model Standards for Adult Education Programs* (California, 1992) and is the author, co-author, and editor of many ESL materials, including *Teacher Training through Video*, *Parenting for Academic Success: A Curriculum for Families Learning English*, *Crossroads Café*, *Building Life Skills*, *Picture Stories*, *May I Help You?*, and *English That Works*.

Welcome

1 Meet your classmates

Look at the picture. What do you see?

Lesson objective
- Learn the alphabet

Warm-up

- Before class. Write today's lesson focus on the board.
  Welcome unit:
  The alphabet
- Begin class. Books closed. Say: *Welcome to English class.*
- Write your name on the board. Point to it. Say: *My name is _____. I am your teacher.*

Teaching tip
You may have beginning-level Ss in your class who will not understand what you are saying. Be patient. Ss will slowly build up vocabulary and will be able to understand what you are saying.

- Slowly repeat: *My name is _____.* Point to a S. Ask: *What's your name?* If the S doesn't answer, ask different Ss until someone can answer you.

Expansion activity (whole group)

- Bring to class a small, soft object, such as a bean bag, a ball, or a stuffed animal.
- Say: *My name is _____. What's your name?* Toss the object to a S (try to pick a S you think will be able to respond). The S will say: *My name is _____.* Encourage the S to throw the object to another S and ask: *What's your name?* Continue until all Ss have had a chance to say their names and ask other Ss their names.

  Option If you feel this game is too challenging, say your name only; then toss the object to another S, who will say his or her name and toss the object to someone else. Continue until all Ss have said their names.

Presentation

- Books open. Hold up the Student's Book. Direct Ss' attention to the picture on page 2. Point to the two women shaking hands at the back of the library.
- Ask a S to stand up. Hold out your hand for a handshake. Say: *Hello, my name is _____. What's your name?* Elicit: *My name is _____.* Say: *Nice to meet you.* Encourage the S to say: *Nice to meet you, too.*
- Write this conversation on the board.
  A *Hello. My name is _____. What's your name?*
  B *My name is _____.*
  A *Nice to meet you.*
  B *Nice to meet you, too.*
- Point to the conversation on the board. Say each part aloud. Ask Ss to repeat after you.
- Indicate to Ss that they should practice the conversation with a partner. Walk around and help as needed.
- Ask pairs to perform the conversation for the class.
- Direct Ss' attention again to the picture on page 2. Ask Ss: *Where is this?* (a library) *What do you see?* Elicit any vocabulary words that Ss know about the picture, for example: *woman, man, calendar, books, window.*
- Direct Ss' attention to the letters on the side of the library shelves. Ask: *What do you see?* Elicit: *A, B, C, D.*
- Direct Ss' attention to the library hours sign. Ask: *What days is the library open?* (Monday to Saturday) *What time does the library open on Mondays?* (nine o'clock) *What time does the library close on Saturdays?* (six)
- Direct Ss' attention to the calendar behind the librarian. Ask: *What month is this?* (September)
- Direct Ss' attention to the sign at the back of the room. Ask: *When do English classes start?* (Monday, September 17)

Comprehension check

- Hold up the Student's Book. Teach Ss the verb *point* by pointing to the pictures in the book. Ask Ss to point to different items in their books. If Ss need help, they can look at what other Ss are pointing to in their books. Say: *Point to a window. Point to a man. Point to a woman. Point to a table. Point to a computer. Point to a book. Point to the letter "D." Point to a calendar. Point to the number nine.*

Teaching tip
Do not expect Ss to know all the new vocabulary words. These warm-up exercises are intended to find out what Ss already know in English.

Expansion activity (whole group)

- Show Ss items from the picture on page 2 that are in your own classroom. Hold up or point to items and say their names in English. Ask Ss to repeat the words after you, for example: *window, calendar, man.*

Learner persistence (whole group)

- If possible, take your Ss on a tour of your school. Show Ss different rooms in the building. As you are walking, say things such as: *This is the office.* This will help Ss feel more comfortable on their first day of English class.

Welcome

Presentation

- Books open. Direct Ss' attention to the alphabet in Exercise **2A**. Say: *This is the English alphabet.*
- Read the instructions for Exercise **2A** aloud.
- [Class Audio CD1 track 2] Play or read the audio program (see audio script, page T-151). Ss listen and repeat the names of the letters. Repeat the audio program as needed.

Learner persistence *(individual work)*

- [Self-Study Audio CD track 2] Exercise **2A** is recorded on the Ss' self-study CD at the back of the Student's Book. Ss can listen to the CD at home for reinforcement and review. They can also listen to the CD for self-directed learning when class attendance is not possible.

Expansion activity *(student pairs)*

- Ask pairs to read the alphabet to each other. Walk around and help as needed.

Expansion activity *(whole group)*

- Teach Ss the ABC song. This is a fun way for them to learn how to say the names of the letters in English.

Practice

- Direct Ss' attention to the capital letters in Exercise **2B**. Say: *These are capital letters.* Write your name in capital letters on the board. Say: *My name is in capital letters.*
- Read the instructions aloud. Hold up the Student's Book. Point to the example of the letter *A* written in the book. Say: *Write the other letters.*
- Ss complete the exercise individually. Walk around and help as needed.
- Ask several Ss to write the alphabet in capital letters on the board. Ask: *Are the letters correct?* Ask different Ss to correct any errors.
- Focus Ss' attention on the lowercase letters. Say: *These are lowercase letters.* Write your last name in lowercase letters on the board. Say: *My last name is in lowercase letters.*
- Read the instructions aloud. Hold up the Student's Book. Point to the example of the letter *a* written in the book. Say: *Write the other letters.*
- Ss complete the exercise individually. Walk around and help as needed.
- Ask several Ss to write the alphabet in lowercase letters on the board. Ask: *Are the letters correct?* Ask different Ss to correct any errors.

Comprehension check

- Read aloud the second part of the instructions for Exercise **2B**.
- Model the task. Hold up the Student's Book. Ask a S to come to the front of the room. Say: *H.* Encourage the S to point to the letter *H.*
- Ss complete the exercise in pairs. Walk around and help as needed.
- Direct Ss' attention to Exercise **2C** and read the instructions aloud.
- [Class Audio CD1 track 3] Play or read the audio program (see audio script, page T-151). Ss listen and repeat the questions and answers. Repeat the audio program as needed.

Learner persistence *(individual work)*

- [Self-Study Audio CD track 3] Exercise **2C** is recorded on the Ss' self-study CD at the back of the Student's Book. Ss can listen to the CD at home for reinforcement and review. They can also listen to the CD for self-directed learning when class attendance is not possible.

Application

- Read aloud the second part of the instructions for Exercise **2C**.
- Focus Ss' attention on the class list in the exercise. Hold up the Student's Book. Point to the name *Helena.* Say: *Write your classmates' names here.*
- Model the task. Ask a S to stand up. Ask him or her the questions from the conversation. Write his or her name on the board.
- Ss complete the exercise individually. Walk around and help as needed.
- Write a class list on the board. Ask individual Ss to write their classmates' names on the board. Ask: *Are the names spelled correctly?* Ask different Ss to correct the spellings if needed.

Evaluation

- Direct Ss' attention to the lesson focus written on the board.
- Ask Ss to say the alphabet.
- Check off the lesson focus as Ss demonstrate understanding of what they have learned in the lesson.

2 The alphabet

A Listen and repeat.

Aa	Bb	Cc	Dd	Ee	Ff	Gg	Hh	Ii
Jj	Kk	Ll	Mm	Nn	Oo	Pp	Qq	Rr
Ss	Tt	Uu	Vv	Ww	Xx	Yy	Zz	

B Write the letters.

CAPITAL LETTERS									
A *A*	B *B*	C *C*	D *D*	E *E*	F *F*	G *G*	H *H*	I *I*	J *J*
K *K*	L *L*	M *M*	N *N*	O *O*	P *P*	Q *Q*	R *R*	S *S*	T *T*
U *U*	V *V*	W *W*	X *X*	Y *Y*	Z *Z*				

lowercase letters									
a *a*	b *b*	c *c*	d *d*	e *e*	f *f*	g *g*	h *h*	i *i*	j *j*
k *k*	l *l*	m *m*	n *n*	o *o*	p *p*	q *q*	r *r*	s *s*	t *t*
u *u*	v *v*	w *w*	x *x*	y *y*	z *z*				

Talk with a partner. Take turns. Say a letter. Your partner points to the letter.

C Listen and repeat.

A What's your name?
B Helena.
A How do you spell that?
B H-E-L-E-N-A.

Talk to five classmates. Write the names.

Class list

Helena

1. *(Answers will vary.)*
2.
3.
4.
5.

3 Numbers

SELF-STUDY AUDIO CD **A** **Listen and repeat.**

0 zero	1 one	2 two	3 three	4 four	5 five
	6 six	7 seven	8 eight	9 nine	10 ten
	11 eleven	12 twelve	13 thirteen	14 fourteen	15 fifteen
	16 sixteen	17 seventeen	18 eighteen	19 nineteen	20 twenty

Talk with a partner. Take turns. Say a number. Your partner points to the number.

SELF-STUDY AUDIO CD **B** **Listen.** Circle the number you hear.

1. 0 (6) 16
2. 3 7 (20)
3. (1) 10 11
4. 2 5 (15)
5. 1 (9) 17
6. 11 (12) 20
7. 8 (9) 10
8. 3 (5) 13
9. 14 15 (16)

SELF-STUDY AUDIO CD **C** **Listen.** Write the number you hear.

1. 3
2. 8
3. 18
4. 12
5. 1
6. 0
7. 20
8. 4
9. 15
10. 11

D **Write.** Match the number and the word.

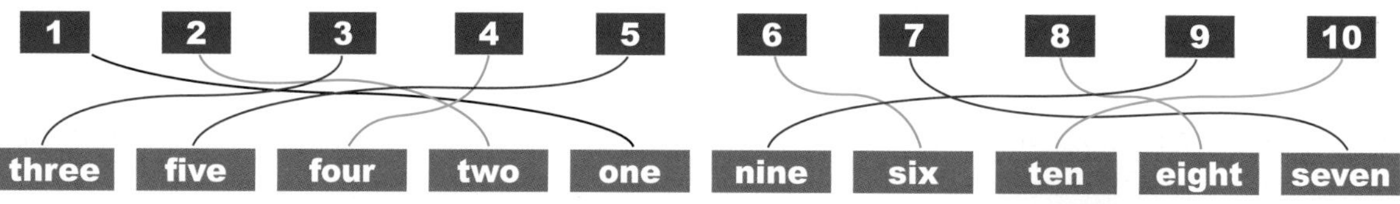

Talk with a partner. Take turns. Spell a number. Your partner says the number.

n-i-n-e

9

Lesson objectives

- Learn the days of the week and the months of the year
- Learn numbers 1–20

Warm-up

- Before class. Write today's lesson focus on the board.
  Welcome unit:
  Days of the week
  Months of the year
  Numbers 1–20
- Begin class. Books closed. Write the word *numbers* on the board. Point to the word. Say it aloud. Ask Ss to repeat after you. Ask: *What numbers do you know in English?* Write any numbers on the board that Ss know.

Teaching tip

Do not expect Ss to know all the new vocabulary words. These warm-up questions are intended to find out what Ss already know about numbers.

Presentation

- Books open. Direct Ss' attention to the numbers in Exercise **3A**. Read the instructions aloud.
- [Class Audio CD1 track 4] Play or read the audio program (see audio script, page T-151). Ss listen and repeat the numbers. Repeat the audio program as needed.

Learner persistence (individual work)

- [Self-Study Audio CD track 4] Exercise **3A** is recorded on the Ss' self-study CD at the back of the Student's Book. Ss can listen to the CD at home for reinforcement and review. They can also listen to the CD for self-directed learning when class attendance is not possible.

Practice

- Read aloud the second part of the instructions for Exercise **3A**.
- Model the task. Hold up the Student's Book. Ask a S to stand. Say a number. The S points to that number.
- Ss complete the activity in pairs. Help as needed.
- Write the numbers *1–20* on the board. Ask pairs to come to the board. One S will say a number. The other S will point to that number on the board.
- Direct Ss' attention to Exercise **3B**. Read the instructions.
- [Class Audio CD1 track 5] Play or read the audio program (see audio script, page T-151). Pause the audio program after the first number. Ask: *What number did you hear?* Elicit: *6*. Hold up the Student's Book. Point to where *6* has been circled in number 1. Say: *Circle the numbers that you hear.*
- [Class Audio CD1 track 5] Play or read the rest of the audio program. Ss listen and circle the numbers that they hear. Repeat the audio program as needed.
- Write the numbers *1–9* on the board. Write a *6* next to number 1. Ask Ss to write the numbers they circled next to the remaining numbers on the board.

Learner persistence (individual work)

- [Self-Study Audio CD track 5] Exercise **3B** is recorded on the Ss' self-study CD at the back of the Student's Book. Ss can listen to the CD at home for reinforcement and review. They can also listen to the CD for self-directed learning when class attendance is not possible.

Practice

- Direct Ss' attention to Exercise **3C**. Read the instructions.
- [Class Audio CD1 track 6] Play or read the audio program (see audio script, page T-151). Pause the audio program after the first number. Ask: *What number did you hear?* Elicit: *3*. Hold up the Student's Book. Point to where *3* is written. Say: *Write the numbers you hear.*
- [Class Audio CD1 track 6] Play or read the rest of the audio program. Ss listen and write the numbers they hear. Repeat the audio program as needed.
- Write the numbers *1–10* on the board. Ask Ss to write the answers on the board. Ask other Ss to correct errors.

Learner persistence (individual work)

- [Self-Study Audio CD track 6] Exercise **3C** is recorded on the Ss' self-study CD at the back of the Student's Book. Ss can listen to the CD at home for reinforcement and review. They can also listen to the CD for self-directed learning when class attendance is not possible.

Comprehension check

- Direct Ss' attention to Exercise **3D** and read the instructions aloud.
- Model the task. Hold up the Student's Book. Point to the number *1*. Then point to the word *one*. Trace the line connecting them with your finger. Say: *Match the number with the word.*
- Ss complete the exercise individually. Help as needed.
- Check answers. Write *1 – one* on the board. Ask Ss to write the numbers in this format from two to ten.
- Read aloud the second part of the instructions for Exercise **3D**. Ask two Ss to read the example aloud.
- Model the task again. Ask a different S to stand up. Spell out the number *ten (T-E-N)*. Encourage the S to respond by saying *ten*.
- Ss complete the exercise in pairs. Help as needed.
- Ask several pairs to perform the exercise for the class.

Warm-up

- Books closed. Show class a calendar. Point to each day on the calendar. Say the day aloud. Ask Ss to repeat.

Presentation

- Books open. Direct Ss' attention to the days of the week in Exercise **4A**.
- [Class Audio CD1 track 7] Play or read the audio program (see audio script, page T-151). Ss listen and repeat the days. Repeat the audio program as needed.
- Read aloud the second part of the instructions for Exercise **4A**.
- Model the task. Hold up the Student's Book. Ask a S to stand up. Say a day of the week. Ask the S to point to that day.
- Ss complete the exercise in pairs. Help as needed.
- Hold up the calendar again. Ask pairs to come to the front of the room. One S will say a day. The other S will point to that day on the calendar.

Learner persistence *(individual work)*

- [Self-Study Audio CD track 7] Exercise **4A** is recorded on the Ss' self-study CD at the back of the Student's Book. Ss can listen to the CD at home for reinforcement and review. They can also listen to the CD for self-directed learning when class attendance is not possible.

Practice

- Point to *Sunday* on the calendar. Say: *This is Sunday.* Write *Sun.* on the board. Say: *This is the short form.*
- Direct Ss' attention to Exercise **4B**. Read the instructions.
- Hold up the Student's Book. Point to the example. Say: *S-U-N-period is the same as Sunday.*
- Ss complete the exercise individually. Help as needed.
- Write the numbers *1–7* on the board. Ask individual Ss to write the days of the week on the board.
- Ask: *Are the days correct?* Ask different Ss to correct the spellings if needed.

Expansion activity *(whole group)*

- Hold up the calendar. Ask: *What day is today?* Elicit the correct response. If no one can answer, point to the correct day on the calendar. Ask a S to read the day.
- Write the word *months* on the board. Point to the word. Say it aloud. Ask Ss to repeat after you.
- Hold up the calendar. Point to the current month. Say: *This is the month right now.*
- Direct Ss' attention to the months in Exercise **4C**. Read the instructions aloud.
- [Class Audio CD1 track 8] Play or read the audio program (see audio script, page T-151). Ss listen and repeat the months after they hear them. Repeat the audio program as needed.
- Read aloud the second part of the instructions for Exercise **4C**. Ask two Ss to read the example aloud.
- Model the task again. Ask a different S to stand. Say the number 2. Have the S say *February.*

> **Teaching tip**
> Encourage Ss to look at the months written in Exercise **4C** to help them remember the names of the months in English.

- Ss complete the exercise in pairs. Help as needed.
- Ask several pairs to perform the exercise for the class.

Learner persistence *(individual work)*

- [Self-Study Audio CD track 8] Exercise **4C** is recorded on the Ss' self-study CD at the back of the Student's Book. Ss can listen to the CD at home for reinforcement and review. They can also listen to the CD for self-directed learning when class attendance is not possible.

Comprehension check

- Write the word *holidays* on the board. Point to the word. Say it aloud. Ask: *What are some holidays in the United States?* Write Ss' responses on the board.
- Focus Ss' attention on Exercise **4D** and read aloud the instructions. Ask two Ss to read the example aloud.
- Ss complete the exercise in pairs. Help as needed.
- Ask several pairs to say the holidays and corresponding months for the rest of the class.

Community building *(whole group)*

- Ask Ss what holidays they celebrate in their countries. Ask them to write the names of the holidays on the board. Say: *Tell us the month of the holiday.*

Evaluation

- Direct Ss' attention to the lesson focus on the board.
- Ask Ss to say the days of the week and months of the year.
- Check off the lesson focus as Ss demonstrate understanding of what they have learned in the lesson.

4 Days and months

SELF-STUDY AUDIO CD

A Listen and repeat.

Sunday	Monday	Tuesday	Wednesday	Thursday	Friday	Saturday

Talk with a partner. Take turns. Say a day. Your partner points to the day.

B **Write** the full spelling.

1. Sun. *Sunday*
2. Mon. *Monday*
3. Tues. *Tuesday*
4. Wed. *Wednesday*
5. Thurs. *Thursday*
6. Fri. *Friday*
7. Sat. *Saturday*

SELF-STUDY AUDIO CD

C Listen and repeat.

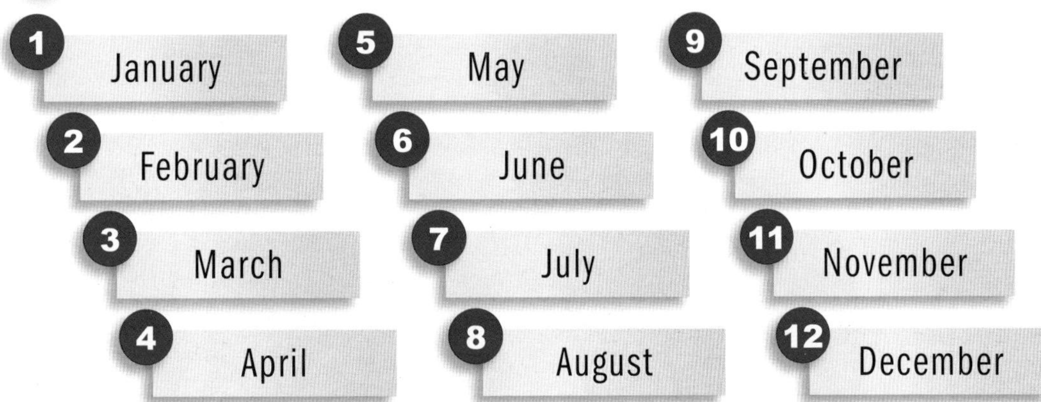

Talk with a partner. Say a number. Your partner says the month.

8

August

D **Talk** with a partner. Tell the month of the holiday.

1. Thanksgiving
2. Halloween
3. New Year's Day
4. Labor Day
5. Mother's Day
6. Father's Day

Lesson A Get ready

1 Talk about the picture

A Look at the picture. What do you see?

B Point to: first name • last name • city
zip code • area code • telephone number

Lesson objectives
- Introduce students to the topic
- Find out what students know about the topic
- Preview the unit by talking about the picture
- Practice key vocabulary
- Practice listening skills

Warm-up and review

- Before class. Write today's lesson focus on the board. *Lesson A: Personal information*
- Begin class. Books closed. Point to the words *Personal information* on the board. Say: *Today's class is about personal information. What is personal information?* Elicit words such as *name, address, telephone number.* Write Ss' responses on the board.
- Point to *name*. Ask Ss: *What is this?* (name) Ask a S: *What is your name?* Elicit response. Repeat with *address* and *telephone number.*

Teaching tip
Do not expect all Ss to be able to respond in English with their addresses and telephone numbers. These warm-up questions are intended to find out which Ss already know how to talk about personal information.

Presentation

- Books open. Set the scene. Direct Ss' attention to the picture on page 6. Say: *Ss are registering for classes at a school.*
- Ask: *What do you see?* Elicit as much information as possible: *school, student, registration, form, man, woman,* etc.
- Direct Ss' attention to the key words in Exercise **1B**. Read each word aloud while pointing to the corresponding item on the registration form. Ask the class to repeat and point.

Teaching tip
The key words are intended to help students talk about the picture and learn some of the vocabulary in the unit.

Comprehension check

- Point to people and items in the picture and ask *Yes / No* questions.
  Is Ricardo a student? (Yes.)
  Is Mr. Clark a man? (Yes.)
  Is Svetlana a teacher? (No.)
  Is Svetlana's last name Kulik? (Yes.)
  Is Svetlana's area code 717? (No.)
  Is this a classroom? (No.)
  Is this an office? (Yes.)
  Is this a registration office? (Yes.)

Teaching tip
Do not expect Ss to answer with more than *Yes* or *No.* The purpose of these questions is to check understanding of new vocabulary.

Practice

- Direct Ss' attention to Exercise **1B**. Model the task. Hold up the Student's Book. Say to a S: *Point to the last name.* The S points to the appropriate line on the registration form.
- Ss in pairs. Say to one S: *Say the words in Exercise 1B.* Say to his or her partner: *Point to the registration form.*
- Ss in small groups. Ask Ss to take turns pointing to and naming different items in the picture. If the word is correct, the group members say *Yes*; if it is incorrect, they say *No.* Walk around and help as needed.

Expansion activity *(whole group)*

- Point to the map pictured behind Mr. Clark. Ask Ss: *What is this?* (It's a map.) Point to your country on the map (or on a larger map, if you have one). Say: *My name is _____. I am from _____.*
- Ask Ss: *What's your name? Where are you from?* Ss can use single word answers. Go around the class until as many Ss as possible have had a chance to answer.

Expansion activity *(whole group)*

- Turn Ss' attention to the filing cabinet right next to the map. Ask Ss: *What is this?* Encourage Ss to say *cabinet* or *filing cabinet.*
- Point to the top drawer. Tell Ss: *A–G means A, B, C, D, E, F, G.* Ask Ss: *What does H–P mean?* (H, I, J, K, L, M, N, O, P) Ask Ss: *What does Q–Z mean?* (Q, R, S, T, U, V, W, X, Y, Z)
- Write on the board:
  1. A–G *2. H–P* *3. Q–Z*
  Ask a S: *What is your first name? What is your last name?* Ask the S: *Where do I write your first name, 1, 2, or 3? Where do I write your last name?*
- Write the S's first and last names in the appropriate columns. Go around the class until as many Ss as possible have had a chance to answer. If necessary, take time to review the letters of the alphabet. Turn to the Welcome unit if additional practice is needed.

Lesson A Get ready

Presentation

- Books closed. Write the name, address, and telephone number of your school on the board. Ask a S to circle the area code. Ask another S to circle the zip code.
- Ask Ss: *What is your area code? What is your zip code?*

Practice

- Books open. Direct Ss' attention to Exercise **2A**. Read the instructions aloud.
- [Class Audio CD1 track 9] Play or read the audio program (see audio script, page T-151). Ss circle the words they hear. Repeat the program as needed.
- Check answers. Ask: *What did you circle?* Ask Ss to write the words on the board. Point to the words. Say: *Repeat after me.* Say each word.
- Ask a S to write the words that were not circled on the board: *city, country, zip code.* Point to the words. Say: *Repeat after me.* Say each word. Listen to Ss' pronunciation and correct as needed.

Culture tip
You may want to ask Ss if they have a middle name. Middle names are not common in many cultures. In some cultures, a middle name is the last name of a parent.

- Direct Ss' attention to the pictures in Exercise **2B**. Hold up the Student's Book. Point to the first picture. Say: *Last name.* Point to the second picture. Ask a S: *What's this?* (first name)
- Continue asking Ss about the rest of the pictures.
- Read aloud the instructions for Exercise **2B**.
- [Class Audio CD1 track 9] Play or read the audio program again. Pause after the first conversation. Ask: *Which picture matches conversation A?* (picture number 6). Point to the handwritten *a* next to number 6. Be sure Ss understand the task. Then play or read the complete audio program. Ss complete the task individually.

Learner persistence *(individual work)*

- [Self-Study Audio CD track 9] Exercises **2A** and **2B** are recorded on the Ss' self-study CD at the back of the Student's Book. Ss can listen to the CD at home for reinforcement and review. They can also listen for self-directed learning when class attendance is not possible.

Comprehension check

- Write the numbers *1–6* on the board. Ask a few Ss to come to the board and write the correct answers to Exercise **2B** next to each number.
- Read aloud the second part of the instructions for Exercise **2B**.
- [Class Audio CD1 track 9] Play or read the audio program again. Pause after each conversation. Point to a letter of the conversation on the board. Ask: *Is this correct?* Ask another S to make any corrections.

Application

- Books closed. Write on the board: *My first name is* _____.
- Complete the sentence using your first name. Read the sentence. Erase your name. Ask a S to come to the board and complete the sentence with his or her first name.
- Direct Ss' attention to Exercise **2C** and read the instructions aloud. Be sure Ss understand the task. Ss complete the exercise individually. Help as needed.

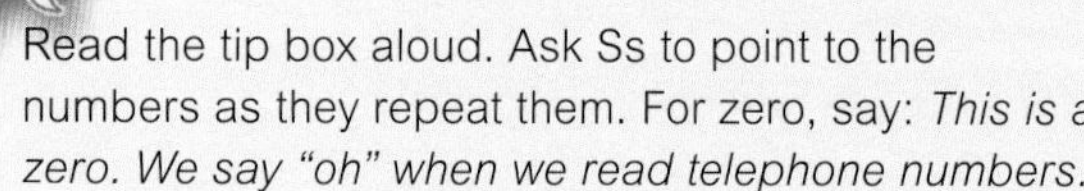

Read the tip box aloud. Ask Ss to point to the numbers as they repeat them. For zero, say: *This is a zero. We say "oh" when we read telephone numbers.*

- Read aloud the second part of the instructions for Exercise **2C**. Ask two Ss to read the example.
- Ss complete the exercise in pairs. Help as needed.

Learner persistence *(student pairs)*

- Ss in pairs. Give each S an envelope. Say: *Ask your partner for personal information. Write your partner's name, address, city, state, and zip code on the envelope.*
- Model the activity with a S. First ask for the S's name and address. Write it on a large envelope you've drawn on the board. Tell the same S: *Now ask me my name and address and write it on your envelope.*
- Tell Ss that the pairs are now "buddies." Explain the word, and tell Ss buddies will help each other in class.
- Collect and save the envelopes, and ask buddies to send assignments to Ss who miss classes.

Evaluation

- Have Ss look at the lesson focus on the board. Ask Ss to give you examples of personal information.
- Check off the lesson focus as Ss demonstrate an understanding of what they have learned in the lesson.

More Ventures *(whole group, pairs, individual)*
Assign appropriate exercises from the *Teacher's Toolkit Audio CD / CD-ROM, Add Ventures,* or the *Workbook.*

2 Listening

SELF-STUDY AUDIO CD **A** **Listen.** Circle the words you hear.

address	country	middle name
area code	first name	telephone number
city	last name	zip code

SELF-STUDY AUDIO CD **B** **Listen again.** Write the letter of the conversation.

1. c

2. e
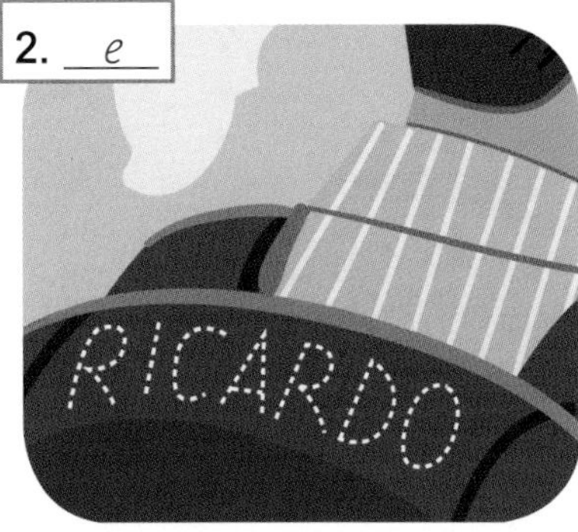

3. b

4. f

5. d

6. a
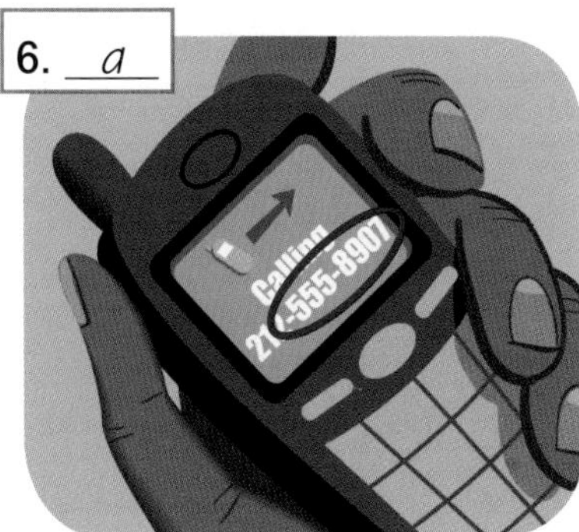

Listen again. Check your answers.

C **Write.** Complete the sentences about yourself.

1. My first name is ___(Answers will vary.)___.
2. My last name is ______________________.
3. My area code is ______________________.
4. My telephone number is ______________________.

Talk with a partner. Talk about yourself.

My first name is Dahlia.

My first name is Yuri.

Saying telephone numbers

Stop at each number. Say *oh* for *zero.*

5 5 5 - 2 0 1 6

five - five - five *two - oh - one - six*

Lesson B What's your name?

1 Grammar focus: possessive adjectives

Questions		
What's	your	name?
What's	his	name?
What's	her	name?
What are	their	names?

Answers	
My	name is Svetlana.
His	name is Steve.
Her	name is Mary.
Their	names are Ted and Rob.

What's = What is

2 Practice

A Write. Complete the sentences.
Use *his*, *her*, or *their*.

1. *A* What's _his_ first name?
   B _His_ first name is Alfred.
2. *A* What's _her_ first name?
   B _Her_ first name is Sue.
3. *A* What's _his_ first name?
   B _His_ first name is Tom.
4. *A* What's _their_ last name?
   B _Their_ last name is Jones.

Listen and repeat. Then practice with a partner.

B Talk with a partner. Look at the student directory.
Change the **bold** words and make conversations.

A What's **his** telephone number?
B **His** telephone number is **555-9314**.

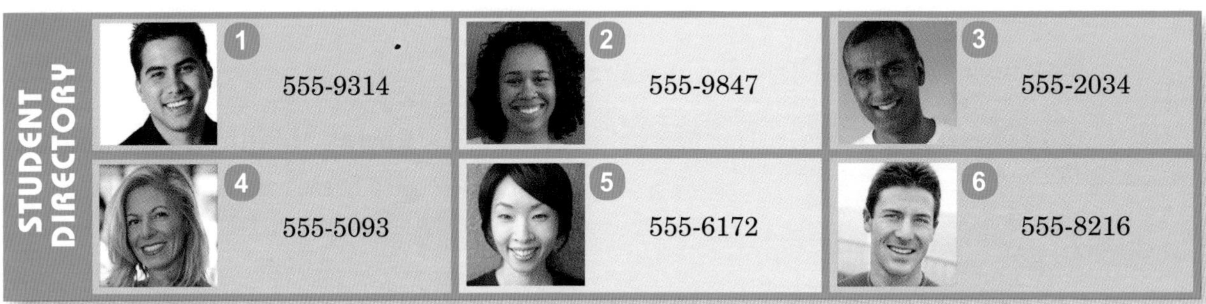

Lesson objectives

- Introduce possessive adjectives
- Practice *Wh-* questions and answers
- Practice saying telephone numbers and spelling names

Warm-up and review

- Before class. Write today's lesson focus on the board.
  Lesson B: Possessive adjectives
  my *his*
  your *her*
  their
- Begin class. Books closed. While pointing to yourself, ask: *What's **my** first name? What's **my** last name?* Write responses on the board: *Your first name is* _____. *Your last name is* _____.
- Ask a S: *What's **your** first name?* (Give extra emphasis to the possessive adjective.) Write the response on the board: *My first name is* _____.
- Ask all the male Ss to stand up. Point to each male S. Ask: *What's **his** first name?* Write on the board: *His first name is* _____. Elicit responses. Then invite Ss to sit.
- Ask all the female Ss to stand up. Point to each. Ask: *What's **her** first name?* Write on the board: *Her first name is* _____. Elicit responses. Then invite Ss to sit.
- Ask any two Ss to stand up. Point to both of them. Ask: *What are **their** first names?* Write on the board: *Their first names are* _____ *and* _____.

Teaching tip

If you have a married couple in your class, ask them to stand in front of the class. Point to them and ask: *What's their last name?* Write the response on the board: *Their last name is* _____.

Presentation

- Books open. Direct Ss' attention to the grammar chart in Exercise **1**. Read the questions and answers aloud. Ask Ss to repeat after you. Point to the contraction *What's*. Hold up one finger and say: *One word = What's*. Hold up two fingers and say: *Two words = What is. They are equal. They are the same*. You could introduce the word *contractions* to talk about these short forms.
- Ss in pairs. Have students practice reading the grammar chart to each other. Say to one S: *Read the questions*. Say to his or her partner: *Read the answers*.

Comprehension check

- Ask Ss questions from the grammar chart. Point to yourself and ask: *What's my name?* Point to a female student and ask: *What's her name?* Continue practicing the different possessive adjectives until Ss show an understanding of the teaching point. If Ss don't know each other's names yet, they can ask: *What's your name?*

Practice

- Direct Ss' attention to Exercise **2A** and read the instructions aloud. Ask two Ss to read the example question and answer. Be sure Ss understand the task.
- Ss complete the exercise individually. Help as needed.
- [Class Audio CD1 track 10] Read aloud the second part of the instructions for Exercise **2A**. Play or read the audio program (see audio script, page T-151). Have Ss check their answers as they listen and repeat. Correct pronunciation as needed.
- Ask Ss to come to the board and write the questions and answers. Ask different Ss to read them aloud. Ask Ss to make any necessary corrections on the board.
- Ss in pairs. Ask Ss to choose role *A* or *B* and practice the questions and answers. Then, have students switch roles and practice again. Walk around and help as needed.

Expansion activity *(small group)*

- Play a name game. Put Ss in groups of five. The first S says his or her name. The second S says the first S's name, then his or her own name. The third S says the first S's name, then the second S's name, then his or her own name. The game continues until all Ss have introduced themselves.

Practice

- Write on the board: *0 1 2 3 4*. Point to *0*. Ask: *What's this?* (zero)
- Point to and read each number aloud. Ask Ss to repeat.
- Write on the board: *(201) 555-1234*. Read the number aloud twice; be sure to pronounce the *0* as "oh." Ask Ss to repeat the numbers after you. Remind Ss that *zero* is pronounced "oh" in telephone numbers.
- Direct Ss' attention to Exercise **2B** and read the instructions aloud. Model the example with a S. As you read *his*, point to the picture of the man in number 1. As you read *555-9314*, point to the phone number next to the man's picture. Be sure Ss understand the task.
- Ss complete the exercise in pairs. Help as needed.
- Ask pairs to perform the conversations for the class.

Expansion activity *(whole group)*

- If you want to expand the grammar presentation, turn to the grammar charts at the back of the Student's Book. Practice making sentences using other possessive pronouns: *our, your* (plural), *its*.

Lesson B What's your name?

Presentation

- Books closed. Ask a S with an unusual name: *What's your first name?* Elicit: *My first name is _____.* Ask: *How do you spell that?* Write the name on the board. Ask: *What's your last name? How do you spell that?* Write the last name on the board.
- Books open. Direct Ss' attention to Exercise **2C** and read the instructions aloud.
- [Class Audio CD1 track 11] Play or read the audio program (see audio script, page T-151). Ask students to read along.
- [Class Audio CD1 track 12] Play or read the audio program (see audio script, page T-151). Listen to Ss' pronunciation as they repeat each line of the conversation. Correct pronunciation as needed.

Teaching tip
A review of pronouncing the letters of the alphabet might be helpful. Write the alphabet on the board. Ask the class to read the entire alphabet aloud.

Practice

- Read aloud the second part of the instructions for Exercise **2C**.
- Write on the board:

First name	*Last name*
Jennifer	*Kent*

- Model the activity. Ask a S his or her name, as in the model conversation. Write the S's first and last name in the appropriate column on the board exactly as he or she spells the name to you.
- Ss complete the task in small groups, using the conversation from Exercise **2C** as a model and their own information. Walk around and help as needed.
- Ask several Ss to write a classmate's first and last name in the appropriate column on the board.

Useful language
Read the tip box aloud and have Ss repeat after you. Have Ss make conversations using the Useful language in place of *How do you spell that?*

Expansion activity *(whole group)*

- Show Ss pictures of famous people. Ask: *What is his / her first name? How do you spell that? What is his / her last name? Please spell that.* Write the names in the chart.

Community building *(whole group)*

- Do the preceding expansion activity using pictures of well-known community people so that Ss learn about them.

Application

- Point to a S and say: *His / Her first name is _____. His / Her last name is _____.*
- Have the S introduce another S in the same way.
- Direct Ss' attention to Exercise **3A** and read the instructions aloud. Ask a S to read the example aloud.

Teaching tip
Tell Ss that after a person is introduced, it is polite to say *Nice to meet you.* The correct response after this is to say *Nice to meet you, too.* Ask Ss to introduce each other in this way.

Culture note
Read the culture note aloud. Ask: *Who has two first names? Who has two last names?* Ask these Ss to write their names on the board.

- Direct Ss to Exercise **3B**. Ask pairs to read the examples.
- Ask different Ss to read the examples again, but say: *This time, use your own names.*
- Ss complete the task in pairs. Help as needed.

Teaching tip
Explain that *Good morning* is a morning greeting. *Hi* and *Hello* are other greetings. *Good night* is not a greeting. We say *good night* only when we're saying good-bye or when we're going to bed. Talk about gestures used with greetings (handshake, hug, kiss, wave, bow) and with whom the gestures are used.

Evaluation

- Direct Ss' attention to the lesson focus written on the board. Show Ss the pictures on page 8. Say: *Make sentences about the people.* (His name is Alfred. Her name is Sue. His telephone number is 555-9314.)
- Check off the items as Ss demonstrate an understanding of what they have learned in the lesson.

More Ventures *(whole group, pairs, individual)*
Assign appropriate exercises from the *Teacher's Toolkit Audio CD / CD-ROM, Add Ventures,* or the *Workbook.*

C **Listen.** Then listen and repeat.

A What's your name?
B **Jennifer Kent.**
A Sorry. What's your first name?
B My first name is **Jennifer**.
A How do you spell that?
B **J-E-N-N-I-F-E-R.**
A OK. What's your last name?
B **Kent. K-E-N-T.**

Useful language
Please spell that.
*How do you spell **Jennifer**?*

Talk in groups. Ask questions and write the names.

First name	Last name
Jennifer	*Kent*
(Answers will vary.)	

3 Communicate

A **Talk** with your classmates. Introduce a classmate.

This is my new classmate. Her first name is Jennifer. Her last name is Kent.

B **Talk** with a partner. Take turns and make new conversations.

A Good morning.
B Good morning.
A My name is Anna Gray. What's your name?
B Kate Harris.
A Nice to meet you.
B Nice to meet you, too.

A Hi. My name is Peter.
B Hi. My name is Alan.
A Nice to meet you, Alan.
B Nice to meet you, too, Peter.

Culture note
Some people have two first names:
Mei-Hwa
Some people have two last names:
Baker-Price

Lesson C Are you from Canada?

1 Grammar focus: subject pronouns; simple present of *be*

Questions

Are you Is he Is she Are they	from Canada?

Answers

Yes,	I am. he is. she is. they are.	No,	I'm not. I'm he isn't. He's she isn't. She's they aren't. They're	from the United States.

I'm = I am He's = He is	She's = She is They're = They are

isn't = is not aren't = are not

2 Practice

A Write. Complete the sentences.

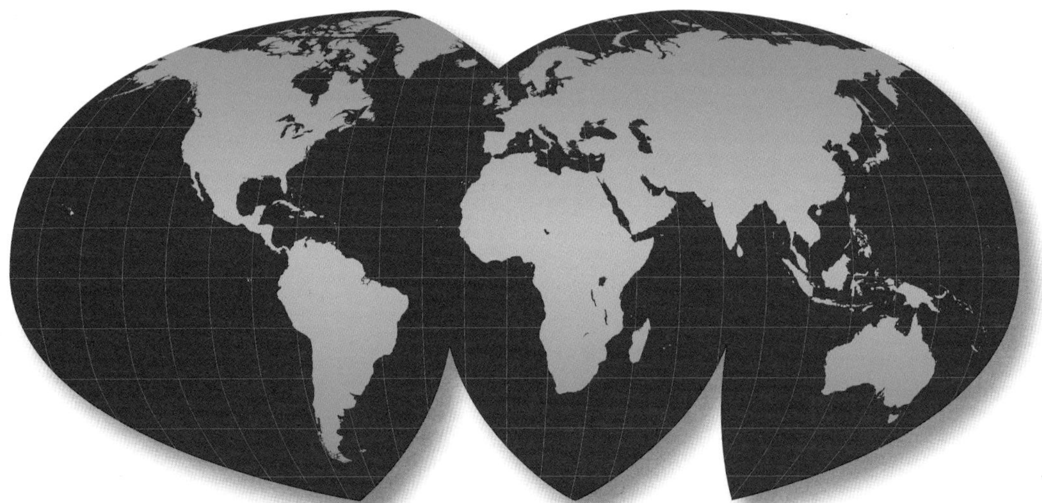

1. **A** Are you from Canada?
   B No, I'm not .
2. **A** Are they from Somalia?
   B Yes, they are .
3. **A** Is she from Russia?
   B Yes, she is .
4. **A** Is he from Mexico?
   B Yes, he is .
5. **A** Is she from China?
   B No, she isn't .
6. **A** Are they from Brazil?
   B No, they aren't .
7. **A** Is he from Ecuador?
   B No, he isn't .
8. **A** Are you from Colombia?
   B Yes, I am .

Listen and repeat. Then practice with a partner.

Lesson objectives

- Introduce simple present of *be* questions, statements, short answers, and contractions
- Review subject pronouns

Warm-up and review

- Before class. Write today's lesson focus on the board.
  Lesson C: Subject pronouns and the verb be

Are you?	*I am*	*I'm not*
Is he?	*He is*	*He isn't*
Is she?	*She is*	*She isn't*
Are they?	*They are*	*They aren't*

- Before class. Bring in a world map, a map of the United States, or a city map and display it at the front of the class. If a map is not available, draw an outline of a world map and a map of the United States on the board.
- Begin class. Books closed. Review Lesson B. Ask different Ss: *What's your name? What's his name* (pointing to a male S)*? What's her name* (pointing to a female)*? What are their names* (pointing to a few Ss)*?*
- Introduce the lesson focus. Point to a place on the map and say: *I'm from* (the United States). Ask different Ss: *Are you?* Elicit: *Yes, I am.* or *No, I'm not.*
- Ask different Ss: *Are you from* _____ (Mexico, China, Ethiopia, etc.)*?* Elicit *Yes / No* answers.

Presentation

- Books open. Direct Ss' attention to the grammar chart in Exercise **1**. Read the questions and answers aloud. Ask Ss to repeat.
- Put Ss in groups of three. Have Ss practice reading the grammar chart to one another.

Contractions

Read the tip box aloud. Point to *I'm*. Say: *This is a contraction. It is short for "I am."* Hold up two fingers and say: *He is*. Put down one finger and say: *He's. This is short for "He is."* Continue to introduce the contractions.

Teaching tip

An explanation of *he's* vs. *his* might be helpful. Write *he's* and *his* on the board. Read the words aloud. Ask Ss to repeat. Correct pronunciation as needed. Explain that *his* is a possessive pronoun: ***His** name is Bill. He's* means *he is*: ***He's** from Mexico.*

Comprehension check

- Review subject pronouns. Ask individual Ss *Yes / No* questions and elicit answers, for example: *Are you from the United States (Korea, Mexico, Ethiopia)? Is he from _____? Is she from _____? Are they from _____?* Elicit *Yes / No* answers. Point to the places on the map.

Practice

- Direct Ss' attention to Exercise **2A**. Ask Ss to look at the map. Ask if they can find Canada on the map. Help Ss locate Canada. Continue for the other countries mentioned in the exercise. Encourage Ss to look for and identify other countries they know.

Teaching tip

On pages 152–153 of the Student's Book, there is a list of countries and nationalities. Ss can use this list to learn names of countries of their classmates.

- Read the instructions aloud.
- Ask two Ss to read the example aloud. Write the example on the board. Be sure Ss understand the task.
- Ss complete the exercise individually. Help as needed.
- Ask Ss to write their answers on the board. Ask different Ss to read the answers aloud. Ask other Ss to correct the answers if needed.
- [Class Audio CD1 track 13] Read the last instruction for Exercise **2A**. Play or read the audio program (see audio script, page T-151). Listen to Ss' pronunciation as they repeat the conversations. Correct pronunciation.
- Say: *Practice with a partner.* Have Ss practice the conversations in pairs. Walk around and help as needed.
- Ask pairs to read the conversations for the class.

Community building *(small group)*

- Before class. For each small group, write the subject pronouns on index cards: *I, you, he, she, they*. Write the names of 12 countries (including the countries represented in the class) on different cards. Keep the two sets of cards separate.
- In class. Ask Ss to take turns choosing one card from each pile and asking a classmate a question using the words on the cards (e.g., *he* and *Colombia* = *Is he from Colombia?*). When the classmate answers, Ss return the cards to the bottom of the two piles and repeat the task until all the cards have been used.
- Ask Ss to introduce their classmates. Review introductions from Lesson B: *This is my new classmate, _____. He is from Colombia.*

Expansion activity *(whole group)*

- If you want to expand the grammar presentation, turn to the grammar charts at the back of the Student's Book. Practice making sentences using other pronouns: *we, you* (plural), *it* with the simple present of *be*.

Lesson C Are you from Canada?

Presentation

- Point to the picture in Exercise **2B**. Ask Ss: *What do you see?* Write responses on the board: *people, camera.*
- Point to each person in the picture. Ask: *Is he / she from* (name of a country)*?* Ss can read the country names on each T-shirt in the picture. Elicit *Yes / No* answers. For *No* answers, encourage Ss to give long answers. (No, he isn't / they aren't. He's / They're from India.) Review long answers in the grammar chart on page 10.

Practice

- Read aloud the instructions for Exercise **2B**. Model the example with two different Ss. You read first. As you read *he,* point to the man in the group picture. As you read *they,* point to the two women in the group picture.
- Model number 1 with a S to be sure Ss understand how to use the group picture and the cues.
- Ss complete the exercise in pairs, taking turns asking and answering questions. Walk around and help as needed.
- Ask pairs to perform their conversations for the class.

Expansion activity (small groups)

- Ask two Ss to stand up. Model the activity with the Ss. Point to one S. Ask the other S: *Is he / she from India?* Elicit: *Yes, he is. / No, he isn't. He's from Mexico.* Continue with more pairs.

Application

- Books closed. Ask a S: *Where are you from,* (S's name)*?* Elicit: *I'm from* (name of country). Ask: *How do you spell that?*
- Write on the board:

<u>Name</u>	<u>Country</u>
(S's name)	*(S's native country)*

  Continue to ask Ss or have Ss ask and answer the questions.
- Direct Ss' attention to Exercise **2C** and read the instructions aloud.
- [Class Audio CD1 track 14] Play or read the audio program (see audio script, page T-152). Listen to Ss' pronunciation as they repeat each line of the conversation. Repeat the program as needed.
- Model the example with a S. The S speaks first. This time, use your own information to answer the question. Make sure Ss understand that they are to answer with their own information.
- Say: *Now practice with a partner.* Help as needed.

> **Useful language**
> Read the tip box aloud. Ask Ss to repeat the questions after you. Model the conversation again using *Where do you come from?* instead of *Where are you from?*

Expansion activity (student pairs)

- Remind Ss about the Useful language box on page 9. Say: *You can say "Please spell that" or "How do you spell* (name of country)*?"*
- Encourage Ss to practice the conversation again, using these different phrases.

Application

- Direct Ss' attention to Exercise **3** and read the instructions aloud.
- Ask two Ss to read the conversation aloud. Then model the task again. Point to a S and say: *This is* (student's name). *Where is she from?* or *Where does she come from?* Have Ss guess by asking and answering *Yes / No* questions until they discover where the S is from. Be sure Ss understand the task.
- Ss complete the exercise in groups. Help as needed.

Learner persistence (small groups)

- Ask Ss to find classmates who come from the same country. Have Ss walk around and ask: *Are you from* (name of their country)*?* Ss write the names of the Ss from the same country. Be sure these Ss speak the same language in their country of origin.
- Put same-language Ss together. If they are comfortable exchanging telephone numbers, have Ss make a telephone directory. If one of the Ss misses class, the other Ss can call to explain the lesson.

Evaluation

- Direct Ss' attention to the lesson focus written on the board. Have Ss turn to the picture in Exercise **2B** and ask and answer questions.
- Have Ss make sentences about their own names and nationalities and those of their classmates.
- Check off the lesson focus as Ss demonstrate understanding of what they have learned in the lesson.

> ***More Ventures*** *(whole group, pairs, individual)*
> Assign appropriate exercises from the *Teacher's Toolkit Audio CD / CD-ROM, Add Ventures,* or the *Workbook.*

B **Talk** with a partner. Change the **bold** words and make conversations.

A **Is he** from **Mexico**?
B Yes, **he is**.

A **Are they** from **the United States**?
B No, **they aren't**. **They're** from **India**.

1. Japan?
2. the United States?
3. Mexico?
4. India?
5. Mexico?
6. Japan?

C **Listen and repeat.** Then practice with a partner.

A Where are you from, **Katia**?
B I'm from **Brazil**.
A **Brazil**? How do you spell that?
B **B-R-A-Z-I-L.**

Useful language
Where are you from?
Where do you come from?

3 Communicate

Talk in groups. Where are your classmates from? Make guesses.

A This is Katia. Where is she from?
B Is she from Colombia?
A No, she isn't.
B Is she from Brazil?
A Yes, she is.

Lesson D Reading

1 Before you read

Talk. Svetlana starts school today. Look at the registration form. Answer the questions.

1. What's her last name?
2. What's her telephone number?

REGISTRATION FORM

Name	*Svetlana Kulik*
Phone	*(707) 555-9073*
Address	*1041 Main Street*
	Napa, California 94558

2 Read

Listen and read.

A New Student

Svetlana Kulik is a new student. She is from Russia. Now she lives in Napa, California. Her address is 1041 Main Street. Her zip code is 94558. Her area code is 707. Her telephone number is 555-9073.

Addresses with 3 numbers
832 Main Street
eight thirty-two

Addresses with 4 numbers
1041 Main Street
ten forty-one

3 After you read

A Read the sentences. Are they correct? Circle *Yes* or *No*.

1. Svetlana is a new teacher. Yes (No)
2. Her last name is Kulik. (Yes) No
3. She is from Colombia. Yes (No)
4. Her address is 1014 Main Street. Yes (No)
5. Her zip code is 94558. (Yes) No
6. Her area code is 555-9073. Yes (No)

Write. Correct the sentences.

1. Svetlana is a new student.

B Write. Answer the questions about Svetlana.

1. What is her last name? *Her last name is Kulik.*
2. Is she from Russia? *Yes, she is.*
3. What is her address? *Her address is 1041 Main Street.*
4. What is her telephone number? *Her telephone number is 555-9073.*

Lesson objectives

- Introduce and read "A New Student"
- Practice using new topic-related words
- Look at addresses with three and four numbers

Warm-up and review

- Before class. Write today's lesson focus on the board.
  Lesson D:
  Read and understand "A New Student"
  Learn words about personal information
- Begin class. Books open. Show Ss the picture on page 6. Point to Svetlana. Ask: *Who is she?* Elicit: *Her name is Svetlana. She is a student.* Point to the registration form. Ask: *What is this?* Elicit: *It's a registration form.*

Teaching tip

It might be helpful to show Ss an example of the registration form that they filled out in order to be in the class. Say: *This is a registration form for our school. What personal information is on this form?*

Presentation

- Direct Ss' attention to the picture in Exercise **1**. Say: *This is Svetlana again. This is her registration form.*
- Read aloud the instructions for Exercise **1**. Ask a S to read the questions aloud. Elicit answers from the class.
- Direct Ss' attention to Exercise **2** and point to the title "A New Student." Ask: *What is this reading about?* Elicit: *It's about a new student.* Say: *Now you will listen to the paragraph.*
- [Class Audio CD1 track 15] Play or read the audio program and ask Ss to read along (see audio script, page T-152). Repeat as needed.

Teaching tip

Here are other ways of presenting the reading: Ss read silently; Ss take turns reading individual sentences aloud to the class; Ss read to each other; Ss listen and repeat the sentences. It might be helpful to remind Ss: *We don't say "zero" with telephone numbers. We say "oh."*

Read the tip box aloud. Say: *We read addresses with three numbers like this: eight thirty-two Main Street. We read addresses with four numbers like this: ten forty-one Main Street.* Ask Ss to repeat the addresses after you. Have Ss write three- and four-number addresses on the board. Dictate the numbers. Ask other Ss to read the addresses on the board.

Learner persistence *(individual work)*

- [Self-Study Audio CD track 10] Exercise **2** is recorded on the Ss' self-study CD at the back of the Student's Book. Ss can listen to the CD at home for reinforcement and review. They can also listen to the CD for self-directed learning when class attendance is not possible.

Comprehension check

- Read aloud the instructions for Exercise **3A**. Ask a S to read the example aloud.
- Ask: *Is Svetlana a new teacher?* Point to where *No* is circled for number 1. Be sure Ss understand the task.
- Ss complete the exercise individually. Help as needed.
- Check answers with the class.
- Ask Ss to take out a piece of paper. Read aloud the last part of the instructions for Exercise **3A**.
- Model the task of correcting the sentences. Point to *No* for number 1 in Exercise **3A**. Read the sentence aloud. Tell Ss: *This sentence is incorrect. Tell me the correct sentence. Svetlana is a new . . .* (student). Write on the board: *Svetlana is a new student.*
- Ss complete the exercise individually. Help as needed.
- Ask Ss to write their answers on the board. Then ask different Ss to read the answers aloud. Ask: *Are the sentences correct?* Make any necessary corrections on the board.

Practice

- Read aloud the instructions for Exercise **3B**.
- Ask a S to read the first question. Elicit the answer from the class and write it on the board: *Her last name is Kulik.*
- Ss complete the exercise individually. Help as needed.
- Ask individual Ss to write their sentences on the board. Ask: *Are the sentences correct?* Make any necessary corrections on the board.

Expansion activity *(small groups)*

- Before class. Write or type the paragraph "A New Student" on a piece of paper, breaking sentences at the end of each line (*Svetlana Kulik is a new student. She is from . . . Russia. Now she lives in Napa, California. Her . . .* etc.). Cut the sentences out separately. Put each sentence in a different envelope.
- In class. Books closed. Put Ss in small groups. Give each group an envelope.
- Ask Ss to read the sentence in their envelope and guess the next sentence.
- Ask Ss to find the group that has the next sentence. Walk around and help as needed.
- Ss re-create the story. Have one person from each group come to the front of the class. Ss arrange themselves in the order of the story and read their sentence so as to tell Svetlana's story.

Lesson D Reading

Warm-up and review

- Books closed. Introduce new vocabulary. Write these titles on the board.
  Mr. *Miss* *Mrs.* *Ms.*
- Point to the words. Say: *These are titles.* Read each title aloud and ask Ss to repeat. Say: *I am (Mr. / Miss / Mrs. / Ms.)* _____. Write your name on the board.
- Ask Ss to tell you their title and name. If necessary, explain that *Mr.* is for a man, *Ms.* is for a woman, etc.

Culture note
Tell Ss that in American culture, titles are used in formal settings. Teachers in schools and universities are usually called by their title and last name. Teachers in adult education classes are often called by their first name.

- Write *middle name* on the board.
- Ask Ss if they have a middle name and write their full name with the middle name included. Tell Ss that middle names are not common in many cultures. In some cultures, a middle name is the last name of a parent.
- Circle the first letter of the middle name and say: *This is the middle initial.* Rewrite the full name using only the middle initial.

Presentation

- Books open. Direct Ss' attention to the ID card in the picture dictionary. Ask: *What do you see?* Elicit responses such as *a student ID, a first name, a last name, a city, a zip code.*
- Direct Ss' attention to word bank words in Exercise **4A**. Say: *Repeat the words after me.* Say each word. Listen and correct Ss' pronunciation as they repeat.
- Say: *Write the words in the picture dictionary.* Point to the first example, which has been done.
- Ss complete the exercise individually. Help as needed.

Comprehension check

- [Class Audio CD1 track 16] Play or read the audio program (see audio script, page T-152). Ss should check their answers and repeat the words after they hear them. Repeat the audio program if necessary.

Learner persistence *(individual work)*

- [Self-Study Audio CD track 11] Exercise **4A** is recorded on the Ss' self-study CD at the back of the Student's Book. Ss can listen to the CD at home for reinforcement and review. They can also listen to the CD for self-directed learning when class attendance is not possible.

Practice

- Write your school's address on the board. Point to the zip code. Ask: *What is this?* Elicit: *It's the zip code.* Repeat the process with *city* and *state.*
- Show Ss a school ID card or any other ID card that you have. Ask: *What is this?* Elicit: *It's an ID card.* It might be helpful to explain that *ID* stands for "identification." Say: *This card tells who you are.*
- Draw an example of a blank ID card on the board.
- Direct Ss' attention to Exercise **4B** and read the instructions aloud. Explain that Ss will use the words from the picture dictionary to ask questions and make an ID card for their partner.
- Ask two Ss to read aloud the example question and answer. Ask pairs of Ss to ask and answer other questions. Write the answers in the blank ID on the board.
- Ss complete the exercise in pairs. Help as needed.

Teaching tip
If Ss are not comfortable using their real addresses, they can use the school address instead.

Expansion activity *(whole class)*

- Draw several blank ID cards on the board. Ask for volunteers to write on the board.
- Ask other Ss to give information (address, apartment number, signature, title, etc.) for the volunteers to complete the ID card.

Evaluation

- Direct Ss' attention to the lesson focus on the board.
- Put a check mark next to *Read and understand "A New Student."*
- Elicit sentences for each of the vocabulary words in the picture dictionary.
- Check off each part of the lesson focus as Ss demonstrate an understanding of what they have learned in the lesson.

More Ventures *(whole group, pairs, individual)*
Assign appropriate exercises from the *Teacher's Toolkit Audio CD / CD-ROM, Add Ventures,* or the *Workbook.*

4 Picture dictionary Personal information

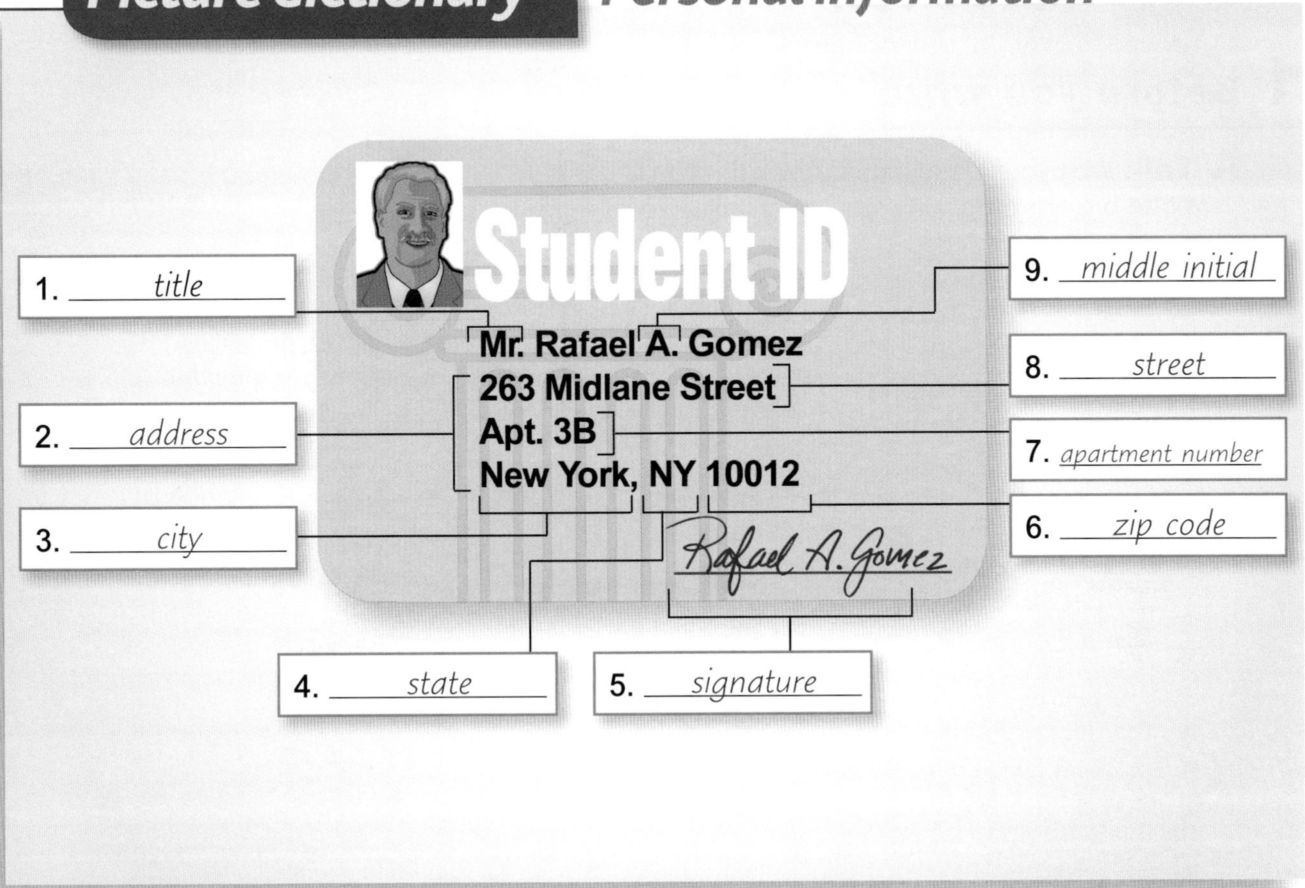

Student ID

Mr. Rafael A. Gomez
263 Midlane Street
Apt. 3B
New York, NY 10012

Rafael A. Gomez

1. title
2. address
3. city
4. state
5. signature
6. zip code
7. apartment number
8. street
9. middle initial

A **Write** the words in the picture dictionary. Then listen and repeat.

address	middle initial	street
apartment number	signature	title
city	state	zip code

Culture note

Use *Mr.* for a man.
Use *Ms.* for a woman.
Use *Mrs.* for a married woman.
Use *Miss* for an unmarried woman.

B **Talk** with a partner. Ask and answer questions. Complete the student ID with your partner's information.

What's your name?

My name is Rafael.

Lesson E Writing

1 Before you write

A Talk with your classmates. Ask questions. Write the answers.

A What's your name?
B My name is **Liliana Lopez**.
A What's your telephone number?
B My telephone number is **555-2904**.
A Where are you from?
B I'm from **Mexico**.

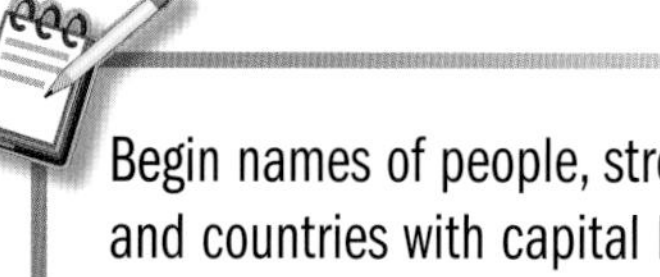

Begin names of people, streets, cities, states, and countries with capital letters.
These are capital letters: *A B C D E*
These are lowercase letters: *a b c d e*

Name	Telephone number	Country
Liliana Lopez	*555-2904*	*Mexico*
(Answers will vary.)		

B Write. Complete the sentences. Use the words in the box.

address	last name	zip code
area code	telephone number	

Svetlana is a new student.

1. Her *last name* is Kulik. She is from Russia.
2. Her *address* is 1041 Main Street.
3. Her *zip code* is 94558.
4. Her *telephone number* is 555-9073.
5. Her *area code* is 707.

Lesson objectives
- Discuss and write about personal information
- Learn about capital letters

Warm-up and review

- Before class. Write today's lesson focus on the board.
  Lesson E:
  Write your first name, last name, address, zip code, telephone number, country
- Begin class. Books closed. Ask a S: *What's your name?* Elicit: *My name is* _____. Ask: *What's your telephone number?* Elicit: *My telephone number is* _____. Ask: *Where are you from?* Elicit: *I'm from* _____.

Teaching tip
If Ss are not comfortable giving out their real telephone numbers, tell them to use the school number.

Presentation

- Books open. Direct Ss' attention to Exercise **1A** and read the instructions aloud.
- Model the conversation with a S. Model the conversation with a different S, but tell the S: *Now use your own name, telephone number, and country.*
- Tell Ss: *Stand up. Talk to your classmates. Write their personal information in the chart.* Walk around and help as needed.
- Check answers with the class. Write these column heads on the board.
  Name　*Telephone number*　*Country*
- Ask different Ss to write one classmate's name, telephone number, and country on the board.
- Call on different Ss. Say: *Tell me about* (name of student). Encourage Ss to make sentences using information from the board, such as: (Name of student) *is from* _____. *Her / His telephone number is* _____.

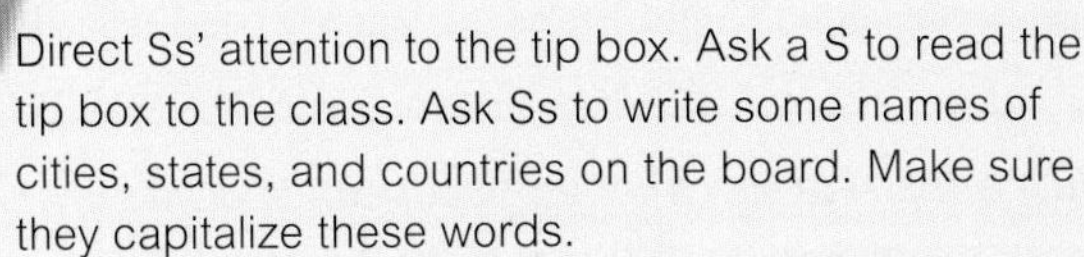

Direct Ss' attention to the tip box. Ask a S to read the tip box to the class. Ask Ss to write some names of cities, states, and countries on the board. Make sure they capitalize these words.

Expansion activity (whole group)

- Ask Ss to add columns to the chart: *Title, Middle initial,* and *Address.*
- Tell Ss: *Talk to your classmates. Write their title, middle initial, and address (or school address).*

Expansion activity (whole group)

- Divide the class into two or three teams for a capital-letter writing game.
- Draw a vertical line (or lines) on the board to divide it into sections. Say: *This is a contest. I will say a name. One person from each team will go to the board and write the name. Remember to use capital letters.*
- Have each team stand in line several feet from its section of the board. Say a name and have the first student in each line go to the board and write the name as quickly as possible, and then go to the back of the line. Use the following names and add some of your own:
  New York
  the United States
  (the name of your city)
  (the name of your state)
  (the name of a street in your city)
  Japan
  India
  Mrs. Smith
  Miss Johnson
- Give a point to the team that writes each name correctly in the shortest time. Then, repeat the process with the next name. Tally the points at the end of the game. The team with the most points wins.

Comprehension check

- Write the following on the board.
  Address:
  Area code:
  Last name:
  Country:
  Telephone number:
  Zip code:
- Ask Ss to come to the board and write an example next to each of the words, for example: *Country: China.*
- Direct Ss' attention to Exercise **1B** and read the instructions aloud. Ask a S to read the example aloud.
- Ss complete the exercise individually. Walk around and help as needed.
- Check answers with the class. Ask Ss to write their sentences on the board. Ask: *Are the sentences correct?* Ask different Ss to make any necessary corrections on the board.

Learner persistence (whole group)

- To engage Ss in the class, ask them to help you. Here are some examples of tasks that Ss can do for you in class.
  Introduce new Ss to the class.
  Take attendance.
  Assist Ss who arrive late.
  Call Ss back from break time.
  Organize parties.
  Straighten the room after class.

Lesson E Writing

Practice

- Direct Ss' attention to Exercise **1C** and point to the paragraph. Say: *This is a paragraph from a class newspaper. What is the title of the paragraph?* Elicit: *Student News*. Tell Ss: *This paragraph is about a student. His name is Pedro.* Point to the corrected lowercase *p* in *Pedro*. Tell Ss: *The paragraph needs capital letters.*
- Read the instructions aloud. Ss complete the exercise individually. Walk around and help as needed.
- Direct Ss' attention to Exercise **1D** and read the instructions aloud. Point to the name *Pedro* in the chart. Point out the capital *P*. Say: *Look at your paragraph about Pedro. Look at the words with capital letters. Complete the chart.*
- Ss complete the chart individually. Walk around and help as needed.
- Check answers with the class. Write the headings from the chart on the board. Ask Ss to fill in the information about Pedro. Make any necessary corrections on the board.

Expansion activity (whole group)

- Write ten sentences on the board. Include names of famous people, addresses, cities, and countries. Write only in lowercase letters. Ask Ss to come to the board. Tell Ss: *Correct these sentences. Use capital letters.*

Application

- Direct Ss' attention to Exercise **2** and read the instructions aloud.
- Model the activity. Write the first sentence on the board using your first name.
- Ss complete the exercise individually. Walk around and help as needed.

Ask Ss to look at the paragraph in Exercise **1C**. Invite Ss to read aloud the first word in each sentence (*He, His, His,* etc.). Ask Ss to circle the capital letter in each of these words. Read the tip box aloud. Have Ss look at their sentences in Exercise **2**. Encourage Ss to check that they have begun each sentence with a capital letter.

Evaluation

- Direct Ss' attention to Exercise **3A** and read the instructions aloud.
- Ss complete the exercise in pairs. Ss read their sentences aloud.
- Walk around and help as needed. Help with pronunciation.
- Read aloud the instructions for Exercise **3B**. This exercise asks Ss to work together and peer-correct their writing. Ask a S to read the questions aloud. Tell Ss to exchange papers and look at their partner's sentences for the answers to the questions. Tell Ss to circle the answers on their partner's note. Walk around and help as needed.
- Ask pairs to answer for the class the questions about their partner's note.

Community building (whole group)

- Help Ss write a class newsletter called *Student News*. Collect the sentences that Ss wrote. Use them to make a newsletter to distribute to the Ss.

Learner persistence (whole group, small groups)

- Make a Useful Language poster for the classroom. Brainstorm ideas on the board. Ask: What are some questions that we use in the English classroom? For example: *How do you _____?* Other suggestions:
  Can you please repeat that?
  Sorry, I don't understand.
  Can you help me?
  Please speak more slowly.
  What does _____ mean?
  Sorry, I don't know.
- Ask a S to make the poster at home, or have small groups make posters in class. Hang the posters on the wall as a reference for Ss.
- Add expressions to the list as Ss learn more English.

More Ventures (whole group, pairs, individual)
Assign appropriate exercises from the *Teacher's Toolkit Audio CD / CD-ROM, Add Ventures,* or the *Workbook*.

C **Write.** Add capital letters.

Student News

pedro is a new student. He is from colombia. His last name is ramirez. His address is 285 pacheco street, houston, texas. His zip code is 77057. His telephone number is 555-7878. His area code is 713.

D **Read** about Pedro again. Complete the chart. Use capital letters.

First name	Last name	City	State
Pedro	Ramirez	Houston	Texas

2 Write

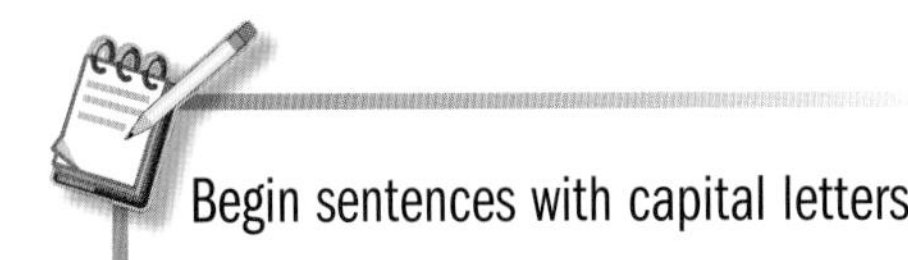

Read the questions and write about yourself.

1. What's your first name? My first name is (Answers will vary.) ________.
2. What's your last name? ________
3. What's your address? ________
4. What's your zip code? ________
5. What's your telephone number? ________
6. Where are you from? ________

3 After you write

A **Read** your sentences to a partner.

B **Check** your partner's sentences.

- What is your partner's name?
- Are the capital letters correct?

Lesson F Another view

1 Life-skills reading

Registration

Please print.

☐ Mr. ☐ Ms. ☐ Mrs.

(1) NAME: ______________________
Last First Middle

(2) ADDRESS: ______________________
Number Street Apt.

(3) ______________________
City State Zip code

(4) TELEPHONE: ______________________
Area code Number

(5) COUNTRY OF ORIGIN: ______________________

(6) ______________________
Signature

A Read the questions. Look at the form. Circle the answers.

1. Where do you print your country of origin?
   a. line 1
   b. line 2
   (c.) line 5
   d. line 6
2. Where do you print your name?
   (a.) line 1
   b. line 3
   c. line 5
   d. line 6
3. Where do you sign your name?
   a. line 1
   b. line 3
   c. line 5
   (d.) line 6
4. Where do you write your zip code?
   a. line 2
   (b.) line 3
   c. line 4
   d. line 5

B Write. Complete the form with your own information.

C Talk in groups. Look at your forms. Ask and answer questions.

What's your last name?

My last name is Hom.

Lesson objectives

- Practice using a registration form
- Review unit vocabulary
- Introduce the projects
- Complete the self-assessment

Warm-up and review

- Before class. Write today's lesson focus on the board.
  Lesson F:
  Read and complete a registration form
  Review vocabulary for personal information
  Complete the self-assessment
- Begin class. Books open. Direct Ss' attention to the registration form in Exercise **1**. Ask: *What is this?* Elicit: *It's a registration form.* Ask: *What words do you see?* (Ss can read aloud some of the words on the form.)
- Review the meaning of any words that Ss do not remember.
- Point to the words *Please print* on the form. Say: *Printing is a way of writing.*

Teaching tip

Model printing versus writing in script. Print your school's address on the board and tell Ss: *This is printing.* Then write your school's address in script and tell Ss: *This is script.*

- Ask: *Where do we use registration forms?* Elicit responses such as: *at school, at the doctor's office.*
- Say: *Look at the form.* Point to the numbers for each line. Ask: *What numbers do you see?* Elicit: *1, 2, 3, 4, 5,* and *6.*
- Ask: *Where do you write your address?* (line 2) *Where do you write your telephone number?* (line 4) *Where do you write your signature?* (line 6)

Presentation

- Read the instructions for Exercise **1A**. This task helps prepare Ss for standardized-type tests they may have to take. Be sure Ss understand the task. Have Ss individually skim for and circle the answers.

Teaching tip

Ss may not know the words *country of origin.* Say: *This is your country. This is where you are from. For example, I am from Canada. Canada is my country of origin.*

Comprehension check

- Check answers with the class. Ask four Ss to read their answers aloud. Ask: *Are the answers correct?* Ask different Ss to correct any errors.

Practice

- Direct Ss' attention to Exercise **1B** and read the instructions aloud.
- Ss fill in the form individually. Walk around and help as needed.

Teaching tip

Ask: *What does apt. mean?* Elicit: *Apartment number.* Some Ss don't have middle names or apartment numbers. Teach them to say: *I don't have a middle name* or *I don't have an apartment number.* Tell them: *Leave that part blank, or empty, on the registration form.*

Expansion activity *(individual work)*

- Practice filling out other application forms. Make copies of application forms from your school. Explain any new vocabulary. Ss complete the forms individually. Go over the forms with the class.

Expansion activity *(whole group)*

- Hand out index cards. Ask each S to write his or her signature on the card. Collect the cards, shuffle, and pass them out again. Ss can match the signature to the correct S.

Application

- Direct Ss' attention to Exercise **1C** and read the instructions aloud. Ask: *What are some questions you can ask your group?* Write their questions on the board, for example:
  What's your last name?
  What's your first name?
  What's your middle name?
- Ss complete the task in small groups. Help as needed.

Expansion activity *(small groups, pairs)*

- Before class. Make two sets of index cards for each group. One set has questions on it; the other has answers to the questions. For example:

Set 1	***Set 2***
What's your name?	*Mary Smith*
Where are you from?	*New York, NY*
What's your area code?	*212*
What's your title?	*Ms.*
What's your middle initial?	*L.*
What's your apartment number?	*3B*

  Shuffle the cards within their sets.
- In class. Give Set 1 and Set 2 of the cards to each group. Say: *Put the questions together with the correct answers.* Walk around and help as needed.

Lesson F Another view

Presentation

- Tell Ss: *In adult ESL classes, we sometimes call teachers by their first name. How do you call a teacher in your country?* Elicit appropriate responses.
- Direct Ss' attention to Exercise **2A** and read the instructions aloud. Ask a S to read the first question aloud. Elicit answers from the class. Repeat with questions 2 and 3.

Practice

- Ask two Ss to come to the front of the class. Say: *This is how we introduce people in English:* (Student number 1), *this is my friend* (student number 2). (Student number 2), *this is my friend* (student number 1).
- Ask another S to stand up. Ask one of the first Ss to introduce the third S to another S in the pair.
- Say: *We usually say, "Nice to meet you" after an introduction*. Write *Nice to meet you* on the board. Point to the words. Say: *Repeat after me*. Correct Ss' pronunciation if needed.
- Point to the picture and conversation in Exercise **2B**. Read each sentence of the conversation aloud and have Ss repeat after you.
- Put Ss in groups of three. Ss practice the conversation, then change roles until everyone is introduced.
- Ask Ss to say the alphabet as you write it on the board. Have Ss repeat the alphabet after you point to and say each letter. Say: *This is alphabetical order.*
- Write a few of the Ss' names on the board. Ask Ss to list the names in alphabetical order and rewrite the names as a model for Exercise **2C**.

Teaching tip

If you notice that Ss are having trouble with certain letters of the alphabet, write those letters separately on the board. Say the name of each difficult letter and ask Ss to repeat. Practice by asking Ss to spell different words in English. For example, write these words on the board and ask Ss to spell them aloud.

address	*signature*
apartment	*state*
city	*title*
country	*zip code*

- Direct Ss' attention to Exercise **2C** and read the instructions aloud. Be sure Ss understand the task. In the left column, Ss write the last name of the people in the group. Then, in the right column, they put those names in alphabetical order.
- Help as needed.
- Ask one S from each group to come to the board to write the name of each group member in alphabetical order.

It might be helpful to bring in a dictionary or a phone book to provide an example of alphabetical listings.

Community building *(whole group)*

- Ss review what they know about their classmates. This will help Ss to bond as a class.
- Model the activity by describing a S in the class. Write sentences on the board: *He is in this English class. He is from Mali. His title is Mr. _____.* (Leave the name blank.) Add other information that has been shared with the class.
- Point to the sentences. Ask a S to read them aloud. Ask: *Who is this student?* Elicit the name of the S.
- Say: *Write about a S in the class. Don't write the name of the student.* Walk around and help as needed.
- Ask Ss to read their descriptions to the class. The class will guess who the sentences are about.

More Ventures *(whole group, pairs, individual)*
Assign appropriate exercises from the *Teacher's Toolkit Audio CD / CD-ROM, Add Ventures,* or the *Workbook.*

Application

Community building

- **Project** Ask Ss to turn to page 136 in their Student's Book to complete the project for Unit 1.

Evaluation

- Before asking Ss to turn to the self-assessment on page 141, do a quick review of the unit. Have Ss turn to Lesson A. Ask the class to call out what they remember about this lesson. Prompt Ss with questions: *What are the conversations about on this page? What vocabulary is in the picture?* Review each lesson quickly.
- **Self-assessment** Read the instructions for Exercise **3**. Ask Ss to turn to the self-assessment page and complete the unit self-assessment.
- If Ss are ready, administer the unit test on pages T-163–T-164 of this Teacher's Edition (or on the *Teacher's Toolkit Audio CD / CD-ROM*). The audio and audio script for the tests are on the *Teacher's Toolkit Audio CD / CD-ROM.*

2 Fun with language

A Talk about names with your classmates.

1. Who do you call by a first name?
2. Who do you call by a title and last name?
3. Who do you call by other names?

B Talk. Read the conversation. Then introduce two classmates to each other.

C Work in a group. Write your last names. Then write your names again in alphabetical order.

Last name	Alphabetical order
(Answers will vary.)	

Alphabetical order is *A* - *B* - *C* order.
Alvarez
Baker
Chang

3 Wrap up

Complete the **Self-assessment** on page 141.

Get ready

At school

1 Talk about the picture

A Look at the picture. What do you see?

B Point to: a book • a desk • a map • a pencil
a clock • an eraser • a pen • a table

Lesson objectives
- Introduce students to the topic
- Find out what students know about the topic
- Preview the unit by talking about the picture
- Practice key vocabulary
- Practice listening skills

Warm-up and review

- Before class. Write today's lesson focus on the board. *Lesson A: At school*
- Begin class. Books closed. Welcome Ss to class and spend a few minutes reviewing Unit 1. Ask different Ss: *What's your name? What's his / her name? Where are you from? Where is he / she from? What's the school address? What's the school's / my phone number?*
- Say: *Today's lesson is about classroom objects. Look around. What do you see?* Elicit: *books, desks, a clock,* etc. Write the words on the board under the lesson focus.
- Point to the words on the board. Read each word aloud and ask Ss to repeat. Point to the items in your classroom. Show and write the names of other items listed in Lesson A to preview the new vocabulary.

Teaching tip
Ask Ss to make labels for common classroom objects. Have Ss put the labels on different objects in the classroom to assist in learning school vocabulary.

Presentation

- Books open. Set the scene. Direct Ss' attention to the picture on page 18. Ask: *What do you see?* Elicit any words Ss know, such as: *dictionary, bookshelf, pencils, calculator.* Write the words on the board. Read each word aloud while pointing to that item in the picture. Ask the class to repeat after you.
- Point to the teacher in the picture and ask: *What's his name?* (Mr. Liang) Help Ss talk about what's happening in the picture: *They're talking. They're coming to class. Her purse is falling. He's preparing the lesson. The lesson is on the board. They're reviewing personal information.*

Teaching tip
Do not expect all Ss to be able to answer the questions. These warm-up questions are meant to show what Ss already know and to draw on Ss' prior knowledge.

- Direct Ss' attention to the key words in Exercise **1B**. Read each word aloud while pointing to the corresponding item in the picture. Ask the class to repeat and point.

Teaching tip
The key words are intended to help Ss talk about the picture and learn some of the vocabulary in the unit.

Comprehension check

- Ask Ss *Yes / No* questions about the picture or about objects in your classroom. Say: *Listen to the questions. Answer "Yes" or "No."*
  Is this a book?
  Is this a table?
  Is this a desk?
  Is this an eraser?
  Is this a pencil?
  Is this a clock?
  Is this a pen?

Practice

- Direct Ss' attention to Exercise **1B**. Model the task. Hold up the Student's Book. Say to a S: *Point to a book.* The S points to the appropriate part of the picture.
- Ss in pairs. Say to one S: *Say the words in Exercise 1B.* Say to his or her partner: *Point to the picture.* Ask several pairs to perform the task for the class to check Ss' understanding.
- Ss complete the exercise in pairs. Walk around and help as needed. When Ss finish, have them change partners and change roles.

Expansion activity (whole group)

- Focus on pronunciation. Write on the board: *book.* Read the word aloud. Ask Ss to repeat. Read the word aloud again while clapping once. Ask Ss to repeat and clap. Say: *"Book" has one syllable.* Write *1* next to *book.*
- Write on the board: *pencil.* Read the word aloud while clapping twice. Ask Ss to repeat and clap. Say: *"Pencil" has two syllables.* Write 2 next to *pencil.*
- Write on the board more words from the picture. Ask Ss to read aloud the items and to clap for each syllable.
- Ask Ss: *How many syllables?* Write the correct number of syllables next to each word.

Expansion activity (whole group)

- Show the Ss a globe (or a world map). Ask: *What is this?* Elicit: *It's a globe.* Write the word on the board. Read the word aloud and ask Ss to repeat after you. Ask: *Where is your country on the globe / map?*
- Ask Ss to come to the front of the class and show their countries on the globe or the map.

Lesson A Get ready

Presentation

- If possible, bring the following items to class: a calculator, an eraser, a pencil, a map, a pen, a book, a notebook, and a ruler. Show the Ss each item. Ask: *What's this?* As Ss respond, write any new words on the board. Read the words aloud and ask Ss to repeat after you. Provide any unknown words.
- If it is not possible to bring items to class, direct Ss' attention to the word bank in Exercise **2A**. Read each word aloud and ask Ss to repeat after you. Use the pictures to clarify the meaning of any unknown words.

Practice

- Direct Ss' attention to Exercise **2A**. Read the instructions.
- [Class Audio CD1 track 17] Play or read the audio program (see audio script, page T-152). Ss circle the words they hear. Repeat the program as needed.
- Check answers. Ask: *What did you circle?* Ask Ss to write the words on the board. Point to the words. Say: *Repeat after me*. Say each word. Listen to Ss' pronunciation and correct as needed.
- Ask a S to write the words that were not circled on the board: *eraser, pencils*. Point to the words. Say: *Repeat after me*. Say each word. Listen to Ss' pronunciation.
- Direct Ss' attention to the pictures in Exercise **2B**. Hold up the Student's Book. Point to the first picture. Say: *Notebook*. Point to the second picture. Ask a S: *What are these?* (rulers)
- Continue asking Ss about the rest of the pictures.
- Read aloud the instructions for Exercise **2B**.
- [Class Audio CD1 track 17] Play or read the audio program again. Pause after the first conversation. Ask: *Which picture matches conversation A?* (picture number 4) Point to the handwritten *a* written next to number 4. Be sure Ss understand the task.
- [Class Audio CD1 track 17] Play or read the complete audio program. Ss complete the exercise individually.

> **Teaching tip**
> It might be helpful to go over the words *drawer, wall,* and *box,* which appear in the audio program. Write the words on the board. Say each word aloud and ask Ss to repeat. Point to the objects in your classroom or in the pictures to clarify the meaning of each word.

Learner persistence (individual work)

- [Self-Study Audio CD track 12] Exercises **2A** and **2B** are recorded on the Ss' self-study CD at the back of the Student's Book. Ss can listen to the CD at home for reinforcement and review. They can also listen for self-directed learning when class attendance is not possible.

Comprehension check

- Write the numbers *1–6* on the board. Ask a few Ss to come to the board and write the correct answers to Exercise **2B** next to each number.
- Read aloud the second part of the instructions for Exercise **2B**.
- [Class Audio CD1 track 17] Play or read the audio program again. Pause the audio program after each conversation. Point to a letter of the conversation on the board. Ask: *Is this correct?* Ask a S to make any necessary corrections on the board.

Application

- Direct Ss to the first picture in Exercise **2C**. Ask: *What's on the desk?* Ask a S to read the example aloud: *Book*.
- Read the instructions aloud. Model the exercise. Point to *clock* in the word bank in Exercise **2C**. Ask: *Where's the clock?* Elicit: *On the table*. Point to the clock in the second picture. Write the word next to number 4.
- Ss complete the exercise individually. Help as needed.
- Check answers with the class. Ask Ss to read their answers aloud. Correct any errors.

Expansion activity (small groups)

- Memory game. Put Ss in small groups. Put several classroom items on a desk in your classroom. Put some items on top of each other. Say: *Look at this desk for 1 minute. Don't write anything. After 1 minute, I will cover the desk. Work with your group. Write everything you saw.*
- When Ss are finished, ask each group to read its list to the class. The group with the most correct items wins.

Evaluation

- Direct Ss' attention to the lesson focus on the board.
- For each item, ask a *Yes / No* question about the picture on page 18, e.g.: *Is there a calculator in the classroom?* (Yes.) Have Ss point to the object as they answer.
- Check off the item as Ss demonstrate an understanding of what they have learned in the lesson.

> ***More Ventures*** (whole group, pairs, individual)
> Assign appropriate exercises from the *Teacher's Toolkit Audio CD / CD-ROM, Add Ventures,* or the *Workbook*.

2 Listening

SELF-STUDY AUDIO CD

A **Listen.** Circle the words you hear.

book	eraser	notebook	pens
calculator	map	pencils	rulers

SELF-STUDY AUDIO CD

B **Listen again.** Write the letter of the conversation.

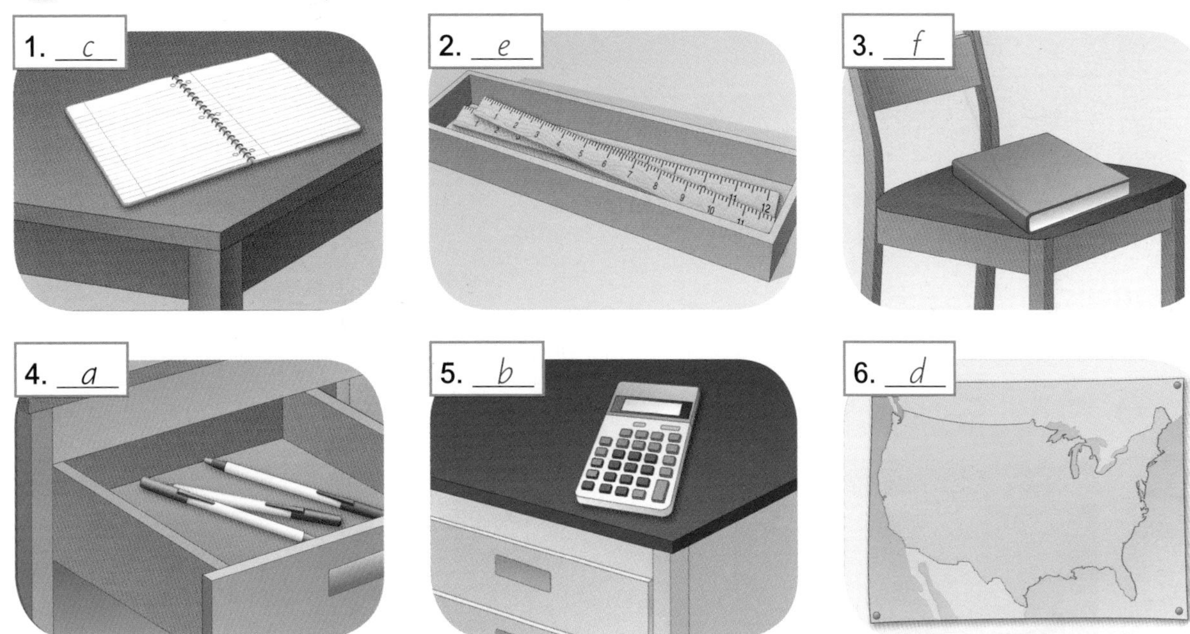

1. c
2. e
3. f
4. a
5. b
6. d

Listen again. Check your answers.

C **Write.** What's on the desk? What's on the table?

book	clock	eraser	notebook	pencil	ruler

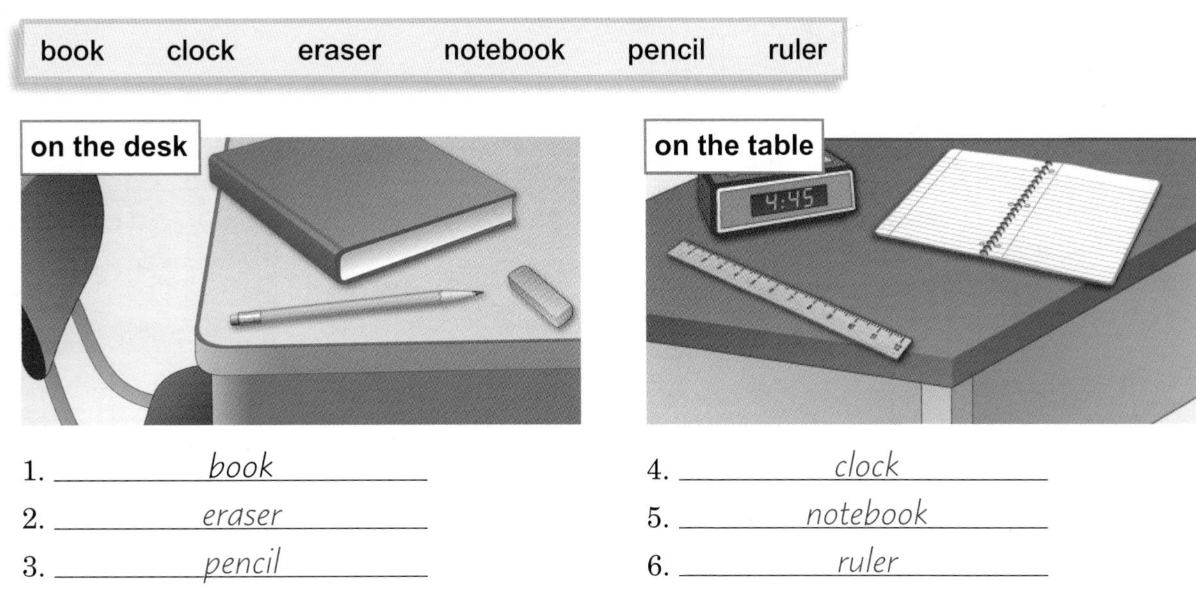

1. book
2. eraser
3. pencil

4. clock
5. notebook
6. ruler

Lesson B

Where is the pen?

1 Grammar focus: prepositions *in* and *on*; *Where is?*

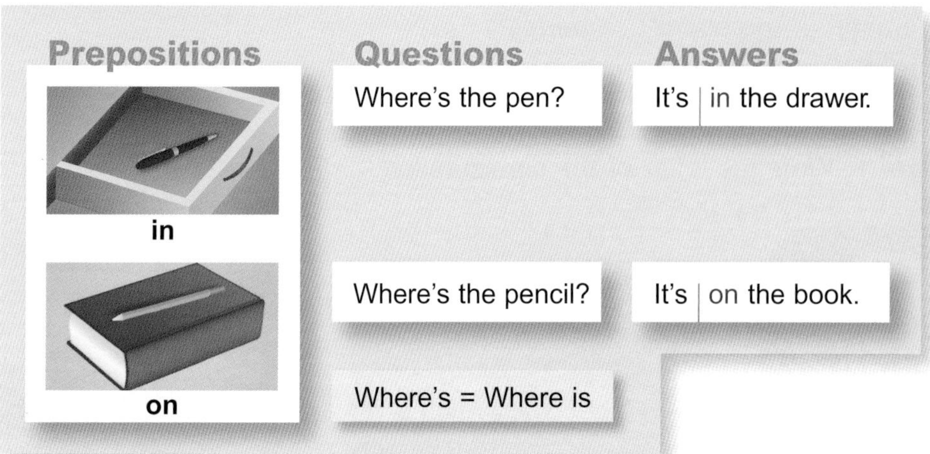

Prepositions	Questions	Answers
in	Where's the pen?	It's in the drawer.
on	Where's the pencil?	It's on the book.
	Where's = Where is	

2 Practice

A Write. Complete the sentences. Use *in* or *on*.

1

A Where's the book?

B It's __on__ the shelf.

2

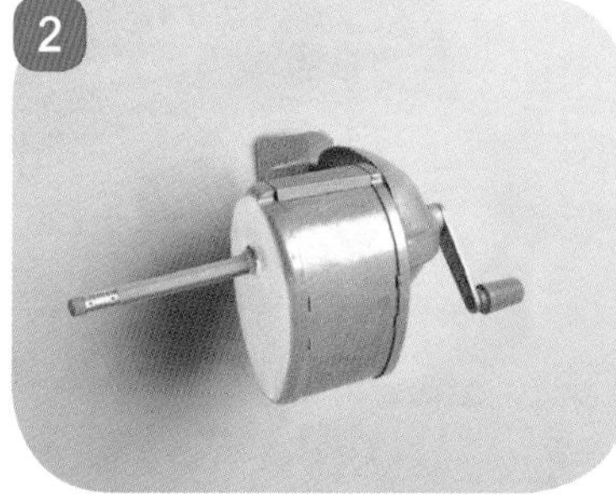

A Where's the pencil sharpener?

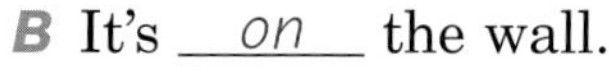

B It's __on__ the wall.

3

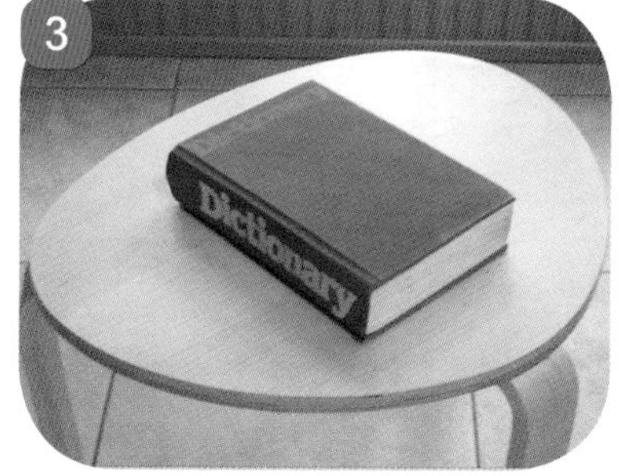

A Where's the dictionary?

B It's __on__ the table.

4

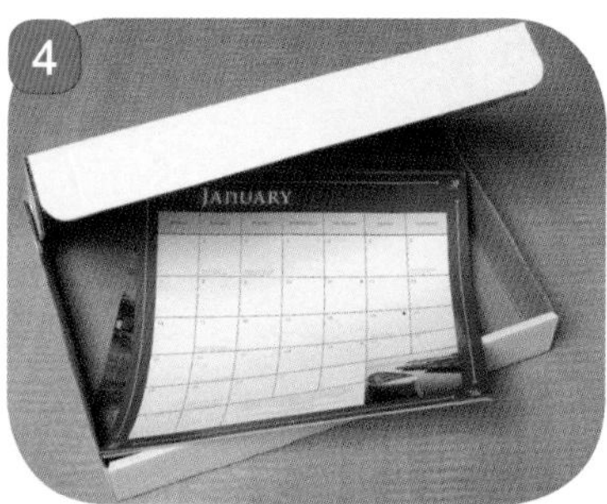

A Where's the calendar?

B It's __in__ the box.

5

A Where's the eraser?

B It's __in__ the drawer.

6

A Where's the calculator?

B It's __in__ the cabinet.

 **Listen and repeat.** Then practice with a partner.

Lesson objectives

- Present and practice the prepositions *in* and *on* and the question *Where is*
- Introduce more school vocabulary
- Practice getting someone's attention

Warm-up and review

- Before class. Write today's lesson focus on the board.
  Lesson B:
  Prepositions — *in* *on*
  Question — *Where is*

> **Teaching tip**
> Bring a bag (any kind) to class for this lesson. You will use it to demonstrate the prepositions *in* and *on.*

- Begin class. Books closed. Review topic vocabulary and introduce new vocabulary in Lesson B by holding up or pointing to classroom items and asking: *What's this?* (a pencil, a dictionary, an eraser, a calendar, etc.)
- Preview *in* and *on*. Show Ss a bag. Write *bag* on the board. Say: *This is a bag.* Take an item, such as a pencil, and place it on top of the bag. Tell Ss: *The pencil is on the bag.* Write the sentence on the board. Then, read the sentence aloud and ask Ss to repeat.
- Put the pencil inside the bag. Tell Ss: *The pencil is in the bag.* Write the sentence on the board. Then, read the sentence aloud and ask Ss to repeat.
- Put the pencil on top of the bag and ask: *Is the pencil **in** the bag or **on** the bag?* (on)
- Put the pencil inside the bag. Ask: *Is the pencil **in** the bag or **on** the bag?* (in)
- Ask a S to come to the front of the room. Say: *Now you ask a question. Use "in" or "on."* The S asks a question. A different S answers the question.

Presentation

- Books open. Direct Ss' attention to Exercise **1** and point to the illustrations next to the grammar chart. Model the example questions and answers with a S. Have the S ask the questions. As you say the answers, point to the object in the picture to make sure the difference between *in* and *on* is clear.

Expansion activity *(student pairs)*

- Practice making sentences with *in* and *on*. Direct Ss' attention to the picture on page 18. Point to the dictionary on the chair in the picture. Ask: *Where's the dictionary?* (The dictionary is on the chair.) Write the sentence on the board.
- Ss in pairs. Ask Ss to make five sentences about the picture using *in* or *on*.
- Check answers with the class. Ask Ss to write their sentences on the board.

Comprehension check

- Show Ss a pencil. Put the pencil on the table. Write on the board: *Where's the pencil?* Read the question aloud and ask Ss to repeat. Call on a S to answer the question. Elicit: *The pencil is on the table* or *It's on the table.* Repeat the process, putting the pencil on or in different places around the classroom.
- Read aloud the instructions for Exercise **2A**.
- Direct Ss' attention to picture number 1. Ask two Ss to read the example question and answer.
- Ss complete the exercise individually. Help as needed.
- [Class Audio CD1 track 18] Read aloud the second part of the instructions for Exercise **2A**. Play or read the audio program (see audio script, page T-152). Have Ss check their answers as they listen and repeat. Correct pronunciation as needed.
- Ask Ss to come to the board and write the answer sentences. Ask different Ss to read the sentences aloud. Ask Ss to make any necessary corrections on the board.
- Ss in pairs. Say: *Now practice with a partner.* Walk around and help as needed.

Expansion activity *(whole group)*

- Question-and-answer practice. Draw this chart on the board. Ask Ss to copy it.

Question with *Where*	Names	Answers

- Say: *Look around the classroom. Write questions about six classroom items. For example, "Where is the clock?" Write the questions in the first column of the chart* (point to the first column).
- Say: *Ask your questions to six different classmates. Write their names in the second column* (point to it). *If necessary, ask "What's your name?" "How do you spell that?" Then write their answers in the third column* (point to it). *For example, "It's on the wall."*
- Model the activity with a S.
- Ss walk around the room and complete the task. Ask individual Ss to come to the board and fill in the chart with some of the information they obtained from their classmates. Go over the chart and correct any errors.

Lesson B Where is the pen?

Practice

- Direct Ss' attention to the picture in Exercise **2B**. Ask: *What do you see?* Elicit appropriate responses to describe the picture. Write the responses on the board.
- Ask a S to come to the board. Read a word from the board and ask the S to circle it. Repeat until Ss understand how to circle the items they hear. Then read aloud the instruction to Exercise **2B**.
- [Class Audio CD1 track 19] Play or read only the first conversation on the audio program (see audio script, page T-152). Ask: *What did you hear?* (calculator) Say: *Circle the calculator in your book.* Check to be sure Ss understand the task.
- [Class Audio CD1 track 19] Play or read the audio program again. Ss complete the task individually. Repeat the audio program as needed.
- Ask: *What did you circle?* Ask Ss to come to the board to write the names of the items they circled.
- [Class Audio CD1 track 19] Play or read the audio program again and ask Ss to check their answers.
- Read aloud the second part of the instructions for Exercise **2B**.
- Model the task. Ask two Ss to read the example conversation. Then repeat the conversation with a S. Substitute a word from the picture in place of *calculator* and prompt the correct response to complete the conversation, for example: *Excuse me. Where's the calendar?*

Teaching tip

Students may not be familiar with the word *bold*. Explain that the bold words in the conversation are darker. In many exercises, Ss are asked to substitute words in place of the bold words.

- Ss complete the exercise in pairs. Walk around and help as needed.
- Ask several pairs to perform their conversations for the rest of the class.

Useful language

Read the tip box aloud. Write on the board: *Excuse me.* Say the words. Ask Ss to repeat after you. You may want to explain that *Excuse me* can be used in several ways: to get attention, to apologize, and to indicate someone is in your way and you would like to get by. Model the different uses for the class.

Expansion activity (student pairs)

- Give Ss 1 minute to study the picture on page 21.
- Books closed. Ask a S: *Where is the _____?* The S tries to remember where this item was in the picture.
- Ss in pairs. Say: *One person looks at the picture and asks questions. The other person tries to remember. Then, the other person asks questions.* Walk around and help as needed.

Application

- Point to an item in the classroom and ask: *Where is the* (name of item)*?* Elicit a response from the class using a preposition of location: *It's on the _____. / It's in the _____.*
- Direct Ss' attention to Exercise **3** and read the instructions aloud. Ask two Ss to read the example. Then, ask them to make up a new example about an item in your classroom.
- Ss ask and answer questions in pairs. Walk around and help as needed.

Expansion activity (group work)

- Practice questions with *What's* and the prepositions *in* and *on*.
- Ask Ss to look at the picture on page 18 and answer your questions: *What's in the drawer?* (a notebook, pens) *What's on the chair?* (a dictionary) *What's in her purse?* (a dollar bill, a pen, etc.) *What's on the cabinet?* (a pencil sharpener, books, a pencil) *What's in his briefcase?* (a cell phone) Introduce new vocabulary if the Ss are ready for it.

Evaluation

- Direct Ss' attention to the lesson focus written on the board. Ask each S to make a sentence using *in* or *on*. Go around the class.
- Ask Ss to make questions using *Where is.*
- Check off each part of the lesson focus as Ss demonstrate an understanding of what they have learned in the lesson.

More Ventures *(whole group, pairs, individual)*
Assign appropriate exercises from the *Teacher's Toolkit Audio CD / CD-ROM, Add Ventures,* or the *Workbook.*

B **Listen.** Circle the items you hear.

Talk with a partner. Look at the picture again. Change the **bold** words and make conversations.

A Excuse me. Where's the **calculator**?
B It's **in the cabinet**.
A Oh, thanks.
B You're welcome.

Useful language
Say *excuse me* to get someone's attention.

3 Communicate

Talk with a partner about your classroom.

Where's the computer?

It's on the table.

Lesson C

Where are the pencils?

1 Grammar focus: singular and plural nouns

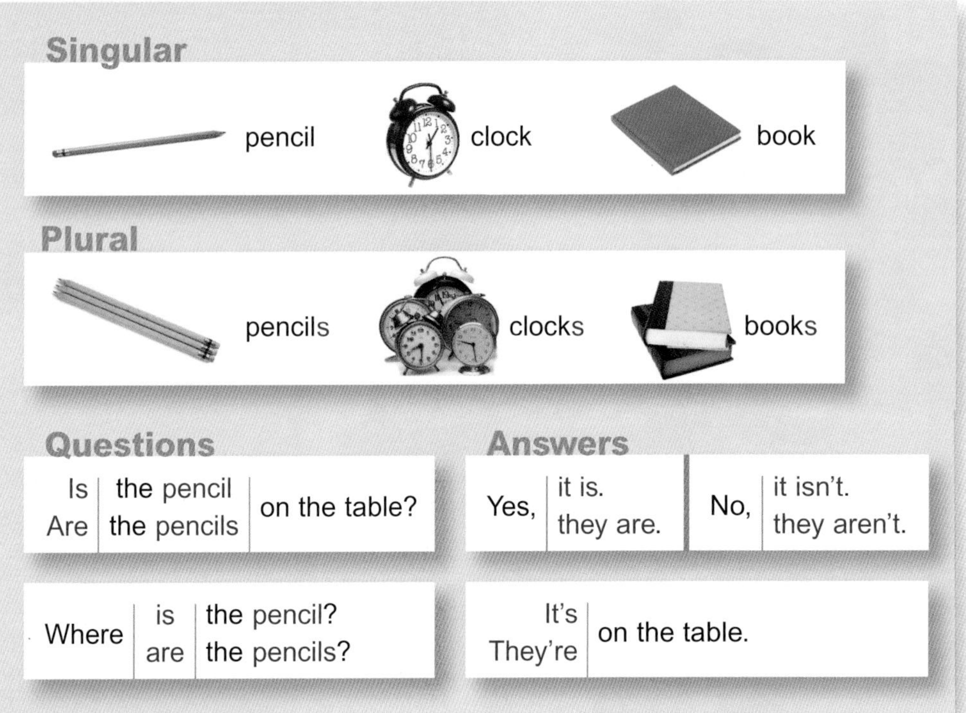

Singular

pencil | clock | book

Plural

pencils | clocks | books

Questions		
Is Are	the pencil the pencils	on the table?

Answers			
Yes,	it is. they are.	No,	it isn't. they aren't.

Where	is are	the pencil? the pencils?

It's They're	on the table.

2 Practice

A Write. Look at the picture. Complete the conversations.

1. **A** Are the ___books___ in the cabinet?
   (book / books)

   B Yes, ___they are___ .

2. **A** Is the ___clock___ in the cabinet?
   (clock / clocks)

   B Yes, ___it is___ .

3. **A** Are the ___rulers___ on the table?
   (ruler / rulers)

   B No, ___they aren't___ .

4. **A** Are the ___pencils___ on the table?
   (pencil / pencils)

   B No, ___they aren't___ .

5. **A** Are the ___calculators___ on the table?
   (calculator / calculators)

   B Yes, ___they are___ .

Listen and repeat. Then practice with a partner.

Lesson objectives
- Introduce singular and plural nouns
- Review topic vocabulary

Warm-up and review

- Before class. Write today's lesson focus on the board.
  Lesson C: Singular and plural nouns
  Is the pencil on the desk? *Yes, it is. / No it isn't.*
  Are the pens on the desk? *Yes, they are. / No, they aren't.*
  Where is the pencil? *It's on the table.*
  Where are the pens? *They're on the table.*
- Begin class. Books closed. Demonstrate *Yes / No* questions with singular and plural nouns. Hold up a pencil. Hold up one finger. Say: *One pencil. Singular.* Put the pencil on a desk. Write on the board:
  Is the pencil on the desk? *Yes, it is. / No, it isn't.*
- Ask: *Is the pencil on the desk?* Elicit: *Yes, it is.*
- Ask: *Is the pencil in the cabinet?* Elicit: *No, it isn't.*
- Hold up two pencils. Hold up two fingers. Say: *Two pencils. Plural.* Emphasize the *-s* ending. Put the pencils on a desk. Write on the board:
  Are the pencils on the desk? *Yes, they are. / No, they aren't.*
- Ask: *Are the pencils on the chair?* Elicit: *No, they aren't.*
- Ask: *Are the pencils on the desk?* Elicit: *Yes, they are.*

Presentation

- Books open. Direct Ss' attention to the grammar chart in Exercise **1** and point to the pencil in the chart. Ask: *Pencil: Singular or plural?* Elicit: *Singular.* Point to and ask about the clock and the book.
- Point to the pencils in the chart. Ask: *Pencils: Singular or plural?* Elicit: *Plural.* Point to and ask about the clocks and the books.
- Read aloud the questions and answers in the grammar chart and ask Ss to repeat.
- Point to the questions you wrote on the board. Underline *it* and *is*. Say: *Use "it" and "is" with a singular noun.* Underline *they* and *are*. Say: *Use "they" and "are" with plural nouns.*
- Write on the board:
  Singular nouns *Plural nouns*
  Write *book, pencil,* and *clock* on the board under *Singular nouns*. Write *books, pencils,* and *clocks* on the board under *Plural nouns*. Say: *Look at the pairs of words.* Circle the plural *-s* ending in the plural words. Have Ss read the words, exaggerating the *-s* ending. Explain that the *-s* makes these words plural.

Contractions
Write on the board: *is not* = *isn't* and *are not* = *aren't*. Ask Ss to repeat the words. Cross off the *o* and show how the word closes up with the insertion of the apostrophe: *isn't / aren't*. Ask Ss to repeat the contractions.

Practice

- Direct Ss' attention to the picture in Exercise **2A**. Ask: *What is singular in the picture?* (cabinet, calendar, clock, lamp, notebook, table) Ask: *What is plural?* (books, calculators, pencils, pens, rulers)
- Ask Ss questions about the picture and elicit responses: *Are the calculators on the table?* Yes, they are. *Are the rulers on the table?* No, they aren't. *Is the clock on the table?* No, it isn't.
- Read the instructions for Exercise **2A** aloud. Ask two Ss to read the example question and answer aloud. Be sure Ss understand the task.
- Ss complete the exercise individually. Walk around and help as needed.
- Check answers with the class. Call on Ss to write the questions and answers on the board. Ask: *Are these sentences correct?* Make any necessary corrections.

Comprehension check

- Read aloud the second part of the instructions for Exercise **2A**.
- [Class Audio CD1 track 20] Play or read the audio program (see audio script, page T-152). Listen to and correct Ss' pronunciation as they repeat the conversations.
- Ss practice the conversations in pairs.

Expansion activity (small groups)

- Ss in small groups. Have Ss identify the singular and plural nouns in the classroom. Write on the board:
  Singular nouns *Plural nouns*
- Say: *Look around the classroom. Tell me a singular noun. Tell me a plural noun.* Elicit one example for each category and write it on the board in the correct column.
- Ask each group to find as many singular and plural items as it can. Say: *Write each word in the correct column on the board.* Walk around and help as needed.
- Check answers with the class.

Expansion activity (whole group)

- Before class. Write each line from Exercise **2A** on a separate index card.
- In class, shuffle the cards and pass them out. Ask Ss to walk around the class and find someone with the answer or question matching their card. When Ss have found their matches, have each pair read their cards aloud.

Lesson C Where are the pencils?

Practice

- Place some items on your desk or on a table in the classroom. Make sure some are singular items and some are plural. Point to the items in turn. Ask the class: *Singular or plural?*
- Point to items on different Ss' desks. Ask: *Where is the* (name of item)*? Where are the* (names of items)*?* Elicit: *It is* (location of item). *They are* (location of items).
- Direct Ss' attention to the picture on page 23. Point to the computer and ask: *Computer: Singular or plural?* (Singular). Repeat for *books, blackboard, maps, pencils, calendar,* and *calculator.*
- Read aloud the instructions for Exercise **2B**. Ask a S to read the example question aloud. Ask: *Why do we say* ***is****?* Elicit: *"Computer" is singular.*
- Ss complete the exercise individually. Walk around and help as needed.
- Ask Ss to read their questions aloud. Write verbs on the board as Ss read their questions. Correct any errors. Then ask Ss to look at the picture in Exercise **2C** and answer the questions from Exercise **2B**: *Where is the computer?* (It's on the desk.) *Where are the notebooks?* (They're in the filing cabinet.) *Where is the calendar?* (It's on the wall.) *Where are the maps?* (They're on the desk.) *Where are the pencils?* (They're on the desk.) *Where is the calculator?* (It's on the filing cabinet.)

Teaching tip
Explain the difference between a *cabinet* and a *filing cabinet.* Tell Ss: *A filing cabinet holds files.* Point to the files pictured inside the filing cabinet on page 18.

- Read aloud the instructions for Exercise **2C**. Be sure Ss understand the task.
- Ss complete the exercise individually. Help as needed.
- Read aloud the second part of the instructions for Exercise **2C**.
- [Class Audio CD1 track 21] Play or read the audio program (see audio script, page T-152). Have Ss correct their sentences as they listen and repeat.
- Ss in pairs. Say: *Now practice with a partner.*
- Walk around and listen to Ss' pronunciation. If you notice any problematic words, write them on the board. When Ss are finished, point to the words on the board. Say: *Listen to the words. Repeat after me.*

Expansion activity (student pairs)

- Turn Ss' attention back to page 22. Ask Ss to make similar conversations using *Where* to ask about the picture in Exercise **2A**.

Application

- Read aloud the instructions for Exercise **3**. Ask two Ss to model the conversation.
- Ss complete the exercise in pairs. Help as needed.

Expansion activity (whole group)

- Play "Ten Questions." Ask a S to sit at the front of the class, facing away from the other Ss. Ask another S to put a classroom item such as a pen or pencil *in* or *on* something in the classroom.
- Tell the first S: *Ask* Yes / No *questions to find out where the item is hidden. You can ask ten questions, for example: Is it in a drawer? Is it on the wall?*
- Once the S has guessed the location, continue the game by hiding a plural object, such as two pens, two erasers, etc. Now the S who is guessing must ask: *Are they on a desk? Are they on a chair?* etc.
- Encourage the class to answer with: *Yes, it is*; *No, it isn't*; *Yes, they are*; or *No, they aren't*.

Expansion activity (whole group)

- Picture description. Draw a picture on a piece of paper. For example, draw a table with classroom objects on it.
- Model the activity. Ask a S to come to the board. Don't show the S your picture. Say: *Draw a table*. The S draws a table on the board. Say: *Draw a book on the table*. The S draws a book on the table.
- Ask Ss to take out a piece of paper. Say: *Listen. I will describe my picture to you. Draw what I say.* Describe your picture. When you are finished, show Ss your picture. Ask: *Is your picture the same or different?*
- Continue by asking a S to draw a new picture.

Evaluation

- Direct Ss' attention to the lesson focus written on the board. Have Ss look at the picture on page 18 and ask and answer questions.
- Check off the lesson focus as Ss demonstrate an understanding of what they have learned in the lesson.

More Ventures *(whole group, pairs, individual)*
Assign appropriate exercises from the *Teacher's Toolkit Audio CD / CD-ROM, Add Ventures,* or the *Workbook.*

B **Write.** Complete the sentences. Use *is* or *are*.

1. Where __is__ the computer?
2. Where __are__ the notebooks?
3. Where __is__ the calendar?
4. Where __are__ the maps?
5. Where __are__ the pencils?
6. Where __is__ the calculator?

C **Write.** Look at the picture. Read the answers. Write the questions.

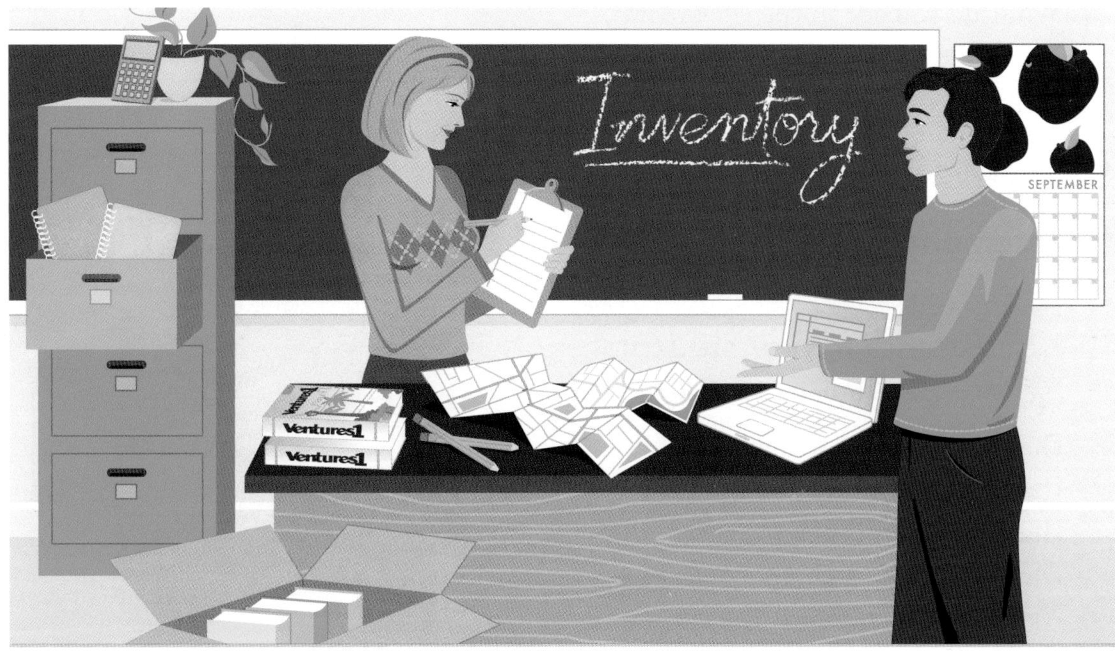

1. **A** Where are the pencils?
   B They're on the desk.
2. **A** Where is the calculator?
   B It's on the filing cabinet.
3. **A** Where is the calendar?
   B It's on the wall.
4. **A** Where is the computer?
   B It's on the desk.
5. **A** Where are the notebooks?
   B They're in the filing cabinet.
6. **A** Where are the books?
   B They're in the box.

Listen and repeat. Then practice with a partner.

3 Communicate

Talk with a partner about things in your classroom.

A Is the map on the desk?
B Yes, it is.
A Are the books on the table?
B No, they aren't.
A Where are they?
B They're in the cabinet.

Lesson D Reading

1 Before you read

Talk. It's the first day of class. Look at the picture. Answer the questions.

1. What do you see in the classroom?
2. Where are the objects?

2 Read

Listen and read.

Attention, new students!

Welcome to your new classroom.

- The computer is on the small table.
- The pencils are in the basket on the desk.
- The erasers are in the basket.
- The books are in the bookcase.
- The calculators are on the bookcase.
- The markers are in the desk drawer.

Look at pictures before you read. They help you understand new words. *Basket* is a new word. Find the basket in the picture.

3 After you read

A Read the sentences. Are they correct? Circle *Yes* or *No*.

1. The computer is on the desk.	Yes	(No)
2. The pencils are in the basket.	(Yes)	No
3. The erasers are in the bookcase.	Yes	(No)
4. The books are in the bookcase.	(Yes)	No
5. The calculators are in the bookcase.	Yes	(No)
6. The markers are in the desk drawer.	(Yes)	No

Write. Correct the sentences.

1. The computer is on the small table.

B Write. Answer the questions about the classroom.

1. Where is the desk? *It's in the classroom.*
2. Where is the basket? *It's on the desk.*

Lesson objectives
- Introduce and read "Attention, new students!"
- Practice using new topic-related words
- Use visual cues to help comprehension

Warm-up and review

- Before class. Write today's lesson focus on the board.
Lesson D:
Read and understand "Attention, new students!"
Learn words about school objects
- Begin class. Books open. Show Ss the picture on page 18. Point to Mr. Liang. Ask: *What's his name?* (Mr. Liang) *Is he a student?* (No, he isn't. He's a teacher.) Point to different Ss in the picture and ask *Is he / she a student?* (Yes, he / she is.) *Are they teachers?* (No, they aren't.)
- Review the prepositions *in* and *on*. Ask: *Where are the pens?* (They're in the drawer.) *Where is the map?* (It's on the wall.) *Where is the pencil sharpener?* (It's on the cabinet.) Continue with other objects pictured on page 18.

Presentation

- Direct Ss' attention to Exercise **1**. Say: *This is Mr. Liang again. This is his classroom.*
- Read aloud the instructions for Exercise **1**. Ask a S to read the questions aloud. Elicit answers from the class.
- Direct Ss' attention to Exercise **2** and point to the title "Attention, new students!" Ask: *What is this reading about?* Elicit: *It's about a new classroom.* Say: *Now you will listen to the paragraph.*
- Tell Ss to use a notebook to keep a running list of new vocabulary words. They can write the definitions or draw a picture next to the words to remember the meanings.
- [Class Audio CD1 track 22] Play or read the audio program and ask Ss to read along (see audio script, page T-152). Repeat the audio program as needed.

Teaching tip

Here are other ways of presenting the reading: Ss read silently; Ss take turns reading individual sentences aloud to the class; Ss read to each other; Ss listen and repeat the sentences.

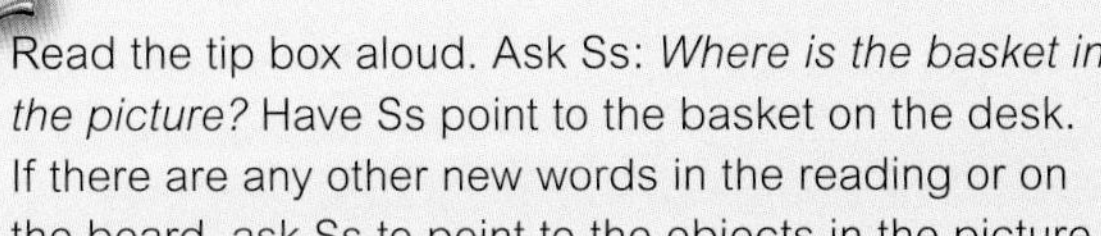

Read the tip box aloud. Ask Ss: *Where is the basket in the picture?* Have Ss point to the basket on the desk. If there are any other new words in the reading or on the board, ask Ss to point to the objects in the picture.

Learner persistence *(individual work)*

- [Self-Study Audio CD track 13] Exercise **2** is recorded on the Ss' self-study CD at the back of the Student's Book. Ss can listen to the CD at home for reinforcement and review. They can also listen to the CD for self-directed learning when class attendance is not possible.

Comprehension check

- Read the instructions for Exercise **3A** aloud. Ask a S to read the example aloud.
- Ask: *Is the computer on the desk?* Point to where *No* is circled for number 1. Be sure Ss understand the task.
- Ss complete the exercise individually. Walk around and help as needed.
- Check answers with the class. Ask Ss to read their sentences and answers aloud.
- Ask Ss to take out a piece of paper. Read aloud the second part of the instructions for Exercise **3A**.
- Model the task of correcting the sentences. Point to *No* for number 1 in Exercise **3A**. Read the sentence aloud. Tell Ss: *This sentence is incorrect. Tell me the correct sentence. The computer is on . . .* (the small table). Write on the board: *The computer is on the small table.*
- Ss complete the exercise individually. Walk around and help as needed.
- Check answers with the class. Ask Ss to write their answers on the board. Then ask different Ss to read the answers aloud. Ask: *Are the sentences correct?* Make any necessary corrections on the board.

Practice

- Read the instructions for Exercise **3B** aloud.
- Ss complete the exercise individually. Walk around and help as needed.
- Check answers with the class. Ask Ss to read their questions and answers aloud.

Lesson D Reading

Warm-up and review

- If possible, bring the following items to class: chalk, a globe, index cards, a marker, notepads, paper clips, a stapler.
- Show each item to the class. Ask: *What is this?* or *What are these?* If Ss don't know the answers, say: *This is a* (name of item) or *These are* (names of items). Point to larger items from the picture dictionary if you have them in your classroom (bulletin board, chalkboard). If you don't have these items, point to the pictures in the book.

Presentation

- Direct Ss' attention to the word bank in Exercise **4A**. Say: *Repeat the words after me.* Say each word. Listen to Ss' pronunciation as they repeat. Correct pronunciation.
- Say: *Write the words in the picture dictionary.* Point to the first example, which has been done.
- Ss complete the exercise individually. Walk around and help as needed.

Comprehension check

- [Class Audio CD1 track 23] Play or read the audio program (see audio script, page T-152). Ss should check their answers and repeat the words after they hear them. Repeat the audio program.

Learner persistence (individual work)

- [Self-Study Audio CD track 14] Exercise **4A** is recorded on the Ss' self-study CD at the back of the Student's Book. Ss can listen to the CD at home for reinforcement and review. They can also listen for self-directed learning when class attendance is not possible.

Community building (small groups)

- Before class, collect catalogs or flyers from an office-supply store and bring them to class.
- In class, write on the board:
  <u>Classroom object</u> <u>Page</u> <u>Price</u>
- Ss in small groups. Model the activity. Locate one of the items from the picture dictionary in the catalog and write its name, page number, and price on the board.
- Ask Ss to find the other items in the catalog and write down the information on a piece of paper.
- Check answers with the class and ask Ss if they found new vocabulary items they want to share with the class.
- Compare prices and determine the best store in which to buy these items.

Application

- Hold up a marker. Put the marker in a drawer. Write on the board: *Where's the marker?* Ask the question aloud. Elicit: *It's in the drawer.*
- Hold up two or more notepads. Put the notepads on a table. Write on the board: *Where are the notepads?* Ask the question aloud. Elicit: *They're on the table.*
- Direct Ss' attention to Exercise **4B** and read the instructions aloud. Point to picture number 1 at the top of the page. Ask a S: *Where's the chalk?* Elicit: *It's on the chalk tray.* Point to picture number 7 and ask: *Where are the paper clips?* Elicit: *They're in the drawer.*

> **Teaching tip**
> Ss will probably not know the words *chalk tray.* If you have a chalk tray in your class, point to it. Say: *This is a chalk tray.*

- Ask two Ss to create another conversation. Be sure Ss pay attention to the correct form of singular and plural sentences.
- Say: *Ask and answer questions about the pictures.* Ss complete the exercise in pairs. Check the answers.

Learner persistence (student pairs)

- Give Ss 5–10 minutes to check in with their classroom buddies. Encourage them to ask their buddies how the class is going for them. Is it easy? Is it hard? Are there problems? This will allow buddies to help each other.

Community building (small groups)

- Ss in small groups. Ask Ss to make a "Welcome to your new classroom" poster for their own classroom. Use the reading on page 24 as a model.
- Collect the group posters and display them in the room.

Evaluation

- Direct Ss' attention to the lesson focus on the board.
- Put a check mark next to *Read and understand "Attention, new students!"*
- Point to classroom objects. Ask Ss *Where* questions for the words in the picture dictionary, for example: *Where is the bulletin board?* (It's on the wall.)
- Check off the lesson focus as Ss demonstrate an understanding of what they have learned in the lesson.

> ***More Ventures*** *(whole group, pairs, individual)*
> Assign appropriate exercises from the *Teacher's Toolkit Audio CD / CD-ROM, Add Ventures,* or the *Workbook.*

4 Picture dictionary Classroom objects

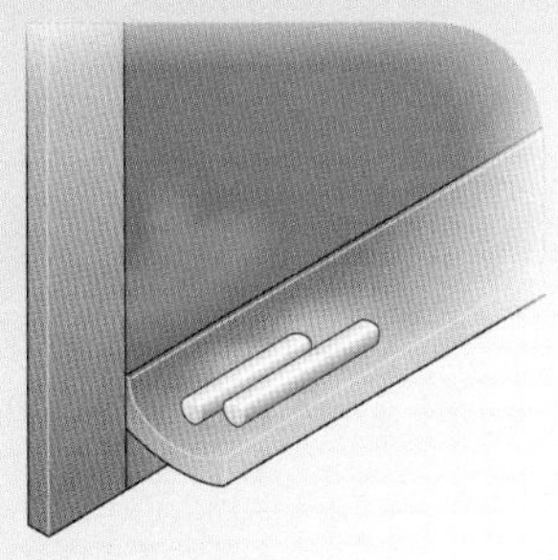

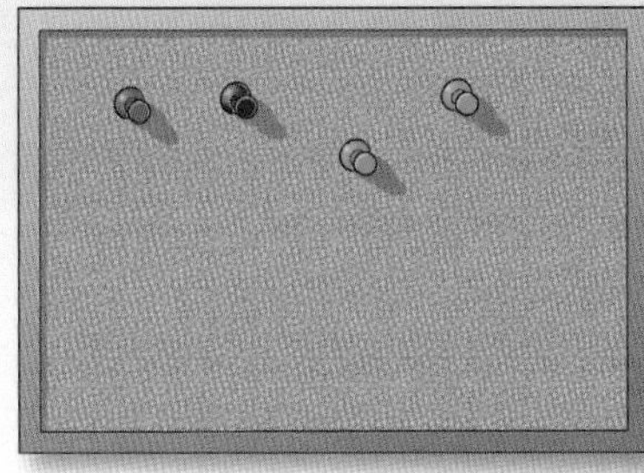

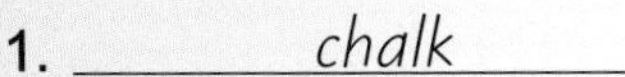

1. chalk
2. notepads
3. bulletin board

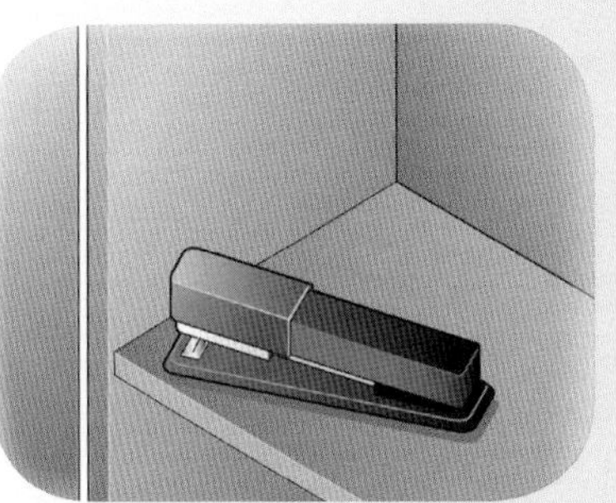

4. chalkboard
5. index cards
6. stapler

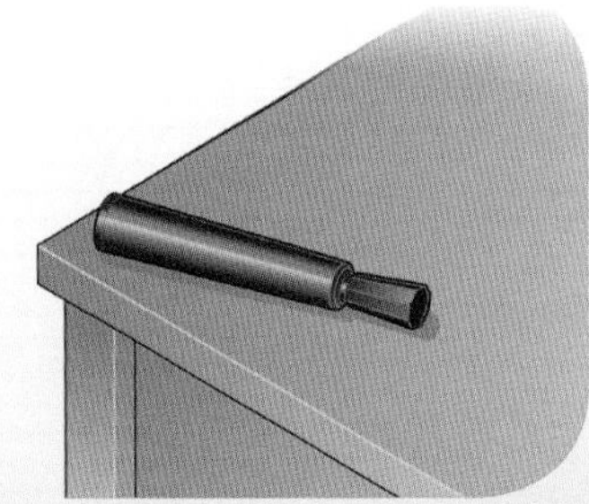

7. paper clips
8. marker
9. globe

A **Write** the words in the picture dictionary. Then listen and repeat.

bulletin board	chalkboard	index cards	notepads	stapler
chalk	globe	marker	paper clips	

B **Talk** with a partner. Look at the pictures and make conversations.

A Where's the chalk?
B It's on the chalk tray.
A Where are the paper clips?
B They're in the drawer.

Writing

1 Before you write

A **Draw.** Choose six objects. Draw two on the desk. Draw two on the table. Draw two in the cabinet. Write the words under the picture.

calculator	clock	globe	notepad	pencil sharpener
calendar	computer	map	pen	ruler
chalk	dictionary	notebook	pencil	stapler

(Answers will vary.) ______________ ______________

______________ ______________ ______________

Talk with a partner. Tell about your picture. Draw your partner's objects.

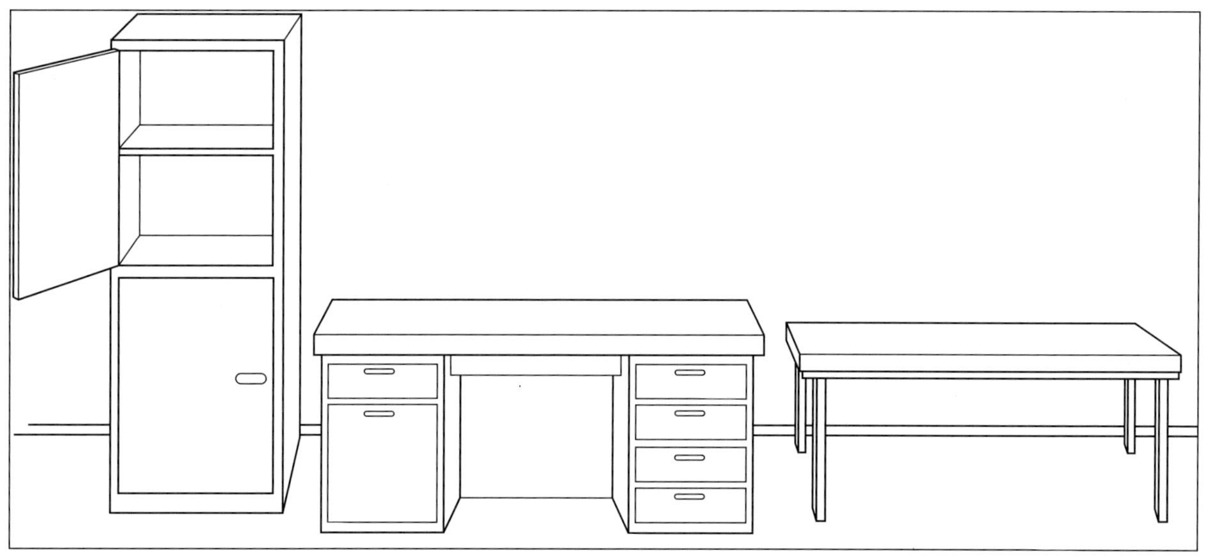

Lesson objectives
- Write about classroom objects
- Learn about capital letters and periods

Warm-up and review

- Before class. Write today's lesson focus on the board.
  Lesson E:
  Write about a classroom
  Start each sentence with a capital letter
  End each sentence with a period
- Begin class. Books closed. Draw a calculator on the board. Ask: *What is this?* When a S guesses correctly, ask him or her to write the word on the board under the picture. Repeat with other vocabulary from the unit (for example, *globe, calculator, clock*).
- Draw several pens on the board. Ask: *What are these?* When a S guesses correctly, ask him or her to write the word on the board under the picture. Repeat with other vocabulary from the unit (for example, *paper clips, markers, notebooks*).

Presentation

- Books open. Point to the words in the word bank in Exercise **1A**. Read each word aloud. Ask Ss to repeat after you. Correct Ss' pronunciation if necessary.

Teaching tip
Whenever possible, use real objects in the classroom to remind Ss of the meaning of this new vocabulary.

- Read aloud the instructions for Exercise **1A**. Say: *Now, in your books you will draw and write the name of classroom objects. How many things will you draw on the desk?* (two) *How many on the table?* (two) *How many in the cabinet?* (two)
- Ss complete the exercise individually. Walk around and help as needed.

Practice

- Read aloud the second part of the instructions for Exercise **1A**. Say: *Talk about your picture. Don't show your partner your picture. Tell your partner what to draw. Your partner will draw your picture.*
- Model the task. Ask a S: *Tell me about one thing in your picture.* Elicit: *The _____ is in / on the _____.* Draw something different. Ask the S: *Is my drawing the same as yours?* Encourage the S to hold up his or her book for the class to compare the two pictures. Don't let the Ss show you the picture. Elicit: *No, it isn't.*
- Erase your drawing and say: *Please repeat.* Elicit: *The _____ is in / on the _____.* Draw on the board whatever the S describes. Ask the S: *Is my drawing the same as yours?* Elicit: *Yes, it is.*
- Ss complete the exercise in pairs. Walk around and help as needed.
- When Ss are finished, say: *Look at your partner's picture. Is it the same? Is it different?*

Expansion activity (student pairs)

- Peer dictation. Before class. Type the following dictation sentences based on the picture on page 18. Some sentences can be silly. Make enough copies for Ss working in pairs.
  Set 1
  1. The globe is on the wall.
  2. The books are on the cabinet.
  3. The map is on the bookcase.
  4. The pencil sharpener is in the cabinet.
  5. The notebooks are on the desk.
  Set 2
  1. The dictionary is on the chair.
  2. The chalkboard is on the wall.
  3. The pencils are in his hand.
  4. The clock is in the drawer.
  5. The erasers are in the basket.
- In class. Ss in pairs. Say: *Take out a piece of paper. Write numbers one to five.* Model the activity by writing numbers *1–5* on the board in a vertical line.
- Say: *I will give you five sentences. Don't show them to your partner. Read the sentences to your partner. Your partner will write the sentences.*
- Walk around and help as needed.
- When Ss are finished, say: *Check your work. Look at your partner's sentences. Are your sentences correct?*
- Direct Ss' attention to the picture on page 18. Write on the board two sentences from the dictation: *The globe is on the wall. The dictionary is on the chair.* Read each sentence and ask: *Is this correct or incorrect?* Ask a S to come to the board and correct the first sentence. (The globe in on the bookshelf.)
- Ask each pair to work together to read the dictation sentences, look at the picture on page 18, and make corrections. The sentences should correctly describe the picture.

Lesson E Writing

Comprehension check

- Direct Ss' attention to the picture in Exercise **1B**. Point to the desk, cabinet, and table. Ask: *What do you see?* (a desk, cabinet, and table)
- Point to the computer. Ask: *What is this?* Elicit: *It's a computer.* Ask: *Where is it?* Elicit: *It's on the desk.* Write on the board: *The computer <u>is</u> <u>on</u> the desk.*
- Write on the board: *The computers _____ _____ the cabinet.* Ask Ss to say the correct sentence. Write the words in the blanks. (are / in) Be sure Ss understand plural / singular and *in / on.*
- Read aloud the instructions for Exercise **1B**.
- Ss complete the exercise individually. Walk around and help as needed.
- Go over answers with the class. Ask Ss to write the complete sentences on the board. Ask different Ss to read them aloud. Ask: *Are the sentences correct?* Have Ss make any necessary corrections on the board.

Teaching tip

Another way to correct the exercise is to put Ss in pairs and have them compare their sentences. If they are different, they can look through the lessons in the unit and discover the correct answers. Walk around and help as needed.

Application

- On the board, draw a chart as for Exercise **2**. Hold up a pen. Ask: *Singular or plural?* (singular) Write *pen* under the *Singular* column. Hold up two pencils. Ask: *Singular or plural?* (plural) Write *pencils* under the *Plural* column. Circle the *-s* in pencils and remind Ss that plural nouns usually end in *-s.*
- Direct Ss' attention to Exercise **2** and read the instructions aloud. Be sure Ss understand the task.
- Ss complete the exercise individually. Walk around and help as needed.
- Ask Ss to read their list of classroom objects. As they read, write the objects in the columns on the board and ask: *Is this right?* Listen and correct for the pronunciation of plural *-s* ending.
- Read aloud the second part of the instructions for Exercise **2**. Ask two Ss to read the example sentences aloud. Say: *Remember to use "is" with singular nouns and "are" with plural nouns. Remember to add* -s *to plural nouns.*
- Ss complete the exercise individually. Walk around and help as needed.

Read the tip box aloud. Remind Ss to use these rules of capitalization and punctuation when writing sentences in English.

Evaluation

- Direct Ss' attention to Exercise **3A** and read the instructions aloud.
- Ss complete the exercise in pairs. Walk around and help as needed. Help with pronunciation.
- Read aloud the instructions for Exercise **3B**. This exercise asks Ss to work together and peer-correct their writing. Ask a S to read the questions aloud. Tell Ss to exchange papers and look at their partner's sentences for the answers to the questions.
- Take a S's book (or paper). Ask the class: *What do I need to check?* (two singular and two plural objects, *is / are, in / on,* capital letters and periods)
- Ss complete the exercise in pairs. Help as needed.
- Ask several Ss to write one of their sentences on the board. Ask different Ss to read them aloud. Ask the questions from Exercise **3B**. Ask other Ss to make any necessary corrections on the board.

Expansion activity *(whole group)*

- Writing competition. Divide the class into two teams. Say: *One person from each team will come to the board. I will tell you a word. You need to write a sentence with that word.*
- Model the activity. Ask a S to come to the board. Say: *Cabinet. Make a sentence with "cabinet."* The S will write a sentence on the board. Ask the class: *Is this sentence correct?* Ask another S to make any necessary corrections on the board.
- Use the words from the word bank on page 26. Call out one word at a time. The person who writes a sentence correctly in the shortest time gets a point. Tally the points at the end of the game. The team with the most points wins.

More Ventures *(whole group, pairs, individual)*
Assign appropriate exercises from the *Teacher's Toolkit Audio CD / CD-ROM, Add Ventures,* or the *Workbook.*

B Write. Look at the picture. Complete the sentences. Use *is* or *are* with *on* or *in*.

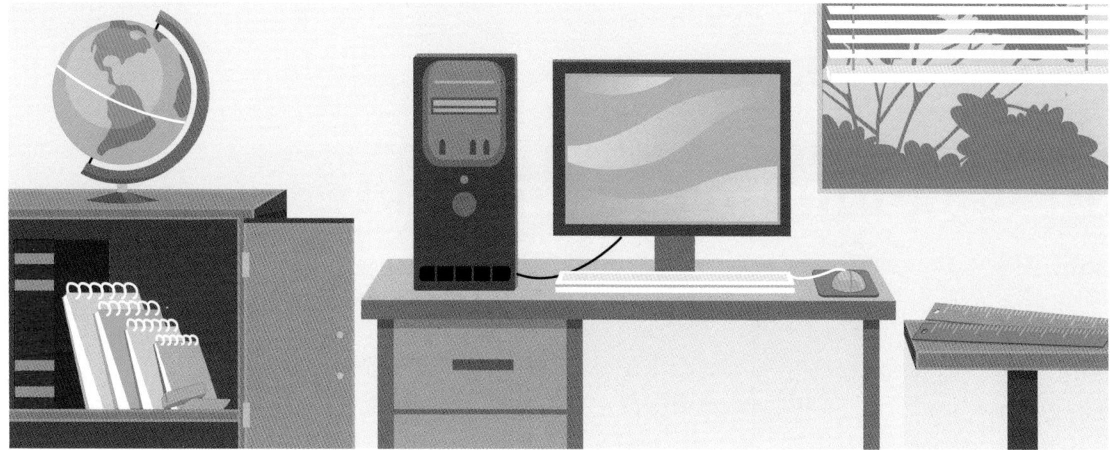

1. The computer *is* *on* the desk.
2. The notepads *are* *in* the cabinet.
3. The book *is* *in* the cabinet.
4. The erasers *are* *in* the cabinet.
5. The globe *is* *on* the cabinet.
6. The rulers *are* *on* the table.

2 Write

Write. Look at your classroom. What do you see? Complete the chart.

Singular	Plural
pen	*pencils*
(Answers will vary.)	

Write one sentence about each object.

1. *The pen is on the desk.*
2. *The pencils are in the drawer.*
3. *(Answers will vary.)*
4.
5.
6.

Start sentences with a capital letter (*A, B, C*). End sentences with a period (**.**).

3 After you write

A Read your sentences to a partner.

B Check your partner's sentences.

- What are four objects in the classroom? Where are they?
- Are the capital letters and periods correct?

Lesson F

Another view

1 Life-skills reading

Classroom Inventory List

Item	Number	Location
calculators	15	in the drawer
computers	1	on the desk
books	5	on the cabinet
erasers	20	in the box
pencils	20	on the table
pens	20	on the table
rulers	25	in the cabinet

A Read the questions. Look at the inventory list. Circle the answers.

1. How many rulers are in the cabinet?
   a. 5
   b. 15
   c. 20
   (d.) 25

2. What's on the desk?
   a. a pen
   b. a book
   (c.) a computer
   d. a calculator

3. Where are the calculators?
   a. in the cabinet
   (b.) in the drawer
   c. on the desk
   d. on the table

4. Where are the books?
   a. on the desk
   (b.) on the cabinet
   c. in the drawer
   d. in the cabinet

B Talk with a partner. Ask and answer questions about the inventory list.

Are the pens on the table?

Yes, they are.

Where are the books?

They're on the cabinet.

Lesson objectives

- Practice reading a classroom inventory list
- Review unit vocabulary
- Introduce the project
- Complete the self-assessment

Warm-up and review

- Before class. Write today's lesson focus on the board.
  Lesson F:
  Read and talk about a classroom inventory list
  Review vocabulary for classroom objects
  Complete the self-assessment
- Begin class. Books closed. Write on the board: *Classroom Inventory List*. Point to the words. Say: *This is a list of items in the classroom.*
- On the board, copy the first two rows from the chart:

Item	*Number*	*Location*
calculators	*15*	*in the drawer*

- Point to *calculators*. Ask: *What item is this?* (calculators) Point to *15*. Ask: *How many calculators are there?* (15) Point to *in the drawer*. Ask: *Where are the calculators?* (They're in the drawer.)
- Review the meaning of any words that Ss do not remember.

Teaching tip

Ss may not be familiar with the question words *How many?* Write them on the board. Say: *"How many?" asks for a number.* Give Ss examples using objects in the classroom.

Presentation

- Books open. Direct Ss' attention to the Classroom Inventory List in Exercise **1**.
- Ask Ss questions using information from the inventory list:
  How many calculators are in the drawer? (15)
  How many pencils are on the table? (20)
  Where are the calculators? (They're in the drawer.)
  Where is the computer? (It's on the desk.)
- Direct Ss' attention to Exercise **1A** and read the instructions aloud. This task helps prepare Ss for standardized-type tests they may have to take. Be sure Ss understand the task. Have Ss individually scan for and circle the answers.
- Ss complete the exercise individually. Walk around and help as needed.

Comprehension check

- Check answers with the class. Ask Ss to read the questions and answers and point to the correct information in the chart.

Practice

- Direct Ss' attention to Exercise **1B** and read the instructions aloud. Call on Ss to read aloud the two examples.

Teaching tip

Remind Ss of the grammar chart in Exercise **1** on page 22. It might help to review asking and answering both *Yes / No* questions and *Where* questions.

- Ss complete the exercise in pairs. Walk around and help as needed. Ask several pairs to ask and answer questions aloud.

Expansion activity *(small groups)*

- Ss in small groups. Say: *Think about another room in our school.* (It can be another classroom, the reception area, a teacher's office, or any other room with which Ss are familiar.) *Ask questions about this room. For example: Is there a computer in the* (name of room)*? Where is it? Write five questions about this room. Ask another group your questions. Do they know the answers?*
- If possible, have Ss go to the other room to see if they have answered the questions correctly.

Lesson F Another view

Presentation

- Books closed. Review the alphabet. Write on the board: *A E I O U*. Point to each vowel. Say each letter and ask Ss to repeat.
- Write these consonants on the board: *J G H K Q V W X Y Z*. Point to each. Say each letter and ask Ss to repeat.

> **Teaching tip**
> If Ss have trouble remembering how to say the names of any of these letters, repeat the above activity several times until they are familiar with the letter names.

- Ask Ss: *What are some objects in our classroom?* When Ss answer, ask: *How do you spell it?* Write the word on the board exactly as the S spells it. Ask the class: *Is that correct?* Make any necessary corrections on the board.

Practice

- Books open. Direct Ss' attention to Exercise **2A** and read the instructions aloud.
- Point to the example in the book. Ask: *Are there pens in our classroom?* Point to the box where *Yes* is checked. Say: *Yes, there are pens in our classroom.*
- Ask Ss for the missing letter in the next word. Write the word on the board and underline the missing letter. (erasers) Write *Yes* / *No* on the board with check boxes below each. Ask: *Are there erasers in our classroom?* Check the correct box. Be sure Ss understand the task.
- Ss complete the exercise in pairs. Help as needed.
- Check answers with the class. Ask individual Ss to write the words on the board.
- Read aloud the second part of the instructions for Exercise **2A**. Point to the *n* in *pens*. Then point to the *n* in the first blank. Point to the word *erasers* on the board. Ask Ss which letter to write in the next blank. (e) Say: *Continue writing the other letters in the blanks.*
- Ss complete the exercise individually. Help as needed.
- Ask a S to write the missing letters from the chart on the board as other Ss work individually. Ask Ss to correct the letters on the board, if necessary.
- Read aloud the third part of the instructions for Exercise **2A**.
- Ask a S to read the question *Where are you?* Say: *Use the letters to answer the question.*
- Help Ss complete the first word. (*in*) Cross off the *i* and *n* from the letters on the board.
- Ss complete the exercise in pairs. Help as needed.
- Ask a S to write the unscrambled answer on the board. (*in the classroom*)

Application

- Ss in small groups. Direct Ss' attention to Exercise **2B** and ask a S to read the instructions aloud.
- Point to the example written in the inventory list. Say: *There are three erasers in the classroom. They are on the shelf.*
- Say: *Continue the list. Walk around the room with your group. How many items can you put on your list?*
- Ss complete the exercise in groups. Help as needed.
- Read aloud the second part of the instructions for Exercise **2B**. Ask a S to read the example aloud. Say: *Choose one person in your group to read your inventory list to the class.* Ss listen and compare lists.

> **Teaching tip**
> To encourage teamwork, before beginning Exercise **2B**, put Ss in groups of three and have Ss choose group tasks. Ask each group to choose one S as recorder to write the list. Choose one S as speaker to talk to the class about their classroom inventory list. Choose one S as accountant to count the items. At the end of the lesson, display a permanent classroom inventory list and assign different groups each week to update the list.

> ***More Ventures*** *(whole group, pairs, individual)*
> Assign appropriate exercises from the *Teacher's Toolkit Audio CD / CD-ROM, Add Ventures,* or the *Workbook.*

Community building

- **Project** Ask Ss to turn to page 136 in their Student's Book to complete the project for Unit 2.

Evaluation

- Before asking Ss to turn to the self-assessment on page 141, do a quick review of the unit. Have Ss turn to Lesson A. Ask the class to tell what they remember about this lesson. Prompt Ss with questions, for example: *What are the conversations about on this page?* Review each lesson quickly.
- **Self-assessment** Read the instructions for Exercise **3**. Ask Ss to complete the unit self-assessment.
- If Ss are ready, administer the unit test on pages T-165–T-166 of this *Teacher's Edition* (or on the *Teacher's Toolkit Audio CD / CD-ROM*). The audio and audio script for the tests are on the *Teacher's Toolkit Audio CD / CD-ROM.*

2 Fun with language

A **Work with a partner.** Complete the words. Are the objects in your classroom?

	Yes	No		Yes	No
pe *n* s	☑	☐	penc *i* ls	☐	☐
e rasers	☐	☐	*m* ap	☐	☐
c *h* alk	☐	☐	*r* uler *s*	☐	☐
no *t* ebo *o* ks	☐	☐	*c* alend *a* r	☐	☐
gl *o* be	☐	☐	*s* tap *l* er	☐	☐

Write the missing letters from the chart.

n e h t o o i m r s c a s l

Write. Unscramble the letters to answer the question.

Where are you? *i n t h e c l a s s r o o m*

B **Work in a group.** Make a classroom inventory list.

Classroom Inventory List		
Item	**Number**	**Location**
erasers	*3*	*on the shelf*
(Answers will vary.)		

Talk. Tell your class about your inventory.

Three erasers are on the shelf.

3 Wrap up

Complete the **Self-assessment** on page 141.

Review

1 Listening

Read the questions. Then listen and circle the answers.

1. What is Juan's last name? (a.) Perez b. Cruz
2. Where is he from? a. Mexico (b.) El Salvador
3. What is his apartment number? a. 1324 (b.) 10
4. What is his zip code? a. 94548 (b.) 94321
5. What is his area code? (a.) 213 b. 555
6. What is his telephone number? (a.) 555-6301 b. 555-0133

Talk with a partner. Ask and answer the questions. Use complete sentences.

2 Grammar

A Write. Complete the story.

A New Student

Layla ___*is*___ (1. is / are) a new student. ___*Her*___ (2. My / Her) last name is Azari. She ___*is*___ (3. is / are) from Iran. She ___*is*___ (4. is / are) a good student. Her pencils and a notebook ___*are*___ (5. is / are) on her desk. A dictionary is ___*in*___ (6. in / at) her bag. Her classmates ___*aren't*___ (7. isn't / aren't) in the classroom now.

B Write. Unscramble the words. Make questions about the story.

1. from / Where / Layla / is / ? *Where is Layla from?*
2. her / What's / name / last / ? *What's her last name?*
3. good / she / a / student / Is / ? *Is she a good student?*
4. in / bag / What / is / her / ? *What is in her bag?*

Talk with a partner. Ask and answer the questions.

Lesson objective

- Review vocabulary, pronunciation, and grammar from Units 1 and 2

Warm-up and review

- Before class. Write today's lesson focus on the board. *Review unit: Review vocabulary, pronunciation, and grammar from Units 1 and 2*
- Begin class. Books closed. Review questions about personal information. Ask individual Ss:
  What's your last name?
  Where are you from?
  What's your address?
  What's your zip code?
  What's your telephone number?
  What's your area code?

Presentation

- Books open. Focus Ss' attention on Exercise **1**. Read the instructions aloud.
- Ask individual Ss to read the questions aloud. Say: *Now listen to the conversation. Circle the correct answers.*
- [Class Audio CD1 track 24] Play or read the audio program (see audio script, page T-153). Ss listen to and circle the answers to the questions. Repeat the audio program as needed.
- Write the numbers *1–6* on the board. Ask individual Ss to write their answers on the board. Ask other Ss: *Are these answers correct?* Have Ss make any necessary corrections on the board.

Practice

- Read aloud the second part of the instructions for Exercise **1**.
- Ss complete the exercise in pairs. Walk around and help as needed.
- Ask several pairs to ask and answer the questions for the rest of the class.
- Write on the board:
  I _____ *You* _____ *She* _____ *He* _____
  We _____ *They* _____
- Model the activity. Point to *I* on the board. Say: *I am a teacher.* Write *am* in the blank next to *I*.
- Ask Ss to continue by writing the correct form of *to be* in the remaining blanks.
- Direct Ss' attention to Exercise **2A**. Read the instructions aloud.
- Ask a S to read aloud the title of the paragraph ("A New Student").
- Ask another S to read aloud the first sentence in the paragraph.
- Ss complete the exercise individually. Walk around and help as needed.
- Write the numbers *1–7* on the board. Ask Ss to come up to the board to write the answers.

Teaching tip

Ask Ss to write only the missing words on the board, not the complete sentences.

- Ask individual Ss to read aloud a sentence from the paragraph. After each sentence, ask: *Is the answer correct?* Ask different Ss to correct any errors.
- Books closed. Write on the board:
  name / is / What / your / ?
- Ask Ss to unscramble the words on the board to make a question. (What is your name?) Write the question on the board.
- Books open. Focus Ss' attention on Exercise **2B**. Read the instructions aloud.
- Ss complete the exercise individually. Walk around and help as needed.
- Write the numbers *1–4* on the board. Ask four Ss to write the unscrambled questions on the board. Ask other Ss: *Are the questions correct?* Ask different Ss to correct any errors.
- Read aloud the second part of the instructions for Exercise **2B**.
- Model the task. Ask a S the first question: *Where is Layla from?* Elicit: *She is from Iran.*
- Ss complete the exercise in pairs. Walk around and help as needed.
- Ask several pairs to ask and answer the questions for the rest of the class.

Warm-up and review

- Write the word *syllables* on the board. Point to the word. Say it aloud. Ask Ss to repeat.
- Underline the syllables in the word *syllable (syll – a – ble).* Clap while you say the word, emphasizing each of the three syllables. Say: *These are syllables.*

Presentation

- Focus Ss' attention on Exercise **3A**. Read the instructions.
- [Class Audio CD1 track 25] Play or read the audio program (see audio script, page T-153). Repeat the audio program as needed.

Practice

- Read aloud the instructions for Exercise **3B**.
- [Class Audio CD1 track 26] Play or read the audio program (see audio script, page T-153). Ss listen and repeat the words they hear in the audio program. Encourage Ss to clap one time for each syllable. Repeat the audio program as needed.

> **Teaching tip**
> Clap with your Ss the first time they repeat the words to show them the correct way to do this exercise.

- Read aloud the second part of the instructions for Exercise **3B**.
- Model the task. Ask a S to stand up. Hold up the Student's Book. Point to the word *map.* Say the word. Ask the S to clap the syllable after you say the word.
- Ss complete the exercise in pairs. Walk around and help as needed.
- Ask several pairs to say the words and clap the syllables for the rest of the class.

  Option Ask the class to pronounce and clap the words.
- Read aloud the instructions for Exercise **3C**.
- [Class Audio CD1 track 27] Model the activity. Play or read only the first word on the audio program (see audio script, page T-153). Ask: *How many syllables did you hear?* (one)
- [Class Audio CD1 track 27] Play or read the audio program. Ss listen and write the number of syllables they hear in each word. Repeat the audio program as needed.
- Write the letters *a–h* on the board. Ask individual Ss to write their answers on the board. Ask: *Are the answers correct?* Ask different Ss to correct.

> **Teaching tip**
> If there are any questions about how many syllables are in each word, clap out the word in question with the class and then count the number of claps for that word.

- Read aloud the second part of the instructions for Exercise **3C**.
- [Class Audio CD1 track 28] Play or read the audio program (see audio script, page T-153). Listen to Ss' pronunciation as they repeat the words and clap out the syllables. Repeat the audio program as needed.

Expansion activity *(small groups)*

- Flash card pronunciation practice. Make a set of ten flash cards for each small group of four or five Ss in your class. On one side of the card, write a word from Unit 1 or 2. On the other side, write the number of syllables in that word.
- Ss in small groups. Give each group a set of cards. Tell Ss to test their classmates by holding up a card with a word on it. The other Ss have to say the word and clap out the correct number of syllables. They will say the number of syllables in the word. Then the person holding the card will show the reverse side of the card to show the S if he or she is correct.

Practice

- Read aloud the instructions for Exercise **3D**.
- Model the task. Look through Units 1 and 2 in the Student's Book. Write a word on the board that isn't in Exercise **3B**. Say: *Find other words to write in the chart.*
- Ss complete the exercise individually. Help as needed.

  Option Ask Ss to write their words on the board.
- Read aloud the second part of the instructions for Exercise **3D**.
- Model the task. Point to the word you wrote on the board. Say it aloud. Ask a S to tell you how many syllables are in the word.
- Ss complete the exercise in pairs. Help as needed.

Evaluation

- Direct Ss' attention to the lesson focus on the board.
- Go around the room. Ask Ss to say a sentence about themselves using the personal information vocabulary they learned in Unit 1.
- Ask Ss to pronounce names of classroom objects and say how many syllables are in each word.
- Check off the items in the lesson focus as Ss demonstrate an understanding of what they have learned in the lesson.

3 Pronunciation: syllables

A **Listen** to the syllables in these words.

•	• •	• • •
name	address	apartment

B **Listen and repeat.** Say the word and clap one time for each syllable.

•	• •	• • •
map	classroom	initial
books	middle	telephone
box	partner	signature
clock	chalkboard	computer
pens	ruler	sharpener
chair	notebook	cabinet
desk	pencil	eraser

Talk with a partner. Take turns. Say a word. Your partner claps for each syllable.

C **Listen** to the words. Write the number of syllables you hear.

a. *1* c. *2* e. *4* g. *1*
b. *2* d. *1* f. *3* h. *2*

Listen again and repeat. Clap one time for each syllable.

D **Write.** Find 10 other words in your book. Make a list.

1. *(Answers will vary.)*	6.
2.	7.
3.	8.
4.	9.
5.	10.

Talk with a partner. Say the words. Your partner says how many syllables.

Friends and family

Lesson A Get ready

1 Talk about the picture

A Look at the picture. What do you see?

B Point to: the mother • the father • the daughter
the son • the grandmother • the grandfather

Lesson objectives
- Introduce students to the topic
- Find out what students know about the topic
- Preview the unit by talking about the picture
- Practice key vocabulary
- Practice listening skills

Warm-up and review

- Before class. Write today's lesson focus on the board.
  Lesson A: Friends and family

brother	*grandfather*	*mother*
daughter	*grandmother*	*sister*
father	*husband*	*son*

- Begin class. Books closed. Say: *Today's class is about the people in your life.* Point to the word *family* on the board. Ask: *What's a family?* Ss may respond with some of the words on the board or with other words they know.
- Show a magazine picture or a photograph of a family, or draw one on the board. Point to the mother in the family. Ask: *Is this the mother or the father?* (the mother) Continue by pointing to other family members and asking questions with *or.*

Teaching tip
Asking *Yes / No* or *or* questions as a warm-up activity is a good idea because the questions are easy to respond to and create a relaxed atmosphere in the classroom.

- Ask: *Who lives with you?* Point to the list of family members on the board. Help Ss answer, if necessary.

Presentation

- Books open. Set the scene. Direct Ss' attention to the picture on page 32. Ask: *What do you see?* Elicit as much vocabulary about the picture as possible and write the words on the board: *phone, lamp, bed, TV, chair,* etc.

Teaching tip
Do not expect all Ss to be able to respond in English. These warm-up activities are meant to identify what Ss already know and to involve Ss in the topic.

- Direct Ss' attention to the key words in Exercise **1B**. Read each word aloud while pointing to the corresponding person in the picture. Ask the class to repeat and point.
- Listen to Ss' pronunciation and repeat the words if needed.

Teaching tip
The key words are intended to help Ss talk about the picture and learn some of the vocabulary of the unit.

Comprehension check

- Ask Ss *Yes / No* questions about the picture. Point to the boy in the top left part of the picture. Ask: *Is he the daughter?* (No.) Point to the girl in the top right part of the picture. Ask: *Is she the daughter?* (Yes.)
- Repeat the procedure with the grandfather, the grandmother, the father, and the mother.

Practice

- Direct Ss' attention to Exercise **1B**. Model the task. Hold up the Student's Book. Say to a S: *Point to the mother.* The S points to the appropriate part of the picture.
- Ss in pairs. Say to one S: *Say the words in Exercise 1B.* Say to his or her partner: *Point to the person in the picture.*
- Ss complete the exercise in pairs. Walk around and help as needed. When Ss finish, have them change partners and change roles.
- Ask several pairs to perform the exercise for the class to check Ss' understanding.

Expansion activity (small groups)

- Bring in a family photograph and pictures of families from magazines.
- Show your family photo. Point to and identify one family member. Say: *This is my* (name of family member). Write on the board: *This is my* _____. Read the sentence aloud. Ask Ss to repeat.
- Point to and identify the other members of your family.
- Ss in small groups. Give pictures of families to the groups. Ss identify the family members in their pictures in their groups.
- Ask Ss to stand up and describe their pictures to the rest of the class. Encourage as many Ss to do this as possible.

Expansion activity (whole group)

- Direct Ss' attention to the rooms in the picture on page 32. Ask: *Where is he?* (in the bedroom) *Where are they?* (in the kitchen / in the living room) *Where is she?* (in the bedroom) Write the names of the rooms on the board. Say each room. Ask Ss to repeat.
- Point to the first picture. Ask: *Who's in the first bedroom?* (son) *Who's in the second bedroom?* (daughter) *Who's in the kitchen?* (mother and grandfather) *Who's in the living room?* (grandmother and father)
- Encourage pairs to ask each other the questions.

Lesson A Get ready

Presentation

- Books open. Direct Ss' attention to the word bank words in Exercise **2A**. Say: *Repeat the words after me.* Point to and say each word aloud. Listen to Ss' pronunciation.
- Ask a married male S: *What's your name? What's your wife's name?* Ask a married female S: *What's your name? What's your husband's name?*
- Write *husband and wife* on the board. Be sure Ss understand the meaning.
- Do the same for *sister and brother.*

Practice

- Read aloud the instructions for Exercise **2A**.
- [Class Audio CD1 track 29] Play or read the audio program (see audio script, page T-153). Ss listen to and circle the words they hear. Repeat the program as needed.
- Check answers. Ask: *What did you circle?* Ask Ss to write the words on the board. Point to the words. Say: *Repeat after me.* Say each word. Listen to Ss' pronunciation and correct as needed.
- Ask a S to write on the board the words that were not circled: *brother, daughter, son.* Point to the words. Say: *Repeat after me.* Say each word.
- Direct Ss' attention to the pictures in Exercise **2B**. Hold up the Student's Book. Point to the first picture. Say: *Who are they?* (the son and the grandfather)
- Continue asking Ss about the rest of the pictures.
- Read aloud the instructions for Exercise **2B**.
- [Class Audio CD1 track 29] Play or read the audio program again. Pause after the first conversation. Ask: *Which picture matches conversation A?* (picture number 4) Point to the handwritten *a* written next to number 4.
- Continue playing the audio program. Ss complete the rest of the exercise individually.

Learner persistence (individual work)

- [Self-Study Audio CD track 15] Exercises **2A** and **2B** are recorded on the Ss' self-study CD at the back of the Student's Book. Ss can listen to the CD at home for reinforcement and review. They can also listen for self-directed learning when class attendance is not possible.

Comprehension check

- Write the numbers *1–6* on the board. Ask a few Ss to come to the board and write the correct answers to Exercise **2B** next to each number.
- Read aloud the second part of the instructions for Exercise **2B**.
- [Class Audio CD1 track 29] Play or read the audio program again. Pause after each conversation. Point to a letter of the conversation on the board. Ask: *Is this correct?* Ask another S to make corrections.

Application

- Say: *I live with* (list people you live with). Ask a S: *Who do you live with?* Continue by asking Ss the same question.
- Direct Ss' attention to Exercise **2C** and read the instructions aloud. Model the task. Write on the board the family members. Draw boxes with check marks next to the family members you live with.
- Ss complete the exercise individually. Walk around and help as needed.
- Read aloud the second part of the instructions for Exercise **2C**. Read the example aloud.
- Ss complete the exercise in small groups.
- When the groups are finished, ask several Ss to tell the class about their families.

Culture tip
You may want to explain that many Americans do not live with their extended families. They usually live with their immediate families, with roommates, or alone.

Learner persistence (small groups)

- Put Ss in small groups according to their countries. Say: *Talk in your group. Prepare to tell the class about how people live in your country. Do they live with friends? Do they live with their extended family?*
- Write on the board: *In* (name of country), *people live with _____.* Have Ss share information.

Evaluation

- Direct Ss' attention to the lesson focus written on the board. Point to the names of family members. Say: *Look at page 32. Make sentences with the words on the board.*
- Check off the items as Ss demonstrate understanding of what they have learned in the lesson.

More Ventures *(whole group, pairs, individual)*
Assign appropriate exercises from the *Teacher's Toolkit Audio CD / CD-ROM, Add Ventures,* or the *Workbook.*

2 Listening

A **Listen.** Circle the words you hear.

brother	grandfather	mother
daughter	grandmother	sister
father	husband	son

SELF-STUDY AUDIO CD **B** **Listen again.** Write the letter of the conversation.

1. c

2. b

3. e

4. a

5. d

6. f

Listen again. Check your answers.

C **Write.** Who lives with you? Check (✓) your answers.

- ☐ my husband
- ☐ my wife
- ☐ my son
- ☐ my daughter
- ☐ my mother
- ☐ my father
- ☐ my sister
- ☐ my brother

Talk about your family. Work in a group.

My husband and my son live with me.
My mother and father live in Ecuador.

Lesson B What are you doing?

1 Grammar focus: present continuous; *Wh-* questions

Questions	
What are you	doing?
What's he	
What's she	
What are they	

Answers	
I'm	reading.
He's	
She's	
They're	

The present continuous = *be* + verb + *-ing*:
read → I am reading.
talk → He is talking.
listen → They are listening.

2 Practice

A Write. Complete the conversations.

A What's she doing?
B She's reading . (read)

A What's he doing?
B He's sleeping . (sleep)

A What are they doing?
B They're eating . (eat)

A What's he doing?
B He's watching TV. (watch)

A What's she doing?
B She's talking . (talk)

A What are you doing?
B I'm studying . (study)

 **Listen and repeat.** Then practice with a partner.

Lesson objective

- Introduce the present continuous and *Wh-* questions

Warm-up and review

- Before class. Write today's lesson focus on the board.
  Lesson B:
  What are you doing? I'm reading.
  What's he doing? He's reading.
  What's she doing? She's reading.
  What are they doing? They're reading.
- Begin class. Books open. Direct Ss' attention to the picture on page 32. Say: *Point to the son.* Ss point. Say: *He's listening to music.* Write the sentence on the board.
- Ask Ss to point to other family members in the picture. Tell them what those family members are doing and write the sentences on the board.
- Pantomime these actions: eating, reading, talking, sleeping, studying, watching TV. Ask Ss to say what you're doing. Write on the board as a cue: *You're* _____. Fill in the verbs as Ss guess. Help with vocabulary as needed.
- Write on the board as cues: *He's* _____. *She's* _____. Ask Ss to pantomime and have the class guess. Fill in the verbs as Ss guess.

Presentation

- Books open. Direct Ss' attention to the grammar chart in Exercise **1**. Read the questions and answers aloud. Ask Ss to repeat.
- Write on the board:
  What's = *I'm =* *he's =* *she's =* *they're =*
- Point to the words. Say: *These are contractions.* Write *I am* after *I'm*. Say: *"I'm" is the same as "I am."* Point to the other contractions. Ask: *What are two words for "he's"?* (he is) Repeat with *she's, they're,* and *What's.*

Comprehension check

- Ask: *What am I doing right now?* Elicit: *You're teaching.* Write on the board: *You are teaching* or *You're teaching.*
- Ask Ss questions about other Ss in the class using *What* and the present continuous. For example, ask one S: *What's* (student's name) *doing?* (He's / She's studying, He's / She's sitting, etc.) Say to the same S: *Now you ask a question about a S in the class.* The S stands up and asks another S what someone else in the class is doing. Write new words on the board.

Practice

- Direct Ss' attention to Exercise **2A** and point to number 1. Ask: *What's she doing?* (She's reading.) Point to *read* in the example. Say: *Use this verb to help you write the answer.* Continue with the other items.
- Read aloud the instructions for Exercise **2A**.
- Ss complete the exercise individually. Walk around and help as needed.
- [Class Audio CD1 track 30] Read aloud the second part of the instructions for Exercise **2A**. Play or read the audio program (see audio script, page T-153). Have Ss check the answers as they listen and repeat. Correct pronunciation as needed.
- Ss in pairs. Say: *Practice the conversations with your partner.* Walk around and help as needed. Write on the board any pronunciation errors that you hear. When Ss are finished practicing in pairs, point to the words on the board. Say: *Listen and repeat after me.*

Expansion activity *(whole group)*

- Tic-tac-toe. Draw a tic-tac-toe grid on the board. Ask the class to tell you some verbs that they learned in today's lesson. Write the verbs in the grid, for example:

read	*eat*	*study*
sleep	*watch*	*talk*
listen		

  Ask Ss to give two more verbs to complete the grid.
- Divide the class into two teams, *X* and *O*. Say: *One person from each team will choose a verb on the board. He or she has to make a sentence with the verb and the present continuous. I will say "correct" or "incorrect." If you are correct, draw an "X" or "O" in the square.*
- The first team to get three *X*s or *O*s in a row (vertically, horizontally, or diagonally) wins the game.

Teaching tip

This game can be played with many grammar points and vocabulary words learned in a lesson. It is a fun way to close a class.

Expansion activity *(whole group)*

- If you want to expand the grammar presentation, turn to the grammar charts at the back of the Student's Book. Practice making sentences using the present continuous and the pronouns *we* and *you* (plural).

Lesson B What are you doing?

Presentation

- Direct Ss' attention to the picture in Exercise **2B**. Ask: *Where are the people?* (They're in the living room.) Ask: *What do you see in the picture?* Write Ss' answers on the board. (baby, mother, couch, bookshelf, TV, etc.)
- Read the instructions aloud. Ask two Ss to read aloud the example conversation.

Teaching tip
Ss may not be familiar with the word *bold*. Explain that the bold words in the conversation are darker. In many exercises, Ss are asked to replace the bold words with other words in the exercise.

Practice

- Model the task. Point to another person in the picture. Ask: *What's he / she doing?* (watching TV, eating, talking on the phone, etc.)
- Ss in pairs. Say: *Ask and answer questions about the picture.* Walk around and help as needed.
- Ask several pairs to perform their conversations in front of the class.
- Books closed. Ask several Ss to stand up. Ask each one in turn: *What are you doing?* Elicit sentences, such as: *I'm standing. / I'm talking. / I'm studying English.*
- Books open. Direct Ss' attention to Exercise **2C** and read the instructions aloud.
- Ss complete the exercise individually. Help as needed.
- Ask Ss to write their answers on the board. Ask different Ss to read the sentences. After each sentence, ask: *Is this correct?* Ask other Ss to correct any errors on the board.

Expansion activity (whole class)

- Total Physical Response. Give Ss commands as a whole group, such as: *Stand up, sit down, open your books, close your books,* etc.
- After each command, ask a S: *What are you doing?* (I am standing / I am sitting / I am opening my book, etc.)

Application

- Books closed. Show Ss a telephone or cell phone. Ask: *What's this?* (It's a telephone / cell phone.)
- Ask: *When the phone rings* (make a ringing noise), *what do you say in English?* (Hello.) Make a ringing noise again. Hand the phone to a S. The S can pick it up and say *Hello*. Write *Hello* on the board.
- Give another S the phone. Make a ringing noise. Encourage the S to say *Hello*. Say: *Hi,* (S's name). *This is* (your name). Write these sentences on the board. Practice with a few more Ss, taking different roles.

Learner persistence (whole class)

- If there are new Ss in the class, include them in this telephone practice exercise. Encourage Ss to ask them *What's your name?* before they practice the conversation. Write their names on the board as a way of introducing them to the class and making them feel welcome.
- Books open. Have Ss' look at the pictures in Exercise **3**. Ask: *What do you see?* (a man and a woman) Ask: *What are they doing?* (They are talking on the phone.)
- Read the instructions aloud. Model the example with a S.
- Ask two Ss to model the example again using their own names and a different verb for *watching TV.*
- Ss practice the example in pairs and then make new conversations. Walk around and help as needed.
- Ask several pairs to perform their conversations.

Culture tip
Many people celebrate birthdays with a party. Big parties often are for the sixteenth, twenty-first, and fiftieth birthdays. Ask Ss if birthdays are celebrated in their families. Ask: *How are they celebrated?*

Expansion activity (whole group)

- If you want to expand the grammar presentation, turn to the grammar charts at the back of the Student's Book. Practice making sentences using the present continuous and the pronouns *we, it,* and *you (plural).*

Evaluation

- Direct Ss' attention to the sentences you wrote on the board at the beginning of the lesson. Ask questions about people in the picture on page 32. For example, point to the mother and ask: *What's she doing?* Elicit answers in the present continuous: *She's cooking.*
- Check off the questions and answers as Ss demonstrate an understanding of what they have learned in the lesson.

More Ventures (whole group, pairs, individual)
Assign appropriate exercises from the *Teacher's Toolkit Audio CD / CD-ROM, Add Ventures,* or the *Workbook.*

B **Talk** with a partner. Point to the picture. Change the **bold** words and make conversations.

A What**'s she** doing?
B **She's listening to music.**

C **Write.** Answer the question.

What are you doing?

I'm (Answers will vary.) ______________________________.

3 Communicate

Talk. Practice with a partner.

A Hello?
B Hi, Ann. This is Paul.
A Oh, hi, Paul.
B What are you doing?
A I'm watching TV.
B Well, today's my birthday. I'm having my party now.
A Now? Oh, no. I forgot!

Make new conversations.

Lesson C

Are you working now?

1 Grammar focus: present continuous; *Yes / No* questions

Questions		Answers			
Are you	working?	Yes,	I am.	No,	I'm not.
Is he			he is.		he isn't.
Is she			she is.		she isn't.
Are they			they are.		they aren't.

Spelling change
drive → driving
take → taking

2 Practice

A Write. Complete the conversations.

1
A Is she *working* (work) now?
B Yes, she is. She's very busy.

2
A Is he *driving* (drive) to work?
B Yes, he is. He's late.

3
A Are they *eating* (eat) lunch now?
B Yes, they are. They're hungry.

4
A Is he *helping* (help) his grandmother?
B Yes, he is. He's really nice.

5
A Is she *taking* (take) a break?
B Yes, she is. She's tired.

6
A Are they *buying* (buy) water?
B Yes, they are. They're thirsty.

Listen and repeat. Then practice with a partner.

Lesson objective

- Introduce *Yes* / *No* questions in the present continuous tense

Warm-up and review

- Before class. Write today's lesson focus on the board.
  Lesson C:
  Are you _____ing? *Yes, I am. / No, I'm not.*
  Is he _____ing? *Yes, he is. / No, he isn't.*
  Is she _____ing? *Yes, she is. / No, she isn't.*
  Are they _____ing? *Yes, they are. / No, they aren't.*
- Begin class. Books closed. Ask a S: *Are you studying English?* Elicit: *Yes, I am.*
- Ask another S: *Are you studying French right now?* Elicit: *No, I'm not.*

Teaching tip

Point to the answer on the board: *Yes, I am.* Say: *In English, we say "Yes, I am." We never say "Yes, I'm."*

Presentation

- Books open. Direct Ss' attention to the grammar chart in Exercise **1**. Say: *This is how we ask Yes / No questions about something we are doing right now.*
- Ask three Ss to stand up. One S reads the questions, one reads the *Yes* answers, and one reads the *No* answers.

Teaching tip

Read the spelling note aloud. Say: *When we change "drive" to "driving" we don't write the "e." This is true for verbs ending in "e." "Take" is another example.*

Expansion activity *(whole group)*

- Ask Ss to brainstorm other verbs that end in *e*. Write the verbs on the board. Ask: *How do we change the spelling when we add "ing"?* Ask Ss to come to the board and add *-ing*. Make sure they don't write the new form with *e*. Some words that Ss might think of are *make, bake*, etc.

Practice

- Direct Ss' attention to the first picture in Exercise **2A**. Point to the woman. Ask: *What is she doing?* (She is working. She is using the computer.)
- Write *busy* on the board. Point to the word and pronounce it. Say: *Repeat the word after me.* Ask: *What does "busy" mean?* If no one knows the answer, say: *"Busy" means that you are doing something.*
- Read the instructions aloud. Ask two Ss to read the example question and answer.
- Ss complete the exercise individually. Help as needed.
- Ask Ss to write the questions on the board. Make sure that Ss spell "driving" and "taking" correctly.
- Read aloud the second part of the instructions for Exercise **2A**.
- [Class Audio CD1 track 31] Play or read the audio program (see audio script, page T-153). Listen to Ss' pronunciation as they repeat the conversations. Correct pronunciation as needed.
- Ss practice the conversations in pairs. Clear up any problems with pronunciation or the meanings of words.
- Ask several pairs to read the conversations for the rest of the class.

Expansion activity *(whole group, pairs, small groups)*

- Question and answer practice. Make copies of this chart. Give one to each S.

Names	What is he or she doing?
John	
Mary	
Sally	
Nancy	
Tim	
James	
Jack	
Lily	
Betty	
Susan	

- Write each of the following sentences on an index card and give one card to each S. If you have more than ten Ss in your class, give cards to pairs, or divide the class into groups of ten and give each group a set of cards. The cards will have the following information on them (one sentence per card):
  John is sleeping. *James is buying gas.*
  Mary is working. *Jack is listening to music.*
  Sally is taking a break. *Lily is watching TV.*
  Nancy is reading. *Betty is talking.*
  Tim is driving to work. *Susan is eating dinner.*
- Write two questions on the board: *What is the name on your card? What is he or she doing?*
- Say: *Look at your card. Then fill in your chart. Ask your classmates the two questions on the board. Write your classmates' answers in the chart.*
- Ss complete the activity individually. Walk around and help as needed. Check answers with the class.

Lesson C Are you working now?

Warm-up and review

- Direct Ss' attention to the lesson focus on the board.

Are you _____ing?	*Yes, I am. / No, I'm not.*
Is he _____ing?	*Yes, he is. / No, he isn't.*
Is she _____ing?	*Yes, she is. / No, she isn't.*
Are they _____ing?	*Yes, they are. / No, they aren't.*

- Hold up the Student's Book. Point to the boy in the picture on page 32. Ask: *Is he sitting?* Elicit: *No, he isn't.*

> **Teaching tip**
> If no one can answer the question, point to *No, he isn't* on the board.

- Continue asking *Yes / No* questions about the other people in the picture using the present continuous.
- Ss in pairs. Say: *Ask your partner questions about the people in the picture.* Walk around and help as needed.

Practice

- Direct Ss' attention to Exercise **2B** and read the instructions aloud. Ask a S to read aloud the example. Say: *Choose the words that go together. Make questions.*
- Ss complete the task individually. Help as needed.
- Ask Ss to write the completed questions on the board. Ask different Ss to read the questions aloud. Ask: *Are the questions correct?* Make corrections on the board.
- Direct Ss' attention to the picture in Exercise **2C**. Ask: *Where are the people?* (in the park) *Who do you see?* (a grandmother, a mother, a father, a sister, a brother, etc.) Read the instructions aloud.
- Point to the example question. Say: *Is he driving to work?* (No.) Point to the check mark in the *No* box.
- Ss complete the exercise individually. Help as needed.
- Read aloud the second part of the instructions for Exercise **2C**.
- Ask two Ss to read the example question and answer aloud. Point to the man in the picture. Ask: *Is he driving to work?* (No, he isn't. He's cooking lunch.)
- Ss complete the exercise in pairs. Walk around and help as needed.

Practice

- Direct Ss' attention to Exercise **3** and read the instructions aloud. Ask Ss to read aloud the example questions and answers.
- Read each of the words in the word bank and ask Ss to repeat after you.

> **Teaching tip**
> Explain the meaning of *act out*. Write the word *tired* on the board. Yawn and lean on the desk and look very tired. Say: *That's what "act out" means.*

- Ss complete the exercise in pairs. Help as needed.
- Ask pairs to perform their conversations for the class.

> **Teaching tip**
> If Ss don't know the words in the word bank, write them on the board. Point to each word and pronounce it. Ask Ss to repeat. Show the meanings of the words by acting them out.

Expansion activity (student pairs)

- **Materials needed** Magazine pictures of people performing everyday actions (eating, sleeping, etc.).
- Ss in pairs. Give a picture to each pair. Write on the board: *What's he doing? What's she doing? What are they doing?*
- Point to the questions. Say: *Ask and answer questions about the picture. When you're finished, give your picture to another pair of students.*
- Help as needed. Continue the activity until all Ss have seen each picture. Ask several pairs to hold up their pictures and ask and answer questions for the class.

Expansion activity (whole group)

- If you want to expand the grammar presentation, turn to the grammar charts at the back of the Student's Book. Practice asking questions using the present continuous and the pronouns *we* and *you* (plural).

Evaluation

- Direct Ss' attention to the lesson focus written on the board. Say: *These questions need verbs.* Elicit appropriate questions, such as: *Are you studying? Is he driving? Is she sleeping? Are they drinking coffee?*
- Check off the lesson focus as Ss demonstrate an understanding of what they have learned in the lesson.

> ***More Ventures*** *(whole group, pairs, individual)*
> Assign appropriate exercises from the *Teacher's Toolkit Audio CD / CD-ROM, Add Ventures,* or the *Workbook.*

B **Match.** Complete the questions.

1. Is she working — f. now?
2. Are you eating — a. lunch?
3. Is he buying — e. a soda?
4. Are they helping — b. their grandmother?
5. Is he driving — c. to work?
6. Is she taking — d. a break?

1. Is she working	a. lunch?
2. Are you eating	b. their grandmother?
3. Is he buying	c. to work?
4. Are they helping	d. a break?
5. Is he driving	e. a soda?
6. Is she taking	f. now?

C **Look** at the picture. Check (✓) *Yes* or *No*.

	Yes	No
1. Is he driving to work?	☐	☑
2. Is he helping his father?	☑	☐
3. Is she talking to her brother?	☑	☐
4. Is she eating lunch?	☑	☐
5. Is she working now?	☐	☑
6. Are they buying soda?	☐	☑

Talk with a partner. Ask and answer questions.

Is he driving to work?

No, he isn't. He's cooking lunch.

3 Communicate

Talk with a partner. Take turns. Act out and guess a word from the box.

tired	thirsty	hungry	busy

driving	studying	eating	working

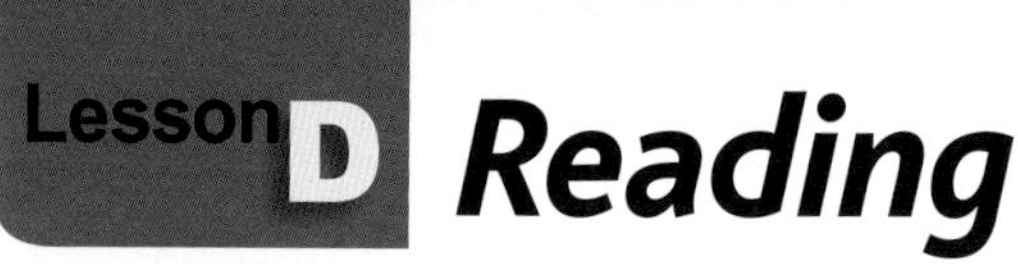

Lesson D Reading

1 Before you read

Talk. Juan is celebrating his 70th birthday. Look at the picture. Answer the questions.

1. What are the people doing?
2. Do you celebrate birthdays? How?

2 Read

SELF-STUDY AUDIO CD

 **Listen and read.**

The Birthday Party

My name is Juan. In this picture, it's my birthday. I am 70 years old. Look at me! I don't look 70 years old. My wife, my daughter, and my grandson are eating cake. My grandson is always hungry. My granddaughter is drinking soda. She's always thirsty. My son-in-law is playing the guitar and singing. Everyone is happy!

Think about the title before you read. This helps you understand the story.

3 After you read

A **Read** the sentences. Are they correct? Circle *Yes* or *No*.

1. Juan is 17 years old.	Yes	(No)
2. Juan is celebrating his birthday with his friends.	Yes	(No)
3. His wife, daughter, and grandson are eating cake.	(Yes)	No
4. His granddaughter is drinking soda.	(Yes)	No
5. His grandson is playing the guitar and singing.	Yes	(No)
6. Everyone is tired.	Yes	(No)

Write. Correct the sentences.

1. Juan is 70 years old.

B **Write.** Answer the questions about Juan's birthday party.

1. What is Juan celebrating? *Juan is celebrating his birthday.*
2. What is his family eating? *His family is eating cake.*
3. What is his granddaughter doing? *His granddaughter is drinking soda.*
4. What is his son-in-law doing? *His son-in-law is playing the guitar.*

Lesson objectives

- Introduce and read "The Birthday Party"
- Practice using new topic-related words
- Look at reading titles

Warm-up and review

- Before class. Write today's lesson focus on the board.
  Lesson D:
  Read and understand "The Birthday Party"
  Learn names of family members:

daughter	*husband*	*son*
granddaughter	*nephew*	*son-in-law*
grandson	*niece*	*wife*

- Begin class. Books open. Show Ss the picture from Lesson A on page 32. Ask: *Do you remember this picture?* Point to the grandfather in the kitchen. Ask: *Who is he?* (He is the grandfather.) *What's he doing?* (He's eating.)
- Say: *The grandfather's name is Juan. Today is his birthday. How old do you think he is?* Ss will guess his age. Ask several Ss: *When is your birthday?* Make sure everyone understands the meaning of *birthday.*

Presentation

- Direct Ss' attention to the picture in Exercise **1**. Ask: *Who do you see in this picture?* (Juan and his family) *What are they doing?* (They are eating cake / celebrating Juan's birthday, etc.)
- Read the instructions and questions for Exercise **1**.
- Ss in pairs. Say: *Ask your partner these two questions. Talk about the picture and birthdays.* Ask several pairs to ask and answer the questions for the class.
- Direct Ss' attention to Exercise **2**. Ask: *What is the title?* ("The Birthday Party") *What is the reading about?* Elicit appropriate answers about a birthday party.
- Ask Ss to read the story individually.

Culture tip

Explain that in many places, people celebrate their birthdays with family and friends. The birthday person's family and friends have a party for him or her. There is a birthday cake, and the birthday person receives presents. Many people send birthday cards or e-mail greetings.

- [Class Audio CD1 track 32] Play or read the audio program and ask Ss to read along (see audio script, pages T-153–T-154). Repeat the program as needed. After Ss listen to the paragraph, they can practice reading it to each other.

Ss may be unfamiliar with some of the words in the reading. Encourage Ss to use visual literacy skills to look at the picture closely to guess the meaning of these words. They can also guess meaning from the title of the reading.

Learner persistence (individual work)

- [Self-Study Audio CD track 16] Exercise **2** is recorded on the Ss' self-study CD at the back of the Student's Book. Ss can listen to the CD at home for reinforcement and review. They can also listen to the CD for self-directed learning when class attendance is not possible.

Comprehension check

- Read aloud the instructions for Exercise **3A**. Ask a S to read the example. Ask: *Is Juan 17 years old?* (No.) Point to the circled *No.*
- Ss complete the exercise individually.
- Check answers with the class.
- Ask Ss to take out a piece of paper. Read aloud the second part of the instructions for Exercise **3A**.
- Model the task of correcting the sentences. Point to *No* for number 1 in Exercise **3A**. Read the sentence aloud. Tell Ss: *This sentence is incorrect. Tell me the correct sentence. Juan is . . .* (70 years old). Write it on the board.
- Ss complete the exercise individually.
- Check answers with the class. Ask Ss to write their corrected sentences on the board and ask other Ss to read them aloud.

Practice

- Direct Ss' attention to the picture in Exercise **1**. Ask questions based on the reading, such as: *What's Juan doing?* (He's celebrating his birthday.) *What's his wife doing?* (She's eating cake.) *Is Juan happy?* (Yes, he is.) *Is his wife sad?* (No, she isn't.)
- Direct Ss' attention to Exercise **3B** and read the instructions aloud.
- Model the task. Ask a S to read the first question aloud. Ask: *What's the answer?* (Juan is celebrating his birthday). Write the sentence on the board.
- Ss complete the exercise individually. Help as needed.
- Check answers with the class. Ask Ss to write their sentences on the board and ask other Ss to read them aloud. Ask: *Are these sentences correct?* Ask Ss to make any necessary corrections on the board.

Learner persistence (individual work)

- Encourage Ss to keep a vocabulary notebook. In addition to writing new words, they can write a sentence with the word, draw a picture to remind them of the meaning, or keep words in categories (family words, party vocabulary, etc.).

Lesson D Reading

Warm-up and review

- Books closed. Write on the board: *family tree*. Point to the words. Ask: *What does this mean?* If Ss do not know the answer, say: *A family tree is a map of your family.*
- Say: *This is my family tree.* Draw a stick figure of yourself on the board. Write your name under it. Add family members you wish to include, drawing lines to show family relationships. Use the family tree on page 39. Point to each person in your family tree and say: *This is my _____.*

Presentation

- Books open. Direct Ss' attention to the family tree in the picture dictionary. Point to Tony (number 5). Say: *This is Tony's family tree.* Ask Ss questions about Tony:
  Is he married? (Yes.)
  Who is his wife? (Yoko)
  Who is Tony's mother? (Cathy)
  Who is Tony's father? (Ted)
  Who is Tony's aunt? (Marta)
  Who are Tony's grandparents? (Sam and Mary)

Practice

- Direct Ss' attention to the word bank in Exercise **4A**.
- Say each word in the word bank and ask Ss to repeat. Correct Ss' pronunciation.
- Model the task. Hold up the Student's Book. Point to Tony and say: *This is Tony.* Point to Cathy and say: *This is his _____.* Elicit: *mother.* Point to Mary and say: *This is his _____.* Elicit: *grandmother.* Point to the word *grandmother* written in the family tree. Say: *Write the words in the picture dictionary.*
- Ss complete the exercise individually. Help as needed.

Culture tip
These relationships may be different for some cultures. If possible, ask same-culture Ss to work together to help each other understand the words used to express these relationships.

Comprehension check

- [Class Audio CD1 track 33] Play or read the audio program (see audio script, page T-154). Ss should check their answers and repeat the words after they hear them. Repeat the audio program if necessary.
- Write the numbers *1–7* on the board in a vertical line. Ask seven Ss to come to the board and write their answers from the picture dictionary.

Learner persistence *(individual work)*

- [Self-Study Audio CD track 17] Exercise **4A** is recorded on the Ss' self-study CD at the back of the Student's Book. Ss can listen to the CD at home for reinforcement and review. They can also listen for self-directed learning when class attendance is not possible.

Useful language
Read the tip box aloud. Explain that these are affectionate ways to address parents and grandparents.

Community building *(whole group)*

- Ask: *What do children call parents and grandparents in your country?* Ask Ss from different countries to tell affectionate names people use for their parents and grandparents.

Practice

- Direct Ss' attention to Exercise **4B** and read the instructions aloud. Model the example with a S. You speak first. Point to Anne in the picture.
- Ss complete the exercise in pairs. Help as needed.
- Ask pairs to perform their conversations. Make sure all the words from the word bank have been practiced.

Expansion activity *(small groups)*

- Divide the class into groups of ten. Say: *Make a family in your group. Who is the grandfather? Who is the grandmother?* Have Ss make comical choices, such as a teenager being a grandparent. Say: *Introduce your "family." "This is my (family member), (name of family member)" = "This is my cousin, Anne."*

Evaluation

- Direct Ss' attention to the lesson focus written on the board. Ask Ss questions about "The Birthday Party," such as: *How old is Juan? Who is eating cake?*
- Point to the words for family members. Elicit sentences for each of the words in the family tree on page 39.
- Check off each part of the lesson focus as Ss demonstrate an understanding of what they have learned in the lesson.

More Ventures *(whole group, pairs, individual)*
Assign appropriate exercises from the *Teacher's Toolkit Audio CD / CD-ROM, Add Ventures,* or the *Workbook.*

4 Picture dictionary Family members

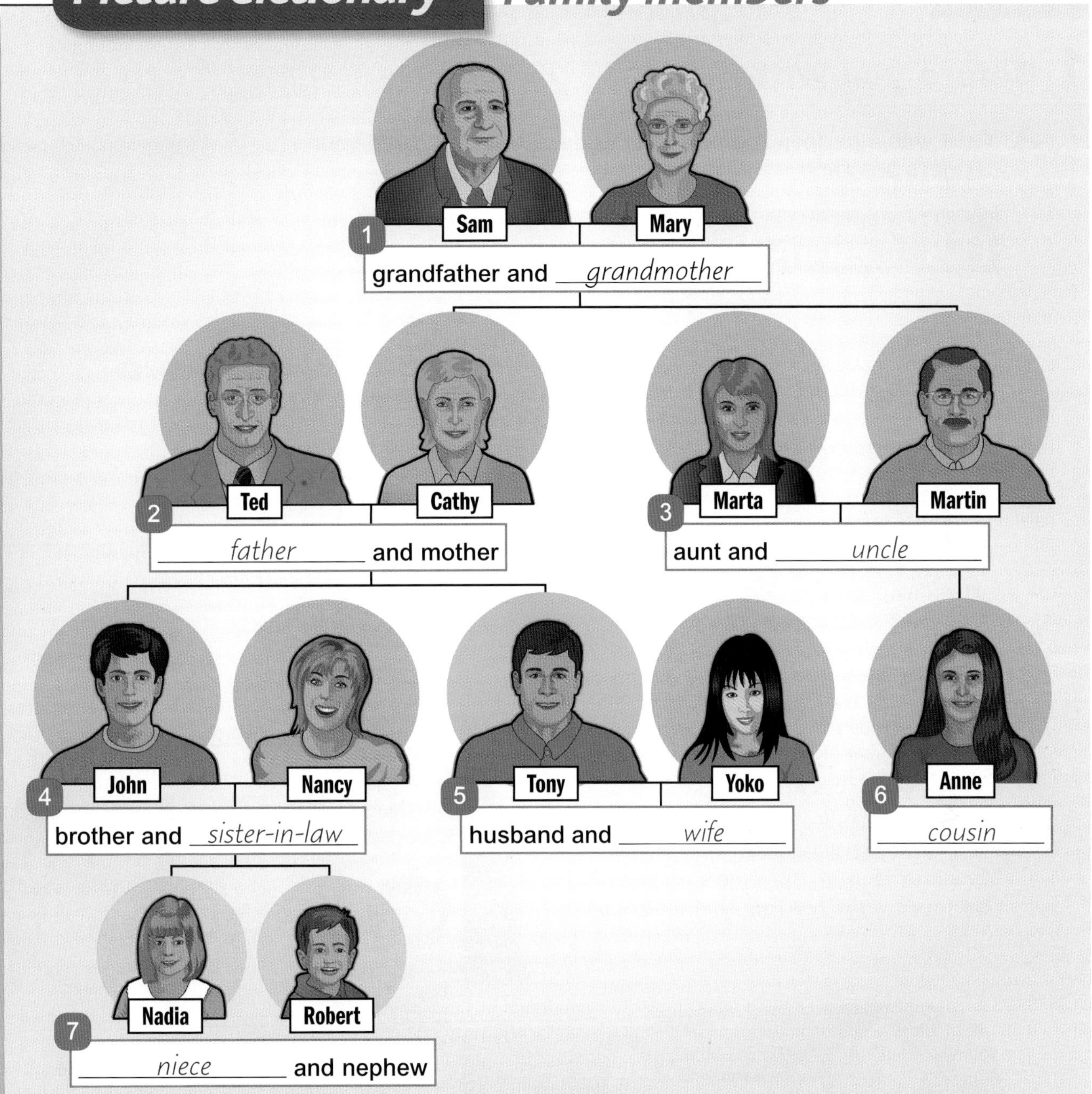

Sam Mary
1 grandfather and grandmother

Ted Cathy
2 father and mother

Marta Martin
3 aunt and uncle

John Nancy
4 brother and sister-in-law

Tony Yoko
5 husband and wife

Anne
6 cousin

Nadia Robert
7 niece and nephew

A  **Write.** Look at Tony. Complete his family tree. Then listen and repeat.

cousin	grandmother	sister-in-law	wife
father	niece	uncle	

B Talk with a partner. Take turns. Ask and answer questions about Tony's family.

Who's Tony's cousin? Anne.

Useful language

Dad is informal for *father*.
Mom is informal for *mother*.
Grandpa is informal for *grandfather*.
Grandma is informal for *grandmother*.

Lesson **E** *Writing*

1 Before you write

A Talk with a partner. Ask and answer the questions. Write your partner's answers.

U.S. Census Bureau

What's your name? ______ *(Answers will vary.)* ______

Are you married or single? ______

Do you have children? ______

How many daughters? ______

How many sons? ______

How many sisters do you have? ______

How many brothers do you have? ______

Useful language

When you have a husband or wife, you say *I'm married.*

When you have no husband or wife, you say *I'm single.*

When you have no children, you say *I don't have any.*

B Read. Then write the words on the picture.

My name is David. I am single.
I live with my sister and her husband.
I have two nieces and one nephew.
In this picture, my nieces are cooking.
My nephew is watching TV.
My sister is studying. She's very smart.
Her husband is reading the newspaper.

Lesson objectives

- Discuss and write about family members
- Learn about writing numbers

Warm-up and review

- Before class. Write today's lesson focus on the board.
  Lesson E:
  Write about your family
  Practice new words: married, single
- Also write on the board:
  What's your name?
  Where are you from?
  Please tell me about your family.
- Begin class. Greet Ss by asking the questions you wrote on the board. Encourage Ss to use the names of family members they learned in Lesson D.
- Point to the words *married* and *single* on the board. Ask Ss: *Who is married? Raise your hand. Who is single?* Demonstrate the meaning of the words by saying, for example: *Oh, you have a husband?* or *You don't have a wife?*

Presentation

- Books open. Direct Ss' attention to the census form in Exercise **1A**.
- Write *U.S. Census Bureau* on the board. Say: *This is an agency that gets information about people in the United States.*

Useful language

Read the tip box aloud. It might be helpful to show someone's wedding ring to the class. Say: (Name of S) *is married.* Point to a single person in the class. Say: (Name of S) *is single.*

Practice

- Read aloud the instructions for Exercise **1A**.
- Ss complete the exercise in pairs. Walk around and help as needed.
- Direct Ss' attention to the picture in Exercise **1B**. Ask: *What is happening in this picture?* (Two girls are cooking, a woman is studying, a man is reading the newspaper, a boy is watching TV, a man is standing.)
- Say: *The man on the right is David. We are going to read about him.*
- Read the instructions aloud.
- Ask Ss to read the paragraph silently.
- Point to the two girls in the picture. Ask: *What are they doing?* (They're cooking.) Write on the board: *My nieces are cooking*. Point to *cooking* in the picture. Say: *Fill in the other blanks with words in the reading.*
- Ss complete the task individually. Walk around and help as needed.
- Check answers with the class. Point to the blanks in the picture and ask questions using the present continuous, for example: *What is David's sister doing?* (studying)

Expansion Activity *(student pairs)*

- Question and answer practice. Say: *Read the paragraph about David again. Then, write some questions for your partner, for example: "Is David reading the newspaper?" (No, he isn't). Write five questions.*

Community building *(small groups)*

- Build a Census Bureau bar graph. Draw a bar graph on the board. Write the numbers *1–10* on the vertical axis. Write the following words on the horizontal axis: *single, married, children, sisters, brothers.*
- Model the activity. Ask five Ss the questions from the Census Bureau form in Exercise **1A**. Total the answers and fill in the bar graph (number of Ss single, number of Ss married, total number of children Ss have, total number of sisters and brothers Ss have).
- In groups of five, have Ss make a Census Bureau bar graph.
- Ss complete the activity in groups. Walk around and help as needed.
- Check the bar graphs with the class.

Lesson E Writing

Presentation

- Books closed. Say: *I am going to draw on the board a picture of my family.*
- Draw the picture. It can be very simple, but be sure the people are doing things such as watching TV or reading a book. Point to each member of your family. Introduce each one and talk about what he or she is doing. Say: *This is my* (name of family member). *He's _____.*
- Write on the board: *What are the people in the picture doing?* Elicit appropriate responses.
- Books open. Direct Ss' attention to the blank picture frame in Exercise **2A**. Read the instructions aloud.
- Ss complete the exercise individually. Help as needed.

Application

- Direct Ss' attention to Exercise **2B** and read the instructions aloud.
- Model the task. Ask each of five Ss to ask you the five questions in Exercise **2B**. Answer the questions. Point to your picture on the board as you answer.
- Ss complete the exercise individually. Walk around and help as needed.

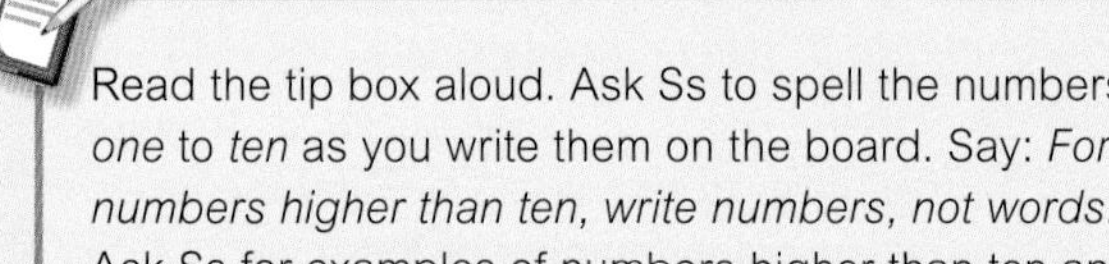

Read the tip box aloud. Ask Ss to spell the numbers *one* to *ten* as you write them on the board. Say: *For numbers higher than ten, write numbers, not words.* Ask Ss for examples of numbers higher than ten and write them on the board as numerals, not words.

Evaluation

- Direct Ss' attention to Exercise **3A** and read the instructions aloud.
- Ss complete the exercise in pairs. Walk around and listen to Ss' pronunciation. Help as needed.
- Read aloud the instructions for Exercise **3B**. This exercise asks Ss to work together and peer-correct their writing. Ask a S to read the questions aloud. Tell Ss to exchange papers and look at their partner's sentences for the answers to the questions. Tell Ss to circle the answers on their partner's paper. Walk around and help as needed.

Expansion activity (small groups)

- **Materials needed** Magazine pictures of families, preferably families doing something active
- Ss in small groups. Give each group a magazine picture. Say: *Write about the family in your picture.*
- Write on the board: *How many people are in the family? Who are the family members? What are they doing?*
- Ss complete the task in groups. Ask one person from each group to come to the front of the class and show the group's picture. Another group member can read the group's sentences to the rest of the class.

Expansion activity (individual work)

- Dictation. Say: *Take out a piece of paper. Write the numbers 1–5 on it. I will read five sentences. Write the sentences on your paper.*
- Dictate the following sentences:
  1. Sam is married.
  2. His wife's name is Mary.
  3. They have a daughter and a son.
  4. They have three grandchildren.
  5. They are happy.
- Ask individual Ss to write the sentences on the board. Ask other Ss to read the sentences aloud. Ask: *Are the sentences correct?* Make any necessary corrections on the board.

Learner persistence (whole class)

- Do a small survey of Ss in your class. Ask: *How much do you speak English outside of class? Five minutes? Half an hour? Many hours?* Congratulate the Ss who speak the most English outside of class.
- Say: *Try to speak more English outside of class. Speak to someone in the grocery store, or call a friend from class and practice speaking English on the phone.*
- Ask Ss to report back to you on their English practice outside of class the next time they are in class with you. Ask: *Was it easy? Was it hard? Why?*

More Ventures *(whole group, pairs, individual)*
Assign appropriate exercises from the *Teacher's Toolkit Audio CD / CD-ROM, Add Ventures,* or the *Workbook.*

2 Write

A **Draw** your family. What are they doing?

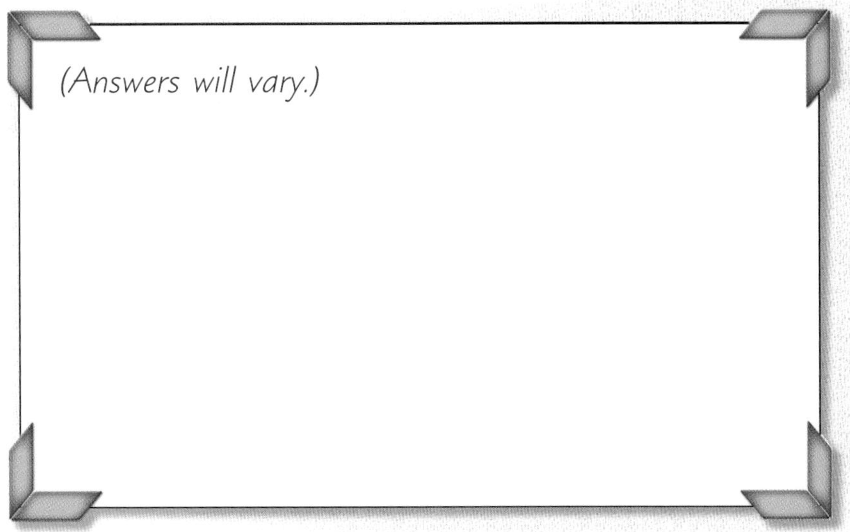

B **Write** about your picture. Answer the questions.

1. What's your name?

   My name is (Answers will vary.) ______ .

2. Are you married or single?

   I'm ______ .

3. Who do you live with?

   I live with ______ .

4. How many are in your family?

   I have ______ .

5. In the picture, what are they doing?

   ______

   ______

   ______

> Spell numbers from one to ten:
> *I have **one** brother.*
> Write all other numbers:
> *I have **11** nieces.*

3 After you write

A **Read** your sentences to a partner.

B **Check** your partner's sentences.

- How many people are in the family?
- Did your partner spell the numbers from one to ten?

Lesson F Another view

1 Life-skills reading

Insurance Application Form				
Last name	**First name**	**Age**	**Male**	**Female**
Parents				
Clark	*Joseph*	*30*	*x*	
Clark	*Rita*	*29*		*x*
Children				
Clark	*Justin*	*10*	*x*	
Clark	*Scott*	*8*	*x*	
Clark	*Carolyn*	*7*		*x*
Clark	*Michael*	*2*	*x*	

A Read the questions. Look at the form. Circle the answers.

1. How many children do Mr. and Mrs. Clark have?
   a. 1
   b. 2
   c. 3
   (d.) 4

2. How many daughters do Mr. and Mrs. Clark have?
   (a.) 1
   b. 2
   c. 3
   d. 4

3. How many sons do Mr. and Mrs. Clark have?
   a. 1
   b. 2
   (c.) 3
   d. 4

4. Who is eight years old?
   a. Carolyn
   b. Justin
   c. Michael
   (d.) Scott

B Talk in groups. Ask and answer questions about the Clark family.

How old is Michael?

He's two years old.

Lesson objectives

- Understand an insurance application form
- Review unit vocabulary
- Introduce the project
- Complete the self-assessment

Warm-up and review

- Before class. Write today's lesson focus on the board.
  Lesson F:
  Read a section of an insurance application form
  Review vocabulary for family members
  Complete the self-assessment
- Also write on the board:
  Children
  Last name First name Age Male Female
- Begin class. Books closed. Ask: *Who has children?* Say to a S who raises his or her hand: *Tell me about your children*. If Ss do not have children, ask about nieces and nephews.
- Fill in the chart on the board with the S's answers. Ask: *What's his / her first name? What's his / her last name? How old is he / she?*
- Ask another S to come to the board. Say: *Ask a S in the class questions about his or her family.* Write the answers on the board.
- Ask questions about the chart on the board, for example:
  How many children does (student's name) *have?*
  How many daughters does (student's name) *have?*
  Who is (age of one of the children) *years old?*

Presentation

- Books open. Direct Ss' attention to the insurance application form in Exercise **1**. Ask:
  What is this? (It's an insurance application form.)
  What is the family's last name? (Clark)
  What are the parents' names? (Joseph and Rita)
  Is Justin a male or female? (male)
  How old is Michael? (two)
- Explain any vocabulary Ss do not understand.

Culture tip

If Ss don't know what insurance is, write on the board some examples of types of insurance. Say: *You can have medical insurance and insurance for your car and house.* In an emergency, insurance companies pay for things. Ask Ss if they have different types of insurance.

Practice

- Direct Ss' attention to Exercise **1A** and read the instructions aloud. This task helps prepare Ss for standardized-type tests they may have to take. Be sure Ss understand the task. Have Ss individually scan for and circle the answers.
- Check answers with the class. Ask Ss to read the questions and their answers aloud. Ask: *Is that answer correct?* Make any necessary corrections.
- Direct Ss' attention to Exercise **1B** and read the instructions aloud. Ask two Ss to read aloud the example question and answer.
- Model the task by pointing to the chart you wrote on the board. Ask questions about the children, for example:
  How old is (child's name)*?* (She's / He's _____ years old.)
  How many sons does (student's name) *have?*
- Ss in groups. Ss ask and answer questions using information from the insurance application form.
- Check answers with the class. Ask Ss in different groups to perform their conversations for the class.

Expansion activity *(student pairs, individual work)*

- Ask Ss to make charts with information about their children (or about themselves and their brothers and sisters if they don't have children).
- Model the exercise by writing these columns on the board:
  Last name First name Age Male Female
  Ss complete the charts individually. Tell Ss to leave the *Age* column blank.
- Ss in pairs. Ss exchange papers with a partner, ask about the age of each child, and then fill in the information.

Teaching tip

Ss may not want to give information about their family. Bring in pictures of families from magazines and ask Ss to make up information about the family in each picture.

Learner persistence *(whole class)*

- Ask if anyone in the class needs extra help with English outside of class. If you have Ss who feel this way, ask Ss in more advanced ESL classes to volunteer to help your Ss after class.

Lesson F

Another view

Presentation

- On the board, draw the head of a man in one column and the head of a woman in another column. Read family member names (*wife, father, nephew,* etc.) from Exercise **2A**. For each name, ask: *Male or female?* Elicit responses and write the names in the correct column.
- Point to the family tree in Exercise **2A**. Ask: *What is this?* (It's a family tree.)
- Read the instructions aloud. Ask a S to read the first sentence aloud. Point to where *Kate* is written next to *Jim*. Say: *Kate is Jim's wife*. Point to where *Carol* is written. Say: *Carol is Jim's sister*. Read item 3: *Sarah is Jim's mother*. Ask Ss to show you where to write *Sarah*.
- Continue with more examples until Ss understand the task.

Useful language
Read the tip box. Say: *We can say, "Jim's wife" or "his wife." We can say, "Carol's son" or "her son."*

Practice

- Ss complete Exercise **2A** in pairs. Help as needed.
- Draw on the board the blank family tree from this exercise. Ask individual Ss to fill in the names.
- Ask the rest of the class: *Are the names correct?* Ask other Ss to make any necessary corrections.
- Direct Ss' attention to Exercise **2B** and read the instructions aloud.

Teaching tip
It might be helpful to remind Ss that they don't need to include their entire extended family in their family tree. They can include only those family members who fit on the page.

- Ss complete the exercise individually. Walk around and help as needed.

Culture tip
You might want to explain to Ss that family trees can look different in different cultures. Ask Ss to think about what they call various family members in their language. Ask Ss to draw a family tree that represents the relationships in their culture.

- Read aloud the second part of the instructions for Exercise **2B**.
- Ss complete the exercise in pairs. Help as needed.
- Ask volunteers to draw their family trees on the board and to tell the class about them.

Learner persistence (whole class)

- Ask Ss: *How can you learn English more quickly?* Brainstorm ideas and write them on the board. Ask a S to write them down and make a poster to display in the classroom. If Ss don't have any ideas, you can suggest:
  Watch TV in English.
  Listen to the radio in English – learn a song!
  Look at English-language magazines.
  Read captions under pictures in the newspaper.
  Read the weather report in the newspaper.
  Make friends with someone who doesn't speak your language.
  Try to speak English outside of class every day!

Community building (whole class)

- If you have Ss in your classes with young children, tell them about family activities that are taking place within your community. Bring in flyers and ads about local events. Encourage your Ss to attend.

More Ventures *(whole group, pairs, individual)*
Assign appropriate exercises from the *Teacher's Toolkit Audio CD / CD-ROM, Add Ventures,* or the *Workbook.*

Application

Community building

- **Project** Ask Ss to turn to page 137 in their Student's Book to complete the project for Unit 3.

Evaluation

- Before asking Ss to turn to the self-assessment on page 142, do a quick review of the unit. Have Ss turn to Lesson A. Ask the class to call out what they remember about this lesson. Prompt Ss, if necessary, with questions, for example: *What are the conversations about on this page? What vocabulary is in the picture?* Continue in this manner to review each lesson quickly.
- **Self-assessment** Read the instructions for Exercise **3**. Ask Ss to turn to the self-assessment page and complete the unit self-assessment.
- If Ss are ready, administer the unit test on pages T-167–T-168 of this *Teacher's Edition* (or on the *Teacher's Toolkit Audio CD / CD-ROM*). The audio and audio script for the tests are on the *Teacher's Toolkit Audio CD / CD-ROM.*

2 Fun with language

A Work with a partner. Read the sentences. Complete Jim's family tree.

1. Kate is Jim's wife.
2. Carol is Jim's sister.
3. Sarah is Jim's mother.
4. Burt is Jim's grandfather.
5. Rose is Jim's grandmother.
6. Bill is Jim's brother-in-law.
7. Todd is Jim's father.
8. Emily is Jim's daughter.
9. Chris is Jim's son.
10. Rob is Jim's nephew.

Useful language

*Jim**'s** wife* → ***his** wife*
*Carol**'s** son* → ***her** son*

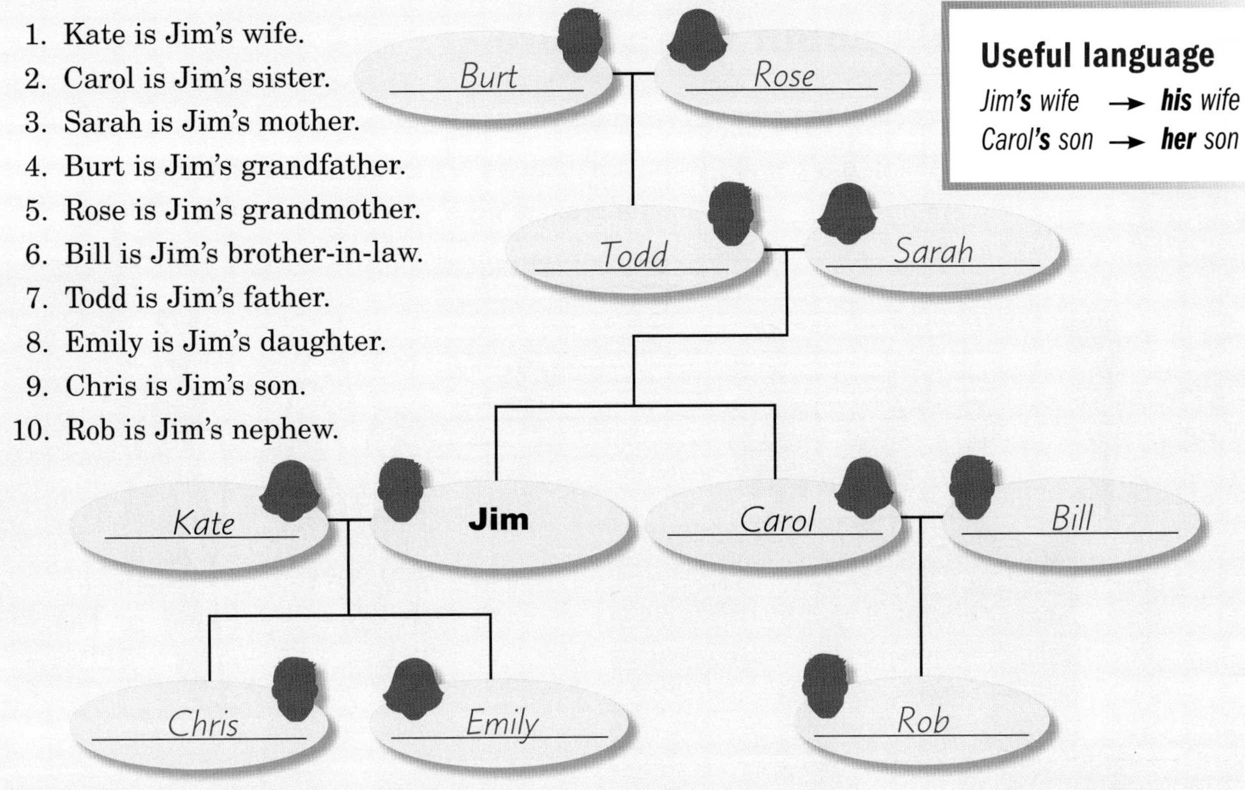

B Draw your family tree.

Talk with a partner. Show your family tree. Talk about your family.

3 Wrap up

Complete the **Self-assessment** on page 142.

Lesson A Get ready

1 Talk about the picture

A Look at the picture. What do you see?

B Point to a person with: a backache • a cough • a headache
a broken leg • an earache • a sore throat

Lesson objectives

- Introduce students to the topic
- Find out what students know about the topic
- Preview the unit by talking about the picture
- Practice key vocabulary
- Practice listening skills

Warm-up and review

- Before class. Write today's lesson focus on the board. *Lesson A: Health problems*
- Begin class. Books closed. Point to the words *Health problems* on the board. Say the words. Ask Ss to repeat them after you. Hold your head as if you have a headache. Ask: *What's my problem?* Elicit: *Headache.* Write it on the board. Ask: *What are some other health problems?* Write Ss' responses on the board. Elicit words such as *backache, earache, stomachache.*

Teaching tip

Do not expect Ss to know all these words. These warm-up questions are meant to show which students already know some of the unit vocabulary and to encourage students to draw on prior knowledge. If Ss do not know any of these words, write the following words on the board: *backache, cough, headache, broken leg, earache, sore throat.*

- Point to the health problems that you elicited from the Ss. Say: *Repeat the words after me.* As you say each word, demonstrate the meaning by acting as if you have the problem. For example, hold your back if the word is *backache.*
- Listen to Ss' pronunciation. Correct pronunciation as needed.

Presentation

- Books open. Set the scene. Direct Ss' attention to the picture on page 44. Ask: *Where is this?* (a hospital / clinic / waiting room) Ask: *What do you see?* Elicit as much vocabulary about the picture as possible: *people, chairs, a man with a broken leg, doctor, nurse,* etc.
- Direct Ss' attention to the key words in Exercise **1B**. Read each word aloud while pointing to a person in the picture who has the corresponding health problem. Ask the class to repeat and point.

Teaching tip

The key words are intended to help students talk about the picture and learn some of the vocabulary in the unit.

Comprehension check

- Ask Ss *Yes / No* questions about the picture. Recycle questions in the present continuous. Say: *Listen to the questions. Answer "Yes" or "No."*
  Point to the picture. Point to the man getting out of the elevator. Ask: *Is he sitting?* (No.)
  Point to the woman talking to her son. Ask: *Is she talking?* (Yes.)
  Point to the doctor or nurse by the reception desk. Ask: *Is he / she cooking?* (No.)
  Point to the woman in the chair holding her head. Ask: *Does she have a headache?* (Yes.)
  Point to the man with a broken leg. Ask: *Does he have a sore throat?* (No.)
  Point to the man who is sneezing. Ask: *Does he have a cold?* (Yes.)
  Point to the woman with a backache. Ask: *Does she have a stomachache?* (No.)
  Point to the boy with the sore throat. Ask: *Does he have a sore throat?* (Yes.)

Teaching tip

Do not expect Ss to answer with more than *Yes* or *No.* The purpose of this exercise is to show that Ss understand the questions you are asking.

Practice

- Direct Ss' attention to Exercise **1B**. Model the task. Hold up the Student's Book. Say to a S: *Point to a person with a backache.* The S points to the appropriate part of the picture.
- Ss in pairs. Say to one S: *Say the words in Exercise 1B.* Say to his or her partner: *Point to the person in the picture.*
- Ss complete the exercise in pairs. Walk around and help as needed. When Ss have finished, have them change partners and change roles.
- Ask several pairs to perform the exercise for the class to check Ss' understanding.

Lesson A Get ready

Presentation

- Before class. On a separate index card, write each of the words from the word bank in Exercise **2A**.
- In class. Books closed. Show each card to the class. Read each card aloud and act out the meaning.
- Shuffle the cards. Give one card to each of nine Ss. Ss act out the health problems. Encourage the other Ss to guess the problems. If Ss have difficulty pronouncing a health problem, write the word on the board and ask students to repeat. Correct Ss' pronunciation as needed.

Practice

- Books open. Direct Ss' attention to Exercise **2A**. Read the instructions aloud.
- [Class Audio CD1 track 34] Play or read the audio program (see audio script, page T-154). Ss circle the words they hear. Repeat the audio program as needed.
- Check answers. Ask: *What did you circle?* Ask Ss to write the words on the board. Point to the words. Say: *Repeat after me.* Say each word. Listen to Ss' pronunciation and correct as needed.
- Ask a S to write the words that were not circled on the board: *broken leg, cold, cough*. Point to the words. Say: *Repeat after me.* Say each word. Listen to Ss' pronunciation and correct as needed.
- Direct Ss' attention to the pictures in Exercise **2B**. Hold up the Student's Book. Point to the first picture. Say: *Sore throat.* Point to the second picture. Ask a S: *What's the health problem?* (headache)
- Continue asking Ss about the rest of the pictures.
- Direct Ss' attention to the instructions for Exercise **2B** and read them aloud.
- [Class Audio CD1 track 34] Play or read the audio program again. Pause after the first conversation. Ask: *Which picture matches conversation A?* (picture number 2) Point to the handwritten *a* written next to number 2. Be sure that Ss understand the task.
- [Class Audio CD1 track 34] Play or read the complete audio program (see audio script, page T-154). Ss complete the rest of the exercise individually.

Learner persistence *(individual work)*

- [Self-Study Audio CD track 18] Exercises **2A** and **2B** are recorded on the Ss' self-study CD at the back of the Student's Book. Ss can listen to the CD at home for reinforcement and review. They can also listen for self-directed learning when class attendance is not possible.

Comprehension check

- Write the numbers *1–6* on the board. Ask a few Ss to come to the board to write the correct answers to Exercise **2B** next to each number.
- Read aloud the second part of the instructions for Exercise **2B**.
- [Class Audio CD1 track 34] Play or read the audio program again. Pause the audio program after each conversation. Point to a letter of the conversation on the board. Ask: *Is this correct?* Ask another S to make any necessary corrections on the board.

Application

- Direct Ss' attention to the picture in Exercise **2C**. Ask two Ss to read the example question and answer aloud.
- Read the instructions. Model the exercise. Point to the word bank in Exercise **2A**. Act out a headache and elicit *headache* from the Ss. Say: *Right.* Then, ask a S to stand up. Tell the S: *Pick a word. Act it out.* Elicit guesses from the Ss until they have the right answer. Say: *Yes.* Continue modeling the task until Ss understand it.
- Ss complete the exercise in pairs. Walk around and help as needed.
- Ask several pairs to act out their conversations for the rest of the class.

Useful language
Read the tip box. Have Ss practice their conversations again, choosing either *Yes* or *Right*. You could also write other ways of saying "yes" on the board and have Ss practice, such as: *Yep, Yeah, Uh-huh, That's correct.*

Evaluation

- Direct Ss' attention to the health problems you wrote on the board at the beginning of the lesson. For each of the vocabulary words, ask a *Yes / No* question about people in the picture on page 44, for example: *Does he have a backache / an earache / a cold /* etc.? Elicit *Yes* or *No* answers.
- Check off each word as Ss demonstrate an understanding of what they have learned in the lesson.

More Ventures *(whole group, pairs, individual)*
Assign appropriate exercises from the *Teacher's Toolkit Audio CD / CD-ROM, Add Ventures,* or the *Workbook.*

2 Listening

A **Listen.** Circle the words you hear.

broken leg	earache	sore throat
cold	fever	sprained ankle
cough	headache	stomachache

B **Listen again.** Write the letter of the conversation.

Listen again. Check your answers.

C **Talk** with a partner. Take turns. Act out and guess the problem.

Useful language
Yes.
Right.

Lesson B *I have a headache.*

1 Grammar focus: simple present of *have*

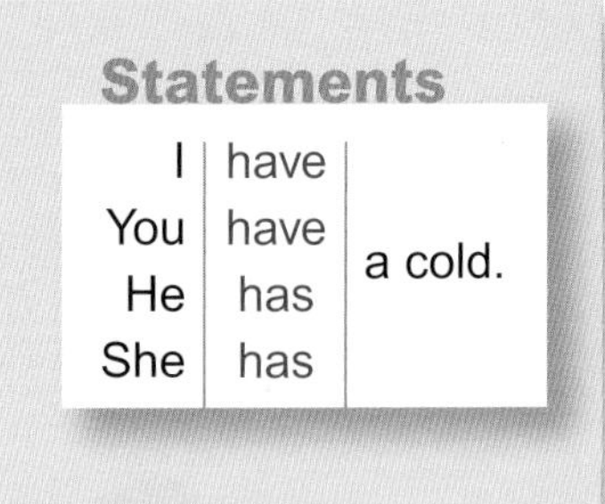

Statements

I	have	a cold.
You	have	
He	has	
She	has	

Useful language

*I have a **terrible** cold.*
*I have a **bad** headache.*

2 Practice

A Write. Complete the sentences. Use *has* or *have*.

1 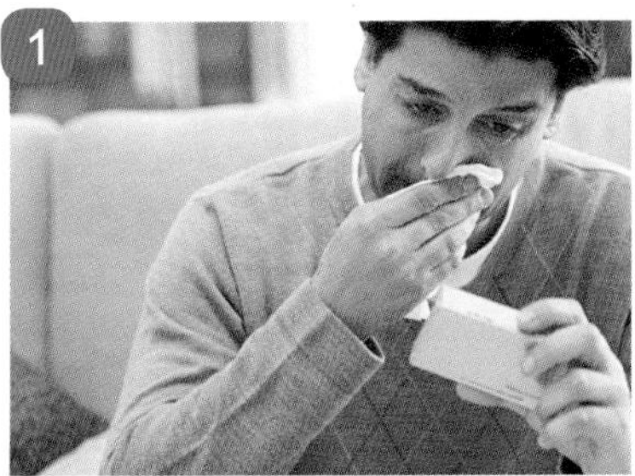

He *has* a terrible cold.

2 

I *have* a headache.

3 

He *has* a backache.

4 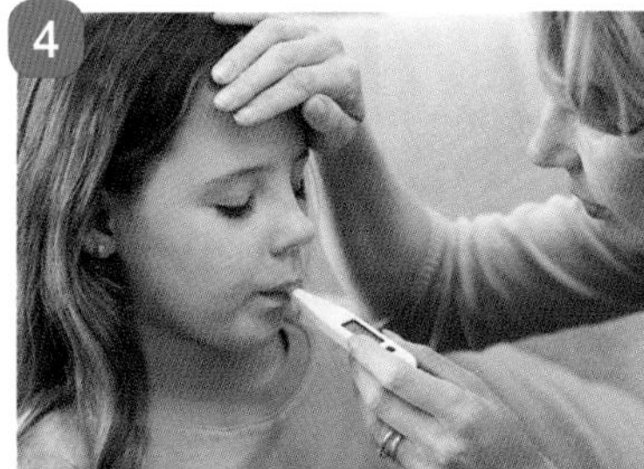

You *have* a fever.

5 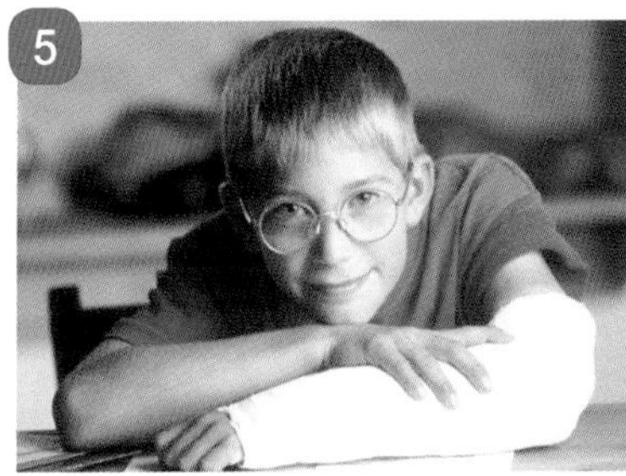

I *have* a broken arm.

6 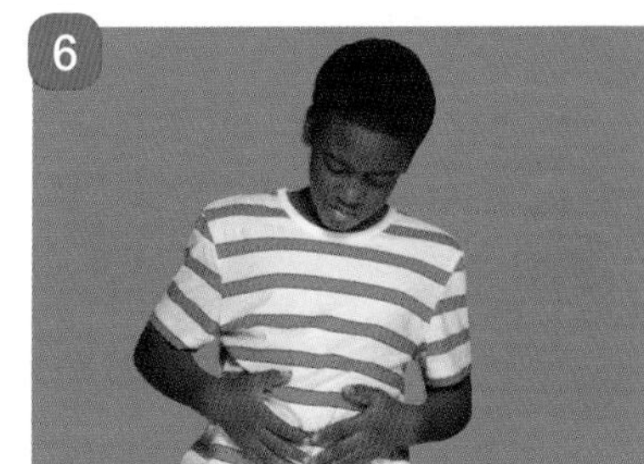

He *has* a stomachache.

7 

She *has* a bad cough.

8 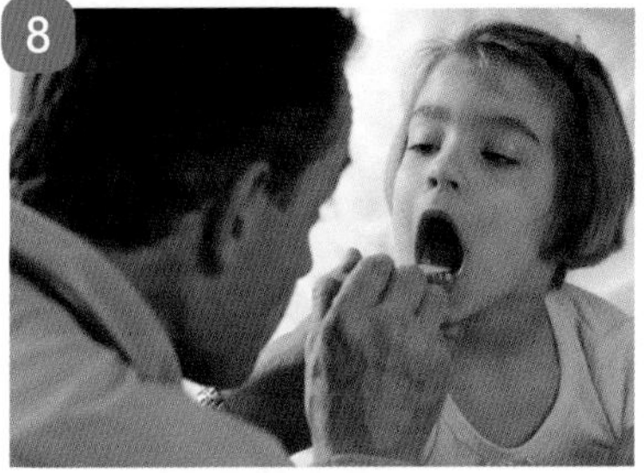

You *have* a sore throat.

9 

She *has* a cut.

 **Listen and repeat.**

Lesson objectives

- Introduce the simple present of *have*
- Talk about common health remedies

Warm-up and review

- Before class. Write today's lesson focus on the board.
  Lesson B: Simple present of have
  I have *You have* *He has* *She has*
- Write *I have a cold* in big letters on a piece of paper.
- Begin class. Review the words for the health problems Ss learned in Lesson A: *backache, cough, headache, broken leg, earache, sore throat*. Write the words for these problems on the board. Have Ss stand and act out the words as you point to them on the board.
- Books closed. Hold up the paper with the sentence *I have a cold*. Act out a cold (sneeze, sniff, cough, etc.). Read the sentence aloud. Ask Ss to repeat.
- Give the paper to a male student. Ask him to read it aloud. Say to him: *You have a cold*. Write the sentence on the board. Ask Ss to repeat. Point to the same student again. Look at the class and say: *He has a cold*. Write the sentence on the board. Ask Ss to repeat.
- Give the paper to a female student. Ask her to read it aloud. Say to her: *You have a cold*. Point to the sentence on the board. Ask Ss to repeat. Point to the same student again. Look at the class and say: *She has a cold*. Write the sentence on the board. Ask Ss to repeat.

Presentation

- Books open. Direct Ss' attention to the grammar chart in Exercise **1**. Read the statements aloud. Ask Ss to repeat.
- Ss in pairs. Have students practice reading the grammar chart to each other while pointing to the appropriate person in the class (*I, You, He, She*).

Comprehension check

- Act out a health problem, point to yourself, and ask, *What's wrong?* Elicit: *You have a* _____. Call on a student to act out a different health problem. Ask: *What's wrong?* Elicit: *She / He has a* _____.

Practice

- Direct Ss' attention to the pictures in Exercise **2A** and point to number 1. Ask: *What's the matter?* Elicit: *He has a terrible cold.*

Useful language

Read the tip box aloud. Focus on the words *terrible* and *bad* to talk about health problems.

- Read aloud the instructions for Exercise **2A**. Be sure students understand the task.
- Ss complete the exercise individually. Walk around and help as needed.

Teaching tip

It might be useful to remind Ss that the verb form *has* is used with *he* and *she*, and *have* is used with *I* and *you.*

- [Class Audio CD1 track 35] Read aloud the second part of the instructions for Exercise **2A**. Play or read the audio program (see audio script, page T-154). Have Ss check their answers as they listen and repeat. Correct pronunciation as needed.
- Ask Ss to come to the board to write the sentences. Ask different Ss to read the sentences aloud. Ask Ss to make any necessary corrections on the board.

Expansion activity (student pairs)

- Write on the board: *What's the matter?* Model the activity with a S. Ask a S to stand up. Hold up the Student's Book with a paper over sentences 1–3. Point to picture number 3. Ask: *What's the matter?* Elicit: *He has a backache.*
- Ss in pairs. Have Ss complete the question-and-answer practice, covering up the answers. Walk around and help as needed.

Expansion activity (whole group)

- If you want to expand the grammar presentation, turn to the grammar charts at the back of the Student's Book. Practice making sentences using the pronouns *we, you* (plural), and *they* with the simple present of *have.*

Lesson B I have a headache.

Presentation

- Books closed. Draw a vertical line down the middle of the board. On the left side, write *Health problems*. On the right side, write *Remedies*. Under *Health problems,* write *headache*. Under *Remedies,* write *aspirin*. Make a list of health problems and remedies on the board.

Teaching tip
Help Ss understand the meaning of *remedies* by translating the word into a common language Ss understand; by explaining that remedies help a problem go away; by asking for additional examples; or by showing real products that help health problems.

- Books open. Direct Ss' attention to the pictures in Exercise **2B**. Add the health problems and remedies to the list on the board if they are not already there. Explain any words Ss don't understand.
- [Class Audio CD1 track 36] Read the instructions aloud. Play or read the audio program (see audio script, page T-154). Listen to Ss and correct pronunciation as needed.

Practice

- Read aloud the second part of the instructions for Exercise **2B**. Ask two Ss to read the example conversation aloud.
- Point to *She has a cut* in Exercise **2B**. Ask another S to read the conversation with you, substituting the correct words for the bold words. Check that Ss understand the task.
- Have Ss complete the exercise in pairs. Walk around and help as needed.
- Ask pairs to perform their conversations in front of the class.

Useful language
Read the tip box aloud. Ask Ss to repeat the questions after you. Have Ss practice the conversation using the useful language: *What's wrong?* and *What's the matter?*

Application

- Write on the board:

Use	*Take*
a heating pad	*vitamin C*
a bandage	*aspirin*
	cough drops

- Point to the first column. Say the complete phrase for each item: *Use a heating pad; use a bandage*. Ask Ss to repeat.
- Point to the second column. Say: *Take*. Gesture to your mouth to indicate that *take* is used for medicine a person swallows, eats, or drinks. Then say the complete phrase for each item: *Take vitamin C; take cough drops*. Ask Ss to repeat.
- Direct Ss' attention to Exercise **3**. Read the instructions aloud. Model the exercise by reading the example aloud with a S. Model the exercise again by working with a different S and using different language, for example: *What's the matter? How are you? What's wrong? I have a cough. I have a backache. Take cough drops. Use a heating pad*. Check that Ss understand the task.
- Have Ss complete the exercise in pairs, taking turns asking and answering. When they finish, have them switch partners and make different conversations. Walk around and help as needed.

Community building *(small groups)*

- Ask Ss to name stores where they find remedies for their health problems. As Ss brainstorm different places in town, write the names of the stores on the board.

Evaluation

- Direct Ss' attention to the phrases with *have* and *has,* which you wrote on the board at the beginning of the lesson. Ask Ss to look at the pictures on page 45 and make sentences using *has*. Ask students to act out health problems and elicit *I have, you have*.
- Check off each phrase as Ss demonstrate an understanding of what they have learned in the lesson.

More Ventures *(whole group, pairs, individual)*
Assign appropriate exercises from the *Teacher's Toolkit Audio CD / CD-ROM, Add Ventures,* or the *Workbook*.

B **Listen and repeat.** Then match.

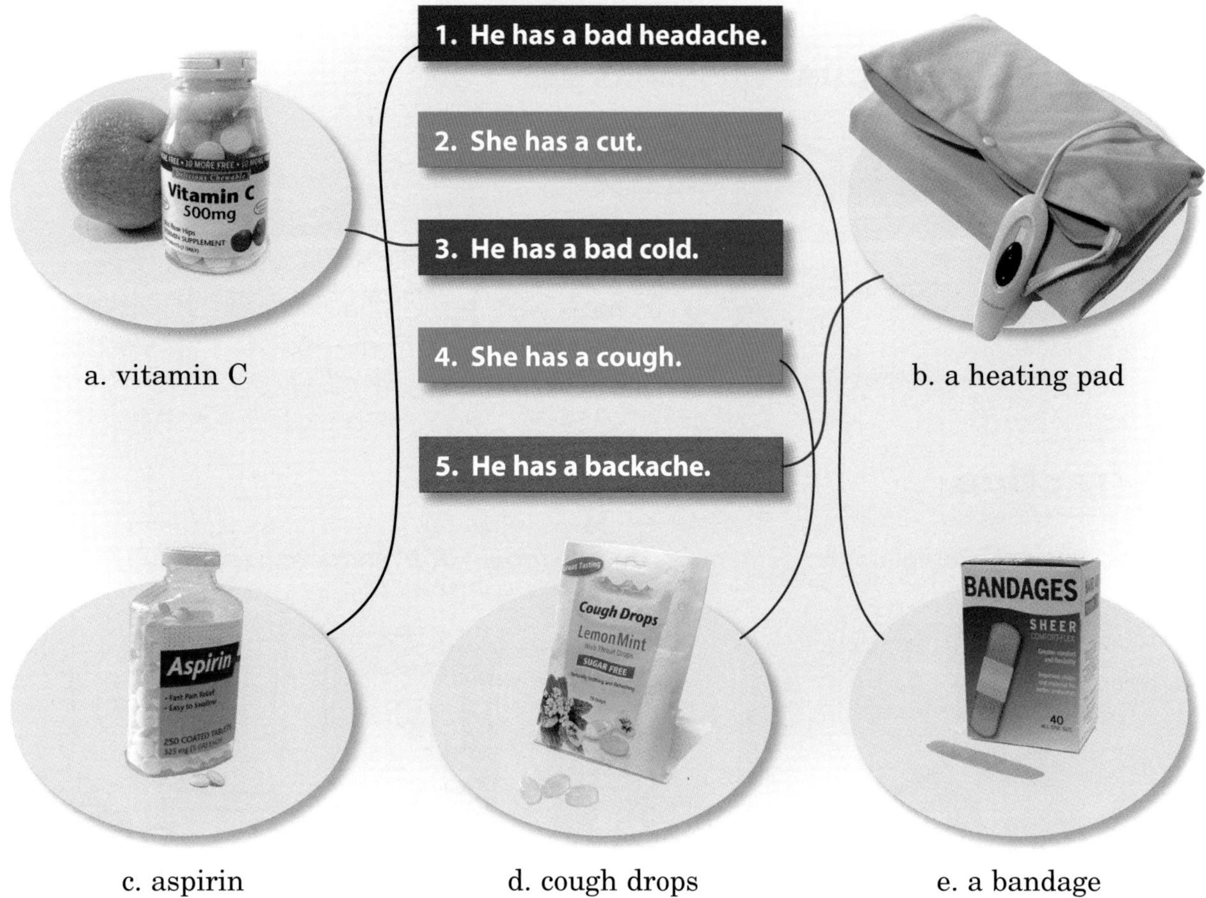

a. vitamin C

b. a heating pad

c. aspirin

d. cough drops

e. a bandage

Talk with a partner. Change the **bold** words and make conversations.

A How **is he**?
B Not so good.
A What's wrong?
B **He has a bad headache.**
A I have **aspirin**.
B Really? Thanks.

Useful language
What's wrong?
What's the matter?

3 Communicate

Talk with a partner. Ask and answer questions.

A What's the matter?
B I have a cold.
A Take vitamin C.

Useful language
Take: *medicine, aspirin, vitamin C, cough drops*
Use: *a bandage, a heating pad*

Lesson C Do you have a cold?

1 Grammar focus: questions with *have*

Questions			Answers					
Do	I	have a fever?	Yes,	you	do.	No,	you	don't.
Do	you			I	do.		I	don't.
Does	he			he	does.		he	doesn't.
Does	she			she	does.		she	doesn't.

don't = do not
doesn't = does not

2 Practice

A Write. Complete the sentences. Use *do*, *does*, *don't*, or *doesn't*.

1. Do I have a fever?
   No, you don't.
2. Does she have a sore throat?
   No, she doesn't.
3. Does he have a cough?
   Yes, he does.
4. Do you have a cold?
   Yes, I do.
5. Does she have the flu?
   Yes, she does.
6. Does she have a sprained ankle?
   No, she doesn't.

Listen and repeat. Then practice with a partner.

Lesson objectives

- Introduce simple present questions with *have*
- Introduce subject and object pronouns

Warm-up and review

- Before class. Write today's lesson focus on the board.
  Lesson C:
  Simple present. Questions and answers with have
  Do you have . . . ? Does he have . . . ?
  Yes, I do. No, I don't.
  Yes, he does. No, he doesn't.
- Before class. Write on index cards the names of all the health problems Ss discussed in Lessons A and B.
- Begin class. Show the Ss the cards and ask them to read aloud the health problems. Then spread the cards out on a table.
- Write on the board: *I have a* _____. Act out one of the health problems. Have a student choose the correct card and make a statement: *You have a* _____. Then have a student act out a different health problem and say: *I have a* _____. Another student chooses the correct card. You say: *He / She has a* _____. Allow students to take on the teacher's role and continue the review.

Presentation

- Books open. Direct Ss' attention to the grammar chart in Exercise **1**. Read each question and answer aloud. Ask Ss to repeat the questions and answers.
- Ss in pairs. Have partners practice reading the grammar chart while pointing to an appropriate person in the class (*I, you, he, she*).

Contractions

Read the tip box aloud. Point to *don't.* Say: *This is a contraction. It is short for "do not."* Point to *doesn't.* Say: *This is short for "does not."*

Comprehension check

- Hold up an index card with the word *backache*. Act as if your back hurts. Ask: *Do I have a backache?* Elicit: *Yes, you do.* Hold up the same card. Ask: *Do I have a stomachache?* Elicit: *No, you don't.*
- Hand one of the index cards to a S. Encourage the S to act out the health problem. Point to the S. Ask the S: *Do you have a headache?* Elicit the appropriate answer from the S. Point to the correct answer on the board if necessary.
- Continue asking and answering the questions by giving cards to different Ss.

Teaching tip

If Ss have trouble pronouncing *do, does, don't,* and *doesn't,* write the words on the board. Point to each word. Say the word and ask Ss to repeat it.

Practice

- Direct Ss' attention to the picture in Exercise **2A**. This scene takes place in a nurse's office in a school. Ask: *Where are the people? Are they in a hospital?* Elicit: *No, they aren't.* Ask: *Are they in a clinic?* (No, they aren't.) *Are they at school?* (Yes, they are.) *Are they in a nurse's office?* (Yes, they are.)
- Point to the girl labeled number 2. Ask: *What's the matter?* Elicit: *She has an earache.* Ask a S to write the sentence on the board.
- Continue asking about the other people in the picture. Have students make guesses. Ask different Ss to write the sentences on the board. Possible answers:

1. He has a fever.	4. He has a cold.
2. She has an earache.	5. She has the flu.
3. He has a cough.	6. She has a sprained ankle.

- Read aloud the instructions for Exercise **2A**.
- Ask two Ss to read the example question and answer aloud. Be sure Ss understand the task. Ss complete the exercise individually. Walk around and help as needed.
- Check answers with the class. Ask Ss to write their answers on the board. Ask different Ss to read the answers aloud. Ask other Ss to make any necessary corrections on the board.
- Read aloud the second part of the instructions for Exercise **2A**.
- [Class Audio CD1 track 37] Play or read the audio program (see audio script, page T-154). Listen to Ss' pronunciation as they repeat the conversations. Correct pronunciation as needed.
- Say: *Practice with a partner.* Have Ss practice the conversations in pairs. Walk around and help as needed.
- Ask several pairs to read the conversations to the rest of the class.

Learner persistence *(whole class)*

- Give Ss your office phone number or e-mail address. Encourage them to call you if they can't come to class. Ask students for reasons they may not be able to attend class. Practice conversations. Help Ss by writing some examples on the board, such as: *I'm sick. / My child is sick. / I have a headache. / I have a doctor's appointment. / I have a cold.*

Lesson C Do you have a cold?

Presentation

- Write on the board: *What's wrong with _____?*
- Direct Ss' attention to the pictures in Exercise **2B**. Point to number 1. Say: *What's wrong with him?* Elicit: *He has a backache*. Write *him* in the blank on the board. Ask Ss to repeat the question after you.
- Point to picture number 2. Say: *What's wrong with her?* Elicit: *She has a cold*. Write on the board: *What's wrong with her?* Ask Ss to repeat the question after you.

> **Useful language**
> Read the tip box aloud. Ask Ss to repeat the words and sentences after you. If Ss want to know the name of the pronouns, point to *he*. Say: *This is a subject pronoun.* Point to *him*. Say: *This is an object pronoun.*

Practice

- Direct Ss' attention to the pictures in Exercise **2B**. Read the instructions aloud.
- Ask two pairs of Ss to read the example conversations aloud. Be sure Ss understand the task.
- Ss complete the exercise in pairs. Walk around and help as needed.
- Ask pairs to say the conversations for each picture.

Application

- Read aloud the instructions for Exercise **3**. Model the example with a S. The S speaks first. Encourage the S to act out the health problem.
- Model the example again. This time, you speak first. Use a different health problem.
- Ss complete the exercise in pairs. Encourage Ss to use different health problems and to take both roles – *A* and *B*.
- Ask different pairs to perform their conversations for the rest of the class.

> **Useful language**
> Read the tip box aloud. Ask Ss to repeat the phrases after you. Have Ss make conversations using *Get some rest* instead of *I hope you feel better.*

Expansion activity (whole group)

- Recycle questions about illnesses. Write on the board: *What's wrong?* Point to the question. Say: *What are some different ways to ask this question?* Write Ss' responses on the board. If no one can answer the question, write these questions on the board:
  What's the matter?
  What's wrong with him / her?
  What's the problem?
  How are you?

Expansion activity (whole class, student pairs)

- Practice useful phrases. Write on the board: *I don't feel well.* Ask Ss: *What are some different ways to say this in English?* Write Ss' responses on the board if they are correct. If Ss cannot think of any other examples, write these phrases on the board:
  I'm not feeling well.
  I'm feeling under the weather.
- Point to the sentences. Say: *These sentences mean "I don't feel well."*
- Read each sentence aloud. Ask Ss to repeat.
- Ss in pairs. Ask Ss to practice their conversations again using the new phrases.

Evaluation

- Direct Ss' attention to the questions and answers you wrote on the board at the beginning of the lesson. Have Ss turn to the picture on page 44 and ask *Yes / No* questions using *Does he / she have . . . ?* about people in the picture. For example, *Does he have a backache / an earache / a cold /* etc.*?* Elicit *Yes* or *No* answers. Ask questions about the Ss: *Do you have a cold? Do you have a broken arm?* Elicit *Yes* or *No* answers.
- Check off the items as Ss demonstrate an understanding of what they have learned in the lesson.

Learner persistence (whole group)

- Brainstorm different ways of keeping up with English lessons when Ss miss a class. Write them on the board, for example: *Practice the last lesson. Do Workbook exercises. Call a classmate and ask about class. Listen and repeat exercises on the self-study CD. Call or e-mail your teacher for help.*

> ***More Ventures*** (whole group, pairs, individual)
> Assign appropriate exercises from the *Teacher's Toolkit Audio CD / CD-ROM, Add Ventures,* or the *Workbook.*

B **Talk** with a partner. Change the **bold** words and make conversations.

A **Mr. Jones** isn't at work today.
B What's wrong with **him**? Does **he** have the flu?
A No, **he doesn't**. **He** has a **backache**.

A **Diana** isn't at work today.
B What's wrong with **her**? Does **she** have the flu?
A No, **she doesn't**. **She** has a **cold**.

Useful language

he → him
she → her
***He** is sick.*
*What's wrong with **him**?*
***She** is sick.*
*What's wrong with **her**?*

1. Mr. Jones

a backache

2. Diana

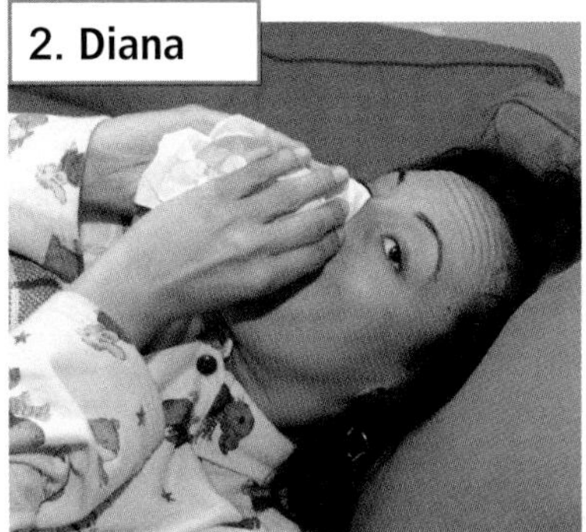

a cold

3. Carl

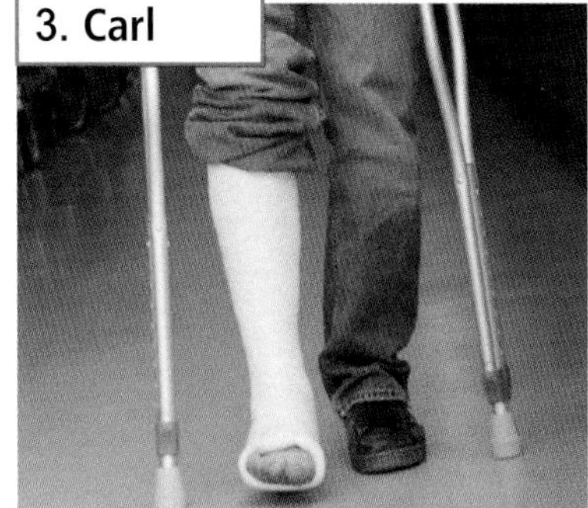

a broken leg

4. Mrs. Leeds

a stomachache

5. Eva

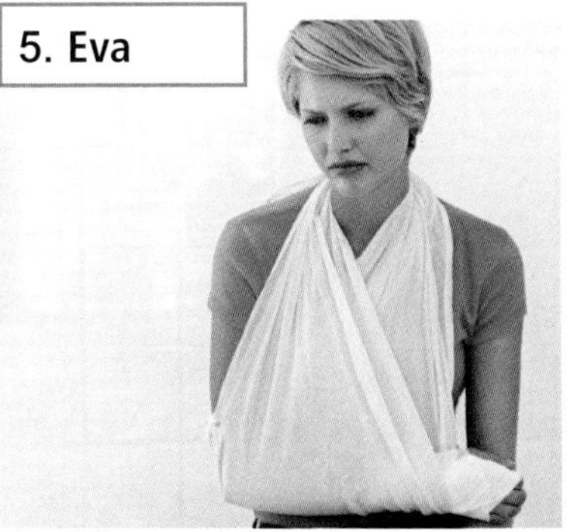

a broken arm

6. Ben

a fever

3 Communicate

Talk with a partner. Take turns and make conversations.

A I don't feel well.
B Do you have a cold?
A No, I don't. I have a sore throat.
B That's too bad. I hope you feel better.

Useful language

Get some rest.
I hope you feel better.

Lesson D Reading

1 Before you read

Talk. Maria is at the health clinic.
Look at the picture. Answer the questions.

1. Who is with Maria?
2. What's wrong?

2 Read

  **Listen and read.**

SELF-STUDY AUDIO CD

The Health Clinic

Poor Maria! Everyone is sick! Maria and her children are at the health clinic today. Her son, Luis, has a sore throat. Her daughter, Rosa, has a stomachache. Her baby, Gabriel, has an earache. Maria doesn't have a sore throat. She doesn't have a stomachache. And she doesn't have an earache. But Maria has a very bad headache!

Look at the exclamation points (!) in the reading. An exclamation point shows strong feeling.

3 After you read

A Read the sentences. Are they correct? Circle *Yes* or *No*.

1. Maria and her children are at school. Yes (No)
2. Luis has a backache. Yes (No)
3. Rosa has a headache. Yes (No)
4. Gabriel has an earache. (Yes) No
5. Maria has a bad headache. (Yes) No
6. Everyone is happy today. Yes (No)

Write. Correct the sentences.

1. Maria and her children are at the health clinic.

B Write. Answer the questions about Maria.

1. Where are Maria and her three children today? *They are at the health clinic.*
2. What's wrong with her baby? *Her baby has an earache.*
3. What's the matter with Maria? *Maria has a very bad headache.*

Lesson objectives

- Introduce and read "The Health Clinic"
- Practice using new topic-related words

Warm-up and review

- Before class. Write today's lesson focus on the board.
  Lesson D:
  Read and understand "The Health Clinic"
  Look at exclamation points
  Learn parts of the body
- Begin class. Books closed. Write *"The Health Clinic"* on the board and read it aloud. Say: *The reading today is about the health clinic.* Ask: *What is a health clinic?* Write Ss' answers on the board. Ask: *Why do you visit a health clinic?* Write Ss' responses on the board. Encourage them to use words they have learned, such as *backache, stomachache, earache, headache, sick.*
- Books open. Remind Ss about Maria and her family from the picture on page 44. Then direct Ss' attention to Exercise **1**. Read the instructions aloud. Ask: *Who is with Maria?* (her two sons and her daughter) Point to the young boy and ask: *What's wrong with him?* (He has a sore throat.) Point to the baby. Ask: *What wrong with him?* (He has an earache.) Point to the little girl. Ask: *What's wrong with her?* (She has a stomachache.)

Presentation

- [Class Audio CD1 track 38] Direct Ss' attention to Exercise **2** and read the instructions aloud. Play or read the audio program and ask Ss to read along (see audio script, page T-154). Repeat as needed.

Teaching tip

Here are other ways of presenting the reading: Ss read silently; Ss take turns reading aloud individual sentences to the class; Ss read to each other; Ss listen and repeat the sentences.

Read the tip box aloud. Write an exclamation point on the board. Say: *This means we say something with excitement.* Write on the board *Stop! Help!* Read the words aloud with emphasis. Ask Ss to repeat.

- Ss in pairs. Say: *Now read the paragraph to your partner. Be sure to use strong feeling to read the sentences that have exclamation points.* Demonstrate by reading *Poor Maria!* with emphasis.

Teaching tip

Explain the different meanings of *poor*: "having little money" or "feeling sorry for a person's condition or situation."

Learner persistence *(individual work)*

- [Self-Study Audio CD track 19] Exercise **2** is recorded on the Ss' self-study CD at the back of the Student's Book. Ss can listen to the CD at home for reinforcement and review. They can also listen to the CD for self-directed learning when class attendance is not possible.

Comprehension check

- Read aloud the instructions for Exercise **3A**. Ask a S to read the example aloud.
- Ask: *Are Maria and her children at school?* (No, Maria and her children are at the health clinic.) Point to where *No* is circled for number 1. Be sure Ss understand the task.
- Ss complete the exercise individually. Help as needed.
- Check answers with the class. Ask Ss to read their sentences and answers aloud.
- Ask Ss to take out a piece of paper. Read aloud the second part of the instructions for Exercise **3A**.
- Model the task of correcting the sentences. Point to *No* for number 1 in Exercise **3A**. Read the sentence aloud. Tell Ss: *This sentence is incorrect. Tell me the correct sentence. Maria and her children are at . . .* (the health clinic). Write on the board: *Maria and her children are at the health clinic.*
- Ss complete the exercise individually. Walk around and help as needed.
- Check answers with the class. Ask Ss to write their answers on the board. Then ask different Ss to read the answers aloud. Ask: *Are the sentences correct?* Make any necessary corrections on the board.

Practice

- Ask Ss questions about the paragraph: *What's wrong with Maria?* (She has a bad headache.) *What's wrong with Gabriel?* (He has an earache.)
- Read aloud the instructions for Exercise **3B**. Ss complete the exercise individually. Help as needed.
- Check answers with the class. Ask Ss to read their questions and answers aloud.

Learner persistence *(whole class)*

- If you have Ss who always arrive late for class or who are frequently absent, try to find out why this is happening. Encourage Ss to attend class regularly and on time. If Ss are having problems with transportation or childcare, try to connect them with a school counselor or classmates who might be able to help them with these issues.

Lesson D Reading

Warm-up and review

- Books closed. Write on the board: *Parts of the body.* Draw a stick figure on the board. Draw a line to the person's head. Ask: *What is this?* Elicit: *It's the head.* Ask the S who answered with the correct word to write *head* on the line.

Teaching tip
If Ss don't know the answer, write *head* on the line indicating the head. Continue by asking about other parts of the body. Use some of the words in the word bank in Exercise **4A**. If Ss don't know the answers, write them on the lines for them.

Presentation

- Books open. Direct Ss' attention to the picture in the picture dictionary. Ask: *What do you see?* (a man, a surfboard) *Where is he?* (at the beach)
- Direct Ss' attention to the word bank in Exercise **4A**. Say: *Repeat the words after me.* Say each word. Listen to Ss' pronunciation as they repeat. Correct pronunciation as needed.
- Say: *Write the words in the picture dictionary.* Point to the first example, which has been done. Be sure Ss understand the task.
- Ss complete the exercise individually. Walk around and help as needed.

Comprehension check

- [Class Audio CD1 track 39] Play or read the audio program (see audio script, page T-154). Ss should check their answers and repeat the words after they hear them. Repeat the audio program if necessary.

Learner persistence *(individual work)*

- [Self-Study Audio CD track 20] Exercise **4A** is recorded on the Ss' self-study CD at the back of the Student's Book. Ss can listen to the CD at home for reinforcement and review. They can also listen to the CD for self-directed learning when class attendance is not possible.

Expansion activity *(whole group)*

- Draw another stick figure on the board. Ask a S to come to the board. Read one of the vocabulary words aloud. Ask the S to write the word on the board next to the correct body part. Continue with different Ss until all the vocabulary words have been written.

Practice

- Write on the board:
  A *What's the matter?*
  B *My shoulder hurts.*
  A *That's too bad.*
- Model the conversation with a S. The S speaks first. Be sure to pretend your shoulder hurts.
- Read aloud the instructions for Exercise **4B**. Model the example conversation with a S. You speak first. Encourage the S to pretend his or her tooth hurts.
- Ss practice the conversation in pairs.
- Say: *Now make up a new conversation.* Be sure Ss understand that they are to use the language in the picture dictionary. Ss complete the activity in pairs.
- Ask several pairs to act out their conversations.

Expansion activity *(whole group)*

- Suggest other ways of expressing sympathy. Ask Ss how they answer: *My tooth hurts.* Write responses on the board – *That's too bad. / I'm sorry. / Feel better.*
- Have Ss practice new conversations using these new ways of expressing sympathy.

Application

- Ss can also review earlier lessons to make dialogs using *I have a / an . . . ache.* Make a list of picture dictionary words that can be used in this way: *backache, earache, headache, stomachache, toothache.*
- Ss can also review earlier lessons to make dialogs using *I have a sprained or broken . . .* Make a list of picture dictionary words that can be used in this way: *finger, foot, hand, leg, shoulder, toe.*

Evaluation

- Direct Ss' attention to the lesson focus you wrote on the board. Ask Ss some questions about "The Health Clinic," such as: *What's wrong with Maria? What's wrong with her sons?* Ask Ss to tell you about the reading.
- Ask individual Ss to stand up. Say: *Show me your* (name of body part listed in the picture dictionary).
- Check off each focus point as Ss demonstrate an understanding of what they have learned in the lesson.

More Ventures *(whole group, pairs, individual)*
Assign appropriate exercises from the *Teacher's Toolkit Audio CD / CD-ROM, Add Ventures,* or the *Workbook.*

4 Picture dictionary Parts of the body

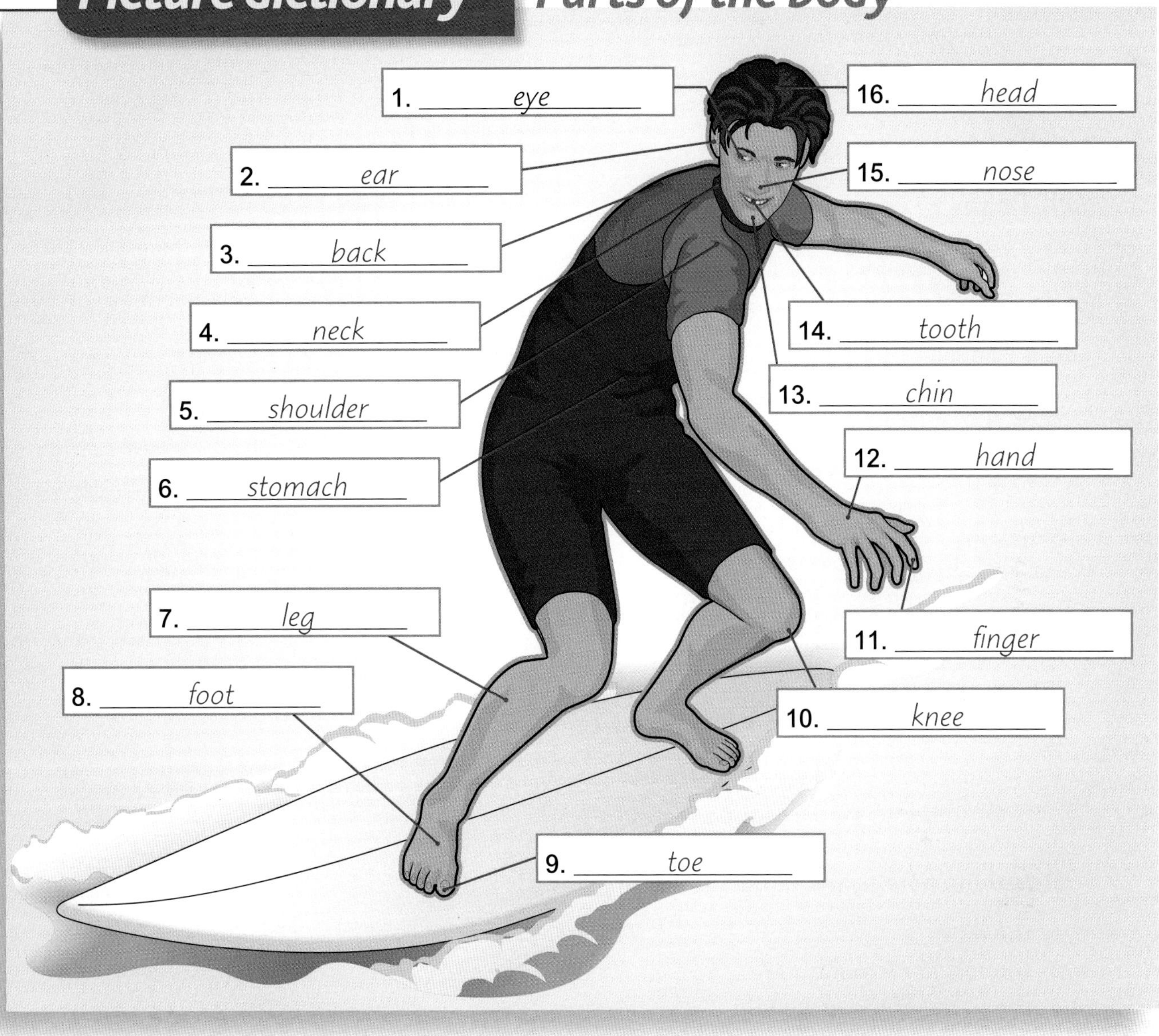
1. eye
2. ear
3. back
4. neck
5. shoulder
6. stomach
7. leg
8. foot
9. toe
10. knee
11. finger
12. hand
13. chin
14. tooth
15. nose
16. head

SELF-STUDY AUDIO CD

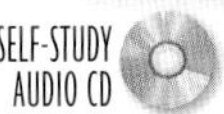

A **Write** the words in the picture dictionary. Then listen and repeat.

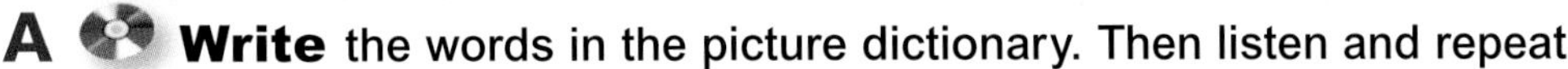

back	ear	finger	hand	knee	neck	shoulder	toe
chin	eye	foot	head	leg	nose	stomach	tooth

B **Talk** with a partner. Change the **bold** word and make conversations.

A What's wrong?
B My **tooth** hurts.
A That's too bad.

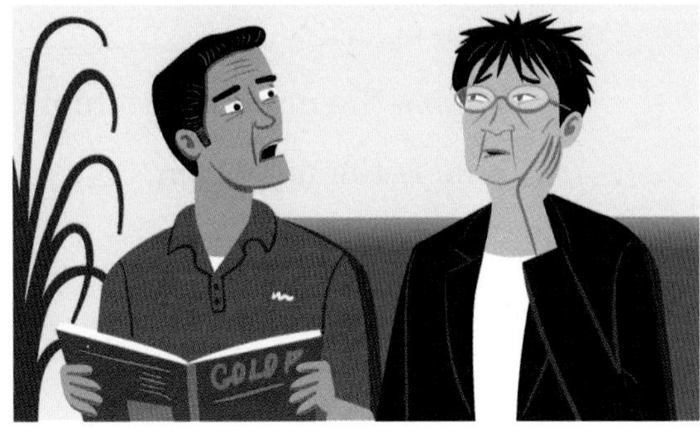

Writing

1 Before you write

A Talk with your classmates.

1. Do you write notes?
2. Who do you write to?

B Read. Luis is sick today. Read the note from his mother to his teacher.

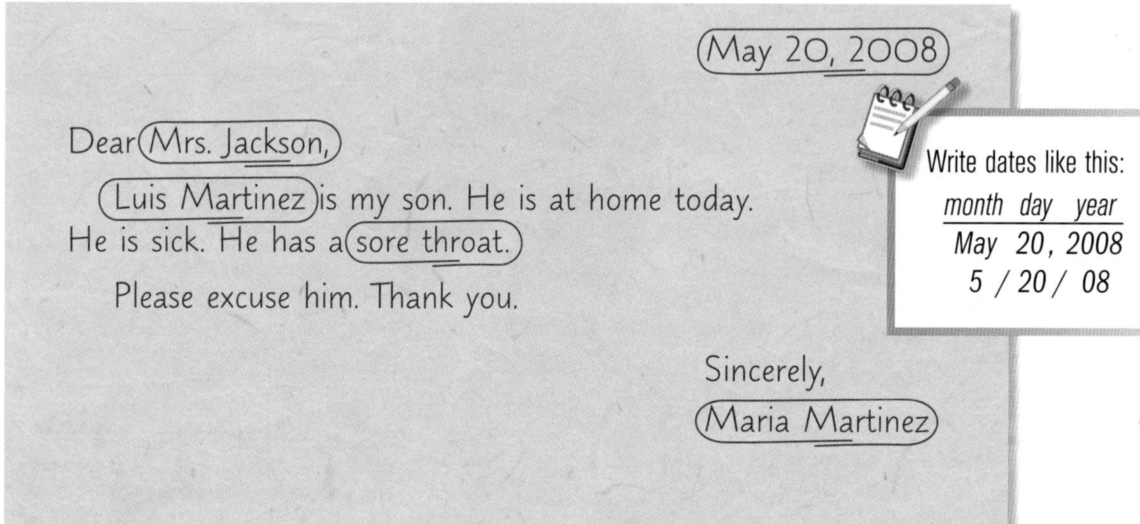

May 20, 2008

Dear Mrs. Jackson,

Luis Martinez is my son. He is at home today. He is sick. He has a sore throat.

Please excuse him. Thank you.

Sincerely,
Maria Martinez

Write dates like this:
month day year
May 20, 2008
5 / 20 / 08

Read the note again. Circle the information.

1. the date
2. the teacher's name
3. the name of the sick child
4. what's wrong
5. the signature

Write. Answer the questions.

1. What is the date? *The date is May 20, 2008.*
2. What is the teacher's name? *The teacher's name is Mrs. Jackson.*
3. Who is sick? *Luis Martinez is sick.*
4. What's the matter with him? *He has a sore throat.*
5. Who is the note from? *The note is from Maria Martinez.*

Lesson objectives

- Write absence notes
- Write dates

Warm-up and review

- Before class. Write today's lesson focus on the board.
  Lesson E:
  Write an absence note
  Learn to write month, day, and year
- Begin class. Books closed. Write *absent* and *absence note* on the board. Point to the words. Say: *"Absent" means "not here."*
- If a S is absent, ask the class: *Where is* (student's name)*?* Write on the board: (Student's name) *is absent.* Point to *absent*. Read the sentence aloud. Ask Ss to repeat.
- Point to *absence note* on the board. Read the words aloud. Say: *A note is like a short letter. An absence note is a short letter. It says you are not here. When you are absent from school, call or write an absence note to the teacher.*
- Review unit vocabulary. Ask Ss reasons for writing an absence note to a teacher, such as: *I have a sick child; I have a broken finger; I have a sore throat; My head hurts.* Write the reasons on the board.

Culture tip

You may want to explain to Ss that American schools expect parents to let them know if their children are not going to be in school. It might be interesting to ask Ss if they have the same policy in their countries, how teachers are informed if a child will not be in school one day, and what happens when Ss miss school too often without an absence note.

Presentation

- Books open. Read aloud the instructions for Exercise **1A**.
- Ask two Ss to read the questions aloud.
- Discuss the answers to the questions with the class.
- Point to the note in Exercise **1B**. Ask: *What is this?* Elicit: *An absence note.* Read the instructions aloud. Ss read the note silently. Explain words Ss don't know.
- Ask Ss: *Who is Mrs. Jackson?* (the teacher) Ask: *Who is Luis?* (Maria's son, the sick student) *Who is Maria?* (the mother) If Ss don't remember Luis and Maria, direct their attention to page 50. Point to Luis. Ask: *What's wrong with him?* (He has a sore throat.)
- Read the note aloud.

Read the tip box aloud. Ask Ss to point to the month, day, and year as they repeat them. Write today's date on the board. Ask a S to read the date; then change it to all numbers.

- Read the second part of the instructions for Exercise **1B**. Say: *Point to the date in the absence note.* After Ss point to the date, say: *Circle the date in your books.*
- Ask a S to write the date from the note on the board. Ask the S to circle the date. Be sure Ss understand the meaning of *circle* and the task.
- Read each of the five items. Ss listen to and circle the information they hear. Walk around and help as needed.

Comprehension check

- Read aloud the final part of the instructions for Exercise **1B**. Ss complete the exercise individually. Help as needed.
- Check answers with the class. Ask Ss to come to the board and write each answer. Ask: *Are these answers correct?* Ask other Ss to correct any errors.

Expansion activity (whole group)

- Review the months of the year. Write on the board:
  Months of the year
  1. January
  2. February
- Ask: *What's next?* Number and write all the months on the board.
- Read the months aloud. Ask Ss to repeat.
- Write on the board: *2-1-08.* Point to the numbers and ask: *What date is this?* (February 1, 2008)
- Ask a S to come to the board. Tell the S: *June 26, 2000.* Encourage him or her to write the date on the board. (June 26, 2000; 6-26-00; 6/26/00)
- Continue with new dates until most Ss have had a chance to write on the board.

Community building (small groups)

- Ask one S in each group to be the recorder. Ask Ss to say their name and their birthday. The recorder writes the name and date of each student on a piece of paper. If Ss don't wish to say the year of their birthday, they can say the month and day but not mention the year.
- Point to (or list) the months on the board. Ask Ss to call out the names of Ss in their group with birthdays in each month. Write the names on the board. Plan a monthly celebration of Ss' birthdays.
- Collect the papers with names and dates for reference.

Lesson E Writing

Practice

- Direct Ss' attention to the format of the absence note on page 52. Ask: *Where do you write the date?* (in the upper right-hand corner) Have Ss point to the date in the note in their books. Ask: *What do you write next?* (the greeting: *Dear* + the name of the teacher) Ask: *What do you write next?* (the body of the note: the name of the S and the health problem) Ask: *What do you write at the end?* (the closing: *Sincerely* + your signature)
- Read aloud the instructions for Exercise **1C**. Ask: *Who is Rosa?* (Maria's daughter) If Ss don't remember, turn to the picture on page 44. Point to the Martinez family. Say: *This is Maria. What's wrong with her?* (She has a headache.) Point to Luis and say: *This is Luis. He is Maria's son. What's wrong with him?* (He has a sore throat.) Point to Rosa and ask: *Who is this?* (Maria's daughter.) *What's wrong with her?* (She has a stomachache.)
- Direct Ss' attention to the words in the word bank on page 53. Say each word aloud. Ask Ss to repeat. Explain any words Ss do not remember.
- Be sure Ss understand the task. Ss complete the exercise individually.
- Ask Ss to compare their note with a partner's. Then ask a S to read the completed note to the class. Ask: *Is the note correct?* Correct any errors.

Application

- Write on the board:

  My son has a _____. _____ is at home. Please excuse _____.

  Ask Ss to fill in the blanks. Accept any health problems. Then write:

  My daughter has a _____. _____ is at home. Please excuse _____.

  Ask Ss to fill in the blanks. Accept any health problems. Remind Ss about the subject and object pronouns *he – him* and *she – her.*
- Read aloud the instructions for Exercise **2**.
- Ss complete the exercise individually. Tell Ss to use today's date and the name of their child and their child's teacher. Walk around and help as needed.

Teaching tip

Some Ss may not have children in school. In that case, you can ask Ss to write a note to you about their husband, wife, friend, or classmate.

Evaluation

- Direct Ss' attention to Exercise **3A** and read aloud the instructions.
- Ss complete the exercise in pairs. Walk around and help as needed. Help with pronunciation.
- Read aloud the instructions for Exercise **3B**. This exercise asks Ss to work together to peer-correct their writing. Ask a S to read the questions aloud. Tell Ss to exchange papers and look at their partner's note for the answers to the questions. Tell Ss to circle the answers on their partner's note. Walk around and help as needed.
- Ask pairs of Ss to answer the questions about their partner's note for the class.

Expansion activity *(student pairs, individual work)*

- Dictate a new note. Have Ss write it on a separate piece of paper. Remind them to use the correct format. Then ask Ss to write it on the board for correction:

  [yesterday's date]

  Dear Mr. Jones,

  Hector Ramirez is my son. He is at home today. He has the flu.

  Please excuse him. Thank you.

  Sincerely,
  Victor Ramirez
- Before class. Make several copies of this letter for Ss to dictate to each other.

  [yesterday's date]

  Dear Mrs. Smith,

  Lucy Lin is my daughter. She is at home today. She has a broken leg.

  Please excuse her. Thank you.

  Sincerely,
  Teresa Lin
- In class. Give copies of a new note to Ss to take turns dictating to each other. Ss can compare their writing to the copies you handed out.

Learner persistence

- If you have any Ss who are absent, ask a S in the class to call or e-mail the Ss and tell them what happened in class. If no one knows the Ss' contact information, ask Ss to explain today's lesson briefly to the absent Ss before class begins next time.

More Ventures *(whole group, pairs, individual)*
Assign appropriate exercises from the *Teacher's Toolkit Audio CD / CD-ROM, Add Ventures,* or the *Workbook.*

C **Write** about Rosa. She is sick, too. Complete the note.

daughter	Dear	home	May 20, 2008	stomachache

May 20, 2008

Dear Mr. O'Hara,

Rosa Martinez is my daughter. She is at home today. She is sick. She has a stomachache.

Please excuse her. Thank you.

Sincerely,
Maria Martinez

2 Write

Write. Imagine your son or daughter is sick today. Complete the note to the teacher.

(Answers will vary.)

Dear ______________,

______________ is my ______________.

______________ is at home today. ______________ is sick.

______________ has a fever.

Please excuse ______________. Thank you.

Sincerely,

____

3 After you write

A **Read** your note to a partner.

B **Check** your partner's note.

- Who is sick? What's the matter?
- Is the date correct?

Lesson F Another view

1 Life-skills reading

Appointment Confirmation
Here is your appointment information.

Patient: J. D. Avona
Medical record number: 9999999
Date: Monday, October 23
Time: 9:10 a.m.
Doctor: William Goldman, MD
Address: Eye Care Clinic
2025 Morse Avenue

Cancellation Information

To cancel only:	To cancel and reschedule:
(973) 555-5645	(973) 555-5210
7 days / 24 hours	Mon–Fri 8:30 a.m. to 5:00 p.m.

A Read the questions. Look at the appointment confirmation card. Circle the answers.

1. What is the doctor's last name?
   a. Avona
   (b.) Goldman
   c. Morse
   d. William
2. What is the appointment for?
   a. ears
   (b.) eyes
   c. nose
   d. throat
3. What is the address?
   a. Monday
   b. MD
   (c.) 2025 Morse Avenue
   d. 2025 Morris Avenue
4. What do you do to reschedule?
   a. call J. D. Avona
   b. call (973) 555-5645
   (c.) call (973) 555-5210
   d. go to the Eye Care Clinic

B Talk with your classmates. Ask and answer the questions.

1. Do you have a doctor?
2. Do you get appointment cards?
3. What information do your appointment cards have?

Lesson objectives
- Practice reading an appointment confirmation card
- Review unit vocabulary
- Introduce the project
- Complete the self-assessment

Warm-up and review

- Before class. Write today's lesson focus on the board.
  Lesson F:
  Read a doctor's appointment card
  Review topic vocabulary
  Complete the self-assessment
- Begin class. Books closed. Write *appointment* on the board. Ask: *What does this mean?* Help Ss if they do not know the meaning. Ask: *Do you have appointments? What kind?* Write Ss' examples on the board: *doctor's appointment, dentist's appointment, appointment with a teacher,* etc.
- Ask: *How do you remember appointments?* (Write the day and time down on paper; have someone remind you; write the date on a calendar; have a good memory; wrap string around your finger, etc.) Write the answers on the board.

Presentation

- Books open. Direct Ss' attention to the appointment confirmation card in Exercise **1A**. Read the instructions aloud. This task helps prepare Ss for standardized-type tests they may have to take. Be sure Ss understand the task. Have Ss individually scan for and circle the answers.

Comprehension check

- Ss should be able to guess what an appointment confirmation card is after doing Exercise **1A**. Say: *This is an appointment confirmation card. What does it do?* or *What is it for?* (It helps you remember an appointment.) *What kind of appointment is this for?* (a doctor's appointment, an eye doctor's appointment) *What is on the card?* (patient's name, doctor's name and address, date and time of the appointment, doctor's phone numbers, etc.)
- Check answers with the class.

Expansion activity *(whole group)*

- Explain vocabulary Ss do not know.
- Ask additional questions about the confirmation card: *Who is the patient for this appointment?* (J. D. Avona) *When is the appointment?* (Monday, October 23) *What time is the appointment?* (9:10 in the morning) *How can you cancel?* (Call 973-555-5645.) *When can you call to reschedule?* (Monday through Friday, 8:30 to 5:00)

Culture tip

Tell Ss that in the United States, you get an appointment card when you make an appointment at the doctor's or dentist's office. Sometimes a card is sent to your home to remind you of your next visit. Other times, you are given the card in the office by the receptionist. It might be interesting to ask Ss if they have these appointment cards in other countries.

Application

- Read aloud the instructions for Exercise **1B**.
- Ss in small groups. Say: *Ask all the people in your group the questions.*
- When Ss are finished, ask one member from each group to report back to the rest of the class about what his or her group discussed.

Expansion activity *(student pairs)*

- Role-play making appointments over the phone. Write the following dialog on the board, or pass out copies you have printed of it.

  A *Hello, Dr. Epstein's office.*
  B *I'd like to make an appointment.*
  A *What's your name?*
  B *My name is _____.*
  A *What's the matter?*
  B *I have a _____.*
  A *Is Monday, October 23, at 9:10 OK?*
  B *Yes, thanks.*
  A *OK. See you then.*
- Model the conversation with a S. Ss practice the conversation with a partner.
- Encourage Ss to change the date and time of the appointment, the name of the doctor, and the reason for the appointment.

Teaching tip

Point out the abbreviation *MD*. Explain that this is the short way of writing the degree for Doctor of Medicine. In talking about or addressing a Doctor of Medicine, you say *Doctor* + last name (Doctor Goldman); you write *Dr. Goldman.*

Lesson F Another view

Warm-up and review

- Review parts of the body. Have Ss call out body parts they have learned. Write the words on the board. Write words from the unit if Ss don't remember them. Point to the words and have Ss point to that part of their body.
- Point to parts of your body and say the right or wrong word. Ask Ss to say *Right* or *Wrong* and give the correct word.

Presentation

- Draw word webs on the board to prepare for Exercise **2A**. Draw three ovals on the board. Write one of these terms in each oval: *Health problems, Remedies,* and *Parts of the body*. Draw four spokes from each oval. Ask students to give you examples for each category and write them near the appropriate spoke. Say: *This is a word web. Word webs help you remember vocabulary.*

Practice

- Read aloud the instructions for Exercise **2A**. Be sure Ss understand the task.
- Direct Ss' attention to the words in the word bank. Say each word aloud. Ask Ss to repeat them.
- Ss work together in small groups to complete the exercise. Walk around and help as needed.
- Check answers with the class. Have Ss write the words in the word webs on the board.
- Read aloud the instructions for Exercise **2B**. Write the word *Clues* on the board. Below *Clues,* write the words *Across* and *Down*. Draw arrows next to the words to indicate the direction.
- Say: *Look at the man. Look at 1 Down.* Ask: *What is it?* (tooth) Point to where *tooth* is written in the puzzle.
- Say: *Look at the woman. Look at 1 Across.* Ask: *What is it?* (toe) Point to where *toe* is written in the puzzle.
- Ss complete the exercise individually. Walk around and help as needed.

Comprehension check

- Read aloud the second part of the instructions for Exercise **2B**. Ss in pairs compare their answers.
- Check answers with the class. Ask individual Ss for answers, for example: *What is number 2 across?* (shoulder) *How do you spell it?*

Expansion activity

- Point to Exercise **2B** and say: *This is a crossword puzzle. Do you like crossword puzzles? Do you do crossword puzzles outside of class? In what language?*
- If Ss have access to computers, play online crossword puzzles. Direct them to Web sites with ESL crossword puzzles, for example:
  iteslj.org/cw/
  a4esl.org/a/c3.html

  Crossword puzzles can be a fun way for Ss to practice their English at home.

Expansion activity

- Play Dictionary. Ss in two teams. Give each team a stack of index cards. Ask each team to write down as many body parts as they can. Collect the cards.
- Have each team select a student-artist. Call the artists to the board. Show them one of the cards. Say: *Draw this.*
- The first team to guess the picture wins a point. Keep score and continue with different artists until all the cards have been used.

> ***More Ventures*** *(whole group, pairs, individual)*
> Assign appropriate exercises from the *Teacher's Toolkit Audio CD / CD-ROM, Add Ventures,* or the *Workbook.*

Application

Community building

- **Project** Ask Ss to turn to page 137 in their Student's Book to complete the project for Unit 4.

Evaluation

- Before asking Ss to turn to the self-assessment on page 142, do a quick review of the unit. Have Ss turn to Lesson A. Ask the class to call out what they remember about this lesson. Prompt Ss, if necessary, with questions, for example: *What are the conversations about on this page? What vocabulary is in the picture?* Continue in this manner to review each lesson quickly.
- **Self-assessment** Read the instructions for Exercise **3**. Ask Ss to turn to the self-assessment page and complete the unit self-assessment.
- If Ss are ready, administer the unit test on pages T-169–T-170 of this *Teacher's Edition* (or on the *Teacher's Toolkit Audio CD / CD-ROM*). The audio and audio script for the tests are on the *Teacher's Toolkit Audio CD / CD-ROM.*

2 Fun with language

A Work in a group. Write the words in the webs.

aspirin	chin	finger	knee	sore throat	toothache
bandage	cough	heating pad	neck	stomachache	vitamin C

Health problems: cough, sore throat, stomachache, toothache

Remedies: aspirin, bandage, heating pad, vitamin C

Parts of the body: chin, finger, knee, neck

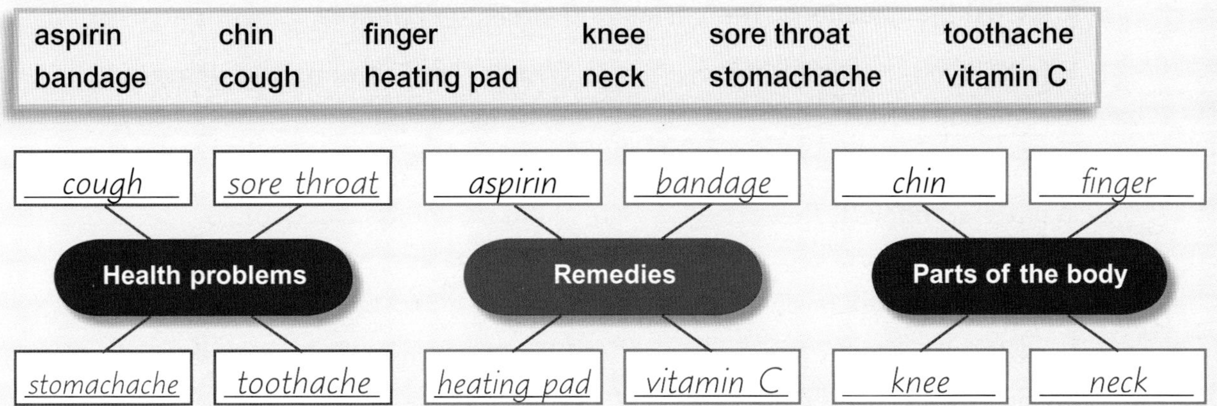

B Write. Look at the clues. Complete the puzzle.

	1. t	o	e		2. s	h	o	u	3. l	d	4. e	r
	o				t				e		y	
	o		5. f	o	o	t			g		e	
	t		i		m			6. h		7. b		
8. c	h	i	n		a			a		a		
			g		c			9. n	e	c	k	
10. k	n	e	e		11. h	e	a	d		k		
			r									

Down ↓

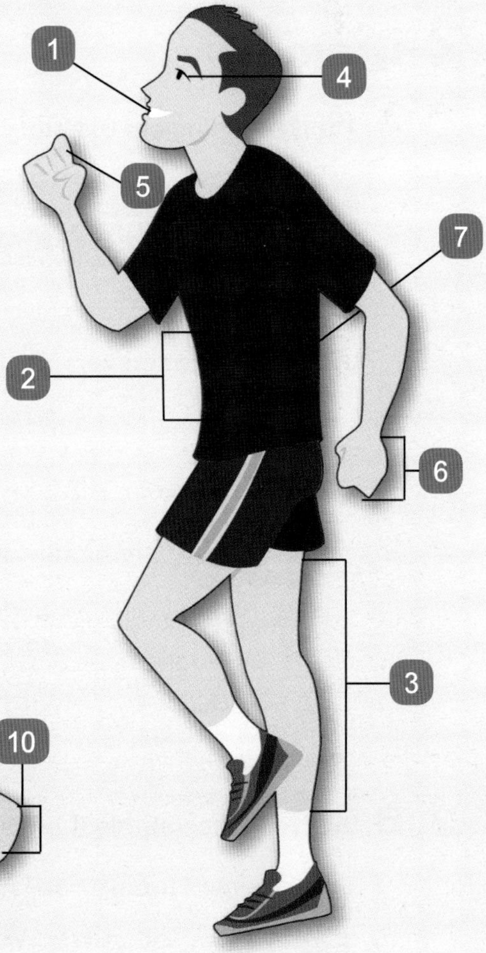

Across →

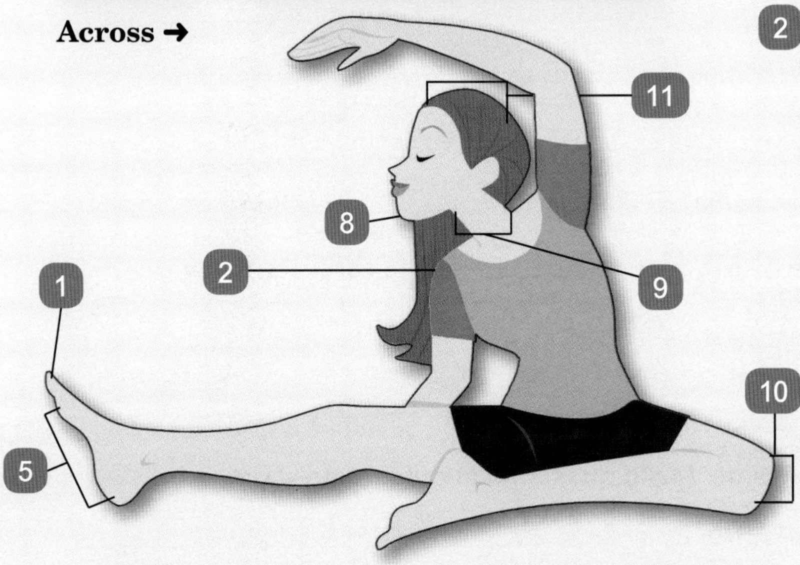

Work with a partner. Check your answers.

3 Wrap up

Complete the **Self-assessment** on page 142.

Review

1 Listening

Read the questions. Then listen and circle the answers.

1. What's wrong with Connie?
   a. She has a backache.
   (b.) She has a headache.
2. What's wrong with Robert?
   (a.) He has an earache.
   b. He has a headache.
3. What's Robert doing?
   (a.) He's talking to the doctor.
   b. He's talking to the children.
4. What's Connie's daughter doing?
   (a.) She's sleeping.
   b. She's watching TV.
5. What's Connie's son doing?
   a. He's eating.
   (b.) He's watching TV.
6. What's wrong with Eddie?
   a. He has an earache.
   (b.) He has a stomachache.

Talk with a partner. Ask and answer the questions. Use complete sentences.

2 Grammar

A Write. Complete the story.

At the Hospital

This week, everyone in Anthony's family is sick. Anthony ___has___ (1. have / has) a wife, a son, and a daughter. Right now, they ___are___ (2. is / are) sitting in a hospital room. Anthony's wife ___has___ (3. have / has) a backache. The nurse ___is___ (4. is / are) giving her medicine. The doctor ___is___ (5. is / are) talking to Anthony. He ___is___ (6. is / are) asking questions about the children. They ___have___ (7. have / has) the flu.

B Write. Unscramble the words. Make questions about the story.

1. Is / home / family / at / Anthony's / ? *Is Anthony's family at home?*
2. is / doing / the nurse / What / ? *What is the nurse doing?*
3. wrong / the children / with / What's / ? *What's wrong with the children?*

Talk with a partner. Ask and answer the questions.

Lesson objective

- Review vocabulary, pronunciation, and grammar from Units 3 and 4

Warm-up and review

- Before class. Write today's lesson focus on the board. *Review unit: Review vocabulary, pronunciation, and grammar from Units 3 and 4*
- Begin class. Books closed. Act as if you have a backache. Ask: *What's the matter?* Elicit: *You have a backache.*
- Give Ss slips of paper with the following health problems written on them: *headache, earache, stomachache.*
- Ask Ss to act out the health problems, one at a time. After each S acts, ask the class: *What's the matter?* Elicit: *He / She has a headache / an earache / a stomachache.*

Presentation

- Books open. Say: *Listen to a story about Connie. What's the matter with Connie and her family?*
- Focus Ss' attention on Exercise **1**. Read the instructions aloud.
- Ask individual Ss to read the questions aloud. Say: *Now listen to the story. Circle the correct answers.*
- [Class Audio CD1 track 40] Play or read the audio program (see audio script, page T-154). Ss listen and circle the answers to the questions. Repeat the audio program as needed.
- Write the numbers *1–6* on the board. Ask individual Ss to write their answers on the board. Ask other Ss: *Are these answers correct?* Have Ss make any necessary corrections on the board.

Practice

- Read aloud the second part of the instructions for Exercise **1**.
- Ss complete the exercise in pairs. Walk around and help as needed.
- Ask several pairs to ask and answer the questions for the rest of the class.
- Write on the board:

  I _____ *You* _____ *She* _____
  He _____ *We* _____ *They* _____
- Model the activity. Point to *I* on the board. Say: *I have a headache.* Write *have* in the blank next to *I.*
- Ask Ss to continue by writing the correct form of *to have* in the remaining blanks.
- Direct Ss' attention to Exercise **2A**. Read the instructions aloud.
- Ask a S to read aloud the title of the paragraph ("At the Hospital.") Ask: *What do you think this story is about?* Elicit an appropriate answer, for example: *It is a story about people at the hospital.*
- Ask another S to read aloud the first sentence in the paragraph.
- Ss complete the exercise individually. Walk around and help as needed.
- Write the numbers *1–7* on the board. Ask Ss to come to the board to write the answers.

Teaching tip

Ask Ss to write only the missing words on the board, not the complete sentences.

- Ask individual Ss to read aloud a sentence from the paragraph. After each sentence, ask: *Is the answer correct?* Ask different Ss to correct any errors.
- Books closed. Write on the board: *doing / is / What / Anthony / ?*
- Ask Ss to unscramble the words on the board to make a question. (What is Anthony doing?) Write the question on the board.
- Books open. Focus Ss' attention on Exercise **2B**. Read the instructions aloud.
- Ss complete the exercise individually. Walk around and help as needed.
- Write the numbers *1–3* on the board. Ask three Ss to write the unscrambled questions on the board. Ask other Ss: *Are the questions correct?* Ask different Ss to correct any errors.
- Read aloud the second part of the instructions for Exercise **2B**.
- Model the task. Ask a S the first question: *Is Anthony's family at home?* Elicit: *No, they aren't.*
- Ss complete the exercise in pairs. Walk around and help as needed.
- Ask several pairs to ask and answer the questions for the rest of the class.

Review

Warm-up and review

- Say: *Now we are going to practice pronunciation.*
- Write the word *syllables* on the board. Ask: *Do you remember what syllables are?* Elicit a *Yes* or *No* answer. Write the word *husband* on the board. Ask: *How many syllables are in this word?* (two) Clap the syllables while you say the word to remind Ss of the syllable counting exercise in the last review unit.

Presentation

- Focus Ss' attention on Exercise **3A**. Read the instructions aloud.
- [Class Audio CD1 track 41] Play or read the audio program (see audio script, page T-154). Repeat the audio program as needed.

Practice

- Read aloud the instructions for Exercise **3B**. Say: *When a word has more than one syllable, one of the syllables is strong.* Point to the word *husband* on the board. Say it aloud. Clap loudly for the first syllable and softly for the second syllable. Underline the first syllable on the board. Say: *This syllable is the strong syllable in "husband."*
- [Class Audio CD1 track 42] Play or read the audio program (see audio script, page T-154). Ss listen and repeat the words they hear. Encourage Ss to clap one time for each syllable in the word, and to clap loudly on the strong syllable. Repeat the audio program as needed.

Teaching tip
Clap with your Ss as they repeat the words to model the correct stress pattern.

- Read aloud the second part of the instructions for Exercise **3B**.
- Model the task. Ask a S to stand up. Hold up the Student's Book. Point to the word *tomorrow* in the first row. Say the word. Ask the S to clap the syllables after you say the word. Make sure the S claps loudly for the strong second syllable.
- Ss complete the exercise in pairs. Walk around and help as needed.
- Ask several pairs to say the words and to clap the syllables for the rest of the class.

  Option Ask the class to work together to pronounce and clap the words.
- Read aloud the instructions for Exercise **3C**.
- [Class Audio CD1 track 43] Play or read only the first word on the audio program (see audio script, page T-155). Ask: *Which is the strong syllable?* (the first syllable) Hold up the Student's Book. Show Ss how the first syllable has a circle over it.
- [Class Audio CD1 track 43] Play or read the audio program. Ss listen and draw a circle over the strong syllable in each word. Repeat the audio program as needed.
- Write the numbers *1–12* on the board. Ask individual Ss to write their answers on the board. Ask: *Are these answers correct?* Ask different Ss to make any necessary corrections.

Teaching tip
If there are any questions about which syllable in a word is the strong syllable, clap out the word with the class, emphasizing the strong syllable.

- Read aloud the instructions for Exercise **3D**.
- Model the task. Look through Units 3 and 4 in the Student's Book. Write a word on the board that isn't in Exercise **3B**, and draw a circle over the strong syllable.
- Ss complete the exercise individually. Walk around and help as needed.

  Option Ask Ss to write their words on the board.
- Read aloud the second part of the instructions for Exercise **3D**.
- Model the task. Point to the word you wrote on the board. Say it aloud. Clap for each syllable, and clap loudly as you say the strong syllable.
- Ss complete the exercise in pairs. Walk around and help as needed.

Evaluation

- Direct Ss' attention to the lesson focus written on the board.
- Go around the room. Ask each S to say a sentence about Connie's family from Exercise **1** on page 56.
- Ask Ss to pronounce the words in Exercise **3B** and say which syllable in each word is the strong syllable.
- Check off the items in the lesson focus as Ss demonstrate an understanding of what they have learned in the lesson.

3 Pronunciation: strong syllables

A **Listen** to the syllables in these words.

happy   fever

B **Listen and repeat.** Clap for each syllable. Clap loudly for the strong syllable.

●	● •	● • •	• ● •
son	cooking	yesterday	tomorrow
wife	homework	grandmother	computer
head	toothache	grandfather	
ear	headache	newspaper	
foot	husband	studying	
leg	daughter	stomachache	

Talk with a partner. Take turns. Say each word. Your partner claps for each syllable.

C **Listen** for the strong syllable in each word. Put a circle over the strong syllable.

1. father
2. earache
3. tired
4. birthday
5. thirsty
6. celebrate
7. finger
8. Brazil
9. repeat
10. elbow
11. reschedule
12. fever

D **Write** eight words from Units 3 and 4. Put a circle over the strong syllable in each word.

1. *(Answers will vary.)*	5.
2.	6.
3.	7.
4.	8.

Talk with a partner. Read the names.

Around town

Lesson A Get ready

1 Talk about the picture

A Look at the picture. What do you see?

B Point to: a grocery store • a library • a restaurant
a hospital • a house • a street

Lesson objectives

- Introduce students to the topic
- Find out what students know about the topic
- Preview the unit by talking about the picture
- Practice key vocabulary
- Practice listening skills

Warm-up and review

- Before class. Write today's lesson focus on the board.
  Lesson A: Around town
  Places in town
- Begin class. Books closed. Point to the words *Places in town* on the board. Ask: *What are some places in town?* Elicit: *stores, the library, schools,* etc. Write Ss' responses on the board.
- Ask:
  Where do you go shopping? (the supermarket / grocery store)
  Where do you mail a letter? (the post office)
  Where do your children play? (the park)
  Where do you eat? (at home, at a restaurant)
  Where do you go if you're sick? (the hospital)
  Where do you go to learn English? (the school)

Teaching tip
Do not expect Ss to know all the new vocabulary words. These warm-up questions are intended to find out what Ss already know about places in town.

Presentation

- Books open. Set the scene. Direct Ss' attention to the picture on page 58. Ask: *What do you see?* Elicit as much vocabulary about the picture as possible: *restaurant, library, hospital, grocery store, school, car,* etc.
- Direct Ss' attention to the key words in Exercise **1B**. Read each word aloud. Ask Ss to repeat the words.

Teaching tip
It might be helpful to explain that a grocery store is like a small supermarket. It might also be helpful to explain the difference between a town and a city. Say: *A town is small. A city is big. Do we live in a town or a city?*

Comprehension check

- Point to items in the picture and ask *Yes / No* questions:
  Is the restaurant busy? (Yes.)
  Are the buses on the street? (Yes.)
  Is the library closed? (No.)
  Is Sandra on Second St.? (Yes.)
  Are the schoolchildren playing ball? (Yes.)
  Is the community center closed? (No.)

Practice

- Direct Ss' attention to Exercise **1B**. Model the task. Hold up the Student's Book. Say to a S: *Point to the grocery store*. The S points to the appropriate store.
- Ss in pairs. Say to one S: *Say the words in Exercise 1B.* Say to the partner: *Point to the places in the picture.*
- Pairs complete the exercise. Help as needed. When Ss have finished, have them change partners and change roles.
- Ask several pairs to perform the exercise for the class to check Ss' understanding.

Expansion activity *(student pairs)*

- Write on the board, in the form of a list, some places in your town or city that you like to frequent, for example: *the library, the mall, Amy's Restaurant.*
- Point to the words. Say: *I like to go to these places in* (name of your town or city). Ask: *Where do you like to go to in* (name of your town or city)*? Make a list with a partner.*
- Ss complete the exercise in pairs. Help as needed.
- Ask pairs to write their lists on the board. Ask Ss to say their lists to the rest of the class.

Expansion activity *(small groups)*

- **Materials needed** A local phone book for each group
- Write on the board the names of some local businesses and restaurants. Include a hospital, library, grocery store, school, community center, and restaurant. Say: *Let's look up the phone numbers for these places in town.*
- Ss complete the task in groups. Ask individual Ss to write the phone numbers of the businesses or restaurants next to their names on the board.

Community building *(student pairs)*

- Talk about favorite places. Write on the board: *What's your favorite _____?*
  bank
  school
  park
  restaurant
  grocery store
- Model the activity. Ask a S: *What's your favorite restaurant?* Elicit an appropriate answer.
- Ss in pairs. Say: *Ask your partner what his or her favorite places in town are. Use the question and the places on the board*. Walk around and help as needed.
- When everyone has finished asking the questions, ask individual Ss to say their favorite places.

Lesson A Get ready

Warm-up and review

- Books closed. Write the name of your school on the board. Point to the words. Say: *This is the name of our school. What places are near the school?*
- Write Ss' responses on the board, for example, the names of drugstores, grocery stores, and restaurants.

Practice

- Books open. Direct Ss' attention to Exercise **2A**. Read the instructions aloud.
- [Class Audio CD1 track 44] Play or read the audio program (see audio script, page T-155). Ss listen to and circle the words they hear. Repeat the audio as needed.
- Check answers. Ask: *What did you circle?* Ask Ss to write the words on the board. Point to the words. Say: *Repeat after me*. Say each word. Listen to Ss' pronunciation and correct as needed.

Expansion activity *(student pairs)*

- Ask a S to write on the board the words they did not circle: *hospital, library, school.*
- Ss in pairs. Say: *Write sentences with these words.*
- Ask Ss to write their sentences on the board. Ask other Ss to read the sentences aloud.

Practice

- Direct Ss' attention to the pictures in Exercise **2B**. Ask: *What do you see in each picture?* (a post office, a park, a drugstore, a bus stop, a museum, a restaurant)
- Write Ss' responses on the board.
- Read aloud the second part of the instructions for exercise **2B**.
- [Class Audio CD1 track 44] Play or read the audio program again. Pause after the first conversation. Ask: *Which picture matches conversation A?* (picture number 3) Point to the handwritten *a* written next to number 3. Be sure Ss understand the task.
- [Class Audio CD1 track 44] Play or read the complete audio program. Ss complete the rest of the exercise individually.

Learner persistence *(individual work)*

- [Self-Study Audio CD track 21] Exercises **2A** and **2B** are recorded on the Ss' self-study CD at the back of the Student's Book. Ss can listen to the CD at home for reinforcement and review. They can also listen for self-directed learning when class attendance is not possible.

Comprehension check

- Write numbers *1–6* on the board. Ask a few Ss to write the answers to Exercise **2B** next to each number.
- Read aloud the second part of the instructions for Exercise **2B**.
- [Class Audio CD1 track 44] Play or read the audio program again. Ask Ss to check their answers. Pause the audio program after each conversation. Point to a letter of the conversation on the board. Ask: *Is this correct?*

Application

- Write *neighborhood* on the board. Ask: *What is this?*
- If no one knows the answer, underline *neighbor.* Say: *Your neighbor is the person who lives near you. Your neighborhood is the area where you live.*
- Have Ss look at Exercise **2C** and read the instructions.
- Direct Ss' attention to the zero written next to *museums.* Say: *If you have no museums in your neighborhood, write a zero. What do you write if you have one museum in your neighborhood?* (1)
- Ss complete the exercise individually. Help as needed.
- Read aloud the second part of the instructions for Exercise **2C**.
- Ask two Ss to read the example question and answer.

> **Useful language**
> Read the tip box aloud. Say: *If you have a zero in Exercise 2C, the answer to the question is "none."*

- Say: *Ask your partner about the places in Exercise 2C.*
- Ss complete the exercise in pairs. Help as needed.

Community building *(whole group)*

- Make a drawing on the board of your school's neighborhood. Draw rectangles and squares for buildings.
- Ask Ss to write the names of the businesses and buildings drawn on the board.

Evaluation

- Direct Ss' attention to the lesson focus on the board. Ask Ss to give you examples of places in town.
- Check off the lesson focus as Ss demonstrate an understanding of what they have learned in the lesson.

> ***More Ventures*** *(whole group, pairs, individual)*
> Assign appropriate exercises from the *Teacher's Toolkit Audio CD / CD-ROM, Add Ventures,* or the *Workbook*.

2 Listening

A **Listen.** Circle the words you hear.

bus stop	library	post office
drugstore	museum	restaurant
hospital	park	school

SELF-STUDY AUDIO CD **B** **Listen again.** Write the letter of the conversation.

1. _c_

2. _e_

3. _a_
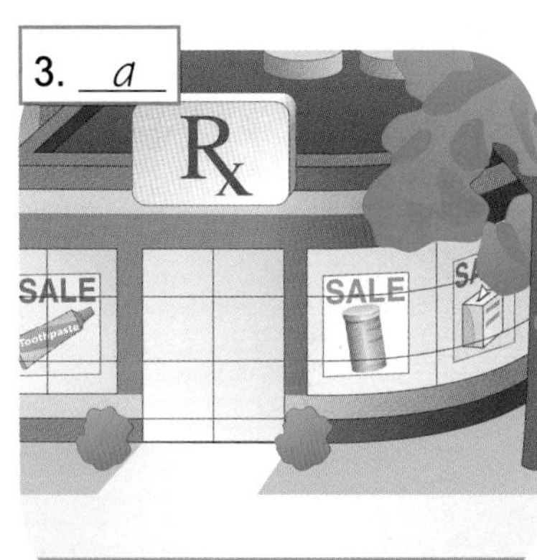

4. _f_

5. _d_

6. _b_

Listen again. Check your answers.

C **Write.** How many places are in your neighborhood? *(Answers will vary.)*

museums	_0_	libraries	_____	schools	_____
drugstores	_____	restaurants	_____	post offices	_____
bus stops	_____	parks	_____	hospitals	_____

Work with a partner. Ask and answer questions.

How many museums are in your neighborhood?

None.

Useful language

When *0* means *not one*, say *none*.

Lesson B *It's on the corner.*

1 Grammar focus: *on, next to, across from, between, on the corner of*

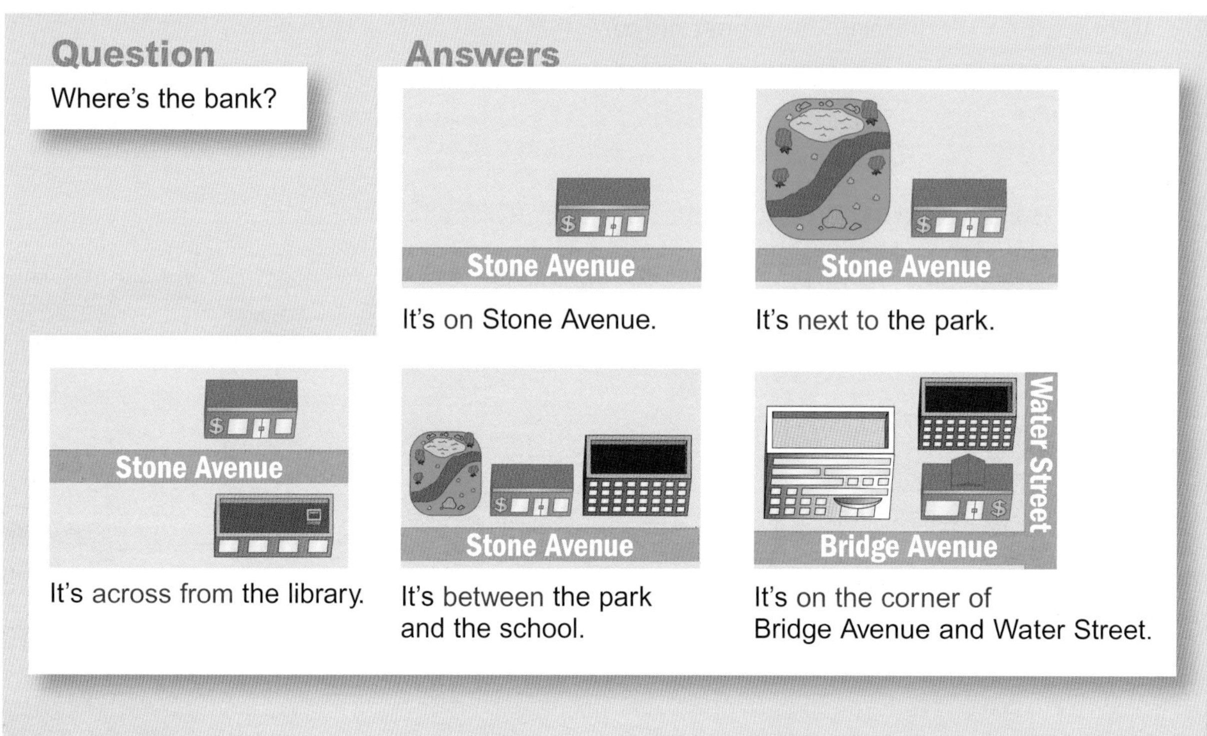

2 Practice

A Write. Look at the map. Complete the sentences.

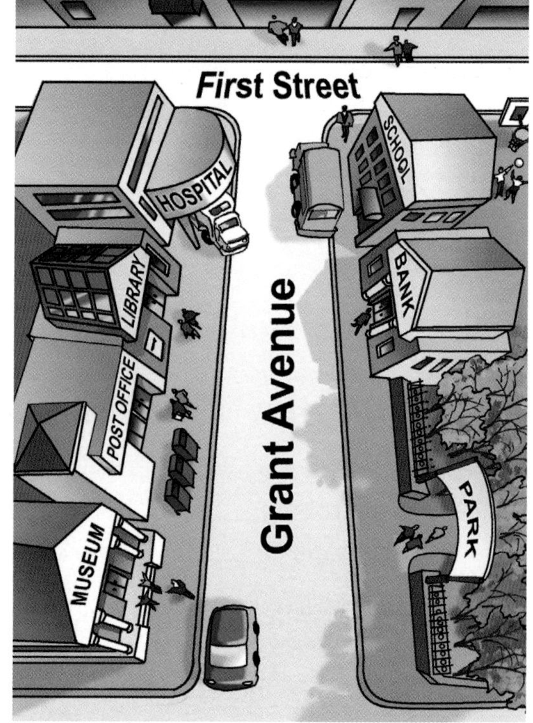

1. ***A*** Where's the park?
   B It's ___next to___ the bank.
2. ***A*** Where's the library?
   B It's ___across from___ the bank.
3. ***A*** Where's the school?
   B It's ___on the corner of___ First Street and Grant Avenue.
4. ***A*** Where's the hospital?
   B It's ___on___ Grant Avenue.
5. ***A*** Where's the bank?
   B It's ___between___ the school and the park.
6. ***A*** Where's the post office?
   B It's ___next to___ the library.

Listen and repeat. Then practice with a partner.

Lesson objective

- Introduce prepositions of location

Warm-up and review

- Before class. Write today's lesson focus on the board.
Lesson B: Prepositions of location:
on, next to, across from, between, on the corner of
- Begin class. Books closed. Draw a simple map on the board, using squares and rectangles for buildings. For example:

drugstore	*restaurant*	*park*
hospital	*museum*	*bus stop*

- Point to the drugstore. Ask: *Where is the drugstore?* Elicit: *It's next to the restaurant.* Ask: *Where is the park?* (It's across from the bus stop). Ask: *Where is the museum?* (It's between the hospital and the bus stop).
- If Ss do not know the answers, point and say: *The drugstore is next to the restaurant. The park is across from the bus stop. The museum is between the hospital and the bus stop.* Draw lines to indicate *next to, across from,* and *between.*

Teaching tip
Do not expect Ss to know all the names of the prepositions yet. This warm-up is intended to find out which Ss already know some of the prepositions.

Presentation

- Books open. Direct Ss' attention to Exercise **1**.
- Hold up the Student's Book. Ask the example question aloud. Say each answer while pointing to the corresponding picture. Ask Ss to repeat each sentence after you.

Contractions
It might be helpful to review contractions. Write on the board: *Where's* = and *It's*= . Ask: *What do these contractions mean?* Ask a S to write the complete forms on the board: *Where is* and *It is.* Say: *We often use contractions in English.* Contractions are short forms.

Practice

- Direct Ss' attention to the map in Exercise **2A**. Ask: *Where's the park in this map?* (It's next to the bank. It's across from the museum and the post office.)
- Read the instructions aloud. Ask two Ss to read aloud the example question and answer.
- Ss complete the exercise individually. Help as needed.
- [Class Audio CD1 track 45] Read the second part of the instructions for Exercise **2A**. Play or read the audio program (see audio script, page T-155). Have Ss check answers as they listen and repeat. Correct pronunciation.
- Ask Ss to come to the board and write the sentences. Ask different Ss to read aloud and correct the sentences.

Expansion activity *(student pairs)*

- Conversation practice about local places. Ask: *What are some places that you go to in our town or city?* Write Ss' responses on the board. Elicit names of local places.
- Ss in pairs. Say: *Use the questions in Exercise 2A as a guide. Ask questions about real places in town. Use "next to," "across from," "between," and "on the corner of" in your answers.* Help as needed.
- Ask pairs to perform the conversations for the class.

Teaching tip
It might be helpful to teach Ss the phrase *I don't know* if they don't know the location of local places.

Expansion activity *(small groups)*

- **Materials needed** Poster board or a large piece of white paper, pencils, rulers, markers
- Perfect-town maps. Explain the meaning of *perfect.* Say: *"Perfect" means "the best."*
- Ss in small groups. Say: *Work with your group. Draw the perfect town. Include places like parks and stores.*
- Model the activity. Draw a simple map on the board. Use rectangles and squares to represent buildings, and include things such as a beach or a large park that you would like to have in your perfect town.
- Ss complete the activity in groups.
- Say: *Now write five sentences about your maps. Use "on," "next to," "across from," "between," and "on the corner of."* Walk around and help as needed.
- Ask groups to come to the front of the class and present their maps of their perfect town. One S from each group can read the sentences, while another S points to the places as they are described.

Expansion activity *(student pairs)*

- Ss in pairs. Say: *Look at page 58. Ask your partner questions with "Where." Your partner will answer with "on," "next to," "across from," "between," and "on the corner of."*
- Walk around and help as needed.

Lesson B It's on the corner.

Warm-up and review

- Books closed. Draw on the board a simple map of your school's location. Include any street names that are near the school. Draw a rectangle to represent the school. Label the building.
- Point to the street that your school is on. Ask a S: *Where's* (name of school)*?* Elicit: *It's on* (name of street).

Presentation

- Books open. Direct Ss' attention to Exercise **2B**. Read the instructions aloud.
- [Class Audio CD1 track 46] Play or read the audio program (see audio script, page T-155). Listen to Ss' pronunciation as they repeat the conversation.

> **Useful language**
> Read the tip box aloud. Ask Ss to repeat the examples after you. Ask a S to read the dialog with you. You begin. Use *Sorry, I didn't get that* instead of *Could you repeat that, please?* Show that both expressions can be used to clarify information.

Practice

- Direct Ss' attention to the pictures in Exercise **2B**. Ask: *What is picture number 1?* (a coffee shop) *What is picture number 2?* (a drugstore) *What is picture number 3?* (a grocery store) Ask: *What do you do at a coffee shop?* (drink coffee, eat lunch, etc.) *At a drugstore?* (buy medicine, etc.) *At a grocery store?* (buy food, etc.)
- Read the instructions aloud. Model the task. Ask a S to practice the conversation with you.
- Ss complete the exercise in pairs. Encourage them to use the different phrases found in the "Useful language" box.
- Ask pairs to perform the conversations for the class.
- Direct Ss' attention to Exercise **3A** and read the instructions aloud.
- Ask two Ss to read the example conversation aloud.
- Direct Ss' attention to the map on page 60. Hold up the Student's Book. Show the map. Point to the school and say: *See. The school is on the corner of First Street and Grant Avenue. It's across from the hospital.*
- Ask two Ss to stand up. Hold up the Student's Book with the map on page 60. Ask one S to describe a location. The other S guesses the location and points to it.
- Ss complete the exercise in pairs. Help as needed.

Application

- On the board, draw the map in Exercise **3B**. Ask a S to draw on the map a post office, a bank, and a restaurant.
- Point to the map on the board. Ask another S: *Where is the bank?* Ask the S to point to the map as he or she gives an appropriate answer.
- Ask two other Ss: *Where is the post office? Where is the restaurant?* Ask the Ss to point to the map as they give appropriate answers.
- Read aloud the instructions for Exercise **3B**.
- Ss draw their maps individually. Help as needed.
- Ss in pairs. Say: *Ask your partner about the places on the map. Is your partner's map the same or different from your map?* Walk around and help as needed.

Expansion activity (student pairs)

- Conversation practice with local street names. Ask: *What are some places that you go to in our town or city?* Write Ss' responses on the board.
- Ss in pairs. Say: *Use the conversation in Exercise 2B as a guide. Make up conversations about real places in our town. Use the real street names.*
- Ask pairs to perform their conversations for the class.

Expansion activity (individual work)

- Dictation. Ask Ss to write the numbers *1–5* in a vertical line in their notebooks. Say: *Listen to the sentences. Write what you hear.* Dictate the following sentences:
  1. The bank is on Second Street.
  2. The library is across from the post office.
  3. The park is between the bank and the school.
  4. The museum is next to the grocery store.
  5. The restaurant is on the corner of Grant Avenue and First Street.
- Ask Ss to write their sentences on the board.

Evaluation

- Direct Ss' attention to the lesson focus on the board. Show Ss the picture on page 58. Say: *Make sentences. Use the prepositions on the board.*
- Check off the items as Ss demonstrate an understanding of what they have learned in the lesson.

> ***More Ventures*** (whole group, pairs, individual)
> Assign appropriate exercises from the *Teacher's Toolkit Audio CD / CD-ROM, Add Ventures,* or the *Workbook.*

B Listen and repeat.

A Excuse me. Where's **Kim's Coffee Shop**?
B It's **on Kent Street**.
A Sorry. Could you repeat that, please?
B It's **on Kent Street**.
A Oh, OK. Thanks.

Useful language
Could you repeat that, please?
Sorry, I didn't get that.

Talk with a partner. Change the **bold** words and make conversations.

1

coffee shop

2
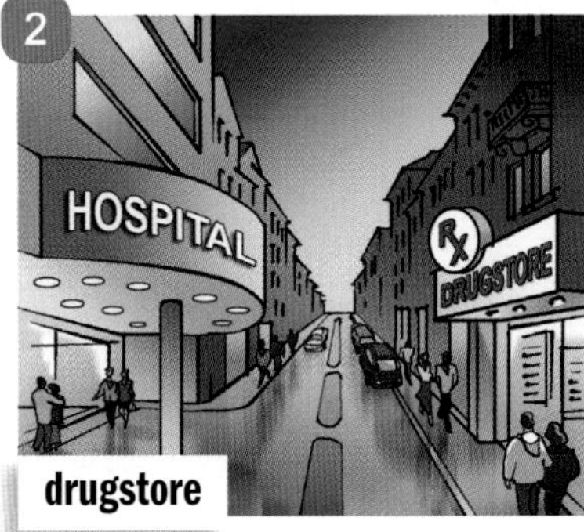

drugstore

3

grocery store

3 Communicate

A **Talk** with a partner. Look at the map on page 60. Give directions. Guess the place.

A It's on the corner of First Street and Grant Avenue. It's across from the hospital.
B The school?
A That's right.

B **Draw** these places on the map. Talk with a partner. Ask and answer questions about your maps.

- bank
- bus stop
- coffee shop
- grocery store
- hospital
- house

Lesson C

Go two blocks.

1 Grammar focus: imperatives

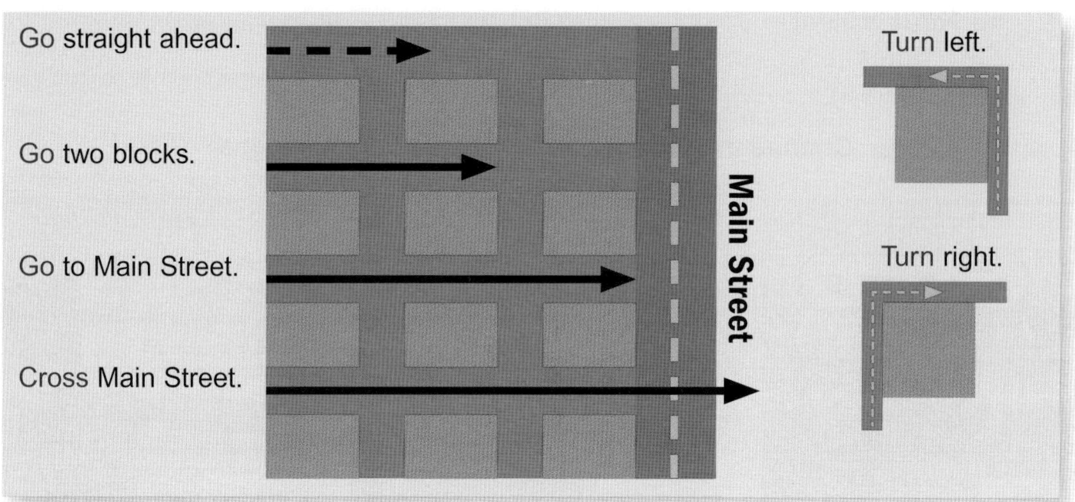

2 Practice

A Write. Match the pictures and the directions.

Cross Union Street.	Go three blocks.	Turn left.
Go straight ahead.	Go to Main Street.	Turn right.

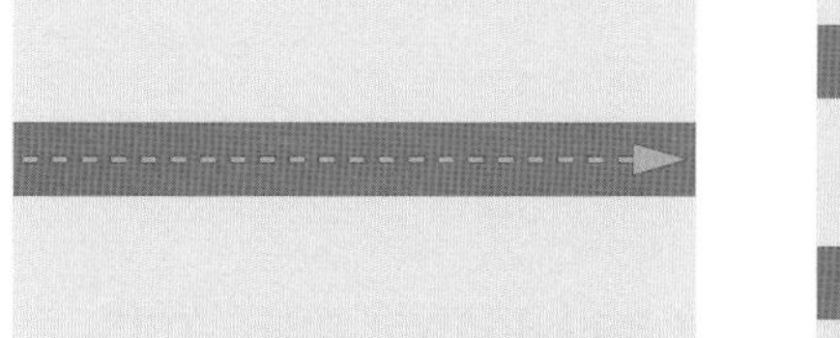

1. *Go straight ahead.*

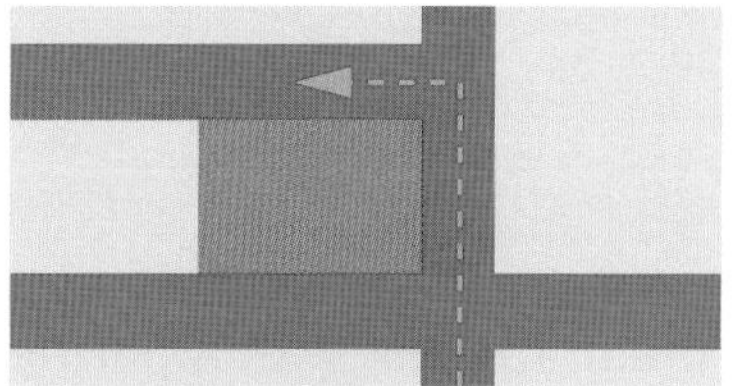

2. *Turn left.*

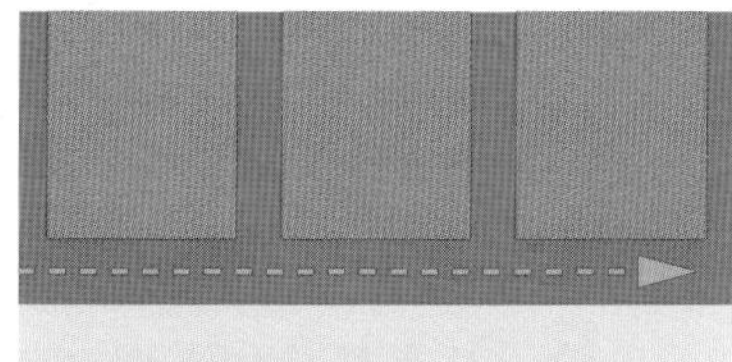

3. *Go three blocks.*

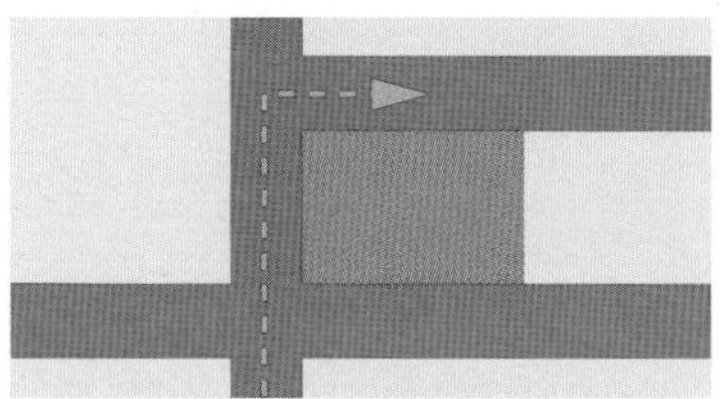

4. *Turn right.*

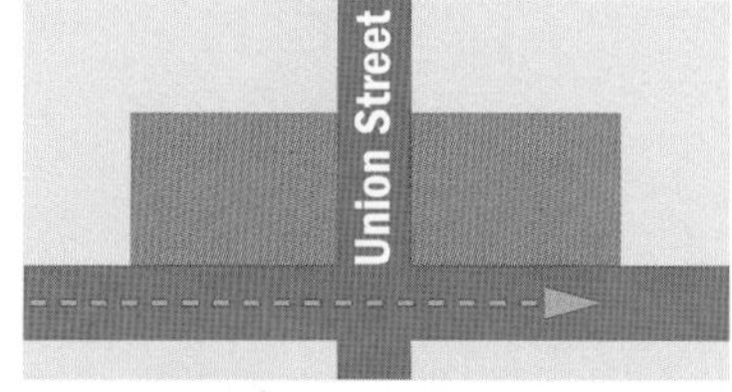

5. *Cross Union Street.*

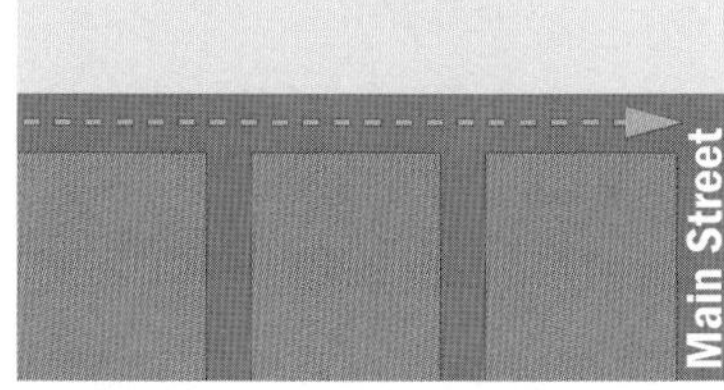

6. *Go to Main Street.*

 **Listen and repeat.**

Lesson objective
- Introduce imperatives

Warm-up and review

- Before class. Write today's lesson focus on the board.
Lesson C: Giving directions
- Begin class. Total Physical Response. Sit in a chair in front of the class. Stand up and say: *Stand up.* (Gesture with your hands to make your point clear.) Wait until the entire class stands up.
- Say: *Sit down.* (Perform the action as a model.)
- Ask an individual S to stand up. Say: *Walk straight ahead.* If the S doesn't know what to do, demonstrate the action. Repeat the procedure with *Walk straight ahead. Turn right. Walk straight ahead. Turn left.*

Teaching tip
If time allows, you can repeat the above commands several times with the whole class or individual Ss to make sure that Ss understand.

Presentation

- Direct Ss' attention to the grammar chart in Exercise **1**.
- Hold up the Student's Book. Read each sentence in the grammar chart while pointing to the corresponding pictures. Ask Ss to repeat after you.

Culture tip
You may want to ask individual Ss how they give directions in their native country. Ask if they use maps or use buildings as guides to give directions. It might be interesting to tell Ss that many people use maps and landmarks to give directions to places.

Comprehension check

- Ask: *Where is the office in our school?* Elicit an appropriate response, such as: *It's over there.* If your school doesn't have an office, ask about another location at your school with which everyone is familiar.

Teaching tip
Accept nonverbal gestures as responses (such as pointing in the correct direction) if Ss cannot articulate the answer to this question.

- Say: *Imagine that we have a new student in our classroom. Give him directions to the office.* Elicit directions, such as: *Turn right, Turn left, Go straight.*
- Write the correct directions on the board for getting to the office.
- Say: *What if the new student asks, "Where is the bathroom?"* Elicit directions, such as: *Turn right, Turn left, Go straight.*

Practice

- Direct Ss' attention to Exercise **2A** and read the instructions aloud.
- Have Ss focus on the word bank. Read each sentence aloud and listen to Ss' pronunciation as they repeat after you. Make sure Ss understand that the sentences can be used to give directions.
- Direct Ss' attention to the picture in number 1. Ask: *What does the picture show?* (Go straight ahead.)
- Ss complete the exercise individually. Walk around and help as needed.
- Read aloud the second part of the instructions for Exercise **2A**.
- [Class Audio CD1 track 47] Play or read the audio program (see audio script, page T-155). Listen to Ss' pronunciation as they repeat the directions. Correct pronunciation as needed.

Expansion activity *(student pairs)*

- Practice giving directions. Direct Ss' attention to the picture on page 58.
- Model the activity. Say: *I will give you directions. Follow my directions with your finger on the map. Where will you go?* Say these directions:
1. Start at the restaurant.
2. Go straight on Second Street.
3. Cross the first street.
4. Go to the first building across the street.
5. Where are you?
Answer: At the Community Center.
Option Hold up the Student's Book and show Ss how you are tracing the route with your finger as you say each direction to the class.
- Ss in pairs. Say: *One person will give directions. The other will follow in the book. Where will you go?* Give Ss time to plan their directions. Walk around and help as needed.
- Ask several Ss to say their directions to the rest of the class. Ask: *What is the final location?*

Community building *(student pairs)*

- Ask Ss to draw a map that includes the school as well as their home or a place near the school. Say: *Choose a partner. Show your partner your map. Tell your partner how to get from the school to your home (or to a place near school).*

Lesson C Go two blocks.

Presentation

- Draw the following map on the board:

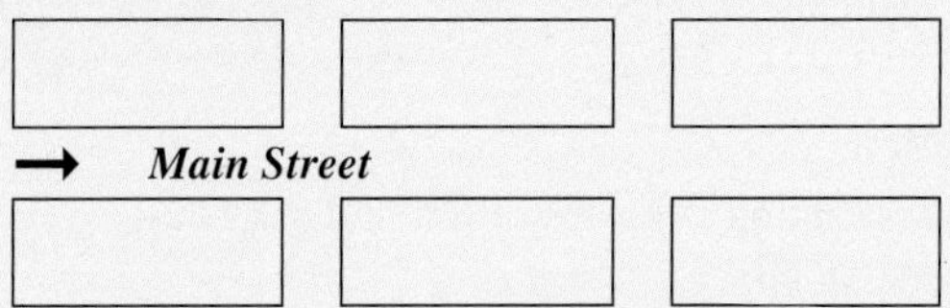

- Ask a S to come to the board. Say: *Point to the arrow. Go straight on Main Street. Go to the third building. Turn left. That is the bank.* Speak slowly as the S traces the path to the bank.

> **Teaching tip**
> If the S has trouble following your directions, trace the direction along with the S.

- Ask the S to label the bank.
- Ask other Ss to stand up. Give them these directions and ask them to label the buildings:
  The post office is next to the bank.
  The museum is across from the post office.
  The museum is between the park and the school.
  The school is on the corner.
  The hospital is across from the school.

  The labeled map will look like this:

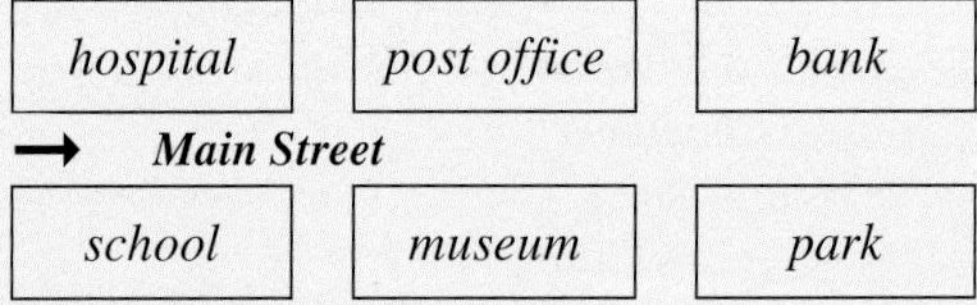

Practice

- Direct Ss' attention to the map in Exercise **2B**. Read the instructions aloud.
- Point to the arrow near the man at the left of the map and say: *Start here.* Ask a S to read the example directions.
- Hold up the Student's Book. Trace the directions as the S reads them. Ask: *Where are you?* (at the DMV)

> **Culture note**
> Read the tip box aloud. It might be interesting to ask Ss if they have been to the DMV.

- Ss complete the exercise individually. Help as needed.
- Read aloud the second part of the instructions for Exercise **2B**. Say: *Check your answers as you listen to the audio program.*
- [Class Audio CD1 track 48] Play or read the audio program (see audio script, page T-155). Listen to Ss' pronunciation as they repeat the sentences and answers. Correct pronunciation as needed.
- Ask: *Were your answers correct?* If Ss got some answers wrong, hold up the Student's Book and trace the route.
- Write on the board: *How do I get to the _____?*
- Point to the words. Say: *This is how you can ask for directions in English.*

> **Teaching tip**
> Point out the use of *Excuse me* to get someone's attention.

- Direct Ss' attention to Exercise **2C** and read the instructions aloud. Ask two Ss to read aloud the conversation.
- Point to the list of locations. Say: *Ask your partner how to get to these places on the map. Then your partner will ask you.* Walk around and help as needed.
- Ask pairs to perform their conversations for the class.

Application

- Direct Ss' attention to the map at the top of page 63. Point to the arrow near the man at the left of the map and say: *Start here. Go straight on Clark Avenue. Cross Grand Street. It's on the right, across from the drugstore. Where am I?* Elicit: *The park.*
- Direct Ss' attention to Exercise **3** and read the instructions aloud.
- Ask two Ss to read the example conversation to the class.
- Ss complete the exercise in pairs. Help as needed.
- Ask pairs to perform their conversations for the class.

Evaluation

- Direct Ss' attention to the lesson focus written on the board. Say: *Look at the picture on page 58. Start at the restaurant. Give directions to the library, hospital, school, and Lee's Store.*
- Check off the lesson focus as Ss demonstrate understanding of what they have learned in the lesson.

> ***More Ventures*** *(whole group, pairs, individual)*
> Assign appropriate exercises from the *Teacher's Toolkit Audio CD / CD-ROM, Add Ventures,* or the *Workbook.*

B **Read** the directions. Look at the map. Write the places.

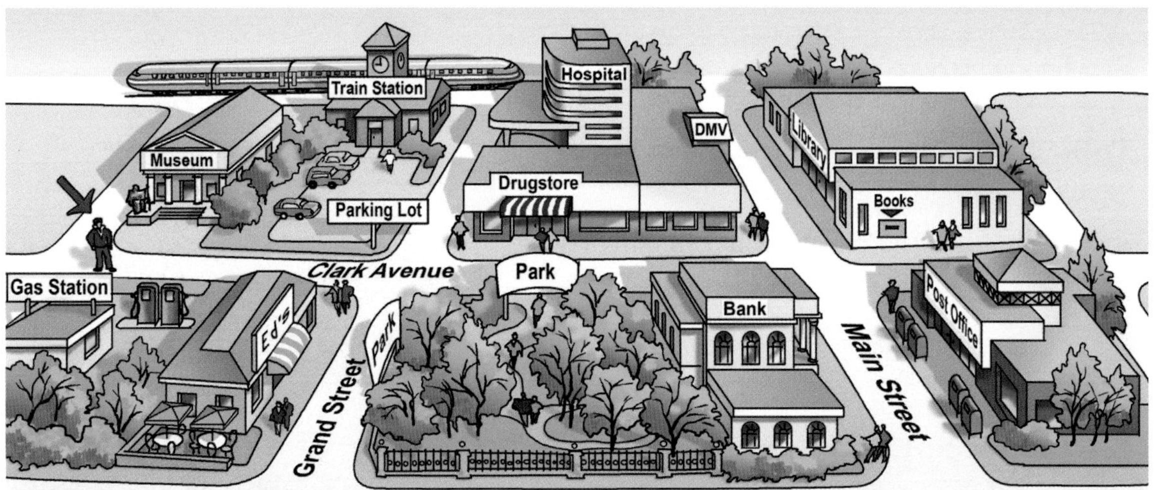

1. Go two blocks. Turn left. It's across from the library. *the DMV*
2. Go straight. Cross Grand Street. Turn right on Main Street. It's across from the post office. *the bank*
3. Go to Grand Street. Turn left. It's next to the parking lot. *the train station*
4. Go one block. Turn right on Grand Street. It's across from Ed's Restaurant. *the park*

Listen and repeat.

C **Talk** with a partner. Look at the map in Exercise B. Change the **bold** words and make conversations.

A Excuse me. How do I get to the **DMV**?
B **Go two blocks. Turn left.**
It's on Main Street.
A OK. **Go two blocks. Turn left.**
It's on Main Street.
B Right.
A Thank you.

Culture note

The DMV is the Department of Motor Vehicles. You can get a driver's license there.

1. DMV
2. parking lot
3. drugstore
4. library
5. hospital
6. post office

3 Communicate

Talk with a partner. Give directions to a building on the map in Exercise B. Your partner names the building.

Go two blocks. Turn left. It's on Main Street.

The DMV.

Lesson D Reading

1 Before you read

Talk. Look at these photos of Sandra's new neighborhood. Answer the questions.

1. What are the places in her neighborhood?
2. What can you do in these places?

2 Read

Listen and read.

Hi Angela,

I love my new house. My neighborhood is great! Here are some pictures.

There is a school on my street. My children go to the school. They like it a lot. There is a community center across from the school. My husband works at the community center. He walks to work. There is a grocery store next to my house. It's a small store, but we can buy a lot of things. There is a good Mexican restaurant on Second Street. It's right across from my house.

I like it here, but I miss you. Please write.

Your friend,
Sandra

When you see pronouns (*he, it, they*), ask *Who is the writer talking about?* Look at the sentences before a pronoun to find the answer.

3 After you read

A Read the sentences. Are they correct? Circle *Yes* or *No*.

1. Sandra lives on Summit Street. Yes (No)
2. There is a school on Sandra's street. (Yes) No
3. There is a community center next to the school. Yes (No)
4. Sandra's husband works at the community center. (Yes) No
5. Sandra's husband drives to work. Yes (No)

Write. Correct the sentences.

1. Sandra lives on Second Street.

B Write. Answer the questions about Sandra's neighborhood.

1. Where is the school? The school is on Sandra's street.
2. Where is the grocery store? The grocery store is next to Sandra's house.
3. Is the restaurant good? Yes, it is.

Lesson objectives

- Read about someone's neighborhood
- Practice using new topic-related words
- Look at pronoun references

Warm-up and review

- Before class. Write today's lesson focus on the board.
Lesson D:
Read a letter about Sandra's neighborhood
Learn new vocabulary about places around town
- Begin class. Books open. Direct Ss' attention to the picture on page 58. Point to Sandra. Ask: *Do you remember Sandra? Where does she live?* (on Second Street) Say: *We are going to read about Sandra's neighborhood.*
- Direct Ss to the pictures in Exercise **1** on page 64. Ask: *What do you see?* (community center, restaurant)
- Read the instructions aloud. Ask two Ss to read aloud the questions. Discuss the answers.

Presentation

- Direct Ss' attention to the letter in Exercise **2**. Ask: *What is this?* (It's a letter.) *Who wrote the letter?* (Sandra) *Who did she write it to?* (Angela)
- Ask Ss to read the letter silently.
- Say: *Now listen to the letter on the audio program.*
- [Class Audio CD1 track 49] Play or read the audio program and ask Ss to read along in their books (see audio script, page T-155). Repeat as needed.

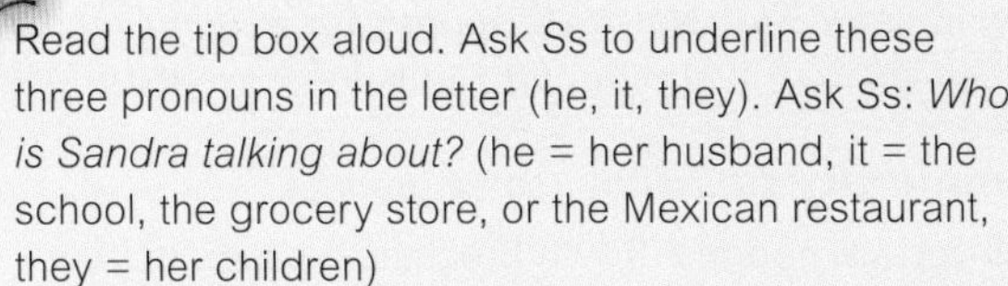

Read the tip box aloud. Ask Ss to underline these three pronouns in the letter (he, it, they). Ask Ss: *Who is Sandra talking about?* (he = her husband, it = the school, the grocery store, or the Mexican restaurant, they = her children)

Expansion activity (individual work)

- Say: *Read Sandra's letter again. Draw her neighborhood. Where is the community center? Where is the Mexican restaurant? The school? Make a map.*
- Ask several Ss to draw their maps on the board. Make sure Ss know that the maps will vary, as directions in the letter are not detailed.

Learner persistence (individual work)

- [Self-Study Audio CD track 22] Exercise **2** is recorded on the Ss' self-study CD at the back of the Student's Book. Ss can listen to the CD at home for reinforcement and review. They can also listen to the CD for self-directed learning when class attendance is not possible.

Comprehension check

- Read aloud the instructions for Exercise **3A**. Ask a S to read the example aloud.
- Ask: *Is this sentence correct?* (No.) *Why not?* (Sandra lives on Second Street.) Point to where *No* is circled for number 1. Be sure Ss understand the task.
- Ss complete the exercise individually. Help as needed.
- Ask individual Ss to read the sentences and their answers aloud. Ask the other Ss: *Do you agree with this answer?*

Practice

- Ask Ss to take out a piece of paper. Read aloud the second part of the instructions for Exercise **3A**.
- Model the task of correcting the sentences. Point to *No* for number 1 in Exercise **3A**. Read the sentence aloud. Tell Ss: *This sentence is incorrect. Tell me the correct sentence. Sandra lives on . . .* (Second Street). Write on the board: *Sandra lives on <u>Second Street</u>.*
- Ss complete the exercise individually. Help as needed.
- Ask Ss to write the corrected sentences on the board.
- Ask other Ss to read the sentences on the board. Ask: *Are the sentences correct?* Ask Ss to make corrections.

Expansion activity (individual work)

- Letter writing. Say: *Write a short letter about your neighborhood to a friend in your country. Use Sandra's letter as a guide.*
- Ss complete the activity individually. Help as needed. Ask several Ss to write their letters on the board.

Practice

- Ask a S to read the first question for Exercise **3B**. *Where is the school?* Elicit: *The school is on Second Street.*
- Read aloud the instructions for Exercise **3B**. Ss complete the exercise individually. Help as needed.
- Check answers with the class. Ask Ss to read aloud their questions and answers.

Culture tip
You may want to ask Ss about their neighborhoods in their countries. Ask them how these neighborhoods differ from the neighborhoods in which they live now.

Expansion activity (student pairs)

- *Yes / No* question practice. Ss in pairs. Say: *With your partner, write five* Yes / No *questions about the letter, for example: Is the community center in Sandra's neighborhood across from the school?* (Yes.)
- When Ss are finished with their questions, ask them to join another pair. Have pairs take turns asking and answering questions.

Lesson D Reading

Warm-up and review

- Books closed. Write on the board: *Places around town.* Ask Ss: *What are some places in our town?* Write Ss' responses on the board. Recycle vocabulary learned in the last lessons; include any new places that Ss think of, for example: *apartment building, store, the mall.*
- If your Ss do not say the following places, write them on the board:

day-care center	*high school*
elementary school	*middle school*
gas station	*park*
hardware store	*university*

- Point to each place on the board. Ask: *What are the names of some of these places in our town?* Elicit names.

Teaching tip
It might be helpful to ask Ss to keep a log of new vocabulary that they learn every day. Encourage them to write down new words and their meanings.

Presentation

- Books open. Direct Ss' attention to the pictures in the picture dictionary. Say: *These are places around town.* Point to picture number 1. Say: *This is a shopping mall.*
- Direct Ss' attention to the word bank in Exercise **4A**. Say: *Repeat the words after me.* Say each word.
- Say: *Write the words in the picture dictionary.* Point to the first example. Be sure Ss understand the task.
- Ss complete the exercise individually. Help as needed.

Comprehension check

- [Class Audio CD1 track 50] Play or read the audio program (see audio script, page T-155). Ss should check their answers and repeat the words after they hear them. Repeat the audio if necessary.

Learner persistence (individual work)

- [Self-Study Audio CD track 23] Exercise **4A** is recorded on the Ss' self-study CD at the back of the Student's Book. Ss can listen to the CD at home for reinforcement and review. They can also listen for self-directed learning when class attendance is not possible.

Expansion activity (small groups)

- Categorizing activity. Draw five columns on the board. Write these headings in the columns: *Places to shop, Places to study, Government places, Places to play, Places to live.* Point to the first heading. Say: *Look at the words in the word bank in Exercise 4A. Put them in the right place. For example, where can we put "an apartment building"?* Elicit: *Places to live.* Write *an apartment building* under the heading *Places to live.*
- Ss in small groups. Ask Ss to copy the headings. Have them agree under which headings to write the words.
- Ask one S from each group to fill in a column on the board. Have Ss add places to the categories.

Culture note
Read the tip box aloud. It might be interesting to ask Ss the ages of elementary school, middle school, and high school students in their countries.

Application

- Ask a S: *What is a place in your neighborhood?* Write the answer. Ask: *Where is it?* Write the answer on the board as a full sentence, for example: *There's a high school in my neighborhood. It's next to the library.*
- Direct Ss' attention to Exercise **4B** and read the instructions aloud. Model the conversation with a S.

Teaching tip
Remind Ss to use the prepositions of location *on, next to, across from, between,* and *on the corner of.*

- Ss in pairs. Say: *Now talk about your neighborhood with your partner.* Walk around and help as needed.

Community building (small groups)

- **Materials needed** Town brochures, paper, markers
- Writing a welcome guide. Ss in small groups. Say: *You are going to write a welcome guide for new people in our town or city. What are some special places?* Write Ss' responses on the board.
- Say: *Write the places of interest in your welcome guide. Write where the places are located. Draw pictures.*

Evaluation

- Have Ss look at the lesson focus. Put a check next to *Read a letter about Sandra's neighborhood.*
- Elicit sentences for each of the words in the word bank in Exercise **4A** on page 65.
- Check off each part of the lesson focus as Ss demonstrate understanding of what they have learned in the lesson.

More Ventures (whole group, pairs, individual)
Assign appropriate exercises from the *Teacher's Toolkit Audio CD / CD-ROM, Add Ventures,* or the *Workbook.*

4 Picture dictionary Places around town

1. *a shopping mall*

2. *a high school*

3. *a day-care center*

4. *a gas station*

5. *a playground*

6. *a police station*

7. *an apartment building*

8. *a hardware store*

9. *a courthouse*

A **Write** the words in the picture dictionary. Then listen and repeat.

an apartment building	a gas station	a playground
a courthouse	a hardware store	a police station
a day-care center	a high school	a shopping mall

B **Talk** with a partner about your neighborhood.

There's a gas station in my neighborhood.

Where is it?

It's across from the bank.

Culture note

Most elementary school students are 5 to 10 years old.

Most middle school students are 11 to 13 years old.

Most high school students are 14 to 18 years old.

Lesson E
Writing

1 Before you write

A **Listen.** Draw the way from the train station to the school.

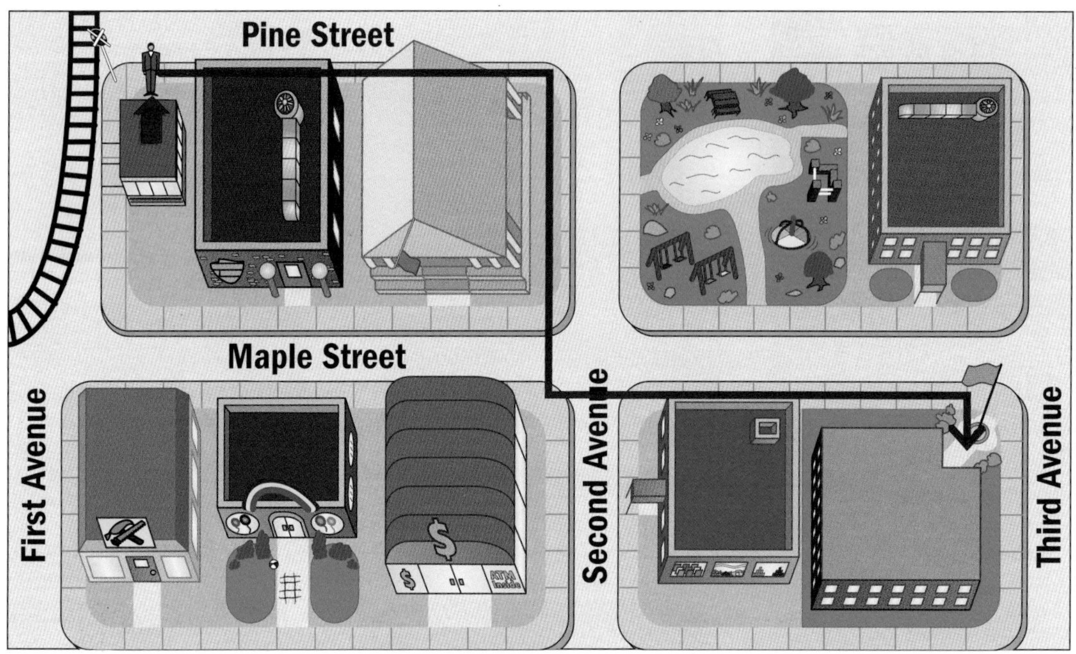

Write. Look at the map. Complete the directions from the train station to the school.

across from	go straight	on the corner of	turn right
cross	one block	straight ahead	

START **1. From the train station, turn right.**

2. *Go straight* **on Pine Street.**

3. *Turn right* **on Second Avenue.**

4. Go *straight ahead* **.**

5. *Cross* **Maple Street. Then turn left.**

6. Walk *one block* **to the corner.**

7. The school is *on the corner of* **Maple Street and Third Avenue.**

FINISH **8. It's** *across from* **the apartment building.**

Talk with a partner. Give different directions to get from the train station to the school.

Lesson objectives

- Discuss and write about neighborhoods
- Write capital letters

Warm-up and review

- Before class. Write today's lesson focus on the board.
  Lesson E:
  Practice writing directions
  Write a capital letter to begin a street name
- Begin class. Books open. Direct Ss' attention to the map in Exercise **1A**. Ask:
  What do you see? (a map)
  What streets are on the map? (Pine Street and Maple Street)
  What avenues do you see? (First Avenue, Second Avenue, and Third Avenue)

Teaching tip

It might be helpful to explain that *avenue* has a meaning similar to *street.*

Presentation

- Hold up the Student's Book. Ask: *Where is the train station?* (It is marked with an arrow.) Ask a S to point to it in your book. Ask: *Where is the school?* Ask another S to point to it in your book.
- Read aloud the instructions for Exercise **1A**. Say: *Find the person at the train station. Take a pen or pencil and draw the way while you listen to the CD.*
- [Class Audio CD1 track 51] Play or read the audio program (see audio script, page T-155). Ss complete the exercise individually. Repeat the audio program as needed.
- Ss in pairs. Say: *Show your map to your partner. Is it the same as your partner's map?* Walk around the room to make sure Ss have drawn the route correctly.

Practice

- Direct Ss' attention to the word bank. Read the words aloud and ask Ss to repeat.
- Read aloud the second part of the instructions for Exercise **1A**. Ask a S to read the first two directions aloud. Ask: *What's next? What do you do on Second Avenue?* Elicit: *Turn right.* Write on the board: *Turn right on Second Avenue.*
- Ss complete the exercise individually. Walk around and help as needed.
- Ask individual Ss to write the sentences on the board. Ask: *Are the directions correct?* Ask other Ss to correct any errors.

  Option If Ss need additional practice with this exercise, ask them to choose a partner. One S will read the directions while the other traces the route on the map with his or her finger. Then ask Ss to switch roles.

Expansion activity *(student pairs)*

- Ss in pairs. Review asking for directions. Say: *Ask your partner questions about different places on the map on page 66. Use the conversation on page 63 as a guide.*
- Ask Ss: *Is there a different way to get from the train station to the school?*
- Read aloud the last part of the instructions for Exercise **1A**.
- Ss complete the exercise in pairs. Walk around and help as needed.
- Ask several pairs to perform their conversations for the rest of the class.
- Ask: *Are the directions correct?* Ask other Ss to make any necessary corrections.

Expansion activity *(student pairs)*

- Point to the map on page 66. Ask: *Where is the apartment building?* Write different answers on the board, for example: *It's across from the school. It's on Maple Street. Say: There is more than one way to say where something is. In this activity we will practice different ways.*
- Ss in pairs. Write on the board: *Where is the _____?* Tell Ss to ask their partners questions about the map. Encourage Ss to say where the buildings are in at least two different ways. Walk around and help as needed.
- Ask several pairs to perform their conversations for the rest of the class.

Expansion activity *(small groups)*

- **Materials needed** One copy of a directory from a local shopping mall for each small group of Ss in your class
- Shopping mall directory reading; writing practice. Give each group a directory and say: *Write directions for someone who is at the mall. Tell him or her where to start and where to finish. For example, tell how to get from a restaurant to a certain store.* Model the activity by telling Ss how to get from one place in the mall to another. Recycle the directions that Ss learned in class (*go straight, turn right, turn left,* etc.).
- When Ss are finished writing, ask one S from each group to read his or her directions to the class. Ask the S not to say the name of the place where the person is going. Have the class trace the route on their shopping mall directories and say where they end up.

Lesson E Writing

Presentation

- Books open. Direct Ss' attention to Exercise **1B** and read the instructions aloud.

Read the tip box aloud. Ask Ss to repeat the street names after you. It might be helpful to ask a S to write on the board the name of the street where your school is. Make sure the S capitalizes the name of the street.

- Ask a S to read aloud the first two lines of the directions. Ask: *Why is Maple Street capitalized?* (It is the name of a street.)

Practice

- Ss complete the exercise individually. Help as needed.
- Ask individual Ss to write each sentence on the board. Ask: *Are the sentences correct? Are the street names capitalized?* Make corrections on the board.

Teaching tip
It might be helpful to recycle the writing tip from the first unit of the Student's Book. Ask: *What other words do we capitalize in English?* Ss can look at the tip box on page 14 to refresh their memory.

Comprehension check

- Draw two columns on the board. Write *Streets* and *Places* as the heading in each column.
- Say: *Name a street near school.* Write the name in the correct column. Say: *Name a place near school.* Write the name in the correct column.
- Direct Ss' attention to Exercise **1C** and read the instructions aloud.
- Ss complete the exercise in pairs. Help as needed.
- Ask Ss for names of streets and places near school and write them in the correct columns on the board.

Application

- Ask Ss to take out a piece of paper.
- Direct Ss' attention to Exercise **2** and read the first part of the instructions aloud.
- Ss complete the exercise individually.

Teaching tip
Offer Ss colored pencils to enhance their maps.

- Walk around and help as needed. Make sure that the places on the map are clearly marked.
- Read aloud the second part of the instructions for Exercise **2**.
- Ss complete the task individually. Help as needed with writing directions.

Evaluation

- Direct Ss' attention to Exercise **3A** and read the instructions aloud.
- Ss complete the exercise in pairs.
- Read aloud the instructions for Exercise **3B**. This exercise asks Ss to work together and peer-correct their writing. Ask a S to read the questions aloud. Tell Ss to exchange papers and look at their partner's sentences for the answers to the questions. Walk around and help as needed.

Community building *(individual work)*

- Ask Ss to post their maps and written directions on the bulletin board.

Learner persistence *(whole group)*

- It is important to tell Ss that what they are doing in class has practical value for life outside the classroom. Remind them that they may have to tell or write directions in English for a friend someday.

Expansion activity *(individual work)*

- Dictation. Dictate the following sentences:
  1. Go straight on Clark Avenue.
  2. Cross Grand Street.
  3. Go past the park.
  4. Turn right on Main Street.
  5. Go to the building across from the bank.
- Ask Ss to write the sentences on the board when they are finished. Ask: *Are these sentences correct?* Correct any errors on the board.
- Ask Ss to look at the map on page 63 and to follow the dictated directions. Where are they at the end of the route? (the post office)

More Ventures *(whole group, pairs, individual)*
Assign appropriate exercises from the *Teacher's Toolkit Audio CD / CD-ROM, Add Ventures,* or the *Workbook.*

B Write. Add capital letters.

Directions to Colgate Adult School

From the courthouse:
Turn left on maple street.
Go to the corner and cross second avenue.
Go straight one block to third avenue.
The school is on the corner of maple street and third avenue.

Street names begin with capital letters:
***M**aple **S**treet*
***S**econd **A**venue*
***N**ational **B**oulevard*

C Write. Work with a partner. Complete the chart. Write four streets near your school. Write four places near your school.

Streets	Places
(Answers will vary.)	

2 Write

Draw a map first. Show directions to your school. Start from a bus stop, a train station, a subway stop, a restaurant, or your home.

Write the directions to your school.

3 After you write

A Read your directions to a partner.

B Check your partner's directions.

- What are the street names?
- Do all the street names have capital letters?

Lesson F

Another view

1 Life-skills reading

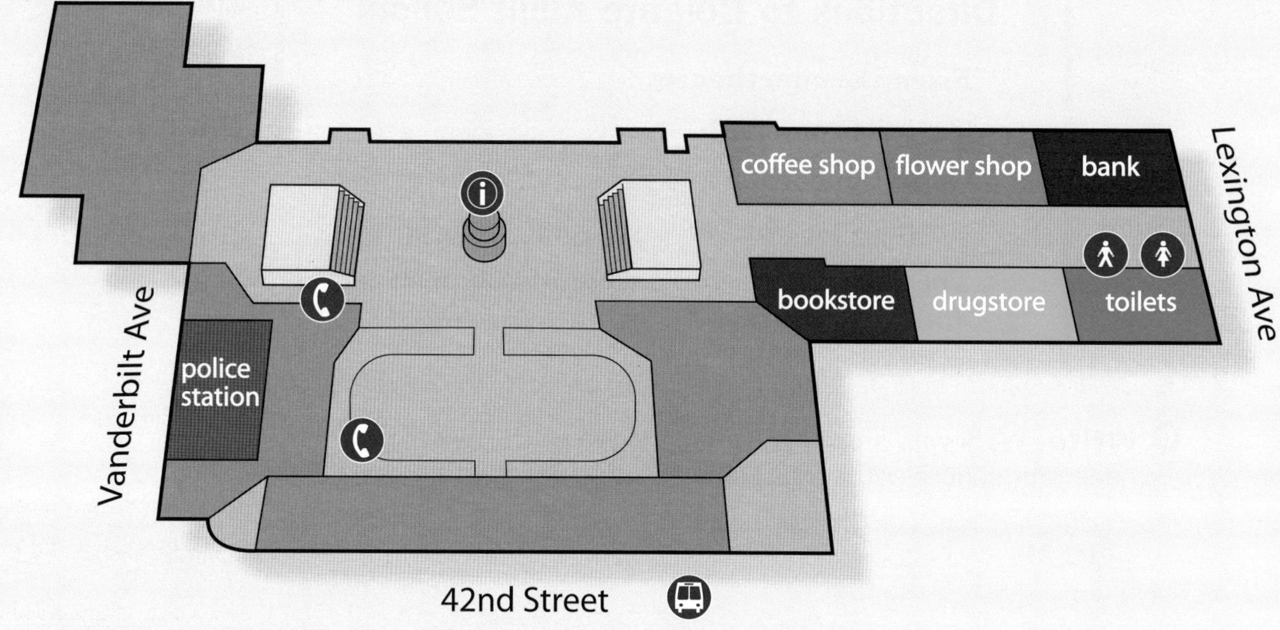

A Read the questions. Look at the map. Circle the answers.

1. Where is the drugstore?
   a. It's between the coffee shop and the bank.
   b. It's on Lexington Avenue.
   (c.) It's next to the bookstore.
   d. It's across from the coffee shop.
2. Where is the bus stop?
   a. It's on Lexington Avenue.
   (b.) It's on 42nd Street.
   c. It's on Vanderbilt Avenue.
   d. It's on the corner of Lexington Avenue and 42nd Street.
3. Where is the police station?
   (a.) It's on Vanderbilt Avenue.
   b. It's on 42nd Street.
   c. It's on Lexington Avenue.
   d. It's on the corner of Lexington Avenue and 42nd Street.
4. Where is the flower shop?
   a. It's next to the police station.
   b. It's across from the bookstore.
   (c.) It's between the coffee shop and the bank.
   d. It's on Vanderbilt Avenue.

B Talk with your classmates. Ask and answer the questions.

1. What places in your neighborhood do you go to every day?
2. Where do you go on the weekend?

Lesson objectives

- Practice using a map
- Review unit vocabulary
- Introduce the project
- Complete the self-assessment

Warm-up and review

- Before class. Write today's lesson focus on the board.
  Lesson F:
  Practice using a map and giving directions
  Review topic vocabulary
  Complete the self-assessment
- Begin class. Books closed. Ask: *Do you ever use maps outside of English class? What kinds of maps do you use?* Elicit appropriate responses, such as: *city maps, mall directories, world maps,* etc.

Teaching tip

It might be helpful to bring some local maps or mall directories to the classroom for Ss to look at.

- Ask: *How do you get to class each day?* Elicit different means of transportation.
- Ask: *Do you use public transportation? Do you need a map to use public transportation?* Elicit appropriate responses.

Presentation

- Books open. Say: *We are going to look at a map of Grand Central Station. Where is Grand Central Station?* (New York City)
- Direct Ss' attention to the map in Exercise **1A**. Ask: *What do you see?* (a drugstore, a bank, Lexington Avenue, etc.)

Teaching tip

Check that Ss understand the words on the map. Ask classmates to help explain these words, or draw on the board representations of these places (for example, a coffee cup, a flower, a dollar sign, a book, etc.). Point out that *Ave* is short for *Avenue*. Ask Ss if they know what is short for *Street*. (St.)

- Read aloud the instructions for Exercise **1A**. This task helps prepare Ss for standardized-type tests they may have to take. Be sure that Ss understand the task. Have Ss individually scan for and circle the answers.

Practice

- Ss complete the exercise individually. Walk around and help as needed.
- Ss in pairs. Say: *Ask and answer the questions with your partner. Are your answers the same or different?*
- Ask several pairs to ask and answer the questions for the rest of the class.

Application

- Read aloud the instructions for Exercise **1B**.
- Ask two Ss to read the questions aloud.
- Ss ask and answer the questions in pairs. Walk around and help as needed.
- Ask several pairs to ask and answer the questions for the rest of the class.

Community building *(whole group, small groups)*

- **Materials needed** Maps and brochures of local places of interest
- Ss in small groups. Ask Ss to look together at a brochure and map of a place in town that they find interesting. List places they would like to visit and find the directions to those places.
- Have Ss work together to write sentences to explain how to get to these places.
- Have one person in each group read the list of places. Write the suggestions on the board. Take a vote on the most interesting place (or the one that is easiest to get to).
  Option If it is feasible, plan a field trip to that place.

Lesson F Another view

Practice

- Direct Ss' attention to the pictures in Exercise **2A**. Ask: *What do you see in the pictures?* Elicit any appropriate responses. Supply words the Ss may not know: *gas pumps, napkins, library, books, grocery cart.*
- Read aloud the first part of the instructions for Exercise **2A**. Be sure Ss understand the task.
- Direct Ss' attention to the words in the word bank. Say each word aloud. Ask Ss to repeat them.
- Ss complete the exercise in pairs. Walk around and help as needed. Ask Ss to tell you the names of the places and write them on the board.
- Read aloud the second part of the instructions for Exercise **2A**. Be sure Ss understand the task.
- Ask a S: *What do you do at the gas station?* The S can read the example answer: *I buy gas at the gas station.*

Teaching tip

Encourage Ss to come up with other answers as well, such as: *I buy snacks at the gas station.*

- Ss complete the exercise individually. Walk around and help as needed.
- Ask Ss what they do at each of the places in the pictures.

Application

- Books closed. Draw several rectangles on the board, like this:

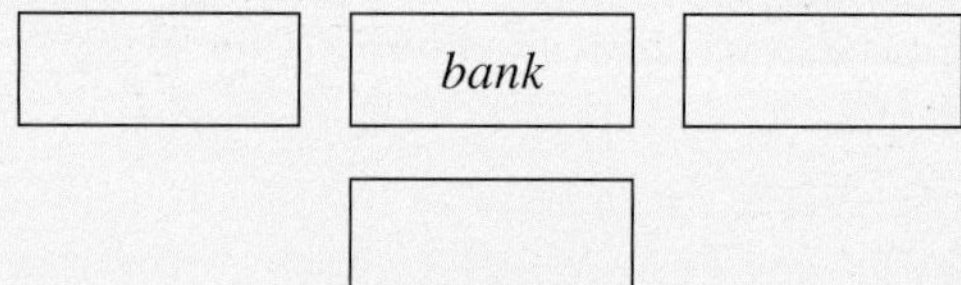

- Ask a S to come to the board. Say: *Listen to the directions. The courthouse is across from the bank. Write "courthouse" on the correct building.* The S will write *courthouse* in the rectangle across from the bank.
- Ask another S to come to the board. Say: *The grocery store is next to the bank, on the right.* The S will write *grocery store* in the rectangle to the right of the bank.
- Ask another S to come to the board. Say: *The bank is between the restaurant and the grocery store.* The S will write *restaurant* in the rectangle to the left of the bank.
- Books open. Direct Ss' attention to Exercise **2B** and read the instructions aloud. Be sure Ss understand the task.
- Ss complete the exercise in groups. Walk around and help as needed.
- Ask Ss to show their maps to Ss from other groups to see if they are the same. Have them work together to correct any discrepencies.

Community Building

- **Project** Ask Ss to turn to page 138 in their Student's Book to complete the project for Unit 5.

More Ventures *(whole group, pairs, individual)*
Assign appropriate exercises from the *Teacher's Toolkit Audio CD / CD-ROM, Add Ventures,* or the *Workbook.*

Evaluation

- Before asking Ss to turn to the self-assessment on page 143, do a quick review of the unit. Have Ss turn to Lesson A. Ask the class to call out what they remember about this lesson. Prompt Ss, if necessary, with questions, for example: *What are the conversations about on this page? What vocabulary is in the picture?* Continue in this manner to review each lesson quickly.
- **Self-assessment** Read the instructions for Exercise **3**. Ask Ss to turn to the self-assessment page and complete the unit self-assessment.
- If Ss are ready, administer the unit test on pages T-171–T-172 of this *Teacher's Edition* (or on the *Teacher's Toolkit Audio CD / CD-ROM*). The audio and audio script for the tests are on the *Teacher's Toolkit Audio CD / CD-ROM.*

2 Fun with language

A Work with a partner. Where do you find these things? Write the words.

gas station   grocery store   library   restaurant

1. *gas station* 2. *restaurant* 3. *library* 4. *grocery store*

Write. What do you do in each place? Write sentences in your notebook.

1. I buy gas at the gas station.

B Work in a group. Solve the map puzzle. Read the clues. Write the names of the places.

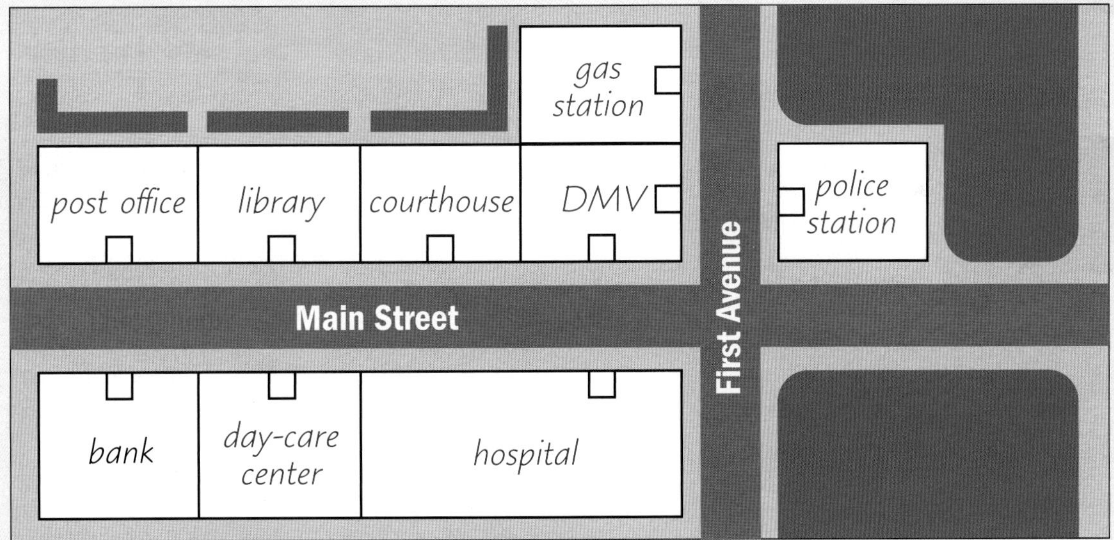

1. The day-care center is between the hospital and the bank.
2. The DMV is across from the hospital, on the corner of Main and First.
3. The courthouse is between the DMV and the library.
4. The post office is next to the library.
5. The gas station is next to the DMV.
6. The police station is across from the DMV.

3 Wrap up

Complete the **Self-assessment** on page 143.

Time

Lesson A Get ready

1 Talk about the picture

A Look at the picture. What do you see?

B Point to a person: eating • talking • taking a nap • drinking coffee
reading a schedule • buying a snack

Lesson objectives

- Introduce students to the topic
- Find out what students know about the topic
- Preview the unit by talking about the picture
- Practice key vocabulary
- Practice listening skills

Warm-up and review

- Before class. Write today's lesson focus on the board.
  Lesson A:
  Vocabulary for daily activities
  Telling time
- Begin class. Books closed. Point to *time* on the board. Say: *Today's class is about time. What things in this room tell time?* Write Ss' responses on the board: *clock, watch.*

Teaching tip
It is important to allow Ss a few moments to think before giving them any help with answers to questions. If Ss don't know the words *clock* or *watch*, allow them to point to the objects. Write the words on the board.

Presentation

- Books open. Set the scene. Direct Ss' attention to the picture on page 70. Ask:
  Who is in the picture? (men and women)
  Where are the people? (They are at work.)
  What room are they in? (the break room, the lunch room)
  What do you see? (a work schedule, a vending machine, posters, a book, hats, etc.)
  What are they doing? (They are standing, talking, sleeping, reading, and eating.)
- Direct Ss to the key words in Exercise **1B**. Read each word aloud while pointing to that action being performed in the picture. Ask Ss to repeat and point.

Comprehension check

- Ask Ss *Yes / No* questions about the picture. Recycle questions in the present continuous. Say: *Listen to the questions. Answer "Yes" or "No."*
  Point to the picture. Ask: *Is this a break room?* (Yes.)
  Point to the woman at the table. Ask: *Is she sitting?* (Yes.)
  Point to the man at the work schedule. Ask: *Is he talking?* (No.)
  Point to the woman sitting under the clock. Ask: *Is she buying a snack?* (No.)

Practice

- Direct Ss' attention to Exercise **1B**. Model the task. Hold up the Student's Book. Say to a S: *Point to a person eating.* Pretend you are eating something to illustrate the meaning. If the S can't find the right picture, ask other Ss to help.
- Ss in pairs. Say to one S: *Say the words in Exercise 1B.* Say to his or her partner: *Point to the picture.*
- Ss complete the exercise in pairs. Walk around and help as needed. When Ss have finished, have them change partners and change roles.

Expansion activity (whole group)

- Vocabulary challenge. Hold up the Student's Book. Say: *Listen to the words I say. Point to them in your books.* Say:
  Point to the clock.
  Point to the work schedule.
  Point to the night checklist.
  Point to the snack machine.
  Point to the flashlight.
  Point to the sandwich.

Expansion activity (whole group)

- Hold up the Student's Book. Point to the picture of the work schedule on page 70. Ask: *What's this?* (It's a work schedule.) If Ss don't know the term, write it on the board. Say the words aloud. Ask Ss to repeat after you.
- Write *hours* on the board. Point to it. Say: *The hours of this class are* (write the schedule of today's class).
- Point to the work schedule in the picture. Ask: *What are Margie's hours?* (M, W, F 8–4; T, Th 10–6)
- If Ss in your class work, ask: *What are your work hours?* Give each working S a chance to say his or her hours to the class.

Teaching tip
A review of the days of the week might be helpful. Show the class a calendar. Ask: *What are the days of the week?* Say the days aloud. Ask Ss to repeat.

Community building (whole group)

- Accessing community information through bulletin boards. Point to the bulletin board in the picture. Ask: *What's this?* (a bulletin board) *Does our school or class have a bulletin board? Where is it?* Ss can point.
- Ask: *What kind of information is on the bulletin board?* Ask a S to look at a bulletin board in the school and report back to the class. Brainstorm different types of announcements and write them on the board, for example: job announcements or class schedules.
- Tell Ss that bulletin boards have a lot of important information on them. Remind Ss to check the bulletin board on a regular basis.

Lesson A Get ready

Presentation

- Write the schedule for your English class on the board. Include beginning and end times and anything else that happens in your class, for example:
  9:00 *Class starts*
  10:30 *Break*
  12:00 *Class ends*
- Books closed. Point to the schedule. Ask: *What time does class start?* (9:00) Say: *That's right. Class starts at 9:00.* Ask: *What time is the break?* (10:30) Say: *Good. At 10:30 we take a break.* Ask: *What time does class end?* (12:00) Say: *Yes, class ends at 12:00.*

Practice

- Books open. Direct Ss' attention to Exercise **2A** and read aloud each phrase in the word bank. Ask Ss to repeat after you. Make each meaning clear by acting out the phrase (pretend to drink a cup of coffee, for example) or by pointing to the actions pictured on page 70.
- Read the instructions aloud. Tell Ss: *Listen to some conversations about time.*
- [Class Audio CD 2 track 2] Play or read the audio program (see audio script, page T-156). Ss listen and circle the phrases they hear. Repeat the audio as needed.
- Check answers. Ask: *What did you circle?* Ask Ss to write the phrases on the board. Point to the phrases. Say: *Repeat after me.* Say each phrase. Listen to Ss' pronunciation and correct as needed.
- Ask a S to write the words that were not circled on the board: *buy a snack, drink coffee, take a nap.* Point to the phrases. Say: *Repeat after me.*
- Direct Ss' attention to the pictures in Exercise **2B**. Hold up the Student's Book. Point to the first picture. Say: *He is reading.* Point to the second picture. Ask a S: *What's he doing?* (He's starting work.) Continue asking Ss about the rest of the pictures. Correct any errors.
- Read aloud the instructions for Exercise **2B**.
- [Class Audio CD2 track 2] Play or read the audio program again. Pause after the first conversation. Ask: *Which picture matches conversation a?* (picture number 6) Point to the handwritten *a* next to number 6. Be sure Ss understand the task.
- [Class Audio CD2 track 2] Play or read the complete audio program. Ss complete the exercise individually.

Learner persistence *(individual work)*

- [Self-Study Audio CD track 24] Exercises **2A** and **2B** are recorded on the Ss' self-study CD at the back of the Student's Book. Ss can listen to the CD at home for reinforcement and review. They can also listen for self-directed learning when class attendance is not possible.

Comprehension check

- Write the numbers *1–6* on the board. Ask a few Ss to come to the board and write the correct answers to Exercise **2B** next to each number.
- Read aloud the second part of the instructions for Exercise **2B**.
- [Class Audio CD2 track 2] Play or read the audio program again. Pause the audio program after each conversation. Point to a letter of the conversation on the board. Ask: *Is this correct?* Ask another S to make any necessary corrections on the board.

Application

- Direct Ss' attention to Exercise **2C**. Focus Ss' attention on the picture in number 1. Ask two Ss to read the example question and answer aloud.
- Read aloud the instructions for Exercise **2C**.
- [Class Audio CD2 track 3] Play or read the audio program (see audio script, page T-156). Listen to Ss' pronunciation. Repeat the audio program if needed.

> **Teaching tip**
> Ss may need help pronouncing numbers such as *fifteen* and *fifty*. Point out that in the "teen" numbers, the emphasis is on the last syllable; in the other numbers (twenty, thirty, etc.), emphasis is on the first syllable.

- Read aloud the second part of the instructions for Exercise **2C**.
- Ss complete the activity in pairs. Help as needed.
- Ask pairs to ask and answer the questions for the class.

Evaluation

- Direct Ss' attention to the lesson focus on the board.
- Ask Ss to look at the picture on page 70. Point to different parts of the picture and ask questions, such as: *What's she doing?* (She's drinking coffee.)
- Draw on the board some clocks with different times. While pointing to the clocks, ask Ss: *What time is it?*
- Check off the items as Ss demonstrate understanding of what they have learned in the lesson.

> ***More Ventures*** *(whole group, pairs, individual)*
> Assign appropriate exercises from the *Teacher's Toolkit Audio CD / CD-ROM, Add Ventures,* or the *Workbook.*

2 Listening

A **Listen.** Circle the words you hear.

buy a snack	eat dinner	start work
catch the bus	get home	take a break
drink coffee	leave for work	take a nap

B **Listen again.** Write the letter of the conversation.

1. e

2. c

3. d

4. b

5. f

6. a

Listen again. Check your answers.

C **Listen** and repeat the times.

What time is it?

It's ten o'clock.

1. ten o'clock

2. ten-thirty

3. six-fifteen

4. five-twenty

5. twelve-fifty

6. two-forty-five

7. seven-thirty

8. nine-oh-five

Talk with a partner. Take turns. Ask and tell the time.

Lesson B What do you do in the evening?

1 Grammar focus: simple present tense; *Wh-* questions

Questions

What	do you do does he do does she do do they do	in the evening?

Answers

I	read.
He	reads.
She	reads.
They	read.

With *he* and *she*:
do → does
exercise → exercises
go → goes
study → studies
watch → watches

2 Practice

A Write. Complete the sentences. Use *do* or *does* and the correct form of the verb.

1

A What *do* they do in the evening?

B They *watch* TV.
(watch / watches)

2

A What *does* he do in the afternoon?

B He *studies* .
(study / studies)

3

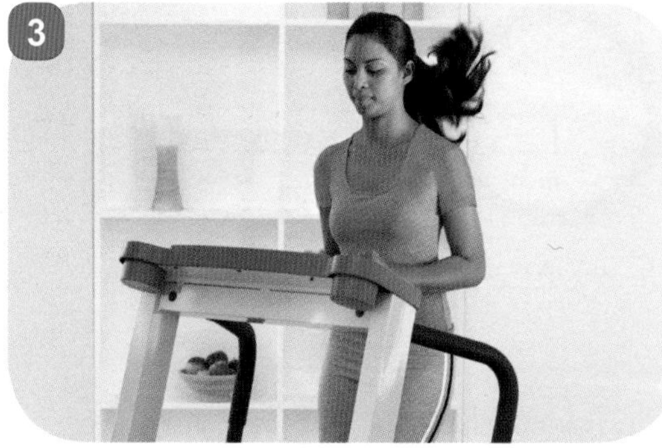

A What *does* she do in the morning?

B She *exercises* .
(exercise / exercises)

4

A What *do* they do on Sunday?

B They *go* to the park.
(go / goes)

 **Listen and repeat.** Then practice with a partner.

Lesson objective

- Introduce the simple present tense and *Wh-* questions

Warm-up and review

- Before class. Write today's lesson focus on the board.
  Lesson B:
  Simple present tense: Describing things you do regularly
  Wh- questions:
  What do you do in the evening? *I read.*
  What does he do in the evening? *He reads.*
- Write *I read in the evening* in big letters on a piece of paper.
- Begin class. Books closed. Hold up the paper with the sentence *I read in the evening.* Pretend to read a book or a newspaper. Read the sentence aloud. Ask Ss to repeat.
- Give the paper to a male student. Ask him to read it aloud. Say to him: *You read in the evening.* Write the sentence on the board. Ask Ss to repeat. Point to the same student. Say to the class: *He reads in the evening.* Write the sentence on the board. Ask Ss to repeat.
- Give the paper to a female student. Ask her to read it aloud. Say to her: *You read in the evening.* Write the sentence on the board. Ask Ss to repeat. Point to the same student. Look at the class and say: *She reads in the evening.* Write the sentence on the board. Ask Ss to repeat.

Teaching tip

Review *morning, afternoon,* and *evening.* Tell Ss: *Morning is before 12:00 noon; afternoon is from noon to around 5:00 p.m.; evening is from 5:00 p.m. until nighttime.*

Presentation

- Books open. Direct Ss' attention to the grammar chart in Exercise **1**. Read the questions and answers aloud. Ask Ss to repeat. Listen to Ss' pronunciation.
- Direct Ss' attention to the Answers column. Point to *He reads* and *She reads.* Say: *Add an "s" to the verb when you answer with "he" or "she."*

Teaching tip

Ss often find it difficult to pronounce *do* and *does.* Say each word. Ask Ss to repeat.

Comprehension check

- Write a few verbs or verb phrases on the board, for example: *study, watch TV, work.*
- Ask: *What do you do in the evening?* Point to one of the verbs on the board so that Ss answer using that verb.
- Repeat the process with *he, she,* and *they.*

Practice

- Read aloud the instructions for Exercise **2A**.
- Direct Ss' attention to the first picture. Model the activity. Ask: *What are they doing in the picture?* Elicit: *They are watching TV.*
- Ask: *What do they do in the evening?* Elicit: *They watch TV.*
- Ss complete the exercise individually. Help as needed.

Teaching tip

If your class asks about spelling, write on the board:

work → works *watch → watches*
study → studies *do → does*

Say: *Usually we just add an "s" for the simple present tense for "he," "she," or "it." But for words that end in "y," we change "y" to "i" and add "-es." We add "-es" after "ch," "sh," and some words that end in "o."*

Comprehension check

- [Class Audio CD2 track 4] Read the second part of the instructions for Exercise **2A**. Play or read the audio program (see audio script, page T-156). Have Ss check their answers as they listen and repeat.
- Ask Ss to come to the board and write the sentences. Ask different Ss to read the sentences aloud. Ask Ss to make any necessary corrections on the board.
- Ss in pairs. Say: *Now practice the conversations.*

Expansion activity *(whole group)*

- Question-and-answer practice. Before class. Make copies of this grid for each S in your class.
- In class. Give each S a copy of the grid. Say: *Walk around the room. Fill in the chart. Ask your classmates questions. Write your classmates' names in the first column. Write their answers in the other three columns.*
- Direct Ss' attention to the example in the grid.

Student's Name	What do you do in the morning?	What do you do in the afternoon?	What do you do in the evening?
Mary	I eat breakfast.	I pick up my children.	I watch TV.

Expansion activity *(whole group)*

- If you want to expand the grammar presentation, turn to the grammar charts at the back of the Student's Book. Practice making sentences using other pronouns.

Lesson B What do you do in the evening?

Presentation

- Write on the board: *What do you do on Saturday?*
  Morning Afternoon Evening
- Point to the question on the board. Ask several Ss: *What do you do on Saturday?* After each response, ask: *Do you do that in the morning, afternoon, or evening?* Write the verb under the appropriate heading on the board.

Expansion activity (small groups)

- Ss in small groups. Say: *Ask the people in your group the question on the board: What do you do on Saturday?* Then, make a chart like the one on the board. Include three columns with *Morning, Afternoon,* and *Evening* as titles. Each group writes its activities in the columns.
- Books open. Direct Ss' attention to the pictures in Exercise **2B**. Point to the first picture. Ask: *What does Jill do on Saturday morning?* Elicit: *She watches TV.* Continue asking about the rest of the pictures.
- Read aloud the instructions for Exercise **2B**. Tell Ss: *Listen to the Wilder family schedule.*
- [Class Audio CD2 track 5] Play or read the audio program (see audio script, page T-156). Ss listen to the family's schedule.
- [Class Audio CD2 track 6] Play or read the audio program again (see audio script, page T-156). Listen to Ss. Correct pronunciation.
- Read aloud the second part of the instructions for Exercise **2B**.
- [Class Audio CD2 track 7] Play or read the audio program (see audio script, page T-156). Ss listen, then talk with a partner.
- Ask two Ss to read the example conversation aloud.
- Ss complete the exercise in pairs. Help as needed.

Teaching tip

Ss may not know the word *bills* in this context. Bring a bill to class or show one from the school office.

- Write *weekend* on the board. Point to the word. Ask: *What is this?* Elicit: *It's Saturday and Sunday.*
- Ask a S: *What do you usually do on Saturday?*
- Ask another S: *What do you always do on Sunday?*
- Direct Ss' attention to Exercise **3** and read the instructions aloud.
- Ask two Ss to read aloud the question and answer.

Useful language

Read the tip box aloud. Ask Ss to repeat the two words after you. It might be helpful to give Ss examples of activities you *usually* and *always* do on the weekend.

- Ss complete the exercise in pairs. Help as needed.
- Ask pairs to ask and answer the questions for the class.

Expansion activity (small groups)

- Writing competition. Divide the class into two teams. Say: *I am going to tell you a word or phrase. One person from each team will go to the board and write a sentence using that word.*
- Model the activity. Ask a S to stand up. Say: *Make a sentence with "Saturday afternoon."* The S goes to the board and writes a sentence that uses that phrase.
- Begin the game. Ask Ss to use these words in their sentences:
  Sunday morning *Thursday morning*
  Saturday evening *Wednesday afternoon*
  Friday evening
- Continue the game by using other days and times. The S who writes the first sentence correctly earns a point.
- Tally the points at the end of the game. The team with the most points wins.

Learner persistence (whole group)

- Ask Ss: *Are your weekends here different from the weekends in your country? What is the same? What is different?* Write answers on the board under two columns labeled *Same* and *Different.*

Evaluation

- Direct Ss' attention to the lesson focus written on the board. Show Ss the pictures on page 73. Point to the first picture. Say: *Ask a question about Jill on Saturday morning.* Elicit: *What does Jill do on Saturday morning?* Ask another S to answer the question. Continue with the rest of the pictures. Go around the room.
- Check off the items as Ss demonstrate an understanding of what they have learned in the lesson.

More Ventures *(whole group, pairs, individual)*
Assign appropriate exercises from the *Teacher's Toolkit Audio CD / CD-ROM, Add Ventures,* or the *Workbook.*

B **Listen** to the Wilder family's schedule. Then listen and repeat.

Listen. Then talk with a partner. Change the bold words and make conversations.

A What does **Jill** do on **Saturday morning**?
B **She** usually **watches TV**.

1. Jill / Saturday morning
2. Mr. and Mrs. Wilder / Saturday evening
3. Mr. and Mrs. Wilder / Saturday morning
4. Jill / Saturday afternoon
5. Mr. and Mrs. Wilder / Saturday afternoon
6. Jill / Saturday evening

3 Communicate

Talk with your classmates. Ask questions about the weekend.

What do you do on Saturday morning?

I usually go to the grocery store.

Useful language

Usually means *most of the time.*
Always means *all of the time.*

Lesson C I go to work at 8:00.

1 Grammar focus: *at*, *in*, and *on* with time; *When* questions

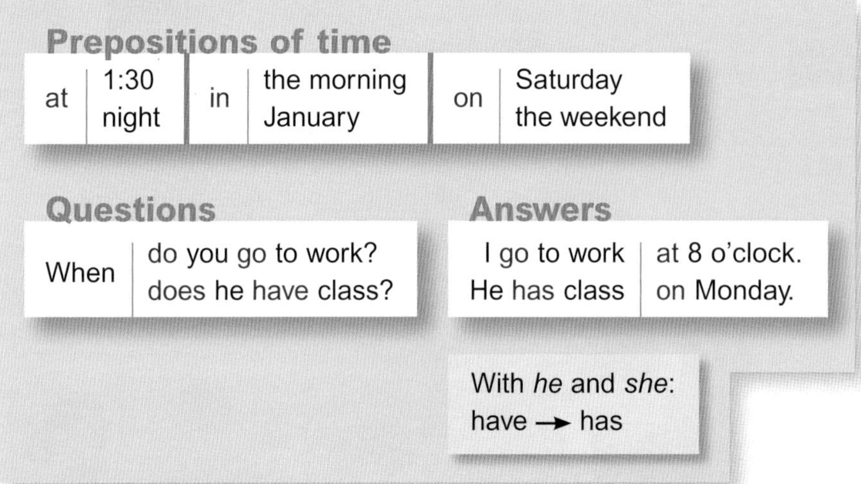

Prepositions of time

at	1:30 night	in	the morning January	on	Saturday the weekend

Questions

When	do you go to work? does he have class?

Answers

I go to work He has class	at 8 o'clock. on Monday.

With *he* and *she*:
have → has

2 Practice

A Write. Complete the sentences.
Use *at*, *in*, or *on*.

1. I have English class ___on___ Tuesday and Thursday.
2. My sister has class ___on___ Saturday.
3. I do homework ___at___ night.
4. My father goes to work ___in___ the morning.
5. He catches the bus ___at___ 8:45.
6. Sometimes my mom goes to PTA meetings ___in___ the evening.
7. I go on vacation ___in___ July.

Culture note

The PTA is the Parent-Teacher Association at a school. Parents and teachers meet in a group to talk about school.

B Write. Read the answers. Complete the questions.

1. ***A*** When ___do___ you ___go___ on vacation?
   B I go on vacation in July.
2. ***A*** When ___does___ your sister ___have___ class?
   B She has class on Saturday.
3. ***A*** When ___does___ your father ___catch___ the bus?
   B He catches the bus at 8:45.
4. ***A*** When ___do___ you ___do___ homework?
   B I do homework at night.

Listen and repeat. Then practice with a partner.

Lesson objective

- Introduce prepositions of time and questions with *When*

Warm-up and review

- Before class. Write today's lesson focus on the board.
  Lesson C:
  "When" questions:
  When do you go to work?
  When does he go to work?
  Prepositions of time:
  at 8:00
  in the morning
  on Sunday
- Begin class. Books closed. Ask: *What time is it?* Elicit an appropriate answer. Write the time on the board. Point to it and say the time. Ask Ss to repeat.
- Ask: *When does this class start? When does this class end? What days do we have this class? What is the date today?* Elicit appropriate answers to the questions.

Teaching tip

Ss will probably not be able to respond with the correct prepositions of time right now. They will learn them when the grammar chart is presented. The purpose of asking the questions is to find out what Ss already know about time, days, and dates.

Presentation

- Books open. Direct Ss' attention to the grammar chart in Exercise **1**. Read aloud each section of the chart. Ask Ss to repeat after you.
- Ss in pairs. Have Ss practice reading to each other the questions and answers in the grammar chart while pointing to an appropriate person in the class (*I, He, She*).

Practice

- Direct Ss' attention to the picture in Exercise **2A**. Ask: *What do you see?* (a woman, a family photo)
- Ask: *Who is in the family photo?* (a mother, a father, two children) Say: *We are going to finish sentences about this family.*
- Read the instructions aloud. Ask a S to read aloud the example sentence.
- Ss complete the exercise individually. Walk around the classroom and help as needed.

Teaching tip

Remind Ss to refer to the grammar chart to find out which preposition of time to use in each of the sentences.

- Ask individual Ss to read the sentences aloud (or write them on the board). Ask: *Are the sentences correct?* Ask other Ss to correct any errors involving prepositions.

Culture note

Read the tip box aloud. Ask Ss with children in school if they attend PTA meetings. Tell them that this is a way for parents to be more involved in their children's education.

Expansion activity *(small groups)*

- Competition. Draw a chart with three columns on the board. Write the prepositions *in, on,* and *at* at the top of the columns.
- Ss in small groups. Say: *Write time phrases in each of the columns.* Model the activity. Write *in September, on Tuesday,* and *at 12:00* in the appropriate column.
- Ss copy the chart onto a piece of paper and write as many time phrases as they can. The team that thinks of the most phrases in 5 minutes wins the competition.
- Ask the winning team to write its time phrases in the columns on the board. The other teams decide whether or not the team used the correct prepositions.

Practice

- Ask the following questions. Elicit appropriate responses.
  When do you get up?
  When do you go to bed?
  When do you go on vacation?
- Say: *Now we are going to write questions about routines.*

Teaching tip

If Ss don't know what a routine is, say: *It's something you do every day.*

- Read aloud the instructions for Exercise **2B**.
- Ss complete the exercise individually. Walk around and help as needed.

Comprehension check

- Read aloud the second part of the instructions for Exercise **2B**.
- [Class Audio CD2 track 8] Play or read the audio program (see audio script, page T-156). Listen to Ss' pronunciation as they repeat the questions and answers. Repeat the audio program if needed.
- Ss practice the conversations in pairs. Walk around and listen to Ss' pronunciation, offering help as needed.
- Ask several pairs to read the conversations to the rest of the class.

Lesson C I go to work at 8:00.

Presentation

- Write on the board: *schedule*. Say the word. Ask Ss to repeat. Ask: *What is a schedule?* If Ss don't know this word, say: *A schedule is what you do for a day, a week, a month, or a year.*
- Ask: *Remember the Wilder family's schedule on page 73?* Have Ss look at page 73.
- Direct Ss' attention to Mrs. Wilder's schedule in Exercise **2C** on page 75. Say: *This is Mrs. Wilder's schedule for the week. What does she do on Sunday?* Elicit: *She rests.*

Teaching tip

It might be helpful to remind Ss that the verb takes an *s* for the third person singular form in the simple present tense. Say: *Don't forget to add an "s" to the verb when you talk about "he," "she," or "it."*

- Ask: *When does Mrs. Wilder go shopping?* Elicit: *She goes shopping on Saturday.*
- Read aloud the instructions for Exercise **2C**. Focus Ss' attention on the conversation. Say: *Listen to the conversation. Read it in your book.*
- [Class Audio CD2 track 9] Play or read the audio program (see audio script, page T-156). Repeat the audio program as needed.

Culture note

Read the tip box aloud. Ask Ss if they do volunteer work at their children's schools or anywhere else. Ask Ss if it is common for people to do volunteer work in their home countries.

- Ask two Ss to read the conversation aloud. Say: *Now change the bold words to make new conversations.*
- Ask two different Ss to model the task by asking about Mrs. Wilder's driving lessons.
- Ss complete the exercise in pairs. Help as needed.
- Ask pairs to ask and answer the questions for the class.

Useful language

Read the tip box aloud. Tell Ss that there are two different ways to talk about lessons and classes. Have Ss look at the schedule and make similar statements about Spanish class and driving lessons. *(She has Spanish class. / She goes to Spanish class.)*

Application

- Direct Ss' attention to Exercise **3** and read the instructions aloud.
- Ask individual Ss to read aloud the items in the list.
- Ss complete the exercise individually. Help as needed.
- Ask several Ss to write their lists on the board. Ask them to read their lists to the class.
- Read aloud the second part of the instructions for Exercise **3**.
- Ask two Ss to read aloud the question and answer.
- Ss complete the exercise in pairs. Help as needed.
- Ask pairs to ask and answer their questions for the class.

Expansion activity *(small groups)*

- Celebrity lists. Say: *Now you are going to think about what a movie star or president might do every week.*
- Ss in small groups. Say: *Think of a famous person. Make a schedule for the person.*
- Model the activity. Ask Ss to tell you the name of a famous person. Write the name on the board. Under the name, write the days of the week. Ask the class: *What do you think this person does on Sunday?* Ask different Ss to write their ideas on the board.
- Ss complete the activity in small groups, using a different famous person. Ask each group to read its list to the class. This can be a humorous activity.

Evaluation

- Direct Ss' attention to the lesson focus on the board.
- Focus Ss' attention on the picture on page 70. Ask Ss to use *When* to make questions about the work schedule. Then ask different Ss to answer the questions, using *at, in,* or *on* correctly. For example: *When does Margie work? She works on Monday, Wednesday, and Friday from 8 a.m. to 4 p.m., and on Tuesday and Thursday from 10 a.m. to 6 p.m.*
- Check off the items as Ss demonstrate understanding of what they have learned in the lesson.

More Ventures *(whole group, pairs, individual)*
Assign appropriate exercises from the *Teacher's Toolkit Audio CD / CD-ROM, Add Ventures,* or the *Workbook.*

C **Listen.** Then talk with a partner. Change the bold words and make conversations.

Mrs. Wilder's Schedule

SUNDAY	MONDAY	TUESDAY	WEDNESDAY	THURSDAY	FRIDAY	SATURDAY
rest	*11:00 a.m. volunteer at the high school*	*7:30 p.m. cooking class*	*2:30 p.m. driving lessons*	*4:00 p.m. Spanish class*	*6:30 p.m. PTA meeting*	*9:00 a.m. go shopping*

A When does Mrs. Wilder **volunteer at the high school**?
B She **volunteers at the high school on Monday**.
A What time?
B At **11:00 in the morning**.

Culture note

Many people in the U.S. do volunteer work in their free time. Volunteers do not receive money for their work.

1. volunteer at the high school
2. take driving lessons
3. have cooking class
4. have Spanish class
5. go shopping
6. go to the PTA meeting

Useful language

*She **has** cooking class on Tuesday.*
*She **goes to** cooking class on Tuesday.*

3 Communicate

Write. What are five things you do every week? Make a list.

1. call my mother
2. go to English class
3. work
4. visit friends
5. go to the grocery store

Talk with a partner. Ask questions about your partner's list.

When do you call your mother?

I usually call my mother on Sunday at nine o'clock at night.

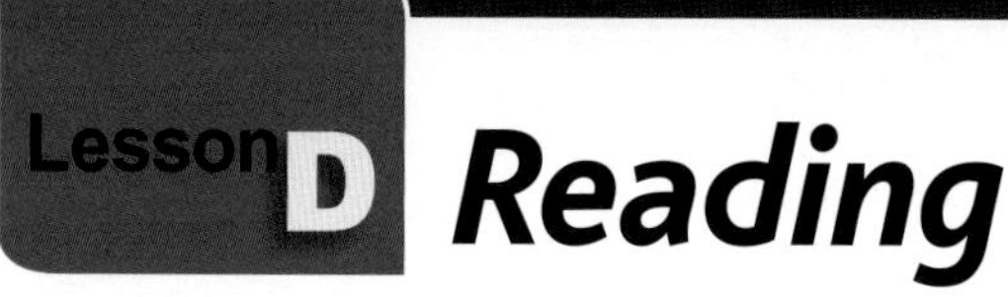

Lesson D Reading

1 Before you read

Talk. Bob has a new job. Look at the picture. Answer the questions.

1. What is Bob wearing?
2. What is his new job?

2 Read

 **Listen and read.**

Meet Our New Employee: Bob Green

Please welcome Bob. He is a new security guard. He works the night shift at the East End Factory. Bob starts work at 11:00 at night. He leaves work at 7:00 in the morning.

Bob likes these hours because he can spend time with his family. Bob says, "I eat breakfast with my wife, Arlene, and my son, Brett, at 7:30 every morning. I help Brett with his homework in the afternoon. I eat dinner with my family at 6:30. Then we watch TV. At 10:30, I go to work."

Congratulations to Bob on his new job!

To help you remember, ask questions as you read:
Who *is this reading about?*
What *is this reading about?*
Where *does Bob work?*
When *does Bob work?*

3 After you read

A Read the sentences. Are they correct? Circle *Yes* or *No*.

1. Bob is a new police officer. Yes (No)
2. He starts work at 7:00 at night. Yes (No)
3. He likes to spend time with his family. (Yes) No
4. Bob helps Brett with his homework. (Yes) No
5. Bob's family eats dinner at 6:30. (Yes) No
6. At 10:30, Bob watches TV. Yes (No)

Write. Correct the sentences.

1. Bob is a new security guard.

B Write. Answer the questions about Bob's schedule.

1. When does Bob eat breakfast with his family? *Bob eats breakfast with his family at 7:30.*
2. Where does Bob work? *Bob works at the East End Factory.*

Lesson objectives

- Introduce and read "Meet Our New Employee: Bob Green"
- Practice using new topic-related words
- Practice discussing daily activities

Warm-up and review

- Before class. Write today's lesson focus on the board:
  Lesson D:
  Read about Bob's schedule
  Discuss daily activities
  Ask questions with "When"
- Begin class. Books closed. Ask Ss: *Do you have a job? Where do you work?* Write Ss' workplaces on the board.
- Ask several working Ss: *When do you work every day? When do you finish work?* Elicit appropriate responses.
- Books open. Have students recall the picture of Bob they saw on page 70. Then focus Ss' attention on Exercise **1**. Read the instructions aloud. Ask: *What is Bob wearing?* (a cap, glasses) Point to the word on Bob's cap and ask: *What is his new job?* (He is a security guard.)

Presentation

- Direct Ss' attention to the reading in Exercise **2**. Ask a S to read the title aloud. Ask: *What is an employee?* (a worker)
- Read aloud the instructions for Exercise **2**.
- [Class Audio CD2 track 10] Play or read the audio program, and ask Ss to read along (see audio script, page T-156). Repeat as needed.

Read the tip box aloud. Explain to Ss that asking and answering *Wh-* questions as they read will help them better understand a reading passage.

Expansion activity *(student pairs)*

- Ss in pairs. Ask Ss to take turns reading the paragraphs to each other.
- Walk around and listen to Ss' pronunciation as they are reading. If you notice they are having difficulty with certain words, write them on the board.
- When Ss finish, point to the words on the board. Say the words and ask Ss to repeat.

Learner persistence *(individual work)*

- [Self-Study Audio CD track 25] Exercise **2** is recorded on the Ss' self-study CD at the back of the Student's Book. Ss can listen to the CD at home for reinforcement and review. They can also listen to the CD for self-directed learning when class attendance is not possible.

Comprehension check

- Read aloud the instructions for Exercise **3A**. Ask a S to read the example aloud. Ask: *Is Bob a new police officer?* (No. Bob is a new security guard.) Point to where *No* is circled for number 1. Be sure Ss understand the task.
- Ss complete the exercise individually. Walk around and help as needed.
- Check answers with the class. Ask Ss to read their sentences and answers aloud.
- Ask Ss to take out a piece of paper. Read aloud the second part of the instructions for Exercise **3A**.
- Model the task of correcting the sentences. Point to *No* for number 1 in Exercise **3A**. Read the sentence aloud. Tell Ss: *This sentence is incorrect.* Say: *Tell me the correct sentence. Bob is a new . . .* (security guard) Write on the board: *Bob is a new security guard.*
- Ss complete the exercise individually. Help as needed.
- Check answers with the class. Ask Ss to write their answers on the board. Then ask different Ss to read the answers aloud. Ask: *Are the sentences correct?* Make any necessary corrections on the board.

Expansion activity *(student pairs)*

- *Wh-* question practice. Turn Ss' attention back to the four *Wh-* questions in the tip box.
- Ss in pairs. Ask Ss to take turns asking and answering the questions about the reading.
- When Ss finish, ask four pairs to ask and answer the questions for the class.

Practice

- Direct Ss' attention to Exercise **3B** and read the instructions to the class. Ask two Ss to read the questions aloud.
- Ss complete the exercise individually. Walk around and help as needed.
- Ss in pairs. Say: *Ask your partner the questions. Then your partner will ask you the questions.*
- Walk around and listen to Ss asking and answering the questions.
- Ask several pairs to ask and answer the questions for the rest of the class.

Lesson **D** *Reading*

Warm-up and review

- Books closed. Write on the board: *Daily activities*. Ask Ss: *What are your daily activities?* Write Ss' responses on the board. Recycle vocabulary learned in the last lessons, for example: *I drink coffee* or *I exercise*. Include any new activities that Ss think of, for example: *I get up, I get dressed, I take a shower.*

Teaching tip

The purpose of asking *What are your daily activities?* is to find out which vocabulary words Ss already know and to activate their prior knowledge of the subject. Do not be concerned if Ss are unable to list many daily activities.

Presentation

- Books open. Direct Ss' attention to the pictures in the picture dictionary. Point to picture number 1. Ask: *What does she do every day?* Elicit: *She eats lunch*.
- Direct Ss' attention to the word bank in Exercise **4A**. Say each phrase aloud and ask Ss to repeat. Listen to Ss' pronunciation. Repeat the phrases if necessary.
- Say: *Write the activities in the picture dictionary*. Point to the first example. Be sure Ss understand the task.
- Ss complete the exercise individually. Help as needed.

Comprehension check

- [Class Audio CD2 track 11] Play or read the audio program (see audio script, page T-157). Ss should check their answers and repeat the phrases after they hear them. Repeat the audio program if necessary.

Learner persistence *(individual work)*

- [Self-Study Audio CD track 26] Exercise **4A** is recorded on the Ss' self-study CD at the back of the Student's Book. Ss can listen to the CD at home for reinforcement and review. They can also listen for self-directed learning when class attendance is not possible.

Expansion activity *(individual work, student pairs)*

- Draw a chart with three columns on the board. Write the headings *Morning, Afternoon,* and *Evening* in the columns.
- Ask Ss to copy the columns into their notebooks.
- Say: *Look at the activities in the picture dictionary. Write them in the correct column in your notebook.*
- Model the activity. Ask a S: *Do you eat lunch in the morning, in the afternoon, or in the evening?* Write the Ss' response in the appropriate column on the board.
- Ss complete the activity individually. Help as needed.
- When Ss finish, divide the class into pairs and ask Ss to compare the columns in their charts.

Application

- Write *When* on the board. Hold up the Student's Book. Point to the first picture. Ask: *When do you eat lunch?* Elicit an appropriate answer. Write the question on the board. Say it aloud. Ask Ss to repeat the question.
- Read aloud the instructions for Exercise **4B**. Ask two Ss to read aloud the example question and answer.
- Ss complete the exercise in pairs. Help as needed.
- Ask pairs to ask and answer the questions for the class.

Expansion activity *(individual work)*

- Class survey. Ask Ss to brainstorm questions with *When*, for example: *When do you get up? When do you go to school?* Write Ss' questions on the board.
- Ask Ss to write the questions in their notebook. Say: *Walk around the room. Ask everyone in the class the questions. Write the answers next to the questions.*
- When Ss finish, have them write a paragraph about their classmates, for example: *Nine people in our class get up at 8:00 a.m. Ten people go to school at 9:30 a.m. Three people go to bed in the afternoon.*
- Ask several Ss to read their paragraphs to the class.

Learner persistence *(individual work)*

- If you have Ss who are habitually late or absent, invite them to stay after class. Ask *When* questions to find out why they are late or absent. If Ss have conflicts that cause them to miss class or be late, work together to find a solution to enable them to spend more time in class.

Evaluation

- Direct Ss' attention to the lesson focus on the board. Put a check mark next to *Read about Bob's schedule*.
- Elicit daily activities. Ask Ss to make sentences for each of the illustrations in the picture dictionary on page 77.
- Ask Ss to form questions with *When* about each of the pictures on page 73.
- Check off each part of the lesson focus as Ss demonstrate understanding of what they have learned in the lesson.

More Ventures *(whole group, pairs, individual)*
Assign appropriate exercises from the *Teacher's Toolkit Audio CD / CD-ROM, Add Ventures,* or the *Workbook*.

4 Picture dictionary Daily activities

1. *eat lunch*

2. *take the children to school*

3. *walk the dog*

4. *take a shower*

5. *eat dinner*

6. *go to bed*

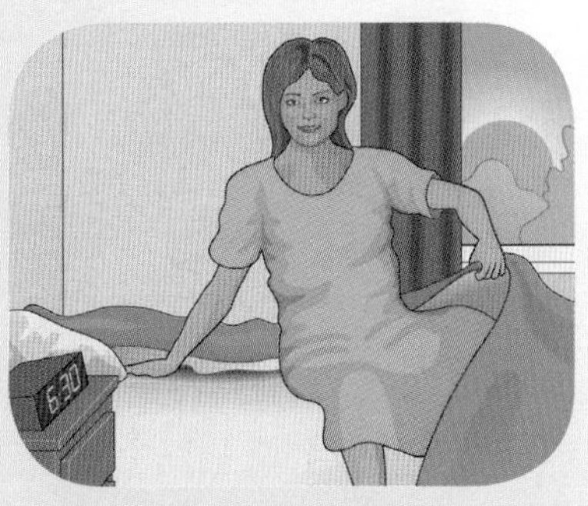

7. *get up*

8. *eat breakfast*

9. *get dressed*

A **Write** the words in the picture dictionary. Then listen and repeat.

eat breakfast	get dressed	take a shower
eat dinner	get up	take the children to school
eat lunch	go to bed	walk the dog

B **Talk** with a partner. Ask and answer questions about your daily activities.

When do you eat breakfast?

I usually eat breakfast at 6:30.

Lesson E **Writing**

1 Before you write

A **Write.** What do you do in the morning, afternoon, and evening? Complete the chart.

Morning	Afternoon	Evening
get up		
get dressed		
(Answers will vary.)		

Talk with a partner about your daily schedule.

What do you do in the morning?

I get up. I get dressed. . . .

Write sentences.

Morning

I get up.

I get dressed.

(Answers will vary.)

Afternoon

Evening

Lesson objective

- Discuss and write about daily routines

Warm-up and review

- Before class. Write today's lesson focus on the board. *Lesson E: Write about your daily routine*
- Begin class. Books closed. Ask: *What do you do every day?* Elicit appropriate responses.

Teaching tip

When you ask this question, call on as many Ss as possible for responses. This will help you ascertain how many Ss have understood the unit so far.

Practice

- Books open. Direct Ss' attention to the chart in Exercise **1A**. Read the instructions aloud.
- Ss complete the exercise individually. Help as needed.
- Read aloud the second part of the instructions for Exercise **1A**. Ask two Ss to read aloud the example question and answer.
- Model the task. Ask Ss what they do in the morning, afternoon, and evening.

  Option Draw a chart on the board that is similar to the one on page 78. Write Ss' responses in the columns of the chart.
- Ss complete the exercise in pairs. Walk around and help as needed.
- Ask several pairs to ask and answer questions about their daily routines for the rest of the class.
- Read aloud the last part of the instructions for Exercise **1A**.
- Model the task. Point to the two examples in the chart *(get up, get dressed)*. Then, write the two example sentences on the board: *I get up. I get dressed.*
- Ss complete the exercise individually. Walk around and help as needed.
- Draw a three-column chart on the board. Write the headings *Morning, Afternoon,* and *Evening* in the columns. Ask each S in the class to write a sentence in one of the columns on the board.
- Ask different Ss to read aloud the sentences on the board. Ask: *Are these sentences correct?* Ask other Ss to correct the sentences if necessary.

Community building (individual work, small groups)

- Ask: *How was your daily routine in your country different from your routine in this country?* Ask Ss to make two lists, titled *My daily routine in my home country* and *My daily routine now.*
- When Ss finish writing, ask them to form small groups and share their lists with their classmates. If possible, ask Ss to sit with Ss from other cultures to form diverse groups.
- When all groups have finished, ask each group to choose one or two Ss to tell the class about their lists.

Culture tip

It is important to be sensitive to your Ss' backgrounds when doing this activity. If some of your Ss left difficult situations in their home countries, they may not feel comfortable participating in this activity. Similarly, if Ss have spent most of their lives in this country, this activity may not be appropriate.

Expansion activity (student pairs)

- Ask: *When do your daily routines change?* Elicit: *When I go on vacation; when there is a special holiday,* etc.
- Ss in pairs. Say: *Talk to your partner. Give him or her an example of a time when you do not do your normal routine. What do you do instead? How is your day different?*
- Ss complete the activity in pairs. Walk around and help as needed, offering feedback and support.
- Ask several pairs to ask and answer the questions for the rest of the class.

Lesson E Writing

Practice

- Draw three vertical lines down the board to make three columns. Write *in, on,* and *at* as headings.
- Review prepositions of time. Say: *I am going to say some time phrases. Tell me in which column to put the phrases – in, on, or at.*
- Say: *The morning.* Point to the board and ask: *Which column?* (in)
- Say the following time phrases. Ask individual Ss to write them in the correct columns on the board:
  the afternoon (in)
  Saturday (on)
  the evening (in)
  March 2 (on)
  the weekend (on)
  10 o'clock (at)
  Friday (on)
- Direct Ss' attention to Exercise **1B** and read the instructions aloud.
- Ask a S to read aloud the title and the first two sentences of "My Daily Schedule."
- When the S fills in the blanks in the second sentence, ask the class: *Is the sentence correct?* Ask another S to correct the prepositions if needed.
- Ss complete the exercise individually. Help as needed.

Read the tip box aloud. Hold up the Student's Book. Show Ss where the two paragraphs in "My Daily Schedule" are indented. Remind Ss to indent each time they begin a new paragraph.

- Ask individual Ss to write their completed sentences on the board.
- Ask: *Are the sentences correct?* Ask different Ss to make any necessary corrections.

Teaching tip
If Ss are having trouble remembering which prepositions to use, direct their attention to the grammar chart on page 74.

Expansion activity *(individual work)*

- Dictation. Ask Ss to take out a piece of paper and write the numbers *1–10* on it. Dictate the following sentences.
  1. *I get up at 7:00 in the morning on weekdays.*
  2. *I get dressed.*
  3. *I eat breakfast at 7:30.*
  4. *I read the newspaper.*
  5. *I drive to work at 8:00.*
  6. *My work starts at 8:30.*
  7. *I work until 5:30 in the evening.*
  8. *I go home.*
  9. *I eat dinner and watch TV.*
  10. *I go to bed at 10:00 p.m.*
- Ask Ss to write their sentences on the board. Ask other Ss: *Are the sentences correct?* Ask different Ss to correct any errors.

Application

- Read aloud the instructions for Exercise **2**.
- Remind Ss to indent when they begin a paragraph.
- Ss complete the exercise individually. Help as needed.

Comprehension check

- Read aloud the instructions for Exercise **3A**.
- Ss complete the exercise in pairs. After a few minutes, encourage Ss to switch roles.
- Read aloud the instructions for Exercise **3B**. This exercise asks Ss to work together to peer-correct their writing. Ask two Ss to read the questions aloud. Tell Ss to exchange papers and look at their partner's paragraphs for the answers to the questions. Help as needed.
- Ask several Ss to read their paragraphs to the class.

Learner persistence *(individual work)*

- If you notice that some Ss have a daily routine that is difficult for them to maintain, talk to the Ss after class. Work together to try to figure out a way that their class or work load can be adjusted so that they will be better able to adapt to their schedules.

Evaluation

- Direct Ss' attention to the lesson focus on the board.
- Ask different Ss to come to the board and write sentences about their daily routine.
- Check off the lesson focus as Ss demonstrate an understanding of what they have learned in the lesson.

More Ventures *(whole group, pairs, individual)*
Assign appropriate exercises from the *Teacher's Toolkit Audio CD / CD-ROM, Add Ventures,* or the *Workbook.*

B Write. Complete the paragraph. Use *in*, *on*, and *at*.

Leave space at the beginning of a paragraph. This space is an *indent*.

Hamid
August 10

My Daily Schedule

Let me tell you about my daily schedule. __On__ Monday, I usually get up __at__ 6:30 __in__ the morning. I eat breakfast and get dressed. __At__ 8:00, I go to work. I work at a department store.

I eat lunch __at__ 12:30. __In__ the afternoon, I take a break __at__ 3:30. I finish work __at__ 5:00. I go to a fast-food restaurant or a coffee shop for dinner. I get home __at__ 6:45 or 7:00. I read __in__ the evening. I go to bed __at__ 10:00.

2 Write

Write a paragraph about your daily schedule.

(Answers will vary.)

3 After you write

A Read your paragraph to a partner.

B Check your partner's paragraph.

- What does your partner do in the evening?
- Is there an indent at the beginning of the paragraph?

Lesson F Another view

1 Life-skills reading

CLASS SCHEDULE: SPRING SEMESTER			
BUSINESS			
Business English	MTuWThF	5:00–7:30 p.m.	3/17–5/22
Keyboarding	MWF	1:00–3:00 p.m.	1/14–5/25
Introduction to Computers	TuTh	10:30–12:30 p.m.	3/17–5/24
Word Processing	TuTh	6:30–9:30 p.m.	3/17–5/24
ENGLISH AS A SECOND LANGUAGE			
ESL Beginning	MTuWThF	8:15–10:15 a.m.	1/15–5/25
ESL Intermediate	MTuWThF	8:15–10:15 p.m.	1/15–5/25
ESL Citizenship	Sat	8:00–10:45 a.m.	1/20–5/19
ESL Citizenship	Sun	7:45–10:30 a.m.	1/21–5/20
ESL Pronunciation	MWF	12:00–1:00 p.m.	3/19–5/25
ESL Writing	MTuWTh	12:00–1:15 p.m.	3/19–5/24

Useful language

M	Monday
Tu	Tuesday
W	Wednesday
Th	Thursday
F	Friday
Sat	Saturday
Sun	Sunday

A Read the questions. Look at the schedule. Circle the answers.

1. What time does the ESL Citizenship class start on Saturday morning?
   a. at 7:45
   (b.) at 8:00
   c. at 8:15
   d. at 10:15

2. When does the Introduction to Computers class start?
   a. on January 15
   b. on February 12
   (c.) on March 17
   d. on March 19

3. When is the ESL Pronunciation class?
   (a.) on Monday, Wednesday, and Friday
   b. on Tuesday and Thursday
   c. on Monday, Tuesday, and Thursday
   d. on Monday, Tuesday, and Wednesday

4. When does the spring semester end?
   a. in January
   b. in February
   c. in March
   (d.) in May

B Talk with a partner. Ask and answer questions about the schedule.

What time does the Business English class start?

It starts at five o'clock.

Lesson objectives
- Practice using a class schedule
- Review unit vocabulary
- Introduce the project
- Complete the self-assessment

Warm-up and review

- Before class. Write today's lesson focus on the board.
  Lesson F:
  Read and answer questions about a class schedule
  Practice using a calendar
  Complete the self-assessment
- Begin class. Books closed. Write on the board: *Class schedule*. Point to the words. Say them aloud and ask Ss to repeat. Ask: *What is our class schedule?* Elicit an appropriate response. Write the class schedule on the board.

Teaching tip
If Ss need help describing the class schedule, ask: *What days does our class meet? What time does our class start and finish? What date did our class begin? What date does it end?* Write Ss' answers on the board.

Option If your program is large enough to have semester course schedules, bring one in and hold it up. Ask: *Where is our class on this schedule?* Ask a S to come to the front of the room to point to your class on the schedule. Highlight the listing. Pass the schedule around so that all Ss can look at it.

Presentation

- Books open. Direct Ss' attention to the class schedule in Exercise **1A**.
- Hold up the Student's Book. Point to the first column in the schedule. Say: *These are the names of the courses.* Point to the second column. Ask: *What is this?* Elicit: *The days that the class meets.*

Useful language
Read the tip box aloud. Explain the word *abbreviation* to Ss. Tell them that we use abbreviations when we want to show a short form of a longer word. It might be helpful to ask Ss if they have seen abbreviations for the days of the week. Ask them where they have seen the abbreviations.

- Point to the third column. Ask: *What is this?* Elicit: *The time that the class meets.*
- Point to the fourth column. Ask: *What is this?* Elicit: *The dates that the class meets.*
- Point to the title of the schedule. Ask: *What semester is this schedule for?* Elicit: *Spring semester.*

Teaching tip
It might be helpful to go over the four seasons of the year. Write on the board: *fall, winter, spring, summer.* Say each season as you point to it. Ask Ss to repeat the season. If Ss need to review seasons further, show them a calendar. Ask them which months fall into the different seasons where they live.

- Ask: *Which kinds of courses are on this schedule?* Elicit: *Business and English as a Second Language courses.*
- Ask: *Which business courses are on the schedule?* Elicit: *Business English, Keyboarding, Introduction to Computers, and Word Processing.*
- Ask: *Which ESL courses are on the schedule?* Elicit: *Beginning, Intermediate, Citizenship, Pronunciation, and Writing.*

Teaching tip
It might be helpful to give a course description of the courses listed in the class schedule if Ss are unsure of the meaning of the class titles.

- Read the instructions for Exercise **1A**. This task helps prepare Ss for standardized-type tests they may have to take. Be sure Ss understand the task. Have Ss individually scan for and circle the answers.
- Check answers with the class.

Practice

- Read aloud the instructions for Exercise **1B**. Ask two Ss to read the example question and answer aloud.
- Ss complete the exercise in pairs. Help as needed.
- Ask pairs to ask and answer the questions for the class.

Expansion activity (small groups)

- **Materials needed** Sample class schedules, ideally from your school, but they may be from other schools
- Ss in small groups. Practice reading a class schedule. Give each group a class schedule.
- Say: *Ask your classmates questions about the class schedule. Use the examples on page 80 to help you.*
- Walk around and help as needed.
- Ask pairs from each group to ask and answer the questions about the class schedules.

Learner persistence (small groups)

- To motivate Ss to keep up with their English studies, encourage them to look through course catalogs to see other English courses they could take in the future.

Lesson F Another view

Presentation

- Show the class a wall calendar. Review the months of the year by turning to each month. Point to the names of the months. Read them aloud and ask Ss to repeat.

Practice

- Direct Ss' attention to Exercise **2A**. Read the instructions aloud. Ask Ss to read the names of the holidays.

Teaching tip

Make sure Ss understand the basic purpose of each holiday listed in this exercise. If Ss haven't heard of any of the holidays, give a brief explanation.

- Ss in small groups. Give a calendar to each group or ask Ss to use their own.
- Model the task. Ask a S to show the class where January 1 is on the calendar. Ask: *What day of the week is New Year's Day?* Elicit an appropriate response.
- Ss complete the exercise in small groups. Help as needed.
- Ask Ss to write their answers on the board. Ask the rest of the class: *Are the dates on the board correct?*

Teaching tip

Ask Ss to use their calendars to show the day and dates of the holidays to Ss who may need help.

Expansion activity (whole group)

- Birthday line and calendar follow-up. Write on the board: *When is your birthday?* Point to the words. Ask a S the question. Write his or her birthday on the board.
- Say: *Ask everyone in the class when his or her birthday is. Line up in the order of your birthdays. For example, a January birthday will come at the beginning of the line and a December birthday will come at the end of the line.*
- Walk around and help as Ss arrange themselves in the correct order according to the calendar.
- When the line is made, ask everyone to tell his or her birthday in turn. Confirm that the order is correct.
- Ask Ss to write their birthdays on the class calendar so that you can acknowledge your Ss' birthdays!

Teaching tip

It might be helpful to go over the difference between *day* and *date*. Ask Ss to write today's day and date on the board to illustrate the difference.

Practice

- Direct Ss' attention to Exercise **2B** and read the instructions.
- Ss complete the exercise in small groups.
- Write the numbers *1–4* on the board. Ask individual Ss to come to the board to write their answers.
- For extra speaking practice, point to the dates written on the board and say them aloud. Ask Ss to repeat.
- Read aloud the instructions for Exercise **2C**.
- Ss complete the chart individually. Help as needed.
- Say: *Now you are going to talk about different holidays.* Read aloud the second part of the instructions for Exercise **2C**. Ask four Ss to read the questions aloud.
- Ss complete the exercise in small groups using the information they wrote in their charts. Help as needed.
- Ask several Ss to ask and answer the questions aloud.

Community building

- Be sure to represent all the cultures and nationalities in your class by asking a S from each culture to answer the questions about the holidays that they celebrate.

Application

Community building

- **Project** Ask Ss to turn to page 138 in their Student's Book to complete the project for Unit 6.

More Ventures *(whole group, pairs, individual)*
Assign appropriate exercises from the *Teacher's Toolkit Audio CD / CD-ROM, Add Ventures,* or the *Workbook.*

Evaluation

- Before asking Ss to turn to the self-assessment on page 143, do a quick review of the unit. Have Ss turn to Lesson A. Ask the class to call out what they remember about this lesson. Prompt Ss, if necessary, with questions, for example: *What are the conversations about on this page? What vocabulary is in the picture?* Continue in this manner to review each lesson quickly.
- **Self-assessment** Read the instructions for Exercise **3**. Ask Ss to turn to the self-assessment page and complete the unit assignment.
- If Ss are ready, administer the unit test on pages T-177–T-178 of this *Teacher's Edition* (or on the *Teacher's Toolkit Audio CD / CD-ROM*). The audio and audio script for the test are on the *Teacher's Toolkit Audio CD / CD-ROM.*

2 Fun with language

A Work in a group. Look at a calendar for this year. Find the holidays. Write the day of the week for each holiday.

Holiday	When	Day of the week
New Year's Day	January 1	1. *(Answers will vary.)*
Valentine's Day	February 14	2. ______________
Independence Day	July 4	3. ______________
Veterans Day	November 11	4. ______________

B Work in a group. Look at a calendar for this year. Find the holidays. Write the date for each holiday.

Holiday	When	Date this year
Mother's Day	2nd Sunday in May	1. *(Answers will vary.)*
Father's Day	3rd Sunday in June	2. ______________
Thanksgiving Day	4th Thursday in November	3. ______________
Labor Day	1st Monday in September	4. ______________

C Write. Do you celebrate other holidays? Write three other holidays.

Holiday	When	Date this year
(Answers will vary.)		

Talk with your classmates. Ask and answers questions about the holidays.

1. What is the name of the holiday?
2. When is it?
3. What do you eat on this holiday?
4. What do you do on this holiday? How do you celebrate?

3 Wrap up

Complete the **Self-assessment** on page 143.

1 Listening

Read the questions. Then listen and circle the answers.

1. Where is the DMV?
   (a.) on Broadway
   b. on Fifth Avenue
2. What is the address number?
   a. 550
   (b.) 515
3. Is the DMV between the coffee shop and the grocery store?
   a. Yes, it is.
   (b.) No, it isn't.
4. Is the DMV between the bank and the coffee shop?
   (a.) Yes, it is.
   b. No, it isn't.
5. Is the DMV across from the hospital?
   (a.) Yes, it is.
   b. No, it isn't.

Talk with a partner. Ask and answer the questions. Use complete sentences.

2 Grammar

A Write. Complete the story.

Kate's Day

Kate is very busy. She's a wife, a mother, and a volunteer at the library. *In* (1. In / On) the morning, she *has* (2. has / have) breakfast with her husband. *At* (3. At / In) 8:30, she takes the children to school. Her house is *on the corner of* (4. on / on the corner of) Tenth and Pine. The school is *across from* (5. across from / between) the post office. At 3:30, Kate *gets* (6. get / gets) her children from school. The family *eats* (7. eat / eats) dinner at 6:00. In the evening, they *watch* (8. watch / watches) TV.

B Write. Unscramble the words. Make questions about the story.

1. morning / Kate / do / What / does / the / in / ? *What does Kate do in the morning?*
2. school / Where / the / is / ? *Where is the school?*
3. get / When / children / does / her / Kate / ? *When does Kate get her children?*
4. What time / the family / eat / dinner / does / ? *What time does the family eat dinner?*

Talk with a partner. Ask and answer the questions.

Lesson objective
- Review vocabulary, pronunciation, and grammar from Units 5 and 6

Warm-up and review

- Before class. Write today's lesson focus on the board. *Review unit: Review vocabulary, pronunciation, and grammar from Units 5 and 6*
- Begin class. Books closed. Ask Ss: *What's the address of our school?* Elicit an appropriate answer.
- Ask: *What is next to our school?* Elicit an appropriate answer.
- Ask: *Is the DMV next to our school?* Elicit a *Yes* or *No* answer.

Presentation

- Books open. Say: *Listen to a conversation about places.*
- Focus Ss' attention on Exercise **1**. Read the instructions aloud.
- Ask individual Ss to read the questions aloud. Say: *Now listen to the conversation. Circle the correct answers.*
- [Class Audio CD 2 track 12] Play or read the audio program (see audio script, page T-157). Ss listen and circle the answers to the questions. Repeat the audio program as needed.
- Write the numbers *1–5* on the board. Ask individual Ss to write their answers on the board. Ask other Ss: *Are these answers correct?* Have Ss make any necessary corrections on the board.

Practice

- Read aloud the second part of the instructions for Exercise **1**.
- Ss complete the exercise in pairs. Walk around and help as needed.
- Ask several pairs to ask and answer the questions for the rest of the class.
- Write on the board:
  I _____ *You* _____ *She* _____ *He* _____
  We _____ *They* _____
- Model the activity. Point to *I* on the board. Say: *I eat lunch every day.* Write *eat* in the blank next to *I*.
- Ask Ss to continue by writing the correct form of *to eat* in the remaining blanks.
- Direct Ss' attention to Exercise **2A**. Read the instructions aloud.
- Ask a S to read aloud the title of the paragraph ("Kate's Day"). Ask: *What do you think this story is about?* Elicit an appropriate answer, for example: *It is a story about things Kate does every day.*
- Ask another S to read aloud the first sentence in the paragraph.
- Ss complete the exercise individually. Walk around. Help as needed.
- Write the numbers *1–8* on the board. Ask Ss to come up to write the answers on the board.

Teaching tip
Ask Ss to write on the board only the missing words, not the complete sentences.

- Ask individual Ss to read aloud a sentence from the paragraph. After each sentence, ask: *Is the answer correct?* Ask different Ss to correct any errors.
- Books closed. Write on the board:
  eat / you / for / What / breakfast / do / ?
- Ask Ss to unscramble the words on the board to make a question. (What do you eat for breakfast?) Write the question on the board.
- Books open. Focus Ss' attention on Exercise **2B**. Read the instructions aloud.
- Ss complete the exercise individually. Help as needed.
- Write the numbers *1–4* on the board. Ask four Ss to write the unscrambled questions on the board. Ask other Ss: *Are the questions correct?* Ask different Ss to correct any errors on the board.
- Read aloud the second part of the instructions in Exercise **2B**.
- Model the task. Ask a S the first question: *What does Kate do in the morning?* Elicit: *She has breakfast with her husband.*
- Ss complete the exercise in pairs. Walk around and help as needed.
- Ask several pairs to ask and answer the questions for the rest of the class.

Warm-up and review

- Say: *Now we are going to practice intonation in questions. "Intonation" means your voice goes up or down at the end of a question.*
- Focus Ss' attention on Exercise **3A**. Read the instructions aloud.
- [Class Audio CD 2 track 13] Play or read the first question in the audio program (see audio script, page T-157). Say: *The intonation goes down. Listen again.* Repeat as needed.
- [Class Audio CD 2 track 13] Play or read the second question in the audio program. Say: *The intonation goes up. Listen again.* Repeat as needed.

Presentation

- Direct Ss' attention to Exercise **3B**. Hold up the Student's Book. Point to the arrows going down at the end of the *Wh-* questions. Say: *When you ask a Wh- question, your voice goes down at the end of the question.*
- Point to the arrows going up at the end of the *Yes / No* questions. Say: *When you ask a Yes / No question, your voice goes up at the end of the question.*
- [Class Audio CD 2 track 14] Play or read the audio program (see audio script, page T-157). Ss listen and repeat the questions. Encourage Ss to use the correct intonation as they repeat the questions. Repeat the audio program as needed.

Practice

- Read aloud the instructions for Exercise **3C**.
- Ask individual Ss to read the questions aloud. Say: *The first four questions are Wh- questions. Does your voice go up or down for these questions?* Elicit: *It goes down.* Say: *The next four questions are Yes / No questions. Does your voice go up or down for these questions?* Elicit: *It goes up.*

  Option Say each question and ask Ss to repeat after you as a group. Listen to make sure Ss are using the correct intonation when asking the questions.
- Ss complete the exercise in pairs. Help as needed.
- Read aloud the instructions for Exercise **3D**.
- Ask two Ss to read aloud the example question and answer.
- Ss complete the exercise in pairs. Walk around and help as needed.
- Ask several pairs to ask and answer their questions for the rest of the class.

Expansion activity *(individual work, student pairs)*

- Focus Ss' attention on the story "Kate's Day" on page 82. Say: *Write a story like this about yourself. What do you do every morning, afternoon, and evening?*
- Ss complete the activity individually. Walk around and help as needed.
- Ss in pairs. Say: *Read your story to your partner. Then, your partner will ask you Wh- and Yes / No questions about your story. Be sure to use the correct question intonation.*
- Ss complete the activity in pairs. When one S finishes reading his or her story, encourage the other S to ask questions about it. Then Ss switch roles.

Evaluation

- Direct Ss' attention to the lesson focus written on the board.
- Go around the room. Ask each S to say a sentence about Kate from Exercise **2A** on page 82.
- Ask Ss to read the questions from Exercise **2B** on page 82 and to use the correct intonation.
- Check off the items in the lesson focus as Ss demonstrate understanding of what they have learned in the lesson.

3 Pronunciation: intonation in questions

A **Listen** to the intonation in these questions.

Where is the bank? | Is the bank on Broadway?

When is your class? | Is your class in the morning?

B **Listen and repeat.**

Wh- questions

1. **A** Where is the post office?
   B It's on First Street.
2. **A** What time do they eat dinner?
   B They eat dinner at 6:30.

Yes / No questions

3. **A** Are you from Mexico?
   B Yes, I am.
4. **A** Does he start work at 7:00?
   B No, he doesn't.

C **Talk** with a partner. Ask and answer the questions.

1. What time do you go to bed?
2. When is your birthday?
3. Where is your supermarket?
4. What time is your English class?
5. Do you visit your friends on the weekend?
6. Do you work in the evening?
7. Do you volunteer?
8. Do you watch TV in the afternoon?

D **Write** five questions.

What's your name?

1. *(Answers will vary.)*
2. ______
3. ______
4. ______
5. ______

Talk with a partner. Ask and answer the questions. Use correct intonation.

What's your name? | My name is Teresa.

Get ready

Shopping

1 Talk about the picture

A Look at the picture. What do you see?

B Point to: apples • bananas • bread • cheese • cookies • milk
a cashier • a shopping cart • a stock clerk

Shirley

Dan

Lesson objectives

- Introduce students to the topic
- Find out what students know about the topic
- Preview the unit by talking about the picture
- Practice key vocabulary
- Practice listening skills

Warm-up and review

- Before class. Write today's lesson focus on the board.
  Lesson A: Shopping
  Grocery shopping vocabulary
  Prices
- Begin class. Books closed. Point to the word *Shopping* on the board. Say the word. Ask Ss to repeat it after you. Say: *Today's class is about shopping. Where do you go shopping?* Elicit places to shop, such as: *grocery store, drugstore, shopping mall.*
- Ask: *What do you buy when you go shopping?* Elicit items such as: *food, books, medicine, clothes,* and *groceries.*

Presentation

- Books open. Set the scene. Direct Ss' attention to the picture on page 84. Ask: *Where is this?* (a supermarket or grocery store) Ask: *What do you see?* Elicit as much information as possible: *people shopping, bananas, fruit, vegetables, bread, shopping cart, cashier,* etc.

Teaching tip

Do not expect Ss to know all the new vocabulary words. These questions are intended to find out what Ss already know about shopping vocabulary.

- Direct Ss' attention to the key words in Exercise **1B**. Read each word aloud while pointing to the corresponding item in the picture. Ask the class to repeat and point.

Comprehension check

- Ask Ss *Yes / No* questions about the picture. Say: *Listen to the questions. Answer Yes or No.*
  Is this a grocery store? (Yes.)
  Are there apples at the store? (Yes.)
  Are there eight people in the picture? (No, seven.)
  What fruits and vegetables can you see? (Accept any of the following answers: apples, bananas, oranges, strawberries, pineapples, potatoes, carrots, broccoli, tomatoes, green peppers, and onions.)
  What other groceries do you see? (Accept any possible answer, such as: eggs, bread, cookies, cheese, and chicken.)

Practice

- Direct Ss' attention to Exercise **1B**. Model the task. Hold up the Student's Book. Say to a S: *Point to apples in the picture.* The S points to the appropriate picture.
- Ss in pairs. Say to one S: *Say the words in Exercise 1B.* Say to his or her partner: *Point to the picture.*
- Ss complete the exercise in pairs. Walk around and help as needed. When Ss have finished, have them change partners and change roles.
- Ask several pairs to perform the task for the class to check Ss' understanding.

Expansion activity *(small groups)*

- Discuss grocery shopping. Write on the board:
  Where do you buy groceries?
  When do you go grocery shopping?
  What do you usually buy?
- Direct Ss' attention to the questions on the board. Read them aloud. Ask Ss to repeat them after you.
- Say: *Talk in your small group. Ask and answer the questions on the board.*
- Ss complete the activity in small groups. Walk around and help as needed.
- Ask members of each group to report their answers to the rest of the class.

  Option Shopping survey. Do the expansion activity. Then, tell Ss to take a survey within their small group. *How many people shop at the same store? How many go shopping every day? How many go shopping once a week? How many people go shopping on Sunday? How many people go shopping in the morning? How many usually buy the same items?* After Ss have completed the survey, they can report their findings to the class. Use this as an opportunity to review language from Unit 6.

Lesson A Get ready

Presentation

- Books closed. Write on the board:

  Oranges – 40¢ each *Bananas – $0.25 each*
  Milk – $1.89 *Potatoes – 99¢ / lb*
- Read each line aloud. Ask Ss to repeat. Check that Ss understand the symbols ($, ¢, lb).
- Point to *oranges* on the board. Ask: *How much are oranges?* (40 cents each.) Repeat the same questions for *milk, bananas,* and *potatoes.*
- Books open. Direct Ss' attention to Exercise **2A** and read the instructions aloud.
- [Class Audio CD2 track 15] Play or read the audio program (see audio script, page T-157). Ss listen and circle the words they hear. Repeat the audio program as needed.
- Check answers. Ask: *What did you circle?* Ask Ss to write the words on the board. Point to the words. Say: *Repeat after me.* Say each word.

Expansion activity *(student pairs)*

- Ask Ss to write the words they did not circle on the board: *apples, bananas, cookies, rice.*

Practice

- Direct Ss' attention to Exercise **2B** and read the instructions aloud.
- [Class Audio CD2 track 15] Play or read only conversation *A* on the audio program.
- Ask Ss: *Which picture matches conversation A?* (picture number 3) Hold up the Student's Book. Point to the handwritten *a* next to number 3.
- [Class Audio CD2 track 15] Play or read the complete audio program. Ss complete the exercise individually.

Learner persistence *(individual work)*

- [Self-Study Audio CD track 27] Exercises **2A** and **2B** are recorded on the Ss' self-study CD at the back of the Student's Book. Ss can listen to the CD at home for reinforcement and review. They can also listen for self-directed learning when class attendance is not possible.

Comprehension check

- Write the numbers *1–6* on the board. Ask individual Ss to come to the board and write the correct answers to Exercise **2B** next to each number.
- [Class Audio CD2 track 15] Play or read the audio program again. Pause the audio after each conversation. Point to a letter of the conversation on the board. Ask: *Is this correct?* If not, erase the answer and ask a S to correct it.

Application

- If possible, show Ss a circular from a local grocery store. Point to items in the circular. Ask: *How much is this?*
- Direct Ss' attention to the receipt in Exercise **2C**. Ask: *What do you see?* Elicit: *It's a receipt.* If Ss don't know the word, write it on the board. Say the word. Ask Ss to repeat it.
- Read aloud the instructions for Exercise **2C**.
- Read aloud each food item and price. Ask Ss to repeat the words and prices.
- Ss complete the exercise individually. Help as needed.

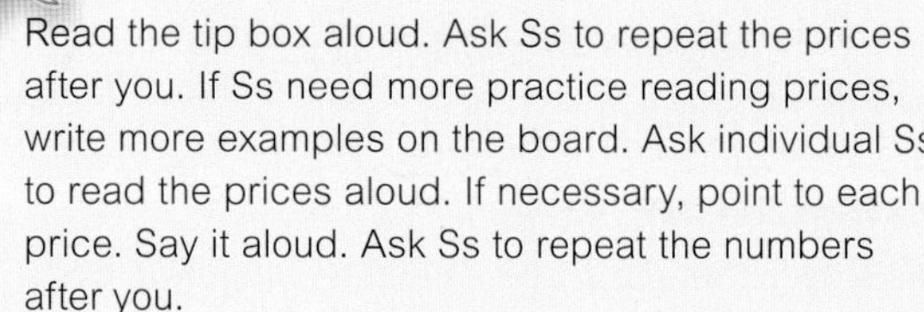

Read the tip box aloud. Ask Ss to repeat the prices after you. If Ss need more practice reading prices, write more examples on the board. Ask individual Ss to read the prices aloud. If necessary, point to each price. Say it aloud. Ask Ss to repeat the numbers after you.

Comprehension check

- Ss in pairs. Say: *Show your total to your partner. Is it the same or different? If they are different, which total is correct?* Ask a S to write the correct total on the board.

Community building *(small groups)*

- Ask Ss to visit their local supermarket or grocery store and record the price in that store of the items pictured on page 84 (carrots, potatoes, bananas, etc). Ask Ss to bring in their results to the next class. Have Ss write the name of the store and the prices on the board. Compare prices and decide which store offers the best values.
- Practice numeracy skills. Put Ss in groups. Ask Ss to look at the prices in one store and use them to calculate the price of a pound of carrots, five apples, and so on. Ask Ss to calculate the total bill and compare their answers for accuracy.

Evaluation

- Direct Ss' attention to the lesson focus on the board.
- Ask Ss to identify items in the picture on page 84.
- Write different prices on the board (*$1.14, $2.59,* etc.). Ask Ss to read the prices aloud.
- Check off the lesson focus as Ss demonstrate understanding of what they have learned in the lesson.

More Ventures *(whole group, pairs, individual)*
Assign appropriate exercises from the *Teacher's Toolkit Audio CD / CD-ROM, Add Ventures,* or the *Workbook.*

2 Listening

SELF-STUDY AUDIO CD

A **Listen.** Circle the words you hear.

apples	(bread)	cookies	(onions)	rice
bananas	(cheese)	(milk)	(potatoes)	(tomatoes)

SELF-STUDY AUDIO CD

B **Listen again.** Write the letter of the conversation.

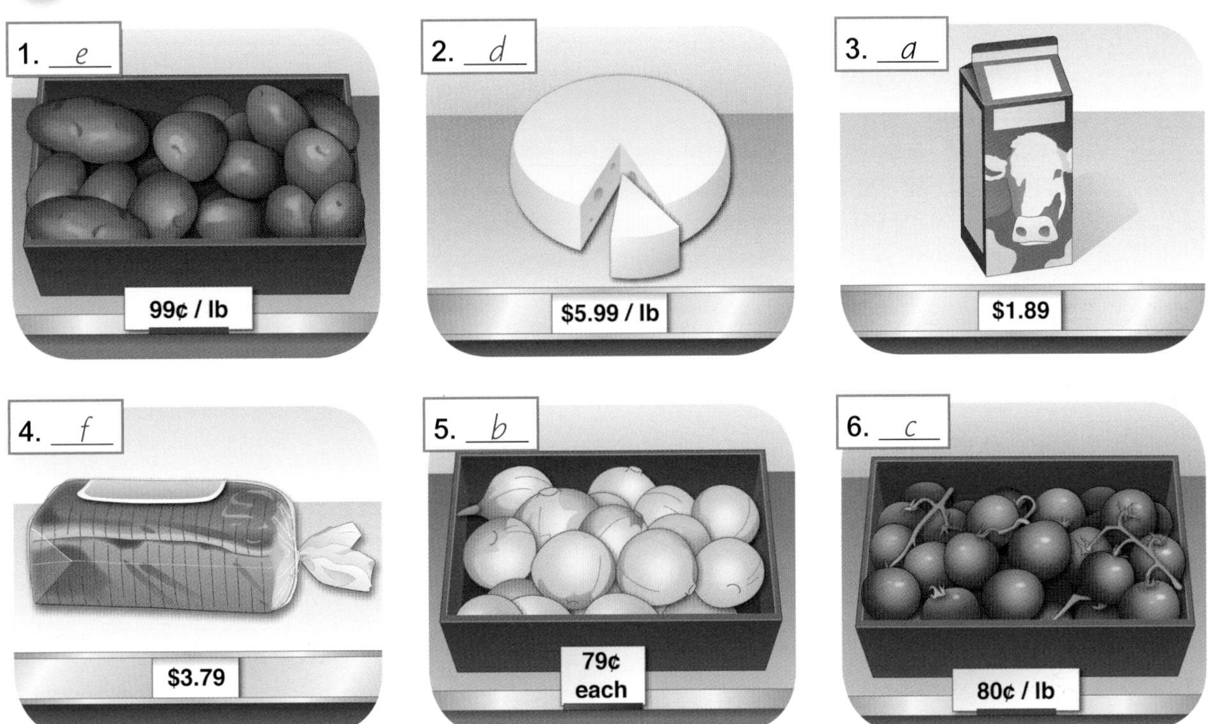

Listen again. Check your answers.

C **Write.** Add the prices of all the items. What is the total?

potatoes - 2lb	$1.98
onions - 1	.79
tomatoes - 3lb	2.40
cheese - 1lb	5.99
bread - 1	3.79
milk - 2	3.78
Total	$ 18.73

Thank you!

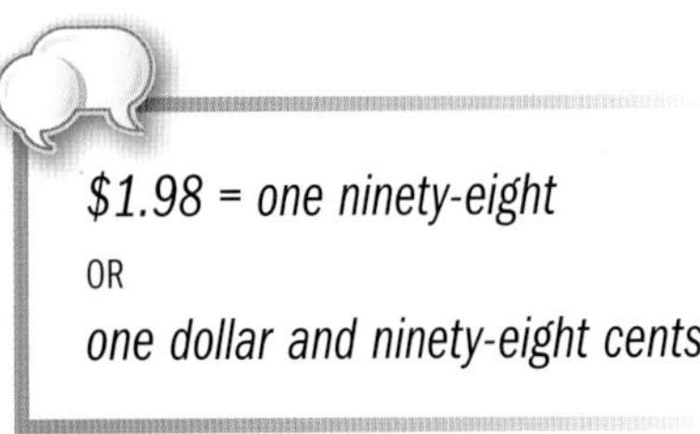

$1.98 = one ninety-eight
OR
one dollar and ninety-eight cents

Lesson B How many? How much?

1 Grammar focus: count / non-count nouns; *How many? / How much?*

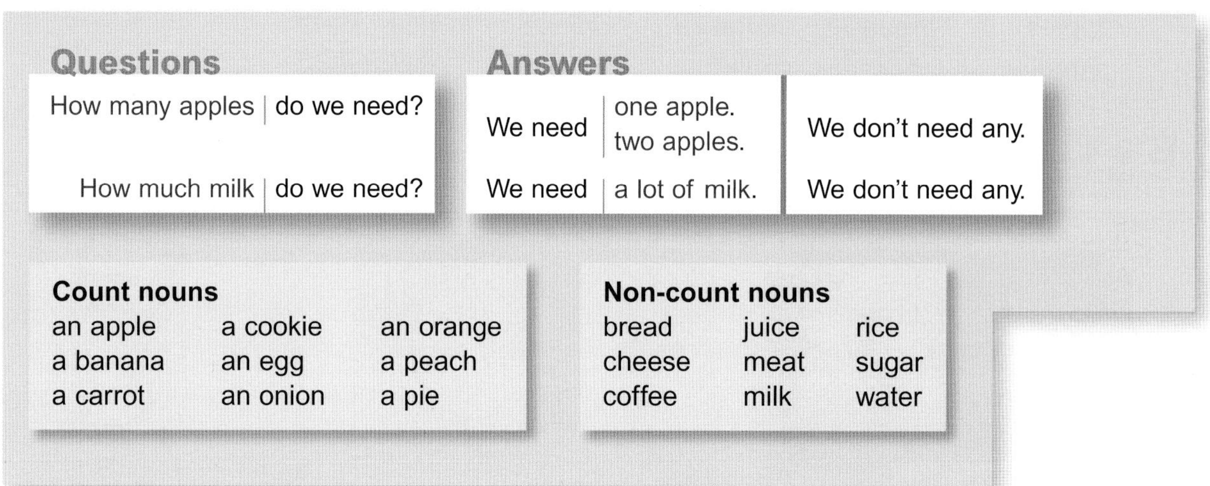

Questions

How many apples	do we need?
How much milk	do we need?

Answers

We need	one apple. two apples.	We don't need any.
We need	a lot of milk.	We don't need any.

Count nouns

an apple	a cookie	an orange
a banana	an egg	a peach
a carrot	an onion	a pie

Non-count nouns

bread	juice	rice
cheese	meat	sugar
coffee	milk	water

2 Practice

A Look at the pictures. Circle only the count nouns.

1 2  3  4

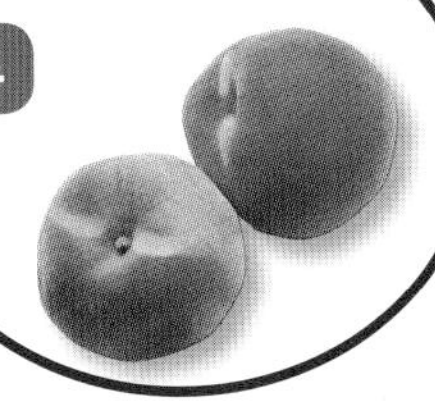

5  6  7  8

9  10  11  12

Listen and repeat.

Lesson objective

- Introduce count and non-count nouns and questions with *How many* and *How much*

Warm-up and review

- Before class. Write today's lesson focus on the board.
  Lesson B:
  Count nouns
  Non-count nouns
  How many?
  How much?
- Begin class. Books closed. Draw a vertical line down the board, making two columns. Ask Ss: *What kind of food do you have in your kitchen?* As Ss respond, write the count items they say in the first column and the non-count items in the second column. For example:

  Food in my kitchen

apples	*milk*
eggs	*bread*
carrots	*juice*
cookies	*rice*

- When you have filled up both columns, ask: *What's the difference between the first column and the second?*

> **Teaching tip**
> It might be helpful to remind Ss that count nouns have the plural *s*. Non-count nouns do not have the plural *s* form.

- Underline all the *s* plurals in the foods in the first column. Say: *You can count all of these items, for example: two eggs, three carrots, four cookies. These are called count nouns.* Point to the words in the lesson focus on the board and label the first column *Count nouns.*
- Point to the food items in the second column. Say: *You can't count these items. These are non-count nouns.* Point to the words in the lesson focus on the board and label the second column *Non-count nouns.*

Presentation

- Books open. Direct Ss' attention to the grammar chart in Exercise **1**. Say the count nouns aloud and ask Ss to repeat after you. Do the same for the non-count nouns.

> **Teaching tip**
> It might be helpful to point out that singular count nouns take the article *a* or *an* in front of them. Explain that if the noun begins with a vowel, the article is *an*. If it begins with a consonant, the article is *a*. Practice by writing count nouns on the board. Ask the class if the article is *a* or *an*.

- Direct Ss' attention to the questions and answers at the top of the grammar chart. Say: *For count nouns we ask "How many?" For non-count nouns we ask "How much?"*
- Read aloud the questions and answers in the grammar chart. Ask Ss to repeat after you.

Comprehension check

- Direct Ss' attention to the picture on page 84.
- Write on the board:
  Count nouns　　*Non-count nouns*
- Say: *Tell me one count noun in the picture.* Elicit: *apple, banana, potato,* etc. Write the word in the correct column.
- Elicit and write one non-count noun, for example: *bread, cheese, milk.*
- Ss in pairs. Ask Ss to copy into their notebooks the columns from the board and then write down all the count and non-count nouns in the picture on page 84. Walk around and help as needed.
- Ask Ss to write their answers in the columns on the board. Count nouns can include: *bananas, potatoes, cookies, apples, shopping carts.* Non-count nouns can include: *bread, cheese, milk,* etc.

> **Teaching tip**
> Ss may want to know whether *person* is a count or a non-count noun. Explain that it is a count noun, but the plural form is usually *people.*

Practice

- Read aloud the instructions for Exercise **2A**.
- Ss complete the exercise individually. Walk around and help as needed.
- Ask individual Ss to say which count nouns they circled, and ask *How many?* questions about the pictures. For example: *How many carrots do you see?*

  Option Ask Ss to write the count nouns they circled in the correct column on the board. Ask them to write the non-count nouns they didn't circle in the second column.
- [Class Audio CD2 track 16] Read the second part of the instructions for Exercise **2A**. Play or read the audio program (see audio script, page T-157). Have Ss listen and repeat. Correct pronunciation as needed.

Lesson B How many? How much?

Presentation

- Books closed. Write on the board: *apples*. Ask: *Is this a count noun or a non-count noun?* Elicit: *It's a count noun.*
- Write on the board: *How many apples do you need?* Read the question aloud. Ask Ss to repeat after you.
- Write on the board: *milk*. Ask: *Is this a count noun or a non-count noun?* Elicit: *It is a non-count noun.*
- Write on the board: *How much milk do you need?* Read the question aloud. Ask Ss to repeat after you.

Practice

- Books open. Direct Ss' attention to Exercise **2B** and read the instructions aloud. Ask two Ss to read the first two examples aloud.
- Ss complete the exercise individually. Help as needed.
- Direct Ss' attention to Exercise **2C** and read the instructions aloud.
- Ss complete the exercise individually. Help as needed.

Comprehension check

- Read aloud the second part of the instructions for Exercise **2C**.
- [Class Audio CD2 track 17] Play or read the audio program (see audio script, page T-157). Listen to Ss' pronunciation as they repeat. Repeat the audio program as needed.
- Check answers with the class. Call on individual Ss to read the questions aloud.
- Direct Ss' attention to Exercise **2D** and read the instructions aloud.
- Model the examples with a S. You speak first.
- Ss complete the exercise in pairs. Help as needed.
- Ask pairs to perform their conversations for the class.

Useful language

Read the tip box aloud. Focus on the questions with *How many* and *How much*. Ask Ss to repeat the questions after you. Then have them answer using *Not many, Not much*, or *A lot*.

Application

- Books closed. Ask: *Do you like to cook?* Elicit *Yes* or *No* responses.
- Ask a S who responded with *Yes*: *What do you like to cook?* Elicit an appropriate response. Continue by asking other Ss what they like to cook.
- Choose one of the responses that requires simple ingredients. Ask: *What do you need for* (name of food item)*?* Write on the board the ingredients the S says.
- Books open. Direct Ss' attention to Exercise **3** and read the instructions aloud. Ask: *Do you make fruit salad at home?*

Teaching tip

Explain that *pretend* means to imagine you are doing something.

- Read aloud the names of the fruit. Ask Ss to repeat.
- Ask two Ss to read aloud the example question and answer.
- Ss complete the exercise in pairs. Help as needed.
- Ask several pairs to perform their conversations for the class. Make sure Ss are using *How much* and *How many* correctly.

Expansion activity *(small groups)*

- **Materials needed** Circulars from local supermarkets
- Ss in small groups. Pass out a circular to each group. Say: *Imagine that you have $100. Plan a party. How many people will you invite? What food will you buy? Make a list of all the items that you are going to buy. They have to be in the supermarket ad, and you can't spend more than $100.*
- When Ss finish, ask one person from each group to write the group's party list on the board. Then ask each group to read its list and the prices to the rest of the class.
- The class can vote for the party that sounds as if it would be the most fun to attend.

Evaluation

- Direct Ss' attention to the lesson focus on the board.
- Show Ss the pictures on page 86. Point to different pictures. Say the words and ask: *Is this a count noun or a non-count noun?* Go around the room.
- Say: *Now ask questions about the pictures. Use "How much" and "How many."*
- Check off the items as Ss demonstrate understanding of what they have learned in the lesson.

More Ventures *(whole group, pairs, individual)*
Assign appropriate exercises from the *Teacher's Toolkit Audio CD / CD-ROM, Add Ventures*, or the *Workbook*.

B Write. Look at the pictures on page 86. Write the food words on the chart.

1. *carrots*	5. *milk*	9. *coffee*
2. *water*	6. *oranges*	10. *apples*
3. *bread*	7. *eggs*	11. *sugar*
4. *peaches*	8. *meat*	12. *pies*

C Write. Complete the questions. Use *many* or *much*.

1. How *many* eggs do we need?
2. How *much* juice do we need?
3. How *much* milk do we need?
4. How *many* pies do we need?
5. How *much* bread do we need?
6. How *many* potatoes do we need?
7. How *much* rice do we need?
8. How *much* meat do we need?

Listen and repeat.

D Talk with a partner. Change the **bold** words and make conversations.

A We need **apples.**
B How **many apples** do we need?
A Two.

1. apples / two
2. milk / not much
3. bananas / five
4. bread / a lot
5. oranges / six
6. cheese / not much
7. eggs / a dozen
8. onions / not many

A We need **milk.**
B How **much milk** do we need?
A **Not much.**

Useful language
How many *do we need?*
You can answer *Not many* OR *A lot.*
How much *do we need?*
You can answer *Not much* OR *A lot.*

3 Communicate

Talk with a partner. Pretend you are making a fruit salad for four friends. Check (✓) six items. Then make conversations.

How many apples do we need?

We need three.

☐ apples	☐ cherries	☐ pineapples
☐ bananas	☐ orange juice	☐ strawberries
☐ blueberries	☐ oranges	☐ sugar

Lesson C Are there any bananas?

1 Grammar focus: *There is / There are*

Statements

There is There are	a banana two bananas	on the table.
There is	bread	on the table.

Questions

Is there Are there	a banana any bananas	on the table?
Is there	any bread	on the table?

Answers

Yes, there	is. are.	No, there	isn't. aren't.
Yes, there	is.	No, there	isn't.

2 Practice

A **Write.** Complete the sentences. Use *there is*, *there are*, *there isn't*, or *there aren't*.

1. ***A*** Is there any bread on the table?
   B Yes, there is.
2. ***A*** Are there any eggs?
   B No, there aren't.
3. ***A*** Is there any juice?
   B Yes, there is.
4. ***A*** Is there any water?
   B No, there isn't.
5. ***A*** Are there any cookies?
   B Yes, there are.
6. ***A*** Are there any bananas?
   B No, there aren't.

Listen and repeat. Then practice with a partner.

B **Write.** Complete the questions. Use *Is there* or *Are there*.

1. ***A*** Is there any meat in the refrigerator?
   B Yes, there is.
2. ***A*** Are there any oranges?
   B Yes, there are.
3. ***A*** Is there any cheese?
   B No, there isn't.
4. ***A*** Is there any coffee?
   B Yes, there is.
5. ***A*** Are there any apples?
   B No, there aren't.
6. ***A*** Are there any cherries?
   B Yes, there are.

Listen and repeat. Then practice with a partner.

Lesson objective
- Introduce *There is* and *There are*

Warm-up and review

- Before class. Write today's lesson focus on the board.
  Lesson C:
  There is / Is there
  There are / Are there
- Begin class. Books closed. Review count and non-count nouns. Show Ss items in the classroom, such as a pencil, a pen, an eraser, and the blackboard. Each time you show an item, ask the class: *Is this a count or a non-count noun?* (All are count nouns.)
- Draw non-count items on the board, such as bread, milk, cheese, and juice. Ask: *Are these count or non-count nouns?* Elicit: *They are non-count nouns.*

Presentation

- Put a pen on a desk. Ask: *Is there a pen on the desk?* (Yes.) Take the pen off the desk. Ask: *Now is there a pen on the desk?* (No.)
- Put two or more pens on the desk. Ask: *Are there any pens on the desk?* (Yes.) Take the pens off the desk. Ask: *Now are there pens on the desk?* (No.)

Teaching tip
Ss may not know this grammar structure yet. Accept simple *Yes / No* answers.

- Books open. Direct Ss' attention to the grammar chart in Exercise **1**. Read aloud each statement, question, and answer. Ask Ss to repeat after you.
- Ss in pairs. Have Ss practice reading the statements, questions, and answers in the grammar chart to each other.

Comprehension check

- Bring in objects to illustrate the grammar points, for example, two apples and a loaf of bread.
- Put one apple on a desk. Say: *There is an apple on the desk*. (Throughout this activity, emphasize the underlined words.) Write the sentence on the board. Ask Ss to repeat.
- Put both apples on the desk and say: *There are two apples on the desk*. Write the sentence on the board. Ask Ss to repeat.
- Take away one of the apples from the desk and ask: *Is there an apple on the desk?* Elicit: *Yes, there is*. Then ask: *Are there two apples on the desk?* Elicit: *No, there aren't*. Put the second apple back on the desk and ask: *Are there two apples on the desk?* Elicit: *Yes, there are*.
- Point to an empty desk. Ask: *Is there any bread on the desk?* Elicit: *No, there isn't*. Put the bread on the desk. Ask: *Now is there any bread on the desk?* Elicit: *Yes, there is*.
- Elicit other short answers using different count and non-count objects.

Practice

- Turn Ss' attention to Exercise **2A** and read the instructions aloud.
- Ss complete the exercise individually. Walk around and help as needed.
- Check answers with the class. Ask Ss to write their answers on the board. Ask different Ss to read the answers aloud. Ask other Ss to make any necessary corrections on the board.
- Read aloud the second part of the instructions for Exercise **2A**.
- [Class Audio CD2 track 18] Play or read the audio program (see audio script, page T-158). Listen to Ss' pronunciation as they repeat the conversations. Correct pronunciation as needed.
- Ss practice the conversations in pairs. Walk around and help as needed.
- Ask several pairs to read the conversations for the rest of the class.
- Direct Ss' attention to Exercise **2B** and read the instructions aloud.
- Ss complete the exercise individually. Walk around and help as needed.
- Check answers with the class. Ask Ss to write their answers on the board. Ask different Ss to read the answers aloud. Ask other Ss to make any necessary corrections on the board.
- Read aloud the second part of the instructions for Exercise **2B**.
- [Class Audio CD2 track 19] Play or read the audio program (see audio script, page T-158). Listen to Ss' pronunciation as they repeat the conversations. Correct pronunciation as needed.
- Say: *Practice with a partner*. In pairs, have Ss practice the conversations. Walk around and help as needed.
- Ask several pairs to read the conversations to the class.

Lesson C Are there any bananas?

Practice

- Direct Ss' attention to the picture in Exercise **2C**. Ask: *What do you see?* Elicit the names of the groceries.
- Read the instructions aloud. Ask a S to read the example sentence aloud. Be sure Ss understand the task.
- Ss complete the exercise individually. Walk around and help as needed.
- Check answers with the class. Ask Ss to write their sentences on the board. Ask different Ss to read them aloud. Ask other Ss to make any necessary corrections on the board.

Comprehension check

- Read aloud the second part of the instructions for Exercise **2C**.
- [Class Audio CD2 track 20] Play or read the audio program (see audio script, page T-158). Listen to Ss' pronunciation as they repeat the sentences. Correct pronunciation as needed.

> **Useful language**
> Read the tip box aloud. Review the words by pointing to the objects in the picture in Exercise **2C**. Have students use the count words to tell how many of an item they see.

Application

- Direct Ss' attention to the picture in Exercise **2D**. Ask: *What do you see?* Elicit: *A bag of sugar, six bottles of water, three boxes of tea,* etc.
- Read the instructions aloud. Ask four Ss to read aloud the example conversations.
- Ss complete the exercise in pairs. Walk around and help as needed.
- Ask several pairs to ask and answer the questions for the rest of the class.
- Read aloud the instructions for Exercise **3**. Write on the board: *There is . . .* or *There are . . .*
- Ask a S the first question. Point to the words on the board to indicate that the S should use this structure when answering the question.
- Ss complete the exercise in pairs. Walk around and help as needed.
- Ask several pairs to ask and answer the questions for the rest of the class.

  Option After Ss have worked in pairs, ask them to team up with another pair. They can continue the exercise by asking the new Ss the questions in Exercise **3**.

Expansion activity (small groups)

- Memory game. Before playing this game, briefly review the vocabulary from this lesson, for example: *a carton of apple juice, a bottle of water, three boxes of tea,* etc.
- Ask Ss to sit in groups of five to seven. Say: *Tell your group something you have in your kitchen. The next person will repeat what you say and then tell the group what he or she has in the kitchen.* Give Ss an example:
  S1 *In my kitchen, I have two bottles of water.*
  S2 *In his kitchen, he has two bottles of water, and I have one carton of milk.*
  S3 *In his kitchen, he has two bottles of water, she has one carton of milk, and I have one bag of rice.*

  Keep playing until everyone has had a chance to participate. Ask one S from each group to try to remember everything the group members have said.

Learner persistence (whole group)

- Ask the class: *What is there to help you improve your English?* Encourage Ss to answer using *There is* and *There are*. Talk about resources available to Ss, for example: *There are volunteers who can help you in class. There are dictionaries on the shelf. There are students in a more advanced class who can help you with your homework.*

Evaluation

- Direct Ss' attention to the lesson focus written on the board.
- Focus Ss' attention on the picture on page 84. Say: *Ask questions. Use "Is there" and "Are there."* Go around the room. Then ask Ss to answer the questions using *There is* and *There are.*
- Check off the items as Ss demonstrate understanding of what they have learned in the lesson.

> ***More Ventures*** *(whole group, pairs, individual)*
> Assign appropriate exercises from the *Teacher's Toolkit Audio CD / CD-ROM, Add Ventures,* or the *Workbook.*

C **Write.** Complete the sentences. Use *There is* or *There are*.

> **Useful language**
> You can count words like *loaf*, *carton*, *box*, *bottle*, *package*, *can*, and *bag*.
> Use these words with non-count nouns.

1. There is one loaf of bread.
2. There are two cartons of apple juice.
3. There are three boxes of tea.
4. There are four bottles of water.
5. There is one package of ground meat.
6. There are six cans of soda.
7. There is one bag of flour.
8. There are two packages of cheese.

Listen and repeat.

D **Talk** with a partner. Look at the picture. Make conversations.

1. rice	3. milk	5. tea	7. sugar
2. soda	4. coffee	6. cheese	8. water

3 Communicate

Talk with a partner. Ask and answer these questions.

1. What is in your refrigerator?
2. What is on your kitchen shelves?

Lesson D Reading

1 Before you read

Talk. Shirley and Dan are shopping. Look at the picture. Answer the questions.

1. Where are they?
2. What are they doing?

2 Read

 **Listen and read.**

Regular Customers

Shirley and Dan are regular customers at SaveMore Supermarket. They go to SaveMore three or four times a week. The cashiers and stock clerks at SaveMore know them and like them. There are fruit and vegetables, meat and fish, and cookies and cakes in the supermarket. But today, Shirley and Dan are buying apples, bananas, bread, and cheese. There is one problem. The total is $16.75. They only have a ten-dollar bill, 5 one-dollar bills, and three quarters!

When you don't understand a word, look for clues.
Do you understand *regular customer*?
Clue: They go to SaveMore *three or four times a week.*

3 After you read

A Read the sentences. Are they correct? Circle *Yes* or *No*.

1. Shirley and Dan go to SaveMore three or four times a day. Yes (No)
2. They are regular customers at SaveMore Supermarket. (Yes) No
3. The cashiers and stock clerks know them. (Yes) No
4. Shirley and Dan are buying meat and fish. Yes (No)
5. Shirley and Dan have $16.00. Yes (No)

B Write. Correct the sentences.

1. *Shirley and Dan go to SaveMore three or four times a week.*

C Write. Answer the questions about Shirley and Dan.

1. How much money do Shirley and Dan have? *Shirley and Dan have $15.75.*
2. How many quarters do they have? *They have three quarters.*
3. How much more money do they need? *They need one dollar more.*

Lesson objectives

- Introduce and read "Regular Customers"
- Practice using new topic-related words
- Use reading clues to help comprehension

Warm-up and review

- Before class. Write today's lesson focus on the board.
  Lesson D:
  Read and understand "Regular Customers"
  Learn new vocabulary about shopping
- Begin class. Books closed. Write on the board: *regular customer.* Ask a S: *Where do you usually go grocery shopping?* Elicit an appropriate answer. Write the name of the store on the board. Point to it. Say: (Name of S) *is a regular customer at* (name of store). Continue by asking several more Ss where they like to shop.
- Remind Ss about the grocery store they saw in the picture on page 84. Then focus Ss' attention on Exercise **1** on page 90. Read the instructions aloud. Point to the picture and ask: *Where are they?* (at the grocery store, at the checkout) Ask: *What are they doing?* (shopping, buying groceries, paying for food).

Presentation

- Direct Ss' attention to Exercise **2**. Read the instructions aloud.
- [Class Audio CD2 track 21] Play or read the audio program and ask Ss to read along (see audio script, page T-158). Repeat the audio program as needed.

> Read the tip box aloud. Ask Ss if they understand what *regular customer* means. It might be helpful to have a discussion about context clues and how they help you find the meanings of words. Ask Ss if they can sometimes figure out the meaning of a new word without using a dictionary.

- Have Ss tell if there are any words in the reading that they don't understand. Ask if they can figure out the meaning of the words by looking for clues to help them.

Teaching tip

Ss may not know the meaning of the word *bill* as it is used in this context. It might be helpful to ask a S to read the last sentence in the paragraph. Ask Ss what a ten-dollar bill could be. If Ss can't figure out the meaning, draw a ten-dollar bill on the board.

Learner persistence *(individual work)*

- [Self-Study Audio CD track 28] Exercise **2** is recorded on the Ss' self-study CD at the back of the Student's Book. Ss can listen to the CD at home for reinforcement and review. They can also listen to the CD for self-directed learning when class attendance is not possible.

Comprehension check

- Read aloud the instructions for Exercise **3A**. Ask a S to read the example aloud.
- Ask: *Do Shirley and Dan go to SaveMore three or four times a day?* (No, they go to SaveMore three or four times a week.) Point to where *No* is circled for number 1. Be sure Ss understand the task.
- Ss complete the exercise individually. Walk around and help as needed.
- Check answers with the class. Ask Ss to read their sentences and answers aloud.
- Ask Ss to take out a piece of paper. Read the instructions for Exercise **3B**.
- Model the task of correcting the sentences. Point to *No* for number 1 in Exercise **3A**. Read the sentence aloud. Tell Ss: *This sentence is incorrect. Tell me the correct sentence. Shirley and Dan go to SaveMore three or four times a . . .* (week). Write on the board: *Shirley and Dan go to SaveMore three or four times a week.*
- Ss complete the exercise individually. Walk around and help as needed.
- Check answers with the class. Ask Ss to write their answers on the board. Then ask different Ss to read the answers aloud. Ask: *Are the sentences correct?* Make any necessary corrections on the board.

Practice

- Ask Ss questions about the paragraph: *How much money do they have?* ($15.75) *How much more do they need?* ($1)
- Direct Ss' attention to Exercise **3C** and read aloud the instructions.
- Ss complete the exercise individually. Walk around and help as needed.
- Check answers with the class. Ask Ss to read aloud their questions and answers.

Teaching tip

It might be helpful to remind Ss that we use the question words *How many* for count nouns and *How much* for non-count nouns, such as *money.*

Lesson D Reading

Warm-up and review

- Books closed. Find out what Ss know about the new vocabulary by asking questions that use the new words. Ss can answer the questions by raising their hands. If possible, show Ss the items that you ask about (use fake ATM and credit cards or draw pictures of them on the board). Ask:
  How many of you have an ATM card?
  How many of you have a checking account?
  How many of you have a credit card?
- Write *money* on the board. Ask: *What are some different amounts of money?* Write Ss' responses on the board. Elicit: *penny, nickel, dime, quarter, half-dollar, one-dollar bill, five-dollar bill, ten-dollar bill, twenty-dollar bill.*

Teaching tip
Do not be surprised if Ss do not know the new words. This exercise is meant to show you if your Ss already know some of the vocabulary in this lesson.

Presentation

- Books open. Focus Ss' attention on the pictures in Exercise **4**. Say: *These are pictures of different types of money.*
- Direct Ss' attention to the word bank in Exercise **4A**. Say: *Repeat the words after me.* Say each word. Listen to Ss' pronunciation as they repeat. Correct pronunciation.
- Say: *Write the words in the picture dictionary.* Point to the first example, which has been done. Be sure Ss understand the task.
- Ss complete the exercise individually. Help as needed.

Comprehension check

- [Class Audio CD2 track 22] Play or read the audio program (see audio script, page T-158). Ss should check their answers and repeat the words after they hear them. Repeat the audio program if necessary.

Learner persistence *(individual work)*

- [Self-Study Audio CD track 29] Exercise **4A** is recorded on the Ss' self-study CD at the back of the Student's Book. Ss can listen to the CD at home for reinforcement and review. They can also listen for self-directed learning when class attendance is not possible.

Expansion activity *(whole group)*

- **Materials needed** Examples of the items in the picture dictionary (a fake ATM card, a penny, a dollar bill, etc.)
- Guessing game. Ss practice guessing what their classmates are hiding behind their backs. Model the activity by spreading out the money and cards on the desk in front of the class. Ask all the Ss in the class to close their eyes. Invite a S to come to the front of the class and choose one item. Instruct the S to hold the item behind his or her back.
- Tell Ss to open their eyes. Ask the S: *Is there a one-dollar bill in your hand?* Elicit: *Yes, there is* or *No, there isn't.* Elicit more questions from the class until someone guesses correctly. Then invite that S to the front of the class to choose another item while the other class members close their eyes. Elicit another round of questions.

Practice

- Direct Ss' attention to the first set of pictures in Exercise **4B**. Ask: *What do you see?* (a dollar bill and four quarters) Say: *A dollar bill is the same as four quarters.*
- Continue by asking Ss about the remaining sets of pictures. Elicit: *A quarter is the same as two dimes and a nickel. A twenty-dollar bill is the same as two ten-dollar bills. A half-dollar is the same as two quarters.*
- Read the instructions aloud. Ask two Ss to read the example conversation.

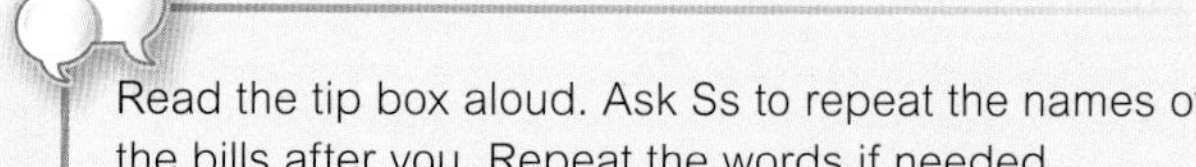

Read the tip box aloud. Ask Ss to repeat the names of the bills after you. Repeat the words if needed.

- Ss practice the conversations in pairs. Help as needed.
- Ask pairs to perform their conversations for the class.

Evaluation

- Direct Ss' attention to the lesson focus on the board.
- Put a check mark next to *Read "Regular Customers."* Elicit sentences for the words in the picture dictionary.
- Check off each part of the lesson focus as Ss demonstrate an understanding of what they have learned in the lesson.

More Ventures *(whole group, pairs, individual)*
Assign appropriate exercises from the *Teacher's Toolkit Audio CD / CD-ROM, Add Ventures,* or the *Workbook.*

4 Picture dictionary Money

1. a penny

2. a nickel

3. a dime

4. a quarter

5. a half-dollar

6. a one-dollar bill

7. a five-dollar bill

8. a ten-dollar bill

9. a twenty-dollar bill

10. a check

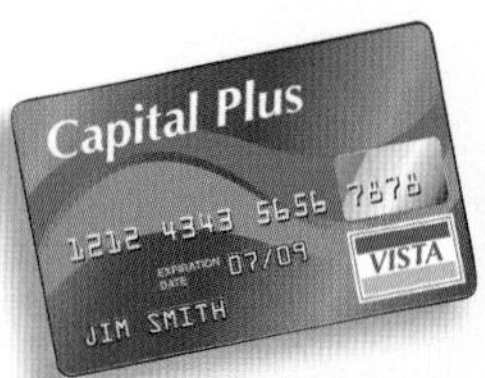

11. a credit card

12. an ATM card

A **Write** the words in the picture dictionary. Then listen and repeat.

an ATM card	a dime	a nickel	a quarter
a check	a five-dollar bill	a one-dollar bill	a ten-dollar bill
a credit card	a half-dollar	a penny	a twenty-dollar bill

B **Talk** with a partner. Look at the pictures.
Change the **bold** words and make conversations.

A Do you have change for **a dollar**?
B Sure. What do you need?
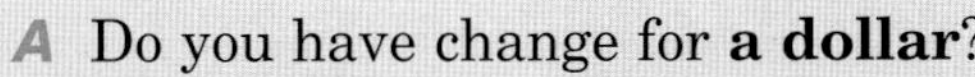
A I need **four quarters**.
B Here you are.

You can say:
a one-dollar bill OR *a dollar*
a five-dollar bill OR *five dollars*
a ten-dollar bill OR *ten dollars*

1
 = 

2
 = 

3

4

Lesson E Writing

1 Before you write

A Talk with a partner. Ask and answer questions.

1. When do you go shopping?
2. What are the names of some supermarkets in your neighborhood?
3. What do you usually buy at the supermarket?

B Read the note. Make a shopping list.

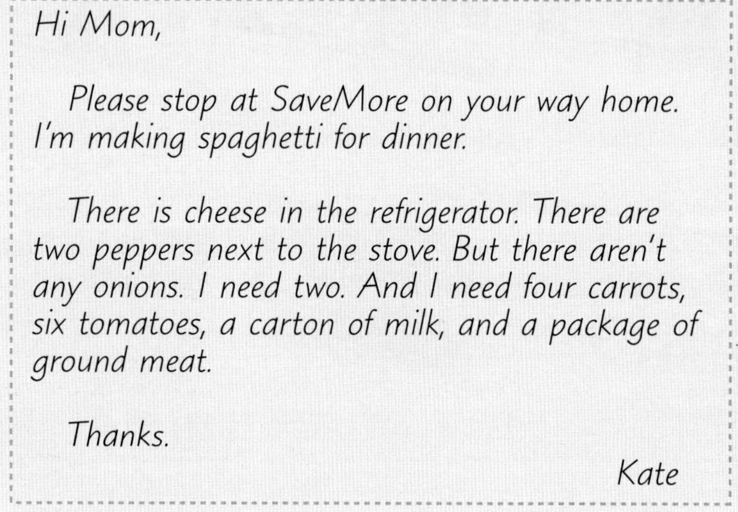

Hi Mom,

Please stop at SaveMore on your way home. I'm making spaghetti for dinner.

There is cheese in the refrigerator. There are two peppers next to the stove. But there aren't any onions. I need two. And I need four carrots, six tomatoes, a carton of milk, and a package of ground meat.

Thanks.

Kate

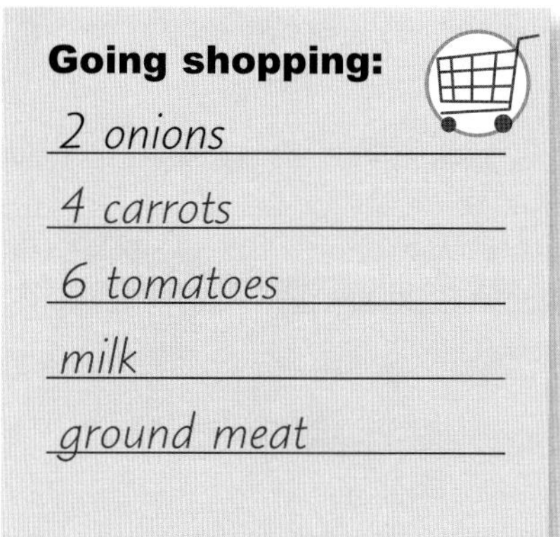

Going shopping:

2 onions
4 carrots
6 tomatoes
milk
ground meat

C Write. Look at the picture. What is she buying? Write the words.

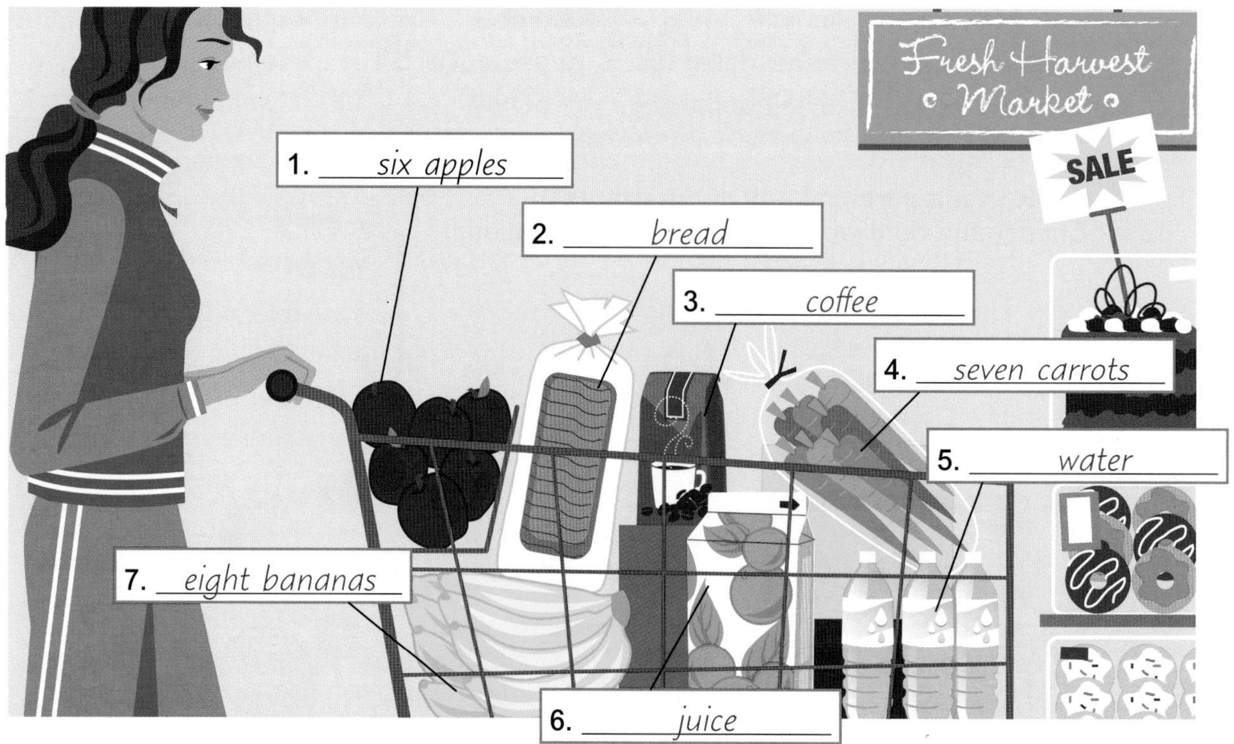

Lesson objective

- Discuss and write about shopping at the supermarket

Warm-up and review

- Before class. Write today's lesson focus on the board. *Lesson E: Write a note about food shopping*
- Begin class. Books closed. Ask Ss: *In your family, who goes grocery shopping?* Elicit appropriate responses.
- Ask: *Do you like to go grocery shopping? Why or why not?* Elicit appropriate responses.

Presentation

- Books open. Direct Ss' attention to Exercise **1A**. Read the instructions aloud.
- Ask three Ss to read the questions aloud.
- Ss complete the exercise in pairs. Encourage Ss to take notes on their partner's answers.

> **Teaching tip**
> To answer the first question, it might be helpful to refer Ss to page 74 in Unit 6 to review prepositions of time.

- Ask several pairs to ask and answer the questions for the rest of the class.

  Option Ask Ss to report their partner's responses to the class, for example: *My partner goes shopping on Saturday morning. There is only one supermarket in her neighborhood. It is SaveMore Supermarket. She usually buys milk, eggs, and rice at the supermarket.*

Practice

- Direct Ss' attention to Exercise **1B** and read the instructions aloud.
- Write *Shopping list* on the board. Point to the words. Say them aloud and ask Ss to repeat after you. Ask: *What is this?* Elicit: *It's a list of food you need to buy at the supermarket.*
- Ask: *Do you make a list before you go to the supermarket?* Elicit *Yes* or *No* answers.

  Option Encourage Ss to make their shopping lists in English to help them practice food vocabulary.
- Ask Ss to read the note silently.
- Ss in pairs. Say: *Now read the note to your partner. Then your partner will read it to you.* Walk around and help as needed.
- Direct Ss' attention to the "Going shopping" list to the right of the note. Say: *Work with your partner. Write the items that Mom needs to buy at the store.*
- Check answers with the class. Ask individual Ss to write the shopping list on the board. Ask: *Is the list correct?* Ask different Ss to make any necessary corrections to the list.
- Direct Ss' attention to the picture in Exercise **1C**. Ask: *Where is the woman?* (She is at the Fresh Harvest Market.) *What do you see?* (The woman is shopping. She is buying apples, bread, coffee, etc.)
- Read aloud the instructions for Exercise **1C**. Ask a S to read the example aloud.
- Ss complete the exercise individually. Walk around and help as needed.
- Write the numbers *1–7* on the board. Ask individual Ss to write their answers on the board. Ask: *Are the answers correct?* Ask different Ss to correct any errors.

Expansion activity *(student pairs)*

- Review *How much / How many*. Direct Ss' attention to the picture in Exercise **1C**. Ask: *How many apples is she buying?* (six)
- Ss in pairs. Say: *Ask your partner questions about the food the woman is buying. Use "How much" or "How many."*
- Ss complete the activity in pairs. Walk around and help as needed.
- Ask several pairs to ask and answer their questions for the rest of the class.

Expansion activity *(student pairs)*

- Matching exercise. Practice using amounts from page 89. Copy the following lists on the board, making two columns:

A bag of	*bread*
A bottle of	*sugar*
A box of	*meat*
A can of	*water*
A carton of	*milk*
A loaf of	*cereal*
A package of	*beans*

- Ask pairs to copy the lists into their notebooks and then match the phrases on the left with the food items on the right. Tell Ss that there may be more than one correct answer.
- When Ss finish, ask them to come to the board and draw lines connecting the items together.

Lesson E Writing

Practice

- Direct Ss' attention to Exercise **1D** and read the instructions aloud.
- Ask: *What's a comma?* If Ss don't know the word, draw a large comma on the board and point out the comma after the greeting in the note.

Read the tip box aloud. Tell Ss that when there is a comma in a sentence, it is a signal to the reader to pause. Ask several Ss to read aloud the example sentence in the tip box. Make sure they pause after each comma in the sentence.

- Ss complete the exercise individually. Walk around and help as needed.
- Ask five Ss each to write a sentence from the note on the board, adding commas correctly.
- Ask different Ss to read the sentences aloud. Ask: *Are the commas in the correct places?* Ask Ss to correct any punctuation errors on the board.
- Ask: *Do you ever write notes to people in English? What kinds of notes do you write? Who do you write the notes to?* Elicit appropriate responses.
- Say: *We are going to practice writing a note in English.*
- Direct Ss' attention to the blank notepaper in Exercise **2**. Read the instructions aloud.

Teaching tip

If Ss need help getting started with the note, tell them to use the notes on pages 92 and 93 as examples. It might also be helpful to remind Ss that they need to indent each paragraph in the note.

Comprehension check

- Read aloud the instructions for Exercise **3A**. Ss complete the exercise in pairs. Walk around and help as needed. Help with pronunciation.
- Read aloud the instructions for Exercise **3B**. This exercise asks Ss to work together to peer-correct their writing. Ask a S to read the questions aloud. Tell Ss to exchange papers and look at their partner's note for the answers to the questions. Tell Ss to circle the answers on their partner's note.
- Ss complete the exercise in pairs. Walk around and help as needed.
- Ask pairs to answer the questions about their partner's note for the class.

Learner persistence *(whole group)*

- Encourage Ss to practice writing notes or e-mails to each other in English. Tell Ss that this kind of writing practice will help to improve their English skills and will be useful in the workplace.

Expansion activity *(individual work)*

- Dictation. Tell Ss to take out a piece of paper. Dictate the following note:

  Dear Sam,
  Can you get some groceries for me?
  I need lettuce, tomatoes, and carrots.
  I need rice, beans, and a package of meat.
  I also need milk, juice, and a bottle of soda.
  Thanks so much,
  Sarah

- Ask Ss to write the note on the board when they have finished. Ask: *Are these sentences correct?* Make any necessary corrections. Be sure Ss use commas and other punctuation correctly in the note.

Evaluation

- Direct Ss' attention to the lesson focus written on the board.
- Have students reread the note about food shopping on page 92, pausing at commas.
- Check off the lesson focus as Ss demonstrate an understanding of what they have learned in the lesson.

More Ventures *(whole group, pairs, individual)*
Assign appropriate exercises from the *Teacher's Toolkit Audio CD / CD-ROM, Add Ventures,* or the *Workbook.*

D **Write.** Correct the note. Add commas.

Hi Roberto,

I'm making dinner tonight, but I need a few more groceries. I need a package of meat,an onion,a green pepper,three tomatoes, and a bag of rice. I also need a carton of milk, two bottles of apple juice,six cans of soda, and a carton of orange juice. Oh, and one more thing – a dozen eggs.

Thanks. See you tonight.

Iris

Put a comma (**,**) after each item when there is a list of three or more items.

*Please buy five oranges***,** *two apples***,** *and a peach.*

2 Write

Write a note asking someone to go shopping for you.

(Answers will vary.)

3 After you write

A **Read** your note to a partner.

B **Check** your partner's note.

- What food does your partner need?
- Are the commas correct?

Lesson F Another view

1 Life-skills reading

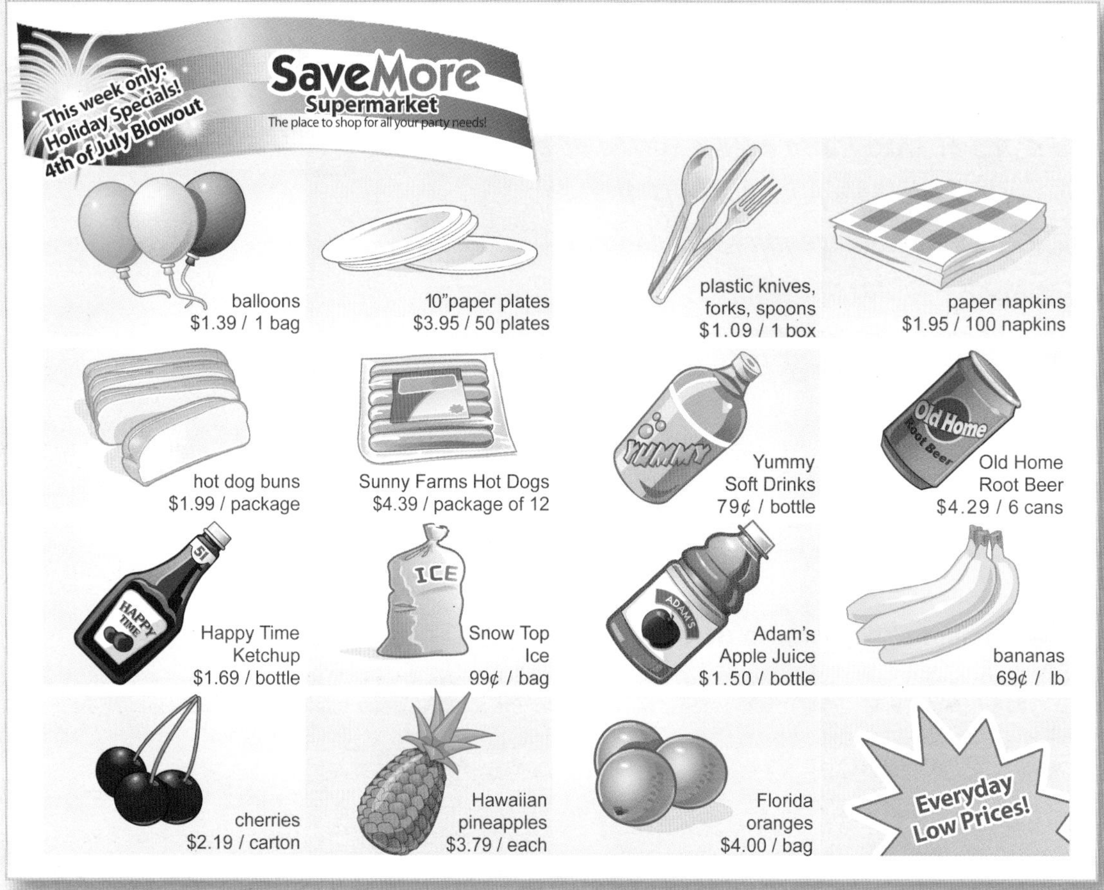

A Read the questions. Look at the ad. Circle the answers.

1. What's the name of the store?
   a. SaveMore Supermarket
   b. The Place to Shop
   c. This week only
   d. Fourth of July Blowout
2. How much are paper plates?
   a. 10¢
   b. $1.39
   c. $3.95
   d. $4.49
3. How much are Florida oranges?
   a. 50¢
   b. $1.00
   c. $2.00
   d. $4.00
4. How much are Yummy Soft Drinks?
   a. 79¢
   b. $1.19
   c. $1.58
   d. $2.37

B Talk in a group. Ask about the prices of different items in the ad.

How much are the bananas?

They're sixty-nine cents a pound.

Lesson objectives

- Practice reading a supermarket advertisement
- Learn about the food pyramid
- Review unit vocabulary; introduce the project
- Complete the self-assessment

Warm-up and review

- Before class. Write today's lesson focus on the board.
  Lesson F:
  Understand a supermarket advertisement
  Learn about the food pyramid
  Complete the self-assessment
- If possible, bring some local supermarket ads to class.
- Begin class. Books closed. Write on the board: *advertisement*. Point to the word and pronounce it. Show the supermarket ads to the class (or write *Shop at SaveMore!* on the board). Say: *These are advertisements.* Erase the last part of *advertisements* on the board, leaving the word *ad*. Say: *This is the short form. People usually say "ad" instead of "advertisement."*
- Ask: *Do you look at supermarket ads?* Elicit a *Yes* or *No* response. Ask: *Do you use supermarket ads in your countries?* Elicit a *Yes* or *No* response.

Presentation

- Books open. Direct Ss' attention to the ad in Exercise **1**. Ask: *What is this?* Elicit: *It's a supermarket ad.*

Expansion activity (whole group)

- Review the Speaking Tip on page 85. Point to each price in the ad and ask a S to read it aloud, using the two variations ($1.39 = *one thirty-nine* or *one-dollar and thirty-nine cents*).

Practice

- Direct Ss' attention to Exercise **1A** and read the instructions aloud. Be sure Ss understand the task. Have Ss individually scan for and circle the answers.
- Ask four Ss to write their answers on the board. Ask: *Are the answers correct?* Ask different Ss to make any necessary corrections on the board.

Teaching tip

This exercise is meant to prepare Ss to take standardized tests. It might be helpful to go over some test-taking skills, such as the importance of reading the questions first and scanning the ad for relevant information. Another test-taking skill would be for Ss to look at the way the questions are ordered (vertically or horizontally). This will help them in a test-taking situation where they are asked to supply their answers in a bubble-in format.

Teaching tip

It might be helpful to go over the different ways to say the price per unit. Tell Ss that if the price is for one type of container, we say *$1.39 a bag* or *$1.09 a box.* If the price is for a certain number of items, we say *$1.95 for 100 napkins* or *$1.99 for eight buns.*

- Read aloud the instructions for Exercise **1B**.
- Ask two Ss to read aloud the example question and answer.
- Ss complete the exercise in small groups. Walk around and help as needed.
- Ask group members to ask and answer the questions for the rest of the class.
- Ask: *Are the prices correct?* Ask different Ss to make any necessary corrections.

Expansion activity (small groups)

- **Materials needed** Advertisements from local supermarkets
- Write on the board:
  1. What is the name of the store?
  2. What do you want to buy? (Choose five count nouns and five non-count nouns.)
  3. How much is each item?
  4. How much is the total?
- Ss in small groups. Pass out an advertisement to each group. Ask Ss to look through the ads and answer the questions on the board.
- When Ss are finished, ask a member from each group to stand up. Other Ss ask them the questions on the board.

Expansion activity (small groups)

- Number and price practice. Direct Ss' attention to the sample ad in Exercise **1**.
- Ss in small groups. Say: *Make a shopping list. Use the items in the ad. Make sure you include multiple amounts of the items, such as two bottles of Happy Time Ketchup, three Yummy Soft Drinks, etc.*
- Tell Ss that when they are finished, they need to total the amount of money they need in order to buy the items. Then they will say their list aloud (without the total) to another group. The other group has to add up the prices, too. Ask the groups to compare their prices. Are they the same or different? Which group has the correct total price?

Lesson F Another view

Application

- Write on the board: *party*. Point to the word. Say: *Imagine that you are going to have a party. What food and drinks will you buy?* Elicit appropriate responses. Write Ss' responses on the board.
- Ask: *How much money do you think you'll need for the party?* Elicit appropriate responses. Write Ss' responses on the board.
- Direct Ss' attention to Exercise **2A**. Read the instructions aloud. Ask four Ss to read the example conversation aloud.
- Ss complete the activity in small groups. Walk around and help as needed.
- Ask one member from each group to read aloud its party shopping list.

  Option Ask each group to write its list on the board, including the total. Ask Ss to vote for their favorite list.

Teaching tip
Make sure Ss are using *How much* and *How many* correctly.

- Books closed. Draw six columns on the board with headings from the food pyramid in Exercise **2B** (*Fats, Oils, and Sweets; Dairy; Meat, Beans, and Eggs; Vegetables; Fruit; Bread, Cereal, and Rice*).
- Ask: *What are some different types of food?* As Ss respond, write their answers in the appropriate columns on the board.
- Point to the columns. Say: *These are the different categories of food in the U.S. food pyramid.*
- Books open. Direct Ss' attention to the food pyramid in Exercise **2B**. Read the instructions aloud.
- Model the task. Hold up the Student's Book. Point to the top of the pyramid. Ask: *What foods do you see in this category?* (oil, chocolate, sugar, cake) Write the words on the board.
- Ss complete the exercise in small groups. Walk around and help as needed.
- Ask Ss to read their answers aloud. Ask: *Are the answers correct?* Ask different Ss to correct any errors.

Expansion activity (student pairs)

- Recipe practice. Ask Ss to write out the ingredients and the instructions for a recipe that they like to make, and have Ss bring the recipe to class.
- Model the activity by writing on the board a simple recipe of your own. If Ss forget to bring in a recipe, or say that they never cook, ask them to make up a simple recipe in class. You could also bring in some basic cookbooks for them to look through.
- Ss in pairs. Say to one S: *Tell your partner your recipe. First, say the ingredients and then the procedure. Your partner will ask you questions, such as: How much salt is there? How many eggs do you use?* Walk around and help as needed.
- When Ss are finished, ask them to change roles.
- Ask several Ss to write their recipes on the board and explain the procedure to the rest of the class.

  Option Another way to do this activity is to ask small groups to create a recipe in class. Then one member of each group will write the recipe on the board, and another member will explain the recipe to the rest of the class.

More Ventures *(whole group, pairs, individual)*
Assign appropriate exercises from the *Teacher's Toolkit Audio CD / CD-ROM, Add Ventures,* or the *Workbook*.

Application

Community building

- **Project** Ask Ss to turn to page 139 in their Student's Book to complete the project for Unit 7.

Evaluation

- Before asking Ss to turn to the self-assessment on page 144, do a quick review of the unit. Have Ss turn to Lesson A. Ask the class to call out what they remember about this lesson. Prompt Ss, if necessary, with questions, for example: *What are the conversations about on this page? What vocabulary is in the picture?* Continue in this manner to review each lesson quickly.
- **Self-assessment** Read the instructions for Exercise **3**. Ask Ss to turn to the self-assessment page and complete the unit self-assessment.
- If Ss are ready, administer the unit test on pages T-179–T-180 of this *Teacher's Edition* (or on the *Teacher's Toolkit Audio CD / CD-ROM*). The audio and audio scripts for the test are on the *Teacher's Toolkit Audio CD / CD-ROM.*

2 Fun with language

A **Work in a group.** Read the ad on page 94. Plan a party.
You have $30.00. What do you want to buy? Make a list. Add the total.

Read your list to the class. What is the total?

B **Work in a group.** What food is in each category? Write some names.

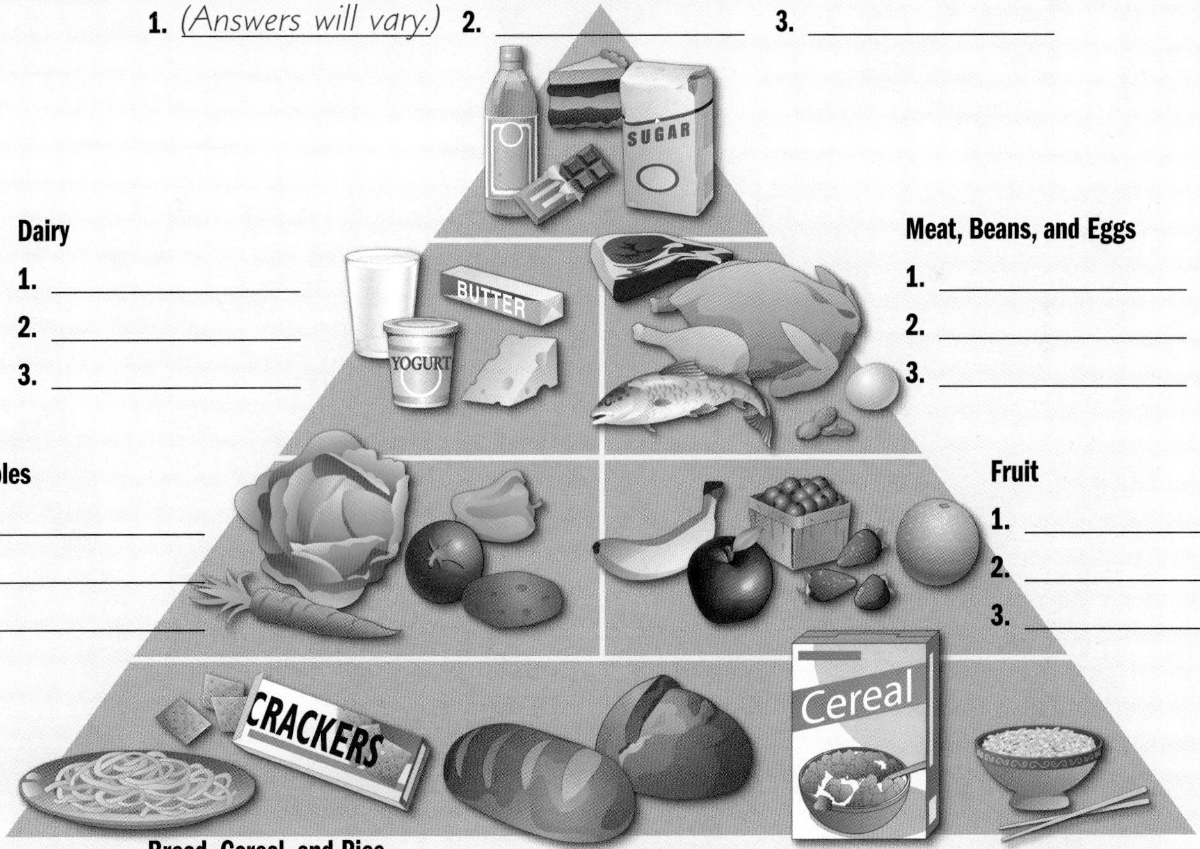

Fats, Oils, and Sweets

1. *(Answers will vary.)* 2. ________ 3. ________

Dairy

1. ________
2. ________
3. ________

Meat, Beans, and Eggs

1. ________
2. ________
3. ________

Vegetables

1. ________
2. ________
3. ________

Fruit

1. ________
2. ________
3. ________

Bread, Cereal, and Rice

1. ________ 2. ________ 3. ________

3 Wrap up

Complete the **Self-assessment** on page 144.

Work

Lesson A Get ready

1 Talk about the picture

A Look at the picture. What do you see?

B Point to: a busboy • a waiter • a construction worker • a cook
a nurse • a nursing assistant • a cashier

Lesson objectives
- Introduce students to the topic
- Find out what students know about the topic
- Preview the unit by talking about the picture
- Practice key vocabulary
- Practice listening skills

Warm-up and review

- Before class. Write today's lesson focus on the board.
  Lesson A:
  Work vocabulary
  Names of occupations
- Begin class. Books closed. Write on the board: *work*. Point to the word. Say: *Today's class is about work. What are some different kinds of jobs?* Elicit occupations and write them on the board.
- Ask Ss: *Do you work?* Elicit *Yes* or *No* answers. Ask Ss who say *Yes*: *Where do you work? What is your job or occupation?* Write Ss' responses on the board.

Presentation

- Books open. Set the scene. Direct Ss' attention to the picture on page 96. Ask: *Where is this?* (a restaurant, a café) Ask: *What do you see?* Elicit as much vocabulary about the picture as possible: *restaurant, waiter, waitress, people eating and drinking, kitchen, tables, chairs.*

Teaching tip
Do not expect Ss to know all the new vocabulary words. These questions are intended to find out what Ss already know about work vocabulary.

- Direct Ss' attention to the key words in Exercise **1B**. Read each word aloud while pointing to the corresponding person in the picture. Ask the class to repeat and point.

Teaching tip
Ss may not be familiar with some of the occupations listed at the top of the page. It might be helpful to hold up the Student's Book and point out each occupation so that the class knows which job each word is describing.

Comprehension check

- Ask Ss *Wh-* questions about the picture. Recycle questions in the present continuous. Ask:
  What is the cook doing? (He is cooking / cutting / grilling food.)
  What is the waiter doing? (He is talking to the customer. / He is working.)
  What is the waitress doing? (She is giving the customer food and a drink.)
  What is the man at the counter doing? (He is eating.)
  What is the electrician doing? (He is working. He is fixing the light.)

Option If you feel Ss need help reviewing more basic *Yes / No* questions, point to people in the picture and ask: *Is he a waiter / cook / construction worker* / etc.? Ss will give a *Yes* or *No* answer.

Practice

- Direct Ss' attention to Exercise **1B**. Model the task. Hold up the Student's Book. Say to a S: *Point to the busboy in the picture.* (The S points to the busboy.)
- Ss in pairs. Say to one S: *Say the words in Exercise 1B.* Say to his or her partner: *Point to the person in the picture.*
- Pairs complete the exercise. Help as needed. When Ss finish, have them change partners and roles.
- Ask several pairs to perform the exercise for the class to check Ss' understanding.

Expansion activity (small groups)

- Ss in small groups. Say: *Choose one of the tables in the picture on page 96. Talk about it in your group. Write three or four sentences about the table in the picture.*
- When Ss finish, ask one person from each group to read the description to the rest of the class. The class tries to guess which table is being described.

Expansion activity (student pairs)

- **Materials needed** Old magazines with pictures of people doing different jobs
- Ss in pairs. Give each pair an old magazine. Say: *Find a picture of someone working. Cut out the picture and glue it onto a piece of paper. Then write about that person. What is his or her name? What is his or her job? What is he or she doing in the picture?*
- Ss complete the activity in pairs. Walk around and help as needed.
- When Ss finish, ask them to post the pictures around the room. Ask Ss to peruse the "gallery" and read the descriptions their classmates have written.

Learner persistence (whole group)

- Ask working Ss: *What's your job? Do you speak English at your job? What are some examples of words you say at work?*
- Work with Ss to find out what types of language help they need in order to do their jobs. If Ss are struggling to speak English at work, try to arrange for them to have a tutor who can focus on specific workplace English in order to help those Ss meet their language needs at work.

Lesson A Get ready

Presentation

- Direct Ss' attention to Exercise **2A**. Read the occupations in the word bank. Ask Ss to repeat.
- Ask questions about the words in the word bank:
  What do truck drivers do? Elicit a response such as: *They drive trucks.*
  What do receptionists do? Elicit a response such as: *They answer the phone and help people.*
- Explain any unfamiliar words.

> **Teaching tip**
> Mention familiar people who have the occupations listed in the word bank. Point out the school receptionist and any other workers Ss may know.

- Direct Ss' attention to the picture on page 96 in Exercise **1**. Ask *Yes / No* questions using the vocabulary words. Say: *Listen to the questions. Answer Yes or No.*
  Is there a busboy in the picture? (Yes.)
  Is there a cashier in the picture? (Yes.)
  Is there an electrician in the picture? (Yes.)
  Is there a receptionist in the picture? (No.)
  Is there a waiter in the picture? (Yes.)
  Is there a nursing assistant in the picture? (Yes.)

Practice

- Direct Ss' attention back to Exercise **2A** and read the instructions aloud.
- [Class Audio CD2 track 23] Play or read the audio program (see audio script, page T-158). Ss listen and circle the words they hear. Repeat the audio program as needed.
- Check answers. Ask: *What did you circle?* Ask Ss to read the words aloud. Hold up the Student's Book. Point to the words that were mentioned in the audio program. Say: *Repeat after me.* Say each word.

Expansion activity (student pairs)

- Ask Ss to look at the words they did not circle. Ask a S to write them on the board: *office worker, receptionist, truck driver.*
- Ss in pairs. Say: *Write sentences with the words that you didn't hear in Exercise 2A.* Help as needed.
- Ask Ss to write their sentences on the board.
- Ask other Ss to read the sentences aloud.

Practice

- Direct Ss' attention to Exercise **2B** and read the instructions aloud. Tell Ss: *Listen to conversation A.*
- [Class Audio CD2 track 23] Play or read the first conversation only on the audio program.
- Ask Ss: *Which picture matches conversation A?* (picture number 2) After Ss respond, hold up the Student's Book. Point to the handwritten *a* next to number 2.
- [Class Audio CD2 track 23] Play or read the complete audio program. Ss complete the exercise individually.

Learner persistence (individual work)

- [Self-Study Audio CD track 30] Exercises **2A** and **2B** are recorded on the Ss' self-study CD at the back of the Student's Book. Ss can listen to the CD at home for reinforcement and review. They can also listen for self-directed learning when class attendance is not possible.

Comprehension check

- Write the numbers *1–6* on the board. Ask individual Ss to come to the board and write the correct answers to Exercise **2B** next to each number.
- Read aloud the second part of the instructions for Exercise **2B**.
- [Class Audio CD2 track 23] Play or read the audio program again. Pause the audio program after each conversation. Point to a letter of the conversation on the board. Ask: *Is this correct?* Make corrections on the board.

Application

- Books closed. Ask Ss: *What are some places that people can work?* Elicit examples such as: *restaurant, hospital.*
- Ask working Ss: *Where do you work?* Elicit responses.
- Books open. Direct Ss' attention to Exercise **2C**.
- Hold up the Student's Book. Point to the words in the word bank. Say each word. Ask Ss to repeat.
- Read aloud the instructions for Exercise **2C**.
- Hold up the Student's Book. Point to the hospital sign. Ask a S to read the example aloud.
- Ss complete the exercise individually. Help as needed.
- Write the numbers *1–6* on the board. Ask Ss to write their answers on the board.

Evaluation

- Direct Ss' attention to the lesson focus on the board. Ask Ss to identify the occupations in the pictures on pages 96 and 97.
- Check off the lesson focus as Ss demonstrate understanding of what they have learned in the lesson.

> ***More Ventures*** (whole group, pairs, individual)
> Assign appropriate exercises from the *Teacher's Toolkit Audio CD / CD-ROM, Add Ventures,* or the *Workbook.*

2 Listening

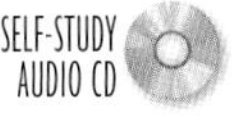

SELF-STUDY AUDIO CD **A** **Listen.** Circle the words you hear.

busboy	electrician	receptionist
cashier	nurse	truck driver
doctor	office worker	waitress

SELF-STUDY AUDIO CD **B** **Listen again.** Write the letter of the conversation.

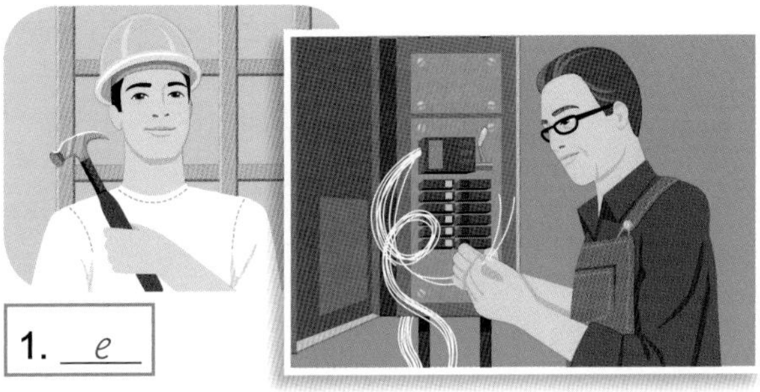

1. e

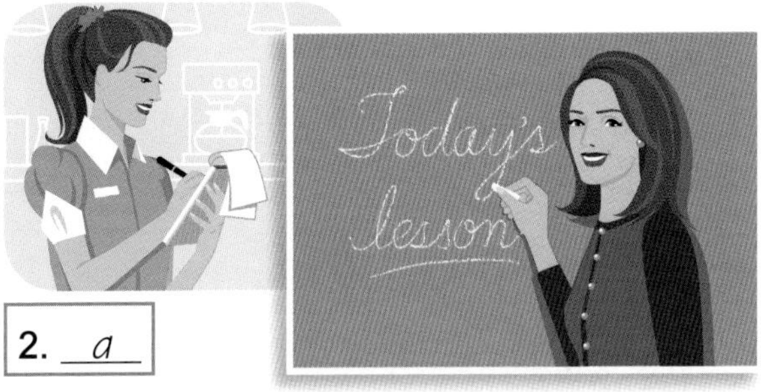

2. a

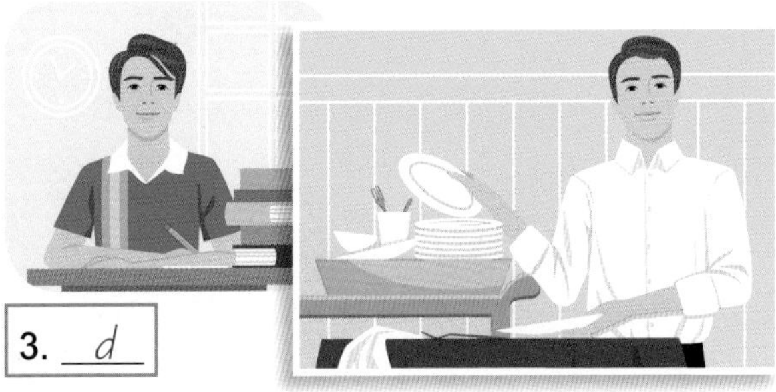

3. d

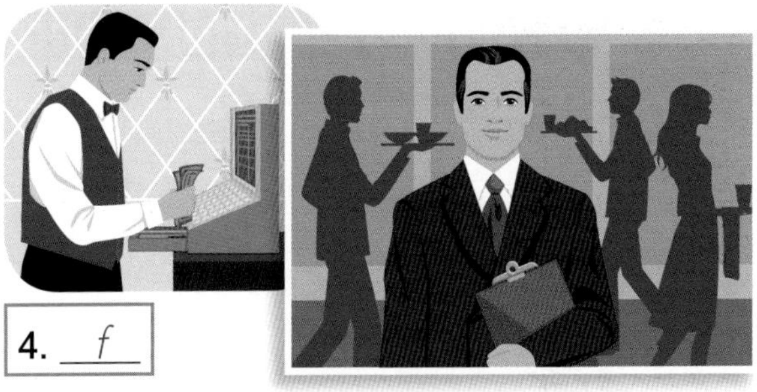

4. f

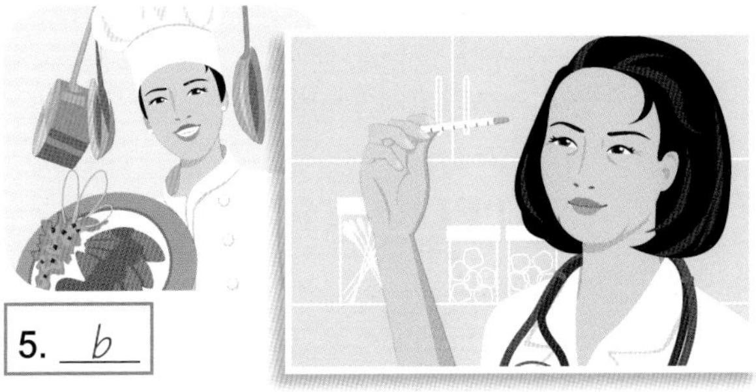

5. b

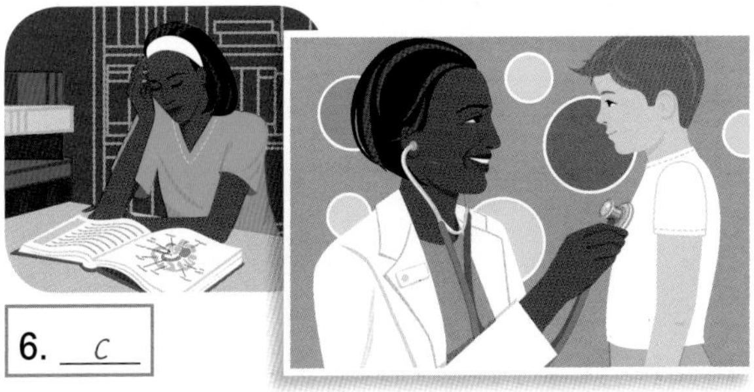

6. c

Listen again. Check your answers.

C **Write.** Where do the people work? Write the words.

busboy cashier doctor nurse receptionist waiter

1. doctor
2. nurse
3. receptionist

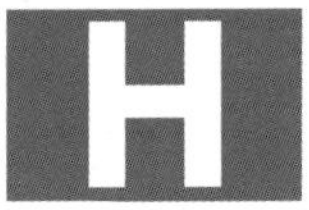

hospital

4. busboy
5. cashier
6. waiter

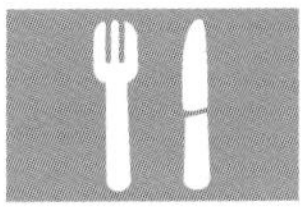

restaurant

Lesson B

I was a teacher.

1 Grammar focus: simple past of *be*

Questions		
Were	you	a student?
Was	he	a student?
Was	she	a student?
Were	they	students?

Answers			
Yes,	I was.	No,	I wasn't. I was a teacher.
	he was.		he wasn't. He was a teacher.
	she was.		she wasn't. She was a teacher.
	they were.		they weren't. They were teachers.

wasn't = was not   weren't = were not

2 Practice

A Write. Look at the pictures. Complete the sentences. Use *is*, *are*, *was*, or *were*.

JOB APPLICATION FORM

Name: Amy Cho

Job History:

2006–Present Nurse

2000–2006 Teacher

1. She ___was___ a teacher before.
   Now she ___is___ a nurse.

2. She ___is___ a manager now.
   She ___was___ a cashier before.

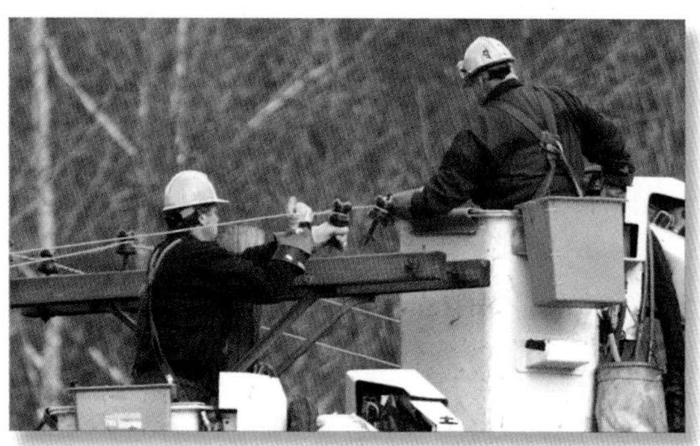

3. They ___were___ students before.
   Now they ___are___ electricians.

APPLICATION FORM

Name: BEN LIAO

Job History:

2006–PRESENT CONSTRUCTION WORKER

2004–2006 WAITER

4. He ___was___ a waiter before.
   Now he ___is___ a construction worker.

Listen and repeat.

Lesson objective

- Introduce the simple past of *be*

Warm-up and review

- Before class. Write today's lesson focus on the board.
  Lesson B:
  The simple past of be:
  was / wasn't
  were / weren't
- Begin class. Books closed. Draw a time line on the board.
  2001 ←——————→ *now*
  student *teacher*
- Point to *student* and *2001*. Say: *I was a student in 2001.* Point to *teacher* and *now*. Say: *I'm a teacher now.* (Modify the information to make it accurate about yourself, or speak about a fictitious third person: *Betty was a student in 2001. She's a teacher now.*)
- Write the sentences on the board. Read them aloud and ask Ss to repeat.
- Ask: *What about you?* Go around the room. Ask Ss to make sentences about their past and present occupations, for example: *I was a _____ in* (year). *I am a _____ now.*

Teaching tip

Ask Ss to draw a simple time line similar to the one on the board. Tell them to include a date in the past and the present year. Then ask them to write a sentence describing the time line.

Presentation

- Books open. Direct Ss' attention to the grammar chart in Exercise **1**. Read the questions and answers aloud. Ask Ss to repeat.
- Direct Ss' attention to the contractions *wasn't* and *weren't*. Say: *These are contractions.* Say the contractions and the corresponding long forms. Ask Ss to repeat them.

Practice

- Direct Ss' attention to Exercise **2A** and point to number 1. Ask: *Who is applying for a job?* (Amy Cho)
- Point to the last line of the job application form and ask: *What was Amy Cho's job from 2000 to 2006?* Ask a S to read the two example answers aloud.
- Read the instructions aloud. Be sure students understand the task.
- Ss complete the sentences individually. Walk around and help as needed.

Comprehension check

- [Class Audio CD2 track 24] Read aloud the second part of the instructions for Exercise **2A**. Play or read the audio program (see audio script, page T-158). Have Ss check their answers as they listen and repeat. Correct pronunciation as needed.
- Ask Ss to come to the board and write the sentences. Ask different Ss to read the sentences aloud. Ask Ss to make any necessary corrections on the board.

Expansion activity (whole group)

- **Materials needed** Index cards
- Memory game. Give each S an index card. Say: *Write an occupation on your card. It can be a job that you have had in the past, or any job.* Model the activity by writing *waiter* or *waitress* on an index card.
- Ss in a circle. Model the exercise by holding up your card and saying: *I was a waiter / waitress.* Encourage the S to your right to do the same. Go around the circle until everyone has had a chance to show his or her card and to name a past job.
- Write on the board:
  He / She was . . .
  You were . . .
  I was . . .
- Sit in the circle again. Describe the S to your left, by saying: *He / She was a* (name of job). Then describe the S to your right by saying to him or her: *You were a* (name of job). Then describe yourself by saying: *I was a* (name of job). Encourage the student on your right to do the same. Go around the circle until everyone has had a chance to speak.

Expansion activity (whole group)

- If you want to expand the grammar presentation, turn to the grammar charts at the back of the Student's Book. Practice making sentences using the simple past of *be* and the pronouns *we, you* (plural), *it*.

Lesson B *I was a teacher.*

Presentation

- Direct Ss' attention to the pictures in Exercise **2B**. Ask: *Are these pictures of people today? When were these pictures taken?* Hold up the Student's Book. Point to the first picture. Ask: *What was her occupation?* Elicit: *She was a teacher.* Ask: *When?* Make sure Ss understand that she was a teacher in the past.
- Continue by asking about the rest of the pictures:
  What were their occupations? (They were nurses.)
  What was his occupation? (He was a waiter.)
  What were their occupations? (They were doctors.)
  What was his occupation? (He was a cook.)
  What was her occupation? (She was a cashier.)
- Read the instructions aloud. Ask two Ss to read the example conversations aloud.
- Ss complete the exercise in pairs. Walk around and help as needed.
- Ask several pairs to perform their conversations for the class.

Application

- Books closed. Model different ways of asking someone about his or her job. Ask a S: *What's your job?* Elicit: *I'm a _____.*
- Ask another S: *What do you do?* Elicit: *I'm a _____.*
- Ask another S: *What's your occupation?* Elicit: *I'm a _____.*

Teaching tip
It might be helpful to teach Ss a few other occupations, including housewife or stay-at-home parent. Encourage students to look up their past jobs in a bilingual dictionary if they don't know how to say an occupation in English. Encourage nonworking Ss to say: *I am a student* or *I am a housewife* or *I stay at home with my children* or *I'm looking for a job.*

Useful language
Books open. Read the tip box aloud. Ask Ss to repeat the three questions after you. Tell Ss that the questions all have the same meaning.

- Direct Ss' attention to Exercise **3**. Read the instructions aloud. Model the example with a S. The S speaks first.
- Point out the chart below the conversation. Ask a S: *What's the name of the person in the conversation?* Elicit: *Sylvia.* Ask another S: *What's her job?* Elicit: *She's a housewife.* Ask another S: *What was her job before?* Elicit: *She was a receptionist.*
- In groups of four, Ss complete the chart with information about themselves. Walk around and help as needed.
- Read aloud the second part of the instructions for Exercise **3**.
- Ask a S to read the example sentences. As the S reads, hold up the Student's Book and point to the key words in the chart.
- Ss complete the exercise individually. Walk around and help as needed.
- Ask each S to tell you about another student. Elicit appropriate responses.

Expansion activity (small groups)

- **Materials needed** Index cards
- Ss in small groups. Give each group two piles of index cards – six in one pile and ten in the other. Ask Ss to write the subject pronouns on the first set of cards: *I, you, he, she, we,* and *they* (also write these on the board as a reference). Ask Ss to write the names of occupations on a separate set of cards: *truck driver(s), nurse(s), manager(s), office worker(s), electrician(s), student(s), gardener(s), construction worker(s), cashier(s),* and *cook(s).* Tell the groups to keep the two piles separate.
- Model the activity by choosing one card from each pile and making a sentence about yourself or the students, for example: *He wasn't a gardener.* Point to the S to whom you are referring.
- Ask Ss to choose one card from each pile and make a sentence about themselves or their classmates. Repeat the task until everyone has had a chance to make a sentence.

Evaluation

- Direct Ss' attention to the lesson focus written on the board. Elicit affirmative and negative statements using *was* and *were,* for example: *I was a taxi driver. He wasn't a truck driver. They were cooks.*
- Have Ss ask their classmates questions using *Was* and *Were* (*Was he a teacher? Were you a nurse?*) Ask other Ss to answer the questions.
- Check off the items as Ss demonstrate understanding of what they have learned in the lesson.

More Ventures *(whole group, pairs, individual)*
Assign appropriate exercises from the *Teacher's Toolkit Audio CD / CD-ROM, Add Ventures,* or the *Workbook.*

B Talk with a partner. Look at the pictures. Change the **bold** words and make conversations.

1. *A* Was **she a teacher**?
   B Yes, **she** was.

2. *A* Were they **receptionists**?
   B No, they weren't. They were **nurses**.

1. a teacher?

2. receptionists?

3. waiter?

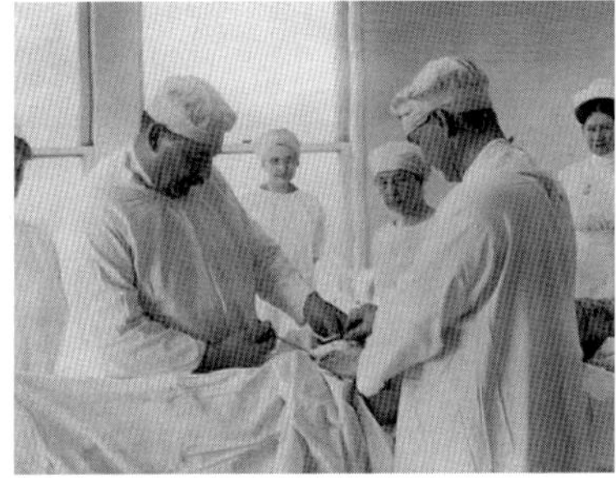

4. electricians?

5. a cook?

6. a cashier?

3 Communicate

Talk with three classmates. Complete the chart.

A Sylvia, what do you do now?
B Now? I'm a housewife.
A Oh, really? Were you a housewife before?
B No, I wasn't. I was a receptionist in a bank.

Useful language

In conversation, *What do you do?* means *What's your job?* OR *What's your occupation?*

Name	Job now	Job before
Sylvia	*a housewife*	*a receptionist*
(Answers will vary.)		

Write two sentences about your classmates. Use information from the chart.

Sylvia is a housewife now. She was a receptionist before.

Lesson C Can you cook?

1 Grammar focus: *can*

Statements			Questions			Answers					
I He She They	can	cook.	Can	you he she they	cook?	Yes,	I he she they	can.	No,	I he she they	can't.

can't = cannot

2 Practice

A Write. Complete the sentences. Use *yes*, *no*, *can*, or *can't*.

1

A Can she speak Spanish?
B Yes, she can.

2

A Can he drive a truck?
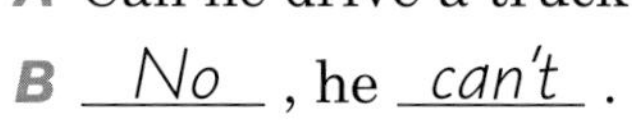
B No, he can't.

3

A Can he fix a car?
B Yes, he can.

4

A Can she paint a house?
B No, she can't.

5

A Can they work with computers?
B No, they can't.

6

A Can you cook?
B Yes, I can.

Listen and repeat. Then practice with a partner.

Lesson objective
- Introduce *can*

Warm-up and review

- Before class. Write today's lesson focus on the board.
  Lesson C: Use "can" to talk about ability
- Begin class. Books closed. Ask Ss: *Can someone in this class play the piano?* If someone in your class answers *Yes,* write a sentence on the board about that person: (Name of S) *can play the piano.*
- Ask: *Can someone in this class play another musical instrument?* If someone in your class answers *Yes,* write a sentence about that S on the board.
- Ask: *Can someone in this class cook Chinese food?* Elicit a negative answer and write a *can't* sentence on the board: (Name of S) *can't cook Chinese food.*
- Ask a S: *Can you drive a car?* Elicit: *Yes* or *No.* Write on the board:
  Can you drive a car?
  Yes, I can. or *No, I can't.*
- Read aloud what you've written on the board. Ask Ss to repeat after you.

Presentation

- Books open. Direct Ss' attention to the grammar chart in Exercise **1**. Read each section aloud. Ask Ss to repeat after you.

Contractions
Focus Ss' attention on the contraction *can't.* Say: *"Can't" is the same as "cannot." It is a contraction.*

- Ss in pairs. Have students practice reading the grammar chart to each other while pointing to an appropriate person (or persons) in the class (*I, You, He, She, They*).

Expansion activity (whole group)

- Write on the board: *Can you _____?*
- Point to the question on the board. Ask: *What questions can you ask your classmates?* Elicit verbs such as *cook, paint, sing,* etc. Write the verbs under the blank on the board.
- Ask two Ss to stand up. Say to one S: *Ask your classmate one of the questions on the board.* Elicit the correct short answer form *Yes, I can* or *No, I can't.* Repeat with a few more pairs of Ss.

Practice

- Direct Ss' attention to the pictures in Exercise **2A**. Hold up the Student's Book. Point to each picture. Ask: *What's happening?* Elicit responses such as: *The teacher is writing on the board; the boy is holding the keys; the man is fixing a car; the girl is walking; the cats are playing; the food is on the counter.*

  Option If you feel that this warm-up question will be too challenging, ask: *What do you see?* Accept single-word answers as Ss point out the items they see in the pictures.
- Read the instructions aloud. Ask two Ss to read aloud the example questions and answers.
- Ss complete the exercise individually. Walk around and help as needed.
- Check answers with the class. Ask Ss to write their answers on the board. Ask different Ss to read the answers aloud. Ask other Ss to make any necessary corrections on the board.

Comprehension check

- Read aloud the second part of the instructions for Exercise **2A**.
- [Class Audio CD2 track 25] Play or read the audio program (see audio script, page T-158). Listen to Ss' pronunciation as they repeat the conversations. Correct pronunciation as needed.
- Ss practice the conversations in pairs. Walk around and help as needed.
- Ask several pairs to read the conversations for the rest of the class.

Expansion activity (small groups)

- Question-and-answer practice. Ss in groups of four to six. Write a checklist on the board using the skills in Exercise **2A**, or elicit other skills from the class, for example:
  ☐ *Speak Spanish?* ☐ *Paint a house?*
  ☐ *Drive a truck?* ☐ *Use a computer?*
  ☐ *Fix a car?* ☐ *Cook?*
- Model the activity by asking a S: *Can you speak Spanish?* Elicit: *Yes, I can* or *No, I can't.* Write on the board: (Name of S) *can / can't speak Spanish.*
- Have Ss ask their classmates questions. Encourage them to write complete sentences based on the answers they receive.
- Check answers with the class. Ask each S to tell the class about a group member, for example: *Tell me about* (name of S).

Expansion activity (whole group)

- If you want to expand the grammar presentation, turn to the grammar charts at the back of the Student's Book. Practice making sentences using *can* and the pronouns *we, you* (plural), *it.*

Lesson C Can you cook?

Presentation

- Books closed. Write on the board: *A teacher can* _____. Elicit possible answers and write them on the board, for example: *teach English, give homework.*
- Write on the board: *A student can* _____. Elicit possible answers and write them on the board, for example: *study, learn, go to school.*
- Books open. Direct Ss' attention to Exercise **2B**. Read aloud the words in the word bank and ask Ss to repeat.
- Explain any new words to Ss.
- Focus Ss' attention on the first picture. Ask: *What's his job?* Elicit: *He's a painter.* Ask: *Can he fix cars in his job?* Elicit: *No, he can't.* Ask: *Can he make food in his job?* Elicit: *No, he can't.* Ask: *Can he paint?* Elicit: *Yes, he can.*
- Read the instructions aloud. Ask a S to read aloud the example. Point to where *paint* is written on the blank.
- Ss complete the exercise individually. Help as needed.
- Check answers with the class. Ask Ss to write their sentences on the board. Ask different Ss to read the sentences aloud. Ask other Ss to make any necessary corrections on the board.
- Read aloud the second part of the instructions for Exercise **2B**.
- [Class Audio CD2 track 26] Play or read the audio program (see audio script, page T-159). Listen to Ss' pronunciation as they repeat the sentences. Correct pronunciation as needed.

Application

- Write on the board: *I'm looking for a job.* Point to the sentence and read it aloud. Ask Ss to repeat after you.
- Ask: *What does this mean?* If Ss don't know, say: *It means you need a job. You don't have a job, but you want one.*
- Direct Ss' attention to Exercise **2C**. Read the instructions.
- Ask two Ss to read the example conversation aloud.
- Ss complete the exercise in pairs. Help as needed.
- Ask pairs to perform their conversations for the class.

Expansion activity (whole group)

- Guessing game. Write on the board the occupations from Exercise **2B**. Elicit other occupations from Ss and write them on the board.
- Invite a S to the front of the class. Write one of the occupations on a piece of paper and show it to the S without letting anyone else see what you have written. Say: *Imagine that this is your job.*
- Model the activity by asking the S about his or her job: *Can you fix cars?* Elicit: *Yes I can* or *No, I can't.*
- Invite Ss to ask *Yes / No* questions until they can guess the occupation. When a S guesses correctly, invite him or her to the front of the room. Continue the game by showing the new S a different occupation and eliciting *Yes / No* questions about the job from the class. If Ss are having trouble guessing, ask a helpful *Yes / No* question as a clue.
- Repeat until all the occupations have been chosen.

Application

- Read aloud the instructions for Exercise **3**. Ask two Ss to ask and answer the sample question aloud.
- Ss complete the exercise in pairs. Help as needed.
- Ask pairs to ask and answer the question for the rest of the class.

Expansion activity (whole group)

- Expand on Exercise **3** by asking Ss to stand up and ask classmates about their skills and abilities. Explain that they need to find other Ss who can do the same things that they can do.
- After they have finished asking the questions, ask Ss to talk to the rest of the class about their shared abilities, for example: *We can speak Spanish. We can type. We can work with computers.*

Evaluation

- Direct Ss' attention to the lesson focus on the board.
- Guide Ss to look carefully at the picture on page 96. Ask: *What can the people in the picture do?* Elicit answers such as: *The electrician can fix the lights. The cook can make lunch. The cashier can take money.*
- Check off the lesson focus as Ss demonstrate understanding of what they have learned in the lesson.

More Ventures (whole group, pairs, individual)
Assign appropriate exercises from the *Teacher's Toolkit Audio CD / CD-ROM, Add Ventures,* or the *Workbook.*

B **Write.** Look at the pictures. Complete the sentences.

build things	paint	take care of children
fix cars	sell	take care of plants

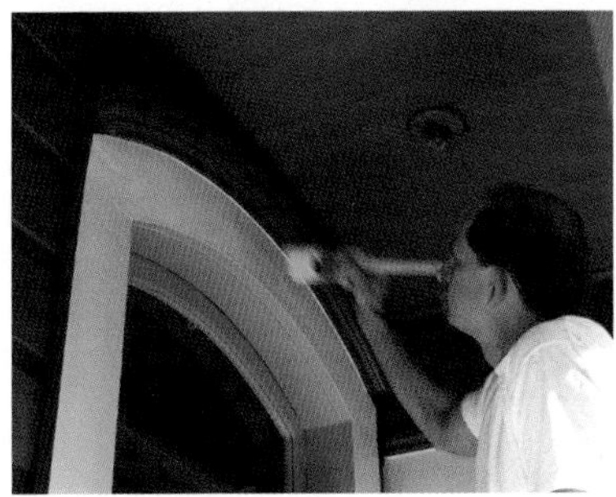

1. A painter can *paint*.

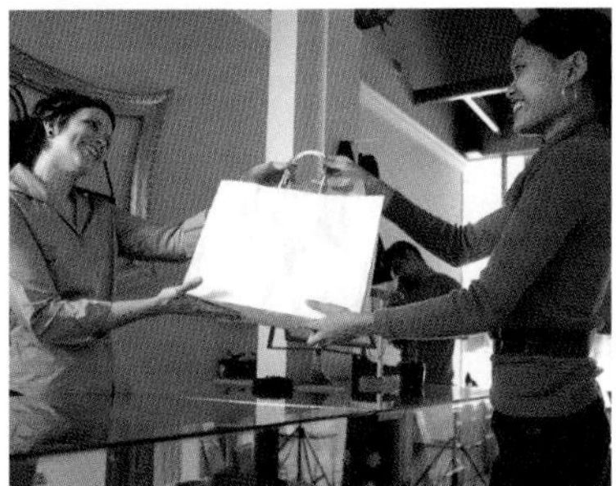

2. A salesperson can *sell*.

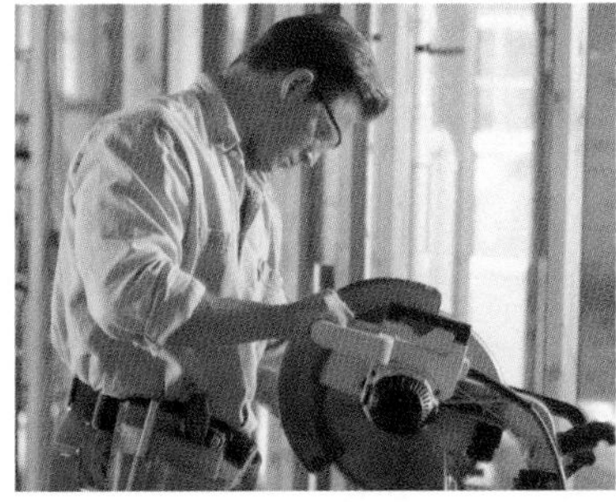

3. A carpenter can *build things*.

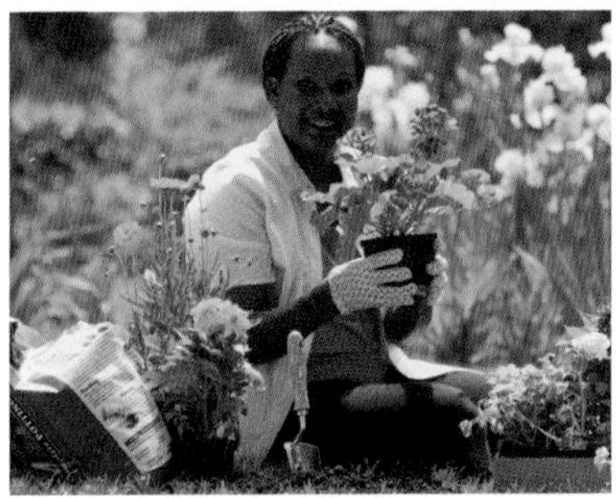

4. A gardener can *take care of plants*.

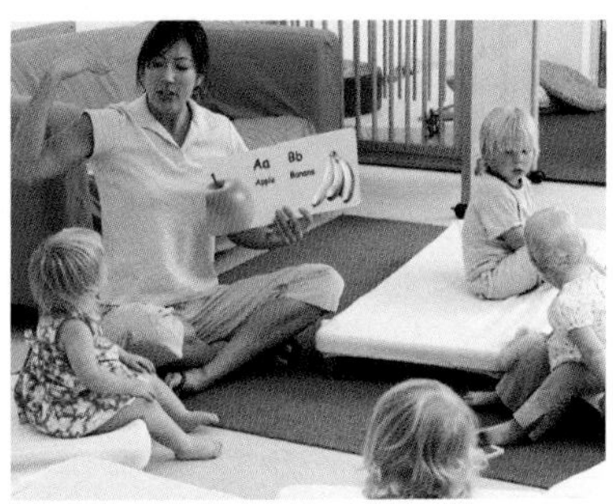

5. A child-care worker can *take care of children*.

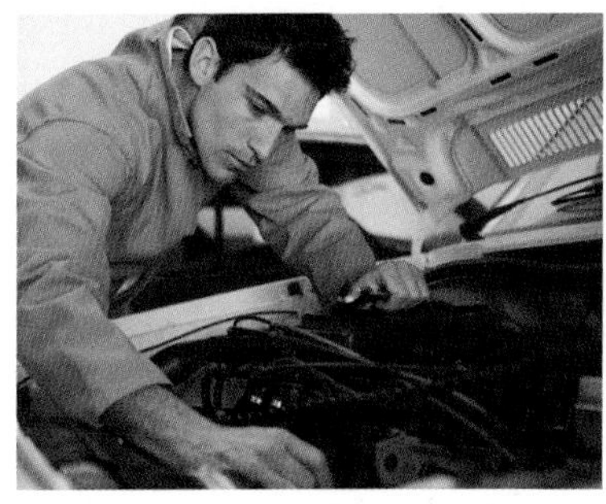

6. An auto mechanic can *fix cars*.

Listen and repeat.

C **Talk** with a partner. Look at the pictures in Exercise B. Change the **bold** words and make conversations.

A Hi. I'm looking for a job. Can you help me?
B What can you do?
A I'm **a painter**. I can **paint** very well.

3 Communicate

Talk with a partner. Ask and answer questions.

What can you do?

I can cook. I can work with computers.

Lesson D **Reading**

1 Before you read

Talk. Mai Linh is looking for a new job. Look at the picture. Answer the questions.

1. Who are the people in the picture?
2. Where are they?
3. What is Mai Linh's volunteer job now?

2 Read

 **Listen and read.**

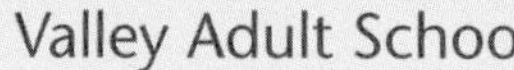

Dear Ms. Carter:

I am writing this letter to recommend my student Mai Linh Lam.

Mai Linh was a teacher in Vietnam. She is looking for a new job in the United States. She is a certified nursing assistant now. She volunteers in a nursing home Monday through Friday from 8:30 to 4:30. She takes care of senior citizens.

Mai has many good work skills. She can write reports. She can help elderly people move around and sit down. She can help them eat. She can also speak English and Vietnamese. These skills are useful in her job, and she is very good at her work.

Sincerely,
Elaine Maxwell

Verb forms can tell you if something happened in the past or is happening now.
*Mai Linh **was** a teacher in Vietnam.*
*She **is looking** for a new job.*

3 After you read

A Read the sentences. Are they correct? Circle *Yes* or *No*.

1. Mai Linh is looking for a job in Vietnam. Yes (No)
2. She volunteers in a hospital. Yes (No)
3. She can write reports. (Yes) No
4. She finishes work at 8:30. Yes (No)
5. She is good at her job. (Yes) No

Write. Correct the sentences.

1. *Mai Linh is looking for a job in the United States.*

B Write. Answer the questions about Mai Linh.

1. What was Mai Linh's job before? *a teacher*
2. Is Mai Linh certified? *Yes, she is.*
3. What are her work skills? *write reports, help elderly people, speak two languages.*

Culture note

For some jobs, you need a certificate. You have to take a test to get the certificate. *I'm certified* means *I have a certificate.*

Lesson objectives
- Introduce and read a letter of recommendation
- Practice using new topic-related words

Warm-up and review

- Before class. Write today's lesson focus on the board.
  Lesson D:
  Read a letter about Mai Linh Lam
  Learn new vocabulary: occupations and workplaces
- Begin class. Books closed. Ask: *Are any of you looking for a job?* Elicit *Yes* or *No* responses.
- Write on the board: *How can you get a job?* Read the question to the class. Write Ss' responses on the board. If Ss don't know how to answer the question, help them by writing these ideas on the board.
  Look at the job ads in the newspaper
  Look at ads on the bulletin board
  Answer an ad in a store (Help Wanted)
  Ask a friend to recommend you
  Look on the Internet
- Ask individual Ss to read the suggestions on the board.
- Write *recommend* on the board. Ask: *What does this mean?* (It means that someone will say you are a good worker.)

Presentation

- Books open. Have Ss' look at Exercise **1**. Read the instructions. Ask: *Who are the people in the picture?* (Mai Linh and a man) *Where are they?* (Harmon Hills Nursing Home) *What is a nursing home?* (It is where older people live.) *What is Mai Linh's volunteer job now?* (She takes care of senior citizens.)

Culture note
You may want to ask Ss if they are familiar with nursing homes. Nursing homes are not common in many cultures. It might be interesting to ask Ss how elderly people live in their countries. You can also ask if any of your Ss work or have ever worked in a nursing home.

- Direct Ss' attention to Exercise **2** and read the instructions aloud.
- Say: *You are going to read a letter of recommendation. Remember that "recommend" means to say someone is a good person for a job.*
- [Class Audio CD2 track 27] Play or read the audio program (see audio script, page T-159). Repeat as needed.
- Identify and explain any words Ss don't understand. Then have Ss reread the letter silently.
- Ask Ss to read the letter aloud. Each S will read a sentence in turn.
- Hold up the Student's Book. Point to the word *certified.* Direct Ss' attention to the culture note near the bottom of the page.

Culture tip
Read the culture note aloud. Ask Ss if they are certified in anything. Give examples of jobs that require certification, such as nursing assistant and teacher.

Read the tip box aloud. Remind Ss that *was* and *were* are the past tense, and *is* and *are* are the present tense. It might be helpful to ask Ss to underline the different forms of *to be* in the letter.

Learner persistence (individual work)

- [Self-Study Audio CD track 31] Exercise **2** is recorded on the Ss' self-study CD at the back of the Student's Book. Ss can listen to the CD at home for reinforcement and review. They can also listen to the CD for self-directed learning when class attendance is not possible.

Comprehension check

- Read aloud the instructions for Exercise **3A**. Ask a S to read the example aloud.
- Ask: *Is Mai Linh looking for a job in Vietnam?* (No, she is looking for a new job in the United States.) Point to where *No* is circled for number 1. Be sure Ss understand the task.
- Ss complete the exercise individually. Help as needed.
- Check answers with the class. Ask Ss to read aloud their sentences and answers.
- Ask Ss to take out a piece of paper. Read the second part of the instructions for Exercise **3A**.
- Model the task of correcting the sentences. Point to *No* for number 1 in Exercise **3A**. Read the sentence aloud. Tell Ss: *This sentence is incorrect. Tell me the correct sentence. Mai Linh is looking for a job in . . .* (the United States). Write on the board: *Mai Linh is looking for a job in the United States.*
- Ss complete the exercise individually. Help as needed.
- Check answers with the class. Ask Ss to write their answers on the board. Ask different Ss to read the answers aloud.

Practice

- Read aloud the instructions for Exercise **3B**.
- Ss complete the exercise individually. Help as needed.
- Check answers with the class. Ask Ss to read their questions and answers aloud.

Lesson D Reading

Warm-up and review

- Books closed. Write on the board: *occupations*. Ask: *What are the names of some occupations?* Write Ss' responses on the board. Elicit the names of occupations learned in this unit and other occupations Ss may know.
- Point to each occupation written on the board. Say the word aloud and ask Ss to repeat after you.

> **Teaching tip**
> Bring in pictures of different occupations from magazines. Try to include the occupations learned in this unit.

Presentation

- Books open. Direct Ss' attention to the pictures in Exercise **4**. Ask: *What are these people doing?* Elicit as much vocabulary as possible, for example: *working, cutting hair, cleaning teeth.*
- Direct Ss' attention to the word bank in Exercise **4A**. Say: *Repeat the words after me.* Say each word. Listen to Ss' pronunciation as they repeat. Correct as needed.
- Say: *Write the words in the picture dictionary.* Point to the first example. Be sure Ss understand the task.
- Ss complete the exercise individually. Walk around and help as needed.

Comprehension check

- [Class Audio CD2 track 28] Play or read the audio program (see audio script, page T-159). Ss should check their answers and repeat the words after they hear them. Repeat the audio if necessary.

Learner persistence *(individual work)*

- [Self-Study Audio CD track 32] Exercise **4A** is recorded on the Ss' self-study CD at the back of the Student's Book. Ss can listen to the CD at home for reinforcement and review. They can also listen for self-directed learning when class attendance is not possible.

Practice

- Direct Ss' attention to the occupations written on the board during the warm-up activity. Point to each occupation. Ask: *Where does this person work?* (For example: *Where does a doctor work? He / She works in a hospital.*)
- Focus Ss' attention on the workplaces listed in Exercise **4B**. Read the words aloud. Ask Ss to repeat after you.

> **Teaching tip**
> Ask Ss if they work in the places listed in this exercise.

- Read the instructions aloud.
- Ss complete the exercise in pairs. Help as needed.
- Write the numbers *1–6* on the board. Ask individual Ss to come to the board to write their answers. Ask different Ss to read the answers.

Practice

- Read aloud the second part of the instructions for Exercise **4B**.
- Model the task. Hold up the Student's Book. Point to one of the pictures in the picture dictionary. Ask two Ss the questions at the bottom of the page.
- Ss complete the exercise in pairs. Help as needed.
- Ask pairs to ask and answer the questions for the class.

Expansion activity *(small groups)*

- **Materials needed** Two sets of index cards (six cards in each set) for each small group of Ss
- Memory game. Ss in small groups. Give each group two sets of six index cards. Ask each group to write the occupations and workplaces from Exercise **4B** on the two sets of cards.
- Tell Ss to shuffle each set of cards and spread the cards face down on a desk or table in neat rows.
- Each S in the group takes turns turning over two cards. If the S turns over an occupation and a workplace that match, he or she can take the cards and continue trying to make a new match.
- The game ends when all matches have been made. The player with the most matches wins the game.

Evaluation

- Direct Ss' attention to the lesson focus on the board.
- Put a check next to *Read a letter about Mai Linh Lam.*
- Focus Ss' attention on page 103. Ask Ss to make sentences about the occupations and workplaces of the people in the picture dictionary.
- Check off each part of the lesson focus as Ss demonstrate understanding of what they have learned in the lesson.

> ***More Ventures*** *(whole group, pairs, individual)*
> Assign appropriate exercises from the *Teacher's Toolkit Audio CD / CD-ROM, Add Ventures,* or the *Workbook.*

4 Picture dictionary Occupations

1. *housekeeper*

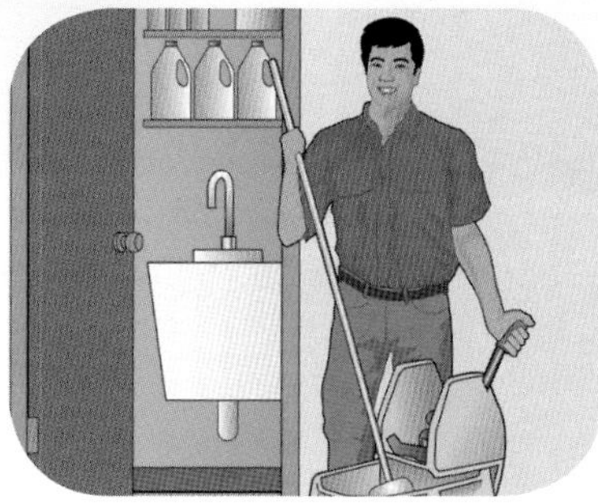

2. *custodian*

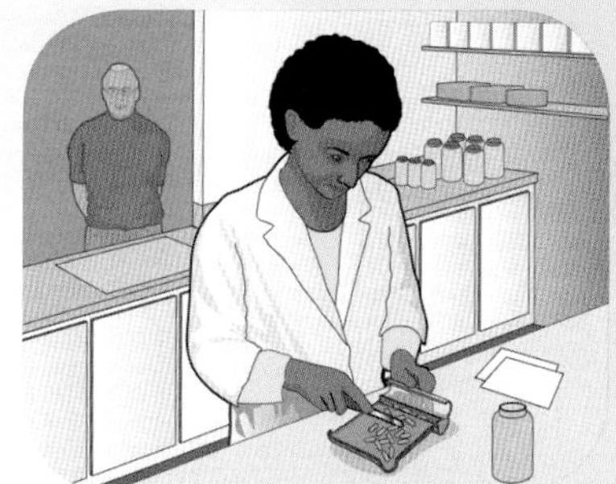

3. *pharmacist*

4. *factory worker*

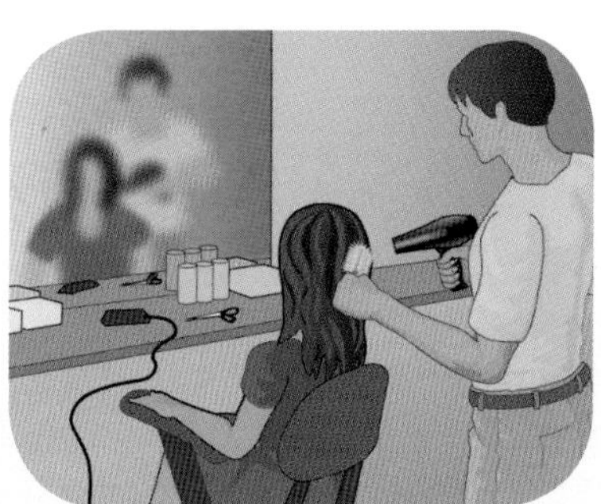

5. *hairstylist*

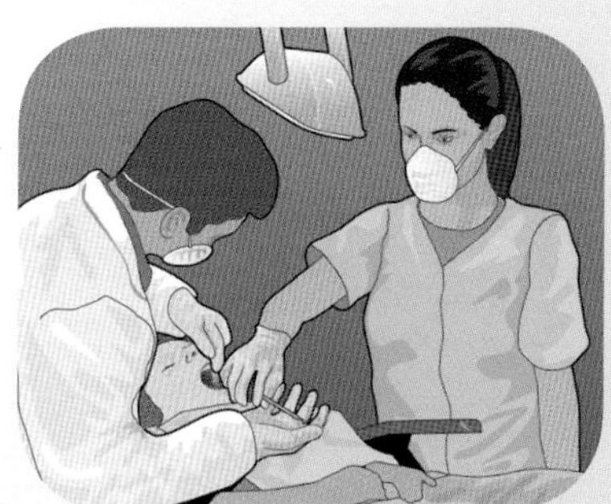

6. *dental assistant*

A **Write** the words in the picture dictionary. Then listen and repeat.

custodian	factory worker	housekeeper
dental assistant	hairstylist	pharmacist

B **Work** with a partner. Match the words in the picture dictionary with the places in the box.

1. a beauty salon *hairstylist*	3. a factory *factory worker*	5. an office building *custodian*
2. a dental office *dental assistant*	4. a hotel *housekeeper*	6. a drugstore *pharmacist*

Talk with a partner. Point to a picture in the dictionary. Ask and answer questions about the occupations.

What's her occupation? — She's a housekeeper.

Where does she work? — She works in a hotel.

Lesson E **Writing**

1 Before you write

A Write. Check (✓) the boxes. *(Answers will vary.)*

	Work skill	Life skill	Both
1. drive	☐	☐	☑
2. cook	☐	☐	☐
3. use a computer	☐	☐	☐
4. housework	☐	☐	☐
5. read to children	☐	☐	☐
6. pay bills	☐	☐	☐
7. shop	☐	☐	☐
8. read a schedule	☐	☐	☐

Talk with a partner.

A What about number 1? Can you drive?
B Yes, I can.
A Is it a work skill or a life skill?
B I think it's both.

B Read. Answer the questions.

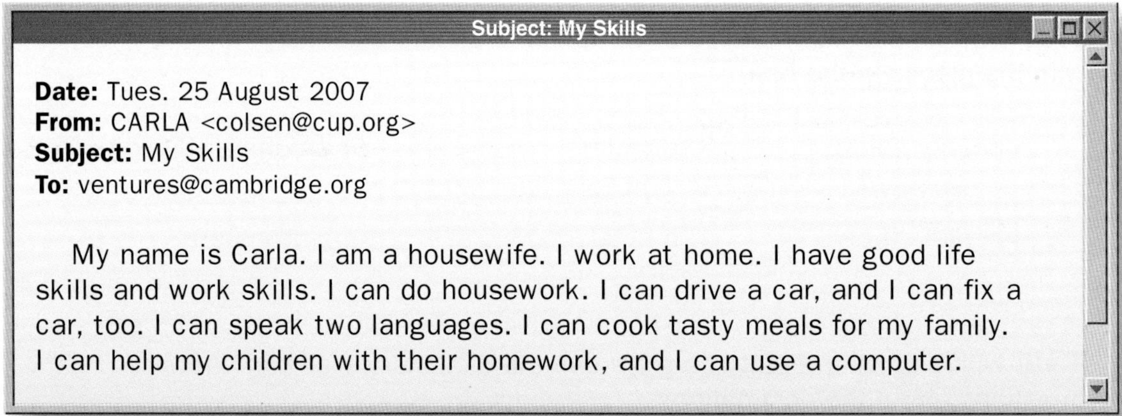

Subject: My Skills

Date: Tues. 25 August 2007
From: CARLA <colsen@cup.org>
Subject: My Skills
To: ventures@cambridge.org

My name is Carla. I am a housewife. I work at home. I have good life skills and work skills. I can do housework. I can drive a car, and I can fix a car, too. I can speak two languages. I can cook tasty meals for my family. I can help my children with their homework, and I can use a computer.

1. What are Carla's life skills? *She can do housework, drive a car, and cook.*
2. What are Carla's work skills? *She can fix a car, speak two languages, and use a computer.*

Lesson objectives

- Discuss and write about work and life skills
- Practice using a dictionary

Warm-up and review

- Before class. Write today's lesson focus on the board.
  Lesson E:
  Write about your skills: What can you do?
- Also write on the board:
  Work skills *Life skills* *Both*
- Begin class. Books closed. Ask: *What skills do you use at work?* (file, use office equipment, cook, etc.) Write one of the skills on the board under *Work skills.*
- Ask: *What skills do you use outside of work?* (shop, help children with homework, etc.) Write one of the skills on the board under *Life skills.*
- Ask: *What skills do you use at work and outside of work?* (use a computer, etc.) Write one of the skills on the board under *Both.*
- Ask Ss to brainstorm more life skills and work skills. Write them in the columns on the board.
- Books open. Direct Ss' attention to Exercise **1A**. Read the instructions aloud.
- Hold up the Student's Book. Point to number 1 (drive). Ask: *Is this a work skill, a life skill, or both?* (both) Point to where *Both* has been checked.
- Ss complete the exercise individually. Walk around and help as needed.
- Focus Ss' attention on the second part of Exercise **1A**. Ask two Ss to read the example conversation aloud.
- Ss complete the exercise in pairs. Walk around and help as needed.
- Check answers by asking individual Ss to say which box they checked. Ask the rest of the class: *Do you agree with this answer?* Allow Ss to discuss any differences of opinion.
- Read aloud the instructions for Exercise **1B**.
- Focus Ss' attention on the e-mail message. Ask: *What is this?* (It's an e-mail message.)
- Ask: *Do you write e-mail messages in English?* Elicit a *Yes* or *No* response.

Teaching tip

Encourage Ss to practice their English outside of class by writing e-mail messages in English.

- Ask questions about the e-mail:
  What's the date? (Tuesday, August 25th, 2007)
  Who is it from? (Carla)
  What is the subject? (My life skills and work skills)
  Who is the e-mail to? (Ventures)
- Ask Ss to read the e-mail silently and then write answers to the questions.
- Ss in pairs. Say: *Ask your partner the questions. Then your partner will ask you the questions.* Ask several pairs to ask and answer the questions for the rest of the class.

Expansion activity *(whole group)*

- Practice statements with *He can* and *She can*. Point to a student. Say: *He can* _____. Write the sentence on the board. Read it aloud.
- Encourage a S to make a sentence about another S in the class. Continue going around the class until everyone has had a chance to describe another student.

Expansion activity *(small groups)*

- Read a classified section. Give each S a copy of a classified section from a local newspaper.
- Write on the board:
  1. Find five different jobs.
  2. Find five different job skills.
  3. Find five different companies.
- Model the activity by pointing to an ad, reading it aloud, and listing the information on the board.
- Ss in small groups. Ss answer the questions in a small group.
- Check answers with the class. Elicit information from each group.

Lesson E Writing

Practice

- Books closed. Write on the board: *I'm a _____. I work at _____.* Fill in the first blank with *teacher.* Fill in the second blank with the name of your school.
- Read the sentences aloud. Ask Ss to repeat after you.

> **Teaching tip**
> Remind Ss to capitalize names of businesses. Write a name of a local company on the board as an example. Elicit other examples and write the names on the board as Ss spell the names aloud.

- Books open. Direct Ss' attention to Exercise **2A** and read the instructions aloud.
- Ss complete the exercise individually. Walk around and help as needed.
- Check answers by asking Ss to write their sentences on the board. Check for correct capitalization.
- Write on the board:
  I can _____.
  I can _____.
- Fill in the blanks with two skills you have. Read the sentences aloud. Ask Ss to repeat after you.
- Direct Ss' attention to Exercise **2B** and read the instructions aloud.
- Ss complete the exercise individually. Walk around and help as needed.
- Check answers by asking each S to read aloud one of his or her skills.
- Read aloud the instructions for Exercise **2C**.
- Direct Ss' attention to the e-mail in Exercise **1B** on page 104. Say: *Write a paragraph like this one. Write about your own skills.*
- Remind Ss to capitalize the names of businesses.
- Ss complete the exercise individually. Walk around and help as needed.

  Option Write a paragraph about your own skills. Model the activity by reading it to the class before Ss write their own paragraphs.

Read the tip box aloud. Remind Ss that correct spelling, capitalization, and punctuation are very important in helping to make writing clear.

Comprehension check

- Read aloud the instructions for Exercise **3A**.
- Ss complete the exercise in pairs. Walk around and help as needed. Help with pronunciation.
- Read aloud the instructions for Exercise **3B**. This exercise asks Ss to work together and peer-correct their writing. Ask a S to read the questions aloud. Tell Ss to exchange papers and find the answers to the questions. Tell Ss to circle the answers on their partner's note.
- Walk around and help as needed.
- Ask pairs to answer the questions about their partner's note for the class.

Expansion activity (whole group)

- Sentence writing competition. Divide the class into two teams. Say: *I will say an occupation. One person from each team will come to the board and write a sentence using that occupation. Try to include skills. The first person to write a correct sentence will get one point.*
- Model the activity. Say the word *doctor.* Write on the board: *A doctor can take care of people.*
- Use the occupations from the picture dictionary. Tally the points. The team with the most points wins the game.

Evaluation

- Direct Ss' attention to the lesson focus written on the board.
- Ask different Ss to come to the board and write some examples of their work skills and life skills. Encourage Ss to make sentences with *can*.
- Check off the lesson focus as Ss demonstrate an understanding of what they have learned in the lesson.

> ***More Ventures*** (whole group, pairs, individual)
> Assign appropriate exercises from the *Teacher's Toolkit Audio CD / CD-ROM, Add Ventures,* or the *Workbook.*

2 Write

A Write about your job. Complete the sentences.

I am a ______ *(Answers will vary.)* ______ .

I work at ________________________ .

B Write. What are your life skills and work skills? Make a list.

(Answers will vary.)

C Write a paragraph about your skills.

(Answers will vary.)

Check your spelling. Use a dictionary if necessary. Correct spelling is important in writing.

3 After you write

A Read your paragraph to a partner.

B Check your partner's paragraph.

- What are your partner's life skills?
- What are your partner's work skills?
- Is the spelling correct?

Lesson F Another view

1 Life-skills reading

APPLICATION FOR EMPLOYMENT

1 Name ______________________ (FIRST, LAST)
2 Soc. Sec. No. 000-99-9103
3 Address ______________________ (STREET)
______________________ (CITY, STATE, ZIP)
4 Phone (_____) ______________
5 Are you 16 years or older? Yes __ No __
6 Position desired ______________

EMPLOYMENT HISTORY (List most recent job first.)

	Dates	Employer Name and Address	Position
7			
8			
9			

10 **Important:** Show your Social Security card at the time you present this application.

A Read the questions. Look at the job application. Circle the answers.

1. Where do you write the job you want?
   a. line 5
   (b.) line 6
   c. line 8
   d. line 10

2. Where do you write your job now?
   a. line 5
   (b.) line 7
   c. line 8
   d. line 9

3. What do you show with your application?
   a. a library card
   b. a photograph
   c. a driver's license
   (d.) a Social Security card

4. Where do you write your phone number?
   (a.) line 4
   b. line 5
   c. line 8
   d. line 9

B Write. Complete the form with your own information.

C Talk with a partner about your form.

My name is Mario Rivera. My address is 613 Apple Road, Los Angeles, California. I'm looking for a job. The job I want is construction worker.

Lesson objectives

- Understand and complete a job application
- Learn new words to describe occupations
- Review unit vocabulary; introduce the project
- Complete the self-assessment

Warm-up and review

- Before class. Write today's lesson focus on the board.
  Lesson F:
  Read and fill out a job application
  Learn adjectives that describe occupations
  Complete the self-assessment
- Begin class. Books closed. Ask Ss: *Have you ever applied for a job in the U.S.?* Elicit *Yes* or *No* responses. Ask Ss who say *Yes*: *What did you do to apply for the job?* If Ss don't know how to reply, write on the board: *fill out a job application.*
- Underline the words *job application* written on the board. Say the words aloud. Ask Ss to repeat. Ask: *What is this?* Elicit an appropriate response. If Ss don't know, focus Ss' attention on the job application (application for employment) on page 106.

Presentation

- Books open. Hold up the Student's Book. Point to the job application in Exercise **1**. Ask Ss: *What's this?* Elicit: *It's an application for employment* or *a job application.*
- Point to the top portion of the job application. Ask: *What information does this part of the application ask for?* Elicit: *Name, address, Social Security number,* etc.

Teaching tip

It might be helpful to explain the terms *Social Security number* and *position desired.* Tell Ss that a Social Security number is a number issued by the government that you must have in order to get a job in the United States; *position desired* means the job you want to get by filling out the application form.

- Focus Ss' attention on the Employment History portion of the job application. Say: *This is where you write the jobs you've had in the past.*
- Hold up the Student's Book. Point to the most recent job. Say: *This is the last job that you've had.*
- Point to numbers 7–9 on the application form. Say: *This is where you describe other jobs that you've had. You list the last job first.* Write an example on the board of a past job, for example:
  9/01–5/05 The Shoe Factory Salesperson
- Point to each part of the job description. Say: *These are the dates that I worked. This was the name and address of the employer. This was the name of my job.*
- Direct Ss' attention to Exercise **1A**. Read the instructions aloud. This task helps prepare Ss for standardized-type tests they may have to take. Be sure Ss understand the task. Have Ss individually scan for and circle the answers.
- Check answers with the class. Write the numbers *1–4* on the board. Ask four Ss to write their answers on the board. Ask: *Are these answers correct?* Ask other Ss to correct any errors.
- Direct Ss attention to Exercise **1B**. Read the instructions aloud.

Teaching tip

Review writing dates and addresses. Remind Ss to write dates in the order of month, day, and year. Also remind Ss to write their street number, the street name, and then the apartment number on one line; they write the city, state, and zip code on the next line. Write examples on the board.

- Point out the example in number 2 on the application form. Tell Ss they should make up a Social Security number for the activity and that they can make up a phone number if they don't want to use their real telephone number.
- Ss complete the exercise individually. Walk around and help as needed.
- Direct Ss' attention to Exercise **1C** and read the instructions aloud. Ask a S to read aloud the example.
- Ss in pairs. Walk around and listen to Ss' pronunciation. Write difficult words on the board. When Ss finish, say the words aloud. Ask Ss to repeat after you.
- Ask several Ss to tell the class about their forms.

Expansion activity *(individual work)*

- Filling out different employment applications. Ask Ss to gather job applications from local businesses, or collect them yourself.
- Make copies for the class and have Ss work in groups to fill out the information. Discuss any unfamiliar terms.

Lesson F Another view

Presentation

- Focus Ss' attention on the pictures in Exercise **2A**. Hold up the Student's Book. Point to the first picture. Ask: *What does she do?* (She's a student.) Ask: *Where is she?* (She's at school.)
- Point to the second picture. Ask: *What does he do?* (He's an office worker.) Ask: *Where is he?* (He's at the office.)
- Point to the third picture. Ask: *What's her job?* (She's a painter.) Ask: *Where is she?* (She's in a house.)
- Read the instructions aloud.
- Ask three Ss to read aloud the questions.
- Ss complete the exercise in pairs.

Teaching tip

If Ss are unfamiliar with the adjectives in this exercise, encourage them to look up the words in a dictionary.

Practice

- Write on the board: *child-care worker.*
- Point to the words on the board. Ask: *Is this job easy or difficult?* Responses will vary. Ask: *Is it boring or fun?* Responses will vary. Ask: *Is it dangerous or safe?* Responses will vary.
- Read aloud the instructions for Exercise **2B**.
- Ss complete the chart in pairs. Help as needed.
- Write on the board: *opinions.* Point to the word. Say it. Ask Ss to repeat. Ask: *What does this word mean?* If Ss don't know, say: *Opinions are what people think. Not everyone agrees with other people's opinions.*
- Read aloud the second part of the instructions for Exercise **2B**. Ask three Ss to read the examples aloud.
- Ss complete the exercise in small groups. Help as needed.
- Ask each small group to choose one occupation. One person from each group will give his or her opinion and then say whether the group agrees or disagrees.

Expansion activity (whole group)

- Opinion survey. Before class. Make a copy of the following grid for each S in your class.

Opinions	Agree	Disagree
Driving is fun.		
Homework for this class is easy.		
Cooking is fun.		
Using a computer is boring.		
Doing housework is boring.		

- In class. Give each S a copy of the grid. Say: *Stand up and walk around the class. Say the opinions to classmates. Ask them if they agree or disagree.*
- Model the activity. Ask a S to stand up. Say: *Driving is fun. Do you agree or disagree?* Put a check mark in the appropriate column to record the S's answer.
- When Ss have finished talking to their classmates, ask them to report their findings, for example: *Ten people think driving is fun. Twelve people think it is boring.* Ask several Ss to report their findings to the class.

Learner persistence (whole group)

- Ask the class: *Do you think this class is easy or difficult?* If any Ss say that they find the class to be very difficult, talk to them after class. Find out where the problem areas are, and encourage Ss to work with another S or a tutor after class.

More Ventures *(whole group, pairs, individual)*
Assign appropriate exercises from the *Teacher's Toolkit Audio CD / CD-ROM, Add Ventures,* or the *Workbook.*

Application

Community building

- **Project** Ask Ss to turn to page 139 in their Student's Book and complete the project for Unit 8.

Evaluation

- Before asking Ss to turn to the self-assessment on page 144, do a quick review of the unit. Have Ss turn to Lesson A. Ask the class to call out what they remember about this lesson. Prompt Ss, if necessary, with questions, for example: *What are the conversations about on this page? What vocabulary is in the picture?* Continue in this manner to review each lesson quickly.
- **Self-assessment** Read the instructions for Exercise **3**. Ask Ss to turn to the self-assessment page and complete the unit self-assessment.
- If Ss are ready, administer the unit test on pages T-181–T-182 of this *Teacher's Edition* (or on the *Teacher's Toolkit Audio CD / CD-ROM*). The audio and audio scripts for the test are on the *Teacher's Toolkit Audio CD / CD-ROM.*

2 Fun with language

A **Work with a partner.** Talk about the pictures.

1. Is this **easy** or **difficult**?

2. Is this **boring** or **fun**?

3. Is this **dangerous** or **safe**?

B **Work with a partner.** Complete the chart. Use the words from Exercise A.

Occupation	Word to describe it
1. construction worker	*difficult*
2. salesperson	*(Answers will vary.)*
3. housewife	
4. cashier	
5. pharmacist	
6. waiter / waitress	
7. hairstylist	
8. (your job) ________________	

Work in a group. Talk about your opinions. Do you agree with your classmates? Why? Why not?

I think a construction worker has a difficult job.

I think a construction worker has a dangerous job.

I agree. I think it's a dangerous job.

3 Wrap up

Complete the **Self-assessment** on page 144.

Review

1 Listening

Read the questions. Then listen and circle the answers.

1. What did Carlos do before?
   (a.) He was an office worker.
   b. He was a construction worker.
2. What does Carlos do now?
   a. He is an office worker.
   (b.) He is a construction worker.
3. When does Carlos buy groceries?
   a. every Tuesday
   (b.) every Thursday
4. Where is Carlos right now?
   (a.) at SaveMore Supermarket
   b. at work
5. What is he buying at the supermarket?
   a. milk, tea, bread, and eggs
   (b.) milk, cheese, bread, and eggs
6. How much are the groceries?
   (a.) $11.75
   b. $7.75

Talk with a partner. Ask and answer the questions. Use complete sentences.

2 Grammar

A Write. Complete the story.

Peter

Peter _was_ (1. is / was) a waiter in his country. Now he _is_ (2. is / was) a cashier. He can do many things. He _can_ (3. can / can't) use a cash register. He _can_ (4. can / can't) use a computer, too. But Peter has two problems. First, he _can't_ (5. can / can't) speak English well. Second, he works a lot of hours. He _can't_ (6. can / can't) find time to go to school.

B Write. Unscramble the words. Make questions about the story.

1. a / teacher / Was / Peter / country / his / in / ? _Was Peter a teacher in his country?_
2. use / cash register / a / Can / he / ? _Can he use a cash register?_
3. speak / well / English / Can / he / ? _Can he speak English well?_
4. he / construction worker / Is / now / a / ? _Is he a construction worker now?_

Talk with a partner. Ask and answer the questions.

Lesson objective
- Review vocabulary, pronunciation, and grammar from Units 7 and 8

Warm-up and review

- Before class. Write today's lesson focus on the board. *Review unit: Review vocabulary, pronunciation, and grammar from Units 7 and 8*
- Begin class. Books closed. Write on the board: *How much* *How many*
- Ask Ss to brainstorm questions that begin with *How much* and *How many*, for example: *How much milk do you have? How many eggs do you need?*

Presentation

- Books open. Focus Ss' attention on Exercise **1**. Read the instructions aloud.
- Ask individual Ss to read the questions aloud. Say: *Now listen to a story about Carlos. Circle the correct answers.*
- [Class Audio CD2 track 29] Play or read the audio program (see audio script, page T-159). Ss listen and circle the answers to the questions. Repeat the audio program as needed.
- Write the numbers *1–6* on the board. Ask individual Ss to write their answers on the board. Ask other Ss: *Are these answers correct?* Have Ss make any necessary corrections on the board.

Practice

- Read aloud the second part of the instructions for Exercise **1**.
- Ss complete the exercise in pairs. Help as needed.
- Ask several pairs to ask and answer the questions for the rest of the class.
- Write on the board:
  I _____ *You* _____ *She* _____ *He* _____
  We _____ *They* _____
- Model the activity. Point to *I* on the board. Say: *I was a student.* Write *was* in the blank next to *I*.
- Ask Ss to continue by writing the correct form of *to be* in the remaining blanks.
- Direct Ss' attention to Exercise **2A**. Read the instructions aloud.
- Ask a S to read aloud the title of the paragraph ("Peter"). Say: *This is a story about Peter. He is a cashier. What do you think he can do?* Elicit answers such as: *He can use a cash register; he can give change.*
- Ask another S to read aloud the first sentence in the paragraph.
- Ss complete the exercise individually. Walk around and help as needed.
- Write the numbers *1–6* on the board. Ask Ss to come to the board to write the answers.

Teaching tip
Ask Ss to write on the board only the missing words, not the complete sentences.

- Ask individual Ss to read aloud a sentence from the paragraph. Ask: *Are the answers correct?* Ask Ss to correct any errors.
- Books closed. Write on the board: *you / speak / Can / English / ?*
- Ask Ss to unscramble the words on the board to make a question. (Can you speak English?) Write the question on the board.
- Books open. Focus Ss' attention on Exercise **2B**. Read the instructions aloud.
- Ss complete the exercise individually. Walk around and help as needed.
- Write the numbers *1–4* on the board. Ask four Ss to write the unscrambled questions on the board. Ask other Ss: *Are the questions correct?* Ask different Ss to correct any errors.
- Read aloud the second part of the instructions in Exercise **2B**.
- Model the task. Ask a S the first question: *Was Peter a teacher in his country?* Elicit: *No, he wasn't.*
- Ss complete the exercise in pairs. Walk around and help as needed.
- Ask several pairs to ask and answer the questions for the rest of the class.

Review

Warm-up and review

- Ask: *How do we usually make words plural in English?* Elicit: *Add an "s" to the word.*
- Say: *There are different ways to pronounce the plural "s" in English. Sometimes it sounds like /s/, sometimes it sounds like /z/, and sometimes it sounds like /ɪz/.*

Presentation

- Focus Ss' attention on Exercise **3A**. Read the instructions aloud.
- [Class Audio CD2 track 30] Play or read the audio program (see audio script, page T-159). Repeat as needed.
- Ask: *Did you hear the different ways the "s" was pronounced in each word?* Elicit a *Yes* or *No* response.

  Option If Ss ask for the rule for how to pronounce the plural *s* sound correctly, tell them that it depends on the ending letters or sound of the singular form of the noun. Nouns ending with a voiceless sound such as /k/ or /t/ have a plural that sounds like /s/. Nouns ending in voiced sounds such as /n/ or /r/ have a plural that sounds like /z/. Nouns ending in /s/ or similar sounds (the sibilants) have a plural that sounds like /ɪz/.
- Read aloud the instructions for Exercise **3B**.
- [Class Audio CD2 track 31] Play or read the audio program (see audio script, page T-159). Ss listen and repeat the words. Encourage Ss to use the correct plural pronunciation as they repeat the words. Repeat the audio program as needed.

Practice

- Read aloud the second part of the instructions for Exercise **3B**.
- Model the task. Say the word *assistants*. Then make up a sentence with the word, for example: *The assistants are eating lunch.*
- Ss complete the exercise in pairs. Help as needed.
- Ask several Ss to say their sentences for the rest of the class.

  Option Ask Ss to write a sentence on the board for each word. Then ask different Ss to read the sentences aloud, using correct pronunciation.
- Focus Ss' attention on the chart in Exercise **3C**. Read the instructions aloud.
- Say: *Listen to these plural words. Write them in the chart.*
- [Class Audio CD2 track 32] Model the task. Play or read the first word on the audio program (see audio script, page T-159). Say: *bags* /z/ and point to where *bags* has been written in the chart.
- [Class Audio CD2 track 32] Play or read the audio program. Ss listen and complete the chart individually. Help as needed.
- Make a copy of the chart on the board. Ask Ss to fill it in according to the words they wrote in their charts.
- Ask Ss to pronounce each of the words in the chart on the board. Ask: *Is that the correct pronunciation?* Correct any pronunciation errors.
- Read aloud the instructions for Exercise **3D**.
- Ask two Ss to read aloud the example question and answer.

> **Teaching tip**
> It might be helpful to remind Ss about count and non-count nouns. Say: *Use plural count nouns after "there are." Use non-count and singular count nouns after "there is."*

- Ss complete the exercise in pairs. Help as needed.
- Ask several pairs to ask and answer the question for the class. Listen carefully to make sure they are using correct pronunciation.

Expansion activity *(student pairs)*

- Write on the board:
  What items are in the English classroom?
  There are _____. There is _____.
- Say: *Talk about items in the classroom. Be sure to use the correct pronunciation for plural items.*
- Model the activity. Ask a S to ask you the question on the board. Answer by saying: *There are pencils. There is a blackboard,* etc.
- Ss complete the activity in pairs. Walk around and help as needed, offering Ss feedback and support.
- Ask pairs to ask and answer the questions for the class.

Evaluation

- Direct Ss' attention to the lesson focus on the board.
- Go around the room. Ask each S to say a sentence about Carlos from Exercise **1** on page 108.
- Ask Ss to read the words from Exercise **3B** on page 109 and to use the correct pronunciation.
- Check off the items in the lesson focus as Ss demonstrate understanding of what they have learned in the lesson.

3 Pronunciation: the -*s* ending with plural nouns

A **Listen** to the -*s* ending in these plural nouns.

/s/	/z/	/ɪz/
cakes	tomatoes	peaches
hairstylists	electricians	nurses

B **Listen and repeat.**

/s/	/z/	/ɪz/
assistants	bananas	nurses
cooks	cashiers	oranges
students	drivers	packages
mechanics	cookies	boxes
pharmacists	waiters	peaches
books	teachers	waitresses

Talk with a partner. Take turns. Practice the words. Make sentences with the words.

C **Listen**. Complete the chart.

1. bags
2. bottles
3. clerks
4. dimes
5. pages
6. carrots
7. desks
8. sandwiches
9. glasses

/s/	/z/	/ɪz/
clerks	*bags*	*pages*
carrots	*bottles*	*sandwiches*
desks	*dimes*	*glasses*

D **Talk** with a partner. Ask and answer the question. Use correct pronunciation.

What's in your refrigerator?

There are ________________ .

There is ________________ .

Lesson A Get ready

1 Talk about the picture

A Look at the picture. What do you see?

B Point to a person: cleaning the bathroom • emptying the trash
mopping the floor • vacuuming the rug • ironing clothes

Lesson objectives
- Introduce students to the topic
- Find out what students know about the topic
- Preview the unit by talking about the picture
- Practice key vocabulary
- Practice listening skills

Warm-up and review
- Before class. Write today's lesson focus on the board.
Lesson A: Daily living
Household chores
- Begin class. Books closed. Review work and occupations from Unit 8. Ask: *Do you have a job? Do you work?* If Ss answer *Yes,* ask: *What's your occupation?* or *What do you do?* Help Ss with vocabulary they learned in Unit 8 or other vocabulary to identify their occupations.
- Ask: *Where do you work?* Elicit: *I work in a . . . hospital, factory,* etc. Help Ss remember vocabulary from the previous unit or vocabulary to describe their own jobs.

Teaching tip
Ask Ss to list the life skills and work skills needed for particular jobs. Write them on the board. You can use the life skills list to introduce this unit about daily living and household chores.

- Point to the words *household chores.* Say them aloud. Ask Ss to repeat.
- Ask: *What are household chores?* If there is no response, ask: *What work do you do at home?* Write responses on the board: *wash, cook, clean, pay bills,* etc.
- Ask: *Who does the chores in your house?* Elicit various responses from the class.
- Point to the words for chores that you have elicited from Ss. Say: *Repeat the words after me.* As you say each word, demonstrate the meaning by acting as if you are doing the chore.
- Ask: *Who does the chores in your house?* Elicit various responses from the class.

Presentation
- Books open. Set the scene. Direct Ss' attention to the picture on page 110. Ask: *What do you see?* Elicit as much vocabulary about the picture as possible and write the words on the board: *a house, a kitchen, a family, a vacuum cleaner, dishes,* etc.
- Direct Ss' attention to the key words in Exercise **1B**. Read each word aloud while pointing to the person in the picture who is doing the chore. Ask the class to repeat and point.

Comprehension check
- Ask Ss questions about the picture. Recycle vocabulary from past lessons.
Where are the people? (They are in the kitchen and bathroom.)
What is the girl doing? (She's mopping the floor.)
What is the man in the bathroom doing? (He's cleaning.)
What is the boy in the yellow shirt doing? (He's emptying the trash.)
What is the boy in the green shirt doing? (He's ironing clothes.)
What is the boy in the purple shirt doing? (He's vacuuming the rug.)

Practice
- Direct Ss' attention to Exercise **1B**. Model the task. Hold up the Student's Book. Say to a S: *Point to the person cleaning the bathroom.* The S points to the appropriate person in the picture.
- Ss in pairs. Say to one S: *Say the words in Exercise 1B.* Say to his or her partner. *Point to the picture.*
- Ss complete the exercise in pairs. Walk around and help as needed. When Ss finish, have them change partners and change roles.
- Ask several pairs to perform the exercise for the class to check Ss' understanding.

Expansion activity (small groups)
- Cultural reflection. Write these discussion questions on the board:
What chores did you have to do in your home country?
Were they different from the chores you do now?
Many parents think that doing chores is important for children. What's your opinion?
- Ask Ss to discuss the questions in their small groups.
- Ask members of each group to report on their group's discussion to the rest of the class.

Expansion activity (student pairs)
- Interviews about chores. Ss in pairs. Write the following questions on the board:
What chores do you do at home?
What chores do other people in your home do?
- Ss in pairs. Say: *Ask your partner the questions. Then your partner asks you the questions.*
- Ask several pairs to ask and answer their questions in front of the class.

Lesson A Get ready

Presentation

- Books closed. Ask Ss: *What are some other chores you do that are not in the picture on page 110?* Write Ss' responses on the board. Say the chores aloud. Ask Ss to repeat after you. If any Ss don't know what the words mean, ask the Ss who said the chores to act them out.

Practice

- Books open. Direct Ss' attention to Exercise **2A**. Read aloud the vocabulary words in the word bank and ask Ss to repeat after you. For each item, ask: *What does this mean?* You or the Ss can act out the meaning.
- Read aloud the instructions for Exercise **2A**.
- [Class Audio CD2 track 33] Play or read the audio program (see audio script, page T-159). Ss listen and circle the words they hear. Repeat the audio as needed.
- Check answers. Ss write the words on the board.

Expansion activity (student pairs)

- Ask Ss to look at the words they did not circle. Ask a S to write them on the board: *empty, iron, sweep.*
- Ss in pairs. Say: *Write sentences with the words that you didn't hear in Exercise 2A.* Help as needed.
- Ask Ss to write their sentences on the board. Ask other Ss to read the sentences aloud.

Practice

- Direct Ss' attention to the pictures for Exercise **2B**. Hold up the Student's Book and point to the first picture. Say: *Paying bills.* Point to the second picture. Ask a S: *What's he doing?* (mopping)
- Continue asking Ss about the rest of the pictures.
- Read aloud the instructions for Exercise **2B**.
- [Class Audio CD2 track 33] Play or read the audio program again. Pause after the first conversation. Ask: *Which picture matches conversation A?* (picture number 3). Point to the handwritten *a* written next to number 3. Be sure Ss understand the task. Then play or read the complete audio program for Ss to complete the exercise individually.

Learner persistence (individual work)

- [Self-Study Audio CD track 33] Exercises **2A** and **2B** are recorded on the Ss' self-study CD at the back of the Student's Book. Ss can listen to the CD at home for reinforcement and review. They can also listen for self-directed learning when class attendance is not possible.

Comprehension check

- Write the numbers *1–6* on the board. Ask individual Ss to come to the board and write the correct answer next to each number.
- Read aloud the second part of the instructions for Exercise **2B**.
- [Class Audio CD2 track 33] Play or read the audio program again. Pause the audio program after each conversation. Point to a letter of the conversation on the board. Ask: *Is this correct?*

Application

- Write on the board: *clean.* Ask Ss: *What can you clean?* Elicit responses such as: *the blackboard, the house,* and *the bathroom.* Write responses on the board under *clean.*
- Direct Ss' attention to the word bank in Exercise **2C**. Read each word aloud. Ask Ss to repeat. Ask Ss if they have any questions about word meanings.
- Read aloud the instructions for Exercise **2C**.
- Hold up the Student's Book. Point to *iron.* Ask: *What can you iron?* Elicit responses such as: *a dress, a shirt.*
- Ss complete the exercise in pairs. Help as needed.
- Copy the chart onto the board. Ask individual Ss to write their answers in the correct columns.

Expansion activity (small groups)

- **Materials needed** Index cards with words from the word bank in Exercise **2C** written on them
- Charades relay race. Ask Ss to review the word bank words in Exercise **2A**. Then have them close their books.
- Divide the class into three teams. Ask one S from each team to read the chore on the index card silently. When you say *Go,* each S acts out the chore for his or her team.
- Another S from each team will stand at the board and write the chore that team members are guessing. The first team that writes the chore correctly wins a point. The team with the most points wins.

Evaluation

- Direct Ss' attention to the lesson focus on the board. Ask Ss to identify the chores in the pictures on pages 110 and 111.
- Check off the lesson focus as Ss demonstrate understanding of what they have learned in the lesson.

More Ventures (whole group, pairs, individual)
Assign appropriate exercises from the *Teacher's Toolkit Audio CD / CD-ROM, Add Ventures,* or the *Workbook.*

2 Listening

A **Listen.** Circle the words you hear.

clean	mop	sweep
empty	paint	vacuum
iron	pay	wash

B **Listen again.** Write the letter of the conversation.

Listen again. Check your answers.

C **Write.** Work with a partner. Put the words from the box in the correct category.

a bill	the floor	a shirt	the trash
a dress	the rug	a ticket	the wastebasket

iron	empty	vacuum	pay
a dress a shirt	the trash the wastebasket	the floor the rug	a bill a ticket

Lesson B I dusted the living room.

1 Grammar focus: simple past with regular verbs

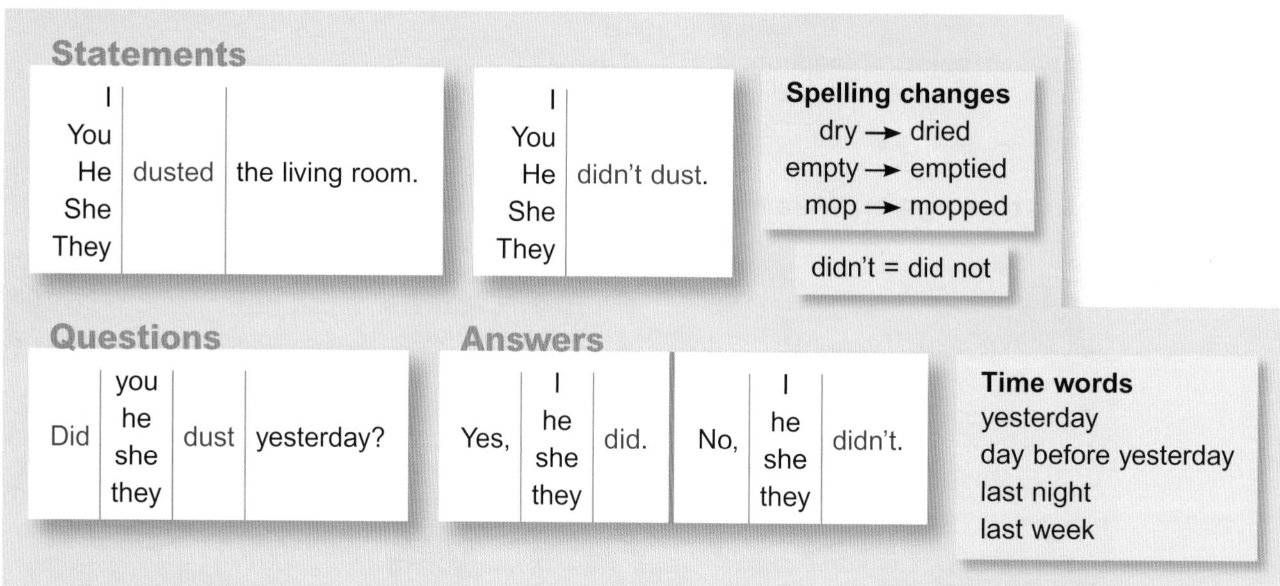

Statements

I You He She They	dusted	the living room.

I You He She They	didn't dust.

Spelling changes
dry → dried
empty → emptied
mop → mopped

didn't = did not

Questions

Did	you he she they	dust	yesterday?

Answers

Yes,	I he she they	did.

No,	I he she they	didn't.

Time words
yesterday
day before yesterday
last night
last week

2 Practice

A Write. Look at the picture. Complete the sentences.

1. Yousef *cooked* dinner. (cook)
2. He *didn't clean* the kitchen. (clean)
3. He *dusted* the shelves. (dust)
4. He *didn't wash* the dishes. (wash)
5. He *ironed* the shirts. (iron)
6. He *didn't empty* the trash. (empty)

 **Listen and repeat.**

Lesson objective
- Introduce the simple past with regular verbs

Warm-up and review

- Before class. Write today's lesson focus on the board. *Lesson B: The simple question in the past with regular verbs*
- Begin class. Books closed. Write on the board: *the past.* Say the words aloud. Ask Ss to repeat after you. Ask: *What are some time words that mean the past?* (If Ss don't respond, write *yesterday* on the board. Elicit more past time words from Ss, such as: *last night, last week, last year, two years ago,* etc.)
- Ask: *Did you sweep the floor last night? Did you empty the trash yesterday? Did you iron your clothes last week?* Elicit *Yes* or *No* responses.

> **Teaching tip**
> Do not expect Ss to answer with *Yes, I did* or *No, I didn't,* as they have not yet been introduced to this answer form. At this point, Ss can answer with simple *Yes* or *No* answers.

Presentation

- Books open. Direct Ss' attention to the grammar chart in Exercise **1**. Read the statements, questions, and answers aloud. Ask Ss to repeat.
- Ss in pairs. Have Ss practice reading the grammar chart to each other while pointing to the appropriate person in the class (*I, You, He, She, They*).

> **Teaching tip**
> Direct Ss' attention to the spelling changes written in the grammar chart. Say: *If you change a verb to the simple past tense, there are some spelling changes.* If your Ss are interested in knowing the rules for spelling changes for regular past tense verbs, write the following on the board: *Change the "y" to "i" in verbs that end in "y" (as in "dried"). Double the consonant in verbs spelled with a single vowel followed by a single consonant (as in "mopped").*

> **Teaching tip**
> Focus Ss' attention on the time words in the chart in Exercise **1**. Say: *These are time words about the past.* Say the words aloud. Ask Ss to repeat.

Practice

- Direct Ss' attention to the picture for Exercise **2A**. Ask: *What do you see?* Elicit responses such as: *A man is eating; there is an ironing board and two shirts; there are dirty dishes.*
- Read the instructions aloud. Ask a S to read the first two examples to the class.
- Ss complete the exercise individually. Walk around and help as needed.

Expansion activity (whole group)

- If you want to expand the grammar presentation, turn to the grammar charts at the back of the Student's Book. Practice making affirmative and negative sentences using the simple past tense.

Comprehension check

- Read aloud the second part of the instructions for Exercise **2A**.
- [Class Audio CD2 track 34] Play or read the audio program (see audio script, page T-159). Have Ss check their answers as they listen and repeat. Correct pronunciation as needed.
- Ask Ss to come to the board and write the sentences. Ask different Ss to read the sentences aloud. Ask Ss to make any necessary corrections on the board.
- Ask Ss to read the sentences aloud. Check their pronunciation of the past tense word endings.

Lesson B I dusted the living room.

Practice

- Direct Ss' attention to the picture in Exercise **2B**. Ask: *What happened? What chores did they do?* Elicit various responses, for example: *Mr. Ramirez mopped the floor; Monica vacuumed; Mrs. Ramirez emptied the trash.*
- Read the instructions aloud. Ask two Ss to read aloud the example question and answer.
- Ss complete the exercise individually. Refer Ss to the grammar chart on page 112 for help with short answers. Walk around and help as needed.
- [Class Audio CD2 track 35] Read aloud the second part of the instructions for Exercise **2B**. Play or read the audio program (see audio script, page T-160). Listen to Ss and correct their pronunciation as needed.

  Option Ask: *Were your answers correct?* Ask other Ss to correct any errors.
- Ss ask and answer the questions in pairs. Walk around and help as needed.
- Ask pairs to perform their conversations for the class.

Application

- Read aloud the instructions for Exercise **3**. Ask two Ss to read the example question and answer aloud.
- Focus Ss' attention on the chart. Read each chore aloud. Ask Ss to repeat after you.
- Model the task. Ask a S: (name of S), *did you cook dinner last night?* If the response is *Yes,* write the S's name in the chart. If the response is *No,* continue asking until a S says *Yes.*

> **Teaching tip**
> It might be helpful to remind Ss that the form of the verb in questions in the simple past tense doesn't change – it is used in the base form along with *did.*

- Ss walk around and talk to classmates. Walk around and help as needed.
- Ask Ss to tell you which of their classmates did the chores that are listed in the chart.

Expansion activity *(whole group)*

- Vocabulary review. Write the following on the board:
  Mow the _____.
  Dust the _____.
  Mop the _____.
  Dry the _____.
  Wash the _____.
  Empty the _____.
- Review the vocabulary on the board (Ss probably do not know the verb *mow*). Say: *When the grass is too high, you have to mow the _____.* Elicit: *mow the lawn.*
- Ss copy the sentences and individually fill in the blanks.
- Ask several Ss to fill in the blanks on the board.
- Ss in pairs. Say: *Ask your partners if they did any of the chores on the board. Remember to use the correct question form in the past.*
- Ask several pairs to ask and answer their questions for the rest of the class.

Evaluation

- Direct Ss' attention to the lesson focus written on the board. Go around the class and elicit questions and affirmative and negative answers about the pictures in Exercise **2B** on page 111.
- Check off the lesson focus as Ss demonstrate an understanding of what they have learned in the lesson.

> ***More Ventures*** *(whole group, pairs, individual)*
> Assign appropriate exercises from the *Teacher's Toolkit Audio CD / CD-ROM, Add Ventures,* or the *Workbook.*

B **Write.** Look at the picture. Answer the questions.

1. *A* Did Mr. Ramirez mop the floor?
   B Yes, he did.
2. *A* Did Mrs. Ramirez empty the trash?
   B Yes, she did.
3. *A* Did Mr. and Mrs. Ramirez wash the dishes?
   B No, they didn't.
4. *A* Did Roberto dry the dishes?
   B Yes, he did.
5. *A* Did Luis vacuum the rug?
   B No, he didn't.
6. *A* Did Monica vacuum the rug?
   B Yes, she did.

Listen and repeat. Then practice with a partner.

3 Communicate

Talk with your classmates. Write their names in the chart.

Anna, did you cook dinner last night?

Yes, I did.

Find a classmate who:	Classmate's name
cooked dinner last night	(Answers will vary.)
emptied the trash yesterday	
washed the dishes every night last week	
dried the dishes the day before yesterday	
vacuumed last weekend	
ironed clothes last week	

Lesson C I paid the bills.

1 Grammar focus: simple past with irregular verbs

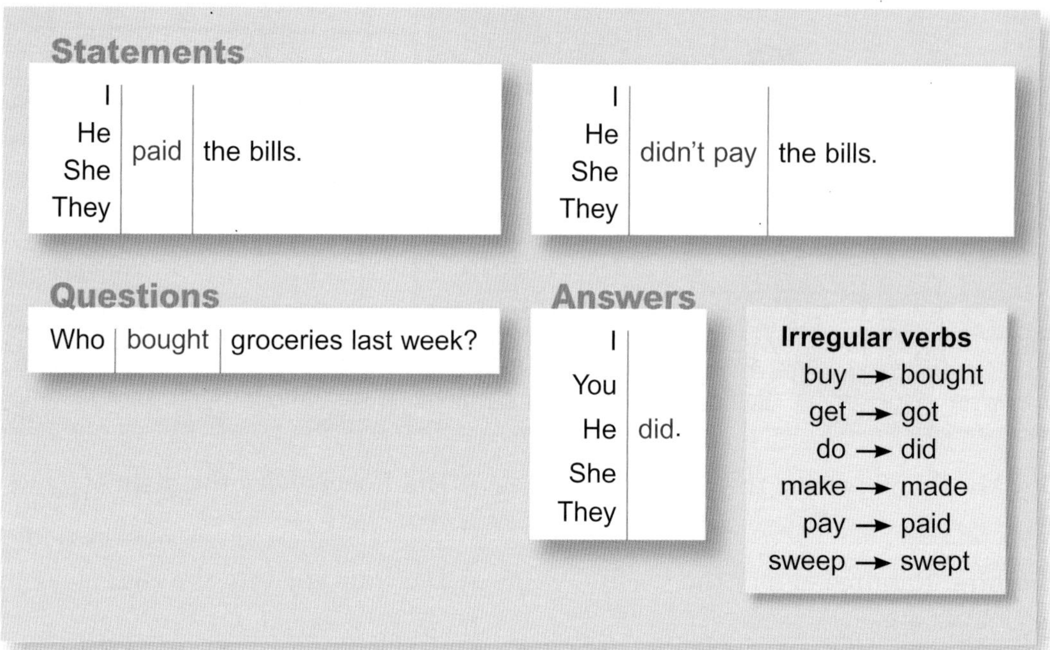

Statements

I He She They	paid	the bills.

I He She They	didn't pay	the bills.

Questions

Who	bought	groceries last week?

Answers

I You He She They	did.

Irregular verbs

buy → bought
get → got
do → did
make → made
pay → paid
sweep → swept

2 Practice

A Write. Look at the pictures. Complete the sentences.

Last night, Linda had to pay the bills. But first, she ___bought___ (1. buy) groceries after work. She ___paid___ (2. pay) $15. She ___got___ (3. get) home, and she ___made___ (4. make) dinner. She ___made___ (5. make) soup and salad. After dinner, she was very tired. She ___swept___ (6. sweep) the kitchen floor, but she ___didn't pay___ (7. not pay) the bills!

Listen and check your answers.

Lesson objective
- Introduce the simple past with irregular verbs

Warm-up and review

- Before class. Write today's lesson focus on the board. *Lesson C: The simple question in the past with irregular verbs*
- Begin class. Books closed. Ask: *Did you clean your house last weekend?* Elicit a *Yes* or *No* response.
- Ask Ss who answer with *Yes*: *What did you do when you cleaned your house?* Elicit appropriate responses, recycling vocabulary from the last lesson.
- Write *-ed* on the board. Say: *Remember that regular verbs in the past end in "-ed."*
- Write on the board:

Present tense	*Past tense*
clean	
cook	
dust	
iron	
vacuum	
wash	
mop	
empty	
dry	

- Ask: *What is the past tense of these verbs?* Ask Ss to write the answers on the board. (All of these are regular verbs, and the past tense form ends in *-ed*.)
- Say: *We also have many verbs that don't end in "-ed" in the past tense. These are called irregular verbs.* Write *irregular* on the board.

Presentation

- Books open. Direct Ss' attention to the grammar chart in Exercise **1**. Read the affirmative and negative statements aloud. Ask Ss to repeat.
- Focus Ss' attention on the questions and answers in the chart. Say: *When we want to find out which person did something, we start with the question word "who."* Read the questions and answers aloud. Ask Ss to repeat.
- Hold up the Student's Book. Point to the list of irregular verbs in the grammar chart. Say: *These are examples of irregular verbs in English. You can find a longer list of irregular verbs on page 149 in your Student's Book.*
- Read aloud the present tense and the past tense forms of the verbs. Ask Ss to repeat them after you. Check Ss' pronunciation. Repeat the words if needed.

Teaching tip

It might be helpful to suggest that Ss make flash cards with the present tense form of a verb on one side and the past tense form on the other side. Encourage Ss to test themselves by guessing the past tense form of the verbs and then checking to see if they are right.

Practice

- Direct Ss' attention to the pictures in Exercise **2A**. Hold up the Student's Book. Point to the first picture. Ask: *What do you see?* Elicit responses such as: *A woman is buying groceries.* Continue by asking about the other pictures. Elicit responses such as: *She is cooking; she is sleeping.*
- Read the instructions aloud. Ask a S to read the first two sentences aloud.
- Ss complete the exercise individually. Walk around and help as needed.

Expansion activity *(whole group)*

- If you want to expand the grammar presentation, turn to the grammar charts at the back of the Student's Book. Practice making sentences using irregular past tense verbs.

Comprehension check

- Read aloud the second part of the instructions for Exercise **2A**. Say: *Check your answers as you listen to the audio.*
- [Class Audio CD2 track 36] Play or read the audio program (see audio script, page T-160). Listen to Ss' pronunciation as they repeat the sentences. Repeat the audio program as needed.
- Ss in pairs. Say: *Now practice reading the paragraph with a partner. First one S will read the paragraph, and then the other S will read it.* Walk around and help as needed.

Learner persistence *(individual work)*

- Encourage Ss to keep a journal. Ask them to write in the journal as often as possible. Their journal can include a paragraph describing what they did during the day or the day before. Exercise **2A** can be a model. Encourage Ss to use a dictionary to help discover new words and the past tense form of verbs.

Lesson C I paid the bills.

Presentation

- Books closed. Write *bulletin board* on the board. Point to it. Ask: *Do you remember what this is?* Elicit an appropriate definition, for example: *You can put notes and ads on a bulletin board.* Ss may also respond by pointing to a bulletin board in the classroom.
- Books open. Focus Ss' attention on the bulletin board in the picture. Ask: *What is on the bulletin board?* Elicit: *Notes from family members.*
- Ask questions about the notes:
  What did Erica do? (She vacuumed the rug in the living room.)
  What did Dad do? (He cut the grass.)
  What did Sasha do? (He got the mail and made the beds.)
  What did Mom do? (She did the laundry.)
- Read aloud the instructions for Exercise **2B**.
- Ask four Ss to read the notes aloud.
- Focus Ss' attention on the questions below the bulletin board. Ask two Ss to read the question and example answer.
- Ss complete the exercise individually. Walk around and help as needed.

Comprehension check

- Read the instructions aloud. Say: *Check your answers as you listen to the audio program.*
- [Class Audio CD2 track 37] Play or read the audio program (see audio script, page T-160). Listen to Ss' pronunciation as they repeat the questions and answers. Repeat the audio program as needed.
- Say: *Now practice the questions and answers with a partner.* Ss complete the exercise in pairs. Walk around and help as needed.
- Ask several pairs to ask and answer the questions for the class.

Application

- Read the instructions aloud for Exercise **3**.
- Direct Ss' attention to the chores listed in the exercise. Read each chore aloud. Ask Ss to repeat after you.
- Model the task. Ask a S: *Did you pay bills yesterday?* Elicit a *Yes* or *No* response. Say: *If your partner says "Yes," put a check mark in the box next to the chore.* Draw a box on the board and mark it with a check.
- Ss complete the exercise in pairs. Walk around and help as needed.
- Ask pairs to ask and answer the questions for the rest of the class. Make sure that Ss use the correct form for questions in the simple past tense.

  Option If your Ss need more writing practice, ask them to write the questions on the board. Ask other Ss to read the questions aloud. Correct any errors.
- Ss in small groups. Read aloud the second part of the instructions for Exercise **3**.
- Ask three Ss to read the example question and answers aloud.
- Ss complete the exercise in small groups. Walk around and help as needed.
- Ask several pairs to ask and answer questions about chores for the class.

Expansion activity *(individual work)*

- Write about your partner. Ask Ss to write paragraphs based on the information they learned about their classmates' chores. Write a general topic sentence on the board to get them started, for example: *My classmate does many different chores. For example, yesterday . . .* Ask Ss to continue the paragraph by writing about what their partner did yesterday, using the paragraph on page 114 as a model.

Evaluation

- Direct Ss' attention to the lesson focus written on the board.
- Focus Ss' attention on the pictures on page 114. Go around the room. Ask Ss to ask and answer questions about the pictures, using irregular verbs in the simple past tense.
- Check off the lesson focus as Ss demonstrate understanding of what they have learned in the lesson.

More Ventures *(whole group, pairs, individual)*
Assign appropriate exercises from the *Teacher's Toolkit Audio CD / CD-ROM, Add Ventures,* or the *Workbook.*

B Write. Look at the notes. Answer the questions.

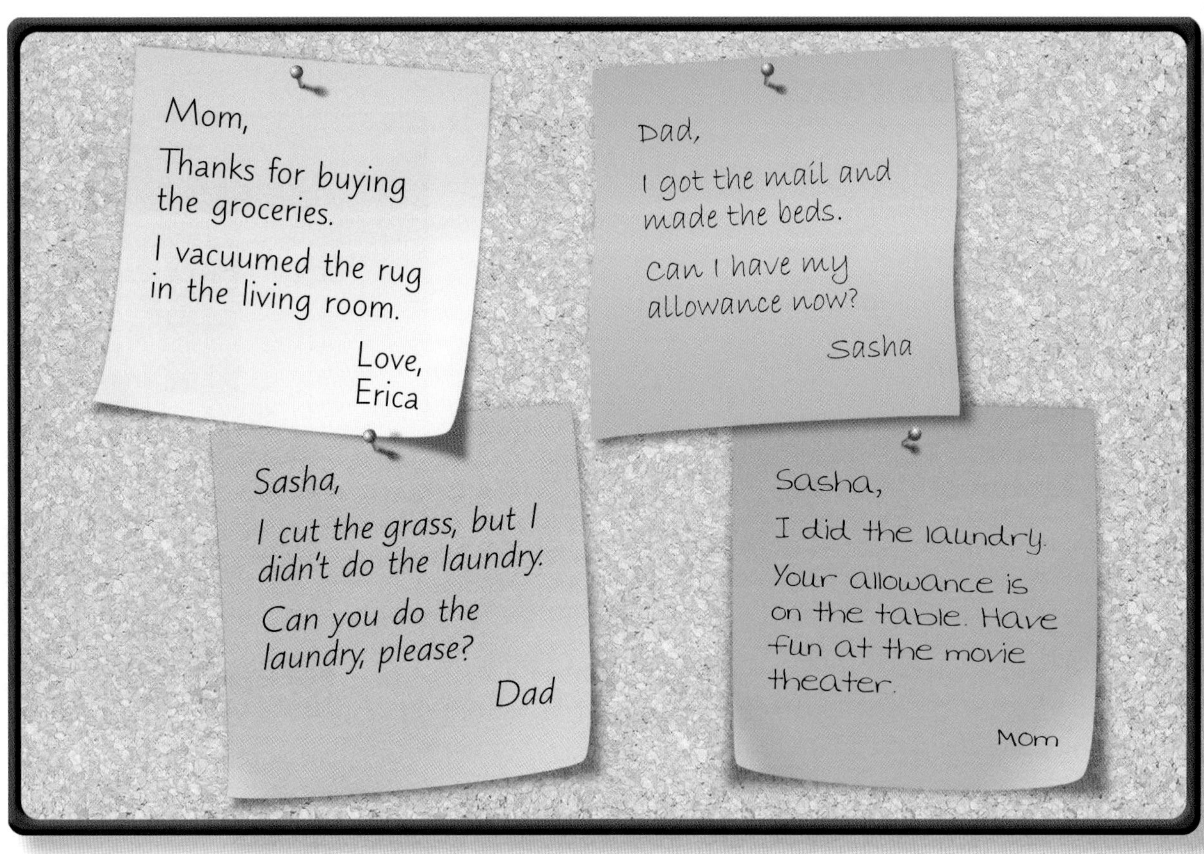

1. **A** Who bought the groceries?
   B *Mom did.*
2. **A** Who made the beds?
   B *Sasha did.*
3. **A** Who vacuumed the rug?
   B *Erica did.*
4. **A** Who got the mail?
   B *Sasha did.*
5. **A** Who cut the grass?
   B *Dad did.*
6. **A** Who did the laundry?
   B *Mom did.*

Listen and repeat. Then practice with a partner.

3 Communicate

Talk with a partner. What chores did you do yesterday? Check (✓) the boxes.

☐ paid the bills ☐ did the laundry ☐ swept the floor ☐ washed the dishes
☐ bought the groceries ☐ made the bed ☐ got the mail ☐ vacuumed the rug

Work in groups. Ask and answer questions.

Who paid the bills yesterday?

I did.

I didn't.

Lesson D Reading

1 Before you read

Talk. Mark is writing a note. Look at the picture. Answer the questions.

1. Where is he?
2. What do you think Mark is writing about?

2 Read

SELF-STUDY AUDIO CD

Listen and read.

Dear Karen,

Welcome home! We were very busy today. Jeff ironed the clothes. Chris emptied the trash. Sharon mopped the floor. Ben vacuumed the rug and dusted the furniture. The house is clean for you!

I cooked dinner. There is food on the stove.

Your husband,
Mark

Good readers ask themselves questions before they start reading, such as *Who wrote the letter?*

3 After you read

A Read the sentences. Are they correct? Circle *Yes* or *No*.

1. Jeff washed the clothes.	Yes	(No)
2. Sharon swept the floor.	Yes	(No)
3. Ben vacuumed the rug.	(Yes)	No
4. Karen cooked dinner.	Yes	(No)
5. Chris emptied the trash.	(Yes)	No

Write. Correct the sentences.

1. Jeff ironed the clothes.

B Write. Answer the questions about the note.

1. Who dusted the furniture? *Ben dusted the furniture.*
2. Did Sharon empty the trash? *No, she didn't.*
3. Who is Karen? *Karen is Mark's wife.*

Lesson objectives
- Read a note about family chores
- Practice using new topic-related words
- Practice reading strategies

Warm-up and review

- Before class. Write today's lesson focus on the board.
Lesson D:
Read a note about family chores.
Learn new vocabulary: household objects
- Begin class, Books open. Direct Ss' attention to the picture in Exercise **1**. Ask: *What do you see?* Elicit appropriate responses, for example: *A man is writing a note.*
- Ask: *Do you write notes at home?* Elicit *Yes* or *No* responses. If Ss say *Yes,* ask: *Who do you write notes to? What do you write notes about?* Responses will vary.

Presentation

- Read aloud the instructions for Exercise **1**. Ask: *Where is he?* (at home, in the kitchen) Point to the note and ask: *What do you think Mark is writing about?* Responses will vary.

Expansion activity *(student pairs)*

- Question practice. Say: *Look at the picture in Exercise 1. Ask more questions about the man in the picture.* Ss write questions in pairs, for example: *What is he wearing?*
- Say: *Join another pair of Ss. Ask the other Ss your questions. Then answer the questions.*
- Have pairs ask and answer their questions for the class.

Practice

- Read aloud the instructions for Exercise **2**.
- [Class Audio CD2 track 38] Play or read the audio program (see audio script, page T-160). Ask Ss to read along. Repeat as needed.

Read the tip box aloud. Encourage Ss to ask themselves "*Wh-*" questions before reading something.

Expansion activity *(individual work, small groups)*

- "Wh-" question-and-answer practice. Ss in small groups. Ask: *What are some "Wh-" question words in English?* Write Ss' responses on the board; for example:
What When Why Where Who
- Say: *Use these question words to write some questions about the note in Exercise 2.*
- Ss write questions individually; then they ask and answer the questions in small groups. Check comprehension by asking Ss from each group to stand up and ask Ss in other groups their questions.

Learner persistence *(individual work)*

- [Self-Study Audio CD track 34] Exercise **2** is recorded on the Ss' self-study CD at the back of the Student's Book. Ss can listen to the CD at home for reinforcement and review. They can also listen to the CD for self-directed learning when class attendance is not possible.

Comprehension check

- Remind Ss of the content of the reading and recycle vocabulary by asking: *What chores did the family do?* (ironed the clothes, emptied the trash, mopped the floor, vacuumed the rug, dusted the furniture, cooked dinner)
- Read aloud the instructions for Exercise **3A**. Ask a S to read the example aloud.
- Ask: *What did Jeff do?* (ironed the clothes) Point to where *No* is circled for number 1.
- Ss complete the exercise individually. Help as needed.
- Check answers with the class. Ask Ss to read their sentences and answers aloud.
- Ask Ss to take out a piece of paper. Read aloud the second part of the instructions for Exercise **3A**.
- Model the task of correcting the sentences. Point to *No* for number 1 in Exercise **3A**. Read the sentence aloud. Tell Ss: *This sentence is incorrect. Tell me the correct sentence. Jeff . . .* (ironed the clothes). Write on the board: *Jeff ironed the clothes.*
- Ss complete the exercise individually. Help as needed.
- Check answers with the class. Ask Ss to write their answers on the board. Then ask different Ss to read the answers aloud.

Practice

- Ask Ss questions about the note in Exercise **2**. *Who dusted the furniture?* (Ben dusted the furniture.) *Did Sharon empty the trash?* (No, Chris emptied the trash.)
- Read the instructions aloud for Exercise **3B**. Ss complete the exercise individually. Help as needed.
- Check answers with the class.

Expansion activity *(whole group, individual work)*

- Review the words for family members in Unit 3. Write *family* on the board. Ask Ss to tell you about their family. Write the family words on the board.
- Ask Ss to look at the note in Exercise **2** and tell you about the family members. Accept any accurate answer.

Lesson D Reading

Warm-up and review

- Books closed. Write on the board: *household objects.* Point to the words. Say them aloud. Ask Ss to repeat after you. Ask: *What are some examples of household objects?* Elicit appropriate responses, for example: a *mop, a broom, a stove.* Write Ss' responses on the board.
- Point to each object written on the board. Say the names of the objects aloud. Ask Ss to repeat after you.

  Option Bring in pictures of different household objects from magazines. Try to include the objects learned in this unit. Show Ss the pictures and ask: *What's this?* Write Ss' responses on the board.

Presentation

- Books open. Direct Ss' attention to the pictures in the picture dictionary. Say: *These are pictures of different household objects.*
- Direct Ss attention to the word bank in Exercise **4A**. Say: *Repeat the words after me.* Say each word. Listen to Ss' pronunciations as they repeat. Correct pronunciation as needed.

Practice

- Say: *Write the words in the picture dictionary.* Point to the first example, which has been done. Be sure Ss understand the task.
- Ss complete the exercise individually. Walk around and help as needed.

Comprehension check

- [Class Audio CD2 track 39] Play or read the audio program (see audio script, page T-160). Ss should check their answers and repeat the words after they hear them. Repeat the audio program if necessary.

Learner persistence *(individual work)*

- [Self-Study Audio CD track 35] Exercise **4A** is recorded on the Ss' self-study CD at the back of the Student's Book. Ss can listen to the CD at home for reinforcement and review. They can also listen to the CD for self-directed learning when class attendance is not possible.

Application

- Read aloud the instructions for Exercise **4B**.
- Ask a S: *What can you do with an iron?* Elicit appropriate responses such as: *iron a shirt.*
- Hold up the Student's Book. Point to the handwritten *d* next to number 1. Say: *You can iron with an iron.*

Teaching tip
It might be helpful to point out that some words can be both nouns and verbs, such as *iron* and *vacuum.*

- Ss complete the exercise individually. Help as needed.
- Write the numbers *1–7* on the board. Ask individual Ss to come to the board to write their answers.
- Ask Ss: *Do you agree with the answers on the board?* Ask different Ss to correct any errors.

Expansion activity *(small groups)*

- Write these questions on the board:
  What can you do with a broom?
  What can you do with an iron?
  What can you do with a mop?
  What can you do with a stove?
- Ss in small groups. Tell Ss to ask their groups the questions on the board. (These questions recycle *can* from Unit 8.) Ask several Ss to ask and answer the questions for the rest of the class.

Learner persistence *(individual work)*

- Encourage Ss to keep a journal and to write in it as often as possible. Ask Ss to keep a list of chores they do every day.
- Encourage Ss to check a dictionary for the names of chores they do not know and to share those names with the class at the next class meeting.

Evaluation

- Direct Ss' attention to the lesson focus on the board. Put a check mark next to *Read a note about family chores.*
- Focus Ss' attention on page 117. Ask Ss to make sentences about the objects in the picture dictionary.
- Check off the lesson focus as Ss demonstrate understanding of what they have learned in the lesson.

More Ventures *(whole group, pairs, individual)*
Assign appropriate exercises from the *Teacher's Toolkit Audio CD / CD-ROM, Add Ventures,* or the *Workbook.*

4 Picture dictionary Household objects

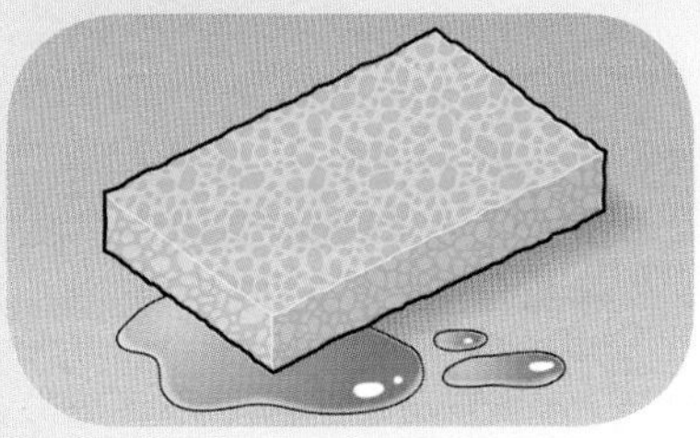

1. *a sponge*

2. *a mop*

3. *a vacuum cleaner*

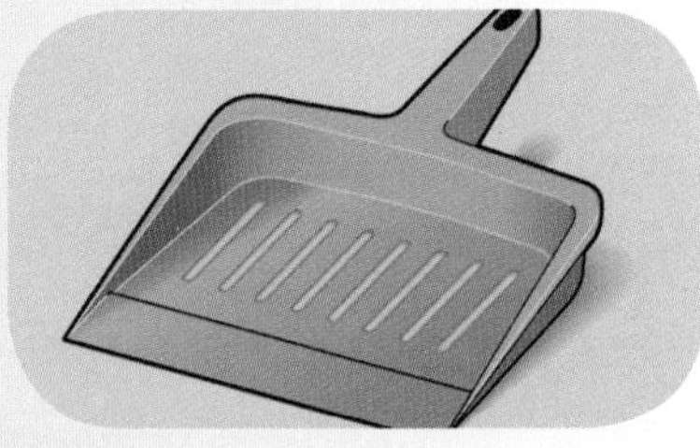

4. *a dustpan*

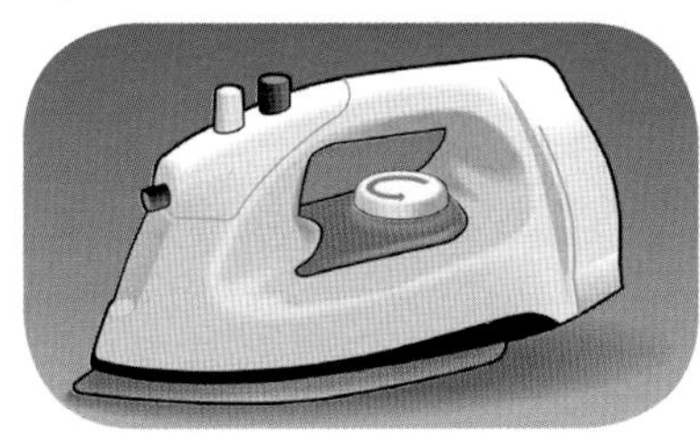

5. *an iron*

6. *a broom*

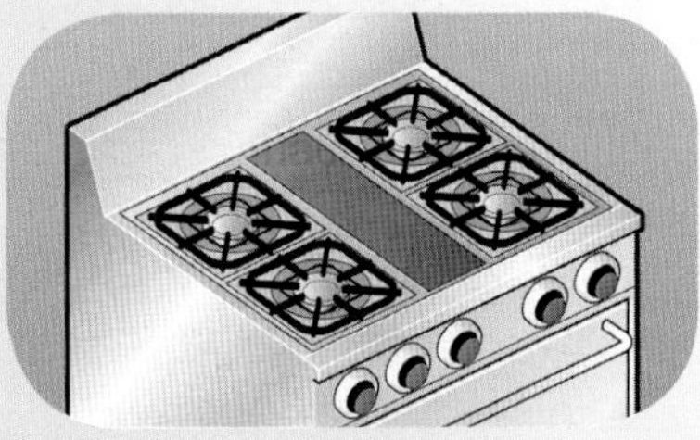

7. *a stove*

8. *a lawn mower*

9. *a bucket*

A **Write** the words in the picture dictionary. Then listen and repeat.

a broom	an iron	a sponge
a bucket	a lawn mower	a stove
a dustpan	a mop	a vacuum cleaner

B **Write.** Match the objects with the actions.

1. an iron *d* — a. vacuum
2. a sponge *f* — b. sweep
3. a stove *e* — c. mop
4. a lawn mower *g* — d. iron
5. a mop *c* — e. cook
6. a vacuum cleaner *a* — f. wash
7. a broom *b* — g. cut grass

Lesson E Writing

1 Before you write

A Talk with a partner. Ask and answer the questions.

1. Who does the chores in your home? What chores?
2. Are there special times to do those chores?
3. How do you feel about chores?

B Talk. Interview three classmates. Write two chores each person did last week and one chore they didn't do.

Name	Chores you did	Chores you didn't do
Katia	*bought the groceries* *walked the dog*	*didn't vacuum the rugs*
(Answers will vary.)		

C Write. Complete the note. Use past tense forms of the verbs.

Dear Mom,

I ___*bought*___ (1. buy) milk from the supermarket. It's in the refrigerator. I also ___*dusted*___ (2. dust) the shelves and ___*swept*___ (3. sweep) the floor, but I didn't ___*wash*___ (4. wash) the dishes. Did you ___*buy*___ (5. buy) a new sponge? Did you ___*vacuum*___ (6. vacuum) the rug yesterday? I also ___*made*___ (7. make) my bed.

See you later,

Irina

Lesson objective
- Discuss and write about chores

Warm-up and review

- Before class. Write today's lesson focus on the board.
  Lesson E:
  Discuss chores
  Write a note about chores you did and didn't do
- Begin class. Books closed. Point to the word *chores* on the board. Ask Ss to think of as many chores as possible. Write their responses on the board.

Presentation

- Books open. Read aloud the instructions for Exercise **1A**. Ask three Ss to read the questions aloud.
- Discuss the answers with the class.
- Write on the board: *interview*. Point to the word. Say it aloud. Ask Ss to repeat after you. Ask: *What does this mean?* Elicit a response such as: *It means asking someone questions and getting answers.*
- Say: *You are going to interview three of your classmates about the chores they did and didn't do at home.*
- Direct Ss' attention to Exercise **1B** and read the instructions aloud.
- Model the task. Ask a S: *What chores did you do last week? What chores didn't you do?* Write the S's responses on the board.
- Ss complete the exercise individually. Encourage Ss to stand up and walk around the room while they ask other Ss the questions.
- Ask Ss to read aloud the information about their classmates.

  Option Draw three columns on the board. Write the headings from the chart in the columns. Ask Ss to come to the board to fill in information about their classmates.
- Direct Ss' attention to the note in Exercise **1C**. Read the instructions aloud. Ask a S to read the first two sentences aloud.
- Ss complete the exercise individually. Walk around and help as needed.
- Write the numbers *1–7* on the board. Ask individual Ss to write their answers on the board.
- Ask different Ss to read the sentences aloud. Ask: *Are these answers correct?* Ask different Ss to correct any errors on the board.

Expansion activity *(student pairs)*

- Chores checklist: "Before Visitors Arrive."
- Say: *Do you do chores before people come to visit you at home? We're going to make a list of those chores. List between seven and ten chores.*
- Model the activity. Write on the board: *Before Visitors Arrive*. Try this "think aloud" to help students list one or two chores they would do to prepare for guests:

  Well, my kitchen floor is dirty, so I will mop it before my visitors arrive.

  Write *mop the kitchen floor* on the board.
- Ss work individually and make a list of everything they need to do before someone comes to visit their home.
- Ss compare their lists in pairs. Encourage them to discuss which chores they like and which ones they don't like.
- Review the lists as a class, or ask Ss to post them around the room.

Expansion activity *(student pairs)*

- Peer dictation. Before class. Make copies of the following sentences. Half of your Ss will get one set of sentences, and the other half will get the other set of sentences.

  Set 1
  1. I mopped the floor yesterday.
  2. I didn't wash the dishes.
  3. I paid the bills last night.

  Set 2
  1. I walked the dog today.
  2. I didn't cook dinner.
  3. I didn't buy the groceries.
- In class. Ss in pairs. Give one person in each pair Set 1 sentences and ask that person to dictate the sentences to his or her partner. Give the partner a copy of the Set 2 sentences to dictate.
- When Ss finish, ask them to check their work by comparing their sentences to the ones in the handouts.

Lesson E Writing

Practice

- Direct Ss' attention to the verbs in the word bank in Exercise **1D**. Say each verb aloud. Ask Ss to repeat after you. Ask: *What is the past tense of each of these verbs?* For example: *Buy*. Elicit: *bought*.

  Option Ask Ss to come to the board to write the past tense form of the verbs in the word bank. Then point to each one and say it aloud. Ask Ss to repeat after you.
- Read aloud the instructions for Exercise **1D**.
- Ask a S to read the first sentence in the note.
- Ss complete the exercise individually. Walk around and help as needed.

> Read the tip box aloud. Encourage Ss to use the verb charts on page 149 as reference materials for the simple past of regular and irregular verbs.

- Go around the room. Ask individual Ss to read a sentence from the note. Ask: *Is the answer correct?* Ask other Ss to correct any errors.
- Ss in pairs. Say: *Read the note to your partner. Then listen while your partner reads the note to you.*

Expansion activity (whole group)

- Gender roles and chores. Write on the board:
  1. Are there chores that only women in your family do?
  2. Are there chores that only men do?
  3. What is your opinion about different chores for women and men?
- Ss answer the questions in small groups.
- Ask one S from each group to report to the class on the group's discussion.
- Direct Ss' attention to Exercise **2** and read the instructions aloud.
- Ss complete the exercise individually. Walk around and help as needed.

Comprehension check

- Read aloud the instructions for Exercise **3A**. Ss complete the exercise in pairs. Walk around and help as needed. Help with pronunciation.
- Read aloud the instructions for Exercise **3B**. This exercise asks Ss to work together to peer-correct their writing. Ask a S to read the questions aloud. Tell Ss to exchange papers and look at their partner's note for the answers to the questions. Tell Ss to circle the answers on their partner's note. Help as needed.
- Ask pairs to answer the questions about their partner's note for the class.

Expansion activity (student pairs)

- Job interview role-plays. Say: *Imagine that you have a job interview. One person will be the interviewer. The other person is looking for a job. Make up a conversation about your work skills.*
- Write the following example conversation on the board or distribute the conversation in a handout:
  INTERVIEWER: Good morning.
  APPLICANT: Good morning.
  INTERVIEWER: I see you are applying to be a waiter at my restaurant. What experience do you have?
  APPLICANT: I worked at another restaurant for two years.
  INTERVIEWER: What did you do at the restaurant?
  APPLICANT: I took orders. I brought the food. I cleaned the tables.
  INTERVIEWER: Did you use the cash register?
  APPLICANT: Yes, I did.
  INTERVIEWER: Can you start tomorrow?
  APPLICANT: Yes, I can.
  INTERVIEWER: Welcome to my restaurant!
- Ask two Ss to read the conversation aloud. Say: *Now make a similar conversation about a different kind of job.*
- Ss complete the activity in pairs. Walk around and help as needed.
- Ask several pairs to perform their job interviews for the class.

Evaluation

- Direct Ss' attention to the lesson focus written on the board. Ask different Ss to come to the board to write the chores they did and didn't do yesterday.
- Check off the lesson focus as Ss demonstrate understanding of what they have learned in the lesson.

> ***More Ventures*** (whole group, pairs, individual)
> Assign appropriate exercises from the *Teacher's Toolkit Audio CD / CD-ROM, Add Ventures,* or the *Workbook*.

D **Write.** Complete the note. Use the correct past tense form.

buy	cook	dry	mop	pay	sweep	walk	wash

Hi Tom,

I ___cooked___ dinner for you. It's on the stove. I ___washed___ the dishes, but I didn't ___dry___ them. Sorry, I didn't have time. I ___bought___ a new broom at the store. I ___swept___ the kitchen floor with it. I ___mopped___ the floor, too, with the new mop. I didn't ___walk___ the dog.

Did you ___pay___ the bills? It's the end of the month. Please remember.

I'll see you tonight.

Love,
Mary

Check your past tense verb forms. Use the chart on page 149.

2 Write

Write a note to a family member. Write the chores you did and didn't do.

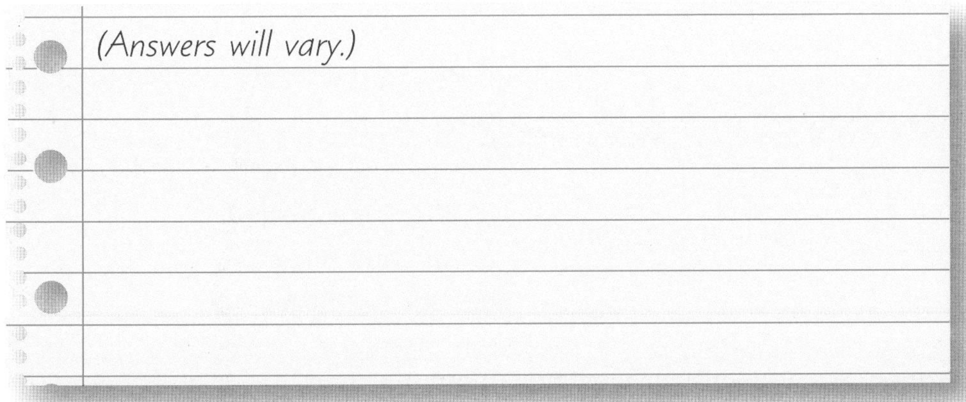

3 After you write

A **Read** your note to a partner.

B **Check** your partner's note.

- What are two chores your partner wrote about?
- Are the past tense forms correct?

Lesson F Another view

1 Life-skills reading

SaveMore Supermarket

JOB DUTIES

Duties	Employee	Initials	Time Completed
Sweep the floor.	Joshua Liu	JL	9:15 p.m.
Mop the floor.	Kim Casey	KC	9:30 p.m.
Mop the floor.	Roger Brown	RB	9:30 p.m.
Clean the bathroom.	Ann Hamilton	AH	8:30 p.m.
Empty the trash cans.	Steve Johnson	SJ	8:45 p.m.
Turn off the lights.	Victor Morales	VM	10:00 p.m.
Lock the doors.	Victor Morales	VM	10:00 p.m.

A Read the questions. Look at the chart. Circle the answers.

1. Who swept the floor?
   a. Ann
   b. Victor
   c. Kim and Roger
   (d.) Joshua
2. When did Steve empty the trash cans?
   a. at 8:30 p.m.
   (b.) at 8:45 p.m.
   c. at 9:15 p.m.
   d. at 10:00 p.m.
3. Did Victor turn off the lights?
   (a.) Yes, he did.
   b. No, he didn't. He swept the floor.
   c. No, he didn't. He cleaned the bathroom.
   d. No, he didn't. He mopped the floor.
4. Who mopped the floor?
   a. Kim and Victor
   b. Steve and Joshua
   c. Ann and Roger
   (d.) Kim and Roger

B Talk with a partner. Ask and answer questions about the chart.

Who locked the doors?

Victor did.

Did Steve empty the trash?

Yes, he did.

Lesson objectives

- Read and discuss a job duties chart
- Review unit vocabulary
- Introduce the project
- Complete the self-assessment

Warm-up and review

- Before class. Write today's lesson focus on the board.
Lesson F:
Read a job duties chart
Review topic vocabulary
Complete the self-assessment
- Begin class. Books closed. Write on the board: *job duties*. Say: *Job duties are things you do at work.* Ask: *What are some duties you have to do for your job?* Elicit appropriate responses, such as: *I open the store, clean the floors,* etc. Write the responses on the board.
- Ask Ss to brainstorm different occupations. Elicit responses such as: *waiter, doctor, nurse.* Point to each one. Ask: *What are his or her job duties?* Elicit appropriate responses such as: *A waiter has to take orders and bring customers food; a doctor has to take care of people; a nurse has to give people medicine.*

  Option If most of your Ss work, ask pairs to discuss and list their job duties, and then report their partner's job duties to the rest of the class.

Presentation

- Books open. Direct Ss' attention to the job duties chart in Exercise **1**. Ask questions about the chart:
What do you see? (a job duties chart)
What supermarket is this from? (SaveMore Supermarket)
What are the duties? (sweep the floor, mop the floor, etc.)
What does "employee" mean? (worker)
What are "initials"? (the first letter of someone's first and last name)
Do you have a chart like this at work? (Yes or No)
How is it different? (Responses will vary.)
How is it the same? (Responses will vary.)
- Ask different Ss to read aloud the job duties for each employee. Model the activity by talking about Joshua Liu: *Joshua Liu has to sweep the floor. His initials are JL. He completed his work at 9:15 p.m.*

Teaching tip
It might be helpful to write your own initials on the board as an example for Ss.

Practice

- Read aloud the instructions for Exercise **1A**. This task helps prepare Ss for standardized-type tests they may have to take. Be sure Ss understand the task. Have students individually scan for and circle the answers.
- Check answers with the class.
- Direct Ss' attention to Exercise **1B** and read the instructions aloud. Ask four Ss to read aloud the example questions and answers.
- Ss complete the exercise in pairs. Walk around and listen to Ss' pronunciations. Write difficult words on the board.
- When Ss finish, say the words aloud. Ask Ss to repeat after you.

Expansion activity *(small groups)*

- Question practice. Ss in small groups. Say: *On a piece of paper, write five questions about the job duties chart. Work together with your group.*
- Ss complete the activity in their groups. Walk around and help as needed.
- When Ss are finished, ask them to exchange papers with another group. Ss then write answers to the questions and return them to the original group. Ask Ss to check the answers.
- For a greater challenge, ask Ss to answer the questions without the help of the books – but they'll need time to study the chart beforehand!

Expansion activity *(small groups)*

- Make a job duties chart for another workplace. Ss in small groups. Say: *Think of another workplace, or use your own place of work. Write a job duties chart for that workplace. Think of all the jobs that need to get done. Use the chart in Exercise 1 as an example.*
- Ss complete the activity in small groups. Walk around and help as needed.
- When Ss finish, ask them to show their charts to other groups. Alternatively, ask them to post the charts around the room.

Community building *(whole group)*

- Ask: *What kinds of duties do you have as Ss?* Write Ss' responses on the board, for example: *do our homework, study, listen in class.*
- Ask: *How can you help me in the classroom? What are some job duties that you can do?* Elicit responses such as: *make photocopies, erase the board, push in the chairs after class, clean up any trash.*
- Write the duties on the board. Encourage Ss to help you with these tasks before, during, and after class.

Lesson F Another view

Warm-up and review

- Books closed. Recycle new vocabulary learned in Lesson D by asking: *What are some household items?* Elicit responses such as: *mop, iron, vacuum, sponge.*
- Ask: *Where can you buy these items?* Elicit appropriate responses.

Presentation

- Books open. Focus Ss' attention on the word bank in Exercise **2A**. Say each word aloud. Ask Ss to repeat.
- Read the instructions aloud. Point out the example in number 1.
- Ss complete the exercise in pairs. Walk around and help as needed.
- Write the numbers *1–8* on the board. Ask individual Ss to come to the board to write the name of each object.
- Ask different Ss to read aloud the answers on the board. Ask: *Are the answers correct?* Ask other Ss to correct any errors.

Expansion activity (student pairs)

- Descriptive writing practice. Ss in pairs. Say: *Describe one of the objects from Exercise 2A. Don't use the name of the object. Later, you will read your description to the class. The class will guess which object you are describing.*
- Model the activity. Say: *It is soft. You can use it to wash dishes. What is it?* Elicit: *It is a sponge.*
- Ss complete the activity in pairs. Then they read their description to the rest of the class, and the other Ss will guess which object they are describing.

Application

- Write on the board: *clothing label.* Point to the words. Say them aloud. Ask: *What is this?* If possible, bring in a piece of clothing. Show Ss the label.
- Ask: *What information do you find on a clothing label?* Elicit appropriate responses, such as: *the material and the washing instructions.*
- Focus Ss' attention on the picture in Exercise **2B**. Ask: *What do you see?* Elicit responses such as: *I see a man. He is holding a shirt. He is looking at the clothing label.*
- Read aloud the instructions for Exercise **2B**. Ask a S to read the example instruction aloud: *Wash in cold water.* Ask: *Which symbol means wash in cold water?* Elicit: *number 1.* Hold up the Student's Book and point to where the line has been drawn from the first symbol to the washing instructions.

Expansion activity (student pairs)

- **Materials needed**
  1. Seven to ten articles of clothing, each with a number; the clothes should be made of different kinds of materials and have clear clothing labels on them.
  2. A copy of the following grid for each pair of Ss.

Type of clothing	Material	Washing instructions
1. shirt	cotton	Wash in warm water.

- Go over the different types of material (*cotton, polyester, wool, silk,* etc.). Write the words on the board.
- Review different washing instructions. Write Ss' examples on the board (see Exercise **2B** for examples).
- Place the clothing on different desks in the room. Say: *Read each clothing label and fill in your charts.*
- Ss complete the exercise in pairs. Help as needed.

Application

Community building

- **Project** Ask Ss to turn to page 140 in their Student's Book to complete the project for Unit 9.

More Ventures (whole group, pairs, individual)
Assign appropriate exercises from the *Teacher's Toolkit Audio CD / CD-ROM, Add Ventures,* or the *Workbook.*

Evaluation

- Before asking Ss to turn to the self-assessment on page 145, do a quick review of each lesson in the unit. Have Ss turn to Lesson A. Ask the class to call out what they remember about this lesson. Prompt Ss with questions, for example: *What are the conversations about on this page? What vocabulary is in the picture?*
- **Self-assessment** Read the instructions for Exercise **3**. Ask Ss to turn to the self-assessment page and complete the unit self-assessment.
- If Ss are ready, administer the unit test on pages T-183–T-184 of this *Teacher's Edition* (or on the *Teacher's Toolkit Audio CD / CD-ROM*). The audio and audio scripts for the tests are on the *Teacher's Toolkit Audio CD / CD-ROM.*

2 Fun with language

A Work with a partner. What are these things? Write the words.

a broom	an iron	a mop	a stove
a dustpan	a lawn mower	a sponge	a vacuum cleaner

1. an iron
2. a sponge
3. a stove
4. a mop

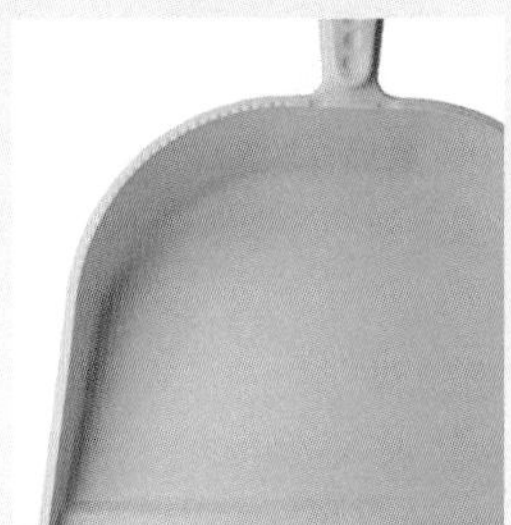

5. a lawn mower
6. a broom
7. a dustpan
8. a vacuum cleaner

B Work with a partner. Match.

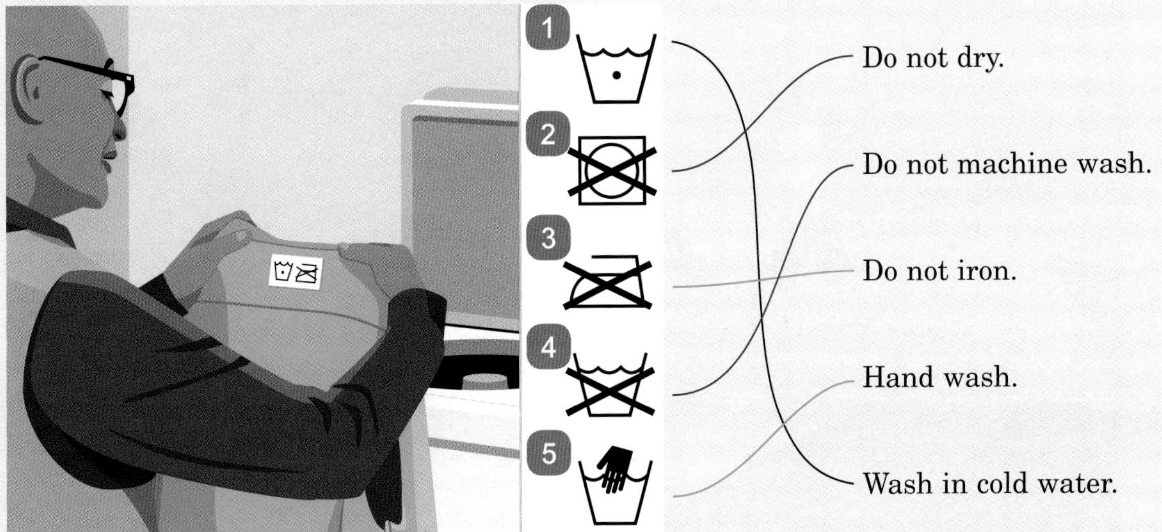

3 Wrap up

Complete the **Self-assessment** on page 145.

Leisure

Lesson A Get ready

1 Talk about the picture

A Look at the picture. What do you see?

B Point to these activities: camping • fishing • hiking • canoeing
swimming • picnicking

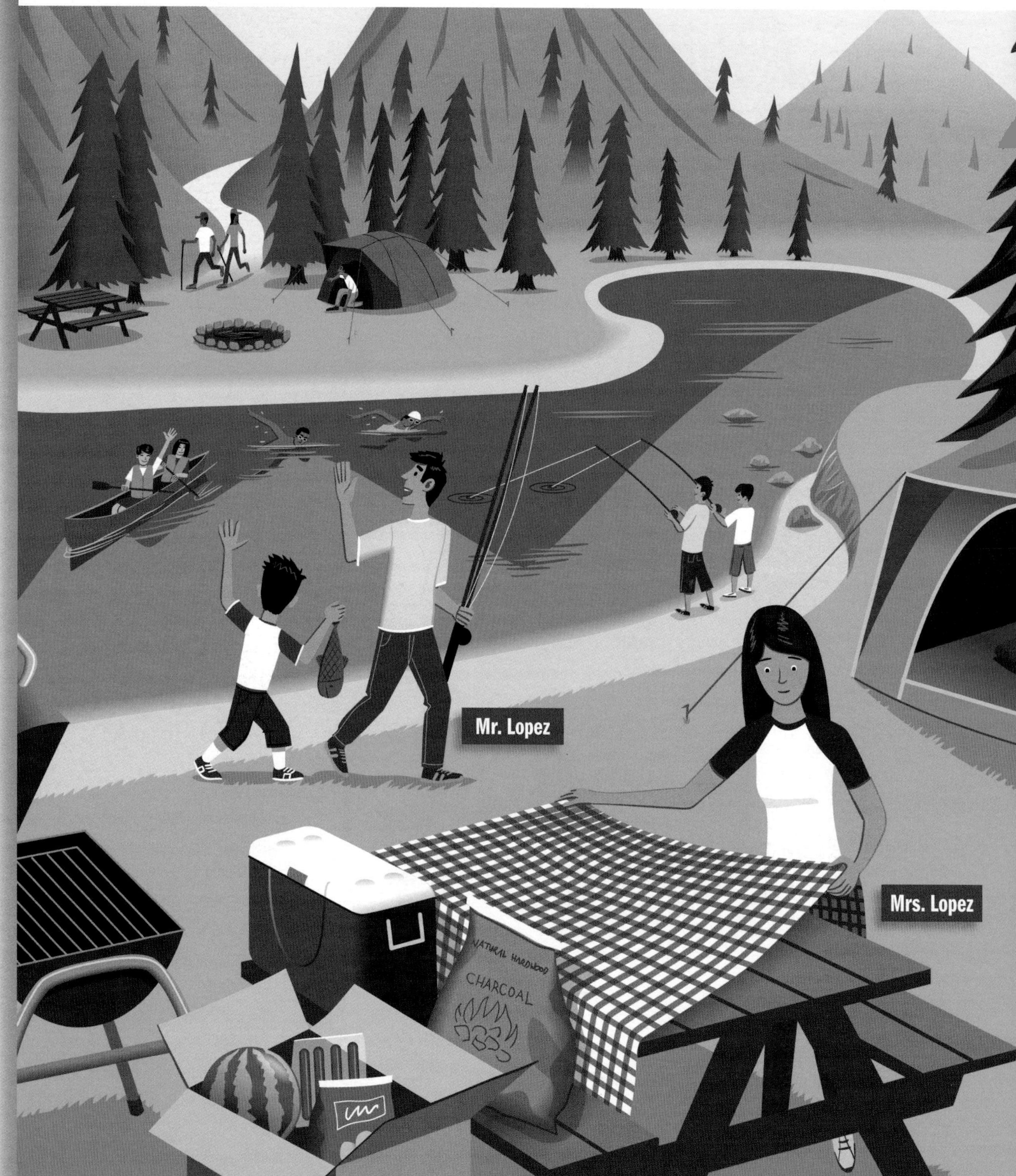

Lesson objectives

- Introduce students to the topic
- Find out what students know about the topic
- Preview the unit by talking about the picture
- Practice key vocabulary
- Practice listening skills

Warm-up and review

- Before class. Write today's lesson focus on the board. *Lesson A: Vocabulary for leisure activities*
- Begin class. Books closed. Write on the board: *leisure.* Point to the word. Say it aloud. Ask Ss to repeat it.
- Say: *Leisure activities are things you do in your free time. In my free time, I go swimming.* Act out *swimming.* Ask: *What do you do in your free time?* Elicit responses such as: *go to the movies, read, watch TV.* Ask: *What are some leisure activities you can do outside?* Elicit responses such as: *hike, swim, play soccer.*

Presentation

- Books open. Set the scene. Direct Ss' attention to the picture on page 122. Ask: *What do you see?* Elicit as much vocabulary about the picture as possible: *people, a lake, mountains, picnic tables, tents,* etc.
- Direct Ss' attention to the key words in Exercise **1B**. Read each word aloud while pointing to the item in the picture and to the person or persons doing the activity. Ask the class to repeat and point.

Teaching tip

Do not expect Ss to know all the new vocabulary words. These warm-up questions are intended to find out what Ss already know about vocabulary pertaining to leisure activities.

Teaching tip

Ss may not be familiar with some of the leisure activities listed at the top of the page. It might be helpful to hold up the Student's Book and point out each activity so that Ss know which word you are describing.

Comprehension check

- Ask Ss *Yes / No* questions about the picture. Recycle grammar and vocabulary from past lessons. Say: *Listen to the questions. Answer "Yes" or "No."*
  Is this a campground? (Yes.)
  Are these mountains? (Yes.)
  Is this a lake? (Yes.)
  Are people fishing? (Yes.)
  Are they swimming? (Yes.)
  Are they shopping? (No.)
  Are they playing soccer? (No.)
  Is Mrs. Lopez ironing? (No.)

Practice

- Direct Ss' attention to Exercise **1B**. Model the task. Hold up the Student's Book. Say to a S: *Point to people who are camping.* The S points to the appropriate part of the picture.
- Ss in pairs. Say to one S: *Say the words in Exercise 1B.* Say to his or her partner. *Point to the activity in the picture.*
- Ss complete the exercise in pairs. Walk around and help as needed. When Ss finish, have them change partners and change roles.
- Ask several pairs to perform the exercise for the class to check Ss' understanding.

Expansion activity *(student pairs)*

- Vacation discussion. Write on the board: *Where do you want to go on vacation? Why?*
- Ss in pairs. Say: *Ask your partner the two questions on the board. Then your partner will ask you the questions.*
- When Ss finish, ask pairs to form a group of four. Say: *Now ask the questions to your new group members.* Walk around and help as needed.

Lesson A Get ready

Presentation

- Books closed. Ask Ss: *What leisure activities are not in the picture on page 122?* Write Ss' responses on the board. Say the words aloud. Ask Ss to repeat after you. If anyone in the class doesn't know what the words mean, ask the Ss who said the leisure activities to explain them through actions or words.

Teaching tip
It is important to give Ss opportunities to explain words and other aspects of English to their classmates. This gives them confidence and helps them improve their English.

Practice

- Books open. Direct Ss' attention to Exercise **2A**. Read aloud the words in the word bank and ask Ss to repeat after you. For each item, ask: *What does this mean?* Ss can use actions to explain the meanings. Model the activity by pretending to swing a bat for *play ball.*
- Read aloud the instructions for Exercise **2A**.
- [Class Audio CD2 track 40] Play or read the audio program (see audio script, page T-160). Ss listen and circle the words they hear. Repeat the audio program as needed.
- Check answers. Ask: *What did you circle?* Ask Ss to write the words on the board. Point to the words. Say: *Repeat after me.* Say each word.

Expansion activity (student pairs)

- Ask Ss to look at the words they did not circle. Ask a S to write them on the board: *go canoeing, play ball, read.*
- Ss in pairs. Say: *Write sentences with the words that you didn't hear in Exercise 2A.* Help as needed.
- Ask Ss to write their sentences on the board. Ask other Ss to read the sentences aloud. Ask: *Are these sentences correct?* Ask different Ss to correct any errors.

Practice

- Direct Ss' attention to the instructions for Exercise **2B** and read them aloud.
- [Class Audio CD2 track 40] Play or read the audio program again. Pause after the first conversation. Ask: *Which picture matches conversation A?* (picture number 4). Point to the handwritten *a* written next to number 4. Be sure Ss understand the task. Then play or read the complete audio program. Ss complete the exercise individually.

Learner persistence (individual work)

- [Self-Study Audio CD track 36] Exercises **2A** and **2B** are recorded on the Ss' self-study CD at the back of the Student's Book. Ss can listen to the CD at home for reinforcement and review. They can also listen for self-directed learning when class attendance is not possible.

Comprehension check

- Write the numbers *1–6* on the board. Ask individual Ss to come to the board to write the correct answers to Exercise **2B** next to each number.
- Read aloud the second part of the instructions for Exercise **2B**.
- [Class Audio CD2 track 40] Play or read the audio program again. Pause the audio program after each conversation. Point to a letter of the conversation on the board. Ask: *Is this correct?*

Application

- Ask Ss: *What did you do last summer?* Elicit leisure activities, for example: *I went camping.*
- Direct Ss' attention to Exercise **2C** and read the instructions aloud.
- Read each activity aloud. Ask Ss to repeat after you. Explain the meaning of any unfamiliar words.
- Ss complete the exercise individually. Help as needed.
- Read aloud the second part of the instructions for Exercise **2C**. Ask two Ss to read the example conversation aloud.
- Ss complete the exercise in pairs. Help as needed.
- Ask several pairs to ask and answer their questions for the rest of the class.

Evaluation

- Direct Ss' attention to the lesson focus on the board. Ask Ss to identify the leisure activities in the pictures on pages 122 and 123.
- Check off the lesson focus as Ss demonstrate understanding of what they have learned in the lesson.

More Ventures *(whole group, pairs, individual)*
Assign appropriate exercises from the *Teacher's Toolkit Audio CD / CD-ROM, Add Ventures,* or the *Workbook.*

2 Listening

A **Listen.** Circle the words you hear.

go camping	go hiking	play ball
go canoeing	go picnicking	read
go fishing	go swimming	rest

B **Listen again.** Write the letter of the conversation.

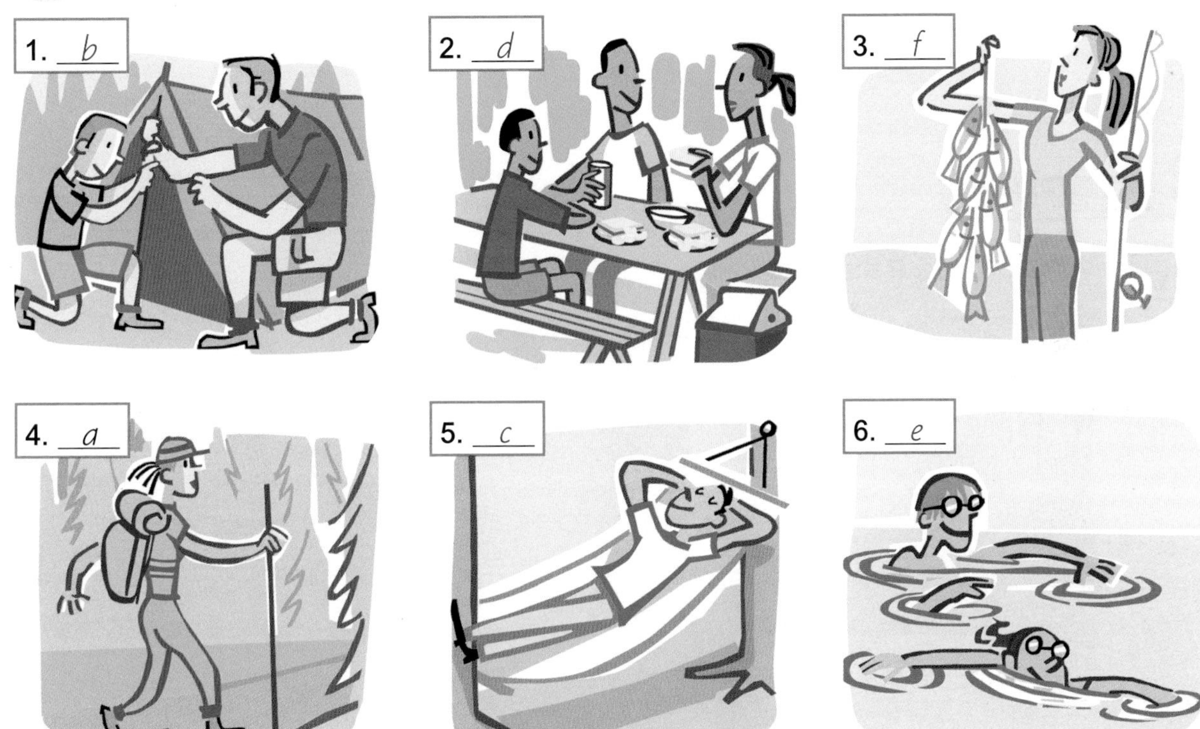

Listen again. Check your answers.

C **What** do you do on your vacation? Check (✓) the boxes.

- ☐ go camping
- ☐ go fishing
- ☐ go hiking
- ☐ go swimming
- ☐ (other) ____________
- ☐ read books
- ☐ rest
- ☐ spend time with my family
- ☐ volunteer
- ☐ (other) ____________

Talk with a partner. Ask and answer questions.

What do you do on your vacation?

I go hiking, swimming, and spend time with my family.

Lesson B What did you do yesterday?

1 Grammar focus: simple past with irregular verbs

Questions

	did you do	
	did he do	
What	did she do	yesterday?
	did you do	
	did they do	

Answers

I	
He	
She	went swimming.
We	
They	

Irregular verbs

drive → drove	ride → rode
eat → ate	see → saw
go → went	sleep → slept
have → had	take → took
read → read	write → wrote

2 Practice

A Write. Answer the questions.

1. **A** What did Mr. Brown do?
   B He went fishing.
   (go fishing)

2. **A** What did Carl do?
   B He went hiking.
   (go hiking)

3. **A** What did Gina do?
   B She went swimming.
   (go swimming)

4. **A** What did Mrs. Brown do?
   B She went riding.
   (go riding)

5. **A** What did Carl and Gina do?
   B They went camping.
   (go camping)

6. **A** What did Mr. and Mrs. Brown do?
   B They went canoeing.
   (go canoeing)

 **Listen and repeat.** Then practice with a partner.

Lesson objective
- Introduce the simple past with irregular verbs

Warm-up and review

- Before class. Write today's lesson focus on the board.
  Lesson B: The simple past with irregular verbs
- Begin class. Books closed. Review questions in the past tense by asking Ss *Yes / No* questions about last weekend.
  Did you buy groceries last weekend?
  Did you go to a restaurant last weekend?
  Did you go camping last weekend?
  Did you eat pizza last weekend?
  Did you take a nap last weekend?
  Elicit *Yes* or *No* responses.
- Write on the board:
  What did you do yesterday?
  I went fishing.
- Point to the question and answer on the board. Read them aloud. Ask Ss to repeat after you.

Presentation

- Books open. Direct Ss' attention to the grammar chart in Exercise **1**. Read the questions and answers aloud. Ask Ss to repeat.
- Direct Ss' attention to the list of irregular verbs. Say: *Irregular verbs do not end in "-ed" in the past tense. The words change completely.*
- Say each verb aloud in the present and past tense. Listen to Ss as they repeat the verbs after you.

Expansion activity (student pairs)

- Past tense practice. Ss in pairs. Ask Ss to practice the irregular past tense verbs on page 124. One S will read the present form, and the other S will read the past form. After a few minutes, ask Ss to switch roles. After a couple of rounds, Ss should practice without looking at the book.

Expansion activity (whole group)

- Review verb phrases, such as: *go camping / went camping; go fishing / went fishing.*
- Write on the board:
  What did you do yesterday?
  I _____ camping.
- Elicit an answer for the blank: *went*. Fill in the blank and read the question and answer aloud. Ask Ss to repeat after you.
- Ask the question again. Encourage Ss to use the key words from page 122, such as: *went fishing, went hiking, went swimming.*

Practice

- Direct Ss' attention to the pictures for Exercise **2A**. Point to number 1. Ask: *What did he do?* Elicit: *He went fishing.*
- Read the instructions aloud.
- Ss complete the exercise individually. Help as needed.

Comprehension check

- [Class Audio CD2 track 41] Read aloud the second part of the instructions for Exercise **2A**. Play or read the audio program (see audio script, page T-160). Have Ss check their answers as they listen and repeat.
- Ask Ss to come to the board to write the sentences. Have different Ss read the sentences aloud. Ask Ss to make any necessary corrections on the board.
- Ss ask and answer the questions in pairs. Help as needed.
- Ask pairs to perform their conversations for the class.

Expansion activity (individual work)

- Before class. Make copies of the following grid for each of your Ss.

Name of student	What did you do last weekend?

- In class. Give each S a copy of the grid. Tell Ss to walk around and ask eight classmates what they did last weekend. In the first column, Ss should write the name of each S they talk to; in the second column, they should write what the S did last weekend.
- When Ss finish, ask them to report their findings.

Expansion activity (whole group)

- If you want to expand the grammar presentation, turn to the grammar charts at the back of the Student's Book. Practice asking and answering questions using irregular verbs in the simple past tense.

What did you do yesterday?

Practice

- Direct Ss' attention to Exercise **2B**.
- Ask Ss to give you the past tense for the verbs in the word bank. Write them on the board.
- Ask Ss to read the sentences in Exercise **2B** and identify words they don't know. Encourage other Ss to help explain the meaning of the words.
- Read the instructions aloud. Ss complete the exercise individually.
- Ask Ss to write the sentences on the board. Ask other Ss to read the sentences aloud. Ask: *Are the sentences correct?* Have Ss correct any errors on the board.
- Write on the board: *schedule*. Point to the word. Say it aloud and ask Ss to repeat. Say: *A schedule tells you what to do on different days of the week.*
- Focus Ss' attention on the schedule in Exercise **2C**. Ask: *What kind of schedule is this?* Elicit: *It's Jeff Yu's vacation schedule.*
- Read the instructions for Exercise **2C** aloud.
- Model the task. Hold up the Student's Book. Point to *Sun* (Sunday).
- Ask a S the example question. The student reads the example answer aloud.
- Ss complete the exercise in pairs. Walk around and help as needed.

Application

- Read aloud the instructions for Exercise **3**. Ask two Ss to read aloud the example question and answer.
- Model the task. In the chart, write *Sarah* after *Name,* and write *read a book* after *last night*.
- Ss ask and answer questions with three classmates. Walk around and help as needed.
- Ask several Ss to report what their classmates did last night, yesterday morning, the day before yesterday, and last weekend.

Expansion activity *(individual work)*

- Write about classmates. Say: *Write complete sentences about your classmates' activities last weekend. Use the chart from Exercise 3.*
- Model the example activity by writing on the board: *Sarah read a book last night.*
- Ss write sentences individually. Walk around and help as needed.
- Check answers with the class. Ask Ss to write complete sentences on the board. Ask: *Are the sentences correct?* Ask different Ss to correct any errors.

Evaluation

- Direct Ss' attention to the lesson focus written on the board. Walk around the class and elicit questions and affirmative and negative answers about the schedule in Exercise **2C** on page 125.
- Check off the lesson focus as Ss demonstrate an understanding of what they have learned in the lesson.

More Ventures *(whole group, pairs, individual)*
Assign appropriate exercises from the *Teacher's Toolkit Audio CD / CD-ROM, Add Ventures,* or the *Workbook.*

B **Write.** Complete the sentences. Use the correct past tense form.

eat	go	go swimming	ride	write

1. We *went swimming* in the swimming pool last weekend.
2. I *rode* my bike yesterday.
3. Silvia *wrote* e-mails to all her friends last week.
4. They *ate* dinner very late last night.
5. We *went* picnicking last Sunday.

C **Talk** with a partner. Look at the schedule. Change the **bold** words and make conversations.

Jeff Yu's Vacation Schedule

Sun	Mon	Tues	Wed	Thurs	Fri	Sat
go to the museum	drive to the lake	ride my motorcycle	take swimming lessons	go hiking	go picnicking in the park	go to the movies

A What did Jeff do on **Sunday**?
B He **went to the museum**.

3 Communicate

Talk with three classmates. Complete the chart.

Sara, what did you do last night?

I read a book.

What did you do	**Name:**	**Name:**	**Name:**
last night?			
yesterday morning?			
the day before yesterday?			
last weekend?			

Lesson C What are you going to do?

1 Grammar focus: future tense with *be going to*

Questions

What	are you is he is she are they	going to	do tomorrow?

Answers

I'm He's She's They're	going to	take a trip.

Time words
today
tomorrow
tonight
next week
next month

2 Practice

A Write. Read the schedule. Answer the questions.

1. **A** What's Marta going to do next Monday?
   B She's *going to take her exams* .
2. **A** What's Paco going to do next Tuesday?
   B He's *going to play soccer* .
3. **A** What's Alfredo going to do next Wednesday?
   B He's *going to go hiking* .
4. **A** What are Mr. and Mrs. Santiago going to do next Thursday?
   B They're *going to go swimming* .
5. **A** What are Alfredo and Marta going to do next Friday?
   B They're *going to go to a party* .
6. **A** What's the family going to do next weekend?
   B They're *going to take a trip* .

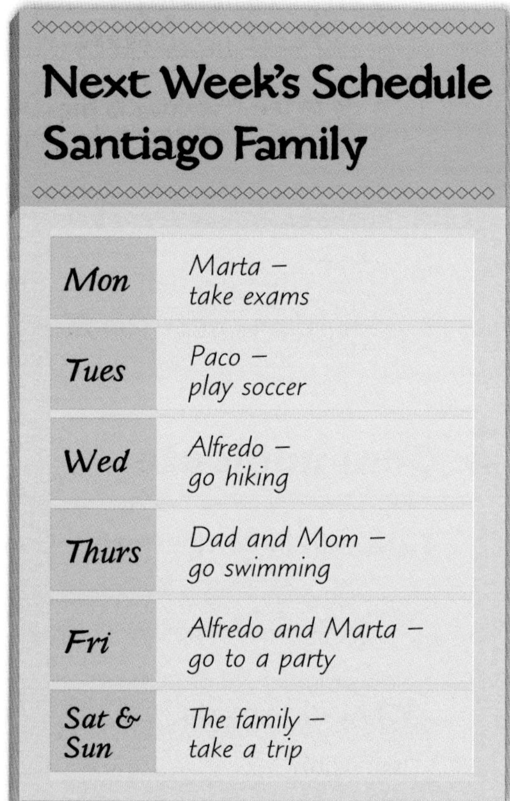
Next Week's Schedule
Santiago Family

Mon	Marta – take exams
Tues	Paco – play soccer
Wed	Alfredo – go hiking
Thurs	Dad and Mom – go swimming
Fri	Alfredo and Marta – go to a party
Sat & Sun	The family – take a trip

Listen and repeat. Then practice with a partner.

Lesson objective

- Introduce the future tense with *be going to*

Warm-up and review

- Before class. Write today's lesson focus on the board. *Lesson C: Ask and answer questions in the future tense with "be going to"*
- Begin class. Books closed. Review vocabulary from Lesson B. Ask: *What did you do last weekend?* Elicit: *I went swimming, I went shopping.* If possible, point to last weekend on a calendar.
- Write on the board:
  What are you going to do next weekend?
  I'm going to study.
- Read the question and answer aloud. Ask Ss to repeat. If possible, point to next weekend on a calendar.
- Ask several Ss: *What are you going to do next weekend?* Write their answers on the board: *I'm going to* _____.

Teaching tip

It might be helpful to explain that we use *be going to* + the base form of the verb to form statements in the future tense.

Presentation

- Books open. Direct Ss' attention to the grammar chart in Exercise **1**. Say: *This is the future tense with "be going to."*
- Read the questions and answers aloud. Ask Ss to repeat after you.
- Focus Ss' attention on the time words next to the grammar chart. Read the words aloud and ask Ss to repeat after you. Say: *These words are about the future.*
- Ask Ss to make sentences with *be going to* and the time words written in the grammar chart.

Practice

- Direct Ss' attention to the Santiago family's schedule for next week in Exercise **2A**.
- Ask: *What do you see?* Elicit: *Next week's schedule for the Santiago family.*
- Read aloud the instructions for Exercise **2A**. Ask two Ss to read aloud the example question and answer.
- Model the task. Hold up the Student's Book. Point to *Mon* on the schedule. Ask: *What day is this?* (Monday) *What's Marta going to do next Monday?* (take exams)
- Ss complete the exercise individually. Walk around and help as needed.

Comprehension check

- Read aloud the second part of the instructions for Exercise **2A**.
- [Class Audio CD2 track 42] Play or read the audio program (see audio script, page T-161). Have Ss check their answers as they listen and repeat.
- Ask Ss to come to the board to write the answers. Have different Ss read the answers aloud. Ask Ss to make any necessary corrections on the board.
- Ss ask and answer the questions in pairs. Help as needed.
- Ask pairs to perform their conversations for the class.

Expansion activity *(whole group)*

- If you want to expand the grammar presentation, turn to the grammar charts at the back of the Student's Book. Practice making sentences about the future using *be going to.*

Lesson C What are you going to do?

Practice

- Direct Ss' attention to the picture in Exercise **2B**. Hold up the Student's Book. Point to each person in the picture and ask Ss to brainstorm what that person is going to do. Elicit responses such as: *Maybe Brian is going to go to the beach.*
- Read the instructions aloud. Ask two Ss to read the example conversation.
- Ss complete the exercise in pairs. Help as needed.
- Ask pairs to ask and answer the questions for the class.

> **Useful language**
> Read the tip box aloud. It might be helpful to brainstorm more examples of this type of sentence and ask Ss to write the sentences on the board.

Expansion activity *(small groups)*

- Ss in small groups. Say: *Imagine that you are waiting for the bus like the people in the picture in Exercise 2B. Write a sentence about each person in your group. Then your group will stand up and act out what they are going to do. The rest of the class has to guess what each person is going to do.*

Application

- Write on the board:
  Name   *Next weekend*
- Ask a S: (Name of S) *What are you going to do next weekend?* Elicit: *I'm going to . . .* Write the S's name in the *Name* column and the activity he or she is going to do in the *Next weekend* column. Ask several other students the same question and write their names and plans on the board.
- Focus Ss' attention on Exercise **3** and read the instructions aloud. Ask two Ss to read aloud the example conversation.
- Hold up the Student's Book. Point to *Yuri* and *fix the car* in the chart.
- Encourage Ss to stand up, walk around, and ask and answer the questions with their classmates. Remind Ss to write the information in their charts.
- Check answers with the class by asking Ss to describe what one of their classmates is going to do next weekend.

Expansion activity *(individual work, small groups)*

- Goals. Ask Ss to think about what their goals are for the next year. Explain that a goal is something important that you want to do. Say: *Let's talk about the future. What are three things you want to do in your life?* Write three examples on the board of your own goals, for example: *I'm going to learn French; I'm going to exercise more; I'm going to spend more time with my family.*
- Ask Ss to write three goals using *be going to*. Walk around and help as needed.
- Ss in small groups. Say: *Show your group members your goals for the future. Who has the same goals? Who has different goals?*
- Ask members from each group to report to the class what they have learned about the Ss in their group.

  Option An alternative way of doing this activity is to ask Ss to write their goals on a piece of paper. Tell Ss you are going to read their goals to the rest of the class. Collect the papers and shuffle them. Read Ss' goals to the class without saying the Ss' names. The rest of the Ss must guess which Ss wrote the goals.

Expansion activity *(individual work, small groups)*

- Writing exercise. Say: *Take out a piece of paper. Write three sentences about the future. Write two true statements and one false statement. You will read your sentences to a small group of Ss. The Ss have to guess which statement is not true.*
- Model the activity. Read three sentences about yourself to the class, for example:
  I'm going to visit my mother next week
  I'm going to cook Chinese food tonight.
  I'm going to go to Mexico this summer.
- Read the sentences to the class. Ask: *Which sentence do you think is not true?* After Ss guess, tell them whether they are right.
- Ss work individually to write the sentences. Then Ss get together with a small group to complete the exercise.

Evaluation

- Direct Ss' attention to the lesson focus on the board.
- Focus Ss' attention on the picture on page 127. Go around the room. Ask Ss to ask and answer questions about the picture using the future tense with *be going to*.
- Check off the lesson focus as Ss demonstrate understanding of what they have learned in the lesson.

> ***More Ventures*** *(whole group, pairs, individual)*
> Assign appropriate exercises from the *Teacher's Toolkit Audio CD / CD-ROM, Add Ventures,* or the *Workbook.*

B **Talk** with a partner. Change the **bold** words and make conversations.

A What**'s Brian** going to do today?
B **He's going to go to the beach.**
A That sounds like fun.

1. Brian / go to the beach
2. Ali / go shopping
3. Lisa / play soccer
4. Hiro and Lee / go fishing
5. Andrea / take a trip
6. Ray / go to a birthday party

Useful language
You can say:
I'm going to go fishing. OR
I'm going fishing.

3 Communicate

Talk to your classmates. Write their names and activities in the chart.

Yuri, what are you going to do next weekend?

I'm going to fix my car.

Name	Next weekend
Yuri	*fix the car*
(Answers will vary.)	

Lesson D Reading

1 Before you read

Talk. Mrs. Lopez sent a picture of her family to a friend. Look at the picture. Answer the questions.

1. Who are the people in the picture?
2. What did they do?
3. What are they going to do next?

2 Read

  **Listen and read.**

Dear Ming,

Last weekend, we went camping in the mountains. I went hiking. My husband and our sons went fishing. They also went swimming in the lake. We all had a great time!

Tonight we're going to eat fish for dinner. After dinner, we're going to watch a movie. Later tonight, we're going to be very busy. We are going to do the laundry. With three boys, we have a lot of dirty clothes!

See you soon,
Maria

Look for words that show past or future time to help you understand.
Last weekend

3 After you read

A Read the sentences. Are they correct? Circle *Yes* or *No*.

1. Last weekend, the Lopez family went shopping. Yes (No)
2. Mrs. Lopez went hiking. (Yes) No
3. Mr. Lopez and his wife went fishing. Yes (No)
4. The Lopez family is going to eat pizza for dinner. Yes (No)
5. After dinner, they are going to watch a movie. (Yes) No
6. They have a lot of clean clothes. Yes (No)

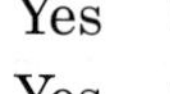

Write. Correct the sentences.

1. Last weekend, the Lopez family went camping.

B Write. Answer the questions about the Lopez family.

1. Who went fishing? *Mr. Lopez and his sons went fishing.*
2. Who went swimming in the lake? *Mr. Lopez and his sons went swimming in the lake.*
3. Is the Lopez family going to be busy tonight? *Yes, they are.*

Lesson objectives

- Introduce and read a note about leisure activities
- Practice using new topic-related words
- Practice reading strategies

Warm-up and review

- Before class. Write today's lesson focus on the board.
  Lesson D:
  Read a note about leisure activities
  Learn new vocabulary: sports
- Begin class. Books closed. Ask: *Remember the Lopez family from the picture on page 122? What did they do last weekend?* Elicit responses, such as: *They went fishing, hiking, camping,* etc.
- Books open. Remind Ss about the Lopez family in the picture on page 122. Then, read aloud the instructions for Exercise **1**. Ask: *Who are the people in the picture?* (Mr. and Mrs. Lopez's three sons) Point to the boys and ask: *What did they do?* (They went fishing; they caught fish.) Ask: *What are they going to do next?* (cook the fish; eat the fish)

Presentation

- Direct Ss' attention to Exercise **2**. Say: *Read the letter that Maria Lopez wrote to her friend Ming.*
- Ss read the letter silently.

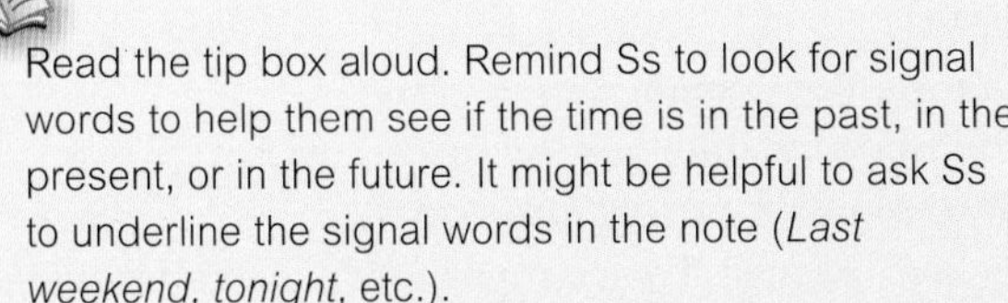

Read the tip box aloud. Remind Ss to look for signal words to help them see if the time is in the past, in the present, or in the future. It might be helpful to ask Ss to underline the signal words in the note (*Last weekend, tonight,* etc.).

- [Class Audio CD2 track 43] Play or read the audio program and ask Ss to read along (see audio script, page T-161). Repeat as needed.

  Option Explain any words Ss don't understand. Then have Ss reread the letter silently.
- Ask individual Ss to read aloud a sentence from the note.

Learner persistence *(individual work)*

- [Self-Study Audio CD track 37] Exercise **2** is recorded on the Ss' self-study CD at the back of the Student's Book. Ss can listen to the CD at home for reinforcement and review. They can also listen to the CD for self-directed learning when class attendance is not possible.

Comprehension check

- Read aloud the instructions for Exercise **3A**. Ask a S to read the example aloud.
- Ask: *Last weekend, did the Lopez family go shopping?* (No, they went camping.) Point to where *No* is circled for number 1. Be sure Ss understand the task.
- Ss complete the exercise individually. Help as needed.
- Check answers with the class. Ask Ss to read the sentences and answers aloud.
- Ask Ss to take out a piece of paper. Read aloud the second part of the instructions for Exercise **3A**.
- Model the task of correcting the sentences. Point to *No* for number 1 in Exercise **3A**. Read the sentence aloud. Tell Ss: *This sentence is incorrect. Tell me the correct sentence. Last weekend, the Lopez family went . . .* (camping). Write on the board: *Last weekend, the Lopez family went camping.*
- Ss complete the exercise individually. Help as needed.
- Check answers with the class. Ask Ss to write their answers on the board. Then ask different Ss to read the answers aloud.

Practice

- Ask Ss questions about the letter in Exercise **2**: *Who went fishing?* (Mr. Lopez and his sons went fishing.) *Who went swimming?* (Mr. Lopez and his sons went swimming.)
- Read aloud the instructions for Exercise **3B**. Ss complete the exercise individually. Help as needed.
- Check answers with the class. Ask Ss to read their questions and answers aloud.
- Ask individual Ss to write their answers on the board. Ask different Ss to read the sentences aloud. Ask: *Are the sentences correct now?* Ask Ss to correct the sentences if needed.

Expansion activity *(student pairs)*

- Expand on the sentence correction in Exercise **3A** by asking Ss to write sentences with *didn't*. For example, for the first sentence Ss could write: *Last weekend, the Lopez family went camping. They didn't go shopping.*
- Write the example sentence on the board. Tell Ss to write sentences with *didn't* for the rest of the sentences they corrected.
- Ask individual Ss to write the negative statements on the board.

Learner persistence *(individual work)*

- Ask Ss to look back at the Lesson D: Reading pages in their Student's Book to find the Reading tips. Make a list of the tips on the board.
- Encourage Ss to copy the list and use it as they read outside of class. Explain that the tips offer strategies to help them become better readers.

Lesson D Reading

Warm-up and review

- Books closed. Write on the board: *Sports*. Point to the word. Say it aloud. Ask Ss to repeat after you. Ask: *What are some examples of sports?* Elicit appropriate responses, such as: *basketball, baseball, football, soccer.*

Teaching tip
You can bring in pictures from magazines of people playing different sports. Show the Ss the pictures and ask: *What sport is this?* Write Ss' responses on the board.

- Point to each sport written on the board. Say the word aloud and ask Ss to repeat after you.
- Ask questions about sports. Responses will vary.

Presentation

- Books open. Direct Ss' attention to the pictures in the picture dictionary Say: *These are pictures of different sports.*
- Direct Ss attention to the word bank in Exercise **4A**. Say the words aloud using *play* with each sport in the first box and *go* with each word in the second box. Ask Ss to repeat after you. Listen to Ss' pronunciation and repeat the words if necessary.

Practice

- Say: *Write the words in the picture dictionary.* Point to the first example, which has been done. Be sure Ss understand the task.
- Ss complete the exercise individually. Walk around and help as needed.

Comprehension check

- [Class Audio CD2 track 44] Play or read the audio program (see audio script, page T-161). Ss should check their answers and repeat the words after they hear them. Repeat the audio program if necessary.

Learner persistence *(individual work)*

- [Self-Study Audio CD track 38] Exercise **4A** is recorded on the Ss' self-study CD at the back of the Student's Book. Ss can listen to the CD at home for reinforcement and review. They can also listen to the CD for self-directed learning when class attendance is not possible.

Application

- Read aloud the instructions for Exercise **4B**. Ask two Ss to read aloud the example conversation.
- Ss complete the exercise individually. Walk around and help as needed.
- Ask several pairs to ask and answer the questions for the class.

Culture note
Read the culture note aloud. It might be interesting to ask Ss which sport they prefer, soccer or football. If it is football season, bring in a newspaper and encourage Ss to follow the sport in the paper every day. Have Ss pick different teams to support.

Expansion activity *(student pairs)*

- Question-and-answer practice – past tense review. Write on the board:
  play / watch
  Did you play basketball last weekend?
  Did you watch basketball last weekend?
  Did you play baseball last weekend?
  Did you watch baseball last weekend?
- Write on the board:
  go / watch
  Did you go skiing last weekend?
  Did you watch skiing last weekend?
  Did you go surfing last weekend?
  Did you watch surfing last weekend?
- Ss in pairs. Say: *Ask your partner the questions on the board. Then your partner will ask you the questions.* Walk around the classroom and help as needed.
- Ask several pairs to ask and answer the questions for the rest of the class.

  Option Dictate the questions to Ss. Then have them ask their partner the questions.

Evaluation

- Direct Ss' attention to the lesson focus written on the board.
- Put a check mark next to *Read a note about leisure activities.*
- Focus Ss' attention on page 129. Ask Ss to make sentences about the sports in the picture dictionary.
- Check off each part of the lesson focus as Ss demonstrate understanding of what they have learned in the lesson.

More Ventures *(whole group, pairs, individual)*
Assign appropriate exercises from the *Teacher's Toolkit Audio CD / CD-ROM, Add Ventures,* or the *Workbook.*

4 Picture dictionary Sports

1. *football*

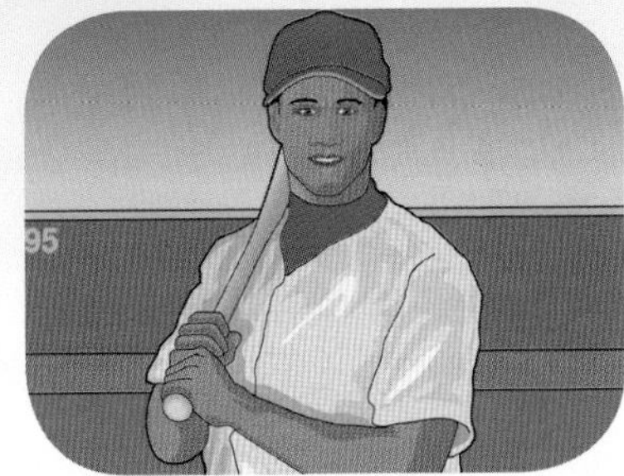

2. *baseball*

3. *basketball*

4. *Ping-Pong*

5. *ice hockey*

6. *soccer*

7. *surfing*

8. *ice-skating*

9. *skiing*

A **Write** the words in the picture dictionary. Then listen and repeat.

Use *play* with these words:		
baseball	football	Ping-Pong
basketball	ice hockey	soccer

Use *go* with these words:		
ice-skating	skiing	surfing

B **Talk** with a partner. Look at the pictures and make conversations.

What's he going to do?

He's going to play football.

Culture note

In the United States, football and soccer are different sports.

Lesson E Writing

1 Before you write

A Talk with four classmates. Ask questions. Write the answers.

A Where did you go on your last vacation?
B I went to Arizona.
A Who did you go with?
B I went with my wife.
A What did you do?
B We went to the Grand Canyon.

Name	Where?	Who with?	Did what?
Omar	Arizona	wife	visited the Grand Canyon
(Answers will vary.)			

B Read Maria's note. Answer the questions.

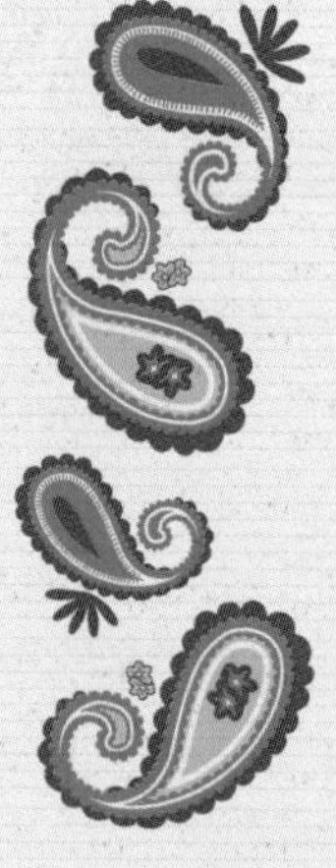

Dear Colleen,

I had a nice vacation. I went to Oregon. I went camping with my family. I read a book and rested. I went hiking. My husband and sons went fishing. We ate fish for dinner every night.

Next year, we are going to drive to New York. We are going to visit my mother and see the Statue of Liberty.

Did you have a nice vacation? What are you going to do on your next vacation?

See you soon,
Maria

1. Where did Maria go on vacation? *She went to Oregon.*
2. What did Maria do? *She went camping, read a book, rested, and went hiking.*
3. What did her husband and sons do? *They went fishing.*
4. Where is Maria's family going next year? *They are going to go to New York.*
5. What are they going to do? *They are going to visit Maria's mother and see the Statue of Liberty.*

Lesson objectives
- Discuss and write about your past and future vacations
- Write paragraphs

Warm-up and review

- Before class. Write today's lesson focus on the board. *Lesson E: Discuss and write about your past and future vacations*
- Begin class. Books closed. Write on the board: *vacation.* Say the word aloud. Ask Ss to repeat. Ask: *Where do you like to go on vacation?* Elicit responses. Write Ss' responses on the board.
- Ask individual Ss: *Where did you go on your last vacation?* Elicit appropriate responses. Write Ss' responses on the board.

Presentation

- Books open. Direct Ss' attention to Exercise **1A**. Read the instructions aloud.
- Ask two Ss to read the example conversation aloud.
- Direct Ss' attention to the chart in Exercise **1A**. Hold up the Student's Book. Point to the name *Omar.* Say: *Write your classmates' names and answers in the blank spaces. Omar went to Arizona with his wife. They went to the Grand Canyon.* Point to each word in the chart as you say it aloud.
- Encourage Ss to walk around the classroom to complete the exercise. Help Ss as needed.
- Copy the grid onto the board. Ask individual Ss to write their answers in the blank spaces. Then ask them to talk about a classmate's last vacation. Elicit a response such as: *Klara went to Mexico with her sister last year. They visited their hometown.*

Expansion activity *(student pairs)*

- **Materials needed** Advertisements for vacation destinations from a travel magazine
- Vacation role-play. Hold up one of the advertisements. Ask Ss: *Where is this?* Elicit an appropriate response, or tell Ss which place it is. Say: *Imagine you're going to go there on your next vacation. What are you going to do during your vacation?* Encourage Ss to make sentences starting with *We are going to . . .* Write the sentences on the board.
- Ss in pairs. Ask each pair of Ss to choose one of the advertisements. Tell Ss to write ten sentences using *be going to.* Walk around and help as needed.
- Ask pairs to hold up their vacation destinations and describe what they are going to do when they get there.

Practice

- Books closed. Ask Ss the following questions. Responses will vary.
  Do you write notes when you go on a trip?
  Who do you write to?
  What do you like to write about?
- Books open. Direct Ss' attention to the note in Exercise **1B**. Read the instructions aloud.
- Ask Ss to read the note silently.
- When Ss finish their silent reading, ask them to read the note to a partner. Ask the partners to switch roles. Walk around and help as needed.
- Direct Ss' attention back to Exercise **1B** ad have them write answers to the questions.

Comprehension check

- Write the numbers *1–5* on the board. Ask Ss to write their answers on the board. Ask other Ss to read the answers aloud. Ask: *Are the answers correct?* Ask different Ss to correct any errors.

Learner persistence *(whole group)*

- A field trip with your class. Go to a place that is well known in your city, town, or community. Before going, bring brochures to class for Ss to look through. Ask Ss: *What are we going to do when we get there? What are we going to see? Why is this place interesting?*
- When Ss return from the field trip, ask them to write a paragraph about their experiences. Have them use the past tense. The writing will help your Ss bond as a class, and it will also help them recycle past and future tense forms.

Lesson E Writing

Presentation

- Books closed. Ask Ss to brainstorm some *Wh-* question words. Elicit: *Who, What, Why, When, Where*. Ask a S to write the responses on the board.
- Write on the board: *Your last vacation*. Point to the *Wh-* words. Say: *What are some questions you can ask about someone's last vacation?* Elicit questions such as: *Where did you go on your last vacation? Who did you go with? What did you do?* Ask Ss to write the questions on the board.

Teaching tip

Some Ss in your class may not have been able to take a vacation because of their personal situations. Rather than discuss their own vacation, bring in pictures of people on simple family vacations. Ask Ss to discuss and write about the pictures rather than about themselves.

Practice

- Books open. Focus Ss' attention on the questions in Exercise **2A**.
- Read each question aloud and ask Ss to repeat.
- Read the instructions aloud.
- Ss complete the exercise individually. Help as needed.

Application

- Read the instructions for Exercise **2B**. Tell Ss to use the note on page 130 as a guide for their writing.

Teaching tip

Refer Ss to the note on page 130. Point out that the first paragraph is written in the past tense and the second paragraph is written in the future tense.

- Model the first sentence of a letter by eliciting information from a S and writing on the board:
  Dear (student's friend's name),
  I had a nice vacation. I went to (name of destination).

Read the tip box aloud. Guide Ss to begin a new paragraph when changing their ideas from one tense to another. Remind Ss to indent each new paragraph.

- Ss complete the exercise individually. Help as needed.

Comprehension check

- Read aloud the instructions for Exercise **3A**. Ss complete the exercise in pairs. Help as needed.
- Read aloud the instructions for Exercise **3B**. This exercise asks Ss to work together to peer-correct their writing. Ask a S to read the questions aloud. Tell Ss to exchange papers and look at their partner's letter for the answers to the questions. Have Ss circle the answers. Help as needed.
- Ask pairs to answer the questions about their partner's letter for the class.

Expansion activity *(whole group)*

- Tic-tac-toe game. Draw a tic-tac-toe grid on the board. Ask Ss to brainstorm verbs. Put each verb in a different section of the grid, for example:

see	*hike*	*fix*
fish	*play*	*go*
take	*ride*	*write*

- Divide the class into two teams, *X* and *O*. Say: *One person from each team will choose a verb on the board. He or she has to make a sentence in the past tense with that verb. If the sentence is correct, I will put an "X" or an "O" in that square. The first team to get three Xs or Os in a row (vertically, horizontally, or diagonally) wins.*
- Continue playing after the first game. This time, ask Ss to make sentences in the future tense. Another alternative is to ask Ss to use the verbs to make questions in the past tense or the future tense. Ask Ss to change the verbs each time they play a new game.

Evaluation

- Direct Ss' attention to the lesson focus on the board.
- Have Ss look at the picture on page 122. Ask different Ss to come to the board and write sentences about the picture in the past tense and the future tense.
- Check off the lesson focus as Ss demonstrate understanding of what they have learned in the lesson.

More Ventures *(whole group, pairs, individual)*
Assign appropriate exercises from the *Teacher's Toolkit Audio CD / CD-ROM, Add Ventures,* or the *Workbook.*

2 Write

A Write. Answer the questions.

1. Where did you go on your last vacation?

   (Answers will vary.)

2. Who did you go with?

3. What did you do?

4. Where are you going to go on your next vacation?

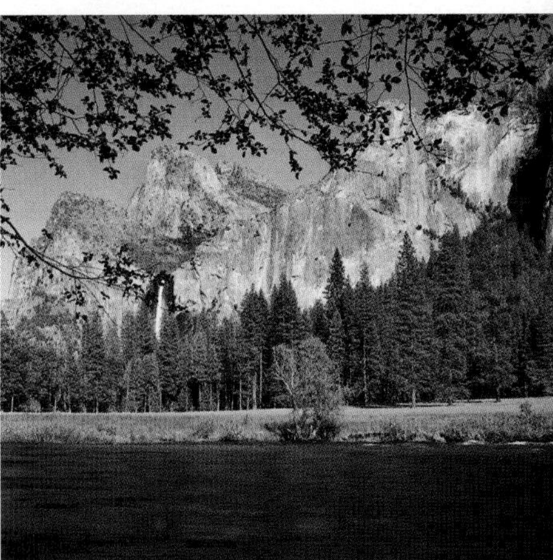

5. Who will you go with?

6. What are you going to do?

B Write a letter about your vacations. Use the information from Exercise A.

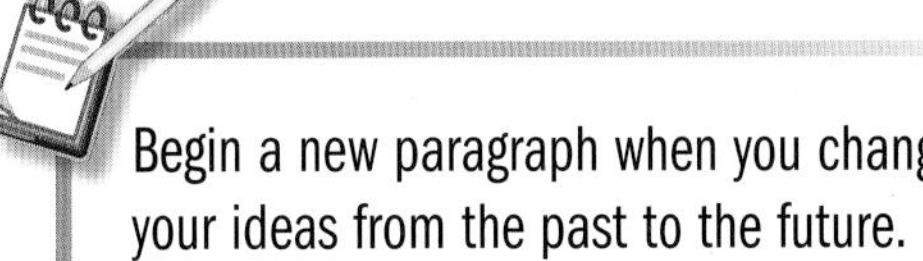

Begin a new paragraph when you change your ideas from the past to the future.

3 After you write

A Read your letter to a partner.

B Check your partner's letter.

- What are the past activities?
- What are the future activities?
- Are there different paragraphs for past and future activities?

Lesson F Another view

1 Life-skills reading

Saturday TV Schedule

	6:00	7:00	8:00	9:00
CHANNEL 7	Local news	Soccer		Swimming competition
CHANNEL 9	Cooking show	Boating program	*Great Places to Hike*	*Strange Animals*
CHANNEL 14	National news	Movie: *Camp Sunshine*		*Kids' Favorite Vacations*
CHANNEL 18	World news	*Fantastic Fishing*	Dancing competition	
CHANNEL 23	*Outdoor Adventures*	Baseball		

A Read the questions. Look at the TV schedule. Circle the answers.

1. On what channel are they going to show a movie?
   a. on Channel 9
   (b.) on Channel 14
   c. on Channel 18
   d. on Channel 23

2. When is *Outdoor Adventures* going to be on?
   (a.) at 6:00 p.m.
   b. at 7:00 p.m.
   c. at 8:00 p.m.
   d. at 9:00 p.m.

3. What are they going to show at 9 p.m. on Channel 9?
   a. *Great Places to Hike*
   b. *Kids' Favorite Vacations*
   c. *Fantastic Fishing*
   (d.) *Strange Animals*

4. How many channels are going to show the news at 6 p.m.?
   a. one channel
   b. two channels
   (c.) three channels
   d. five channels

B Talk with your classmates. Ask and answer the questions.

1. What did you watch on TV last night?
2. What are you going to watch on TV tomorrow night?
3. What are your favorite TV programs?
4. What do your family members watch on TV?

Lesson objectives

- Read and discuss a TV schedule
- Review unit vocabulary
- Introduce the project
- Complete the self-assessment

Warm-up and review

- Before class. Write today's lesson focus on the board.
  Lesson F:
  Read and discuss a TV schedule
  Review topic vocabulary
  Complete the self-assessment
- Begin class. Books closed. Ask questions about TV habits. Responses will vary.
  Do you watch TV?
  What programs do you like to watch?
  What time and day do you watch your favorite programs?
  Do you use a TV guide or TV schedule?

Presentation

- Books open. Direct Ss' attention to Exercise **1A**. Read the instructions aloud. This task helps prepare Ss for standardized-type tests they may have to take. Be sure Ss understand the task. Have Ss individually scan for and circle the answers.
- Check answers with the class. Write the numbers *1–4* on the board. Ask individual Ss to come to the board to write their answers.
- Ask: *Are the answers correct?* Ask other Ss to correct any errors on the board.

Practice

- Read aloud the instructions for Exercise **1B**.
- Ss ask and answer the questions in small groups. Walk around and help as needed.
- Ask several Ss to talk about a classmate's answers. Encourage them to make sentences, such as:
  (S's name) *watched _____ last night. She's going to watch _____ tomorrow night. Her favorite TV program is _____. Her family watches _____ on TV.*

Expansion activity (small groups)

- **Materials needed** Enough copies of your local TV schedule to give to each small group in your class (or a copy of one page of the TV schedule)
- Ss in small groups. Give each group a copy of the local TV schedule.
- Write the following question starters on the board:
  What time _____?
  What channel _____?
  What day _____?
- Ask Ss to write questions with their group about the TV schedule. Walk around and help as needed.
- Ask groups to exchange questions and to find the answers in their TV schedules.
- Ask several Ss from each group to stand up and ask and answer some of their questions for the class.

Expansion activity (student pairs)

- Movie review. Write on the board:
  1. What movie did you see recently? Tell your partner the name and type of movie you saw.
  2. What movie are you going to see next? Why?

Teaching tip

It might be helpful to brainstorm types of movies and write them on the board: *drama, action, romance, mystery, comedy,* etc.

- Ss in pairs. Say: *Ask your partner the questions on the board. Then your partner will ask you the questions.*
- Ss complete the activity in pairs. Walk around and help as needed.
- Ask several pairs to ask and answer the questions for the rest of the class.

Learner persistence (whole group)

- Encourage Ss to watch TV in English. Tell them that this will help them improve their English.

Lesson F Another view

Presentation

- Focus Ss' attention on the picture in Exercise **2A**. Ask: *What do you see?* Elicit responses such as: *Two women are talking; one woman is sitting; the other woman is standing.*
- Read the instructions aloud. Ask two Ss to read aloud the example dialog. Encourage the S reading part B to act out the activities (*go dancing* and *play soccer*).
- Ss in small groups. Say: *Change the bold words.* Ask about different activities. Remind Ss to act out the activities.
- Ss complete the exercise in small groups. Walk around and help as needed.
- Ask each group to perform a conversation for the class.

Practice

- Focus Ss' attention on the pictures in Exercise **2B**. Hold up the Student's Book. Point to each picture and say the name of the item. Ask Ss to repeat.
- Read aloud the instructions for Exercise **2B**.

Teaching tip
It might be helpful to tell Ss that *equipment* means the things you need to play a sport. Ask Ss about the sports they play. Ask if those sports require special equipment.

- Focus Ss' attention on the sports listed in the center of the exercise. Read each sport aloud. Ask Ss to repeat. Listen to Ss' pronunciation. Correct pronunciation as needed.
- Model the task. Hold up the Student's Book. Point to number 1, *baseball*. Ask: *Which equipment goes with this sport?* Elicit: *g, a baseball and bat*. Point to the handwritten letter *g* in the Student's Book.
- Ss complete the exercise in pairs. Walk around and help as needed.
- Write the numbers *1–8* on the board. Ask individual Ss to come to the board to write the answers.
- Ask: *Are these answers correct?* Ask different Ss to correct any errors.

Expansion activity (whole group)

- Before class. Make copies of the following chart for each S in your class.

Student's name	What is your favorite sport?	Did you play it last weekend?	Are you going to play it this weekend?
Kevin	tennis	Yes, he did.	No, he isn't.

- In class. Give each S a copy of the chart. Say: *You are going to interview six of your classmates. Stand up and walk around the room.* Hold up a copy of the chart. Point to *Kevin*. Say: *This is the student's name.* Point to the questions. Say: *These are the questions.*
- Model the activity. Ask a S the questions. Write his or her answers in your copy of the chart.
- Each S completes the exercise. Help as needed.
- Copy the chart onto the board. Ask individual Ss to come to the board to write some of their answers on the chart.

Application

Community building

- **Project** Ask Ss to turn to page 140 in their Student's Book to complete the project for Unit 10.

More Ventures *(whole group, pairs, individual)*
Assign appropriate exercises from the *Teacher's Toolkit Audio CD / CD-ROM, Add Ventures,* or the *Workbook.*

Evaluation

- Before asking Ss to turn to the self-assessment on page 145, do a quick review of each lesson in the unit. Have Ss turn to Lesson A. Ask the class to call out what they remember about this lesson. Prompt Ss with questions: *What are the conversations about on this page? What vocabulary is in the picture?*
- **Self-assessment** Read the instructions for Exercise **3**. Ask Ss to turn to the self-assessment page and complete the unit self-assessment.
- If Ss are ready, administer the unit test on pages T-185–T-186 of this *Teacher's Edition* (or on the *Teacher's Toolkit Audio CD / CD-ROM*). The audio and audio scripts for the tests are on the *Teacher's Toolkit Audio CD / CD-ROM.*

2 Fun with language

A **Work in a group.** What are you going to do next weekend? Do the activity in front of the group. Your classmates ask questions. Answer *Yes, I am* or *No, I'm not*.

A Are you going to **go dancing** next weekend?
B No, I'm not.
A Are you going to **play soccer** next weekend?
B Yes, I am.

B **Work with a partner.** Match the equipment with the sport.

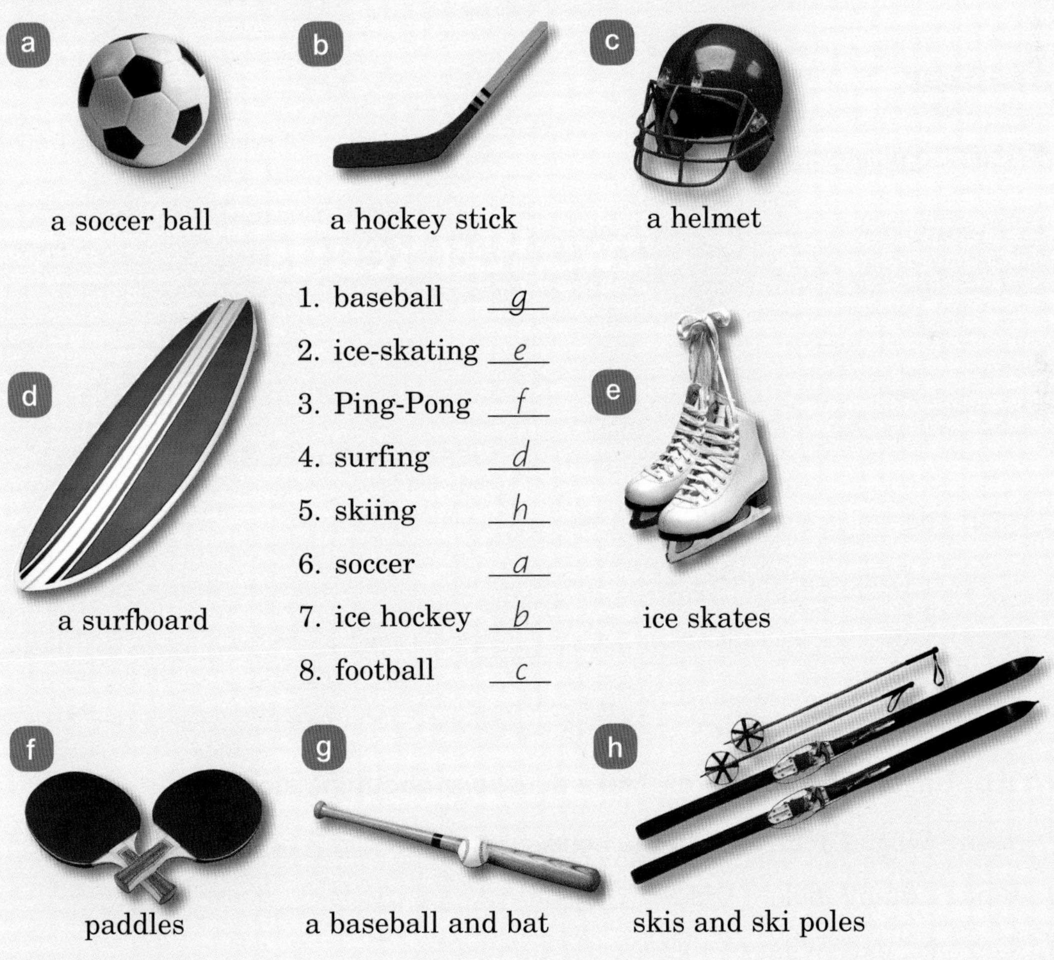

a — a soccer ball
b — a hockey stick
c — a helmet
d — a surfboard
e — ice skates
f — paddles
g — a baseball and bat
h — skis and ski poles

1. baseball <u>g</u>
2. ice-skating <u>e</u>
3. Ping-Pong <u>f</u>
4. surfing <u>d</u>
5. skiing <u>h</u>
6. soccer <u>a</u>
7. ice hockey <u>b</u>
8. football <u>c</u>

3 Wrap up

Complete the **Self-assessment** on page 145.

Review

1 Listening

Read the questions. Then listen and circle the answers.

1. When did Melissa's family go picnicking?
   a. on Saturday
   (b.) on Sunday
2. What did they eat in the park?
   a. hot dogs
   (b.) hamburgers
3. When did Ivan's family do their chores?
   (a.) on Saturday
   b. on Sunday
4. Did Ivan wash the dishes?
   a. Yes, he did.
   (b.) No, he didn't.
5. What did Ivan's wife do?
   a. She washed the clothes.
   (b.) She vacuumed the rugs.
6. Who dusted the furniture?
   a. Tommy
   (b.) Lisa

Talk with a partner. Ask and answer the questions. Use complete sentences.

2 Grammar

A Write. Complete the story.

Two Weekends

Sam and Jenny *had* (1. have / had) a big party last weekend. On Saturday morning, Jenny *cleaned* (2. clean / cleaned) the house and *made* (3. make / made) dinner. Sam *emptied* (4. empty / emptied) the trash and *swept* (5. sweep / swept) the patio.

Next weekend, they're going to *drive* (6. drive / drove) to the mountains. Sam is going to *go* (7. go / went) fishing. Jenny is going to *go* (8. go / went) swimming in a lake.

B Write. Unscramble the words. Make questions about the story.

1. clean / When / Jenny / did / the house / ? *When did Jenny clean the house?*
2. dinner / Sam / make / Did / ? *Did Sam make dinner?*
3. Sam / do / did / What / ? *What did Sam do?*
4. next / do / going to / they / What / are / weekend / ? *What are they going to do next weekend?*

Talk with a partner. Ask and answer the questions.

Lesson objective

- Review vocabulary, pronunciation, and grammar from Units 9 and 10

Warm-up and review

- Before class. Write today's lesson focus on the board. *Review unit: Review vocabulary, pronunciation, and grammar from Units 9 and 10*
- Begin class. Books closed. Ask Ss to brainstorm *Wh-* question words. Elicit: *Who, What, Why, When, Where.* Write the questions on the board.
- Point to the words on the board. Say: *Ask some questions in the past tense using these words.* Elicit questions, such as: *What did you do yesterday? When did you go to bed last night?* Write Ss' responses on the board.

Presentation

- Books open. Focus Ss' attention on Exercise **1**. Read aloud the instructions.
- Ask individual Ss to read the questions aloud. Say: *Now listen to the conversation. Circle the correct answers.*
- [Class Audio CD2 track 45] Play or read the audio program (see audio script, page T-161). Ss listen and circle the answers to the questions. Repeat the audio program as needed.
- Write the numbers *1–6* on the board. Ask individual Ss to write their answers on the board. Ask other Ss: *Are these answers correct?* Have Ss make any necessary corrections on the board.

Practice

- Read aloud the second part of the instructions for Exercise **1**.
- Ss complete the exercise in pairs. Help as needed.
- Ask several pairs to ask and answer the questions for the rest of the class.
- Write on the board:

dry__	*empty__*	*mop__*
dust__	*pay__*	*go__*
read__	*eat__*	*drive__*

- Ask: *What is the past tense form of these verbs?* Model the activity by writing *dried* next to *dry.*
- Ask Ss to continue by writing the correct past tense form of the verbs in the remaining blanks.
- Direct Ss' attention to Exercise **2A**. Read the instructions aloud.
- Ask another S to read aloud the first sentence in the paragraph.
- Ss complete the exercise individually. Help as needed.
- Write the numbers *1–8* on the board. Ask Ss to come to the board to write the answers.

Teaching tip

Ask Ss to write on the board only the missing words, not the complete sentences.

- Ask individual Ss to read aloud a sentence from the paragraph. Ask: *Are the answers correct?* Ask Ss to correct any errors.
- Books closed. Write on the board:
  weekend / do / What / Jenny / did / last ?
- Ask Ss to unscramble the words on the board to make a question. (What did Jenny do last weekend?) Write the question on the board.
- Books open. Focus Ss' attention on Exercise **2B**. Read the instructions aloud.
- Ss complete the exercise individually. Help as needed.
- Write the numbers *1–4* on the board. Ask four Ss to write the unscrambled questions on the board. Ask other Ss: *Are the questions correct?* Ask different Ss to correct any errors.
- Read aloud the second part of the instructions in Exercise **2B**.
- Model the task. Ask a S the first question: *When did Jenny clean the house?* Elicit: *on Saturday morning.*
- Ss complete the exercise in pairs. Walk around and help as needed.
- Ask several pairs to ask and answer the questions for the rest of the class.

Warm-up and review

- Ask: *What is the ending for regular verbs in the past tense?* (-ed)
- Say: *Not all verbs ending in "-ed" are pronounced in the same way. Some endings sound like /d/; some sound like /t/; and some sound like /ɪd/.*

Presentation

- Focus Ss' attention on Exercise **3A**. Read the instructions aloud.
- [Class Audio CD2 track 46] Play or read the audio program (see audio script, page T-161). Repeat as needed.
- Ask: *Did you hear the different ways the "-ed" ending was pronounced for each word?* Elicit a *Yes* or *No* response.

  Option If Ss ask for the rule for how to pronounce the *-ed* ending correctly, tell them that it depends on the ending letters or sound of the verb. Say: *When verbs end with voiceless sounds such as* /k/, /p/, /sh/, or /ch/, *the past tense ending sounds like* /t/. *When verbs end with voiced sounds such as* /n/, /y/, *or* /m/, *the past tense ending sounds like* /d/. *When verbs end with* /t/ *or* /d/, *the past tense ending sounds like* /ɪd/.
- Read aloud the instructions for Exercise **3B**.
- [Class Audio CD2 track 47] Play or read the audio program (see audio script, page T-161). Ss listen to and repeat the words. Encourage Ss to use the correct pronunciation for the *-ed* ending as they repeat the words. Repeat the audio program as needed.
- Focus Ss' attention on the chart in Exercise **3C**. Read the instructions aloud.
- Say: *Listen to these past tense verbs and check the ending that you hear.*
- [Class Audio CD2 track 48] Play or read the audio program (see audio script, page T-161). Ss listen and complete the chart individually. Walk around the classroom and help as needed.
- When Ss finish, ask them to pronounce the words and say which column they checked. Ask the rest of the class: *Did you check the same column?* Correct any errors.

  Option As a group, ask Ss to say the verbs. Make sure they pronounce the *-ed* endings correctly.

Practice

- Read aloud the second part of the instructions for Exercise **3C**.
- Model the task. Read aloud the word *studied*. Then make up a sentence, for example: *I studied last night*.
- Ss complete the exercise in pairs. Walk around and help as needed.
- Ask several Ss to say their sentences for the rest of the class.

  Option Ask Ss to write a sentence on the board for each word. Then ask different Ss to read the sentences to the class, using correct pronunciation.
- Read aloud the instructions for Exercise **3D**.
- Ask two Ss to read aloud the example questions and answers. Encourage Ss to use both regular and irregular verbs in their responses.
- Ask several pairs to ask and answer the questions for the rest of the class. Listen carefully to make sure they are using correct pronunciation.

Expansion activity *(whole group)*

- Pronunciation practice. Divide the class into two teams. Ask a S from one team to write a sentence on the board in the past tense. If the sentence is written correctly, give the team one point. Then, ask a S from the other team to read the sentence aloud. If the student reads it correctly with appropriate pronunciation, give that team one point. Continue in this way until each team has written and pronounced several sentences.
- At the end of the game, add up the points. The team with the most points wins the competition.

Evaluation

- Direct Ss' attention to the lesson focus written on the board.
- Go around the room. Ask each S to say a sentence about Ivan from Exercise **1** on page 134.
- Ask Ss to read the words from Exercise **3C** on page 135 and use the correct pronunciation.
- Check off the items in the lesson focus as Ss demonstrate understanding of what they have learned in the lesson.

3 **Pronunciation:** the *-ed* ending in the simple past

A **Listen** to the *-ed* ending in these past tense verbs.

/d/	/t/	/ɪd/
cleaned He cleaned his house.	**cooked** They cooked dinner.	**dusted** I dusted the living room.
dried I dried all the dishes.	**talked** She talked on the phone.	**folded** He folded his clothes.
emptied They emptied the trash.	**washed** She washed the car.	**painted** They painted the house.

B **Listen and repeat.**

/d/	/t/	/ɪd/
exercised	camped	celebrated
played	fished	folded
turned	walked	visited

C **Listen** and check (✓) the correct column.

	/d/	/t/	/ɪd/		/d/	/t/	/ɪd/
1. studied	☑	☐	☐	5. waited	☐	☐	☑
2. ironed	☑	☐	☐	6. hiked	☐	☑	☐
3. mopped	☐	☑	☐	7. vacuumed	☑	☐	☐
4. rested	☐	☐	☑	8. worked	☐	☑	☐

Talk with a partner. Take turns. Make a sentence with each verb.

D **Talk** with a partner. Ask and answer the questions. Use correct pronunciation.

1. What did you do last weekend?
2. What did you do yesterday?

Last weekend, I . . .

Yesterday, I . . .

Projects

Overview

The projects on pages 136–140 in the *Ventures* Student's Book are optional material to be used at the completion of a unit. There is one project per unit, and most of the projects can be completed in one class period.

Projects are valuable activities because they extend students' learning into a real-world context. They work within the unit topic, but they also go beyond the Student's Book.

These projects are designed to be fun and practical, with the goal of helping students become more independent while learning to live in a new culture and speak a new language.

Project set-up and materials

Projects may be done in class as a group activity or outside of class, individually.

There is a reference at the end of each unit in this Teacher's Edition to remind teachers about the projects. Some projects will need the teacher to gather simple materials to be used in class. For example, some require large poster paper, index cards, or authentic materials such as supermarket ads and copies of the local telephone directory. In order to complete other projects, students will need access to a computer that is linked to the Internet.

Skills learned through the projects

Students learn different skills through these projects. For example, half the projects involve use of the Internet. Students search for information using key words. This is an essential skill that most students will need to use in English. In addition, the projects encourage students to practice other essential life skills, such as working collaboratively to make a poster or a book, looking up information on community resources, and learning to manage their time better by making a time-management calendar.

Community building and learner persistence

Ventures projects help build community inside and outside the classroom as students work together, using materials such as local newspapers and telephone directories to find information. Building community, in turn, helps to promote learner persistence. As students apply essential life skills, they will become more confident in their English skills and will be more motivated to come to class to learn additional skills that will help them in daily life.

Popular names

A Use the Internet.

Find popular names for girls and for boys.

Keywords U.S. baby names | popular names for girls | popular names for boys

B Make two lists.

Write 10 names for girls.
Write 10 names for boys.

Girls' names	Boys' names
1. Julie	1. Christopher
2. Sarah	2. Michael
3. Susan	3. Thomas

C Share your information.

Make a class poster.
Write all the names from your lists.
Write the names in alphabetical order.
What are the class's favorite names?
Take a class vote.

School employee chart

A Make a list.

What are some jobs at your school? Write the jobs.

Jobs at our school
1. teacher
2. principal
3. custodian

B Talk to a school employee.

Ask these questions. Write the answers.

1. What's your first name?
2. What's your last name?
3. What's your title?
4. What's your job?

C Share your information.

Make a class wall chart.
Talk about the people.

School employees

First name	Last name	Title	Job
Diego	Cruz	Dr.	Principal
Eve	Smith	Ms.	Secretary

UNIT 3

Electronic greeting card

A Make a list.

Write the birthdays of eight people you know.
Who has the next birthday?
Circle the name.

Wang	July 10
Mr. Wilson	Aug. 21
Luz	Nov. 16

B Use the Internet.

Find a free electronic card.

Keywords electronic cards | free e-cards | electronic birthday cards

Write a message.
Print a copy.
Send your card.

C Share your information.

Show the copy of the card to your classmates.

UNIT 4

Health and emergency information

A Check (✓) the places and people that are important to you.

☐ Ambulance	☐ Doctor	☐ Hospital
☐ Emergency	☐ Dentist	☐ Poison Control
☐ Fire Department	☐ Health Clinic	☐ (other) ______

B Make an information card.

Write the important names on a card.
Find their phone numbers.
Write the numbers on the card.

Ambulance	911
Emergency	911
Doctor	555-1222
Dentist	555-9037
Health Clinic	555-1234

C Share your information.

Show your card to your classmates.
Add addresses and phone numbers of other important places and people.

UNIT 5

Community directory

A Use the Internet.

Find information about places in your community.

Keywords (name of your town) (name of the place)

B Make a chart.

Write addresses and phone numbers of important places.

Place	Address	Telephone number
Collinsville Museum	44 Maple Street	555-4589
Collinsville Public Library	12 Main Street	555-9023

C Share your information.

Show your chart. Talk about the places.

UNIT 6

Business hours

A Make a list.

Write the names of three stores in your town.

B Make a chart.

Look for the stores in the telephone book.
Find the address and telephone number.
Then call. Ask these questions. Write the answers.

1. What days are you open?
2. What time do you open?
3. What time do you close?

C Share your information.

Make a wall chart.
Talk about the stores.

Store	Address	Telephone	Hours
ABC Grocery	2840 Main Street	555-6320	Tuesday – Saturday 7:00 a.m.–9:00 p.m. Sunday 8:00 a.m.–5:00 p.m.
Pam's Pizza	632 Garden Road	555-6789	Monday – Saturday 11:00 a.m.–11:00 p.m. Closed Sunday

Comparison shopping

A Write a one-week grocery list.

Include food, drinks, and other items you need.

B Find grocery ads from two stores.

Look in this week's paper or in the mail.
OR Go to the store to get the ad.

C Check the ads.

Write prices from each ad on your list.

D Share your information.

Show a classmate your grocery list.
Talk about the prices.
Which store is better for you?

Groceries	A&D Market	Ted's Food
bread	$1.99	?
milk	$2.50	?
bananas	59¢/lb	69¢/lb
lettuce	$1.50	?
onions	$1.29/lb	$1.19
potato chips	?	$2.49
soda	6/$2.00	6/$1.79
ice cream	$3.49	$3.79
toilet paper	6 rolls $4.00	8 rolls $5.00

Job-description search

A Use the Internet.

Look for three jobs you want to learn about.

Keywords (name of job), job description | job description, (name of job)

B Find information about the jobs.

Look at the job descriptions.
Choose one job. Take notes.

Computer Technician
Works with computer hardware, software, and networks.

C Answer these questions.

1. What skills do you need for the job?
2. Do you need special training?
3. Do you need a degree or a certificate?
4. Is this job good for you?

D Share your information.

Find a picture of the job.
Paste it on a piece of paper.
Write information about the job.
Make a class booklet.

UNIT 9

Time-management calendar

A Make a weekly calendar.

Use one or two sheets of notebook paper.

B Write on your calendar.

Write your work schedule.
Write your chores.
Write your study time.
Write other appointments or events.

C Share your information.

Show your calendar.
Talk about your schedule.

Monday

7:00 make breakfast and lunches
8:15 take children to school
9:00 to 5:00 work
6:00 make dinner
7:00 wash dishes
9:00 put children to bed
10:30 study

Tuesday

7:00 make breakfast and lunches
7:30 take out the garbage
8:15 take children to school
9:00 to 5:00 work
7:00 English class

UNIT 10

Public parks

A Use the Internet.

Find the public parks near your home.

Keywords local parks (your city) | public parks (your city) | recreation areas (your city)

B Take notes. Answer these questions.

1. What are the names of the parks?
2. What are the addresses of the parks?
3. What activities do they have there?

C Make a chart.

Write the information you found.

Name of park	Address	Activities
Solomon Park	First Avenue and Cherry Hill Road	bicycling, canoeing, swimming, picnicking

D Share your information.

Show your chart to the class.
Talk about your favorite park and the activities.

Self-assessments

Overview

Each unit of *Ventures 1* Student's Book ends with a self-assessment. Self-assessments allow students to reflect on what they have learned and to decide whether they need more review of the material.

How self-assessments help students

- It is not possible for English language teachers to teach students all the English they need to know. Therefore, it is important that teachers help students develop strategies for learning and for measuring their learning. One important strategy is self-assessment. With self-assessment, students become aware of their own learning and focus on their own performance. Being able to self-assess is important for developing learner autonomy. It is that autonomy that will equip students for lifelong learning.
- Self-assessment allows students to participate in the assessment process. Responsibility for learning shifts from the teacher to the students as self-assessment makes the students more aware of their role in learning and monitoring their own performance.
- Self-assessment can also contribute to learner persistence. Learners will continue to attend classes when they have verification that learning has taken place. They can measure this learning when they complete the self-assessment checklists.

How self-assessments help teachers

- Teachers can use the results of the self-assessments to identify areas that need further instruction or review. Teachers can use the results of this assessment to meet with students and discuss items that have been mastered as well as those that need further study.
- The information on the self-assessment forms can also be used at the beginning of the unit to identify and discuss the learning objectives of the unit. In this way, students will have a clear understanding of the learning goals. If they know what the learning objectives are, they can better focus on their learning. This results in greater learner gains, which is gratifying to both students and teachers.

Self-assessment in *Ventures*

- Each self-assessment asks students to check the words they have learned and the skills and functions they feel they have mastered. Students then decide if they are ready to take the unit test to confirm this acquisition of unit language. The self-assessments are in checklist form, making it easier for lower-level students to check off how they feel they are progressing.
- If students feel they need additional study for a particular unit, the *Ventures* series provides additional practice in the Workbook and *Add Ventures*.
- The *Teacher's Toolkit Audio CD / CD-ROM* contains the same self-assessments that are found in the Student's Book. However, on the CD-ROM, each unit's self-assessment is on its own page and can be printed, distributed to and completed by the student after each unit, and placed in his or her learner portfolio. It can also be given to students to keep as a personal record of their progress.

Self-assessments

Unit 1 Personal information

A Vocabulary Check (✓) the words you know.

☐ address	☐ city	☐ last name	☐ street
☐ apartment number	☐ country	☐ middle name	☐ telephone number
☐ area code	☐ first name	☐ state	☐ zip code

B Skills and functions Read the sentences. Check (✓) what you know.

I can use possessive adjectives: *What's **your** name? **My** name is _____ .*		I can read addresses with three or four numbers.	
I can use subject pronouns: *Is **she** from _____ ? Yes, **she** is. No, **she** isn't.*		I can complete a form with my personal information.	
I can begin names of people and places with capital letters.		I can list names in alphabetical order.	

C What's next? Choose one.

☐ I am ready for the unit test. ☐ I need more practice with ____________________ .

Unit 2 At school

A Vocabulary Check (✓) the words you know.

☐ book	☐ chalkboard	☐ map	☐ pencil
☐ calculator	☐ desk	☐ marker	☐ ruler
☐ calendar	☐ eraser	☐ notebook	☐ stapler

B Skills and functions Read the sentences. Check (✓) what you know.

I can use the prepositions ***in*** and ***on***: *It's **on** the _____ . It's **in** the _____ .*		I can read and understand an inventory list.	
I can use singular and plural nouns: *The **pen** is on the desk. The **pencils** are on the table.*		I can start sentences with a capital letter and end them with a period.	
I can look at a picture to help understand new words.		I can say ***excuse me*** to get someone's attention.	

C What's next? Choose one.

☐ I am ready for the unit test. ☐ I need more practice with ____________________ .

Unit 3 Friends and family

A Vocabulary Check (✓) the words you know.

☐ aunt	☐ father	☐ husband	☐ son
☐ brother	☐ grandfather	☐ mother	☐ uncle
☐ daughter	☐ grandmother	☐ sister	☐ wife

B Skills and functions Read the sentences. Check (✓) what you know.

I can use the present continuous: ***I am studying***.		I can use the title to understand a story.	
I can ask *yes* / *no* questions about the present: ***Are** you **eating**?*		I can spell the numbers from one to ten.	
I can identify family members.		I can read a form with personal information on it.	

C What's next? Choose one.

☐ I am ready for the unit test. ☐ I need more practice with ______________________ .

Unit 4 Health

A Vocabulary Check (✓) the words you know.

☐ backache	☐ cough	☐ fever	☐ sore throat
☐ broken leg	☐ cut	☐ headache	☐ sprained ankle
☐ cold	☐ earache	☐ medicine	☐ stomachache

B Skills and functions Read the sentences. Check (✓) what you know.

I can use the simple present of ***have***: *I **have** a headache. He **has** a cold.*		I can look for exclamation points when reading.	
I can ask questions with ***have***: ***Do** you **have** a headache?*		I can write an excuse note about a sick child.	
I can write dates correctly.		I can read an appointment card.	

C What's next? Choose one.

☐ I am ready for the unit test. ☐ I need more practice with ______________________ .

Unit 5 Around town

A Vocabulary Check (✓) the words you know.

☐ bank	☐ grocery store	☐ parking lot	☐ restaurant
☐ bus stop	☐ hospital	☐ playground	☐ shopping mall
☐ drugstore	☐ library	☐ post office	☐ train station

B Skills and functions Read the sentences. Check (✓) what you know.

I can use the prepositions ***on***, ***next to***, ***across from***, ***between***, and ***on the corner of***.		I can give someone directions to places.	
I can use imperatives: ***Turn*** *right.* ***Go straight*** *two blocks.*		I can understand the pronouns (***I***, ***he***, ***it***, ***they***) in a paragraph.	
I can read a map.		I can capitalize street names.	

C What's next? Choose one.

☐ I am ready for the unit test. ☐ I need more practice with ______________________.

Unit 6 Time

A Vocabulary Check (✓) the words you know.

☐ buy	☐ get home	☐ study	☐ talk
☐ drink	☐ leave for work	☐ take a break	☐ watch TV
☐ eat	☐ read	☐ take a nap	☐ work

B Skills and functions Read the sentences. Check (✓) what you know.

I can use ***at***, ***in***, and ***on*** with time: *The meeting is* ***in*** *March. It is* ***on*** *Monday. It is* ***at*** *1:00.*		I can ask questions to understand what I read: *Who, what, where, when?*	
I can ask ***Wh-*** questions about the present: ***What*** *does he do in the evening?*		I can indent when starting a paragraph.	
I can talk about daily activities: *I eat dinner in the evening.*		I can read a class schedule.	

C What's next? Choose one.

☐ I am ready for the unit test. ☐ I need more practice with ______________________.

Unit 7 Shopping

A Vocabulary Check (✓) the words you know.

☐ apples	☐ check	☐ nickel	☐ quarter
☐ bananas	☐ credit card	☐ one-dollar bill	☐ shopping cart
☐ cashier	☐ dime	☐ penny	☐ supermarket

B Skills and functions Read the sentences. Check (✓) what you know.

I can ask questions using ***How many*** and ***How much***: ***How many*** *eggs do we have?* ***How much*** *coffee do we have?*		I can make sentences using ***There is*** and ***There are***: ***There is*** *rice on the shelf.* ***There are*** *two boxes of tea on the shelf.*	
I can find clues to understand new words.		I can use commas when listing three or more items.	
I can identify U.S. money.		I can read a shopping ad.	

C What's next? Choose one.

☐ I am ready for the unit test. ☐ I need more practice with _______________ .

Unit 8 Work

A Vocabulary Check (✓) the words you know.

☐ busboy	☐ electrician	☐ nurse	☐ receptionist
☐ cashier	☐ housekeeper	☐ nursing assistant	☐ salesperson
☐ construction worker	☐ housewife	☐ office worker	☐ truck driver

B Skills and functions Read the sentences. Check (✓) what you know.

I can use the simple past of ***be***: ***Were*** *you a student? Yes, I* ***was****. No, I* ***wasn't****.*		I can understand past and present when I read.	
I can use ***can***: *He* ***can*** *cook. She* ***can't*** *drive a truck.*		I can use a dictionary to check my spelling.	
I can write about my life skills and work skills.		I can complete an employment application.	

C What's next? Choose one.

☐ I am ready for the unit test. ☐ I need more practice with _______________ .

Unit 9 Daily living

A **Vocabulary** Check (✓) the words you know.

☐ broom	☐ dust	☐ mop	☐ sweep
☐ bucket	☐ empty	☐ paint	☐ vacuum
☐ do laundry	☐ iron	☐ pay the bills	☐ wash the dishes

B **Skills and functions** Read the sentences. Check (✓) what you know.

I can use the simple past with regular verbs: *They **dusted** yesterday. They **didn't vacuum**.*		I can use the simple past with irregular verbs: *She **paid** the bills. He **didn't make** dinner.*	
I can ask questions about what I am reading.		I can check my past tense verb forms when writing.	
I can read a note about daily chores.		I can read a job-duties chart.	

C **What's next?** Choose one.

☐ I am ready for the unit test. ☐ I need more practice with ______________________ .

Unit 10 Leisure

A **Vocabulary** Check (✓) the words you know.

☐ baseball	☐ fishing	☐ ice-skating	☐ soccer
☐ basketball	☐ football	☐ picnicking	☐ surfing
☐ camping	☐ hiking	☐ skiing	☐ swimming

B **Skills and functions** Read the sentences. Check (✓) what you know.

I can talk about the past using irregular verbs: *What **did** you **do** last weekend? I **went** to the park.*		When I read, I can look for words that show time.	
I can talk about the future using ***be going to***: *I **am going to** play soccer tomorrow.*		I can begin a new paragraph when changing from the past to the future tense.	
I can read a letter about a person's vacation.		I can read a TV schedule.	

C **What's next?** Choose one.

☐ I am ready for the unit test. ☐ I need more practice with ______________________ .

Reference

Present of *be*

Affirmative statements

I'm	from Somalia.
You're	
He's	
She's	
It's	
We're	
You're	
They're	

I'm	=	I am	It's	=	It is
You're	=	You are	We're	=	We are
He's	=	He is	You're	=	You are
She's	=	She is	They're	=	They are

Yes / No questions

Am	I	from Guatemala?
Are	you	
Is	he	
Is	she	
Is	it	
Are	we	
Are	you	
Are	they	

Short answers

Yes,	you are.	No,	you aren't.
	I am.		I'm not.
	he is.		he isn't.
	she is.		she isn't.
	it is.		it isn't.
	you are.		you aren't.
	we are.		we aren't.
	they are.		they aren't.

Present continuous

Affirmative statements

I'm	eating.
You're	
He's	
She's	
It's	
We're	
You're	
They're	

Yes / No questions

Am	I	eating?
Are	you	
Is	he	
Is	she	
Is	it	
Are	we	
Are	you	
Are	they	

Short answers

Yes,	you are.	No,	you aren't.
	I am.		I'm not.
	he is.		he isn't.
	she is.		she isn't.
	it is.		it isn't.
	you are.		you aren't.
	we are.		we aren't.
	they are.		they aren't.

Wh- questions

What	am	I	doing?
	are	you	
	is	he	
	is	she	
	is	it	
	are	we	
	are	you	
	are	they	

Answers

You're	eating.
I'm	
He's	
She's	
It's	
You're	
We're	
They're	

Possessive adjectives

Questions

What's	my your his her its our your their	address?

Answers

Your My His Her Its Your Our Their	address is 10 Main Street.

Simple present

Affirmative statements

I	work.
You	work.
He	works.
She	works.
It	works.
We	work.
You	work.
They	work.

Negative statements

I You He She It We You They	don't don't doesn't doesn't doesn't don't don't don't	work.

Yes / No questions

Do Do Does Does Does Do Do Do	I you he she it we you they	work?

Short answers

Yes,	you I he she it you we they	do. do. does. does. does. do. do. do.	No,	you I he she it you we they	don't. don't. doesn't. doesn't. doesn't. don't. don't. don't.

Wh- questions

What	do do does does does do do do	I you he she it we you they	do at 7:00?

Answers

You	work.
I	work.
He	works.
She	works.
It	works.
You	work.
We	work.
They	work.

Simple present of *have*

Affirmative statements

I	have	a cold.
You	have	a cold.
He	has	a cold.
She	has	a cold.
It	has	a cold.
We	have	colds.
You	have	colds.
They	have	colds.

Negative statements

I	don't have	a cold.
You	don't have	a cold.
He	doesn't have	a cold.
She	doesn't have	a cold.
It	doesn't have	a cold.
We	don't have	colds.
You	don't have	colds.
They	don't have	colds.

Yes / No questions

Do	I	have	a cold?
Do	you		a cold?
Does	he		a cold?
Does	she		a cold?
Does	it		a cold?
Do	we		colds?
Do	you		colds?
Do	they		colds?

Short answers

Yes,	you	do.	No,	you	don't.
	I	do.		I	don't.
	he	does.		he	doesn't.
	she	does.		she	doesn't.
	it	does.		it	doesn't.
	you	do.		you	don't.
	we	do.		we	don't.
	they	do.		they	don't.

Simple past of *be*

Affirmative statements

I	was	a teacher.
You	were	a teacher.
He	was	a teacher.
She	was	a teacher.
We	were	teachers.
You	were	teachers.
They	were	teachers.

Negative statements

I	wasn't	a cashier.
You	weren't	a cashier.
He	wasn't	a cashier.
She	wasn't	a cashier.
We	weren't	cashiers.
You	weren't	cashiers.
They	weren't	cashiers.

Yes / No questions

Was	I	a teacher?
Were	you	a teacher?
Was	he	a teacher?
Was	she	a teacher?
Were	we	teachers?
Were	you	teachers?
Were	they	teachers?

Short answers

Yes,	you	were.	No,	you	weren't.
	I	was.		I	wasn't.
	he	was.		he	wasn't.
	she	was.		she	wasn't.
	you	were.		you	weren't.
	we	were.		we	weren't.
	they	were.		they	weren't.

Simple past of regular and irregular verbs

Affirmative statements

I You He She It We You They	cooked. slept.

Negative statements

I You He She It We You They	didn't	cook. sleep.

Yes / No questions

Did	I you he she it we you they	cook? sleep?

Short answers

Yes,	you I he she it you we they	did.	No,	you I he she it you we they	didn't.

Wh- questions

What	did	I you he she it we you they	do?

Answers

You I He She It You We They	cooked. slept.

Regular verbs

Add *-ed*: cook → cooked, dust → dusted, talk → talked, wash → washed

Irregular verbs

break → broke	get → got	ride → rode	sweep → swept
buy → bought	go → went	run → ran	swim → swam
do → did	have → had	see → saw	take → took
drink → drank	make → made	sell → sold	wear → wore
drive → drove	pay → paid	sit → sat	write → wrote
eat → ate	read → read	sleep → slept	

Can

Affirmative statements

I You He She It We You They	can	help.

Negative statements

I You He She It We You They	can't	help.

Yes / No questions

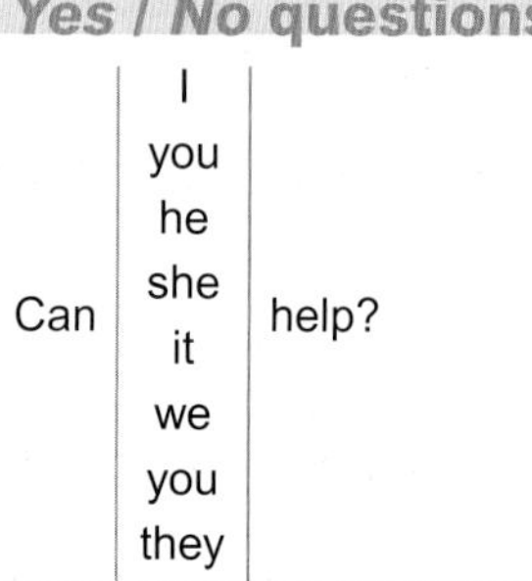

Can	I you he she it we you they	help?

Short answers

Yes,	you I he she it you we they	can.

No,	you I he she it you we they	can't.

Future – *be going to*

Affirmative statements

I'm You're He's She's It's We're You're They're	going to	play.

Negative statements

I'm You're He's She's It's We're You're They're	not going to	play.

Wh- questions

What	am I are you is he is she is it are we are you are they	going to do tomorrow?

Answers

You're I'm He's She's It's You're We're They're	going to	play.

Welcome

Page 3, Exercise 2A – CD 1, Track 2

A, B, C, D, E, F, G, H, I, J, K, L, M, N, O, P, Q, R, S, T, U, V, W, X, Y, Z

Page 3, Exercise 2C – CD 1, Track 3

A What's your name?
B Helena.
A How do you spell that?
B H-E-L-E-N-A.

Page 4, Exercise 3A – CD 1, Track 4

Zero, one, two, three, four, five, six, seven, eight, nine, ten, eleven, twelve, thirteen, fourteen, fifteen, sixteen, seventeen, eighteen, nineteen, twenty

Page 4, Exercise 3B – CD 1, Track 5

1. six
2. twenty
3. one
4. fifteen
5. nine
6. twelve
7. nine
8. five
9. sixteen

Page 4, Exercise 3C – CD 1, Track 6

1. three
2. eight
3. eighteen
4. twelve
5. one
6. zero
7. twenty
8. four
9. fifteen
10. eleven

Page 5, Exercise 4A – CD 1, Track 7

Days: Sunday, Monday, Tuesday, Wednesday, Thursday, Friday, Saturday

Page 5, Exercise 4C – CD 1, Track 8

Months: January, February, March, April, May, June, July, August, September, October, November, December

Unit 1: Personal information

Lesson A: Get ready

Page 7, Exercises 2A and 2B – CD 1, Track 9

Conversation A
A What's your telephone number?
B My telephone number is 555-8907.

Conversation B
A What's your area code?
B My area code is 213.

Conversation C
A What's your last name?
B My last name is Clark.

Conversation D
A What's your address?
B My address is 1041 Main Street.

Conversation E
A What's your first name?
B My first name is Ricardo.

Conversation F
A What's your middle name?
B My middle name is Juan.

Lesson B: What's your name?

Page 8, Exercise 2A – CD 1, Track 10

1. *A* What's his first name?
   B His first name is Alfred.
2. *A* What's her first name?
   B Her first name is Sue.
3. *A* What's his first name?
   B His first name is Tom.
4. *A* What's their last name?
   B Their last name is Jones.

Page 9, Exercise 2C – CD 1, Track 11

A What's your name?
B Jennifer Kent.
A Sorry. What's your first name?
B My first name is Jennifer.
A How do you spell that?
B J-E-N-N-I-F-E-R.
A OK. What's your last name?
B Kent. K-E-N-T.

Page 9, Exercise 2C – CD 1, Track 12

A What's your name?
B Jennifer Kent.
A Sorry. What's your first name?
B My first name is Jennifer.
A How do you spell that?
B J-E-N-N-I-F-E-R.
A OK. What's your last name?
B Kent. K-E-N-T.

Lesson C: Are you from Canada?

Page 10, Exercise 2A – CD 1, Track 13

1. *A* Are you from Canada?
   B No, I'm not
2. *A* Are they from Somalia?
   B Yes, they are.
3. *A* Is she from Russia?
   B Yes, she is.
4. *A* Is he from Mexico?
   B Yes, he is.
5. *A* Is she from China?
   B No, she isn't.
6. *A* Are they from Brazil?
   B No, they aren't.
7. *A* Is he from Ecuador?
   B No, he isn't.
8. *A* Are you from Colombia?
   B Yes, I am.

Page 11, Exercise 2C – CD 1, Track 14

A Where are you from, Katia?
B I'm from Brazil.
A Brazil? How do you spell that?
B B-R-A-Z-I-L.

Lesson D: Reading

Page 12, Exercise 2 – CD 1, Track 15

A New Student

Svetlana Kulik is a new student. She is from Russia. Now she lives in Napa, California. Her address is 1041 Main Street. Her zip code is 94558. Her area code is 707. Her telephone number is 555-9073.

Page 13, Exercise 4A – CD 1, Track 16

1. title
2. address
3. city
4. state
5. signature
6. zip code
7. apartment number
8. street
9. middle initial

Unit 2: At school

Lesson A: Get ready

Page 19, Exercises 2A and 2B – CD 1, Track 17

Conversation A
A Where are the pens?
B They're in the drawer.

Conversation B
A Where is the calculator?
B It's on the desk.

Conversation C
A Where is the notebook?
B It's on the table.

Conversation D
A Is the map on the wall?
B Yes, it is.

Conversation E
A Are the rulers in the box?
B Yes, they are.

Conversation F
A Is the book on the chair?
B Yes, it is.

Lesson B: Where is the pen?

Page 20, Exercise 2A – CD 1, Track 18

1. ***A*** Where's the book?
B It's on the shelf.
2. ***A*** Where's the pencil sharpener?
B It's on the wall.
3. ***A*** Where's the dictionary?
B It's on the table.
4. ***A*** Where's the calendar?
B It's in the box.
5. ***A*** Where's the eraser?
B It's in the drawer.
6. ***A*** Where's the calculator?
B It's in the cabinet.

Page 21, Exercise 2B – CD 1, Track 19

1. ***A*** Excuse me. Where's the calculator?
B It's in the cabinet.
A Oh, thanks.
B You're welcome.
2. ***A*** Excuse me. Where's the pen?
B It's on the table.
A Oh, thanks.
B You're welcome.
3. ***A*** Excuse me. Where's the pencil sharpener?
B It's in the cabinet.
A Oh, thanks.
B You're welcome.
4. ***A*** Excuse me. Where's the eraser?
B It's on the table.
A Oh, thanks.
B You're welcome.

Lesson C: Where are the pencils?

Page 22, Exercise 2A – CD 1, Track 20

1. ***A*** Are the books in the cabinet?
B Yes, they are.
2. ***A*** Is the clock in the cabinet?
B Yes, it is.
3. ***A*** Are the rulers on the table?
B No, they aren't.
4. ***A*** Are the pencils on the table?
B No, they aren't.
5. ***A*** Are the calculators on the table?
B Yes, they are.

Page 23, Exercise 2C – CD 1, Track 21

1. ***A*** Where are the pencils?
B They're on the desk.
2. ***A*** Where is the calculator?
B It's on the filing cabinet.
3. ***A*** Where is the calendar?
B It's on the wall.
4. ***A*** Where is the computer?
B It's on the desk.
5. ***A*** Where are the notebooks?
B They're in the filing cabinet.
6. ***A*** Where are the books?
B They're in the box.

Lesson D: Reading

Page 24, Exercise 2 – CD 1, Track 22

Attention, new students!
Welcome to your new classroom.
The computer is on the small table.
The pencils are in the basket on the desk.
The erasers are in the basket.
The books are in the bookcase.
The calculators are on the bookcase.
The markers are in the desk drawer.

Page 25, Exercise 4A – CD 1, Track 23

1. chalk
2. notepads
3. bulletin board
4. chalkboard
5. index cards
6. stapler
7. paper clips
8. marker
9. globe

Review: Units 1 and 2

Page 30, Exercise 1 – CD 1, Track 24

A Good morning, class. We have a new student today. His name is Juan.
B Hello, Juan.
A Do you want to ask Juan some questions?
C What's your last name?
D My last name is Perez. P-E-R-E-Z.
E What's your middle name?
D Ricardo.
F Where are you from?
D I'm from El Salvador.
C Where do you live?
D My address is 350 Lincoln Avenue, apartment 10. The zip code is 94321.
A Very good. Any other questions?
F What's your telephone number?
D 213-555-6301.
A Welcome, Juan.

Page 31, Exercise 3A – CD 1, Track 25

name
address
apartment

Page 31, Exercise 3B – CD 1, Track 26

map	ruler
books	notebook
box	pencil
clock	initial
pens	telephone
chair	signature
desk	computer
classroom	sharpener
middle	cabinet
partner	eraser
chalkboard	

Page 31, Exercise 3C – CD 1, Track 27

a. from	e. Colombia
b. China	f. Canada
c. student	g. talk
d. name	h. city

Page 31, Exercise 3C–CD 1, Track 28

a. from	e. Colombia
b. China	f. Canada
c. student	g. talk
d. name	h. city

Unit 3: Friends and family

Lesson A: Get ready

Page 33, Exercises 2A and 2B – CD 1, Track 29

Conversation A

A Hello?
B Hi, Louisa. This is Mrs. Brown. Is your grandmother home?
A Yes, she is. She's watching TV.

Conversation B

A Hello?
B Hi, this is Mr. Cho. Is your father home?
A Yes, he is, but he's sleeping right now.

Conversation C

A Hello?
B Hi, Carlos. This is Mr. Ramos. Is your grandfather there?
A Yes, he is, but he's eating right now.

Conversation D

A Hello?
B Hi, this is Angela. Is your mother there?
A Yes, she is. But she's busy. She's cooking dinner.

Conversation E

A Hello?
B Hi, Carlos. This is Mary. Is your sister home?
A Yes, she is, but she's studying.

Conversation F

A Hello?
B Hello. This is Dr. Smith's office. Is your husband home?
A Yes, he is, but he's resting.

Lesson B: What are you doing?

Page 34, Exercise 2A – CD 1, Track 30

1. ***A*** What's she doing?
B She's reading.
2. ***A*** What's he doing?
B He's sleeping.
3. ***A*** What are they doing?
B They're eating.
4. ***A*** What's he doing?
B He's watching TV.
5. ***A*** What's she doing?
B She's talking.
6. ***A*** What are you doing?
B I'm studying.

Lesson C: Are you working now?

Page 36, Exercise 2A – CD 1, Track 31

1. ***A*** Is she working now?
B Yes, she is. She's very busy.
2. ***A*** Is he driving to work?
B Yes, he is. He's late.
3. ***A*** Are they eating lunch now?
B Yes, they are. They're hungry.
4. ***A*** Is he helping his grandmother?
B Yes, he is. He's really nice.
5. ***A*** Is she taking a break?
B Yes, she is. She's tired.
6. ***A*** Are they buying water?
B Yes, they are. They're thirsty.

Lesson D: Reading

Page 38, Exercise 2 – CD 1, Track 32

The Birthday Party

My name is Juan. In this picture, it's my birthday. I am 70 years old. Look at me! I don't look 70 years old. My wife, my daughter, and my grandson are eating cake. My grandson is always hungry. My granddaughter is drinking soda. She's always thirsty. My son-in-law is playing the guitar and singing. Everyone is happy!

Page 39, Exercise 4A – CD 1, Track 33

1. grandfather and grandmother
2. father and mother
3. aunt and uncle
4. brother and sister-in-law
5. husband and wife
6. cousin
7. niece and nephew

Unit 4: Health

Lesson A: Get ready

Page 45, Exercises 2A and 2B – CD 1, Track 34

Conversation A
A What's the matter?
B I have a headache.
A Oh, I'm sorry.

Conversation B
A What's the matter?
B I have a fever.
A Get some rest.

Conversation C
A What's the matter?
B I have a sprained ankle.
A Oh, I'm sorry.

Conversation D
A What's the matter?
B I have a stomachache.
A Oh, that's too bad.

Conversation E
A What's the matter?
B I have a sore throat.
A I hope you feel better.

Conversation F
A What's the matter?
B I have an earache.
A Oh, that's too bad.

Lesson B: I have a headache.

Page 46, Exercise 2A – CD 1, Track 35

1. He has a terrible cold.
2. I have a headache.
3. He has a backache.
4. You have a fever.
5. I have a broken arm.
6. He has a stomachache.
7. She has a bad cough.
8. You have a sore throat.
9. She has a cut.

Page 47, Exercise 2B – CD 1, Track 36

1. *A* He has a bad headache.
B Take aspirin.
2. *A* She has a cut.
B Use a bandage.
3. *A* He has a bad cold.
B Take vitamin C.
4. *A* She has a cough.
B Take cough drops.
5. *A* He has a backache.
B Use a heating pad.

Lesson C: Do you have a cold?

Page 48, Exercise 2A – CD 1, Track 37

1. *A* Do I have a fever?
B No, you don't.
2. *A* Does she have a sore throat?
B No, she doesn't.
3. *A* Does he have a cough?
B Yes, he does.
4. *A* Do you have a cold?
B Yes, I do.
5. *A* Does she have the flu?
B Yes, she does.
6. *A* Does she have a sprained ankle?
B No, she doesn't.

Lesson D: Reading

Page 50, Exercise 2 – CD 1, Track 38

The Health Clinic

Poor Maria! Everyone is sick! Maria and her children are at the health clinic today. Her son, Luis, has a sore throat. Her daughter, Rosa, has a stomachache. Her baby, Gabriel, has an earache. Maria doesn't have a sore throat. She doesn't have a stomachache. And she doesn't have an earache. But Maria has a very bad headache!

Page 51, Exercise 4A – CD 1, Track 39

1. eye	9. toe
2. ear	10. knee
3. back	11. finger
4. neck	12. hand
5. shoulder	13. chin
6. stomach	14. tooth
7. leg	15. nose
8. foot	16. head

Review: Units 3 and 4

Page 56, Exercise 1 – CD 1, Track 40

Connie and her family are at home today. They're not at work or at school. Connie has a headache. Her husband, Robert, has an earache. He's talking to the doctor on the phone. Connie's daughter is sleeping. Her son, Eddie, is in the living room. He's watching TV. He has a stomachache.

Page 57, Exercise 3A – CD 1, Track 41

happy	fever

Page 57, Exercise 3B – CD 1, Track 42

son	husband
wife	daughter
head	yesterday
ear	grandmother
foot	grandfather
leg	newspaper
cooking	studying
homework	stomachache
toothache	tomorrow
headache	computer

Page 57, Exercise 3C – CD 1, Track 43

1. father
2. earache
3. tired
4. birthday
5. thirsty
6. celebrate
7. finger
8. Brazil
9. repeat
10. elbow
11. reschedule
12. fever

Unit 5: Around town

Lesson A: Get ready

Page 59, Exercises 2A and 2B – CD 1, Track 44

Conversation A

A Excuse me. Where's the drugstore?
B The drugstore? It's on Fifth Avenue.

Conversation B

A Excuse me. Where's Low's restaurant?
B Low's restaurant? It's on Fifth Avenue. Go straight two blocks.

Conversation C

A Excuse me. Where's the post office?
B The post office is on Summit Street.

Conversation D

A Excuse me. Where's the museum?
B The museum? It's on Maple Avenue. Go straight one block.

Conversation E

A Excuse me. Where's the park?
B The park is on the corner of Maple and Summit.

Conversation F

A Excuse me. Where's the bus stop?
B The bus stop? It's on Orange Avenue. Go one block and turn left.

Lesson B: It's on the corner.

Page 60, Exercise 2A – CD 1, Track 45

1. *A* Where's the park?
B It's next to the bank.
2. *A* Where's the library?
B It's across from the bank.
3. *A* Where's the school?
B It's on the corner of First Street and Grant Avenue.
4. *A* Where's the hospital?
B It's on Grant Avenue.
5. *A* Where's the bank?
B It's between the school and the park.
6. *A* Where's the post office?
B It's next to the library.

Page 61, Exercise 2B – CD 1, Track 46

A Excuse me. Where's Kim's Coffee Shop?
B It's on Kent Street.
A Sorry. Could you repeat that, please?
B It's on Kent Street.
A Oh, OK. Thanks.

Lesson C: Go two blocks.

Page 62, Exercise 2A – CD 1, Track 47

1. Go straight ahead.
2. Turn left.
3. Go three blocks.
4. Turn right.
5. Cross Union Street.
6. Go to Main Street.

Page 63, Exercise 2B – CD 1, Track 48

1. *A* Go two blocks. Turn left. It's across from the library.
B The DMV.
2. *A* Go straight. Cross Grand Street. Turn right on Main Street. It's across from the post office.
B The bank.
3. *A* Go to Grand Street. Turn left. It's next to the parking lot.
B The train station.
4. *A* Go one block. Turn right on Grand Street. It's across from Ed's Restaurant.
B The park.

Lesson D: Reading

Page 64, Exercise 2 – CD 1, Track 49

Hi Angela,

I love my new house. My neighborhood is great! Here are some pictures.

There is a school on my street. My children go to the school. They like it a lot. There is a community center across from the school. My husband works at the community center. He walks to work. There is a grocery store next to my house. It's a small store, but we can buy a lot of things. There is a good Mexican restaurant on Second Street. It's right across from my house.

I like it here, but I miss you. Please write.

Your friend,
Sandra

Page 65, Exercise 4A – CD 1, Track 50

1. a shopping mall
2. a high school
3. a day-care center
4. a gas station
5. a playground
6. a police station
7. an apartment building
8. a hardware store
9. a courthouse

Page 66, Exercise 1A – CD 1, Track 51

From the train station, turn right. Go straight on Pine Street. Turn right on Second

Avenue. Go straight ahead. Cross Maple Street. Then turn left. Walk one block to the corner. The school is on the corner of Maple Street and Third Avenue. It's across from the apartment building.

Unit 6: Time

Lesson A: Get ready

Page 71, Exercises 2A and 2B – CD 2, Track 2

Conversation A

A Congratulations on your new job.
B Thanks.
A So when do you leave for work?
B I leave at ten-thirty.
A At night?
B Right.

Conversation B

A What time do you eat dinner?
B We eat dinner at six-thirty.

Conversation C

A What time do you start work?
B I start work at eleven o'clock at night.

Conversation D

A What time do you catch the bus?
B I catch the bus at ten-forty-five.

Conversation E

A What time do you take a break?
B I take a break at two-forty-five.

Conversation F

A What time do you get home?
B I get home around seven-thirty.
A In the morning?
B Right.

Page 71, Exercise 2C – CD 2, Track 3

1. ***A*** What time is it?
B It's ten o'clock.
2. ***A*** What time is it?
B It's ten-thirty.
3. ***A*** What time is it?
B It's six-fifteen.
4. ***A*** What time is it?
B It's five-twenty.
5. ***A*** What time is it?
B It's twelve-fifty.
6. ***A*** What time is it?
B It's two-forty-five.
7. ***A*** What time is it?
B It's seven-thirty.
8. ***A*** What time is it?
B It's nine-oh-five.

Lesson B: What do you do in the evening?

Page 72, Exercise 2A – CD 2, Track 4

1. ***A*** What do they do in the evening?
B They watch TV.
2. ***A*** What does he do in the afternoon?
B He studies.
3. ***A*** What does she do in the morning?
B She exercises.
4. ***A*** What do they do on Sunday?
B They go to the park.

Page 73, Exercise 2B – CD 2, Track 5

On Saturday morning, Jill watches TV.
On Saturday afternoon, she plays soccer.
On Saturday evening, she listens to music.
On Saturday morning, Mr. and Mrs. Wilder go shopping.
On Saturday afternoon, they work in the garden.
On Saturday evening, they pay bills.

Page 73, Exercise 2B – CD 2, Track 6

On Saturday morning, Jill watches TV.
On Saturday afternoon, she plays soccer.
On Saturday evening, she listens to music.
On Saturday morning, Mr. and Mrs. Wilder go shopping.
On Saturday afternoon, they work in the garden.
On Saturday evening, they pay bills.

Page 73, Exercise 2B – CD 2, Track 7

What does Jill do on Saturday morning?
She usually watches TV.

Lesson C: I go to work at eight o'clock.

Page 74, Exercise 2B – CD 2, Track 8

1. ***A*** When do you go on vacation?
B I go on vacation in July.
2. ***A*** When does your sister have class?
B She has class on Saturday.
3. ***A*** When does your father catch the bus?
B He catches the bus at 8:45.
4. ***A*** When do you do homework?
B I do homework at night.

Page 75, Exercise 2C – CD 2, Track 9

A When does Mrs. Wilder volunteer at the high school?
B She volunteers at the high school on Monday.
A What time?
B At eleven in the morning.

Lesson D: Reading

Page 76, Exercise 2 – CD 2, Track 10

Meet Our New Employee: Bob Green

Please welcome Bob. He is a new security guard. He works the night shift at the East End Factory. Bob starts work at

11:00 at night. He leaves work at 7:00 in the morning.

Bob likes these hours because he can spend time with his family. Bob says, "I eat breakfast with my wife, Arlene, and my son, Brett, at 7:30 every morning. I help Brett with his homework in the afternoon. I eat dinner with my family at 6:30. Then we watch TV. At 10:30, I go to work."

Congratulations to Bob on his new job!

Page 77, Exercise 4A – CD 2, Track 11

1. eat lunch
2. take the children to school
3. walk the dog
4. take a shower
5. eat dinner
6. go to bed
7. get up
8. eat breakfast
9. get dressed

Review: Units 5 and 6

Page 82, Exercise 1 – CD 2, Track 12

A Excuse me. Where is the DMV?

B It's at 515 Broadway. It's between the bank and the coffee shop.

A Oh, on Broadway. Across from the hospital?

B Yes, that's right.

A OK. Thank you.

B You're welcome. Good luck.

Page 83, Exercise 3A – CD 2, Track 13

A Where is the bank?

B Is the bank on Broadway?

A When is your class?

B Is your class in the morning?

Page 83, Exercise 3B – CD 2, Track 14

Wh- questions

1. ***A*** Where is the post office?
B It's on First Street.

2. ***A*** What time do they eat dinner?
B They eat dinner at 6:30.

Yes/No questions

3. ***A*** Are you from Mexico?
B Yes, I am.

4. ***A*** Does he start work at 7:00?
B No, he doesn't.

Unit 7: Shopping

Lesson A: Get ready

Page 85, Exercises 2A and 2B – CD 2, Track 15

Conversation A

A We need some milk. Is there any milk on sale?

B Yes. Milk is a dollar eighty-nine.

A A dollar eighty-nine? That's cheap.

B How much do we need?

A A lot.

Conversation B

A We need some onions. Are there any onions on sale?

B Yes. Onions are seventy-nine cents each.

A Seventy-nine cents? That's expensive!

B How many do we need?

A Only one.

Conversation C

A We need some tomatoes. Are there any tomatoes on sale?

B Yes, tomatoes are eighty cents a pound.

A Eighty cents? That's cheap.

B How many do we need?

A A lot.

Conversation D

A We need some cheese. Is there any cheese on sale?

B Yes. Cheese is five ninety-nine a pound.

A Five ninety-nine? That's expensive!

B How much do we need?

A Not much.

Conversation E

A We need some potatoes. Are there any potatoes on sale?

B Yes. Potatoes are ninety-nine cents a pound.

A Ninety-nine cents? That's cheap.

B How many do we need?

A A lot.

Conversation F

A We need some bread. Is there any bread on sale?

B Yes, bread is three seventy-nine.

A Three seventy-nine? That's expensive!

B How much do we need?

A Not much.

Lesson B: How many? How much?

Page 86, Exercise 2A – CD 2, Track 16

Count nouns

1. carrots	7. eggs
4. peaches	10. apples
6. oranges	12. pies

Non-count nouns

2. water	8. meat
3. bread	9. coffee
5. milk	11. sugar

Page 87, Exercise 2C – CD 2, Track 17

1. How many eggs do we need?
2. How much juice do we need?
3. How much milk do we need?
4. How many pies do we need?
5. How much bread do we need?
6. How many potatoes do we need?
7. How much rice do we need?
8. How much meat do we need?

Lesson C: Are there any bananas?

Page 88, Exercise 2A – CD 2, Track 18

1. *A* Is there any bread on the table?
   B Yes, there is.
2. *A* Are there any eggs?
   B No, there aren't.
3. *A* Is there any juice?
   B Yes, there is.
4. *A* Is there any water?
   B No, there isn't.
5. *A* Are there any cookies?
   B Yes, there are.
6. *A* Are there any bananas?
   B No, there aren't.

Page 88, Exercise 2B – CD 2, Track 19

1. *A* Is there any meat in the refrigerator?
   B Yes, there is.
2. *A* Are there any oranges?
   B Yes, there are.
3. *A* Is there any cheese?
   B No, there isn't.
4. *A* Is there any coffee?
   B Yes, there is.
5. *A* Are there any apples?
   B No, there aren't.
6. *A* Are there any cherries?
   B Yes, there are.

Page 89, Exercise 2C – CD 2, Track 20

1. There is one loaf of bread.
2. There are two cartons of apple juice.
3. There are three boxes of tea.
4. There are four bottles of water.
5. There is one package of ground meat.
6. There are six cans of soda.
7. There is one bag of flour.
8. There are two packages of cheese.

Lesson D: Reading

Page 90, Exercise 2 – CD 2, Track 21

Regular Customers

Shirley and Dan are regular customers at SaveMore Supermarket. They go to SaveMore three or four times a week. The cashiers and stock clerks at SaveMore know them and like them. There are fruit and vegetables, meat and fish, and cookies and cakes in the supermarket. But today, Shirley and Dan are buying apples, bananas, bread, and cheese. There is one problem. The total is $16.75. They only have a ten-dollar bill, 5 one-dollar bills, and three quarters!

Page 91, Exercise 4A – CD 2, Track 22

1. a penny
2. a nickel
3. a dime
4. a quarter
5. a half-dollar
6. a one-dollar bill
7. a five-dollar bill
8. a ten-dollar bill
9. a twenty-dollar bill
10. a check
11. a credit card
12. an ATM card

Unit 8: Work

Lesson A: Get ready

Page 97, Exercises 2A and 2B – CD 2, Track 23

Conversation A

A What does she do?
B She's a teacher.
A Really? What did she do before?
B She was a waitress.

Conversation B

A What does she do?
B She's a nurse.
A Really? What did she do before?
B She was a cook.

Conversation C

A What does she do?
B She's a doctor.
A What did she do before?
B She was a medical student.

Conversation D

A What does he do now?
B He's a busboy.
A What did he do before?
B He was a student.

Conversation E

A What does he do?
B Now? He's an electrician.
A What did he do before?
B He was a construction worker.

Conversation F

A What does he do?
B He's a manager at a restaurant.
A Really? What did he do before?
B He was a cashier.

Lesson B: I was a teacher.

Page 98, Exercise 2A – CD 2, Track 24

1. *A* She was a teacher before.
   B Now she is a nurse.
2. *A* She is a manager now.
   B She was a cashier before.
3. *A* They were students before.
   B Now they are electricians.
4. *A* He was a waiter before.
   B Now he is a construction worker.

Lesson C: Can you cook?

Page 100, Exercise 2A – CD 2, Track 25

1. *A* Can she speak Spanish?
   B Yes, she can.
2. *A* Can he drive a truck?
   B No, he can't.
3. *A* Can he fix a car?
   B Yes, he can.
4. *A* Can she paint a house?
   B No, she can't.

5. *A* Can they work with computers?
   B No, they can't.
6. *A* Can you cook?
   B Yes, I can.

Page 101, Exercise 2B – CD 2, Track 26

1. A painter can paint.
2. A salesperson can sell.
3. A carpenter can build things.
4. A gardener can take care of plants.
5. A child-care worker can take care of children.
6. An auto mechanic can fix cars.

Lesson D: Reading

Page 102, Exercise 2 – CD 2, Track 27

Dear Ms. Carter:

I am writing this letter to recommend my student, Mai Linh Lam.

Mai Linh was a teacher in Vietnam. She is looking for a new job in the United States. She is a certified nursing assistant now. She volunteers in a nursing home Monday through Friday from 8:30 to 4:30. She takes care of senior citizens.

Mai has many good work skills. She can write reports. She can help elderly people move around and sit down. She can help them eat. She can also speak English and Vietnamese. These skills are useful in her job, and she is very good at her work.

Sincerely,
Elaine Maxwell

Page 103, Exercise 4A – CD 2, Track 28

1. housekeeper
2. custodian
3. pharmacist
4. factory worker
5. hairstylist
6. dental assistant

Review: Units 7 and 8

Page 108, Exercise 1 – CD 2, Track 29

Carlos was an office worker in his native country. Now, he is a construction worker. Every Thursday after work, Carlos buys groceries. Right now, he is shopping at SaveMore Supermarket. He is buying milk, cheese, bread, and a dozen eggs. His groceries cost $11.75. There is a ten-dollar bill and two quarters in his pocket. Good thing he has a credit card!

Page 109, Exercise 3A – CD 2, Track 30

/s/: cakes, hairstylists
/z/: tomatoes, electricians
/ɪz/: peaches, nurses

Page 109, Exercise 3B – CD 2, Track 31

/s/

assistants	mechanics
cooks	pharmacists
students	books

/z/

bananas	cookies
cashiers	waiters
drivers	teachers

/ɪz/

nurses	boxes
oranges	peaches
packages	waitresses

Page 109, Exercise 3C – CD 2, Track 32

1. bags	6. carrots
2. bottles	7. desks
3. clerks	8. sandwiches
4. dimes	9. glasses
5. pages	

Unit 9: Daily living

Lesson A: Get ready

Page 111, Exercises 2A and 2B – CD 2, Track 33

Conversation A
A Did you wash the clothes?
B Yes, I did.
A When?
B I washed them yesterday.

Conversation B
A Did you pay the bills?
B Yes, I did.
A When?
B I paid them last night.

Conversation C
A Did you clean the bathroom?
B Yes, I did.
A When?
B This morning.

Conversation D
A Did you vacuum the rug?
B No, I didn't.
A Please do it now.
B OK.

Conversation E
A Did you paint the wall?
B No, I didn't.
A Please do it now.
B OK.

Conversation F
A Did you mop the floor?
B No, I didn't.
A Please do it now.
B All right.

Lesson B: I dusted the living room.

Page 112, Exercise 2A – CD 2, Track 34

1. Yousef cooked dinner.
2. He didn't clean the kitchen.
3. He dusted the shelves.
4. He didn't wash the dishes.
5. He ironed the shirts.
6. He didn't empty the trash.

Page 113, Exercise 2B – CD 2, Track 35

1. *A* Did Mr. Ramirez mop the floor?
   B Yes, he did.
2. *A* Did Mrs. Ramirez empty the trash?
   B Yes, she did.
3. *A* Did Mr. and Mrs. Ramirez wash the dishes?
   B No, they didn't.
4. *A* Did Roberto dry the dishes?
   B Yes, he did.
5. *A* Did Luis vacuum the rug?
   B No, he didn't.
6. *A* Did Monica vacuum the rug?
   B Yes, she did.

Lesson C: I paid the bills.

Page 114, Exercise 2A – CD 2, Track 36

Last night, Linda had to pay the bills. But first, she bought groceries after work. She paid fifteen dollars. She got home, and she made dinner. She made soup and salad. After dinner, she was very tired. She swept the kitchen floor, but she didn't pay the bills!

Page 115, Exercise 2 – CD 2B, Track 37

1. *A* Who bought the groceries?
   B Mom did.
2. *A* Who made the beds?
   B Sasha did.
3. *A* Who vacuumed the rug?
   B Erica did.
4. *A* Who got the mail?
   B Sasha did.
5. *A* Who cut the grass?
   B Dad did.
6. *A* Who did the laundry?
   B Mom did.

Lesson D: Reading

Page 116, Exercise 2 – Track 38

Dear Karen,

Welcome home! We were very busy today. Jeff ironed the clothes. Chris emptied the trash. Sharon mopped the floor. Ben vacuumed the rug and dusted the furniture. The house is clean for you!

I cooked dinner. There is food on the stove.

Your husband,
Mark

Page 117, Exercise 4A – Track 39

1. a sponge
2. a mop
3. a vacuum cleaner
4. a dustpan
5. an iron
6. a broom
7. a stove
8. a lawn mower
9. a bucket

Unit 10: Leisure

Lesson A: Get ready

Page 123, Exercises 2A and 2B – Track 40

Conversation A

A Hi, Diego!
B Oh! Hi, Carla. How are you? You look tired.
A Oh, no, I'm OK. I went hiking yesterday.
B Hey, I'm going to go hiking next weekend.

Conversation B

A Hi, Nicholas. How are you?
B Oh, pretty good. What's new with you?
A Well, we went camping last weekend.
B Really? We're going to go camping next month.

Conversation C

A Hey, Bill. How are you?
B Terrific. I was on vacation all last week.
A Really? What did you do?
B Nothing. I just needed to rest.

Conversation D

A Hi, Shawn. Where were you yesterday?
B I went with my family to Lookout Park. We went picnicking.
A Really? I'm going to go picnicking there next weekend.
B Well, watch out for the bees!

Conversation E

A Lidia, where were you yesterday?
B It was so hot, we went swimming at the lake.
A Really? I'm going to go swimming next weekend.
B Have fun!

Conversation F

A Hey, Barbara, where did you get those fish?
B I went fishing this morning.
A Really? I'm going to go fishing tomorrow.
B Good luck.

Lesson B: What did you do yesterday?

Page 124, Exercise 2A – CD 2, Track 41

1. *A* What did Mr. Brown do?
   B He went fishing.
2. *A* What did Carl do?
   B He went hiking.
3. *A* What did Gina do?
   B She went swimming.
4. *A* What did Mrs. Brown do?
   B She went riding.
5. *A* What did Carl and Gina do?
   B They went camping.
6. *A* What did Mr. and Mrs. Brown do?
   B They went canoeing.

Lesson C: What are you going to do?

Page 126, Exercise 2A – CD 2, Track 42

1. *A* What's Marta going to do next Monday?
   B She's going to take her exams.
2. *A* What's Paco going to do next Tuesday?
   B He's going to play soccer.
3. *A* What's Alfredo going to do next Wednesday?
   B He's going to go hiking.
4. *A* What are Mr. and Mrs. Santiago going to do next Thursday?
   B They're going to go swimming.
5. *A* What are Alfredo and Marta going to do next Friday?
   B They're going to go to a party.
6. *A* What's the family going to do next weekend?
   B They're going to take a trip.

Lesson D: Reading

Page 128, Exercise 2 – CD 2, Track 43

Dear Ming,

Last weekend, we went camping in the mountains. I went hiking. My husband and our sons went fishing. They also went swimming in the lake. We all had a great time!

Tonight we're going to eat fish for dinner. After dinner, we're going to watch a movie. Later tonight, we're going to be very busy. We are going to do the laundry. With three boys, we have a lot of dirty clothes!

See you soon,
Maria

Page 129, Exercise 4A – CD 2, Track 44

1. football
2. baseball
3. basketball
4. Ping-Pong
5. ice hockey
6. soccer
7. surfing
8. ice-skating
9. skiing

Review: Units 9 and 10

Page 134, Exercise 1 – CD 2, Track 45

A Hi, Melissa.
B Oh, hi, Ivan!
A How was your weekend?
B It was OK. On Sunday, we went picnicking in the park.
A Really? That's great. What did you eat?
B Just hamburgers. What about you? How was your weekend?
A Well, on Saturday, we all did our chores at home. I cut the grass. My wife vacuumed the rugs. My son, Tommy, washed the clothes, and my daughter, Lisa, dusted the furniture.
B Wow! You were really busy!

Page 135, Exercise 3A – CD 2, Track 46

/d/
cleaned: He cleaned his house.
dried: I dried all the dishes.
emptied: They emptied the trash.

/t/
cooked: They cooked dinner.
talked: She talked on the phone.
washed: She washed the car.

/ɪd/
dusted: I dusted the living room.
folded: He folded his clothes.
painted: They painted the house.

Page 135, Exercise 3B – CD 2, Track 47

/d/
exercised
played
turned

/t/
camped
fished
walked

/ɪd/
celebrated
folded
visited

Page 135, Exercise 3C – CD 2, Track 48

1. studied
2. ironed
3. mopped
4. rested
5. waited
6. hiked
7. vacuumed
8. worked

Tests

Overview

The unit tests, midterm test, and final test help teachers assess students' mastery of the material in the *Ventures 1* Student's Book.

- Each of the ten unit tests covers one unit.
- The midterm test covers Units 1–5.
- The final test covers Units 6–10.
- Each test assesses listening, grammar, reading, and writing, with real-life documents incorporated into the reading and writing sections.

Students' performance on the tests helps to determine what has been successfully learned and what may need more attention. Successful completion of a test can also give students a sense of accomplishment.

Getting ready for a test

- Plan to give a unit test shortly after students have completed a unit and have had time for a review. The midterm should follow completion of Unit 5 and the review lesson for Units 5 and 6. The final test should follow completion of Unit 10 and the review lesson for Units 9 and 10. Tell students when the test will be given. Encourage students to study together and to ask you for help if needed.
- Explain the purpose of the test and how students' scores will be used.
- Prepare one test for each student. The tests may be photocopied from the Teacher's Edition, starting on page T-163, or printed from the *Teacher's Toolkit Audio CD / CD-ROM.*
- Schedule approximately 30 minutes for each unit test and 1 hour for the midterm and final tests. Allow more time if needed.
- Locate the audio program for each test's listening section on the *Teacher's Toolkit Audio CD / CD-ROM.* The CD is a hybrid. It will work in both a stereo and a computer CD-ROM drive.

Giving a test

- During the test, have students use a pencil and an eraser. Tell students to put away their Student's Books and dictionaries before the test.
- Hand out one copy of the test to each student.
- Encourage students to take a few minutes to look through the test without answering any of the items. Go through the instructions to make sure students understand them.
- Tell students that approximately 5 minutes of the unit test (10 minutes of the midterm and final tests) will be used for the listening section.
- When playing the listening section of the test, you may choose to pause or repeat the audio program if you feel that students require more time to answer. The audio script appears in the Teacher's Edition on page T-191. The script can also be printed from the *Teacher's Toolkit Audio CD / CD-ROM* and read aloud in class.

Scoring

- You can collect the tests and grade them on your own. Alternatively, you can have students correct their own tests by going over the answers in class or by having students exchange tests with a partner and correcting each other's answers. The answer key is located in the Teacher's Edition on page T-193. It can also be printed from the *Teacher's Toolkit Audio CD / CD-ROM* Tests menu or the "View" button.
- Each test has a total score of 100 points. Each unit test has five sections worth 20 points each. The midterm and final tests have eight sections worth 10 or 15 points each.

Track list for test audio program

Track 1: Introduction
Track 2: Unit 1 Test
Track 3: Unit 2 Test
Track 4: Unit 3 Test
Track 5: Unit 4 Test
Track 6: Unit 5 Test
Track 7: Midterm Test, Section A
Track 8: Midterm Test, Section B
Track 9: Unit 6 Test
Track 10: Unit 7 Test
Track 11: Unit 8 Test
Track 12: Unit 9 Test
Track 13: Unit 10 Test
Track 14: Final Test, Section A
Track 15: Final Test, Section B

Name: ______________________

Date: ______________

Score: ______________

Personal information

A Listening

Listen. Circle the words you hear.

1. first name	middle name	4. address	area code
2. apartment number	telephone number	5. last name	zip code
3. area code	zip code		

B Grammar

Complete the sentences. Use *His, Her,* or *Their.*

1. __________ address is 14 Parker Street.

2. __________ first name is Keiko.

3. __________ telephone number is 555-8870.

4. __________ last name is Jones.

5. __________ middle name is Layla.

C Grammar

Write the correct word.

1. ________________ from the Ukraine.
   (They / They're)
2. ________________ from Mexico.
   (He's / His)
3. ________________ address is 82
   (Her / She's)
   Washington Street.
4. She ________________ from Pakistan.
   (aren't / isn't)
5. ________________ last name is Kamau.
   (Their / They're)

Name: ______________________________

Date: ______________________

D Reading

Read the paragraph. Read the sentences. Are they correct? Circle *Yes* or *No.*

A New Student

Peter Tran is a new student. He's from Vietnam. Now he lives in Miami, Florida. His address is 1513 Orange Avenue. His zip code is 33135. His telephone number is 555-5667. His area code is 305.

1. Peter's last name is Vietnam. Yes No
2. He lives in Miami, Florida. Yes No
3. His zip code is 1513. Yes No
4. His telephone number is 555-5667. Yes No
5. His area code is 305. Yes No

E Writing

Complete the form with your own information.

Registration

Please print.

☐ Mr. ☐ Ms. ☐ Mrs.

(1) NAME: ______________________________
Last First Middle

(2) ADDRESS: ______________________________
Number Street Apt.

(3) ______________________________
City State Zip code

(4) TELEPHONE: ______________________________
Area code Number

(5) COUNTRY OF ORIGIN: ______________________________

____
Signature

Name: ____________________

Date: ____________________

Score: ____________________

At school

A Listening

Listen. Circle the words you hear.

1. paper	stapler	4. erasers	pens
2. calculator	computer	5. marker	pencil
3. drawer	ruler		

B Grammar

Look at the picture. Write the correct word.

1. The computer is __________ (in / on) the desk.
2. The dictionary is __________ (in / on) the cabinet.
3. The map is __________ (in / on) the wall.
4. The calculators are __________ (in / on) the cabinet.
5. The books are __________ (in / on) the desk.

C Grammar

Write the correct word.

1. They __________ (are / is) on the table.
2. Where __________ (are / is) the calendar?
3. It __________ (are / is) on the wall.
4. The dictionaries __________ (are / is) on the desk.
5. __________ (Are / Is) the pencil in the box?

Name: ______________________

Date: ______________________

D Reading

Read the paragraph. Read the sentences. Are they correct? Circle *Yes* or *No.*

In the Classroom

Mr. Parker is a teacher. He's in his classroom. His students are at home. His books are in the bookcase. The calculator is in the drawer. The computer is on the table. The pencils are in the basket on his desk.

1.	Mr. Parker is at home.	Yes	No
2.	His students are in the classroom.	Yes	No
3.	The computer is in the bookcase.	Yes	No
4.	The calculator is in the drawer.	Yes	No
5.	The pencils are in the basket.	Yes	No

E Writing

Write sentences about the picture.

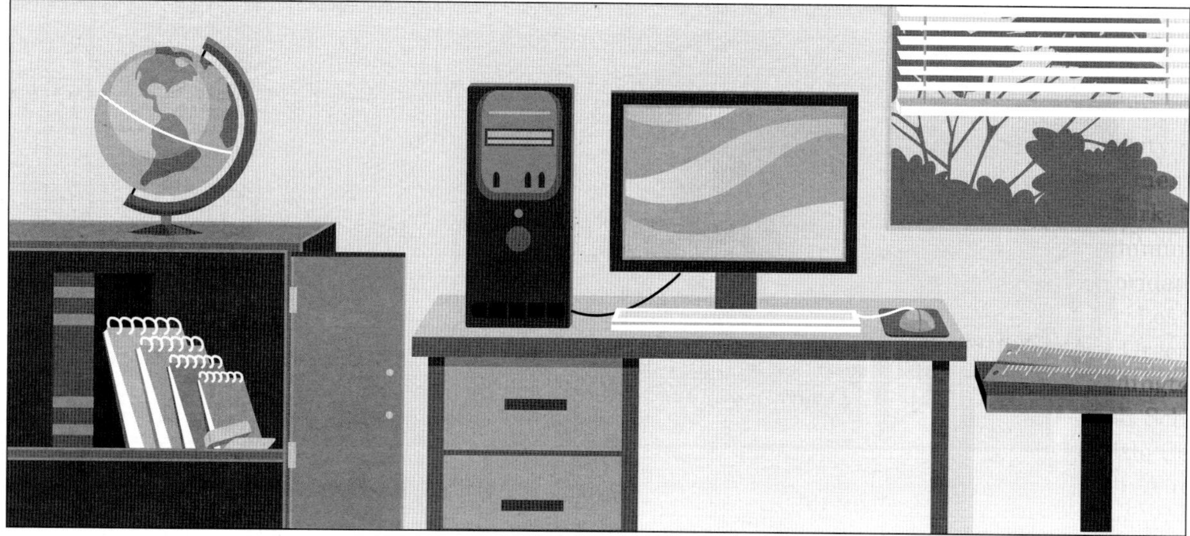

The book is in the cabinet.

1. ______________________
2. ______________________
3. ______________________
4. ______________________
5. ______________________

Name: ______________________

Date: ______________________

Score: ______________________

Friends and family

A Listening

Listen. Circle the words you hear.

1. grandfather grandmother
2. father mother
3. nephew niece
4. grandson son
5. sister sister-in-law

B Grammar

Complete the conversations.

1. ***A*** What are you doing?
   B I ______________________ (study).
2. ***A*** What is she doing?
   B She ______________________ (read).
3. ***A*** What is he doing?
   B He ______________________ (watch) TV.
4. ***A*** What are they doing?
   B They ______________________ (talk).
5. ***A*** What is she doing?
   B She ______________________ (sleep).

C Grammar

Complete the conversations.

1. ***A*** Is she ______________________ (work) now?
   B No, she isn't. She's walking to work.
2. ***A*** Are they ______________________ (eat) now?
   B No, they aren't. They're studying.
3. ***A*** Are they ______________________ (buy) water now?
   B Yes, they are. They're thirsty.
4. ***A*** Is he ______________________ (help) his wife now?
   B Yes, he is. He's cooking dinner.
5. ***A*** Are you ______________________ (take) a break now?
   B Yes, I am. I'm tired.

Name: ______________________

Date: ______________________

D Reading

Complete the paragraph. Use the words in the box.

birthday	eating	family	grandson	taking

The Birthday Party

Today is Alberto's ________ (1.). He is 70 years old. He lives in Mexico. He is celebrating his birthday with his family. His wife, his son, and his ________ (2.) are ________ (3.) cake. His daughter-in-law is ________ (4.) a picture of the ________ (5.).

E Writing

Answer the questions. Use complete sentences.

Insurance Application Form				
Last name	First name	Age	Male	Female
Parents				
Clark	Joseph	30	x	
Clark	Rita	29		x
Children				
Clark	Justin	10	x	
Clark	Scott	8	x	
Clark	Carolyn	7		x
Clark	Michael	2	x	

Who is 30 years old?

Joseph is 30 years old.

1. Who is eight years old?

____

2. How old is Mrs. Clark?

____

3. How many children do Mr. and Mrs. Clark have?

____

4. How many daughters do Mr. and Mrs. Clark have?

____

5. How many sons do Mr. and Mrs. Clark have?

____

Name: ______________________________

Date: ______________________

Score: __________

Health

A Listening

Listen. Write the letter of the conversation.

1. ____

2. ____

3. ____

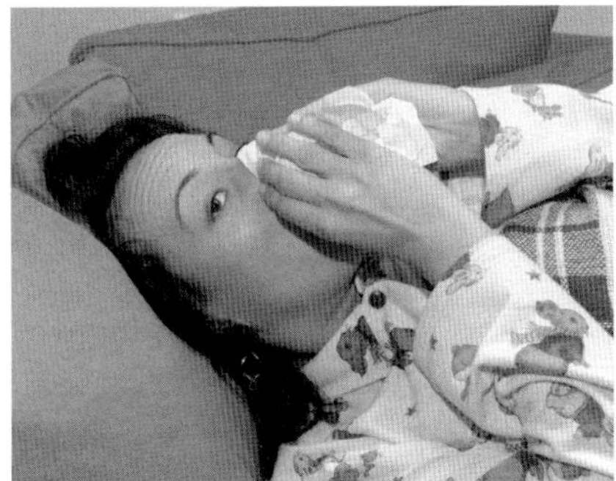
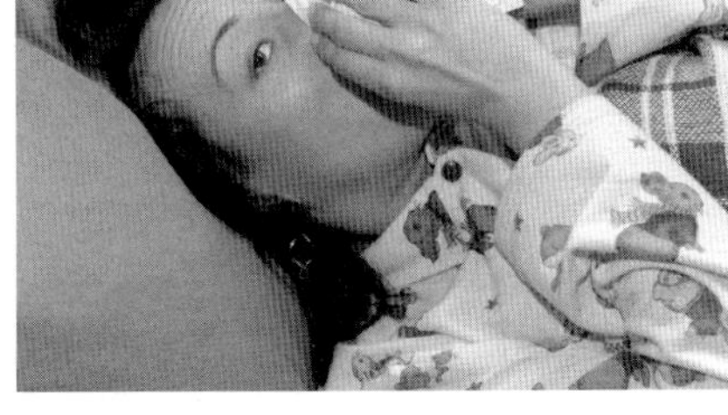
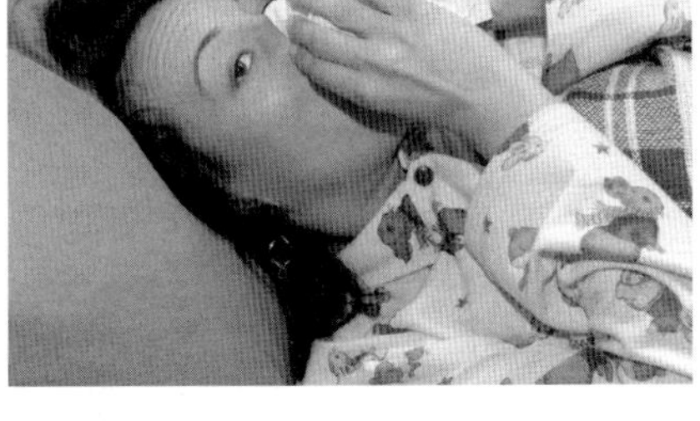

4. ____

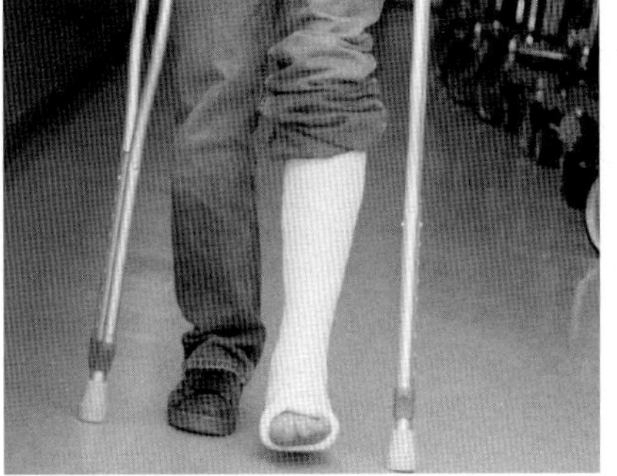

5. ____

B Grammar

Write the correct word.

1. He ________________ a cold. (has / have)
2. They ________________ sore throats. (has / have)
3. You ________________ a fever. (has / have)
4. I ________________ a cut. (has / have)
5. She ________________ a headache. (has / have)

C Grammar

Write the correct word.

1. No, I ________________. (doesn't / don't)
2. ________________ he have the flu? (Do / Does)
3. Yes, he ________________. (do / does)
4. ________________ she have a sprained ankle? (Do / Does)
5. No, she ________________. (doesn't / don't)

Name: ____________________

Date: ____________________

D Reading

Complete the paragraph. Use the words in the box.

aren't	flu	has	have	wrong

Everyone's Sick!

Mrs. James is in her classroom. Her students ______________ (1.) in the classroom. They're at the health clinic. What's ______________ (2.)? Gabriel and Marta ______________ (3.) earaches. Norma ______________ (4.) a headache. Peter has the ______________ (5.).

E Writing

Complete the letter. Use the words in the box.

Dear	fever	January 14, 2008	Sincerely	Thank you

______________ (1.)

______________ (2.) Mrs. Phillips,

Simon Cho is my son. He is at home today. He is sick. He has a ______________ (3.).

Please excuse him. ______________ (4.).

______________ (5.),

Lily Cho

Name: ______________________

Date: ______________________

Score: ______________

TEST UNIT 5 Around town

A Listening

Listen. Circle the words you hear.

1. park school
2. drugstore hardware store
3. bus stop courthouse
4. apartment museum
5. post office restaurant

B Grammar

Complete the sentences. Use *Cross, Go,* or *Turn.*

1. ______________ Fifth Avenue.
2. ______________ left at the post office.
3. ______________ straight to the hospital.
4. ______________ the street by the mall.
5. ______________ right.

C Grammar

Write the correct word.

1. The grocery store is across ________________ the school.
(from / to)
2. The bank is ________________ the drugstore and the coffee shop.
(between / on)
3. Turn right ________________ Main Street.
(on / to)
4. It's on the corner ________________ Fourth Street and Grand Avenue.
(between / of)
5. The restaurant is ________________ the courthouse.
(next to / on)

Name: ____________________

Date: ____________________

D Reading

Read the paragraph. Read the sentences. Are they correct? Circle *Yes* or *No.*

Behnam's Town

Behnam and his family live in a small town. They have an apartment on Second Avenue. There's a supermarket. It's on the corner of Second and Main. The school is between the park and the library. It's on Third Street. There aren't any museums in their town. The family takes a train to the city to visit the museums.

1.	Behnam's family lives on Second Avenue.	Yes	No
2.	There's a supermarket on the corner of Second and Main.	Yes	No
3.	The school is next to the museum.	Yes	No
4.	The library is on Second Avenue.	Yes	No
5.	There are museums in their town.	Yes	No

E Writing

Write sentences about the places on the map. Use *across from, between, next to, on,* and *on the corner of.*

The school is on the corner of First Street and Grant Avenue.

1. ____

2. ____

3. ____

4. ____

5. ____

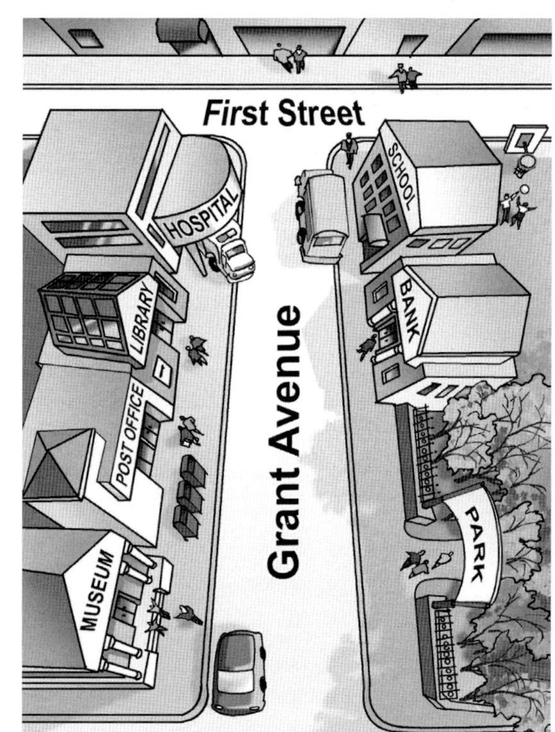

Name: ______________________

Date: ______________________

Score: ____________

MIDTERM TEST Units 1–5

A Listening

Listen. Circle the words you hear.

1. brother mother
2. book eraser
3. cousins sons
4. earache headache
5. ankle leg

B Listening

Listen. Circle the sentences you hear.

1. It's on Pine Street. It's on the shelf.
2. I have a fever. I have the flu.
3. Yes, it is. Yes, they are.
4. No, they aren't. Yes, they are.
5. She's hungry. She's working.

C Grammar

Write the correct word.

1. ________________ he from Russia?
   (Does / Is)
2. The maps are ________________ the table.
   (in / on)
3. Are you ________________?
   (study / studying)
4. ________________ Mrs. Jones have a backache?
   (Do / Does)
5. Go two blocks. ________________ left.
   (Turn / Turning)

Name: ______________________

Date: ______________

D Grammar

Match the questions with the answers.

1. Where are they from? ____
2. Are they eating? ____
3. What are they doing? ____
4. Do they have stomachaches? ____
5. Where are the erasers? ____

a. They're on the table.
b. They're from China.
c. Yes, they do.
d. Yes, they are.
e. They're taking a break.

E Reading

Read the questions. Circle the answers.

Insurance Application Form				
Parents				
Last Name	First Name	Age	Male	Female
Kent	Tom	40	x	
Kent	Abby	36		x
Children				
Kent	Anthony	11	x	
Kent	Kate	8		x
Kent	Susan	4		x

1. What is their last name?
   a. Abby
   b. Kent
   c. Parents
   d. Tom
2. How many children do Tom and Abby have?
   a. 1
   b. 2
   c. 3
   d. 4
3. How many daughters do they have?
   a. 1
   b. 2
   c. 3
   d. 4
4. Who is four years old?
   a. Abby
   b. Anthony
   c. Susan
   d. Tom
5. Who is Tom's son?
   a. Abby
   b. Anthony
   c. Kate
   d. Susan

Name: ______________________

Date: ______________

F Reading

Read the e-mail. Read the sentences. Are they correct? Circle *Yes* or *No.*

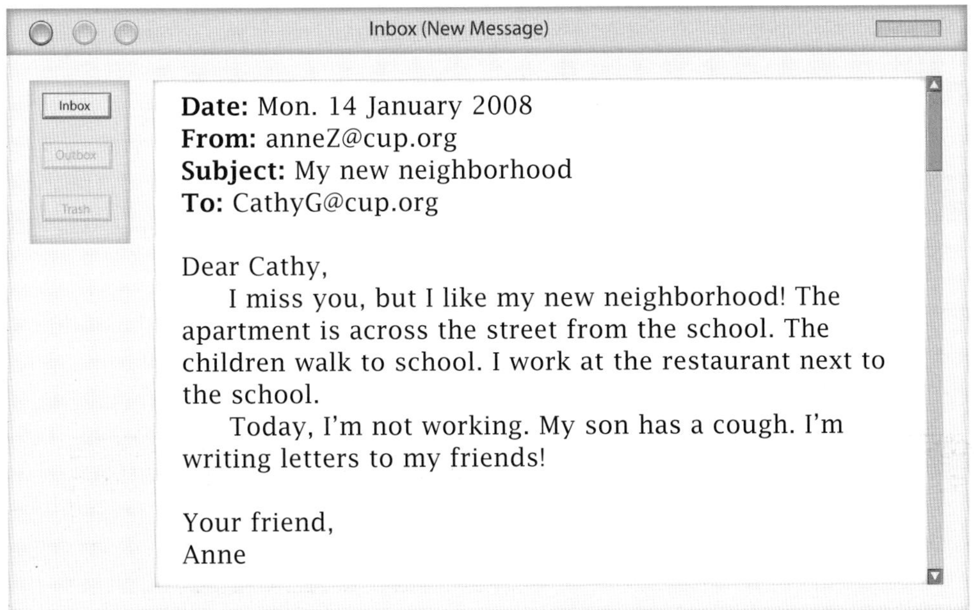
Inbox (New Message)

Inbox
Outbox
Trash

Date: Mon. 14 January 2008
From: anneZ@cup.org
Subject: My new neighborhood
To: CathyG@cup.org

Dear Cathy,

I miss you, but I like my new neighborhood! The apartment is across the street from the school. The children walk to school. I work at the restaurant next to the school.

Today, I'm not working. My son has a cough. I'm writing letters to my friends!

Your friend,
Anne

1. The school is on Anne's street.	Yes	No
2. Anne works at the school.	Yes	No
3. Today, Anne is at the restaurant.	Yes	No
4. Anne's son is sick.	Yes	No
5. Anne's son has a fever.	Yes	No

G Writing

Complete the note. Use the words in the box.

daughter	excuse	fever	June	Sincerely

_____________ 23, 2008
1.

Dear Mrs. Spencer,

Yoko is my _____________ *. She is at home today. She*
2.
is sick. She has a _____________ *.*
3.

Please _____________ *her. Thank you.*
4.

_____________,
5.
Mrs. Uchida

Name: ____________________

Date: ____________________

H Writing

Answer the questions. Use complete sentences.

U.S. Census Bureau

What's your name? *Jorge Costa*

Are you married or single? *Married*

Do you have children? *Yes*

How many daughters? *2*

How many sons? *0*

How many sisters do you have? *2*

How many brothers do you have? *2*

1. Is Mr. Costa married or single?

   ____

2. How many children does Mr. Costa have?

   ____

3. How many daughters does Mr. Costa have?

   ____

4. How many sons does Mr. Costa have?

   ____

5. How many brothers and sisters does Mr. Costa have?

   ____

Name: ______________________

Date: ______________________

Score: ______________________

Time

A Listening

Listen. Circle the times you hear.

1. 10:00 12:00
2. 10:20 3:20
3. 5:50 8:15
4. 7:45 11:45
5. 6:30 6:45

B Grammar

Write the correct word.

1. She ________________ English. (studies / study)
2. He ________________ in the evening. (exercise / exercises)
3. I ________________ shopping on Fridays. (go / goes)
4. They ________________ on Monday. (work / works)
5. Mr. and Mrs. Smith ________________ the bills on Sunday. (pay / pays)

C Grammar

Complete the sentences. Use *at, in,* or *on.*

1. I work ________ the evening.
2. My sister watches TV ________ night.
3. He does his homework ________ the weekend.
4. They usually volunteer ________ December.
5. She takes driving lessons ________ Tuesday.

Name: ______________________________

Date: ____________________

D Reading

Read the paragraph. Read the sentences. Are they correct? Circle *Yes* or *No.*

Blanca's Schedule

Blanca has a busy schedule. She gets up at 5:00 in the morning. She eats breakfast with her son, Marlon, at 6:00. She takes Marlon to school at 7:30. She goes to her English class from 9:00 in the morning to 12:00. Then she cleans the house and goes shopping. Marlon gets home from school at 3:00. Blanca helps Marlon with his homework in the afternoon. Her husband, Tony, gets home at 6:00. They eat dinner at 6:30. Marlon goes to bed at 9:00. And Blanca does her homework from 9:00 to 10:00.

1. Blanca goes shopping in the morning. Yes No
2. Blanca goes to English class at 9:00. Yes No
3. Tony helps Marlon with his homework. Yes No
4. Tony, Blanca, and Marlon eat dinner at 6:30. Yes No
5. Blanca goes to bed at 9:00. Yes No

E Writing

Write a paragraph about your daily schedule. Use the paragraph in Section D as a model.

____

____

____

____

____

____

____

____

____

____

____

Name: ______________________

Date: ______________________

Score: ______________________

Shopping

A Listening

Listen. Write the letter of the conversation.

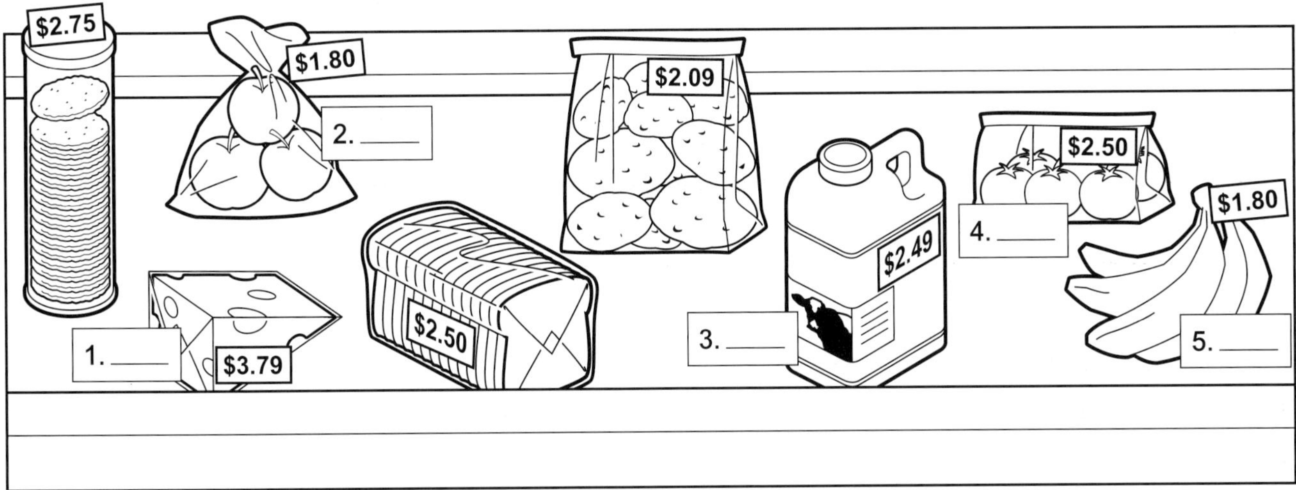

B Grammar

Write the correct word.

1. How ______________ pies do we need?
   (many / much)
2. How ______________ rice do we need?
   (many / much)
3. How ______________ eggs do we need?
   (many / much)
4. How ______________ potatoes do we need?
   (many / much)
5. How ______________ meat do we need?
   (many / much)

C Grammar

Complete the sentences. Use *there is, there are, there isn't,* or *there aren't.*

1. ***A*** Are there any cookies?
   B Yes, ______________________.
2. ***A*** Is there any cheese?
   B No, ______________________.
3. ***A*** Is there any coffee?
   B Yes, ______________________.
4. ***A*** Is there any water?
   B No, ______________________.
5. ***A*** Are there any eggs?
   B No, ______________________.

Name: ____________________

Date: ____________________

D Reading

Complete the note. Use the words in the box.

bottles	loaf	package	rice	supermarket

Hi Pablo,

Please go to the ____________ (1.) tonight.
Please buy a ____________ (2.) of bread, a bag of ____________ (3.), and six ____________ (4.) of water.
Also, we need a ____________ (5.) of hot dogs.

Thanks!

Rosa

E Writing

Write a note. Use the note in Section D as a model.

____

____

____

____

____

____

____

____

____

____

____

Name: ______________________

Date: ______________________

Score: ______________

Work

A Listening

Listen. Circle the words you hear.

1. construction worker   truck driver
2. nurse   waitress
3. cashier   gardener
4. customer   doctor
5. receptionist   teacher

B Grammar

Complete the sentences. Use *are, is, was,* or *were.*

1. Now she __________ a nurse.
2. Now they __________ electricians.
3. They __________ students before.
4. He __________ a construction worker before.
5. Now he __________ a teacher.

C Grammar

Complete the sentences. Use *can* or *can't.*

1. __________ they work with computers?
2. No, they __________.
3. __________ she fix a car?
4. Yes, she __________.
5. No, she __________.

Name: ______________________________

Date: ____________________

D Reading

Read the paragraph. Read the sentences. Are they correct? Circle *Yes* or *No.*

Hyun's Skills

Hyun is looking for a job. She was a cook in her native country. Now she is looking for a job in a restaurant. She has many work skills. She can make food. She can serve food. She can use a cash register. She can count money and give change. Hyun has life skills, too. She speaks Korean, Chinese, and English. She can talk with many customers!

1. Hyun was a nurse. Yes No
2. She's a doctor now. Yes No
3. She can make food. Yes No
4. She can use a cash register. Yes No
5. She can speak Korean, Chinese, and English. Yes No

E Writing

Write a paragraph about your skills. Write about two work skills and two life skills.

____

____

____

____

____

____

____

____

____

____

____

Name: ____________________

Date: ____________________

Score: ____________________

Daily living

A Listening

Listen. Write the letter of the conversation.

B Grammar

Complete the sentences. Use the past tense.

1. She ____________ (dry) the dishes last night.
2. I ____________ (iron) my clothes yesterday.
3. They ____________ (mop) the floor last weekend.
4. He ____________ (empty) the trash last night.
5. You ____________ (clean) the kitchen yesterday.

C Grammar

Complete the sentences. Use the past tense.

1. Sam ____________ (make) breakfast this morning.
2. She ____________ (get) home late last night.
3. He ____________ (sweep) the floor last week.
4. Sheila ____________ (cut) the grass yesterday.
5. They ____________ (do) the laundry last night.

Name: ______________________________

Date: ______________________

D Reading

Read the paragraph. Read the sentences. Are they correct? Circle *Yes* or *No.*

Chores

Marcelo and Angela are brother and sister. Marcelo is 16 years old. Angela is 14 years old. Last Saturday, Angela washed the clothes, dusted the furniture, and swept the floors. She ironed the clothes, vacuumed the rugs, and made dinner for her family. Last Saturday, Marcelo cut the grass and took out the trash. Their parents were happy!

1. Angela made dinner.	Yes	No
2. Angela went shopping.	Yes	No
3. Marcelo took out the trash.	Yes	No
4. Marcelo cut the grass.	Yes	No
5. Their parents weren't happy.	Yes	No

E Writing

Write sentences about the picture.

1. ____
2. ____
3. ____
4. ____
5. ____

Name: ______________________

Date: ______________________

Score: ______________________

Leisure

A Listening

Listen. Write the letter of the conversation.

1. ______ 2. ______ 3. ______ 4. ______ 5. ______

B Grammar

Complete the sentences. Use the past tense.

1. I ______________ (ride) my bicycle last Sunday.
2. Sara ______________ (read) a book last night.
3. They ______________ (go) swimming last weekend.
4. He ______________ (write) e-mails yesterday.
5. She ______________ (drive) to the beach on Thursday.

C Grammar

What's the Shimoda family going to do? Complete the sentences.

1. On Thursday, Hiro ____.
2. On Tuesday, Harumi ____.
3. On Monday, Hideki ____.
4. On Friday, Yoniko and Hiro ____.
5. On Wednesday, everyone ____.

Shimoda Family Schedule

Mon	*Hideki – study English*
Tues	*Harumi – play soccer*
Wed	*Everyone – watch a movie*
Thurs	*Hiro – fix the car*
Fri	*Yoniko and Hiro – go to a birthday party*

Name: ______________________

Date: ______________________

D Reading

Complete the story. Use the words in the box.

go	going	ice hockey	sports	went

Sports Fans

Nancy and her husband love ________ (1.). Tonight, they are going to watch two teams play ________ (2.). They love that game. Last year, they ________ (3.) to see their city's team a lot. When the games start this year, they're ________ (4.) to go again.

Nancy and her husband also love to be outdoors. They like to ________ (5.) hiking in the fall.

E Writing

Write sentences about the picture.

Andrea is going to take a trip.

1. ______________________
2. ______________________
3. ______________________
4. ______________________
5. ______________________

Name: ______________________

Date: ______________________

Score: ______________________

Units 6–10

A Listening

Listen. Circle the words you hear.

1. 7:20 11:30
2. $15.99 $16.95
3. cheap meat
4. carpenter electrician
5. camping trash

B Listening

Listen. Circle the jobs you hear.

1. auto mechanic salesperson
2. child-care worker factory worker
3. gardener painter
4. carpenters office workers
5. nurse salesperson

C Grammar

Write the correct word.

1. We have a vacation ______________ December.
   (in / on)
2. ______________ there any bottles of water?
   (Are / Is)
3. What ______________ she do in the afternoon?
   (do / does)
4. They ______________ teachers before.
   (was / were)
5. ______________ going to go to a party tomorrow.
   (We / We're)

Name: ____________________

Date: ____________

D Grammar

Match the questions with the answers.

1. Were you a waiter? ____
2. What can you do? ____
3. What did you do yesterday? ____
4. What are you going to do today? ____
5. Can you make dinner? ____

a. Yes, I was.
b. I went to a museum.
c. I'm going to go swimming.
d. No, I can't.
e. I can use a computer.

E Reading

Read the questions. Circle the answers.

Day-Care Center Work Schedule		
	Days of the Week	Hours
Sally	Tu Th	12:00–8:00 p.m.
	Sat Sun	10:00 a.m.–3:00 p.m.
Dan	Tu Th F	9:00 a.m.–5:00 p.m.
Megan	M W F	12:00–8:00 p.m.
	Sat	9:00 a.m.–5:00 p.m.
Juan	M W	9:00 a.m.–5:00 p.m.
	Sat Sun	12:00–5:00 p.m.

1. How many people work at the day-care center?
   a. four
   b. five
   c. eight
   d. ten
2. When does Juan start on Saturday?
   a. 9:00 a.m.
   b. 10:00 a.m.
   c. 12:00
   d. 5:00 p.m.
3. Who works until 8:00 p.m. on Monday and Wednesday?
   a. Dan
   b. Juan
   c. Megan
   d. Sally
4. What time does Sally go to work on Saturday and Sunday?
   a. 9:00 a.m.
   b. 10:00 a.m.
   c. 12:00
   d. 3:00 p.m.
5. Who doesn't work on the weekend?
   a. Dan
   b. Juan
   c. Megan
   d. Sally

Name: ____________________

Date: ____________________

F Reading

Read the e-mail. Read the sentences. Are they correct? Circle *Yes* or *No.*

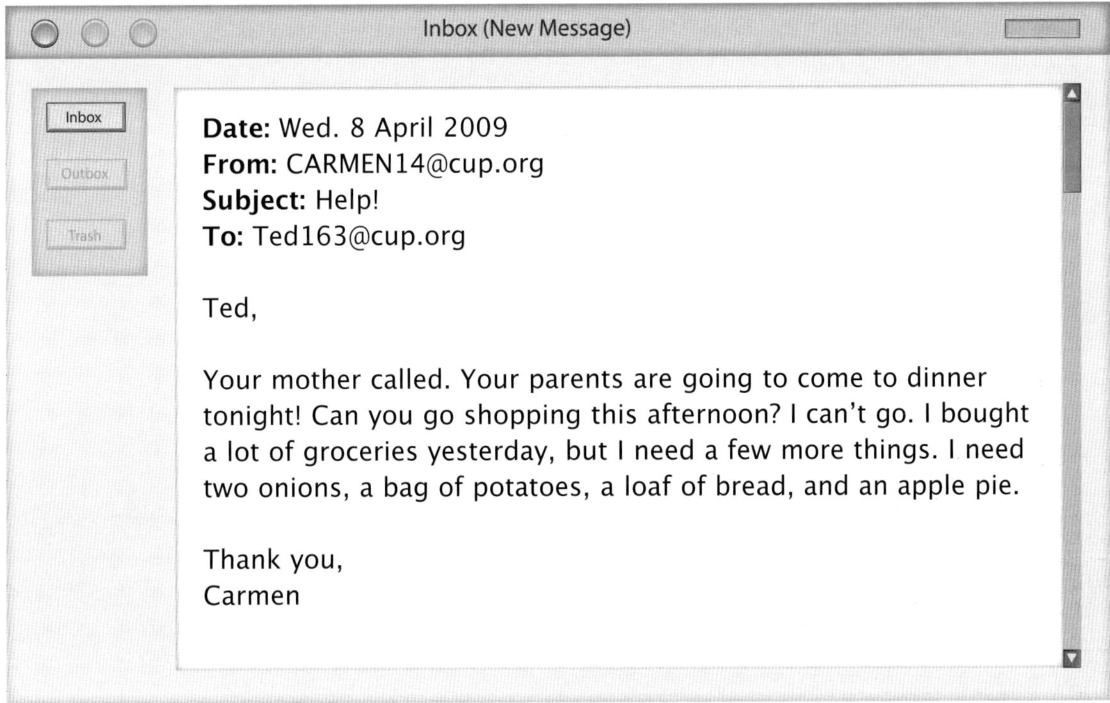

1. Carmen's mother called. Yes No
2. Carmen can go shopping this afternoon. Yes No
3. Carmen went shopping yesterday. Yes No
4. Carmen needs tomatoes. Yes No
5. Ted's parents are going to eat dinner with Ted and Carmen. Yes No

Name: ______________________

Date: ______________________

G Writing

Read about George. Then complete the job application with his information.

This is George Pappas. He is 20 years old. He lives at 2045 Taraval Street, New Orleans, Louisiana. His zip code is 70112. His telephone number is 555-7843. The area code is 504. His Social Security number is 000-67-3859.

JOB APPLICATION

Name: ______________ ______________
1. First 2. Last

Address: ______________________________
3. Street

______________ ______________ ______________
4. City 5. State 6. Zip

Soc. Sec. No. ______________________________
7.

Phone: (__________) ______________________
8. 9.

Are you 19 years or older? Yes ☐ No ☐
10.

H Writing

Write a paragraph about your skills. Write about two work skills and two life skills.

____

____

____

____

____

____

____

____

____

Tests audio script

This audio script contains the listening portions of the *Ventures 1* unit tests, midterm test, and final test. A printable copy is available on the *Teacher's Toolkit Audio CD / CD-ROM.* You can play the audio program using the *Teacher's Toolkit Audio CD / CD-ROM* in a computer or a stereo, or you can read the script aloud.

Unit 1: Personal information

Track 2

A Listening

Listen. Circle the words you hear.

1 *A* What's your first name?
B My first name is Jane.

2 *A* What's your telephone number?
B My telephone number is 555-8907.

3 *A* What's your area code?
B My area code is 213.

4 *A* What's your address?
B My address is 1013 Main Street.

5 *A* What's your zip code?
B My zip code is 07480.

Unit 2: At school

Track 3

A Listening

Listen. Circle the words you hear.

1 *A* Where is the stapler?
B It's in the drawer.

2 *A* Is the calculator in the desk?
B Yes, it is.

3 *A* Where's the ruler?
B It's in the box.

4 *A* Where are the erasers?
B They're in the drawer.

5 *A* Is the marker on the chair?
B Yes, it is.

Unit 3: Friends and family

Track 4

A Listening

Listen. Circle the words you hear.

1 *A* Hi, Mary. This is Mr. Smith. Is your grandfather home?
B Yes, he is. He's watching TV.

2 *A* Hi, this is Mrs. Cho. Is your mother home?
B Yes, she is, but she's eating right now.

3 *A* Hi, Mr. Ramos. This is Marta. Is your niece home?
B Yes, she is, but she's sleeping now.

4 *A* Hi, Mr. Brown. This is Bridget. Is your son home?
B Yes, he is, but he's studying right now.

5 *A* Hi, Harumi. Is your sister-in-law home?
B No, she isn't.

Unit 4: Health

Track 5

A Listening

Listen. Write the letter of the conversation.

Conversation A
A What's the matter?
B Carl has a broken leg.

Conversation B
A What's the matter?
B Mrs. Leeds has a stomachache.

Conversation C
A What's the matter?
B Diana has a cold.

Conversation D
A What's the matter?
B Mr. Jones has a backache.

Conversation E
A What's the matter?
B Ben has a fever.

Unit 5: Around town

Track 6

A Listening

Listen. Circle the words you hear.

1 *A* Excuse me. Where's the park?
B The park is on Jefferson Street.

2 *A* Excuse me. Where's the drugstore?
B The drugstore? It's on Duane Avenue.

3 *A* Excuse me. Where's the bus stop?
B The bus stop is on Carriage Lane.

4 *A* Excuse me. Where's the museum?
B The museum? It's on Orange Avenue.

5 *A* Excuse me. Where's the restaurant?
B The restaurant is on Pine Street.

Midterm Test Units 1–5

Track 7

A Listening

Listen. Circle the words you hear.

1 *A* Hi, Mary. This is Mrs. Li. Is your mother home?
B Yes, she is. But she's studying right now.

2 *A* Where's the book?
B It's in the drawer.

3 *A* Hi, Luis. This is Mrs. Ramirez. Are your cousins home?
B Yes, they are. They're playing right now.

4 *A* What's the matter?
B I have an earache.

5 *A* What's wrong?
B My ankle hurts.

Track 8

B Listening

Listen. Circle the sentences you hear.

1 *A* Where's the dictionary?
B It's on the shelf.

2 *A* What's the matter?
B I have the flu.

3 *A* Is the calculator on the desk?
B Yes, it is.

4 *A* Are they thirsty?
B Yes, they are.

5 *A* What's your mother doing?
B She's working.

Unit 6: Time

Track 9

A Listening

Listen. Circle the times you hear.

1 *A* When do you leave for work?
B I leave at twelve o'clock.

2 *A* What time do you take a break?
B I take a break at three-twenty.

3 *A* When do you eat breakfast?
B I eat breakfast at eight-fifteen.

4 *A* What time do you catch the bus?
B I catch the bus at seven-forty-five.

5 *A* What time do you eat dinner?
B I eat dinner at six-thirty.

Unit 7: Shopping

Track 10

A Listening

Listen. Write the letter of the conversation.

Conversation A
A How many bananas do we have?
B We have five.

Conversation B
A How much cheese do we have?
B We have one piece.

Conversation C
A How many tomatoes do we have?
B We have six tomatoes.

Conversation D
A Are there any apples on sale?
B Yes. Apples are sixty cents each.

Conversation E
A How much milk do we need?
B We need a lot.

Unit 8: Work

Track 11

A Listening

Listen. Circle the words you hear.

1 *A* What does she do?
B She's a truck driver.

2 *A* What did he do before?
B He was a nurse.

3 *A* What does he do now?
B He's a gardener.

4 *A* What does she do now?
B She's a doctor.

5 *A* What did he do before?
B He was a teacher.

Unit 9: Daily living

Track 12

A Listening

Listen. Write the letter of the conversation.

Conversation A
A Did you iron the shirts?
B Yes, I did.

Conversation B
A Did you vacuum the rug?
B No, I didn't.

Conversation C
A Did you pay the bills?
B Yes, I did.

Conversation D
A Did you mop the floor?
B No, I didn't.

Conversation E
A Did you empty the trash?
B No, I didn't.

Unit 10: Leisure

Track 13

A Listening

Listen. Write the letter of the conversation.

Conversation A
A Hi, Mike. How are you?
B Oh, pretty good. I went swimming this morning.

Conversation B
A Hi, Laura. What's new with you?
B Well, I played soccer yesterday.

Conversation C
A Hi, James. Where were you last night?
B I played baseball.

Conversation D
A Hi, Amy. What did you do today?
B I played basketball.

Conversation E
A Hi, Ben. Where were you?
B I was on vacation. I went skiing.

Final Test Units 6–10

Track 14

A Listening

Listen. Circle the words you hear.

1 *A* When does he start work?
B He starts work at eleven-thirty.

2 *A* How much are the groceries?
B The total is fifteen dollars and ninety-nine cents.

3 *A* Is there any meat on sale?
B Yes, there is.

4 *A* What does she do?
B She's an electrician.

5 *A* Hi, Jacob! Where were you last weekend?
B I went camping.

Track 15

B Listening

Listen. Circle the jobs you hear.

1 *A* She's an auto mechanic? What does she do?
B She can fix cars.

2 *A* Is he a child-care worker?
B Yes, he can take care of children.

3 *A* Are you a gardener?
B Yes, I can take care of plants.

4 *A* Are they carpenters?
B Yes, they can build things.

5 *A* Is she a salesperson?
B Yes, she can sell things.

Tests answer key

Each unit test item is 4 points. Unit test sections have five items; therefore, each section is worth 20 points, for a total of 100 points per unit test.

Unit 1: Personal information

A Listening
1. first name
2. telephone number
3. area code
4. address
5. zip code

B Grammar
1. His
2. Her
3. His
4. Their
5. Her

C Grammar
1. They're
2. He's
3. Her
4. isn't
5. Their

D Reading
1. No
2. Yes
3. No
4. Yes
5. Yes

E Writing
Answers will vary. Each item is 4 points. Score for accuracy and spelling.

Unit 2: At school

A Listening
1. stapler
2. calculator
3. ruler
4. erasers
5. marker

B Grammar
1. on
2. in
3. on
4. in
5. in

C Grammar
1. are
2. is
3. is
4. are
5. Is

D Reading
1. No
2. No
3. No
4. Yes
5. Yes

E Writing
Answers will vary. Each item is 4 points. Score for accuracy, grammar, punctuation, and spelling.

Unit 3: Friends and family

A Listening
1. grandfather
2. mother
3. niece
4. son
5. sister-in-law

B Grammar
1. am studying
2. is reading
3. is watching
4. are talking
5. is sleeping

C Grammar
1. working
2. eating
3. buying
4. helping
5. taking

D Reading
1. birthday
2. grandson
3. eating
4. taking
5. family

E Writing
Answers will vary. Each item is 4 points. Score for accuracy, grammar, punctuation, and spelling.

Possible answers:
1. Scott is eight years old.
2. Mrs. Clark is 29 years old.
3. Mr. and Mrs. Clark have four children.
4. Mr. and Mrs. Clark have one daughter.
5. Mr. and Mrs. Clark have three sons.

Unit 4: Health

A Listening
1. e 2. b 3. d 4. c 5. a

B Grammar
1. has
2. have
3. have
4. have
5. has

C Grammar
1. don't
2. Does
3. does
4. Does
5. doesn't

D Reading
1. aren't
2. wrong
3. have
4. has
5. flu

E Writing
1. January 14, 2008
2. Dear
3. fever
4. Thank you
5. Sincerely

Unit 5: Around town

A Listening
1. park
2. drugstore
3. bus stop
4. museum
5. restaurant

B Grammar
1. Cross
2. Turn
3. Go
4. Cross
5. Turn

C Grammar
1. from
2. between
3. on
4. of
5. next to

D Reading
1. Yes
2. Yes
3. No
4. No
5. No

E Writing
Answers will vary. Each sentence is 4 points. Score for accuracy, capitalization, punctuation, vocabulary, and prepositions.

Midterm Test Units 1–5

A Listening
(2 points per item)
1. mother
2. book
3. cousins
4. earache
5. ankle

B Listening
(3 points per item)
1. It's on the shelf.
2. I have the flu.
3. Yes, it is.
4. Yes, they are.
5. She's working.

C Grammar
(2 points per item)
1. Is
2. on
3. studying
4. Does
5. Turn

D Grammar
(3 points per item)
1. b 2. d 3. e 4. c 5. a

E Reading
(2 points per item)
1. b 2. c 3. b 4. c 5. b

F Reading
(3 points per item)
1. Yes
2. No
3. No
4. Yes
5. No

G Writing
(2 points per item)
1. June
2. daughter
3. fever
4. excuse
5. Sincerely

H Writing
(3 points per item)
Suggested rubric:
3 points: Correctly used capital letters, verb, period
2 points: Missing capital letter, verb, or period
1 point: Missing capital letter and/or verb and/or period
0 points: No attempt

Possible answers:
1. Mr. Costa is married.
2. Mr. Costa has two children.
3. Mr. Costa has two daughters.
4. He doesn't have any sons.
5. Mr. Costa has two sisters and two brothers.

Unit 6: Time

A Listening
1. 12:00
2. 3:20
3. 8:15
4. 7:48
5. 6:30

B Grammar
1. studies
2. exercises
3. go
4. work
5. pay

C Grammar
1. in
2. at
3. on
4. in
5. on

D Reading
1. No
2. Yes
3. No
4. Yes
5. No

E Writing
Answers will vary. This section is worth 20 points. Score for accuracy, grammar, punctuation, and spelling.

Unit 7: Shopping

A Listening
1. b 2. d 3. e 4. c 5. a

B Grammar
1. many
2. much
3. many
4. many
5. much

C Grammar
1. there are
2. there isn't
3. there is
4. there isn't
5. there aren't

D Reading
1. supermarket
2. loaf
3. rice
4. bottles
5. package

E Writing
Answers will vary. This section is worth 20 points. Score for accuracy, grammar, punctuation, and spelling.

Unit 8: Work

A Listening
1. truck driver
2. nurse
3. gardener
4. doctor
5. teacher

B Grammar
1. is
2. are
3. were
4. was
5. is

C Grammar
1. Can
2. can't
3. Can
4. can
5. can't

D Reading
1. No
2. No
3. Yes
4. Yes
5. Yes

E Writing
Answers will vary. This section is worth 20 points. Score for accuracy, grammar, punctuation, and spelling.

Unit 9: Daily living

A Listening
1. c 2. e 3. b 4. a 5. d

B Grammar
1. dried
2. ironed
3. mopped
4. emptied
5. cleaned

C Grammar
1. made
2. got
3. swept
4. cut
5. did

D Reading
1. Yes
2. No
3. Yes
4. Yes
5. No

E Writing
Answers will vary. Each item is 4 points. Score for accuracy, grammar, punctuation, and spelling.

Unit 10: Leisure

A Listening
1. d 2. b 3. a 4. e 5. c

B Grammar
1. rode
2. read
3. went
4. wrote
5. drove

C Grammar
1. is going to fix the car
2. is going to play soccer
3. is going to study English
4. are going to go to a birthday party
5. is going to watch a movie

D Reading
1. sports
2. ice hockey
3. went
4. going
5. go

E Writing
Answers will vary. Each item is 4 points. Score for accuracy, grammar, punctuation, and spelling.

Final Test Units 6–10

A Listening
(2 points per item)
1. 11:30
2. $15.99
3. meat
4. electrician
5. camping

B Listening
(3 points per item)
1. auto mechanic
2. child-care worker
3. gardener
4. carpenters
5. salesperson

C Grammar
(2 points per item)
1. in
2. Are
3. does
4. were
5. We're

D Grammar
(3 points per item)
1. a 2. e 3. b 4. c 5. d

E Reading
(2 points per item)
1. a 2. c 3. c 4. b 5. a

F Reading
(3 points per item)
1. No
2. No
3. Yes
4. No
5. Yes

G Writing
(2 points per item)
1. George
2. Pappas
3. 2045 Taraval Street
4. New Orleans
5. Louisiana
6. 70112
7. 000-67-3859
8. 504
9. 555-7843
10. Yes

H Writing
Answers will vary. This section is worth 15 points. Score for accuracy, grammar, punctuation, and spelling.

Teacher's Toolkit Audio CD/CD-ROM

Overview

The *Teacher's Toolkit Audio CD/CD-ROM* is an additional resource for teachers using the *Ventures 1* Student's Book. The *Teacher's Toolkit Audio CD/CD-ROM* provides reproducible, supplementary materials for use during in-class assessment, whole-class activities, and group work. It provides more than 200 pages of additional material.

What's included in the *Teacher's Toolkit Audio CD/CD-ROM*:

- **Unit tests**, a **midterm test**, and a **final test** with corresponding **answer keys**, **audio scripts**, **audio program**, and instructions for administering and scoring the tests. When browsing the tests, a pop-up window can be opened that shows that test's audio script and answer key. The tests can be reproduced from the *Teacher's Toolkit Audio CD/CD-ROM* or from the printed test pages in the Teacher's Edition. Use a compact disc player or your computer's audio software to access the test audio program on the CD-ROM.
- The **self-assessments** from the *Ventures 1* Student's Book. Each unit self-assessment can be duplicated from the CD-ROM, completed by students, and saved as a portfolio assessment tool.
- **Collaborative Activity Worksheets**. For each lesson in the *Ventures 1* Student's Book, there is a reproducible activity worksheet to encourage collaborative pair and group work in class. On each worksheet screen, there is a pop-up window that can be opened to show the instructions for using the worksheet in class.
- Reproducible **Picture Dictionary Cards**. The **Picture Dictionary Cards** display each vocabulary item from the *Ventures 1* Student's Book Picture Dictionary pages. In addition, there are **Picture Dictionary Worksheets**, **Picture Dictionary Card indexes**, and **Teaching tips**. The Picture Dictionary Cards and Worksheets offer additional unit-by-unit practice of all the vocabulary introduced on the Picture dictionary, Lesson D, Reading pages.
- **Real-life Documents**. Forms and documents introduced in *Ventures 1* Student's Book can be reproduced and completed by students to reinforce necessary life skills.
- A **vocabulary list**. All key vocabulary in *Ventures 1* Student's Book is listed alphabetically, with first occurrence page numbers included for easy reference.
- A **certificate of completion**. To recognize students for satisfactory completion of *Ventures 1,* a printable certificate is included.

Games

Overview

Games provide practice and reinforcement of skills, but in a fun and engaging manner. Students love to play games. Games raise motivation and enjoyment for learning. They can be used as a warm-up, practice, or review activity. The games described below can be adjusted and adapted to the skill level of the class.

1. Stand By

Skills: speaking, listening, writing
Objective: to practice asking and answering questions
Preparation: Write the question and answers on the board. Prepare grids.

- Write a question on the board, for example *What is your favorite day of the week?*
- Write possible answers (*Sunday, Monday, Tuesday . . .*) scattered on the board or taped around the room.
- Ss copy the question and write their answer to the question.
- When students have finished writing, they stand next to the answer that corresponds to their own answer.
- Ss discuss their answer with others who have the same answer, using questions such as *Why is* _____ *your favorite day?* or *What do you like to do on* _____*?*
- Then Ss mingle with the rest of the class, asking the initial question and recording each S's name and response on the grid.
- Use the completed grids to ask Ss questions about the responses. For example, *Does Maria like Monday best? How many students like Wednesday?*
- The questions can be made easier or more difficult, depending on the level of the Ss.

Sample Grid:

Question:	
Student's Name	Answer

2. Match the Leader

Skills: speaking, listening, writing
Objective: to practice giving and following directions
Preparation: Prepare grids with boxes – 3 x 3, 3 x 4, or 3 x 5.

- Ss form groups of four or five and designate one S as the leader.
- Provide the leader with a list of words / items (for example, vocabulary words, shapes, telephone numbers) to be reviewed.
- The leader selects an item from the list and tells group members where to write / draw that item on their grids. (For example, *Write <u>broken leg</u> in the box in the top right corner.*)
- The leader enters the item in the same location on his / her own grid (behind an opened file folder so others can't see it).
- The leader continues through all items until the grid is full.
- The leader then shows his / her grid to the group to use to check their own grids.

Adaptation: Spaces on the grids may be numbered for lower-level Ss. For higher-level Ss, teach location words such as *top, bottom, left, right, next to, between,* and *under.*

3. Round Table

Skills: speaking, writing
Objective: to review vocabulary from a unit
Preparation: none

- Ss form groups of four or five. Each group has a blank sheet of paper.
- Announce the topic, usually the unit topic just completed.
- The first S says a word related to the topic, writes the word on the paper, and passes the paper to the next S.
- That S says a new word related to the topic, enters the word on the paper, and passes the paper to the third S, who continues the process.
- Ss can ask for help from their teammates when they cannot think of a new word to add to the list.
- The paper continues to pass around the table until no one can think of another related word.
- A unique way of scoring is to have one group read its first word. If no other group has that word, the first group receives three points. If any other group has that word, the first group receives one point. The first group continues through its list, one word at a time.

- The other groups mark off the words on their lists as they are heard and record one point for each of those words as they know another group has the same word.
- When the first group finishes reading its list, the second group reads only those words that have not already been mentioned. Again, if other groups have the word, they each score one point; if no other group has the word, the first group scores three points.
- Continue until all groups have accounted for all their words.

4. Bingo

Skills: listening, writing
Objective: to review vocabulary
Preparation: Bingo grids (3 x 3, 3 x 4, 4 x 4 . . .)

- Select enough words to fill a Bingo grid. Read and spell each new word and use it in a sentence.
- Ss write each word randomly on their bingo grids. Lower-level Ss may need to copy the words from the board.
- When the grids are filled, play Bingo.
- The S who shouts "Bingo" first calls the next game.

Adaptation: Depending on the Ss' familiarity with the words, call the words by saying the word, spelling the word, providing a definition or an example, or giving a synonym or an antonym.

5. Picture It

Skill: speaking
Objective: to review vocabulary
Preparation: sets of vocabulary cards (one per group)

- Ss form groups of three or four. Give each group one set of vocabulary cards.
- One S chooses a card but does not tell the group members the word.
- On a piece of paper, this S draws a picture or pictures representing the word. Point out that the S drawing the picture cannot talk or make gestures.
- The other Ss try to guess the word, using the drawings as clues.
- Ss take turns choosing and drawing words until all words are chosen.

Adaptation: Instead of drawing the words, Ss can act out the words for group members to guess.

6. Prediction Bingo

Skills: reading or listening
Objective: to develop the prereading or prelistening strategy of predicting
Preparation: Bingo grids (3 x 3, 3 x 4, 4 x 4 . . .)

- Provide Ss with the title or topic of a selection to be read or heard from an audio recording.
- In each square of the Bingo grid, Ss enter a word related to that topic that they think will appear in the reading or audio.
- Ss listen to the audio or read the text. When they hear or see a word that is on their Bingo grid, they circle it.
- Ss discuss in small groups their choices, both correct and incorrect, and how they relate to the topic.

7. Disappearing Dialog

Skills: speaking, listening, reading, writing
Objective: to practice learning dialogs
Preparation: none

- Write a dialog on the board.
- Go over the dialog with the whole class, then have selected groups say the dialog.
- Next, have Ss practice the dialog in pairs.
- Erase one word from each line of the dialog each time pairs practice, until all words are gone.
- Have volunteers recite the dialog without support from words on the board.
- Then have Ss add words back to the board until all words are again in place.

8. Moving Dialog

Skills: speaking, listening
Objective: to practice using dialogs
Preparation: none

- Ss stand in two lines (*A* and *B*), facing each other as partners.
- Ss in line *A* have one side of a conversation. Ss in line *B* have the other side. At a signal, Ss in line *A* begin the dialog, with Ss in line *B* responding. The dialog may be two or several lines long, depending on the level of the Ss.
- When Ss have completed the dialog, Ss in line *A* move one (or more) people to the left and practice the dialog again with a new partner.
- Ss at the end of the line will move to the beginning of the line to find their new partners.

Adaptation: This exchange may be a simple question and answer (**A:** *What is your name?* **B:** *My name is* _____.) for lower-level Ss.

If necessary, Ss can have a card with the dialog printed on it, but encourage Ss to look up and face their partner when they are speaking.

9. Hear Ye, Hear Ye

Skills: listening or reading
Objective: to refine listening skills
Preparation: a reading text or an audio clip; a file card with a word or phrase from the clip on it (one word or phrase for each S or, if not enough words, use the same word multiple times)

- Select an audio clip or a reading segment.
- Provide each S with a file card containing a word or phrase that occurs one or more times in the clip or reading segment.
- Play or read the segment.
- Ss listen, paying particular attention for their word or phrase. They raise, then lower, their file card each time they hear the word.

Adaptation: The audio may be a song, a lecture, or a dialog. Ss can listen for things other than specific words, such as past tense verbs, numbers, or three-syllable words.

Alternatively, Ss can stand up or sit down when they hear their word, rather than raise their cards.

10. Treasure Hunt

Skills: reading, writing
Objective: to develop the reading skill of scanning
Preparation: Enlarge a reading selection from the Student's Book and cut it into paragraphs. Number each one. Create a handout with questions / items to be found in the reading.

- Post the pieces of the reading around the room.
- Ss, individually or in pairs, go around the room and locate specific information to enter into their handout. For example: *Write the words that begin with sh,* or *Where is Fatima's brother?*
- Ss check their answers by reading or reviewing the completed text in their books and sharing their answers as a class.

Adaptation: A short reading selection can be cut into sentences for lower-level Ss.

Multilevel classroom management

All classrooms are multilevel in some sense. No two students will ever be exactly the same. Learners vary in demographic factors such as culture and ethnicity, personal factors such as a willingness to take risks and differing learning styles, and experiential factors such as background knowledge and previous education. With all these differences, it will always be a challenge to provide useful learning activities for all members of the class. Yet there are some techniques that make working with a multilevel class more manageable.

1. Group work is one of the best ways of working with a multilevel class. Some tasks, such as watching a video, going on a field trip, or describing a picture, can be performed as a whole group. What will change in a multilevel class is the level of expectation of responses following the shared experience. Other tasks can be performed as a whole group, but the tasks are adapted for the students' levels. This could include interviews with varying difficulty of questions or a project such as a class newspaper, where students of differing levels contribute through activities appropriate to their abilities.

   Smaller, homogeneous groups allow students of the same level the opportunity to work together on activities such as a problem-solving task or a group writing activity. Smaller, heterogeneous groups are good for board games or jigsaw activities where the difficulty of the material can be controlled. In *Ventures 1,* the picture cards on the *Teacher's Toolkit Audio CD / CD-ROM* are excellent resources for working with heterogeneous or homogeneous groups. Ideas for how to use the picture cards are also on the CD-ROM.

2. Varying the materials or activities is another help in addressing the issue of multiple levels in the classroom. *Add Ventures,* the multilevel component of *Ventures,* provides activities for learners at differing levels. These can be used in the classroom with heterogeneous or homogeneous groups because the answers are the same for all three levels of worksheets.

3. Self-access centers are another kind of classroom management technique. These centers would be located in corners of the classroom and would provide opportunities for learners to work at varying levels. By providing a variety of materials, which can be color-coded for levels of difficulty, students have the opportunity to make choices as to the level they feel comfortable working on. Students can self-correct with answer keys. In this way, students are working towards more learner autonomy, which is a valuable assistant in a multilevel classroom, and a good start towards promoting lifelong learning skills.

4. Computer-assisted learning, using computers located within the classroom, can provide self-directed learning through software programs geared to a student's individual ability. Most programs provide immediate feedback to students to correct errors and build in a level of difficulty as a student progresses. Like-ability groups of students can rotate their time on the computer, working in pairs, or students can work individually at their own level.

A multilevel classroom, while challenging to the teacher, should offer each learner appropriate levels of instruction according to the learner's abilities, interests, needs, and experiences, and it should be designed to maximize each learner's educational gains. Good management techniques call for the teacher to provide a mixture of whole class, small group, and individual activities, create a learner-centered class by establishing self-access materials, use computers, and incorporate variety in the difficulty of the tasks and materials given to each student.

Authors' acknowledgments

The authors would like to acknowledge and thank focus group participants and reviewers for their insightful comments, as well as CUP editorial, marketing, and production staffs, whose thorough research and attention to detail have resulted in a quality product.

The publishers would also like to extend their particular thanks to the following reviewers and consultants for their valuable insights and suggestions:

Francesca Armendaris, North Orange County Community College District, Anaheim, California; **Alex A. Baez**, The Texas Professional Development Group, Austin, Texas; **Kit Bell**, LAUSD Division of Adult and Career Education, Los Angeles, California; **Rose Anne Cleary**, Catholic Migration Office, Diocese of Brooklyn, Brooklyn, New York; **Inga Cristi**, Pima Community College Adult Education, Tucson, Arizona; **Kay De Gennaro**, West Valley Occupational Center, Woodland Hills, California; **Patricia DeJesus-Lopez**, Illinois Community College Board, Springfield, Illinois; **Magali Apareaida Morais Duignan**, Augusta State University, Augusta, Georgia; **Gayle Fagan**, Harris County Department of Education, Houston, Texas; **Lisa A. Fears**, Inglewood Community Adult School, Inglewood, California; **Jas Gill**, English Language Institute at the University of British Columbia, Vancouver, British Columbia, Canada; **Elisabeth Goodwin**, Pima Community College Adult Education, Tucson, Arizona; **Carolyn Grimaldi**, Center for Immigrant Education and Training, LaGuardia Community College, Long Island City, New York; **Masha Gromyko**, Pima Community College Adult Education, Tucson, Arizona; **Jennifer M. Herrin**, Albuquerque TVI Community College, Albuquerque, New Mexico; **Giang T. Hoang**, Evans Community Adult School, Los Angeles, California; **Karen Hribar**, LAUSD West Valley Occupational Center, Los Angeles, California; **Patricia Ishill**, Union County College, Union County, New Jersey; **Dr. Stephen G. Karel**, McKinley Community School for Adults, Honolulu, Hawaii; **Aaron Kelly**, North Orange County Community College District, Anaheim, California; **Dan Kiernan**, Metro Skills Center, LAUSD, Los Angeles, California; **Kirsten Kilcup**, Green River Community College, Auburn, Washington; **Tom Knutson**, New York Association for New Americans, Inc., New York, New York; **Liz Koenig-Golombek**, LAUSD, Los Angeles, California; **Anita Lemonis**, West Valley Occupational Center, Los Angeles, California; **Lia Lerner**, Burbank Adult School, Burbank, California; **Susan Lundquist**, Pima Community College Adult Education, Tucson, Arizona; **Dr. Amal Mahmoud**, Highline Community College, Des Moines, Washington; **Fatiha Makloufi**, Hostos Community College, Bronx, New York; **Judith Martin-Hall**, Indian River Community College, Fort Pierce, Florida; **Gwen Mayer**, Van Nuys Community Adult School, Los Angeles, California; **Lois Miller**, Pima Community College, Tucson, Arizona; **Vicki Moore**, El Monte-Rosemead Adult School, El Monte, California; **Jeanne Petrus-Rivera**, Cuyahoga Community College, Cleveland, Ohio; **Pearl W. Pigott**, Houston Community College, Houston, Texas; **Catherine Porter**, Adult Learning Resource Center, Des Plaines, Illinois; **Planaria Price**, Evans Community Adult School, Los Angeles, California; **James P. Regan**, NYC Board of Education, New York, New York; **Catherine M. Rifkin**, Florida Community College at Jacksonville, Jacksonville, Florida; **Amy Schneider**, Pacoima Skills Center, Los Angeles, California; **Bonnie Sherman**, Green River Community College, Auburn, Washington; **Julie Singer**, Garfield Community Adult School, Los Angeles, California; **Yilin Sun**, Seattle Central Community College, Seattle, Washington; **André Sutton**, Belmont Community Adult School, Los Angeles, California; **Deborah Thompson**, El Camino Real Community Adult School, Los Angeles, California; **Evelyn Trottier**, Basic Studies Division, Seattle Central Community College, Seattle, Washington; **Debra Un**, New York University, American Language Institute, New York, New York; **Jodie Morgan Vargas**, Orange County Public Schools, Orlando, Florida; **Christopher Wahl**, Hudson County Community College, Jersey City, New Jersey; **Ethel S. Watson**, Evans Community Adult School, Los Angeles, California; **Barbara Williams**; **Mimi Yang**, Belmont Community Adult School, Los Angeles, California; **Adèle Youmans**, Pima Community College Adult Education, Tucson, Arizona.

Ventures Student's Book 1

Illustration credits

Ken Batelman: 19, 59, 85, 89, 95 *(bottom)*

Cybele/Three in a Box: 37 *(top)*, 87

Travis Foster: 45 *(top)*, 78, 100, 111, 123

Chuck Gonzales: 17, 34, 35, 48, 95 *(top)*, 107, 112, 113

Stuart Holmes: 26, 68, 105

Ben Kirchner/Heart Agency: 2, 6, 7, 12, 14, 18, 24, 32, 33, 38, 44, 45 *(bottom)*, 50, 51 *(bottom)*, 58, 64, 70, 71, 76, 84, 90, 96, 102, 110, 116, 122, 128

Jim Kopp: 13, 25, 39, 51 *(top)*, 65, 77, 103, 117, 129

Mar Marube: 36, 37 *(bottom two)*

Frank Montagna: 11, 40, 55, 74, 124

Greg Paprocki: 21, 121, 127

Maria Rabinky: 60 *(bottom)*, 61, 63

Monika Roe: 22, 23, 27, 73, 92, 97, 114, 133

Photography credits

4 ©Fotosearch

5 ©Frank Veronsky

8 *(top)* ©Age fotostock; *(bottom, all)* ©Jupiter Images

9 ©Punchstock

15 ©Punchstock

20 *(all)* ©George Kerrigan

35 *(all)* ©Jupiter Images

46 *(top row, left to right)* ©Jupiter Images; ©Punchstock; ©Punchstock; *(middle row, left to right)* ©Veer; ©H.Benser/Zefa/Corbis; ©Age fotostock; *(bottom row, left to right)* ©David Young-Wolff/Photo Edit; ©Photo Researchers; ©Jupiter Images

49 *(clockwise from top left)* ©Jupiter Images; ©Age fotostock; ©Age fotostock; ©Jupiter Images; ©Alamy; ©Alamy

69 *(left to right)* ©Jupiter Images; ©Istock; ©Istock; ©Jupiter Images

72 *(clockwise from top left)* ©Punchstock; ©Getty Images; ©Punchstock; ©Corbis

81 *(top to bottom)* ©Corbis; ©Getty Images

86 *(top row, all)* ©Jupiter Images; *(middle row)* ©Jupiter Images; ©Jupiter Images; ©Jupiter Images; ©Corbis; *(bottom row)* ©Jupiter Images; ©Jupiter Images; ©Punchstock; ©Punchstock

98 *(top to bottom)* ©Getty Images; ©Shutter Stock

99 *(clockwise from top left)* ©Bettmann/Corbis; ©Underwood Archives/Index Stock; ©John Firth/Getty Images; ©H.Armstrong Roberts/Getty Images; ©Ewing Galloway/Index Stock; ©Corbis

101 *(clockwise from top left)* ©Corbis; ©Fotosearch; ©Punchstock; ©Superstock; ©Masterfile; ©Ed Bock/Corbis

121 *(clockwise from top left)* ©Punchstock; ©Jupiter Images; ©Jupiter Images; ©Jupiter Images; ©Jupiter Images; ©Corbis; ©Jupiter Images; ©Jupiter Images

131 *(both)* ©Corbis

133 *(clockwise from top left)* ©Jupiter Images; ©Corbis; ©Jupiter Images; ©Index Stock; ©Veer; ©Corbis; ©Corbis; ©Punchstock

Ventures Teacher's Edition 1 tests

Illustration credits

Chuck Gonzales: T-172

Greg Paprocki: T-174

Maria Rabinky: T-160

Monika Roe: T-154

Willie Ryan: T-153, T-167

William Waitzman: T-171

Photography credits

T-151 *(clockwise from top left)* ©Jupiter Images; ©Jupiter Images; ©Jupiter Images; ©Jupiter Images; ©Age fotostock

T-157 *(clockwise from top left)* ©Jupiter Images; ©Alamy; ©Jupiter Images; ©Age fotostock; ©Age fotostock

Collaborative Activities

Illustration credits

Laurie Conley: 1, 2, 7, 22, 23, 31, 32, 67, 68, 70, 71
Chuck Gonzales: 14, 55, 21
Ben Kirchner: 20
Monika Roe: 10, 11, 12, 13, 28, 29, 65, 66
William Waitzman: 21, 37, 74
Mark Watkinson: 5, 6, 38, 39, 45, 46
Phil Williams: 57, 58, 78

Picture Dictionary Cards

Illustration credits

Jim Kopp: all illustrations

Ventures 1 Teacher's Toolkit Audio CD / CD-ROM

Minimum System Requirements

Windows XP, 2000

- Intel Pentium processor – minimum 400 MHz
- 128 MB RAM minimum
- Sound card. Speakers or headphones.

Macintosh

- PowerPC processor – minimum 300 MHz
- MacOS OSX
- 64 MB free RAM minimum
- Sound card. Speakers or headphones.

Browsers & Plug-ins

- Flash 8 plug-in or higher
- Mac: Microsoft Internet Explorer 5.2 or a comparable browser
- PC: Microsoft Internet Explorer 6.0 or a comparable browser